# CATALOGUE

OF THE

# GOVERNORS, TRUSTEES, AND OFFICERS,

AND OF THE

# ALUMNI AND OTHER GRADUATES,

OF

# COLUMBIA COLLEGE

(ORIGINALLY KING'S COLLEGE),

IN THE

## CITY OF NEW YORK,

FROM

## 1754 TO 1864.

NEW YORK:
D. VAN NOSTRAND, 192 BROADWAY.
M DCCC LXV.

# CONSPECTUS.



# ABBREVIATIONS.

| | | | |
|---|---|---|---|
| ARCH. | Architect. | ED. | Editor. |
| ART. | Artist. | ENG. | Engineer. |
| AU. | Author. | F. | Farmer. |
| B. | Banker. | M. | Merchant. |
| Br. | Broker. | PUB. | Publisher. |
| CHEM. | Chemist. | REV. | Reverend. |
| C. L. | Counsellor at Law. | T. | Teacher. |

A star (*) prefixed to a name denotes that the individual is deceased. In every case in which the year of the decease is known, it is indicated at the right.

# EXPLANATORY NOTICE.

---

The present catalogue of the Alumni and other graduates of Columbia College is the first in which an attempt has been made to exhibit the professions or occupations of the graduates, the academic distinctions which have been conferred on them, and the offices of honor or responsibility which they have filled. Unfortunately, no contemporaneous record of these things has been kept up at the College; and, until within the last few years, no organization among the graduates themselves has existed, by which such information might have been gathered and preserved. A Society of the Alumni was, however, formed in the year 1854; and that Society, very early after its formation, made an earnest effort, by a correspondence conducted through its officers with very many of the living Alumni, to collect all the important or interesting facts in the personal history of every graduate of the College from the beginning.* This correspondence, which was quite laborious, resulted in the accumulation of much useful material; but the information obtained was of very unequal value, and in many instances the letters of inquiry failed to elicit any reply.

Early in the present academic year, the President of the College was authorized by the Board of Trustees to publish a catalogue without further delay—the belief being entertained that the appearance of this publication would revive in the minds of the graduates a sufficient interest in the subject to induce them, severally, to point out such imperfections as they may discover in it, to correct its inaccuracies, and to supply its deficiencies. In the mean time, however, another effort has been made to secure additional information, by correspondence with members of the classes whose record appeared to be the most incomplete, and this effort has been partially, but only partially, successful.

---

* A Society of the Alumni appears to have earlier existed; but no records of that organization are known to have been preserved.

Such as it is, the catalogue is now finally committed to the press. Copies of it will be sent to all the living Alumni whose residences are known. Those who may not receive it will be promptly supplied, on application to the President, at the College, by mail or otherwise.

Every graduate to whom the catalogue may be sent is earnestly requested, first, to correct and complete his own record, as here presented; and, secondly, to communicate any information he may possess, which the catalogue may not give, in regard to any other graduate or graduates. Such communications may be addressed to the President, and the facts which they embrace will be incorporated into the catalogue in the next edition. Hereafter it is proposed to publish the catalogue triennially.

Four catalogues of the Alumni of Columbia College have been heretofore published, the earliest of which appeared in 1815. The succeeding ones were issued in 1826, 1836, and 1844, respectively. The catalogue of 1815 was prepared and printed in Latin, in the style usual in college triennials. In 1826, Latin was abandoned for English, and this language has been employed in the more recent editions. After some hesitation, it has been determined not to revert, in the present publication, to the primitive style.

A catalogue of King's College—that is to say, of Columbia College before the Revolution—appeared in 1774, printed on a broad sheet. Two copies of this, the only copies known to have been preserved, have recently been discovered in the library of Yale College, one of which has been courteously presented by the librarian of that institution to the library of this.

# GOVERNORS

OF

# KING'S COLLEGE,

## NEW YORK,

AS APPOINTED BY ROYAL CHARTER,

A. D. 1754.

---

THE most Reverend Father in God, THOMAS, Lord Archbishop of Canterbury; and the most Reverend the Lord Archbishop of Canterbury for the time being, *ex officio.*

The Right Honorable DUNK, first Lord Commissioner for Trade and Plantations; and the first Lord Commissioner for Trade and Plantations for the time being, *ex officio.*

The Governor of the Province, *ex officio.*

The eldest Councillor of the Province, *ex officio.*

The Judges of the Supreme Court of Judicature of the Province, *ex officio.*

The Secretary of the Province, *ex officio.*

The Attorney-General of the Province, *ex officio.*

The Speaker of the General Assembly of the Province, *ex officio.*

The Treasurer of the Province, *ex officio.*

The Mayor of the City of New York, *ex officio.*

The Rector of Trinity Church in the City of New York, *ex officio.*

The Senior Minister of the Reformed Protestant Dutch Church in the City of New York, *ex officio.*

The Minister of the Ancient Lutheran Church in the City of New York, *ex officio.*

The Minister of the French Church in the City of New York, *ex officio.*

The Minister of the Presbyterian Congregation in the City of New York, *ex officio.*

The President of the College, *ex officio.*

[The names of those who, at various times, attended meetings of the Governors, by virtue of their office as above, are:—

JOHN CHAMBERS, Second Justice of the Supreme Court of the Province.

WILLIAM KEMPE, Attorney-General of the Province.

ABRAHAM DE PEYSTER, Treasurer of the Province.

EDWARD HOLLAND, Mayor of the City of New York.

HENRY BARCLAY, Rector of Trinity Church, New York.

JOANNES RITZEMA, Senior Minister of the Reformed Protestant Dutch Church, New York.

JOHN ALBERT WEYGAND, Minister of the Ancient Lutheran Ch., New York.

JOANNES CARLE, Minister of the French Church, New York.

SAMUEL JOHNSON, President of the College.

JOHN CRUGER, Jr., Mayor of the City of New York.

DANIEL HORSMANDEN, Third Justice of the Supreme Court of the Province.

JOHN TABOR KEMPE, Attorney-General of the Province.

BENJAMIN PRATT, Chief Justice of the Supreme Court of the Province.

MYLES COOPER, President of the College.

SAMUEL AUCHMUTY, Rector of Trinity Church, New York.

JOHN CRUGER, Speaker of the General Assembly of the Province.

The Archbishop of Canterbury (by proxy).]

ARCHIBALD KENNEDY ................Refused to qualify or to serve.

JOSEPH MURRAY......................Between July, 1756, and May, 1757 (Deceased)

JOSIAH MARTIN....................Between March, 1761, and Oct., 1764 (Removed from the Province)

PAUL RICHARD..........................................

HENRY CRUGER..........................................

WILLIAM WALTON .................Between May, 1768, and March, 1770 (Deceased)

JOHN WATTS..........................................

HENRY BEEKMAN..........................................

PHILIP VERPLANCK.......................................... 1770 (Resigned)

FREDERICK PHILIPSE..........................................

Joseph Robinson........................................

John Cruger........................................

Oliver De Lancey........................................

James Livingston........................................ Deceased 1763

Benjamin Nicoll..................Between Feb., 1760, and April, Deceased 1763

William Livingston....... ........ Refused to qualify or to serve.

Joseph Reade........................................

Nathaniel Marston........................................

Joseph Haynes........................................

John Livingston........................................

Abraham Lodge........................................

David Clarkson........................................

Leonard Lispenard........................................

James De Lancey, Jr........................................

Appointed subsequently, by virtue of the power vested in the Governors by the Charter:

Appointed

1759 Samuel Auchmuty....Having become Rector of Trinity Church, Resigned 1764

1759 Gabriel Ludlow........................................ Resigned 1770

1761 Edward Antill....................Did not qualify or serve.

1762 John Chambers................Between Nov., 1762, and Oct., Deceased 1764

1762 Henry Cuyler........................................

1762 James Duane........................................

1762 William Alexander, Earl of Stirling....................

1763 Charles Ward Apthorpe..........................

1764 Beverley Robinson.............................. Resigned 1770

1764 John Provoost.............Between Aug., 1767, and March, Deceased 1770

1764 Thomas Jones........................................

1764 Archibald Kennedy................Did not qualify or serve.

1770 Roger Morris........................................

Appointed

1770 John Ogilvie, S. T. D. ..............................

1770 Samuel Verplanck ..............................

1770 Goldsborough Banyar ..............................

1770 William Walton ..............................

Subsequently appointed, the date not known:

Charles Inglis, S. T. D. ..............................

Henry White ..............................

Peter Middleton, M. D. ..............................

James Walton ..............................

John Henry Cruger ..............................

John Walton ..............................

## REGENTS OF THE UNIVERSITY,

To whom the Government of the College, under the name of Columbia College, was committed by an Act of the Legislature of the State of New York,

A. D. 1784:

The Governor of the State for the time being, *ex officio*.
The Lieutenant-Governor " "
The President of the Senate " "
The Speaker of the House of Assembly for the time being, *ex officio*.
The Mayor of the City of New York " "
The Mayor of the City of Albany " "
The Attorney-General " "
The President and Professors of the College " "
The Secretary of State " "

Brockholst Livingston,
Robert Harpur,
Walter Livingston,
Christopher Yates,
Anthony Hoffman,
Cornelius Humphrey,
Lewis Morris,
Philip Pell, Jr.,
Matthew Clarkson,
Rutgers Van Brunt,
James Townsend,
Thomas Lawrence,
Henry Wisner,
John Haring,
Christopher Tappan,
James Clinton,

Christopher P. Yates,
James Livingston,
Abraham Bancker,
John C. Dongan,
Ezra L'Hommedieu,
Caleb Smith,
John Williams,
John M'Crea.

And the following, added to the above-named by an Act of Legislature passed November 26, 1784:

John Jay, LL. D.,
Samuel Provoost, S. T. D.,
John H. Livingston, S. T. D.,
John Rodgers, S. T. D.,
John Mason, S. T. D.,
John Ganoe,
John Daniel Gross, S. T. D.,
Johann Christoff Kunze, S. T. D.,
Joseph Delaplaine,
Gershom Seixas,
Alexander Hamilton, LL. D.,
John Lawrence,
John Rutherfurd,
Morgan Lewis,
Leonard Lispenard,
John Cochran, M. D.,
Charles McKnight, M. D.,
Thomas Jones, M. D.,
Malachi Treat, M. D.,
Nicholas Romaine, M. D.,
Peter W. Yates,
Matthew Visscher,
Hunlock Woodruff, M. D.,
George I. L. Dole,
John Vanderbilt,
Thomas Romaine,
Samuel Buel,
Gilbert Livingston,
Nathan Kerr,
Ebenezer Lockwood,
John Lloyd,
Herman Garrison,
Ebenezer Russell.

## TRUSTEES OF COLUMBIA COLLEGE.

The following, appointed by an Act of the Legislature of the State of New York, April 13, 1787, reviving the original Charter with amendments:

| | |
|---|---|
| James Duane | Resigned 1795 |
| Samuel Provoost, S. T. D. | Resigned 1801 |
| John H. Livingston, S. T. D. | Resigned 1810 |
| Richard Varick | Resigned 1816 |
| Alexander Hamilton, LL. D. | Deceased 1804 |
| John Mason, S. T. D. | Resigned 1788 |
| James Wilson | Resigned 1788 |

| | |
|---|---|
| JOHN GANOE* | Retired 1788 |
| BROCKHOLST LIVINGSTON, LL. D. | Deceased 1823 |
| ROBERT HARPUR | Resigned 1795 |
| JOHN DANIEL GROSS, S. T. D. | Resigned 1787 |
| JOHANN CHRISTOFF KUNZE, S. T. D. | Resigned 1792 |
| WALTER LIVINGSTON | Deceased 1797 |
| LEWIS A. SCOTT | Deceased 1798 |
| JOSEPH DELAPLAINE | Declined 1787 |
| LEONARD LISPENARD | Deceased 1790 |
| ABRAHAM BEACH, S. T. D. | Resigned 1813 |
| JOHN LAWRENCE | Deceased 1810 |
| JOHN RUTHERFURD † | Retired 1787 |
| MORGAN LEWIS | Resigned 1804 |
| JOHN COCHRAN, M. D. | Resigned 1794 |
| GERSHOM SEIXAS | Resigned 1815 |
| CHARLES MCKNIGHT, M. D. | Resigned 1787 |
| THOMAS JONES, M. D. | Deceased 1798 |
| MALACHI TREAT, M. D. | Deceased 1795 |
| SAMUEL BARD, M. D. | Resigned 1804 |
| NICHOLAS ROMAINE, M. D. | Resigned 1793 |
| BENJAMIN KISSAM, M. D. | Deceased 1804 |
| EBENEZER CROSBY, M. D. | Deceased 1788 |

And the following, subsequently chosen by virtue of the Act of April 13, 1787, empowering the Trustees then created to fill vacancies:

| Appointed | | |
|---|---|---|
| 1788 | WILLIAM SAMUEL JOHNSON, LL. D. | Resigned 1800 |
| 1788 | RICHARD HARISON, LL. D. | Deceased 1829 |

* This name does not appear on the list of Trustees after March 15, 1788.

† This name does not appear on the list of Trustees after May 20, 1787.

| Appointed |  | |  |
|---|---|---|---|
| 1789 | John Watts | Resigned | 1816 |
| 1790 | William Moore, M. D. | Deceased | 1824 |
| 1793 | Edward Livingston | Resigned | 1806 |
| 1793 | John McKnight, S. T. D. | Resigned | 1795 |
| 1794 | John Cosine | Deceased | 1798 |
| 1795 | Cornelius I. Bogert | Resigned | 1823 |
| 1795 | John M. Mason, S. T. D. | Resigned | 1811 |
| 1795 | Samuel Nicoll, M. D. | Deceased | 1796 |
| 1795 | Edward Dunscomb | Deceased | 1814 |
| 1796 | George C. Anthon, M. D. | Resigned | 1815 |
| 1797 | Philip Livingston | Resigned | 1806 |
| 1799 | John Charlton, M. D. | Deceased | 1806 |
| 1799 | John N. Abeel, S. T. D. | Deceased | 1812 |
| 1799 | James Tillary, M. D. | Deceased | 1815 |
| 1801 | John H. Hobart, S. T. D. | Deceased | 1831 |
| 1802 | Benjamin Moore, S. T. D. | Resigned | 1813 |
| 1804 | Egbert Benson, LL. D. | Resigned | 1814 |
| 1804 | Johann C. Kunze, S. T. D. | Deceased | 1805 |
| 1805 | Gouverneur Morris | Deceased | 1816 |
| 1805 | Jacob Radcliff | Resigned | 1817 |
| 1806 | Rufus King, LL. D. | Resigned | 1824 |
| 1806 | Samuel Miller, S. T. D. | Resigned | 1813 |
| 1807 | Nicholas Evertson | Deceased | 1807 |
| 1808 | De Witt Clinton | Declined | 1808 |
| 1808 | Oliver Wolcott | Resigned | 1816 |
| 1809 | John B. Romeyn, S. T. D. | Deceased | 1825 |
| 1811 | William Harris, S. T. D. | Deceased | 1829 |
| 1811 | Robert Troup, LL. D. | Resigned | 1817 |

| Appointed | | Resigned |
|---|---|---|
| 1812 | Peter A. Jay | 1817 |
| | | Resigned |
| 1812 | John M. Mason, S. T. D | 1824 |
| | | Resigned |
| 1813 | Clement C. Moore, LL. D | 1857 |
| | | Resigned |
| 1813 | Charles Wilkes | 1824 |
| | | Deceased |
| 1815 | David B. Ogden, LL. D | 1849 |
| | | Resigned |
| 1815 | William Johnson, LL. D | 1841 |
| | | Deceased |
| 1815 | John Wells | 1823 |
| | | Retired |
| 1816 | Thomas Y. How, S. T. D | 1818 |
| | | Resigned |
| 1816 | William Henderson | 1823 |
| | | Resigned |
| 1816 | Edward W. Laight | 1851 |
| | | Resigned |
| 1816 | John R. Murray | 1835 |
| | | Resigned |
| 1816 | Wright Post, M. D | 1826 |
| | | Resigned |
| 1817 | Beverley Robinson | 1854 |
| | | Deceased |
| 1817 | Thomas L. Ogden | 1844 |
| | | Resigned |
| 1817 | Nicholas Fish | 1833 |
| | | Resigned |
| 1817 | James Renwick | 1820 |
| | | Resigned |
| 1818 | Samuel F. Jarvis, S. T. D | 1820 |
| | | Deceased |
| 1818 | John T. Irving | 1838 |
| | | Deceased |
| 1820 | David S. Jones, LL. D | 1848 |
| | | Resigned |
| 1821 | Gulian C. Verplanck | 1826 |
| | | Deceased |
| 1822 | Paschal N. Strong | 1825 |
| | | Resigned |
| 1823 | James Kent, LL. D | 1823 |
| | | Deceased |
| 1823 | Peter A. Jay, LL. D | 1843 |
| | | Resigned |
| 1823 | John Duer | 1830 |
| | | Resigned |
| 1824 | Benjamin T. Onderdonk, S. T. D | 1853 |
| | | Deceased |
| 1824 | Lynde Catlin | 1833 |
| | | Resigned |
| 1824 | Jonathan M. Wainwright, S. T. D | 1830 |
| | | Deceased |
| 1824 | Philip Hone | 1851 |

| Appointed | Name | |
|---|---|---|
| 1824 | John Watts, M. D. | Deceased 1831 |
| 1825 | Charles King | Resigned 1838 |
| 1825 | James M. Matthews, S. T. D. | Resigned 1830 |
| 1826 | Samuel Boyd | Resigned 1835 |
| 1828 | William Creighton, S. T. D. | Resigned 1840 |
| 1830 | Gardiner Spring, S. T. D. | |
| 1830 | James Campbell | Deceased 1848 |
| 1830 | William D. Snodgrass, S. T. D. | Resigned 1833 |
| 1830 | John L. Lawrence | Deceased 1849 |
| 1830 | William A. Duer, LL. D. | Resigned 1842 |
| 1830 | John Ferguson | Deceased 1832 |
| 1831 | Edward R. Jones | Resigned 1838 |
| 1832 | William Berrian, S. T. D. | Deceased 1862 |
| 1833 | Ogden Hoffman | Deceased 1856 |
| 1833 | Thomas W. Ludlow | Resigned 1836 |
| 1834 | Samuel Ward | Deceased 1838 |
| 1835 | Peter G. Stuyvesant | Declined 1835 |
| 1836 | Samuel B. Ruggles, LL. D. | |
| 1836 | John Knox, S. T. D. | Deceased 1858 |
| 1837 | Thomas L. Wells | Resigned 1859 |
| 1838 | William R. Williams, S. T. D. | Resigned 1848 |
| 1838 | William H. Harison | Deceased 1860 |
| 1838 | John B. Beck, M. D. | Deceased 1851 |
| 1840 | Hamilton Fish | Resigned 1849 |
| 1840 | William Bard | Deceased 1853 |
| 1842 | William Betts, LL. D. | |
| 1842 | Nathaniel F. Moore, LL. D. | Resigned 1851 |
| 1843 | Benjamin I. Haight, S. T. D. | |

| Appointed | | |
|---|---|---|
| 1845 | Gerrit G. Van Wagenen | Deceased 1858 |
| 1848 | John L. Mason | Resigned 1853 |
| 1848 | William H. Hobart, M. D | Resigned 1855 |
| 1849 | Edward Jones | |
| 1849 | Robert Ray | |
| 1849 | Gouverneur M. Ogden | |
| 1849 | Charles King, LL. D. | |
| 1851 | Hamilton Fish, LL. D | |
| 1851 | Henry James Anderson, M. D., LL. D. | |
| 1851 | Gerard W. Morris | Resigned 1855 |
| 1851 | George H. Fisher, S. T. D. | Resigned 1855 |
| 1853 | Jonathan M. Wainwright, S. T. D., J. C. D. | Deceased 1854 |
| 1853 | Edward L. Beadle, M. D | |
| 1853 | George T. Strong | |
| 1854 | George F. Allen | Deceased 1863 |
| 1854 | Horatio Potter, S. T. D., LL. D., D. C. L. | |
| 1855 | Alexander W. Bradford, LL. D. | |
| 1855 | Mancius S. Hutton, S. T. D | |
| 1856 | Martin Zabriskie | |
| 1856 | John Torrey, M. D., LL. D. | |
| 1858 | Lewis M. Rutherfurd | |
| 1858 | Thomas De Witt, S. T. D. | |
| 1859 | John Jacob Astor, Jr. | |
| 1859 | John C. Jay, M. D | |
| 1860 | William C. Schermerhorn | |
| 1862 | Morgan Dix, S. T. D. | |
| 1864 | Frederick A. P. Barnard, S. T. D., LL. D. | |

## COMMITTEE OF THE TRUSTEES ON THE SCHOOL OF MINES.

### 1865.

William Betts, LL. D., Chairman.
Edward Jones,
George T. Strong,
John Torrey, M. D., LL. D.,
Lewis M. Rutherfurd,
Frederick A. P. Barnard, S. T. D., LL. D.,
Hamilton Fish, LL. D.

#### ASSOCIATE MEMBERS.

Cornelius R. Agnew, M. D.,
George C. Anthon,
Samuel W. Bridgham,
Lewis L. Delafield,
Franklin H. Delano,
William E. Dodge, Jr.,
Jacob P. G. Foster,
Nathaniel P. Hosack,
Robert L. Kennedy,
Baron Robert Ostensacken,
Howard Potter,
Temple Prime,
Percy R. Pyne,
James Renwick,
Otis D. Swan,
Lucius Tuckerman,
George C. Ward.

## TRUSTEES OF THE MEDICAL DEPARTMENT.

### 1860.

| | Deceased |
|---|---|
| John C. Cheesman, M. D. | 1862 |
| Edward G. Ludlow, M. D. | |
| Joseph Delafield | |
| Floyd Smith | |
| Richard M. Blatchford | |
| Edward Delafield, M. D. | |
| John P. Crosby | |
| Gurdon Buck, M. D. | |
| Luther Bradish | 1863 |
| James W. Beekman | |

DANIEL D. LORD

BENJAMIN R. WINTHROP

EDWARD L. BEADLE, M. D.

WICKHAM HOFFMAN

ISAAC WOOD, M. D.

GEORGE W. WRIGHT

FREDERICK A. CONKLING

CHARLES HENSCHEL, M. D.

WASHINGTON MURRAY

HENRY CHAUNCEY, Jr.

SULLIVAN H. WESTON, S. T. D.

WILLIAM BETTS, LL. D.

| | Resigned |
|---|---|
| JOHN JACOB ASTOR, Jr. | 1863 |

GEORGE TALBOT OLYPHANT

JOHN TORREY, M. D., LL. D.

### SINCE APPOINTED.

| Appointed | |
|---|---|
| 1863 | BENJAMIN OGDEN, M. D. |
| 1863 | CAMBRIDGE LIVINGSTON |
| 1864 | JARED LINSLY, M. D. |

## CHAIRMEN

### OF THE BOARD OF GOVERNORS UNDER THE ROYAL CHARTER.

The Governor of the Province, or person next in rank, or Senior Governor, as the case may be.

### OF THE BOARD OF REGENTS, 1784-1787.

The Chancellor of the University.

### OF THE BOARD OF TRUSTEES.

| Appointed | | Resigned |
|---|---|---|
| 1787 | JAMES DUANE | 1795 |
| 1795 | SAMUEL PROVOOST, S. T. D. | 1801 |

| Appointed | | Resigned |
|---|---|---|
| 1801 | JOHN H. LIVINGSTON, S. T. D. | 1810 |
| | | Resigned |
| 1810 | RICHARD VARICK | 1816 |
| | | Deceased |
| 1816 | BROCKHOLST LIVINGSTON, LL. D. | 1823 |
| | | Resigned |
| 1823 | RICHARD HARISON, LL. D. | 1823 |
| | | Deceased |
| 1823 | WILLIAM MOORE, M. D. | 1824 |
| | | Resigned |
| 1824 | NICHOLAS FISH | 1832 |
| | | Deceased |
| 1832 | PETER A. JAY, LL. D. | 1843 |
| | | Deceased |
| 1843 | DAVID B. OGDEN, LL. D. | 1849 |
| | | Resigned |
| 1849 | EDWARD W. LAIGHT | 1850 |
| | | Resigned |
| 1850 | BEVERLEY ROBINSON | 1854 |
| | | Deceased |
| 1854 | JOHN KNOX, S. T. D. | 1858 |
| | | Resigned |
| 1858 | GARDINER SPRING, S. T. D. | 1859 |
| 1859 | HAMILTON FISH, LL. D. | |

## CLERKS

### OF THE BOARD OF GOVERNORS.

Lambert Moore.

### OF THE BOARD OF REGENTS, 1784-1787.

Robert Harpur.

### OF THE BOARD OF TRUSTEES.

| | | Resigned |
|---|---|---|
| 1787 | Robert Harpur | 1795 |
| | | Resigned |
| 1795 | Arbaham Beach, S. T. D. | 1811 |
| | | Resigned |
| 1811 | William Harris, S. T. D. | 1811 |
| | | Resigned |
| 1811 | John B. Romeyn, S. T. D. | 1815 |
| | | Resigned |
| 1815 | Clement C. Moore, LL. D. | 1850 |
| 1850 | William Betts, LL. D. | |

## TREASURERS OF THE COLLEGE.

| Appointed | | |
|---|---|---|
| 1775 | Leonard Lispenard | Resigned 1784 |
| 1784 | Brockholst Livingston, LL. D. | Deceased 1823 |
| 1824 | William Johnson, LL. D. | Resigned 1833 |
| 1833 | John L. Lawrence | Deceased 1849 |
| 1849 | Gerrit G. Van Wagenen | Deceased 1858 |
| 1858 | Gouverneur M. Ogden | |

## PRESIDENTS OF THE COLLEGE

### UNDER THE ROYAL CHARTER.

| | | |
|---|---|---|
| 1754 | SAMUEL JOHNSON, S. T. D. | Resigned 1763 |
| 1763 | MYLES COOPER, LL. D. | Retired 1775 |
| 1775 | BENJAMIN MOORE, A. M. (*pro tempore* in the absence of the President) | Resigned 1776 |

### UNDER THE NEW CHARTER.

| | | |
|---|---|---|
| 1787 | WILLIAM SAMUEL JOHNSON, LL. D. | Resigned 1800 |
| 1801 | CHARLES WHARTON, S. T. D. | Resigned 1801 |
| 1801 | BENJAMIN MOORE, S. T. D. | Resigned 1811 |
| 1811 | WILLIAM HARRIS, S. T. D. | Deceased 1829 |
| 1829 | WILLIAM ALEXANDER DUER, LL. D. | Resigned 1842 |
| 1842 | NATHANIEL F. MOORE, LL. D. | Resigned 1849 |
| 1849 | CHARLES KING, LL. D. | Resigned 1864 |
| 1864 | FREDERICK A. P. BARNARD, S. T. D., LL. D. | |

## PROVOST.

| | | |
|---|---|---|
| 1811 | JOHN M. MASON, S. T. D. | Resigned 1816 |

## FELLOWS.

| Appointed | | Resigned |
|---|---|---|
| 1755 | William Samuel Johnson, A. M. | 1756 |
| | | Resigned |
| 1756 | Leonard Cutting, A. M. | 1763 |
| | | Deceased |
| 1757 | Daniel Treadwell, A. M. | 1760 |
| | | Retired |
| 1762 | Myles Cooper, LL. D. | 1775 |
| | | Retired |
| 1773 | John Vardill, A. M. | 1776 |

## FACULTY OF ARTS.

President Johnson was, at first, sole Instructor.

### PROFESSORS OF MATHEMATICS AND NATURAL PHILOSOPHY.

| | | Deceased |
|---|---|---|
| 1757 | Daniel Treadwell, A. M. | 1760 |
| | | Resigned |
| 1761 | Robert Harpur, A. M. | 1767 |
| | | Deceased |
| 1786 | John Kemp, LL. D. | 1812 |
| | | Resigned |
| 1813 | Robert Adrain, LL. D. | 1825 |

### PROFESSORS OF MORAL PHILOSOPHY.

| | | Promoted |
|---|---|---|
| 1762 | Myles Cooper, A. M. | 1763 |
| | | Resigned |
| 1787 | John Daniel Gross, S. T. D. | 1795 |

### PROFESSORS OF NATURAL PHILOSOPHY.

| | | Retired |
|---|---|---|
| 1765 | Samuel Clossy, M. D. | 1776 |

### PROFESSOR OF NATURAL LAW.

| | | Retired |
|---|---|---|
| 1773 | John Vardill, A. M. | 1776 |

### PROFESSOR OF HISTORY AND LANGUAGES.

| | | Retired |
|---|---|---|
| 1773 | John Vardill, A. M. | 1776 |

### PROFESSORS OF THE FRENCH LANGUAGE.

| | | Retired |
|---|---|---|
| 1784 | John P. Tetard | 1787 |
| | | Resigned |
| 1792 | Villette De Marcellin | 1795 |

## PROFESSORS OF THE GREEK AND LATIN LANGUAGES.

| Appointed | | Resigned |
|---|---|---|
| 1784 | William Cochran, A. M. | 1789 |
| | | Resigned |
| 1789 | Peter Wilson, A. M. | 1792 |
| | | Resigned |
| 1792 | Elias D. Rattoone, S. T. D. | 1797 |
| | | Promoted |
| 1817 | Nathaniel F. Moore, A. M. (Adjunct) | 1820 |
| | | Resigned |
| 1820 | Nathaniel F. Moore, LL. D. | 1835 |
| | | Promoted |
| 1820 | Charles Anthon, A. B. (Adjunct) | 1830 |
| | | Transferred |
| 1830 | Charles Anthon, LL. D. (Jay) | 1857 |
| | | Resigned |
| 1837 | Robert G. Vermilye, A. M. (Adjunct) | 1843 |
| | | Promoted |
| 1845 | Henry Drisler, Jr., A. M. (Adjunct) | 1857 |

In 1857 this Chair was subdivided into two, viz.: the Chair of the Greek Language and Literature, and the Chair of the Latin Language and Literature.

## PROFESSOR OF RHETORIC AND LOGIC.

| | | Resigned |
|---|---|---|
| 1784 | Benjamin Moore, A. M. | 1787 |

## PROFESSOR OF ORIENTAL LANGUAGES.

| | | Resigned |
|---|---|---|
| 1784 | Johann C. Kunze, S. T. D. | 1787 |
| | | Resigned |
| 1792 | Johann C. Kunze, S. T. D. (reappointed) | 1795 |

## PROFESSOR OF THE GERMAN LANGUAGE AND GEOGRAPHY.

| | | Resigned |
|---|---|---|
| 1784 | John Daniel Gross, S. T. D. | 1795 |

## PROFESSOR OF NATURAL PHILOSOPHY AND ASTRONOMY.

| | | Resigned |
|---|---|---|
| 1785 | Samuel Bard, M. D. | 1786 |

## PROFESSOR OF NATURAL HISTORY AND CHEMISTRY.

| | | Resigned |
|---|---|---|
| 1785 | Henry Moyes, LL. D. | 1786 |

## PROFESSOR OF NATURAL HISTORY, CHEMISTRY, AND AGRICULTURE.

| | | Resigned |
|---|---|---|
| 1792 | Samuel L. Mitchill, M. D., LL. D. | 1810 |

## PROFESSOR OF BOTANY.

Appointed — Resigned

1792 Samuel L. Mitchill, M. D., LL. D. .......................... 1795

## PROFESSORS OF LAW.

1793 James Kent, A. M. .......................... Resigned 1798

1823 James Kent, LL. D. .......................... Deceased 1847

1848 William Betts, LL. D .......................... Resigned 1854

## PROFESSOR OF GRECIAN AND ROMAN ANTIQUITIES.

1794 Elias D. Rattoone, S. T. D .......................... Resigned 1797

## PROFESSOR OF GEOGRAPHY.

1795 John Kemp, LL. D. .......................... Deceased 1812

## PROFESSOR OF MORAL PHILOSOPHY AND LOGIC.

1795 John McKnight, S. T. D. .......................... Resigned 1801

## PROFESSOR OF RHETORIC AND BELLES-LETTRES.

1795 John Bisset, A. M. .......................... Resigned 1801

## PROFESSOR OF THE GREEK AND LATIN LANGUAGES AND OF GRECIAN AND ROMAN ANTIQUITIES.

1797 Peter Wilson, LL. D .......................... Resigned 1820

## PROFESSOR OF MORAL PHILOSOPHY, BELLES-LETTRES, AND LOGIC.

1801 John Bowden, S. T. D. .......................... Deceased 1817

## LECTURER IN NATURAL AND EXPERIMENTAL PHILOSOPHY AND CHEMISTRY.

1813 James Renwick, A. M. .......................... Retired 1813

## LECTURER IN MATHEMATICS AND GEOGRAPHY.

1813 Henry Vethake, A. B. .......................... Retired 1813

## PROFESSOR OF MORAL PHILOSOPHY, RHETORIC, AND BELLES-LETTRES.

| Appointed | | Transferred |
|---|---|---|
| 1817 | JOHN MCVICKAR, S. T. D. | 1857 |

The subjects of Intellectual Philosophy and Political Economy were, in 1818, added to this Department. In 1857, the Chair was subdivided into three, viz.: the Chair of Moral and Intellectual Philosophy, the Chair of Ancient and Modern Literature, and the Chair of History and Political Science.

## PROFESSORS OF NATURAL AND EXPERIMENTAL PHILOSOPHY AND CHEMISTRY.

| | | |
|---|---|---|
| 1820 | JAMES RENWICK, LL. D. Emeritus, 1853 | Deceased 1863 |
| 1854 | RICHARD S. MCCULLOH, A. M. | Transferred 1857 |

In 1857, this Chair was subdivided into two, viz.: the Chair of Mechanics and Physics, and the Chair of Chemistry.

## PROFESSOR OF MATHEMATICS, ANALYTICAL MECHANICS, AND PHYSICAL ASTRONOMY.

| | | |
|---|---|---|
| 1825 | HENRY JAMES ANDERSON, M. D. | Resigned 1843 |

## PROFESSORS OF THE ITALIAN LANGUAGE AND LITERATURE.

| | | |
|---|---|---|
| 1826 | LORENZO DA PONTE | Deceased 1837 |
| 1839 | E. FELIX FORESTI, LL. B. | Resigned 1856 |

## PROFESSORS OF THE FRENCH LANGUAGE AND LITERATURE.

| | | |
|---|---|---|
| 1828 | ANTOINE VERREN, A. M. | Resigned 1839 |
| 1839 | FELIX G. BERTEAU, LL. B. | Retired 1856 |

## PROFESSOR OF THE HEBREW LANGUAGE.

| | | |
|---|---|---|
| 1830 | SAMUEL H. TURNER, S. T. D. | Deceased 1861 |

## PROFESSOR OF THE SPANISH LANGUAGE AND LITERATURE.

| | | |
|---|---|---|
| 1830 | MARIANO VELAZQUEZ DE LA CADEÑA, LL. B. | Deceased 1860 |

### LECTURER UPON ELEMENTARY CHEMISTRY.

| Appointed | | Promoted |
|---|---|---|
| 1830 | William H. Ellet, M. D. | 1832 |

### PROFESSORS OF THE GERMAN LANGUAGE AND LITERATURE.

| | | |
|---|---|---|
| 1830 | Frederick C. Schaeffer, S. T. D. | Deceased 1831 |
| 1832 | William Ernenputsch. | Resigned 1832 |

### PROFESSOR OF ELEMENTARY CHEMISTRY.

| | | |
|---|---|---|
| 1832 | William H. Ellet, M. D. | Retired 1833 |

### GEBHARD PROFESSORS OF THE GERMAN LANGUAGE AND LITERATURE.

| | | |
|---|---|---|
| 1843 | John Lewis Tellkampf, J. U. D. | Resigned 1847 |
| 1847 | Henry I. Schmidt, S. T. D. | |

### PROFESSOR OF MATHEMATICS AND ASTRONOMY.

| | | |
|---|---|---|
| 1843 | Charles W. Hackley, S. T. D. | Transferred 1857 |

In 1857, this Chair was subdivided into two, viz.: the Chair of Mathematics and the Chair of Astronomy.

### PROFESSOR OF ELOCUTION.

| | | |
|---|---|---|
| 1844 | John W. S. Hows. | Retired 1857 |

### PROFESSOR OF THE EVIDENCES OF NATURAL AND REVEALED RELIGION.

| | | |
|---|---|---|
| 1857 | John McVickar, S. T. D. | Emeritus 1864 |

### JAY PROFESSOR OF THE GREEK LANGUAGE AND LITERATURE.

| | | |
|---|---|---|
| 1857 | Charles Anthon, LL. D. | |

### PROFESSOR OF THE LATIN LANGUAGE AND LITERATURE.

| | | |
|---|---|---|
| 1857 | Henry Drisler, LL. D. | |

## PROFESSORS OF ASTRONOMY.

| Appointed | | Deceased |
|---|---|---|
| 1857 | Charles W. Hackley, S. T. D. | 1861 |
| 1861 | William Guy Peck, LL. D. | |

## PROFESSORS OF MECHANICS AND PHYSICS.

| | | Expelled |
|---|---|---|
| 1857 | Richard S. McCulloh, A. M.* | 1863 |
| 1863 | Ogden N. Rood, A. M. | |

## PROFESSOR OF CHEMISTRY.

1857 Charles A. Joy, Ph. D.

## PROFESSOR OF HISTORY AND POLITICAL SCIENCE.

1857 Francis Lieber, LL. D.

## PROFESSORS OF MATHEMATICS.

| | | |
|---|---|---|
| 1857 | Charles Davies, LL. D. | Transferred 1859 |
| 1857 | William G. Peck, A. M. (Assistant) | Promoted 1858 |
| 1858 | William G. Peck, A. M. (Adjunct) | Promoted 1859 |

In 1859, this Chair was subdivided into two, viz.: the Chair of Higher Mathematics and the Chair of Pure Mathematics.

## PROFESSOR OF ANCIENT AND MODERN LITERATURE.

| | | Declined |
|---|---|---|
| 1857 | Samuel Eliot, A. M. | 1857 |

The Chair was united with the Chair of Moral and Intellectual Philosophy.

## PROFESSOR OF MORAL AND INTELLECTUAL PHILOSOPHY AND LITERATURE.

1857 Charles Murray Nairne, A. M.

* Expelled October 9, 1863, for having abandoned his post and joined the rebels.

## PROFESSOR OF HIGHER MATHEMATICS.

| Appointed | | |
|---|---|---|
| 1859 | Charles Davies, LL. D. | |

## PROFESSORS OF PURE MATHEMATICS.

| | | |
|---|---|---|
| 1859 | William Guy Peck, LL. D. | |
| 1863 | John H. Van Amringe, A. M. (Assistant) | Promoted 1863 |
| 1863 | John H. Van Amringe, A. M. (Adjunct) | |

---

# TUTORS.

| | | |
|---|---|---|
| 1755 | William Samuel Johnson, A. M. | Resigned 1756 |
| 1756 | Leonard Cutting, A. M. | Resigned 1763 |
| 1785 | John Kemp | Promoted 1786 |
| 1830 | Robert B. Van Kleeck, A. M. | Retired 1831 |
| 1831 | Abraham B. Conger, A. B. | Retired 1833 |
| 1831 | John L. O'Sullivan, A. B. | Retired 1833 |
| 1835 | Robert G. Vermilye, A. M. | Promoted 1837 |
| 1843 | Henry Drisler, Jr., A. M. | Promoted 1845 |
| 1854 | George W. Dean, A. B. | Retired 1854 |
| 1854 | Joseph S. Dodge, A. B. | Retired 1854 |
| 1859 | J. Emory McClintock, A. B. | Resigned 1860 |
| 1860 | J. Howard Van Amringe, A. B. | Promoted 1863 |
| 1864 | Duane S. Everson, A. B. | |

---

# LIBRARIANS.

Till 1837, the duties of Librarian were discharged by one of the Professors.

| | | |
|---|---|---|
| 1837 | Nathaniel F. Moore, LL. D. | Resigned 1839 |

| Appointed | | Resigned |
|---|---|---|
| 1839 | George C. Schaeffer, A. M., M. D. | 1847 |
| | | Deceased |
| 1847 | Lefroy Ravenhill, A. M., M. D. | 1851 |
| 1849 | Stephen R. Weeks (Assistant) | |
| 1851 | William Alfred Jones, A. M. | |

## CHAPLAIN.

The President discharged the duties of this office till 1857.

1857 Cornelius R. Duffie, A. M. ..............................

## FACULTY OF MEDICINE.

### PROFESSORS OF ANATOMY.

| | | Retired |
|---|---|---|
| 1767 | Samuel Clossy, M. D. | 1776 |
| | | Transferred |
| 1792 | Richard Bailey, M. D. | 1793 |
| | | Resigned |
| 1793 | Wright Post, M. D. | 1813 |

### PROFESSOR OF PATHOLOGY AND PHYSIOLOGY.

| | | Retired |
|---|---|---|
| 1767 | Peter Middleton, M. D. | 1776 |

### PROFESSORS OF SURGERY.

| | | Retired |
|---|---|---|
| 1767 | John Jones, M. D. | 1776 |
| | | Transferred |
| 1792 | Wright Post, M. D. | 1793 |
| | | Resigned |
| 1793 | Richard Bailey, M. D. | 1811 |
| | | Resigned |
| 1811 | Valentine Mott, M. D. | 1813 |

## PROFESSORS OF CHEMISTRY AND MATERIA MEDICA.

| Appointed | | Retired |
|---|---|---|
| 1767 | James Smith, M. D. | 1770 |
| 1770 | Peter Middleton, M. D. | Retired 1776 |

## PROFESSORS OF THE THEORY AND PRACTICE OF MEDICINE.

| | | |
|---|---|---|
| 1767 | Samuel Bard, M. D. | Retired 1776 |
| 1795 | William Hamersley, M. D. | Resigned 1813 |

## PROFESSORS OF MIDWIFERY.

| | | |
|---|---|---|
| 1767 | John V. B. Tennent, M. D. | Deceased 1770 |
| 1770 | Samuel Bard, M. D. | Retired 1776 |
| 1785 | Ebenezer Crosby, M. D. | Deceased 1788 |
| 1792 | John R. B. Rogers, M. D. | Resigned 1808 |
| 1808 | Walter C. Buchanan, M. D. | Resigned 1813 |

## PROFESSORS OF CHEMISTRY.

| | | |
|---|---|---|
| 1784 | Samuel Bard, M. D. | Resigned 1785 |
| 1786 | Samuel Bard, M. D. (reappointed) | Resigned 1787 |
| 1792 | Samuel Nicoll, M. D. | Resigned 1792 |
| 1802 | James S. Stringham, M. D. | Resigned 1813 |

## PROFESSORS OF THE INSTITUTES OF MEDICINE.

| | | |
|---|---|---|
| 1785 | Benjamin Kissam, M. D. | Resigned 1792 |
| 1792 | William Hamersley, M. D. | Resigned 1808 |
| 1808 | John C. Osborn, M. D. | Resigned 1813 |

## PROFESSOR OF ANATOMY AND SURGERY.

| | | |
|---|---|---|
| 1785 | Charles McKnight, M. D. | Deceased 1792 |

## PROFESSORS OF THE PRACTICE OF MEDICINE.

Appointed — Resigned
1785 Nicholas Romayne, M. D. .......... 1787
Resigned
1792 Samuel Nicoll, M. D. .......... 1794
Resigned
1794 Edward Stevens, M. D. .......... 1795

## LECTURER IN CHEMISTRY, ASTRONOMY, AND THE PRACTICE OF MEDICINE.

Resigned
1791 Nicholas Romayne, M. D. .......... 1792

## PROFESSORS OF MATERIA MEDICA.

Deceased
1792 William P. Smith, M. D. .......... 1795
Resigned
1811 John C. Osborn, M. D. .......... 1813

## PROFESSOR OF THE PRACTICE OF MEDICINE AND CLINICAL LECTURER.

Deceased
1792 William P. Smith, M. D. .......... 1795

## PROFESSORS OF BOTANY.

Resigned
1792 Richard S. Kissam, M. D. .......... 1793
Resigned
1795 David Hosack, M. D., LL. D., F. R. S. .......... 1811

## DEAN OF THE MEDICAL FACULTY.

Resigned
1792 Samuel Bard, M. D. .......... 1804

## PROFESSOR OF BOTANY AND MATERIA MEDICA.

Resigned
1796 David Hosack, M. D., LL. D., F. R. S. .......... 1811

The Faculty of Medicine ceased in 1813, most of the Professors who composed it having been appointed to professorships in the College of Physicians and Surgeons in the City of New York. In 1860 it was revived, by the adoption of the College of Physicians and Surgeons as the Medical Department of the College.

# FACULTY OF MEDICINE, 1860.

## PROFESSOR OF OBSTETRICS.

Edward Delafield, M. D. .................................... Emeritus 1860

## PROFESSOR OF CLINICAL SURGERY.

Alexander H. Stevens, M. D., LL. D. .......................... Emeritus 1860

## PROFESSOR OF CHEMISTRY AND BOTANY.

John Torrey, M. D., LL. D. .................................... Emeritus 1860

## PROFESSOR OF MATERIA MEDICA AND CLINICAL MEDICINE.

Joseph Mather Smith, M. D. ....................................

## PROFESSOR OF ANATOMY.

Robert Watts, M. D. ....................................

## PROFESSOR OF THE PRINCIPLES AND PRACTICE OF SURGERY AND SURGICAL ANATOMY.

Willard Parker, M. D. ....................................

## PROFESSOR OF OBSTETRICS, THE DISEASES OF WOMEN AND CHILDREN, AND MEDICAL JURISPRUDENCE.

Chandler R. Gilman, M. D. ....................................

## PROFESSOR OF PATHOLOGY AND PRACTICAL MEDICINE.

Alonzo Clark, M. D., LL. D. ....................................

## PROFESSOR OF PHYSIOLOGY AND MICROSCOPIC ANATOMY.

John C. Dalton, Jr., M. D. ....................................

## PROFESSOR OF CHEMISTRY.

Samuel St. John, M. D. ....................................

### ADJUNCT PROFESSOR OF SURGERY.

Thomas M. Markoe, M. D. . . . . . . . . . . . . . . . . . . . . . . . . . . . . . . . . . .

### DEMONSTRATOR OF ANATOMY AND CURATOR OF THE COLLEGE MUSEUM.

Henry B. Sands, M. D. . . . . . . . . . . . . . . . . . . . . . . . . . . . . . . . . . . . . .

### ASSISTANTS.

Foster Swift, M. D. (to Prof. of Obstetrics) . . . . . . . . . . . . . . . . . . . . . . .

William H. Draper, M. D. (to Prof. of Surgery) . . . . . . . . . . . . . . . . . . Resigned 1862

George F. Shrady, M. D. (to Prof. of Surgery) . . . . . . . . . . . . . . . . . . . Resigned 1862

### LIBRARIAN.

Gouverneur M. Smith, M. D . . . . . . . . . . . . . . . . . . . . . . . . . . . . . . . . .

SINCE APPOINTED:

### PROFESSOR OF MILITARY SURGERY AND HYGIENE.

Appointed
1862 William Detmold, M. D. . . . . . . . . . . . . . . . . . . . . . . . . . . . . . . . . .

### ADJUNCT PROFESSOR OF OBSTETRICS.

1863 T. Gailliard Thomas, M. D. . . . . . . . . . . . . . . . . . . . . . . . . . . . . . .

### ASSISTANTS.

1861 Maurice Perkins (to Prof. of Chemistry) . . . . . . . . . . . . . . . . . . . . Resigned 1863

1861 Erskine Mason, M. D. (to Demonstrator of Anatomy) . . . . . . . . .

1862 William H. Carmalt, M. D. (to Prof. of Physiology) . . . . . . . . . .

1863 James L. Little, M. D. (to Prof. of Surgery) . . . . . . . . . . . . . . . . .

---

## FACULTY OF LAW.

### PROFESSOR OF MUNICIPAL LAW.

1858 Theodore W. Dwight, LL. D. . . . . . . . . . . . . . . . . . . . . . . . . . . . .

### PROFESSOR OF MEDICAL JURISPRUDENCE.

Appointed
1860 John Ordronaux, LL. B., M. D. . . . . . . . . . . . . . . . . . . . . . . . . . .

### PROFESSOR OF POLITICAL SCIENCE.

1860 Francis Lieber, LL. D. . . . . . . . . . . . . . . . . . . . . . . . . . . . . . . . . .

### PROFESSOR OF THE ETHICS OF JURISPRUDENCE.

1860 Charles Murray Nairne, A. M. . . . . . . . . . . . . . . . . . . . . . . . . . . .

### WARDEN OF THE LAW SCHOOL.

1864 Theodore W. Dwight, LL. D. . . . . . . . . . . . . . . . . . . . . . . . . . . . . .

---

## FACULTY OF THE SCHOOL OF MINES.

### PROFESSOR OF MINERALOGY AND METALLURGY.

1863 Thomas Egleston, Jr., A. M., E. M. . . . . . . . . . . . . . . . . . . . . . . .

### PROFESSOR OF MINING ENGINEERING.

1864 Francis L. Vinton, E. M. . . . . . . . . . . . . . . . . . . . . . . . . . . . . . . . .

### PROFESSOR OF CHEMISTRY.

1864 Charles F. Chandler, Ph. D. . . . . . . . . . . . . . . . . . . . . . . . . . . . . .

### ASSISTANTS.

1864 William A. Potter, A. B. (in Analytical Chemistry) . . . . . . . . . .

1864 Julius Maier, Ph. D. (in Analytical Chemistry) . . . . . . . . . . . . . .

1864 Albert H. Chester (in Mineralogy) . . . . . . . . . . . . . . . . . . . . . . .

1864 Henry B. Cornwall, A. B. (in General Chemistry.) . . . . . . . . . .

# SENATUS ACADEMICUS.

## 1865.

### TRUSTEES.

| NAMES. | RESIDENCES. |
|---|---|
| WILLIAM C. SCHERMERHORN | 49 West 23d Street. |
| MORGAN DIX, S. T. D. | 50 Varick " |
| FREDERIC A. P. BARNARD, S. T. D., LL. D. | Columbia College. |

---

## TRUSTEES OF THE MEDICAL DEPARTMENT.

| | |
|---|---|
| EDWARD G. LUDLOW, M. D | 49 East 23d Street. |
| JOSEPH DELAFIELD | 475 Fifth Avenue. |
| FLOYD SMITH | 283 West 21st Street. |
| RICHARD M. BLATCHFORD | 6 East 14th " |
| EDWARD DELAFIELD, M. D | 2 East 17th " |
| JOHN P. CROSBY | 31 West 17th " |
| GURDON BUCK, M. D | 121 Tenth " |
| JAMES W. BEEKMAN | 5 East 34th " |
| DANIEL D. LORD | 45 West 19th " |
| BENJAMIN R. WINTHROP | 134 Second Avenue. |
| EDWARD L. BEADLE, M. D | Poughkeepsie. |
| WICKHAM HOFFMAN | |
| ISAAC WOOD, M. D | 68 East 17th Street. |
| GEO. W. WRIGHT | 63 East 23d " |
| FREDERICK A. CONKLING | 103 Tenth " |
| CHARLES HENSCHEL, M. D | 20 East 14th " |
| WASHINGTON MURRAY | 11 East 12th " |
| HENRY CHAUNCEY, Jr. | 25 Washington Sq. |
| SULLIVAN H. WESTON, S. T. D | 30 Laight Street. |
| WILLIAM BETTS, LL. D | 122 East 30th Street. |
| TALBOT OLYPHANT | 18 East 37th " |
| JOHN TORREY, M. D., LL. D. | Columbia College. |
| BENJAMIN OGDEN, M. D | 140 Hester Street. |
| CAMBRIDGE LIVINGSTON | 44 West 22d " |
| JARED LINSLY, M. D | 22 Lafayette Place. |

## OFFICERS OF INSTRUCTION AND GOVERNMENT.

| NAMES. | RESIDENCES. |
|---|---|
| FREDERIC A. P. BARNARD, S. T. D., LL. D. | Columbia College. |
| President. | |
| EDWARD DELAFIELD, M. D. | 2 East 17th Street. |
| President of the Medical Department, and Emeritus Professor of Obstetrics. | |
| JOHN McVICKAR, S. T. D. | 21 West 32d " |
| Emeritus Professor of the Evidences of Christianity. | |
| CHARLES ANTHON, LL. D. | 12 East 37th " |
| Jay Professor of the Greek Language and Literature. | |
| HENRY DRISLER, LL. D. | 226 East 10th " |
| Professor of the Latin Language and Literature. | |
| HENRY I. SCHMIDT, S. T. D. | 94 West 43d " |
| Gebhard Professor of the German Language and Literature. | |
| STEPHEN R. WEEKS | Columbia College. |
| Assistant Librarian. | |
| WILLIAM A. JONES, A. M. | 198 West 20th Street. |
| Librarian. | |
| CORNELIUS R. DUFFIE, A. M. | 233 Lexington Av. |
| Chaplain. | |
| CHARLES A. JOY, Ph. D. | Columbia College. |
| Professor of Chemistry. | |
| FRANCIS LIEBER, LL. D. | 48 East 34th Street. |
| Professor of History and Political Science. | |
| CHARLES DAVIES, LL. D. | Fishkill Landing. |
| Professor of Higher Mathematics. | |
| WILLIAM G. PECK, LL. D. | 29 Tenth Street. |
| Professor of Mathematics and Astronomy. | |
| CHARLES M. NAIRNE, A. M. | 163 West 34th Street. |
| Professor of Moral and Intellectual Philosophy and Literature. | |
| THEODORE W. DWIGHT, LL. D. | 37 Lafayette Place. |
| Professor of Municipal Law, and Warden of the Law School. | |

| NAMES. | RESIDENCES. |
|---|---|
| JOHN ORDRONAUX, LL. B., M. D. <br> Professor of Medical Jurisprudence. | 235 West 23d Street. |
| JOHN H. VAN AMRINGE, A. M. <br> Adjunct Professor of Mathematics, and Secretary of the Faculty of Arts. | 172 Lexington Av. |
| ALEXANDER H. STEPHENS, M. D., LL. D. <br> Emeritus Professor of Clinical Surgery. | 6 Lafayette Place. |
| JOHN TORREY, M. D., LL. D. <br> Emeritus Professor of Chemistry and Botany. | Columbia College. |
| JOSEPH M. SMITH, M. D. <br> Professor of Materia Medica and Clinical Medicine. | 11 East 17th Street. |
| ROBERT WATTS, M. D. <br> Professor of Anatomy. | 42 East 12th " |
| WILLARD PARKER, M. D. <br> Professor of the Principles and Practice of Surgery and Surgical Anatomy. | 37 East 12th " |
| CHANDLER R. GILMAN, M. D. <br> Professor of Obstetrics, Diseases of Women and Children, and Medical Jurisprudence. | 5 East 13th " |
| ALONZO CLARK, M. D., LL. D. <br> Professor of Pathology and Practical Medicine. | 30 East 21st " |
| JOHN C. DALTON, Jr., M. D. <br> Professor of Physiology and Microscopic Anatomy, and Registrar of the Medical Department. | 109 East 21st " |
| SAMUEL St.JOHN, M. D. <br> Professor of Chemistry. | 305 Fourth Avenue. |
| THOMAS M. MARKOE, M. D. <br> Adjunct Professor of Surgery. | 4 East 17th Street. |
| WILLIAM DETMOLD, M. D. <br> Professor of Military Surgery and Hygiene. | 103 Ninth " |
| OGDEN N. ROOD, A. M. <br> Professor of Mechanics and Physics. | Columbia College. |
| THOMAS EGLESTON, Jr., A. M., E. M. <br> Professor of Mineralogy and Metallurgy. | 10 Fifth Avenue. |
| T. GAILLIARD THOMAS, M. D. <br> Adjunct Professor of Obstetrics. | 86 Fifth " |

| NAMES. | RESIDENCES. |
|---|---|
| HENRY B. SANDS, M. D. — Demonstrator of Anatomy and Curator of the Museum. | 64 East 12th Street. |
| ERSKINE MASON, M. D. — Assistant Demonstrator of Anatomy. | 95 East 21st " |
| FOSTER SWIFT, M. D. — Assistant to the Professor of Obstetrics. | 54 West 26th " |
| WILLIAM H. CARMALT, M. D. — Assistant to the Professor of Physiology. | 24 West 23d " |
| JAMES L. LITTLE, M. D. — Assistant to the Professor of Surgery. | 268 West 42d " |
| GOUVERNEUR M. SMITH, M. D. — Librarian of the Medical Department. | 11 East 17th " |
| DUANE S. EVERSON, A. B. — Tutor in Greek and Latin, and Secretary to the President. | 16 West 28th " |
| FRANCIS L. VINTON, E. M. — Professor of Mining Engineering. | 5 Grace Court, Brooklyn Heights. |
| CHARLES F. CHANDLER, Ph. D. — Professor of Chemistry. | 246 East 51st Street. |
| WILLIAM A. POTTER, A. B. — Assistant in Analytical Chemistry. | 16 Gramercy Park. |
| JULIUS MAIER, Ph. D. — Assistant in Analytical Chemistry. | Hoboken. |
| ALBERT H. CHESTER — Assistant in Mineralogy. | Columbia College. |
| HENRY B. CORNWALL, A. B. — Assistant in General Chemistry. | 508 Seventh Avenue. |

# GRADUATES IN ARTS.

## 1758.

*Joshua Bloomer, (Rev.), A. M., S. T. D. 1790.
*Isaac Ogden, Judge Supr. Ct. Canada.
*Josiah Ogden.
*Samuel Provoost, (Rev.), A. M., S. T. D. Univ. Penn. 1786, Regent Univ. N. Y. S. 1784–87, Trustee 1787–1801 and Chairman 1795–1801, Bishop P. E. Ch. N. Y. 1787–1815. *1815
*Joseph Reade.
*Rudolph Ritzema, (Rev.), S. T. D. elsewhere.
*Philip Van Cortlandt, A. M., Lt.-Gov. N. Y.
*Samuel Verplanck, A. M. 1763, Gov. 1770.

8

## 1759.

*Epenetus Townsend, (Rev.), A. M.

## 1760.

*Samuel Bayard, A. M.
*Anthony Hoffman, A. M.
*Philip Livingston, A. M., Trustee 1797–1806.
*John Marston, A. M.
*Robert Watts, A. M.
*Isaac Wilkins, (Rev.), A. M., S. T. D. 1811.

6

## 1761.

*Henry Holland, A. M.
*Anthony Lispenard.
*Henry Van Dyck, (Rev.), A. M. 3

## 1762.

*Edward Antil, A. M.
*Henry Cuyler, A. M.
*John Grinnell.
*Alexander Leslie, A. M.
*Leonard Lispenard, Regent Univ. N. Y. S. 1784–7, Trustee 1787–90. *1790
*William Benj. Nicoll Maverick.
*Daniel Robert, (C. L.)

7

## 1763.

*Barent Cuyler, A. M.
*Abraham De Peyster, A. M.

2

## 1764.

*Richard Harison, (C. L.), A. M., D. C. L. Oxford, Del. to U. S. Constit. Conven. 1787, U. S. Dist.-Atty. N. Y., Recorder N. Y. C., Trustee 1788–1829 and Chairman of the Board 1823. *1829

*John Jay, (C. L.), A. M., LL. D. Harv. 1790 and Brown 1794, Del. to Congr. 1774, 1775, Mem. Prov. Conv. N. Y. 1776, Ch.-Just. N. Y. 1777, Prest. National Congr. 1778, Min. Plen. to Spain 1779, U. S. Peace Comr. 1781–3, U. S. Secy. For. Aff. 1784, Del. to Congr. 1784, Del. to N. Y. Constit. Conven. 1788, Ch.-Just. U. S. 1789–94, U. S. Envoy Ex. to Great Britain 1794, Gov. N. Y. 1795–1801. *1829

2

## 1765.

*Egbert Benson, (C. L.), A. M., LL.D. Union 1799 and Harv. 1808 and Dart. 1811, Tutor Union, Trustee 1804–1814, Atty.-Gen. N. Y., Judge Sup. Ct. N. Y., Ch. Judge U. S. Circuit Ct., Delegate American Congr., Repr. in Congr. *1833

*Richard Grant.

*Robert R. Livingston, (C. L.), A. M. and N. Jers., Recorder N. Y. City 1773, Deleg. Amer. Congr. 1775, 1780, Memb. N. Y. Constit. Conven. 1777, Chancell. N. Y. 1777–1801, U. S. Secy. For. Aff. 1781–3, U. S. Min. Plen. to France 1801–4. *1813

*Henry Lloyd, A. M. 1769.

*Arent Schuyler.

5

## 1766.

*James Barclay, A. M.

*Gerard Beekman, A. M.

*Richard Nicholls Colden.

*Richard D'Olier.

*Edward Nicoll, A. M.

*John Ray, A. M. 1773.

*Henry Rutgers, Capt. U. S. A., N. Y. Assemb.

*John Troup, A. M.

*John Troup, Jr., A. M.

*John Vardill, (Rev.), A. M., Fellow, Prof. Natural Law and History and Languages 1773–6.

*John Watts, A. M., Trustee 1789–1816, Judge Westchester Co. N. Y.

11

## 1767.

*William Laight, A. M.

## 1768.

*Charles Doughty, A. M., M. B. 1772.

*James Ludlow, A. M.

*Benjamin Moore, (Rev.), A. M., S. T. D. 1789, President *pro tem.* 1775–6, Prof. Rhet. and Log. 1784–7, Bishop P. E. Ch. N. Y. 1801–16, President 1801–11, Trustee 1802–13. *1816

*Gouverneur Morris, (C. L.), A. M., Memb. N. Y. Prov. Congr. 1775, Del. to Continent. Congr. 1777, Asst. Supt. Finance 1781–5, Del. to U. S. Constit. Conven. 1787, U. S. Min. to France 1792–4, U. S. Sen. 1800–3, Trustee 1805–16, Canal Com. N. Y. 1810–15. *1816

*John Stevens, (Eng.), A. M. *1838

*Peter Van Schaack, A. M. 1773, Commr. for revising Col. Stat. N. Y. 1773. *1832

*Gulian Verplanck, Speaker House Assemb. N. Y.

7

## 1769.

*Caleb Cooper, A. M. 1771.

## 1770.

*James Creighton, A. M.
*John Doughty, Aide to Gen. Knox U. S. A.
*Jonathan Graham, and Yale 1770.
*Richard Harris, A. M.
*William Hubbard, A. M.
*Stephen Lush, A. M.
*Philip Pell, A. M.

7

## 1771.

*Ichabod Best Barnet, A. M.
*Clement Cooke Clarke, A. M.
*John Copp, A. M.
*Henry De Wint, A. M.
*Thomas Knox.
*John Searle, A. M.

6

## 1772.

*Thomas Barclay, British Commr. under Treaty of 1783, H. B. M. Consul Gen. U. S., Col. H. B. M. Army.
*John Bowden, (Rev.), A. M., S. T. D. 1797, Prof. Mor. Phil., Bell. Lett. and Logic 1801–17. *1817
*John King.
*Nicholas Ogden.
*Peter Roebuck, A. M.
*Andrew Skeene.

6

## 1773.

*Cornelius Bogart.
*Frederick Philipse, Capt. Dragoons, British Army.
*Nathaniel Phillipse.
*Beverley Robinson, Lt.-Col. H. B. M. Army.
*Thomas Shreve.

5

## 1774.

*Isaac Abrahams.
*Robert Auchmuty.
*William Chandler.
*Edward Dunscomb, Officer U. S. Rev. Army, Trustee 1795–1814, Sheriff N. Y. C. 1810–11. *1814
*Nicholas Heyliger.
*John Jauncey.
*Henry Nicoll.
*George Ogilvie.
*John Rapelje.
*Benjamin Seaman.
*Edward Stevens, M. D. elsewhere.
*Robert Troup, (C. L.), LL. D. elsewhere, Maj. U. S. A., Judge U. S. Dist. Ct. N. Y., Trustee 1811–17.

12

## 1775.

*William Amory.
*Richard Auchmuty, Maj.-Gen. H. B. M. Army, India.
*Samuel Auchmuty, K. B., Lt.-Gen. H. B. M. Army.
*William Cock, A. M. 1790.
*Joseph Griswold.
*John W. Livingston.
*Jacobus Remsen.

7

## 1776.

*Samuel Bayard.
*James Devereux.
*Peter Kissam.
*Matthias Nicoll.
*Peter Ogden.
*Marinus Willett, Officer U. S.

Rev. Army, Sheriff N. Y. C. 1784–7, 1791–5, Mayor N. Y. C. 6

---

On the 6th of April, 1776, the College buildings were taken for military purposes. The College did not fully resume its functions till the close of the war; and no degrees were conferred till 1786. The following candidates had been admitted, but did not complete their course on account of the disturbed state of public affairs:

## In 1774.†

*Thomas Atwood.
*John Brickell.
*David Clarkson.
*Samuel Deall.
*James De Peyster.
*John Gaine.
*Alexander Hamilton, A. M. 1788 and Harv. 1792, LL. D. Dart. 1790 and N. Jers. 1791 and Harv. 1792 and Rutgers 1792, Capt. U. S. A. 1776, Lt.-Col. staff of Washington 1777, Memb. Congr. 1782, N. Y. Leg. 1786, Del. to U. S. Constit. Conven. 1787, Secy. Treasury U. S. 1789–95, Maj.-Gen. U. S. A. 1798, Trustee 1787–1804. *1804
*Tristrim Lowther.
*Schuyler Lupton.
*Edward Cornwallis Moncrieff.
*Daniel Moore.
*Paul Randall.
*Jacob Shaw.
*Horatio Smith.
*James Stiles.
*John Whitaker.

## In 1775.†

*Edward Kerin.
*Benjamin Kissam.
*Thomas Groesbeck Lynch.
*Thomas Lambert Moore, A. M. 1790.
*Jacob Morris.
*Augustus Nicoll.
*Marinus Oudenaarde.
*Peter Oudenaarde.

## In 1777.†

*James De Lancey Walton.
*William Walton.

---

## 1786.

*John Bassett, and Yale 1786, (Rev.), A. M., S. T. D. Will. 1804. *1824
*De Witt Clinton, (C. L.), A. M., N. Y. Assemb. 1797, N. Y. Sen. 1798–1802, 1805–1811, U. S. Sen. 1802–4, Mayor N. Y. C. 1803–7, 1809–10, 1811–15, Lt.-Gov. N. Y. 1811–13, N. Y. Canal Commr. 1816–24, Gov. N. Y. 1817–21, 1825–28. *1828
*Abraham Huron, A. M.
*George Livingston.
*Philip H. Livingston, A. M.
*Samuel Smith, A. M.
*Peter Steddiford, (Rev.), A. M.
*Francis Sylvester, (C. L.), A. M.
8

## 1787.

*Samuel Boyd, (C. L.), Trustee 1826–35.
*Nicholas Fonda.
*John C. Ludlow, (C. L.), A. M. 1793.
*Henry C. Van Schaack.
*John W. Yates, (B.)
5

## 1788.

*James Cochran, (C. L.), A.M.
*John Eccles.
*Brandt S. Lupton.

3

## 1789.

*John T. Bainbridge.
*James C. Duane, (C. L.)
*William Hurst.
*Henry Izard.
*William Lupton.
*John Mitchell Mason, (Rev.), A.M. N. Jers. 1794, S.T.D. Univ. Penn. 1804, Trustee 1795–1811, Provost 1811–16, Prest. Dickin. Coll. Penn. 1821–4. *1829
*Matthew Mesier.
*Peter Mesier, (C. L.)
*John Remsen, (C. L.)
*John P. Van Ness, A. M. 1845.

10

## 1790.

*David S. Bogart, and N. Jers. 1791, (Rev.) *1839
*Marmaduke Earle, (Rev.)
*Jonathan Freeman, (Rev.), A. M. N. Jers. 1809. *1822
*George Graham, U. S. Asst. Secy. State 1801–25.
*John Graham.
*Frederick Halsey.

6

## 1791.

Peter Anderson, A. M. 1795, M. D. 1795.
*Anthony Bleecker, (C. L.), A. M. 1797, Examiner in Chancery. *1827
*William Bleecker, (C. L.)
*William T. Broome, A. M. 1797.
*Walter L. Cochran.
*Pierre E. Fleming, A. M. 1797.
William Hendell, (Rev.), S. T. D. 1828.
*Cave Jones, (Rev.), A. M., S. T. D. elsewhere.
Isaac Knevils.
John Knevils.
*Lancaster Lupton.
John W. Mulligan, (C. L.), A. M. 1834.
*Charles Ogden, (M.)
*Thomas L. Ogden, (C. L.), Trustee 1817–44. *1844
*Daniel Paris, (C. L.), N. Y. Sen.
*George Rapelje, (C. L.)
*Frederic Van Horne, (Rev.), A. M. 1791.
*William B. Verplanck.
*Nathan White, (C. L.), A. M. 1791.
*Jesse Woodhull.
*James Woods, (C. L.), A. M. 1804.

21

## 1792.

*Gerard Beekman.
*Cornelius Brower.
*Alexander Hosack, M. D. 1797.
*John B. Johnson.
*James W. Nicholson.
*John L. Norton.
*Jotham Post, Jr., (M.), A.M.
*Alexander Proudfit, (Rev.), A. M. Union 1792, S. T. D. Williams 1812. *1844
*Jacob Sickles.
Samuel Smith.
*George Taylor, (M.)
*William Taylor, (M.)

12

## 1793.

*John Brower.

*George Clinton, Jr., (C. L.), Repr. in Congr.
*William Cutting, (C. L.), Sheriff N. Y. C. 1807–8.
*Cornelius Decker, (M.)
*George I. Eacker, (C. L.), A. M. 1797.
*Samuel Gilford, Jr., (M.)
*Charles D. Gould, (M.), A. M. 1797.
*Robert Heaton, Jr., A. M. 1797, U. S. A.
*John I. Johnson.
*Edward W. Laight, (C. L.), Trustee 1816–51 and Chairman 1849–50.
*Henry W. Ludlow, (F.)
*Henry Masterton, (C. L.)
*Philip Milledoler, (Rev.), A. M. 1797, S. T. D. Univ. Penn., Prof. Theol. and Prest. Rutg. Coll 1825–35. *1852
*John Nicholl, A. M. 1797.
*Robert B. Norton, (C. L.)
*Abraham Ogden, (M.)
*James Parker, (M.), Repr. in Congr.
*Jonathan Pearsee, (C. L.)
*Valentine H. Peters, (M.)
John S. Schermerhorn, (M.)
*Gilbert Smith, M. D. elsewhere.
*Thomas R. Smith, (M.)
*James S. Stringham, A. M. 1797, M. D. Univ. Edinb. 1799, Prof. Chem. 1802–13, Prof. Med. Juris. Coll. Phys. and Surg. N. Y. 1813–17. *1817
*Thomas Thompson.
*Cornelius A. Van Horne, (M.)
*Elias B. Woodward, (C. L.), Judge N. W. Territory.

26

# 1794.

*William Cocks.
*John E. Fisher, (M.)
*John Forbes.
*Levi P. Graham, (C. L.)
*Montgomery Hunt, (C. L.)
*Jacob J. Janeway, (Rev.), A. M.
*Peter Augustus Jay, (C. L.), A. M. and Yale 1798, LL. D. 1835 and Harv. 1831, Trustee 1812–17 and 1823–43 and Chairman 1832, Recorder N. Y. C. 1819–20, Memb. N. Y. Constit. Conven., Prest. N. Y. Hist. Soc. *1843
*Cyrus King, (C. L.), Repr. in Congr.
*Leffert Lefferts, (C. L.), Judge Kings Co. N. Y.
*Jacob O. Mackie, (M.)
*Samuel B. Malcolm, (C. L.)
*Gilbert Milligan, M. D. elsewhere.
*John B. Stringham, M. D. elsewhere.
*Peter G. Stuyvesant, (C. L.), Prest. N. Y. Hist. Soc.
*Thomas Ustick, (C. L.)

15

# 1795.

*George Barculoo, (Rev.)
*Philip Duryee, (Rev.)
*Bernard Elliot.
*John J. Faesch.
*John Ferguson, (C. L.), Mayor N. Y. C. 1815, Naval Off. N. Y., Trustee 1830–32. *1832
*Thomas Herring, (M.), A. M.
*James Inglis, (Rev.) *1820
*Nicholas Jones, (Rev.)
*Adolph C. Lent, A. M., M. D. 1798.
*John B. Linn, (Rev.), A. M., S. T. D. Univ. Penn. *1804
Silvanus Miller, (C. L.), N. Y. Assemb., Surrogate N. Y. C. 1800–20, Examiner in Chanc.
*John H. Meier, (Rev.), A. M. 1804.
*John Morrison.
*Alexander Phœnix, (Rev.)
*Sidney Phœnix.

*Thomas Phœnix, (C. L.), Dist.-Atty. N. Y. C.
*Robert Remsen.
*John Brodhead Romeyn, (Rev.), A. M. Union 1797, S. T. D. N. Jers. 1809, Trustee 1809–25 and Clerk 1811–15, Trustee N. Jers. 1809–25. *1825
*William Ross, (C. L.), Speaker N. Y. Assemb.
*Henry Sands, (C. L.), A. M.
*Benjamin Seaman, (C. L.)
*James B. Temple, Capt. H. B. M. Army.
*Daniel D. Tompkins, (C. L.), N. Y. Assemb. 1801, Memb. N. Y. Constit. Conven. 1801, Repr. in Congr. 1804, Just. Supr. Ct. N. Y. 1804, Gov. N. Y. 1807–17, V.-Pres. U. S. 1817–25. *1825
*Pierre C. Van Wyck, (C. L.), Dist.-Atty. N. Y. C., Rec. N. Y. C.
*Effingham Warner, (Rev.)
*Renssalaer Westerlo.

26

## 1796.

David Barclay.
Henry Cruger, Jr.
Philip Fisher.
*Andrew S. Garr, (C. L.) *1859
*David S. Jones, (C. L.), LL. D. Allegh. Coll. Penn., Corporation Counsel N. Y. C. 1813–16, Trustee 1820–48, Trustee Gen. Theol. Sem. P. E. Ch. 1822–48, Judge Queens Co. N. Y. 1840–1. *1848
*Edward P. Livingston, (C. L.), Lt.-Gov. N. Y. and Regent Univ. N. Y. S.
Samuel Nicholson.
Gouverneur Ogden.
William Rattoone.
*Josiah Shippey, (M.)
*Charles Taylor, (M.)
*William Turk, M. D. elsewhere, U. S. N.
Lawrence Van Buskirk.
Adrian C. Van Slyck.
*John Watts.

15

## 1797.

*William Bard, (M.), Trustee 1840–53. *1853
*Robert Boyd, (C. L.)
*Archibald Bruce, M. D. Edinburgh.
George W. Clinton.
*Henry Kunze.
*Abraham R. Lawrence, (M.), Naval Off. N. Y.
*William Le Conte.
*Isaac A. Van Hook, (Rev.), A. M. 1803.
*William Van Ness, (C. L.), Judge U. S. Circuit Ct. S. Dist. N. Y.

9

## 1798.

*Joseph Bainbridge.
Thomas Bay.
*George Brinckerhoff, (C. L.), A. M.
Jacob Brower, A. M.
*Rudolph Bunner, (C. L.), Repr. in Congr.
David Codwise, (C. L.)
*George Davis, A. M.
*Charles Graham, (C. L.)
*John T. Irving, (C. L.), Trustee 1818–38, Judge Supr. Ct. N. Y. *1838
*Philip L. Jones.
*William B. Keese, (C. L.)
Washington McKnight, (Rev.), A. M. 1804.
*Clement C. Moore, A. M., LL. D. 1829, Trustee 1813–57 and Clerk 1815–50, Prof. Hebrew and Greek Lit. Gen. Theol. Sem. P. E. Ch. N. Y. 1821–50, Emeritus 1850–63. *1863

*Samuel Moore, M. D. elsewhere.
*William Ogden, (M.)
*William Rhinelander, (M.), A. M. 1804.
Lewis Sands.
James Walsh.

18

## 1799.

*John Christie, (Rev.)
*Peter D. Fraligh, (Rev.)
*Lewis Le Conte.
*James Livingston.
*James Lynch, (C. L.), Just. Mar. Ct. N. Y. C.
*T. Thornton Mackaness, A. M.
*James R. Manley, A. M., M. D. 1803, Prest. N. Y. S. Med. Soc. 1825–26. *1851
Alexander Murray.
Philip Myer, (Rev.)
*Stephen Price.
*Samuel Riker, Jr., (C. L.)
*Jacob Schoonmaker, (Rev.), A. M.
*Arthur J. Stansbury, (C. L.)
Peter I. Van Pelt, (Rev.), A. M. 1803.
*Abraham Varick, Jr., (C. L.)
*John V. Varick, (M.)
Arthur M. Walter, A. M.
David Wright.

18

## 1800.

John J. De Peyster.
Samuel Halstead, (M.)
*Philip Hamilton.
Samuel Harris.
John Henry.
John Huyler, A. M.
Robert S. Livingston, (C. L.)
John McKinnon, A. M.
*Nicholas I. Quackenbos, M. D. 1802, A. M.
Thomas W. Rathbone.
*Samson Simson, (C. L.)
*Charles F. Thomas.
*Matthew Tillary, M. D. elsewhere.
John Y. Ward.
*George Wilson, (C. L.), A. M.
*Peter Wilson, (C. L.), A. M. *1826

16

## 1801.

*John Anthon, (C. L.), LL. D. 1861. *1863
Robert Benson, (M.)
*Abraham L. Blauvelt.
*Samuel Bogert.
*Thomas Bolton, (C. L.)
*John Furman.
John Gosman, (Rev.)
*John Nitchie, (C. L.)
*Lewis M. Ogden.
*Henry Schenck.
*Henry H. Schieffelin.
*Gabriel Tichenor.
Gulian Crommelin Verplanck, A. M. 1821, LL. D. 1835 and Amh. 1834 and Hob. 1835, N. Y. Assemb. 1820, Prof. Ev. Christian. Gen. Theol. Sem. P. E. Ch. 1821, Repr. in Congr. 1825–33, N. Y. Sen., Trustee 1821–6, Pres. Commr. Emigr. N. Y. 1846–.
*Samuel Armstrong Walsh, M. D. Coll. Phys. and Surg. N. Y. 1811.
*Gabriel Winter, (C. L.)

15

## 1802.

*Alexander M. Beebe.
*John P. Crosby, and Yale 1802 and N. Jers. 1802. *1806
*John Delafield, (B.)
*William Gardner.
*George W. Gosman.
*Francis L. Harison, (C. L.)
*James Jones.
*Henry Laight, (C. L.)
*Leffert Lefferts, (C. L.)

*Robert Macomb, (C. L.)
*John W. Macomb.
Nathaniel F. Moore, A. M., LL. D. 1825, Adj. Prof. Greek and Lat. Lang. 1817–20 and Prof. 1820–35, Librarian 1837–9, President 1842–9, Trustee 1842–51.
*Archibald McVickar, (C. L.)
*James McVickar, (M.) *1836
Isaac Ogden, (M.)
*William Ogilvie.
*Henry Priest.
*Billopp B. Seaman.
*James Tillary, M. D. elsewhere.
*Hubert Van Wagenen.
20

## 1803.

George H. Atkinson.
John Bay.
John Bowne.
Thomas Crolius.
Augustus Fleming.
*Edward R. Jones, (M.), Trustee 1831–38.
Gouverneur Kemble, (M.), Repr. in Congr., Memb. N. Y. S. Constit. Conven. 1846.
Peter Kemble.
Edward Kemeys.
*John L. Lawrence, (C .L.), N. Y. Assemb., Trustee 1830–49, Treasurer 1833–49, Comptr. N. Y. C. *1849
John Le Conte, M. D. elsewhere.
*George C. Quackenbos, M. D. elsewhere. *1858
*William Remsen, (C. L.)
*Henry F. Rogers, (M.)
Alpheus Sherman, (C. L.), N. Y. Assemb., N. Y. Sen.
*John C. Stevens.
Samuel W. Thomson.
Robert Watts.
18

## 1804.

*Samuel Akerly, A. M.
*John W. Barnum.
*William D. Blackwell.
*George Bryar.
Elisha Camp, (C. L.), Asst. U. S. Dist.-Atty N. Dist. N. Y., Capt. U. S. V. 1812.
*Cornelius T. Demarest, (Rev.), A. M. 1813.
*Jeremiah I. Drake, A. M.
*William Edgar.
*William Gracie, and N. Jers. 1804.
*John T. B. Graham.
*Henry B. Hagerman.
Alexander Hamilton, Col. N. Y. S. 1812, U. S. Consul at Havana, U. S. Boundary Commr.
*Richard N. Harison.
*James D. Livingston.
*William L. Lytton, A. M., M. D. 1807.
John McVickar, (Rev.), A. M. 1818, S. T. D. 1825, Prof. Moral and Int. Phil., Rhetoric, Belle-Lett. and Pol. Econ. 1817–57, Prof. Ev. Nat. and Rev. Relig. 1857–64, Emeritus 1864–.
*Edward Manley.
*John Mitchell.
*Joseph Neilson, A. M. 1805, LL. D. elsewhere, Prof. Languages Rutger's Coll.
*William M. Price.
*Philip Rhinelander.
Samuel Rogers.
*David M. Ross, A. M.
*Robert Seaman.
*John I. Sickles, A. M.
*Thomas D. Smith.
*Charles Stewart.
*John R. Thompson, (Rev.), A. M.
*James Talcott Watson, and Yale 1804 and N. Jers. 1804.
*John Watts, Jr., M. D. Ed-

inburgh 1809, Prof. Pract. of Physic Rutg. Coll. N. J., Pres. Coll. Phys. and Surg. N. Y. 1826–31, Trustee 1824–31. *1831

30

## 1805.

Peter Allaire (M.)
*James Bibby.
*Leonard A. Bleecker.
*William Cock.
*Benjamin U. Coles.
*Joab G. Cooper, (Rev.), A. M.
*James L. Fine.
*James Fleming.
*Alexander Gunn, (Rev.), A. M. and N. Jers. 1805, S. T. D. Allegh. Coll. Penn. *1829
*Richard Hatfield.
James A. Hamilton, LL. D. Hamilton, U. S. Dist.-Atty. N. Y., Secy. State N. Y.
Robert Jaques, A. M.
Thomas Lefferts.
Thomas McGahagan.
*Henry Ustick Onderdonk, (Rev.), A. M., M. D. 1810, S. T. D. 1827, Bishop P. E. Ch. Penn. 1827–58. *1858
*Edmund H. Pendleton, (C. L.), Judge Dutchess Co. N. Y.
Abraham Purdy, A. M. 1810.
*Edward Seaman.
John T. Smith.
*Robert I. Watts.

20

## 1806.

*John V. Bartow, (Rev.), A. M.
*George Boyd, (Rev.) *1850
*John Chrystie.
John P. De Wint.
William E. Dunscomb, (C. L.)
*Gilbert O. Fowler, (C. L.)
*Jonathan B. Gosman, (Rev.)
*James McCullen.
*Robert B. Ancœas McLeod, (Rev.)
*Cornelius Miller, (C. L.)
*David Moore, (Rev.), S. T. D. elsewhere. *1856
*Samuel W. Moore, M. D. 1810. *1854
*Ferris Pell, (C. L.)
*David Quackinbush, M. D. elsewhere.
Samuel B. Romaine, (C. L.), N. Y. Assemb.
*Frederic Roorbach, (C. L.)
*Cornelius Schermerhorn, (C. L.)
*Philip Schuyler, U. S. Consul at Liverpool, N. Y. Assemb. *1865
John A. Smith, (C. L.)
John L. Tillinghast, (C. L.)

20

## 1807.

Egbert Benson, Jr.
John L. Bronk.
John H. Brouwer.
*William E. Burrell, M. D. Coll. Phys. and Surg. N. Y. 1811.
George R. Copland.
Henry S. Dodge, A. M.
Robert Gosman.
John H. Hill, (Rev.), A. M. 1845, Missionary to Greece.
Philip M. Holmes.
Daniel Mack.
*Peter T. Marselis, (C. L.)
William H. Maxwell, A. M. 1827.
Simeon Remsen.
*James Renwick, A. M., LL. D. 1829, Lecturer in Nat. and Exper. Phil. and Chem. 1813, Trustee 1817–20, Prof. Nat. and Exper. Phil. and Chem. 1820–53, Emeritus 1853–63. *1863
George P. Rogers.
Dirck B. Stockholm.

Peter V. C. Tappan.
Cornelius Van Buren.
James Van Cortlandt.
Theodore Van Cortlandt.
Theodore V. W. Varick, A.M.
Philip G. Van Wyck.
Charles A. Williamson.

22

## 1808.

*William Atkinson, (M.)
*William Berrian, (Rev.), S.T. D. 1828, Rector Trinity Parish N. Y. C. 1830–62, Trustee 1832–62. *1862
*Lionel Brown.
*Timothy Clowes.
*Henry M. Francis, A. M., M. D. elsewhere.
*James Inderwick, M. D. elsewhere, U. S. N.
*Robert McCartee, (Rev.), A. M., S. T. D. 1831. *1865
John McKnight, (Rev.)
Hugh Maxwell, (C. L.), A. M. 1816, Dist.-Atty. N. Y. C. 1819–29, U. S. Collector Port of N. Y.
Frederick Muzzy, (C. L.)
John W. Philips, (T.)
*Edward Post, M. D. Edinburgh.
William C. Rhinelander, Jr.
Henry H. Ross, (C. L.)
Gilbert H. Sayres, (Rev.), S. T. D. 1863.
James A. Stevens.
*William Stuart, (M.)
*Daniel Van Mater.
Henry Vethake, A. M., LL. D. 1836, Lect. in Math. and Geog. 1813, Prof. Math. and Nat. Phil. Rutg. Coll. 1813–17 and in Coll. N. Jers. 1817–21 and in Dickinson Coll. 1821–29 and in Univ. N. Y. C. 1832–35, Prest. Washington Coll. Va. 1835–36, Prof. Math. Univ. Penn. 1836–54 and Provost and Prof. Moral and Int. Phil. Univ. Penn. 1854–59.
Peter D. Vroom, Jr., (C. L.), A. M. 1812, LL. D. 1837 and N. Jers. 1850, N. Jers. Legis. 1826–29, Gov. and Chancellor N. Jers. 1829–36, Repr. in Congr. 1838–40, Memb. N. Jers. State Constit. Conven. 1844, U. S. Envoy Ex. and Min. Plen. to Prussia 1853–57.
*Henry Watts.

21

## 1809.

*Thomas S. Aspinwall.
Samuel Berrian.
Edward N. Bibby, M. D. elsewhere.
John Brady, (Rev.), A. M.
*John Cadle, A. M., M. D. Coll. Phys. and Surg. N. Y. 1822.
Gerrit Conrey.
Edward Copland.
*Cornelius R. Duffie, (Rev.), A. M. 1813. *1827
Thomas Duggan.
John Fine, (C. L.), A. M., Memb. N. Y. Assemb., Repr. in Congr., Judge St. Lawrence Co. N. Y.
Alexander Fleming.
Alfred Floyd.
*John Wakefield Francis, A. M., M. D. Coll. Phys. and Surg. N. Y. 1809, LL. D. 1860, Prof. Mat. Med. Univ. N. Y. C. *1861
James N. Gifford, (M.)
Henry Green.
John C. Hamilton, (C. L.)
D. Murray Hoffman, (C. L.), Judge Supr. Ct. N. Y.
Samuel Jackson.
Ravaud Kearny, (Rev.), A. M.
Jackson Kemper, S. T. D. 1829, Bishop P. E. Ch. Wis. 1835–.

*Henry McVickar, (M.)
*Benjamin Tredwell Onderdonk, (Rev.), A.M. 1816, S. T.D. 1826, Trustee 1824–53, Bishop P. E. Ch. N.Y. 1830–61. *1861
Walter F. Osgood, A. M.
Robert J. Renwick.
James Stryker, (C. L.), A. M. 1813, Judge Buffalo N.Y.
William Turnbull.
William E. Wyatt, (Rev.), A. M. 1816, S. T. D. elsewhere.

27

# 1810.

*John Agnew.
*Andrew Anderson, M. D. Coll. Phys. and Surg. N. Y. 1813.
Francis Child, A. M. 1816.
*David A. Clarkson, (M.)
*George Codwise.
William De Peyster.
Israel D. Disosway, (F.)
*Jacob Dyckman, A. M., M. D. Coll. Phys. and Surg. N. Y. 1813.
Robert Emmet, (C. L.), Just. Supr. Ct. N. Y. C.
Theodosius O. Fowler.
*James C. Garrison, A. M. 1816, M. D. elsewhere, U. S. Navy.
Joseph Greenleaf, (C. L.)
*Peter F. Hunn, (C. L.)
*Charles J. Kip.
Horatio G. Lewis.
John M. McDonald, (C. L.)
*John McGregor, (T.)
*Benjamin Moore (M.)
George W. Morton, (C. L.), U. S. Commissioner N.Y. C.
John L. Morton, (F.)
*Ava Neal, (Rev.), A. M.
Waldron B. Post, (M.)
John Slidell, (C. L.), U. S. Dist.-Atty. for La. 1829–33, U. S. Min. to Mexico 1845 and to Central America 1853, Repr. in Congr. and U. S. Sen.
*Francis B. Stevens. *1811
*Richard Stevens, M. D. elsewhere. *1828
*James Stoughton, (C. L.), A. M. *1819
*Paschal N. Strong, (Rev.), A. M. N. Jers. 1818, S. T. D. elsewhere, Trustee 1822–5. *1825
*Jacob Townsend, (C. L.)
*Charles Watts, (C. L.), Judge Dist. Ct. New Orleans. *1850

29

# 1811.

*Gregory T. Bedell, (Rev.), A. M. 1816, S. T. D. elsewhere. *1834
John Brown, (Rev.), A. M. 1815.
John Campbell.
Ebenezer Close, A. M. 1815.
John Covert.
George Douglass.
Jacobus Dyckman.
Charles G. Ferris, A. M. 1816.
*David H. Fraser, A. M. 1815, M. D. Coll. Phys. and Surg. N. Y. 1818. *1818
Richard Freeke.
James W. Gerard, (C. L.), A. M. 1816, LL. D. 1863.
Benjamin Haight, A. M. 1816.
*William H. Harison, Trustee 1838–1860. *1860
William H. Hart.
William Hogan, Repr. in Congr.
Peter V. B. Livingston, U. S. Min. to Cent. America.
Thomas W. Ludlow, Trustee 1833–6.
Jackson Odell.
George B. Purdy.
Charles Rapelye, A. M. 1820.
*John R. Rhinelander, M. D. Coll. Phys. and Surg. N. Y. 1824, Prof. Anat. Coll. Phys. and Surg. 1834–9.

John N. Talman, A. M. 1815.
George J. Watts.

23

## 1812.

Albert Ammerman, (Rev.)
*Matthias Bruen, Jr., (Rev.), A. M.
John A. Burtis.
*William Creighton, (Rev.), S.T.D. 1830, elected Bishop P. E. Ch. N. Y. and declined, Prest. Gen. Conven. P. E. Ch. U. S., Trustee 1828–40. *1865
James F. De Peyster, (M.), Capt. U. S. A. 1814.
*Alexander Duer, (C. L.) *1819
*Richard Duryee, (M.)
*Lindley Murray Hoffman, (M.) *1861
*Ogden Hoffman, (C. L.), Midshipman U. S. N. 1814, Repr. in Congr., Dist.-Atty N. Y. C., Atty.-Gen. N. Y., Trustee 1833–56. *1856
Benjamin R. Kissam, M. D. Coll. Phys. and Surg. N. Y. 1819.
Augustine N. Lawrence, (B.)
*Philip K. Lawrence, A. M. 1818.
*Cornelius Low, (C. L.) *1849
*Peter Mackie, Jr.
Edward McVickar.
*John W. B. Murray, A. M., M. D. elsewhere. *1818
*Matthew C. Paterson, (C. L.), A. M. 1819, Dist.-Atty. N. Y. C.
Jacob A. Robertson, (M.), A. M. 1818.
*John Smyth Rogers, M. D. Coll. Phys. and Surg. N. Y. 1821, Prof. Chem. and Min. Trinity, Prof. Mat. Med. N. Y. Coll. of Pharmacy. *1851
*John A. Sidell, (C. L.)
John B. Stevenson, A. M. 1816, M. D. Coll. Phys. and Surg. N. Y. 1816.
John Swartwout.
*Peter S. Townsend, A. M. 1816, M. D. Coll. Phys. and Surg. N. Y. 1816.
*Egerton L. Winthrop, M. D. Coll. Phys. and Surg. N. Y. 1817. *1834

24

## 1813.

*Henry Anthon, (Rev.), A. M., S. T. D. 1832. *1861
William Bailey.
*John Brodhead Beck, A. M. 1818, M. D. Coll. Phys. and Surg. N. Y. 1817, Prof. Mat. Med. Coll. Phys. and Surg. 1826–51, Trustee 1838–51. *1851
*James J. Bowden, (Rev.)
William Boyd.
*George W. Bruen, (M.), A. M.
Richard F. Cadle, (Rev.), A.M.
Thomas L. Davies.
*Robert Hyslop, (M.) *1816
William Kemble, (M.)
Thomas C. Mitchell, A. M.
Nicholas Morris, Jr., A. M.
Thomas C. Murray, A. M. 1818.
Nathaniel G. Pendleton.
Robert Ray, (C. L.), A. M. 1817, Trustee 1849–.
Alexander H. Robertson, A. M.
*Hugh Smith, (Rev.), A. M., S. T. D. 1838. *1849
John Varick.

18

## 1814.

John H. Ball.
James Brooks.
Cornelius Davis.
*William H. Heyer.
Benjamin Hilton.
Allen Jackson, A. M. 1821.
Henry R. Judah.
*James M. Pendleton, A. M. 1819, M. D. Coll. Phys. and Surg. N. Y. 1818. *1832

Theophilus Russel.
George F. Talman, (C. L.) Corporation Counsel N. Y. C. 1838–9.
Ferdinand Vandewater.
11

# 1815.

Charles Anthon, LL. D. 1831, Adj. Prof. Greek and Latin Lang. 1820–30, Jay Prof. Greek and Latin Lang. 1830–57 and Rect. Gram. School 1830–64, Jay Prof. Greek Lang. and Lit. 1857–.
*James W. Berrian.
*Archibald R. Bogardus.
*Robert G. L. De Peyster, (M.)
*Archibald Gracie, Jr., (M.) *1865
*William S. Heyer, (Rev.), A. M.
*John Hone, Jr., (M.)
*William Ironside.
*John Q. Jones, (C. L.)
*Leonard W. Kip, (C. L.), A. M. 1820. *1863
Philip Mesier Lydig, (M.)
*John L. Mason, (C. L.), A. M., Judge Supr. Ct. N. Y., Trustee 1848–53.
*Francis Morton.
*Frederic W. Rhinelander, (M.)
James I. Roosevelt, Jr., (C. L.), Judge Supr. Ct. N. Y.
*Robert Charles Sands, (Au.), A. M. *1832
*Robert Seney, (Rev.)
*Henry Hamlin Van Amringe, (Rev.), A. M. *1862
James S. Watkins, M. D. Coll. Phys. and Surg. N. Y. 1817.
19

# 1816.

Abel T. Anderson, (C. L.), A. M.
*John D. Campbell, (C. L.), A. M. 1820. *1852
*Richard Codman, (M.) *1847
Frederic De Peyster, Jr., (C. L.), A. M., Milit. Secy. to Gov. Clinton 1825–8, Mastery in Chancery for 17 years, Prest. N. Y. Historical Society.
*Maurice W. Dwight, (Rev.), A. M. 1820, S. T. D. elsewhere.
*James Wallis Eastburn, (Rev.), A. M. *1819
Isaac Ferris, (Rev.), A. M., S. T. D. Union 1833, LL. D. 1853, Chancell. Univ. N. Y. C. 1852–.
John Ireland, Jr., (F.)
*John E. Mowatt, (M.)
*Daniel L. M. Peixotto, A. M. 1823, M. D. Coll. Phys. and Surg. N. Y. 1819.
*Samuel G. Raymond, (C. L.), A. M., Memb. N. Y. Assemb. *1850
John J. Robertson, (Rev.), S. T. D. elsewhere.
*James Romeyn, (Rev.), S. T. D. 1838, elected Prof. of Rhet. Rutg. Coll. and declined.
*John M. Smith, (Rev.), A. M. Prof. in Wesl. Univ. Conn. *1832
*Samuel L. Steer, (F.), Speaker Lower House of Louisiana.
*Thomas M. Strong, (Rev.), A. M. 1820, S. T. D. elsewhere.
*Adrian Vandeveer, A. M., M. D. Coll. Phys. and Surg. N. Y. 1818. *1857
17

# 1817.

*John M. Cannon, (C. L.) *1835
James P. F. Clarke, (Rev.)
*Matthias O. Dayton, (C. L.)
Manton Eastburn, (Rev.), A. M., S. T. D. 1835, Bishop P. E. Ch. Mass. 1842–.
*Isaac Fisher, (Rev.), A. M. *1839
*Seymour P. Funk, (Rev.), A. M. 1821. *1828

Samuel L. Gouverneur.
John Grigg, (Rev.), A. M.
Daniel Phœnix Ingraham, (C. L.), LL. D. 1860, Just. Supr. Ct. N. Y.
*Benjamin Isherwood, A. M., M. D. Coll. Phys. and Surg. N. Y. 1820 *1822
William Lowerre, (C. L.), A. M.
Edmund Ludlow.
*William Minturn.
*John Neilson, Jr., A. M., M. D. Coll. Phys. and Surg. N. Y. 1821. *1858
Meredith Ogden (M.)
*Richard Ray, A. M. *1839
Edward N. Rogers, A. M.
*Samuel D. Rogers, (M.) *1850
18

## 1818.

Henry James Anderson, A. M., M. D. Coll. Phys. and Surg. N. Y. 1824, LL. D. 1850, Prof. of Math. Analyt. Mech. and Phys. Ast. 1825–43, Trustee 1851–.
Daniel Bonnett.
*Richard Varick Dey, (Rev.), A. M. and Yale 1823. *1837
*Frederick Fairlie, (C. L.)
*Peter Forrester, A. M. Rutg., M. D. Coll. Phys. and Surg. N. Y. 1822. *1837
Robert Gracie, and Harv. 1818 and Yale 1825, (M.), A. M.
*Henry Hone, (M.)
Richard F. Kemble, (C. L.)
William Beach Lawrence, A. M. 1823, Secy. U. S. Legat. at London, Governor of R. I.
James Lenox, A. M. and N. Jers. 1821, Trustee N. J. 1823–57.
*John H. Lloyd.
*Alexander B. McLeod.
Gerard W. Morris, (C. L.), Trustee 1851–55.
*John O'Blenis.
George D. Post, (C. L.)
*Clarence D. Sackett, (C. L.)
*William Staley, A. M.
*Abraham D. Wilson, A. M., M. D. Coll. Phys. and Surg. N. Y. 1821.
18

## 1819.

Henry N. Cruger, (C. L.), A. M. 1823.
Gabriel Poillon Disosway, (C. L.), A. M. and Wesl. 1833, Member N. Y. Assembly 1849.
*Peter Dykers, M. D. Coll. Phys. and Surg. N. Y. 1823. *1845
*Andrew Hamersley, M. D. Coll. Phys. and Surg. N. Y. 1823.
Edward P. Heyer, (M.)
Walter E. Heyer, (M.)
William L. Johnson, (Rev.), A. M.
*Charles Jones. *1854
George Jones.
*Henry J. Lowerre, (C. L.), A. M. *1830
George J. Rogers, (M.)
*James H. Roosevelt, (C. L.) A. M.
James S. Rumsey, M. D. Coll. Phys. and Surg. N. Y. 1824.
Richard L. Schieffelin, (C. L.), A. M.
*John L. Suckley, A. M. 1823, M. D. Coll. Phys. and Surg. N. Y. 1823. *1836
Samuel Verplanck, (C. L.), A. M.
Thomas L. Wells, (C. L.), Trustee 1837–59.
*Marinus Willett, Jr., M. D. Coll. Phys. and Surg. N. Y. 1823. *1840
*Richard Wynkoop, (Rev.), A. M.
19

## 1820.

William Betts, (C. L.), A. M., LL. D. 1850, Trustee 1842– and Clerk 1850–, Prof. of Law 1848–54.
*John B. Bleecker, (M.) *1831
Joseph H. Coit, (Rev.), S. T. D. 1855.
Cornelius Ryerrs Disosway, (C. L.), A. M. Wesl. 1838.
*James Johnstone, (C. L.) *1854
Samuel Roosevelt Johnson, (Rev.), A. M., S. T. D. 1848, Prof. Divinity Gen. Theolog. Sem. P. E. Ch.
Henry Lawrence, (M.)
*Philip E. Milledoler, (Rev.), M. D. Coll. Phys. and Surg. N. Y. 1824, A. M. Rutg. 1827.
John Mitchell, (C. L.), A. M.
William Mitchell, (C. L.), A. M., LL. D. 1863, Master in Chancery N. Y. 1840–43, Just. Supr. Ct. N. Y. State 1850–58.
Archibald G. Rogers, (C. L.)
Rutsen Suckley, (C. L.)
*John R. Townsend, (C. L.) *1846

13

## 1821.

*William B. Barnes, (B.)
*Peter A. Cowdrey, (C. L.), A. M. *1852
*Isaac F. Craft, (M.)
William D. Craft, (C. L.)
George H. Fisher, (Rev.), S. T. D. elsewhere, Trustee 1851–55.
*William Forsyth.
William N. Gibert, (C. L.) *1851
Frederic Philipse Gouverneur, (C. L.)
*William P. Hawes, (C. L.), A. M.
*William Inglis, (C. L.), Judge Ct. Common Pleas N. Y. 1839–44. *1863
Pierre M. Irving, (C. L.)
*Thomas Kermit.
*Elisha S. King, (C. L.)
*Isaac Low, A. M.
Stephen H. Meeker, (Rev.), A. M.
William H. Munn, (C. L.), A. M.
Samuel Ogden, (M.)
Edwin Post, (M.)
*Henry A. V. Post.
George Shrady.
*John C. Slack, (T.)
*Charles E. Stagg, (M.)
*Peter Stagg, (C. L.)
*Junius Thompson, A. M. 1825, M. D. Coll. Phys. and Surg. N. Y. 1825.
*John Tiebout, Jr., A. M., M. D. Coll. Phys. and Surg. N. Y. 1825.
*William Turner, A. M., M. D. elsewhere. *1858
*Gerrit G. Van Wagenen, Trustee 1845–58 and Treasurer 1849–58. *1858
*John H. Waddell, A. M.
Henry John Whitehouse, (Rev.), A. M., Bishop P. E. Ch. Ill. 1851–.
George Wilkes, M. D. Coll. Phys. and Surg. N. Y. 1824.

30

## 1822.

George Abeel, (M.)
*George W. Dawson, (M.)
*Peter F. Dustan, (C. L.)
*John M. Glover, A. M. Yale 1825, M. D. Coll. Phys. and Surg. N. Y. 1826. *1832
*Josiah D. Harris, A. M., M. D. Coll. Phys. and Surg. N. Y. 1826. *1833
*Edwin Holt, 1826.
Henry P. Jones, (C. L.)
Theodore F. King, M. D. Coll. Phys. and Surg. N. Y. 1827.
N. Gouverneur Kortwright, (C. L.)

Anson Livingston, (C. L.)
Carroll Livingston.
Edward N. Mead, (Rev.), A. M. 1833, S. T. D. 1861, Secy. Trustees Gen. Theo. Sem.
Adrian H. Müller, (M.)
*Alexander H. Paterson, (M.)
Alfred C. Post, M. D. Coll. Phys. and Surg. N. Y. 1827, Prof. Surgery Univ. N. Y. C.
*John Lloyd Stephens, (C. L.), A. M. 1827, U. S. Special Embassador to Central America 1839, Del. to N. Y. S. Constit. Conven. 1846. *1852
*Thomas W Tucker, (C. L.) *1854
Alfred Wagstaff, M. D. Coll. Phys. and Surgeons N. Y. 1826.
*Alfred A. Weeks, (C. L.) *1847
*Hamilton Wilkes, (F.) *1852
Edward M. Willett, (C. L.), A. M.
William R. Williams, (Rev.), A. M. 1835, S. T. D. 1837, Trustee 1838–48.
Samuel F. Wilson, (C. L.)

23

## 1823.

*Christopher Allen.
Horatio Allen, (Eng.)
*Edward Anthon, (C. L.)
William H. Boyd, A. M., M. D. Coll. Phys. and Surg. N. Y. 1826.
Edward M. Clarke, (C. L.)
Lewis Cruger, (C. L.)
*Edmund B. Elmendorf, (C. L.)
John T. Ferguson, A. M., M. D. elsewhere.
*John B. Foulke, A. M.
*Adolphus N. Gouverneur, (C. L.)
*Edmund Dorr Griffin, (Rev.), A. M.
William F. Havemeyer, (M.), Mayor N. Y. C.
*William D. Henderson, (C. L.), A. M.
Henry A. Heyer, (M.)
John A. Hicks, (Rev.), A. M. 1830.
*James Hosack.
Mancius Smedes Hutton, (Rev.), S. T. D. 1841, Trustee 1855–.
*William L. Keese, (Rev.), A. M.
*Jonathan Lawrence, (C. L.) *1833
*William A. Lawrence, (M.)
Adam D. Logan, (C. L.)
*George B. Ogden, (B.)
John D. Ogden, M. D. elsewhere.
Smith Pyne, (Rev.), S. T. D. elsewhere.
*Andrew K. Robertson.
*Noel Robertson, (Rev.)
*Grenville A. Sackett, (C. L.)
Charles J. Smith, (C. L.)
James H. Titus, (M.), A. M., Memb. N. Y. Assemb.

29

## 1824.

Benjamin Aycrigg, (Eng.), A. M. 1839, Chief Engineer Penn.
*Robert Barker.
Alexander M. Burrill, (C. L.)
*Edward C. Crary, (M.)
William A. Curtis, (Rev.), A. M. 1838.
Benjamin Drake, A. M., M. D. Coll. Phys. and Surg. N. Y. 1828.
William Duer, (C. L.), Repr. in Congr. 1849–51, U. S. Consul at Valparaiso.
*William H. Ellet, M. D. elsewhere, Lect. on Element. Chem. 1830–32, Prof. Element. Chem. 1832–33, Prof. Chem. Mineral. and Geol. S. C. Coll. 1835–48. *1859
James T. Gibert, A. M., M. D. elsewhere.
Jacob T. Gilford, M. D. Coll. Phys. and Surg. Geneva.

*Timothy R. Green, (C. L.), A. M. 1834. *1840
John K. Hardenbrook, A. M., M. D. elsewhere.
Dayton Hobart, (C. L.), A. M.
*William H. Hobart, A. M., M. D. Coll. Phys. and Surg. N. Y. 1829, Trustee 1848–55. *1857
Pierre Paris Irving, (Rev.)
*George W. Johnson, (F.) *1856
William H. Lupp, (C. L.), A. M.
*Elias J. Marsh, A. M., M. D. Coll. Phys. and Surg. N. Y. 1828. *1850
Hamilton Morton, (C. L.), A. M. 1834.
*Waddington Ogden, (M.)
*Henry Perkins, A. M., M. D. elsewhere.
*Alexander Robertson, A. M., M. D. elsewhere.
Daniel C. Schermerhorn.

23

## 1825.

George P. Cammann, M. D. elsewhere.
*James A. M. Gardner, A. M., M. D. Coll. Phys. and Surg. N. Y. 1829.
Nathaniel Marius Graves, (M.)
Robert W. Harris, (Rev.), A. M., S. T. D. 1849.
*Jacob Harsen, A. M. 1829, M. D. Coll. Phys. and Surg. N. Y. 1829. *1863
*William E. Laight.
Alexander S. Leonard, (Rev.), A. M. 1847, S. T. D. 1859.
John McKeon, (C. L.), A. M. 1831, N. Y. Assemb. 1831, Repr. in Congr. 1834–37, Dist.-Atty. N. Y. C. 1845–51, U. S. Dist.-Atty. N. Y. 1853.
Isaac T. Minard.
Edward E. Mitchell, (M.)
Walter Nichols.
William Peshine.
William Phyfe.
Anthony L. Robertson, (C. L.), Asst. Vice-Chancellor N. Y. S., Just. Supr. Ct. N. Y.
*Ferdinand Sands, (M.)
John J. Schermerhorn.
John F. Smith.
Wessell S. Smith, (C. L.), N. Y. Assemb.
Oliver S. Strong, (M.)
Peter Wilson, (C. L.)
William Wilson, M. D. Coll. Phys. and Surg. N. Y. 1829.

21

## 1826.

Charles E. Anderson.
William A. Clarke.
John M. Guion, (Rev.)
John W. Hamersley, A. M.
Nathaniel Pendleton Hosack, and Harv. 1826.
Gabriel F. Irving.
*Robert Kelly.
Francis M. Kip.
John N. McLeod, (Rev.)
Joshua S. March.
Thomas H. Merry, Jr.
William H. Milnor, M. D. Coll. Phys. and Surg. N. Y. 1832.
Thomas R. Minturn.
Henry Morris.
Richard L. Morris, M. D. Coll. Phys. and Surg. N. Y. 1830.
John B. Norsworthy.
Hewlett R. Peters, (Rev.)
Daniel Phœnix Riker.
Beverley Robinson, Jr.
William H. Roosevelt.
*Daniel Seymour.
Abraham A. Slover, Jr.
Gerrit H. Van Wagenen.
Harris Wilson.

24

## 1827.

Jonathan Trumbull Backus, (Rev.), A. M., S. T. D. Union 1847.

Jacob Sperry Baker, (M.)
William Sperry Baker, M. D. Coll. Phys. and Surg. N. Y. 1831.
Thomas Hazard Barker (B.)
Henry Neilson Brush.
John P. Crosby, (C. L.), Trust. Med. Dept. 1860–.
William Henry Crosby, (C. L.), Prof. Greek and Latin Lang. Rutg. Coll. 1841–9, Acting Prof. Lat. Lang. and Lit. 1859–60.
Henry Augustus Du Bois, M. D. Coll. Phys. and Surg. N. Y. 1830, LL. D. Yale 1864, Memb. Conn. Acad. Arts and Sciences, Memb. Geolog. Soc. France.
Edward Dunscomb, (M.)
*Edward Bristed Eastburn. *1830
Hamilton Fish, (C. L.), A. M., LL. D. 1850, Trustee 1840– and Chn. Board 1859–, Repr. in Congr. 1843–5, Lt.-Gov. N. Y. 1847–9, Gov. N. Y. 1849–51, U. S. Sen. 1851–7.
*Michael Floy, Jr., A. M. *1837
John Murray Forbes, (Rev.), A. M., S. T. D. 1847 and from Pope Pius IX.
*John Henry Hobart Haws, (C. L.), Repr. in Congr. 1851–3. *1858
John Clarkson Jay, M. D. Coll. Phys. and Surg. N. Y. 1831, Trustee 1859–.
Joshua Jones, (C. L.)
Abraham Beakley Labagh, (F.)
*Alfred Ludlow. *1831
Charles McFarlan, N. J. Sen. 1846.
Henry J. Morton, (Rev.), A. M., S. T. D. Univ. Penn. 1844, Trustee Univ. Penn.
*Jonathan Nathan, (C. L.), Master in Chanc. N. Y. 1840–5. *1863
Henry Onderdonk, Jr., (T.), A. M. 1833.
Laughton Osborn, (Au.)
*Samuel Penny, Jr., (Rev.) *1853
Minturn Post, M. D. Univ. Penn. 1832.
James M. Quin, 1830, M. D. elsewhere, A. M. 1833.
Charles Rhind, Jr., (M.)
*Henry Rogers, Jr., (C. L.) *1840
*Edwin Sands. *1828
*Robert M. Sands, (C. L.) *1835
John Schermerhorn.
*Theodore A. Swords, (C. L.) *1841
Joseph C. Wallace, (F.)
William Winter, (C. L.)
*Grenville Temple Winthrop, and Yale 1827 and Bowd. 1827, (C. L.), A. M., Memb. Mass. Leg. 1840. *1852

35

## 1828.

*William Bayley, (Art.) *1857
*Edmund D. Barry, Jr.
*Jonas Butler, (C. L.) *1858
George Catlin, (C. L.), Dist.-Atty. Richmond Co. N. Y.
Thomas W. Christie, (C. L.)
Thomas T. Devan, (Rev.), A. M., M. D. Coll. Phys. and Surg. N. Y. 1831.
Cornelius Dubois, Jr., (M.)
Edmund Embury, (Rev.), A. M. 1833.
George Gilford.
Robert Goelet.
Alexander N. Gunn, A. M., Rutg. 1832, M. D. Coll. Phys. and Surg. N. Y. 1833.
Benjamin I. Haight, (Rev.), A. M., S. T. D. 1846, Trustee 1843–, Prof. Past. Theol. and Pulp. Eloq. Gen. Theol. Sem. P. E. Ch. and Rector Burlington Coll. 1846.
Henry S. Hoyt.
*Mortimer Livingston, (M.) *1857
Austin L. S. Main, M. D. Coll. Phys. and Surg. N. Y. 1832.
*John A. Morrill, (C. L.)
George B. Neill.
*John M. Ogden. *1836

Joel B. Post, (M.)
Barzillai Slosson, (C. L.), Dist.-Atty. Ontario Co. N. Y.
Samuel S. St. John, (T.), A. M. 1834.
Lewis Thibou, (Rev.)
John L. Vandervoort, A. M., M. D. Coll. Phys. and Surg. N. Y. 1832.
Robert Boyd Van Kleeck, (Rev.), A. M., Tutor 1830–1.
William W. Van Wagenen, (C. L.), A. M. 1834.
A. Robertson Walsh, (M.)
William Walton, (Rev.), A. M. 1836, S. T. D. 1852, Instr. in Hebrew Gen. Theol. Sem. P. E. Ch.
*Richard Whiley, Jr., (C. L.)
Martin R. Zabriskie, (C. L.), Trustee 1856–.

29

## 1829.

*George F. Allen, (Eng.), Trustee 1854–63. *1863
*Theodore A. Bailey, (C. L.)
Thomas E. Blanch, (C. L.), Dist.-Atty. Rockland Co. N. Y.
*James A. Carter, M. D. Coll. Phys. and Surg. N. Y. 1832.
Alfred W. Craven, (Eng.)
Robert J. Dillon, (C. L.), Counsel to Corp. N. Y. C. 1853–6.
*Benjamin S. Downing, M. D. Coll. Phys. and Surg. N. Y. 1832.
William Edgar.
*James Heyward, M. D. elsewhere.
John T. Irving, Jr., (C. L.)
Richard H. Ogden, (C. L.)
Samuel Ogden, (C. L.)
Thomas W. Ogden.
*John D. Ogilby, Prof. Lang. Rutg. Coll. 1832–40, Prof. Eccles. Hist. Gen. Theol. Sem. P. E. Ch. 1841–51. *1851
*Peter A. Schermerhorn.
*Theodore Sedgwick, Jr., (C. L.), U. S. Dist.-Atty. N. Y.
Charles R. Swords, (C. L.)
*Robert Tucker, M. D. Coll. Phys. and Surg. N. Y. 1832.
John D. Van Buren, (C. L.)
*Fanning S. Worth, (T.)

20

## 1830.

*John B. Boggs.
James Bowdoin, (C. L.)
Robert L. Cutting, (Br.)
John Delafield, Jr., (C. L.), A. M. 1837.
Hugh T. Dickie, (C. L.), Judge Sup. Ct. Ill.
*Benjamin T. Ferguson, (C. L.) *1836
Lewis C. Gunn, (Ed.)
*Nicholas C. Heyward. *1852
George Ireland, Jr., (C. L.)
Edward Jones, M. D. Coll. Phys. and Surg. 1834, Trustee 1849–.
*John T. Kneeland, M. D. Coll. Phys. and Surg. N. Y. 1833. *1838
Henry Ledyard, Secy. U. S. Legation at Paris 1839–42, and Chargé d'Aff. 1842–44, Mayor Detroit, Mich. 1855, Mich. Sen. 1857.
*B. Franklin Miller, (C. L.) *1837
Henry C. Murphy, (C. L.), Mayor Brooklyn N. Y., Repr. in Congr., Memb. N. Y. Constit. Conven. 1846, U. S. Min. at the Hague.
Henry Nicoll, (C. L.), Repr. in Congr., Memb. N. Y. Constit. Conven. 1846.
Charles H. Ogden, (M.)
William Steele, (M.), M. D. Coll. Phys. and Surg. N. Y. 1833.
Willliam D. Waddington, (C. L.)
George W. Wright, (C. L.)

19

## 1831.

James Bolton, A. M. 1835, M. D. Coll. Phys. and Surg. N. Y. 1836.
Peter S. Chauncey, (Rev.), A. M. 1836, S. T. D. Univ. N. Y. C.
*James Chrystie.
Abraham B. Conger, A. M., Tutor 1831–3, N. Y. Sen., Prest. N. Y. S. Agricult. Soc.
William E. Eigenbrodt, (Rev.), A. M. 1835, S. T. D. 1855, Prof. Past. Theol. Gen. Theol. Sem. P. E. Ch.
*Robert Emory, (Rev.), A. M., S. T. D. 1846, Prof. Anc. Lang. Dickin. Coll. 1834–9, and Prest. Dickin. 1842–8. *1848
*Petrus Stuyvesant Fish, A. M. *1834
*John B. Gallagher, (Rev.) *1849
John P. Hone.
Bradish Johnson, (M.)
Charles R. King, M. D. Univ. Penn. 1834.
*James Joseph Macneven. *1832
James M. Morgan.
Gideon S. Nichols, (F.)
John L. O'Sullivan, A. M., Tutor 1831–3, U. S. Min. Portugal.
John Punnett, A. M., M. D. elsewhere.
*John B. Purroy, (C. L.), A. M., Consul for Venezuela, N. Y. *1859
*Richard W. Redfield, A. M. 1838. *1846
Edwin M. Taylor, (Eng.), State Eng. Virginia.
Francis Tomes, Jr., (M.)
Robert G. Vermilye, (Rev.), A. M. 1836, Tutor 1835–7, Ad. Prof. Greek and Lat. Lang. 1837–43, Prof. Christ. Theol. in Theol. Instit. Conn.
*Lloyd Saxbury Waddell. *1832
Samuel Ward, Jr., A. M. 1835.
Robert Watts, Jr., A. M., M. D. Coll. Phys. and Surg. N. Y. 1835, Prof. Anatomy.

24

## 1832.

Henry T. Anthony, (M.)
Walter Avery, (M.)
Horatio Bogert, (C. L.), A. M. 1836.
William L. Boyd, (M.), A. M.
George Carvill, Jr., (M.)
*John Chrystie, (M.) *1856
*Henry S. Dodge, (C. L.), A. M. *1855
*Daniel G. F. Fanshaw. *1833
James Heard, Jr., (M.), A. M. 1836.
Alexander C. Hilman, (Rev.)
*Nicholas W. Hoffman, (M.) *1843
*Aaron Jarvis, A. M., M. D. Coll. Phys. and Surg. N. Y. 1835. *1859
William T. Johnson, (C. L.), A. M.
Philip L. Jones, M. D. Coll. Phys. and Surg. N. Y. 1835.
*John J. C. Kane, (C. L.) *1854
Frederick W. Miller, (Rev.)
Stephen Reed, Jr., (C. L.), A. M.
*Thomas A. Richmond, (C. L.), A. M. *1859
William C. Russel, (C. L.), A. M.
Henry J. Ruggles, (C. L.)
Erasmus P. Smith, (C. L.)
John E. Stillwell, M. D. Coll. Phys. and Surg. N. Y. 1836.
Frederick L. Talcott, (M.)
Philip W. Thomas, (C. L.)
Jonathan Thompson, Jr., (M.), A. M. 1836.
Frederick Townsend, (C. L.)
*Russell N. Townsend, (C. L.) *1837
William S. Verplanck.

28

## 1833.

*Stephen D. Allen, M. D. elsewhere. *1840

James Barrow, Jr., (M.)
*John S. Bartlett.
Jackson Bolton, M. D. elsewhere.
James Constable, (C. L.)
Richard Cox, (Rev.), A. M.
John F. Delaplaine, Jr., (C. L.)
*Pierre C. De Peyster, (M.) *1854
*John M. Gelston.
Charles Hall, (M.), A. M. 1838.
John Jay Jenkins, (C. L.)
*Philip Kearney, Jr., Major U. S. A. 1847, Brig.-Gen. U. S. V. 1861 and Maj.-Gen. 1862. *1862
*Francis P. Lee, (Rev.), A. M. *1847
*Samuel B. McVickar. *1837
*James W. Metcalf, M. D. elsewhere. *1856
Gouverneur M. Ogden, (C. L.), Trustee 1849– and Treasurer 1858–.
Henry B. Renwick, Examr. U. S. Pat. Off.
William R. Renwick, (M.)
Bruce Schermerhorn.
Edward Slosson, (C. L.)
John G. Smedberg, (F.)
*Robert Spencer, (C. L.)
Abraham G. Thompson, Jr., A. M., M. D. Coll. Phys. and Surg. N. Y. 1837, N. Y. Assemb. 1847 and 1857.
James A. Williams, (Rev.), A. M., S. T. D. 1863.

24

# 1834.

William M. Allen, (C. L.), A. M.
James W. Beekman, (C. L.), A. M. 1838, N. Y. Assemb. 1848, N. Y. Senate 1848–51, Trustee Med. Dept. 1860–.
Edward H. Bryar, A. M. 1838.
William B. Casey, M. D. elsewhere.
James M. Cockroft, (M.)
William Cockroft, M. D. Coll. Phys. and Surg. N. Y. 1838.
*John Conger, A. M., M. D. Coll. Phys. and Surg. N. Y. 1838.
Isaac C. Delaplaine, (C. L.), A. M.
William Demarest, (Rev.), A. M.
William Dennis, (Rev.)
*William Dodge, (C. L.), A. M., N. Y. Assemb. *1858
William M. Gillespie, (Eng.), A. M., LL. D. 1859 and Univ. Nashville 1857, Prof. Civ. Eng. Union Coll. 1845–.
John S. Heard, M. D. Coll. Phys. and Surg. N. Y. 1837.
Henry Heyward, A. M. 1838.
Benjamin S. Huntington, (Rev.), A. M. 1839.
William Henry Hyde, (M.)
Samuel E. Johnson, (C. L.) Judge Kings Co. N. Y.
William G. King.
Alexander Major, (M.)
Richard E. Mount, Jr., (C. L.)
*Philip Rhinelander.
Robert S. Swords, (C. L.)
Anthony Ten Broeck, (Rev.)
Lloyd Windsor, (Rev.)

24

# 1835.

Jedediah Blakeney Auld, (C. L.), A. M.
Romaine Dillon, (C. L.), Secy. U. S. Legation, Brazil.
Evert A. Duyckinck, (Au.), A. M.
Benigno Gener, (C. L.)
Thomas Buchanan Gilford, (C. L.)
Andrew S. Hamersley, A. M. 1839.
Orlando Harriman, Jr., (Rev.), A. M.
William Heard, (M.)
*Joshua E. Jones.
*Charles C. Lee.
John W. C. Leveridge, (C. L.), A. M. 1839.

Charles H. Lyon, (M.), A. M.
*Joseph McIntyre.
Charles D. Mead, (C. L.), A. M. 1839.
William Mulligan, A. M.
*Alexander Palachè, (M.)
George Q. Pomeroy, (C. L.)
John H. Riker, (C. L.)
William H. Taggard, (C. L.)
Ludlow Thomas, (Br.)
*John R. Thurman, Repr. in Congr. 1849–51. *1854
*Russell Trevett, (Rev.), A. M., S.T.D. 1855, Prof. Anc. Lang. St. James, Md. *1865
William H. Wilson, (T.), A. M.
Christian Zabriskie, (M.)
24

## 1836.

Newbold Edgar.
Christodoulos L. M. Evangeles, (T.)
*George William Fash, (Rev.), A. M. 1840.
John Graham, (C. L.)
Giles Mumford Hillyer, (C. L.), A. M., Repr. in Congr.
John Henry Hobart, (Rev.), S. T. D. 1856.
Edward Hoffman, (C. L.)
John Jay, (C. L.), A. M.
William Alfred Jones, (Au.), A. M., Librarian 1851–.
*Edward Huger Laight, (M.)
James Philips Lake.
George Harrison Lynch, (C. L.)
*Henry McVickar, (Rev.)
Daniel McLaren Quackinbush, (Rev.)
James Renwick, Jr., (Arch.), A. M.
Charles Seymour, (Rev.), A. M.
William Thompson.
*Henry Ward, Jr., A. M.
George Gilfert Waters, (C. L.), A. M.
Harvey Augustus Weed, (C. L.), A. M.
James Willis Wilson, (C. L.), A. M.
21

## 1837.

*Charles Aldis, (Rev.), A. M. *1857
Samuel Blatchford, (C. L.)
Nathaniel W. Chittenden, (C. L.), A. M.
John W. Clark, (Rev.)
Samuel Cockroft.
*J. Wallace Collet, A. M. 1841.
*Stephen Douglass, (Rev.), A. M. *1857
Henry P. Fessenden, (C. L.)
Anthony Halsey, (B.), A. M.
*Benjamin H. Jarvis, (C. L.)
William H. Leggett, (T.)
John McMullen, (T.), A. M.
*Charles D. March.
*William J. Masterton, (M.)
George L. Nevius, (M.)
Charles E. Shea, (C. L.), A. M.
Jesse A. Spencer, (Rev.), A. M., S. T. D. 1852, Prof. Lat. and Orient. Lang. Burlington Coll. 1850–51.
*David P. Thomas, (C. L.)
John I. Tucker, (Rev.), S. T. D. 1858.
*George S. Van Cleef.
John Vanderbilt, Jr., (C. L.), N. Y. Sen., Judge Kings Co. N. Y.
*Samuel H. Whitlock, (M.)
*Alexander S. Wotherspoon, M. D. Coll. Phys. and Surg. N. Y. 1841, U. S. A. *1854
23

## 1838.

Frederic Anthon, (C. L.)
Edward Anthony, (M.)
Mancer M. Backus, (M.), A. M. Geneva 1841.
Thomas C. Cooper.
Richard H. Douglass.
Isaac V. Fowler, (C. L.), A. M. 1842.

John Hone.
Philip Hone, Jr.
Benjamin T. Kissam, (C. L.), A. M. 1851.
John Mason Knox, (C. L.), A. M.
Jeremiah Larocque, (C. L.)
Alfred M. Loutrel.
*William B. Moffat, A. M., M. D. Coll. Phys. and Surg. N. Y. 1842.
*Benjamin Romaine, Jr., (C. L.) *1841
William E. Snowden, (Rev.)
Charles Spear, (Br.)
George Templeton Strong, (C. L.), Trustee 1853–, Treas. U. S. San. Comm.
William R. Travers, (Br.)
Henry Hall Ward, (B.)
*Francis Marion Ward, A. M. 20
Nathaniel B. Hoxie, (C. L.), A. M.
Frederick Hughson.
Charles Ingersoll, (C. L.)
Daniel D. Lord, (C. L.), Trustee Med. Dep. 1860–.
Joseph Rich Mann, (Rev.), A. M. 1844, S. T. D. N. Jers. 1862.
Edwin A. Nichols, (Rev.)
*John Pirnie, Jr., A. M.
*Peter B. Pirnie, A. M.
George W. Quackenbos, A. M.
Edward S. Renwick, A. M.
James W. Walsh, (M.) 25

## 1839.

Charles E. Anthon, A. M. 1853, Prof. Hist. Free Acad. N. Y. C.
George C. Anthon, Prof. Greek Univ. N. Y. C.
John Jacob Astor, Jr., Trustee 1859–, Col. U. S. Vols.
Allen H. Brown.
*James C. R. Brown.
John E. Burrill, Jr., (C. L.), A. M. 1843.
Frederic A. Cairns.
*Arthur Carey, (Rev.), A. M. *1844
John Carey, Jr., (Eng.), A. M.
*George J. Cornell, (C. L.), A. M., Speaker N.Y. Assemb.
Henry Drisler, Jr., A. M., LL. D. 1860, Tutor 1843–45, Adj. Prof. Greek and Lat. Lang. 1845–57, Prof. Lat. Lang. and Lit. 1857–.
Richard S. Emmet, (C. L.)
James Walker Fowler, (C. L.), A. M.
Harvey D. Ganse, (Rev.), A. M. 1844.

## 1840.

Charles Bancroft, (Rev.), A. M., S. T. D. 1861.
Samuel Bowden, A. M.
Gerard S. Boyse.
Charles Bülow Bucknor, (C. L.), A. M.
James Farley Clark, A. M.
Edward N. Crosby.
William Forrest, Jr., A. M.
James G. Graham, (C. L.), A. M.
Ogden Hoffman, Jr., (C. L.), Judge U. S. Dist. Ct. California.
Lydig M. Hoyt.
Alfred G. Jones, A. M.
Robert L. Kennedy, A. M.
Edward H. Lawrence.
Benjamin C. Leveridge, A. M. 1844.
Levi A. Lockwood, (C. L.), A. M.
Dwight E. Lyman.
John M. Mason (C. L.), A. M.
Thomas C. Meyer.
Alonzo C. Monson, A. M.
Obadiah Newcomb, Jr.
William Nicoll.
George W. Pell, A. M. 1852.
Jotham Post, M. D. Coll. Phys. and Surg. N. Y. 1845.
Ellis Potter, Jr.

Worthington Romaine, (C. L.), A. M.
William C. Schermerhorn, A. M., Trustee 1860–.
Peter Shapter, Jr., A. M.
Peter R. Strong, A. M.
Owen Sweeny, A. M., M. D. Coll. Phys. and Surg. N. Y. 1845.
Van Brunt Wyckoff, M. D. Coll. Phys. and Surg. N. Y. 1845.
Joseph W. Winans, A. M.

31

## 1841.

Daniel H. Beadel.
*Edward L. Chichester.
John H. Clark.
George W. Collord, (T.), A. M.
*Frederick Cunningham.
Richard V. De Peyster, (B.)
Thomas B. Dibblee, (C. L.), A. M.
Cornelius Roosevelt Duffie, (Rev.), A. M., Chaplain 1857–.
William W. Duffield, (Eng.)
James Emott, Jr., (C. L.), Just. Sup. Ct. N. Y.
Herman T. E. Foster, (F.)
Oliver Wolcott Gibbs, A. M. M. D. Coll. Phys. and Surg. N. Y. 1845, Prof. Chem. and Phys. Free Acad. N. Y., Prof. Chem. Harv.
Thomas S. Griffing.
Jacob B. Jewett, (C. L.)
*William Kemble, Jr., A. M. *1845
James Hall Mason Knox, (Rev.), A. M., S. T. D. 1861.
Joseph E. Lawrence, (Ed.)
Robert Le Roy, Jr., (Br.)
John H. Mortimer, (M.)
Israel Moses, A. M., M. D. Coll. Phys. and Surg. N. Y. 1845.
Edward D. Nelson, (M.), A. M.
John H. Parish, (C. L.)
William L. Peck, (Rev.), A. M. 1857.
John Rankin, (C. L.)
Jones Rogers.
George M. Root, (Eng.), A. M.
Robert G. Simpson, (C. L.)
Augustus L. Smith, (F.)
William L. Smith, (F.)
John J. Townsend, (C. L.), A. M.
*Robert D. Van Voorhis.

31

## 1842.

*Hector C. Ames, Attaché U. S. Leg. Madrid.
*William G. Banks, (C. L.), A. M.
*Abraham S. Brouwer, (C. L.)
Benjamin F. Clark, (F.)
William H. Ebbets, (C. L.)
Frederick Frye, (C. L.), A. M.
William H. Harison, (Rev.), A. M.
Abram S. Hewitt, (M.), A. M., Secy. and Direct. Cooper Union N. Y. C.
Julius S. Hitchcock, (M.)
Robert Jaffray, Jr.
William S. Kernochan, (C. L.)
*Richard M. Lawrence, Jr., (M.)
Livingston K. Miller, (C. L.), A. M. 1846.
Clement Moore, (A. M.)
*George L. Newton, (C. L.), A. M.
Robert M. Olyphant, (M.)
Wheelock H. Parmly, (Rev.), A. M.
William J. Paulding.
James H. Phinney.
*Edward E. Potter, Brig.-Gen. U. S. Vols.
*Zebedee Ring, Jr., (C. L.)
Oliver E. Roberts, (M.), A. M.
Washington Rodman, (Rev.)
Silas Weir Roosevelt, (C. L.)
David R. Stanford, (M.)
John B. Stevens, (C. L.)
William P. Stewart, (C. L.), A. M. 1848.

John Sym, (Rev.)
Elisha W. Teakle.
David Thomson, Jr., (M.), A. M.

30

## 1843.

*Benjamin N. Aymar.
Samuel P. Bell, (C. L.)
Thomas C. T. Buckley, (C. L.), A. M.
William E. Bunker, (M.)
John W. Dana, M. D. Coll. Phys. and Surg. N. Y. 1846.
William C. Duncan, (Rev.), A. M., S. T. D. 1857.
Benjamin H. Franklin, (M.)
Albert Gallatin, Jr., (C. L.), A. M.
James W. Gerard, Jr., (C. L.), A. M.
William B. Lawrence, Jr.
Edward Z. Lewis.
William McCune, (F.)
Henry P. McGown, (C. L.)
*Robert K. Moffet.
William R. Morgan.
John C. Philip, M. D. Coll. Phys. and Surg. N. Y. 1847.
George P. Quackenbos, (T.), A. M.
Charles Reynolds, (Rev.), A. M.
John H. Ross, M. D. Coll. Phys. and Surg. N. Y. 1847.
Matson Meier Smith, (Rev.), A. M., S. T. D. 1863.
John B. Stevens, (C. L.)
*John Thomson, M. D. Coll. Phys. and Surg. N. Y. 1847. *1856
Cornelius Van Vorst, Jr., (C. L.)

23

## 1844.

Clement W. Al Burtis.
*John B. Arden, M. D. Coll. Phys. and Surg. N. Y. 1848.
Robert B. Campbell.
Jacob P. Giraud Foster, (C. L.)
Samuel Hollingsworth, A. M.
N. Bergasse Labau.
Charles W. Lawrence.
Edward McGee.
William B. Minturn, M. D. Coll. Phys. and Surg. N. Y. 1848.
William T. Moore.
Peter M. Pirnie.
Edward H. Swan.
Otto W. E. Van Tuyl, M. D. Coll. Phys. and Surg. N. Y. 1847.
Charles W. Whiley.

14

## 1845.

John K. Adams.
James Anderson.
Francis S. Cottenet.
John Drake, A. M. 1851.
George B. Draper, A. M.
George T. Elliot, Jr., A. M. 1849.
John J. Elmendorf, (Rev.), A. M.
William A. Falls.
George Irving.
George A. Jones.
Samuel T. Jones.
John W. Leavitt.
Alexander McCue.
Charles A. Minton.
Samuel B. R. Nichols.
David B. Ogden, Jr.
Henry Onderdonk.
*Lefroy Ravenhill, A. M. 1849, M. D. Coll. Phys. and Surg. N. Y. 1849, Librarian 1847–51. *1851
Aaron B. Reid.
Stephen K. Stanton.
*John A. Taggard. *1865
Frederick S. Tallmadge, (C. L.), A. M. 1849.
Pierre M. Van Wyck.
Henry P. Wainwright.

24

## 1846.

*R. S. Carden Abbott, A. M.
G. Mortimer Belden, A. M. 1850.
Beverley Robinson Betts, (Rev.), A. M.
Edward C. Bogert, (M.)
Henry A. Bogert, (C. L.), A. M.
Arthur Bronson.
Elias G. Brown, (C. L.), A. M.
William J. Frost, (Rev.), A. M.
William B. Harison, (C. L.)
Charles B. Hoffman, (B.)
William H. Hudson.
John G. Hyer, (C. L.)
*William M. Johnston, (M.)
John Grenville Kane, (C. L.), A. M.
Edwin M. Kellogg, M. D. elsewhere.
John L. Lefferts, (C. L.)
Jeremiah Loder, (C. L.), A. M.
Charles S. McKnight.
William A. McVickar, (Rev.), A. M. 1850.
Frederick Nash, A. M., M. D. Coll. Phys. and Surg. N. Y. 1850.
William Whittingham Olssen, (Rev.), A. M. 1850.
Edward M. Peck, (Rev.), A. M.
James Thomson, (C. L.), A. M.
Alexander G. Tyng.

24

## 1847.

*Cornelius D. Blake, (C. L.), A. M.
John H. Bolton, (M.)
Henry P. Campbell, (M.), A. M.
John Winthrop Chanler, (C. L.), N. Y. Assemb. 1858–9, Repr. in Congr.
William S. Coffey, (Rev.), A. M.
Wilhelmus B. Conger, (M.)
Carroll Dunham, M. D. Coll. Phys. and Surg. N. Y. 1850.
John W. Ehninger, (Art.)
Robert Holden, A. M., Prof. Burlington Coll. N. Jers. 1849–51.
*Arthur M. Jones.
John S. Lane, (M.), A. M.
Isaac Lawrence, (C. L.), A. M.
William S. Ludlum, (Rev.), A. M.
John S. McLaren, (B.)
Clarence G. Mitchell, (C. L.), A. M.
*Timothy G. Mitchell, A. M., Prof. Burl. Coll. N. Jers. 1849–57. *1857
John Moneypenny, Jr., M. D. Coll. Phys. and Surg. N. Y. 1850.
John Wells Moore, (Rev.), A. M. 1860.
John Neilson, (M.)
Benjamin A. Onderdonk.
Frederic W. Rhinelander, (M.)
Joseph K. Riggs, (B.)
James F. Ruggles, (C. L.)
Archibald M. Stone, (Rev.)
Israel Leander Townsend, (Rev.), A. M.
Robert Travis, Jr., (Rev.), A. M.
Francis Van Rensselaer, (F.)
Tompkins Westervelt, (C. L.)

28

## 1848.

Theodorus B. Bronson, (C. L.), A. M.
Horace W. Carpentier, (C. L.)
Ralph L. Cook, (M.)
Lyman D. Demaray, (M.)
Richard M. De Mille, (C. L.), A. M.
Morgan Dix, (Rev.), A. M., S. T. D. 1862, Rector Trinity Parish N. Y. 1862–, Trustee 1862–.
George Clinton Farrar, (M.), A. M.

Joseph W. Harper, (Pub.), A. M.
Leslie Irving, (C. L.)
Henry W. Johnson, (C. L.)
Levi M. Kellogg.
Cornelius L. King, Capt. U. S. A.
George M. Klots, (M.)
Edward Leavenworth.
Theodore F. Lewis, (M.), A. M.
John Lockwood, Jr., (T.)
*Lewis Morris.
Peter Wilson Ostrander, (C. L.), A. M.
William C. Pell, (C. L.)
Columbus B. Rogers, (C. L.)
Thomas P. St. John.
Otis D. Swan, (C. L.), LL. B. Harv. 1850.
Isaac Van Winkle, (C. L.), A. M.
Benjamin C. Wetmore, (C. L.)
*Joseph M. White, (M.)

25

## 1849.

Cornelius R. Agnew, M. D. Coll. Phys. and Surg., N. Y. 1852, Memb. U. S. San. Comm.
William E. Armitage, (Rev.), A. M.
William Astor.
*Edward C. Babcock.
Norman A. Beach.
Charles H. Brown.
Churchill J. Cambreling, (C. L.)
*Baldwin Dix.
George L. Freeman, M. D. elsewhere.
Henry De Coste Hanners.
William A. Hardenbrook, (T.)
John Vernor Henry, (M.), A. M.
William H. Herriman.
Lewis A. Kemper.
William Morrow Knox, A. M. 1855, M. D. Coll. Phys. and Surg. N. Y. 1854.
Joseph Larocque, (C. L.)
David Porter Lord, (M.)
Charles A. Magnes.
*E. Bowman Miner, M. D. elsewhere.
Daniel Morrelle, A. M. 1855.
Aaron Ogden, (C. L.), A. M.
Henry Parish, Jr.
John P. Pemberton, M. D. 1864.
George C. Pollen.
Charles E. Rhinelander.
S. D. Routh.
J. Frederick Schroeder, Jr., (Rev.)
Ezra K. Sherwood.
John Shrady, Jr., A. M. 1858, M. D. 1861.
John Drake Skidmore, (M.), A. M.
Prosper M. Wetmore, Jr.
John Jay White, (M.)

32

## 1850.

John M. Aims.
Matthew M. Blunt, Major U. S. A.
George W. Byron, (M.)
Malcolm Campbell, (C. L.)
Galen A. Carter.
James Starr Clark, (Rev.), A. M.
Frederic R. Coudert, (C. L.)
J. F. Delaplaine Cornell, (Rev.)
Archibald F. Cushman, (C. L.)
Edwin W. Edwards.
Thomas L. Harison.
John Sebastian Bach Hodges, (Rev.), A. M.
Walter R. T. Jones, (M.)
Adolphe Le Moyne, Jr., (B.)
Frederick L. Purroy.
Erskine M. Rodman, (Rev.), A. M.
Joseph Sands, (Arch.)
George F. Seymour, (Rev.), A. M.
Charles Augustus Silliman, (M.), A. M., LL. B. 1860.

John E. C. Smedes, A. M.
William H. Terry.
Edward Forbes Travis.
Evan T. Walker, (M.)

23

## 1851.

John H. Anthon, (C. L.), A. M., N. Y. Assemb., Asst. Dist.-Atty. N. Y. C., Prof. Med. Jurisp. N. Y. Coll. Med.
Henry M. Bedford, M. D. elsewhere.
Stewart M. Brown, (B.)
Charles Arms Cook.
*William T. Cornell.
John De Ruyter, Jr., (M.)
James De Koven, (Rev.), Prest. Racine Coll. Wis.
Legh R. Dickinson, (Rev.)
William H. Draper, A. M., M. D. Coll. Phys. and Surg. N. Y. 1855, Asst. to Prof. Surgery.
Edward S. Hoffman, M. D. Coll. Phys. and Surg. N. Y. 1855, Surgeon U. S. V.
Henry B. Johnson.
Nicholas F. Ludlum.
John G. McNary, (T.)
George A. Seaman.
William R. Smith.
A. Henry Thurston, A. M., M. D. elsewhere, Surgeon U. S. V.
Charles H. Ward, (B.), A. M. 1864.
William G. Ward, (B.)
Merritt H. Wellman, A. M.
J. Walter Wood.
David Augustus Wright.

21

## 1852.

*John Bennem, (Rev.) *1858
Charles Ludlow Bogert, (Arch.), A. M.
James L. Brown, M. D. elsewhere.
Henry W. Clark, (C. L.), A. M.
*John Wakefield Francis, Jr., M. D. elsewhere. *1855
John W. Harper, (Pub.), A. M.
George H. Hinton, A. M.
John Augustine Hows, (Art.), A. M.
Ansel N. Kellogg, (Ed.)
Lea Luquer, (C. L.), A. M.
Archibald Bleecker McDonald, Jr., (Arch.), A. M.
Samuel L. Mitchill, Jr., (M.), A. M.
James M. Morris, (C. L.)
Charles De Gray Mount, A. M.
Washington R. Nichols, (C. L.)
Charles O'Dowd.
John H. Pell, (C. L.), A. M.
George C. Pennell, (Rev.), A. M.
Robert Ray, Jr., A. M., M. D. Coll. Phys. and Surg. N. Y. 1856.
James Renwick Smedberg, (Eng.), A. M.
Richard F. Stevens.
Henry A. Tailer, (C. L.), A. M.
Eugene Thorn.
William E. Thorn, (C. L.)
Eustace Trenor, A. M., M. D. Coll. Phys. and Surg. N. Y. 1856.
John Trenor, Jr., A. M., M. D. Coll. Phys. and Surg. N. Y. 1856.
Richard H. Tucker, (C. L.)

27

## 1853.

*Cornelius Van Alen Anderson, A. M., M. D. Coll. Phys. and Surg. N. Y. 1857. *1862
William Irving Clark, (M.)
George Washington Dean, (Rev.), A. M. 1861, Tutor 1854.
Joseph Smith Dodge, Jr., A. M., M. D. Coll. Phys. and Surg. N. Y. 1856, Tutor 1854.

Daniel Embury, Jr., (M.), A. M.
*William Emerson, Jr., (C. L.), A. M.
William George Farrington, (Rev.), A. M.
Isaac J. Greenwood, Jr., (Chem.), A. M. 1857.
Albert Ward Hale, (Eng.), A. M. 1862.
Abram S. Jackson, (C. L.), A. M.
William Allen Johnson, (Rev.)
John A. Kernochan, (M.)
Delancy W. Knevels, (M.), A. M. 1857.
Edward W. Laight, (M.)
Thomas McCarty, (C. L.), A. M.
William J. Osborne, (C. L.)
St. Clair Smith, (C. L.)
*Washington Irving Tibbitts.. *1853
Archibald Somerville Van Duzer, (C. L.), A. M.

19

## 1854.

George Washington Bacon, (Rev.), (T.), A. M., LL. B. 1862.
Cullen L. Carter, (F.)
Henry M. Congdon, (Arch.)
*Charles B. Cromwell, (C. L.)
Francis A. De Wint, (C. L.), A. M. 1860.
Elias G. Drake, Jr., (C. L.), A. M.
Leicester K. Ely, (B.)
Carleton Moses Herrick, (C. L.), A. M., LL. B. 1860.
Edward Kirkland, (Br.), U. S. Vols.
George C. Kissam, M. D. Coll. Phys. and Surg. N. Y. 1857.
John V. Lewis, (Rev.), A. M.
Cutler C. McAllister, A. M.
Elias J. Marsh, M. D. Coll. Phys. and Surg. N. Y. 1858.
Henry C. Marvin, (C. L.), A. M.
James S. Merriam.
Charles E. Morgan, M. D. Coll. Phys. and Surg. N. Y. 1857.
Orlando H. Morris, (C. L.), Col. U. S. Vols.
Henry C. Murphy, Jr., (C. L.), A. M. 1860.
Peter J. Neefus, (F.)
*James C. Parker, Jr., (C. L.), A. M., Lieut. U. S. Vols. *1862
Charles S. Pomeroy, (M.), A. M.
George V. Pomeroy, Jr., (M.), A. M.
William J. Sayres, (C. L.), A. M. 1862.
Reginald H. Smith, (Arch.), A. M.
Benjamin Strong.
Gardiner Thompson, (B.)
J. Condit Trippe, (M.)
Marvin R. Vincent, (Rev.), A. M., Prof. Lat. Troy Univ.
Stewart L. Woodford, (C. L.), Col. U. S. Vols.
Jeremiah L. Zabriskie, (C. L.)

29

## 1855.

Gunning S. Bedford, Jr., (C. L.), A. M.
Edward Cammann, (C. L.) A. M.
Benjamin L. Curtis, (M.), A. M.
Charles Da Costa, (C. L.), A. M.
William Dean, (C. L.), A. M.
Lewis L. Delafield, (C. L.), A. M.
Philip A. Embury, (M.), A. M.
Edward O. Harmon, (M.)
James R. Hosmer, (C. L.)
Walter Knight, M. D. elsewhere.
Charles E. Miller, A. M., M. D. elsewhere.
David B. Miller, A. M., M. D. Coll. Phys. and Surg. N. Y. 1858.
George J. Murphy, A. M. 1860.

George A. Ostrander, A. M., M. D. Coll. Phys. and Surg. N. Y. 1858.
William A. Perry, (Eng.), A. M.
George A. Schieffelin, (C. L.), A. M.
Oscar Smedberg, (C. L.), A. M.
Herbert B. Turner, (C. L.), A. M.
John G. Wendel.

19

## 1856.

William Warren Ayres, A. M.
Edwin S. Babcock, (C. L.), A. M., Col. U. S. V.
Charles A. Bacon, A. M. 1863.
Albert H. Baldwin, (Art.), A. M.
Eastburn Benjamin, (C. L.), A. M.
Marshall S. Bidwell, Jr.
William Pell Bogert, (F.)
Abbott Brown, (M.), A. M. 1863.
Henry J. Cammann, (M.), A. M. 1863.
Charles N. Clark, (B.), A. M., U. S. V.
Edward C. Clement, A. M. 1860.
Whittingham Cox, (M.), A. M. 1860, U. S. V.
Robert L. Cutting, Jr., (C. L.), A. M.
Maturin L. Delafield, (M.), A. M.
Walter Gregory.
Francis Hendricks, (M.), A. M. 1861.
William Hyslop, (C. L.), A. M. Capt. U. S. V.
Ambrose C. Kingsland, Jr., (M.), A. M. 1861.
George L. Kingsland, (M.), A. M. 1861.
Leonard W. Kip, Jr., A. M.
Peter I. Labagh, (C. L.), A. M.
Thomas T. Lawrence.
David B. Lee.
Hermon F. Lee.
Alexis Emerson McIlvaine, (M.)
Joseph Meeks, (C. L.), A. M.
Robert B. Minturn.
Richard C. Moore, Jr.
Mandeville Mower, A. M.
James G. Osborne, A. M.
G. Wendell Prime.
William J. Seabury, (C. L.), A. M.
William F. Shepard, (C. L.)
Alexander M. Stanton, (Br.), A. M.
Russel Stebbins, Jr., (M.)
*Thomas Suffern, Jr., *1857
Charles C. Suydam, (C. L.), A. M., U. S. V.
David G. Thompson, Jr., (Br.), A. M. 1860.
John W. Timpson, (C. L.), A. M.
William Gracie Ulshoeffer, (C. L.), Capt. U. S. V.
William T. Van Riper, (C. L.), A. M.
John Francis Walton, (C. L.), A. M.
James Weeks, (M.), U. S. V.
Elbert M. Willett, (C. L.), A. M.
Howell L. Williams, Jr., A. M.

45

## 1857.

William S. Boardman, A. M.
*Morgan L. S. Brower, A. M.
Richard S. Dana, A. M.
Henry E. Davies, Jr., (C. L.), A. M., Brig.-Gen. U. S. V. and Bvt. Maj.-Gen.
Samuel W. Francis, A. M.
Elbridge T. Gerry, (C. L.), A. M.
George G. Haven, A. M.
James B. Herrick, A. M.
Philip W. Holmes, A. M.
Oliver Phelps Jackson, A. M.

William Hamett Martin, A. M., M. D. 1861.
Erskine Mason, A. M., M. D. 1860, Asst. Dem. Anat. 1861–.
*W. Carey Massett, A. M., Lt.-Col. U. S. V. *1862
Mytton Maury, A. M.
Pierre McCarty, A. M.
Henry B. Nott.
Richard T. Packwood, A. M.
Theodore Parkman, A. M.
Goold H. Redmond.
Charles E. Sears, A. M.
James H. Slipper, A. M.
William Renwick Smedberg, A. M., Capt. U. S. A.
Edgar P. Smith, A. M.
James T. Tailer, A. M.
William R. Talbot, A. M.
Daniel S. Tuttle, (Rev.) A. M.
William B. Winslow, A. M.
27

## 1858.

Wyllys P. Baxter, A. M.
Henry Woodward Cooper, A. M., LL. B. 1860.
Stephen B. M. Cornell, A. M.
Lewis A. Curtis.
Daniel Sickles Duvall, LL. B. 1860.
Jacob A. Geissenhainer, A. M.
Harmon Hendricks, A. M.
Henry L. Jones, (Rev.), A. M.
Henry C. Kinney, (Rev.), A. M.
Nicholas Luquer, Jr.
Philip Mesier Lydig, Jr., LL. B. 1861, Capt. U. S. V.
D. Ledyard Mallison.
James R. Manley, A. M.
Charles H. Marshall, Jr., A. M.
William J. Marvin, A. M. 1864.
Benjamin Pell.
A. G. Richards.
Robert K. Richards.
Henry C. Riley.
James W. Romeyn, A. M.
Thomas F. Thatcher.
Gilbert T. Totten, A. M., M. D. 1861.
Hubert Van Wagenen.
Francis C. Wainwright, (Rev.) A. M.
John Ward, Jr., LL. B. 1860, A. M. 1864.
25

## 1859.

Edward H. Anderson, (C. L.), A. M.
Richard Smith Bacon, (T.), A. M., LL. B. 1862.
Thomas J. Benjamin, A. M.
John Crosby Brown, (B.), A. M.
Edward F. Browning, A. M.
Elisha S. Caldwell, (C. L.), A. M.
Frank P. Church, (Ed.), A. M.
Gouverneur Cruger, A. M.
William F. Cushman, A. M.
John William Duer, LL. B. 1861.
Cortlandt De Peyster Field, A. M.
John Frederick Gesner, A. M.
Irving Grinnell, 1862, A. M. 1862.
E. Treadwell Hustace.
William Jay, Jr., A. M.
Charles A. Jackson, Jr., A. M.
James P. Lacombe, A. M.
William Lummis, A. M.
J. Emory McClintock, A. M., Tutor 1859–60.
George William Maynard.
James Frederic Moore, A. M., M. D. elsewhere.
Stephen Whitney Phœnix, A. M., LL. B. 1863.
William L. Raymond, A. M.
*Stephen R. Reynolds, A. M. Major U. S. V. *1864
William T. Sabine, A. M.
Oscar E. Schmidt, A. M.
J. Augustus Slipper, A. M.
Thomas F. Trenor, A. M.

Gabriel Mead Tooker, A. M., LL. B. 1861.
Robert Boyd Van Kleeck, Jr., A. M., LL. B. 1862.
William D. Walker, (Rev.), A. M. 1863.
Edward N. Whitehouse, A. M.
Henry B. Whitehouse, A. M.

33

## 1860.

Robert P. Barry, 1865, Capt. U. S. A.
Richard G. Benjamin, A. M.
Clarence S. Brown, A. M., Major U. S. V.
J. Lorillard Cammann, A. M.
Howard Clarkson.
Walter Livingston Clarkson, A. M., LL. B. 1863.
Edgar M. Cullen, A. M., Col. U. S. V.
Charles De Ruyter, (M.), A. M., LL. B. 1862, U. S. V.
Eugene Du Bois.
J. Haven Emerson, A. M.
George R. Fearing, Capt. U. S. V.
Robert Goelet, Jr., A. M., LL. B. 1862.
Joseph Greenleaf, Jr., (Rev.), A. M.
Edward L. Greenwood, (C. L.)
Laban Gardner Hopkins, A. M., LL. B. 1862, LL. M. 1864.
Edmund Abdy Hurry, A. M., LL. B. 1862.
*John William Jenks, Lieut. U. S. V. *1861
Edward R. Jones.
Herbert Kettell, A. M.
*Augustus F. King, U. S. V. *1862
David Lydig, A. M.
Samuel K. Lyon, A. M.
Thomas H. Messenger, A. M.
George Mason Miller, A. M., LL. B. 1862, Capt. U. S. V.
Augustus Newbold Morris, A. M., LL. B. 1864.
Richard Lewis Morris, Jr., A. M., Lieut. U. S. A.
Robert Dillon Nesmith, A. M., M. D. Univ. N. Y. C. 1862.
Thomas Ludlow Ogden, A. M., LL. B. 1862.
Robert Troup Pell, A. M., LL. B. 1863, U. S. V.
Eugene Hall Pomeroy, A. M., LL. B. 1862, U. S. V.
Edward P. Robins.
James S. Satterthwaite, A. M.
John W. Southack, Jr., A. M., M. D. Bellevue Med. Coll. N. Y. 1865.
Abraham Suydam, A. M.
*Frederick A. Tracy, Lieut. U. S. A. *1863
John Howard Van Amringe, A. M., Tutor 1860–63, Adj. Prof. Maths. 1863–.
George Waddington, LL. B. 1862.
William Fitzhugh Whitehouse, A. M.
Pierre Washington Wildey, A. M., LL. B. 1863.
Egerton L. Winthrop, A. M.

40

## 1861.

James Benkard, Jr., A. M., Capt. U. S. V.
William Alexander Boyd, (C. L.), A. M., Lieut. U. S. V.
George Herbert Carey, A. M., LL. B. 1863.
William Halsted Caswell, (M.), A. M.
Henry Dudley, A. M.
John Gihon, Jr., (M.), A. M.
Langdon Greenwood, (C. L.), A. M.
Edward Haight, Jr., A. M., Capt. U. S. V.
Charles Coolidge Haight, A. M., Capt. U. S. V.
William Richards Hillyer, A. M., Capt. U. S. V.

Elisha Horton, Jr., (C. L.), A. M.
Reuben Wing Howes, Jr., (Rev.), A. M.
Walter Bowne Lawrence, (C. L.), A. M.
Albert McNulty, Jr., A. M., LL. B. 1864.
Edward Mitchell, A. M.
Gratz Nathan, (C. L.), A. M.
Frank Alleyne Otis, A. M., LL. B. 1864.
*Richard Cornelius Ray, Lieut. U. S. V. *1863
William Alexander Rice, (C. L.), A. M., U. S. V.
Erastus Barnes Rudd, A. M., LL. B. 1863.
William Henry Russell, Jr., A. M., Capt. U. S. V.
Thomas Taunton Sabine, A. M., M. D. 1864.
Harry Augustus Schermerhorn, A. M.
Thomas Henry Sill, (Rev.), A. M.
George Lansing Taylor, (Rev.), A. M.
Henry A. Coit Taylor, A. M.
John Ayscough Tucker, A. M.
Stephen Hague Turnbull, (C. L.), A. M.
Joseph Mason Turner, A. M.
William Mansfield Van Wagenen, (Rev.), A. M.
Luis Puertas Walton, A. M.
Isaac Johnson Ward, (C. L.), A. M.
Samuel Baldwin Ward, A. M., M. D. Alex. Med. Coll., Surg. U. S. A.
Edward Walter West, (C. L.), A. M., Col. U. S. V.
Frederick Cope Whitehouse, A. M.
Albert Beach Whitney, A. M. M. D. Univ. N. Y. C. 1863.

36

# 1862.

Edward Robert Atwill, (Rev.)
Francis Babcock.
Robert Erskine Bartow.
William Harbert Benjamin.
Henry Carrington Bolton.
John Thomas Burr.
Robert Bage Canfield.
Leslie Chase.
John Lawrence Churchill.
*Charles Ernest Congdon. *1862
Nathaniel Ellsworth Cornwall, Jr., (T.)
John Halsey Curtis.
Walter Cutting, Capt. U. S. V. 1862–3 and Maj. 1863–.
Henry Ammi Dows.
James Gore King Duer.
Peter Forrester.
Charles Dudley Fuller.
George Wolfe Gillespie, (Eng.)
Louis Haight.
William Augustus Ogden Hegeman, LL. B. 1864.
Burrall Hoffman, LL. B. 1864.
Laurence Yvonnet Hopkins.
William Henry Jackson.
Charles Sigourney Knox.
William Elliott Laight.
William Gerard Lathrop, Jr., (C. L.)
George Anderson Lawrence.
William Henry Martin.
*Henry Howard Marvin, Lt.-Col. U. S. Eng. 1862–3. *1863
Cornelius Berrian Mitchell.
John Fulton Berrian Mitchell, Capt. U. S. V.
Charles Walton Ogden, LL. B. 1864.
*David Burr Olyphant. *1864
*Edward Mesnard Pell, *1863
Richard Varick Pell, M. D. elsewhere.
*Gerardus Post, LL. B. 1864. *1864
Russell Harper Root, LL. B. 1864.
Charles Ames Spencer, (T.)
Foster Thayer, M. D. elsewhere, U. S. N.

Charles Rockland Tyng.
John A. Vanderpoel.
Francis Willis.
William Henry Willis, Jr.
Leroy Milton Yale, M. D. elsewhere.

44

## 1863.

James Herman Aldrich.
William Cornell Binns.
Daniel Frederick Boardman.
William Brevoort Bolmer.
Melville Brown.
Thomas Tileston Bryce.
Charles Frederick Clarke.
Freeman Clarkson.
William Peshine Douglass.
Clifford Faitoute Eagle, Lieut. U. S. A.
George Wilson Ferguson.
William Redwood Fisher.
Randall Cook Hall.
Richard Mentor Henry.
Stephen Ferris Holmes.
Henry Augustus Hurlbut, Jr.
Peter Augustus Jay.
Emile Henry Lacombe.
William Scott Leggat.
Lewis Henry Lighthipe.
Le Grand Lockwood, Jr.
Thomas Morwood McLean, Jr.
Rockwood McQuesten.
William Matthews Martin.
Dan Marvin, Jr.
William Anderson Mitchell.
Stuyvesant Fish Morris.
James Murray.
Hiram Hunt Nazro.
Thomas Bellamy Newby.
George Henry Owen.
James Brinckerhoff Pell.
George Decatur Pond.
Robert Emmet Robinson.
Philip Justice Sands.
Henry Yates Satterlee.
Walter Satterlee.
William Barnewall Schermerhorn.
Rutherfurd Stuyvesant.
Charles William Terrett.
Stephen Howard Thayer, Jr.
Robert Schuyler Tucker.
Frank Roe Van Buren.
Frederick Brinsmade Van Kleeck.
Egbert Ward.
Sylvester Ward.
Ellsworth Westervelt.
Willard Parker Worster.

48

## 1864.

John Magnus Adams.
David Wylie Alexander.
William Gardiner Appleton.
Reginald Heber Bartow.
Gerard Beekman.
John Neilson Beekman.
Walston Hill Browne.
Thomas Baird Browning.
Charles Stedman Bull.
John Frederick Butterworth.
William Henry Butterworth.
J. Ackerman Coles.
Henry Bedinger Cornwall.
Edmund Dewees Davidson.
Theodore Frelinghuysen Cornell Demarest.
Matthew Brinckerhoff Du Bois.
Duane Shuler Everson, Tutor 1864–.
Henry Floy.
William Newton Goddard.
Thomas Hays Harmer.
Hiram Lyman Huston.
Frederick Wendell Jackson.
Charles Henry Kaufman.
Jonas Butler Kissam.
Joseph Bayley Lawrence.
Isidor Mayer.
Alfred Perry McClellan.
John Brainard Morgan.
William Franklin Mott.
Howard Osterhoudt.
Henry Hills Parker.
Frederick William Stevens.
Arthur Pemberton Sturges.
Albert Edward Valentine.
Isidor Walz.
Marinus Willett, Jr. 36

# GRADUATES IN MEDICINE,

EXCEPT THOSE PREVIOUSLY NAMED AS GRADUATES IN ARTS.

## 1769.

*Samuel Kissam.
*Robert Tucker.

2

## 1771.

*Benjamin Onderdonk.
*Michael Sebring.

2

## 1772.

*John Augustus Graham.
*Uzal Johnson.
*James Muirson.
*Richard Udall.
*William Winterton.

5

## 1773.

*Jabez Doty.

## 1774.

*Samuel Nicoll.

## 1793.

*Samuel Borrowe.
John B. Hicks.
Jotham Post.
Willett Taylor, Jr.
Joseph Youle.

5

## 1794.

David G. Abeel.
Peter Irving.
Henry Mead.

3

## 1795.

William M. Ross.
Timothy F. Wetmore.

2

## 1796.

Alexander Anderson.
*Winthrop Saltonstall, Yale 1793. *1802

2

## 1797.

William Bay.

## 1802.

*Joseph Bailey.
*Jacob V. Brower.
Richard L. Walker.

3

## 1803.

Isaac Foster.
Samuel Scofield.

## 1804.

William Barrow.
Ezekiel Ostrander.
Daniel D. Walters.

## 1805.

Thomas Cock, Prof. Anat. and Physiol. Rutg. Coll. N. Jers., V.-Prest. Coll. Phys. and Surg. N. Y. 1827–55 and Prest. 1855–58.
Benjamin Kissam.

## 1806.

*Valentine Mott, LL. D. elsewhere, Prof. Surg. 1811–13, Prof. Surg. Coll. Phys. and Surg. N. Y. 1813–26 and in Rutg. Med. Coll. N.Y. 1826–30, Prof. Surg. and Relative Anat. Univ. N. Y. C. 1830–65. *1865

## 1807.

Alire R. Delile.

## 1810.

Robert Morrell.

## 1860.

Thomas Henry Allen.
Galusha Birchard Balch.
George Burr Banks.
Phanet Coe Barker.
William Comstock Bennett, Yale 1858.
2 John Caruthers Bogardus.
Samuel White Briggs.
Orlo Myron Bump.
Charles Carrington.
Seth Lyman Chase.
Robert Cooper.
Charles Henry Covell.
3 Juan Bautista Ponce De Leon.
Frank Wadsworth Doolittle.
Philo Judson Farnsworth, and Univ. Verm.
William Baldwin Fletcher.
Edward Irving Ford.
Otis W. Gibson.
Walter James Hadden.
Joseph Lawrence Hicks.
Courtland Hoppin.
David Kennedy.
2 Daniel Avery Langworthy.
William Whipple Leavitt.
James Lawrence Little.
James Gifford McKee.
Thomas Knowlton Marcy.
David Matthews.
Robert Wisner Morse.
Archibald Finn Mudie.
George Andrew Mursick.
William Sheldon Clark Perkins.
Howard Pinkney.
Oren Day Pomeroy.
James Henry Pooley.
Peter Prius.
John George Ryerson.
Charles Mase Samson.
O. Henry Seeds.
Benjamin Avery Segur.
Eldridge Gilbert Seymour.
Dwight Delavan Stebbins.
George Miller Sternberg.
William Harrison Studley.
George Edwin Summers.
Charles James Taggart.
William Faulds Thoms.
Julius Vaughan.
Edmund Carlyle Ver Meulen.

Joel Addington Warren.
Augustus Purdy Williams.
51

## 1861.

George Badger.
William Badger.
John Conner Barron.
Thomas Barrow.
John Philip Benkard.
William Alexander Betts.
William Blundell.
A. Norton Brockway.
Ryckman D. Bogert.
Basil Brown Brashear.
Samuel Nelson Brayton.
William McQueen Bryce.
Edmund Shackelford Carew.
George William Carleton.
William Henry Carmalt, Asst. to Prof. Physiol. 1862–.
Charles Carter.
Matthew Chalmers, Yale 1858 and A. M. Yale.
John Francis Hamlin Chipman.
George Rogers Cutter.
F. Munson Coan.
Henry Munson Dean.
Louis George De Blois.
Daniel McComb Devendorf.
John Abbott Douglass.
Albert Fairfax.
Benjamin Franklin Fogg.
Winfield Scott Fuller.
Franklin Benjamin Galbraith.
Josiah H. Goddard.
James Grange.
Theodore E. Hamilton.
Jerome Hibbard.
Henry M. Hitchcock.
Edgar Holden.
John T. Kennedy.
Charles John Kipp.
Thompson Bailey Lewis.
Seth Stephen Lounsbery.
Henry Munson Lyman.
Carrington McFarlane.
Edward Gardner Marshall.
B. Ellis Martin.
Theodore Millspaugh.
Richard H. Moore.
Alfred North.
James H. Noyes.
Andrew T. Pearsall.
William B. Pierce.
Henry Sylvanus Plympton.
Alfred Edgar Martindale Purdy.
Charles H. Reynolds.
Charles Douglas Rigby.
John W. Robie.
Heber Smith.
Normand Smith.
Norman Leslie Snow.
Frederick Dennis Sturges.
Charles Henry Suydam.
Garrett W. Veeder Van Voast.
Maus Rosa Vedder.
Edwin Fletcher Ward.
Robert Watts, Jr.
William Lamont Wheeler.
John Phillips Payson White.
Charles M. Wight.
Benjamin Franklin Wilson.
66

## 1862.

George Pierce Andrews.
Cyrus Ebenezer Baker.
George Page Bassett.
William Whitfield Bowlby.
George Marsden Brennan.
John Weston Brennan.
Sidney Rogers Burnap.
Garabed Caloosdian.
John Ely Carey.
Thomas Knowlton Chandler.
Abel Blood Conant.
William Arthur Conover.
Henry White Cook.
James Russell Cumming.
William Floyd Cushman.
Rem Lefferts Disbrow.
Barnard Douglass Eastman.
William Eddy.
Henry Marlyn Field.
Frank Pierce Foster.
Gustavus Scott Franklin.
William James Gilfillan.

William Henry Harlin.
Solomon E. Hasbrouck.
Jonathan Havens.
Andrew H. Hershey.
George Hopkins.
Lewis Slocomb Horton.
Numon N. Horton.
John Andrew Jaume.
William Malcom James.
Dan Lee Jewett.
Eldridge Monroe Johnson.
Joseph Dodson Lomax.
William S. Ludlum.
Frederick Wentworth Mercer.
William Thomas Nealis.
Edward Monroe Norwood.
George Herschel Olmsted.
William Browne Orchard.
Edmund Morris Pease.
George Porter.
William Chardavoyne Pryer.
Nathaniel B. Reber.
Jasper Godsvenor Reynolds.
John A. Robinson.
William H. Rockwell, Jr.
Frank H. Roof.
George Schuyler Rugg.
Henry Thatcher Sears.
Samuel Francis Shaw.
Franklin Staples.
Thomas Hunt Stilwell.
John L. Swift.
Amazias Walter Tryon.
Edwin Morrison Ward.
Richard Halsted Ward.
James H. Wheeler.
Merrit H. Wilson.

59

## 1863.

William Bruce Almon.
Wendell Abraham Anderson.
Alonzo Brayton Ball, Yale 1860.
John Sterling Bird.
Joseph Bird.
Lewis Henry Bodman.
Wesley M. Carpenter.
George Augustus Christie.
Edward Cowles.
Albert E. Croucher.
Rezin Pollard Davis.
Walter De Forest Day.
Francis Delafield, Yale 1860.
Samuel Demarest, Jr.
George Clinton Dewey.
John Elderkin, Yale 1852 and A. M. Yale.
George M. Engs.
David Osburn Farrand.
Jacob T. Field.
Samuel A. Fitch.
De Witt C. Fowler.
Walter R. Gillette.
Frank West Goodall.
Wait Robbins Griswold, Yale 1844.
Charles Everett Hall.
Frank Granger Hasbrouck.
John Cornelius Hasbrouck.
David Webb Hodgkins.
Edward Kelly Hogan.
James Hutchinson.
Woolsey Johnson.
Charles S. Kittredge.
William Lee.
Elias Lester.
Irving W. Lyon.
Henry Emmet McCartin.
Theodore A. McGraw.
David Magie, Jr.
George Van Rensselaer Merrill.
Martin Alexander Miller.
Lucius Mills.
Sherman Morse.
John D. Nicoll.
Wilbur Fisk Nutten.
Patrick Pendergast.
Charles Leander Pierce.
Peter Van Schaack Pruyn.
Burr Schermerhorn.
Abner Orimel Shaw.
Amos Shaw, Jr.
Andrew Jackson Smith.
Joseph George Smith.
Thomas Thompson.
Jacob Francis Tourtelotte.
Lewis Arnold Tracy.
Samuel D. Wadsworth.
De Witt Webb.

Walter Henry Wentworth.
Lewis Westfall.
Benjamin Wilson.
Gustavus S. Winston.
Lockwood De F. Woodruff.
62

## 1864.

Samson American.
Theophilus H. Andress.
George W. Baker.
Philip H. Barton.
William Hunter Birckhead.
John Bedell Boss.
Richard B. Brown.
George J. Bucknall.
J. Otis Burt.
Adolphe Carit.
Francis P. Casey.
Samuel F. Chapin.
Albert T. Chapman.
Charles De Cockerille.
George W. Currier.
A. Thomas Cuzner.
Henry A. Danker.
Henry A. Darby.
Albert Austin Davis.
Henry J. Devlin.
Dwight Dudley.
George H. Dunbar.
Francis D. Edgerton, and elsewhere.
Henry C. Eno.
D. Darwin Everett.
Edward Farrell.
Archelaus G. Field, and elsewhere.
Luther P. Fitch.
John H. Furman.
A. McI. Gregory.
David L. Haight.
John C. Holmes.
William W. Hoppin, Jr.
John C. Hooper.
George W. Hosmer.
Edward G. Janeway.
Joseph E. Janvrin.
William H. Kinney.
Henry M. Knowles.
William Baldwin Linsly.
William A. Lockwood.
William M. McKay.
James W. McLane.
Daniel E. McSweeny.
George J. Northrop.
George B. Oakes.
Henry E. Ogden.
Benjamin M. Page.
James L. Phillips.
Henry F. Piffard.
Stephen C. Powell.
Alfred Pryor.
Charles S. Robert.
Stephen W. Roof.
Allen S. Russell.
John P. Schenck, Jr.
William F. Scoresby.
Edward C. Seguin.
Charles E. Simmons.
H. Lyle Smith.
Montross L. Smith.
William R. Stilwell.
Freman Stoddard.
George W. Stout.
Edward W. Thompson.
William Thurman.
Elbert P. Tibbals.
John R. Todd.
Platon Vallejo.
Augustus Van Cortlandt.
Frederick D. Vanderhoof.
William P. Warren.
Lathrop P. Weaver.
George G. Wheelock.
J. Elias Whitehead.
Thomas Wight.
William S. Willis.
77

# GRADUATES IN LAW,

EXCEPT THOSE PREVIOUSLY NAMED AS GRADUATES IN ARTS.

## 1860.

Daniel Pratt Baldwin, Mad. Univ.
George Van Nest Baldwin, A. M. Rutg. Coll.
Robert Henry Boorman.
Bradbury Chandler Chetwood, Burlingt. Coll.
Edward Salstonstall Dakin, Ham. Coll.
Van Buren Dutton.
*William Sprague Ely. *1862
Harry Allen Grant, Ham. Coll.
Robert Chadwick Hutchings, N. Jers., N. Y. Assemb. 1861–3.
William Henry Ingersoll.
*Isaac Henry Kirby, Univ. N. Y. C. *1862
Charles McLean Knox, Major U. S. V.
Francis Lewis Lowndes.
William Creighton Meade, A. M. St. James' Coll.
William Stevens Newell.
Julius Harris Ranney, Free Acad. N. Y. C.
Fenton Rockwell.
Walter Seabury Sands, Free Acad. N. Y. C.
John Cornell Schenck.
Samuel Farland Simpson.
Theodore Murray Squires.
Philip Lee Wilson, Lieut. U. S. V.

22

## 1861.

Smith Bloomfield, A. M. Free Acad. N. Y. C.
Miles Standish Bromley.
Herman Washington Bruen.
Nathaniel Barto Cooke, Yale 1859.
Cornelius Jay Du Bois, Capt. U. S. V.
Jas. McLaren Breed Dwight, Yale 1846 and A. M. Yale.
Sidney Stewart Henop.
Benjamin Franklin Lee, Jr. Will. 1858.
Seth Miller Murdock, Harv. 1858 and A. M. Harv.
William Henry Owen, A. M. Bowd., Capt. U. S. V.
Robert Willets Pearsall.
Temple Prime.
Henry Everett Russell, N. Jers. 1859 and A. M. N. Jers.
Frederick Scoville, Univ. N. Y. C., Lieut. U. S. V.
Robert Noxon Toppan, Harv. 1858 and A. M. Harv.
James Raymond Weeks, Lafayette Coll.
Charles Hornblower Woodruff, Yale 1858.

17

## 1862.

Charles Wesley Bangs.

George Alexander Black, Free Acad. N. Y. C.
Daniel Webster Bond.
*Edward Carrington, Jr., Yale 1859, Lieut. U. S. V. *1865
John Townsend Conolly, Lieut. U. S. V.
William Miller Denman, Free Acad. N. Y. C.
Frederic James De Peyster, Free Acad. N. Y. C., LL. M. 1864.
Robert Thomas Brown Easton, Free Acad. N. Y. C.
Edward Clarence Fraser.
Charles Henry Hatch, Yale 1859.
Stephen Burdett Hyatt, Free Acad. N. Y. C.
Sidmon Thorne Keese, Yale 1860.
Edgar Ketchum, Jr., Free Acad. N. Y. C.
Bruce Moffatt.
Augustus White Nicoll, Univ. N. Y. C.
William O'Mullen.
John O'Neil, Jr.
George Percy.
James Edward Ryan.
John Bailey Storm, LL.M. 1864.
John Simpson Walker.
Henry Kirke White, Sci. B. Free Ac. N. Y. C.
Albert Wyckoff, Lieut. U. S. V.

23

## 1863.

James Bruen Andrews, Yale 1861.
John Campbell Broderick.
Willett Bronson, Williams 1861.
William Campbell.
George Chalmers, Yale 1861.
Paris Garner Clark, Jr.
Andrew Kirkpatrick Cogswell, Rutger's.
Richard William Ely, Univ. N. Y. C.
William Henry Fuller, Yale 1861.
Edward Douglas Gale.
Frederick Gallatin, Univ. N. Y. C.
John Lyon Gardiner.
Eugene Terry Gardner.
Francis Joseph Holahan, St. John's.
Edwin Francis Hyde, Free Acad. N. Y. C.
Peter Duncan Kenny.
Francis Edward Kernochan, Yale 1861.
Carleton White Miller.
John Pell.
Charles Osborne Phelps.
George Dwight Phelps, Jr., Yale 1860.
William Walter Phelps, Yale 1860.
William Rounds Potter.
Josiah Collins Pumpelly, Rutger's.
George Washington Sandford.
Eugene Schuyler, Ph. D. Yale 1861.
Jacob Shrady, Univ. N. Y. C.
Archibald Walker Spier, Free Acad. N. Y. C.
James Steers, Free Acad. N. Y. C.
James Ayres Taber.
Ernest Tuckerman.
Morris Ashhurst Tyng, Will. 1861.
George Edmondson Walker.
Josiah Otis Ward.
Edmund Wetmore, Harv. 1860.

35

## 1864.

Richard Armstrong.
William Philip Arnold.
Henry Sandford Bellows.
Henry Brodhead, Yale 1859.
Eldred Absalom Carley, Free Acad. N. Y. C.

Thomas Bernard Connery, St. John's.
George Campbell Cooper, Free Acad. N. Y. C.
Abel Crook, Will. 1862.
Hiram Robert Dixon.
Jeremiah Donovan.
John Esler Eckerson.
Washington White Ellsworth.
Lemuel Edward Evans.
Joseph Fettretch.
Jacob Alfred Gross.
Frank Harris, Christian Bros. Mri.
Andrew Josephus Hennion.
William Myers Hoes, Will. 1861.
Henry Holt, Yale 1862.
Harlow Mather Hoyt, Free Acad. N. Y. C.
Hamilton Bailey Humes.
Charles Nichols Judson, Yale 1862.
William Platt Ketcham, Yale 1862.
Arthur Malachi Lee, Free Acad. N. Y. C.
Franklin McVeagh, Yale 1862.
Joseph Augustus Marsh.
Luther Ainsworth Milbank.
Horatio Woodhull Mills.
Israel Minor, Jr., Yale 1862.
Charles Hoskins Mundy.
William Henry Newschafer, Free Acad. N. Y. C.
Henry Delafield Phelps, Trin. Coll.
Albert Alfred Reuwee.
James Richards, N. Jers. 1858.
Van Ness Roosevelt.
Merwin Rushmore.
Elliot Sanford, Amh. 1861.
Adolph Lewis Sanger, Free Acad. N. Y. C.
John Le Grand Schaffer.
William Arnet Seaman.
Thomas Buckman Shoemaker.
William Shrady.
William Vanderbilt Simpson.
William Edwin Slocum, B. S. Free Acad. N. Y. C.
Jacob Philip Solomon.
Frederick William Stevens, Yale 1858.
John Stout.
Sidney Harrison Stuart, Jr., B. S. Free Acad. N. Y. C.
Frederick Swarts.
William Robert Syme, Univ. N. Y. C.
Richard Terheun Van Boskerck, Free Acad. N. Y. C.
Julius Sylvester Walsh, St. Joseph's.
Frederick Augustus Ward, Yale 1862.
Robert Kelley Weeks, Yale 1862.
William Leggett Whiting.
Miron Winslow, Jr.
Buchanan Winthrop, Yale 1862.
Samuel Purdy Wright.

58

# HONORARY GRADUATES,

AND

# GRADUATES OF OTHER COLLEGES

WHO HAVE BEEN ADMITTED IN COLUMBIA COLLEGE TO THE SAME DEGREE.

## 1758.

*Daniel Isaac Brown, N. Jers. 1753, A. M. and N. Jers.

*Samuel Brown, Yale 1749, A. M. and Yale. *1778

*Isaac Browne, (Rev.), Yale 1729, A. M. and Yale. *1786

*Thomas Bradbury Chandler, (Rev.), Yale 1745, A. M. and Yale and Oxford 1753, S. T. D. 1767 and Oxford 1766. *1790

*Leonard Cutting, (Rev.), Cambridge, A. M., Tutor 1756–63.

*Samuel Fayerweather, (Rev.), Harv. 1743, A. M. and Yale 1753 and Oxford 1756 and Cambridge. *1781

*Carey Ludlow, A. M.

*John McKesson, N. Jers. 1753, A. M. and N. Jers.

*David Matthews, N. Jers. 1754, A. M.

*Cyrus Punderson, Yale 1755, A. M. and Yale. *1789

*Ebenezer Punderson, Yale 1755, A. M. and Yale. *1809

*Daniel Treadwell, Harv. 1754, A. M. and Harv., Fellow and Prof. Math. and Nat. Phil. 1757–60. *1760

*Timothy Wetmore, A. M.



## 1759.

*William Hanna, (Rev.), A. B. and N. Jers. 1790, A. M. 1765 and Yale 1768 and N. Jers.

## 1761.

*John Beardsley, (Rev.), A. B., A. M. 1768.

*William Jackson, A. M. and Yale 1763 and N. Jers. 1771 and Univ. Utrecht. *1813

*William Samuel Johnson, Yale 1744, A. M. and Yale and Harv. 1747, J. C. D. Ox. 1766, LL. D. Yale 1788, Del. to Col. Congr. 1765, Judge Supr. Ct. Conn. 1772, Del. to Congr. 1774, Memb. Council Conn. 1780, Repr. in Congr. 1784–7, Memb. U. S. Constit. Conven. 1787, President 1787–1800, U. S. Sen. 1788. *1819

*Samuel Andrew Peters, (Rev.), Yale 1757, A. M. and Yale, LL. D. elsewhere. *1826

*Samuel Seabury, (Rev.), Yale 1748, A. M. and Yale, S. T. D. Ox., Bishop P. E. Ch. Conn. 1784–96. *1796

*James Scovill, (Rev.), Yale 1757, A. M. and Yale. *1808
*Agur Treadwell, (Rev.), A. B. and Yale 1760, A. M. Yale.
*Edward Winslow, (Rev.), Harv. 1736, A. M. and Harv. *1784
8

# 1762.

*Samuel Andrews, (Rev.), Yale 1759, A. M. *1818
*Richard Clarke, (Rev.), A. B. and Yale 1762, A. M. 1766 and Yale. *1824
*William Cornelius George, A. B. and Yale 1762.
*Robert Harpur, Glasgow, A. M., Prof. Math. and Nat. Phil. 1761–7, Regent Univ. N. Y. S. and Clerk of Board 1784–7, Trustee and Clerk of Board 1787–95, Secy. St. N. Y.
*Bela Hubbard, (Rev.), Yale 1758, A. M. and Yale, S. T. D. Yale 1804. *1812
*Robert McKean, (Rev.), A. M.
*Ebenezer Parmele, Yale 1758, A. M. and Yale. *1802
7

# 1764.

*Matthew Cushing, Harv. 1739, A. M. and Harv., Librarian Harv. *1779
*Samuel Giles, A. B.
2

# 1765.

*Jeremiah Leaming, (Rev.), Yale 1745, A. M. and Yale, S. T. D. 1789. *1804

# 1767.

*Samuel Auchmuty, (Rev.), A. B. Harv. 1745 and A. M. Harv. 1746, S. T. D. and Oxford 1766. *1777
*Ephraim Avery, (Rev.), Yale 1761, A. M. and Yale. *1776
*George Glentworth, M. D. Edinb., A. M.
*Charles Inglis, (Rev.), A. M., S. T. D. elsewhere, Bishop P. E. Ch. Nov. Scot., Governor.
*Hugh Neill, A. M.
*John Ogilvie, (Rev.), Yale 1748, A. M. and Yale, S. T. D. 1770 and Aberd. *1774
*John Tyler, (Rev.), A. B. and Yale 1765, A. M. 1769 and Yale. *1823
7

# 1768.

*Samuel Bard, M. D. and Edinb. 1765, Prof. Theor. and Pract. Med. 1767–76 and Midw. 1770–6, Prof. Chem. 1784–5, 1786–7, Dean Med. Fac. 1792–1804, LL. D. N. Jers. 1815. *1821
*Samuel Clossy, M. D. and Trin. Coll. Dub., Prof. Anat. 1767–76.
*Myles Cooper, (Rev.), Oxford, LL. D. and Ox., Prof. Mor. Phil. 1762–3, Fellow 1762–75, President 1763–75. *1785
*John Jones, M. D. and Rheims, Prof. Surg. 1767–76.
*Peter Middleton, M. D. and St. And., Prof. Path. and Physiol. 1767–76 and Mat. Med. and Chem. 1770–6, Governor 1775.
5

## 1769.

*Ebenezer Kneeland, (Rev.), Yale 1761, A. M. and Yale. *1777

## 1770.

*Thomas Barton, (Rev.), A. M.
*Robert Blackwell, (Rev.), A. B. and N. Jers. 1768, A. M. N. Jers., S. T. D. N. Jers. and Univ. Penn. 1788.

2

## 1771.

*Jonathan Boucher, (Rev.), A. M.

## 1772.

*Edmund Fanning, Yale 1757, A. M. and Yale and Harv. 1764, J. C. D. Oxford 1774, LL. D. Yale 1803 and Dart. 1803, Lt.-Gov. Nov. Scot., Gov. Prince Edw. Isl. *1818

## 1773.

*Isaac Hunt, Phila., A. M.
*Joseph Lamson, (Rev.), Yale 1741, A. M. and Yale. *1773
*John Marshall, (Rev.), A. M.
*Harry Monroe, (Rev.), A. M.
*John Stuart, (Rev.), A. M.

5

## 1774.

*Lucas Babcock, Yale 1755, A. M. and Yale. *1777
*George Panton, (Rev.), Aberd., A. M.
*James Sayre, (Rev.), Phila., A. M.
*William Tryon, LL. D., Governor of the Province of New York.

4

## 1787.

*James Hardie, A. B., A. M. 1790.

## 1788.

*Robert Annan, (Rev.), A. M.
*William Cochran, (Rev.), Trin. Coll. Dub., A. M., Prof. Greek and Lat. Lang. 1784–9.
*Robert Charles Johnson, Yale 1783, A. M. and Yale. *1806
*Peter Schuyler Livingston, A. B. and Yale 1789 and N. Jers. 1789 and Harv. 1790, A. M. 1791. *1807
*Samuel Latham Mitchill, M. D. Univ. Edinb. 1786, A. M., LL. D. elsewhere, Memb. N. Y. Assemb. 1790–2 and 1797–9, Prof. Bot. 1792–5 and Prof. Nat. Hist. Chem. and Agricult. 1792–1801, Repr. in Congr. 1801–3 and 1810–12, U. S. Sen. 1804–10, elected Prof. Chem. Coll. Phys. and Surg. N. Y. 1807 and declined, Prof. Nat. Hist. Coll. Phys. and Surg. N. Y. 1808–20 and Prof. Bot. and Mat. Med. 1820–6, Vice-Prest. Rutg. Med. Coll. N. Y. 1826–30. *1831
*Daniel C. Verplanck, A. M.
*John W. Watkins, A. M.

7

## 1789.

*Roger Alden, Yale 1773, A. M. and Yale. *1836

*Abraham Beach, (Rev.), Yale 1757, S. T. D., Trustee 1787–1813 and Clerk 1795–1811. *1828
*John Daniel Gross, (Rev.), S. T. D., Regent Univ. N. Y. S. 1784–7, Trustee 1787–92, Prof. Germ. Lang. and Geogr. 1784–95 and Prof. Mor. Phil. 1787–95.
*James Rutsen Hardenbergh, (Rev.), A. M. N. Jers. 1770, S. T. D., Prest. Rutg. Coll. *1790
*Samuel William Johnson, Yale 1779, A. M. and Yale. *1846
*William Linn, (Rev.), N. Jers. 1772, S. T. D. *1808
6

## 1790.

*Henry Maeller, (Rev.), A. M.
*James Proudfit, (Rev.), A. M.
2

## 1793.

*Ebenezer Dibble, (Rev.), Yale 1734, S. T. D. *1799
*Andrew Jaffray, (Rev.), S. T. D.
*Samuel Jones, Jr., A. B. and Yale 1790, LL. D. 1826 and Union 1841, N. Y. Assemb. 1812–14, Rec. N. Y. C. 1823, Chancellor N. Y. 1826–8, Ch.-Just. Supr. Ct. N. Y. 1828–47, Just. Supr. Ct. 1847–9. *1853
*William Ogilvie, LL.D., Prof. Human. Univ. Aberd.
4

## 1794.

*Richard Channing Moore, (Rev.), A. M., S. T. D. Dart. 1805, Bishop P. E. Ch. Va. 1814–41. *1841

## 1795.

John Campbell, A. M.
*John Coffin, Dart. 1791, A. M. and Dart. and N. Jers. 1791 and Yale 1798. *1852
2

## 1797.

*James Kent, Yale 1781 and A. M. Yale, LL. D. and Harv. 1810 and Dart. 1819, N. Y. Leg. 1790–94 and 1796, Prof. Law 1793–98 and 1823–47, Mast. in Chanc. N. Y. C. 1793, Recorder N. Y. C. 1797, Judge Sup. Ct. N. Y. 1798–1814 and Ch.-Just. N. Y. 1804–14, Chanc. N. Y. 1814–23, Trustee 1823. *1847
*Samuel Andrew Law, (Rev.), Yale 1792, A. M. and Yale and N. Jers. 1797. *1845
2

## 1798.

William Best, (Rev.), A. M.
William Scott, (Rev.), A. M.
Andrew Smith, A. M.
Robert G. Wetmore, (Rev.), A. M.
4

## 1800.

Joakam Freeman, (Rev.), A. M.

## 1802.

William Duke, (Rev.), A. M.
*James Kemp, (Rev.), S. T. D., Bishop P. E. Ch. Maryland 1814–27. *1827
2

## 1804.

Edmund D. Barry, (Rev.), A. M.
Edward Jenkins, (Rev.), S. T. D. and Brown Univ. 1803.
James Larzelere, (Rev.), A. M.
Peter Stryker, (Rev.), A. M.

4

## 1805.

Clement Merriam, (Rev.), A. M.

## 1806.

*William James Macneven, M. D. and Univ. Vienna 1783, Prof. Mat. Med. Rutg. Med. Coll. N. Y. *1841

## 1809.

Abraham Bronson, (Rev.), A. M.

## 1811.

*John Croes, (Rev.), A. M. N. Jers. 1797, S. T. D., Bishop P. E. Ch. N. Jers. 1815–32. *1832
James Hall, (Rev.), S. T. D.
*William Harris, (Rev.), Harv. 1786 and A. M. Harv., S. T. D. and Harv. 1811, President 1811–29, Trustee 1811–29 and Clerk 1811. *1829

3

## 1815.

*Frederic Beasley, (Rev.), N. Jers. 1797 and A. M. N. Jers., S. T. D. and Univ. Penn. 1815, Tutor N. Jers. 1798–1800, Provost Univ. Penn. 1815. *1845

## 1816.

*John Schureman, (Rev.), Rutg. Coll. 1795 and A. M. Rutg. and N. Jers. 1801, S. T. D., Prof. Eccles. Hist. and Past. Theol. in Theol. Sem. N. Brunsw. N. J. *1818

## 1818.

*Robert Adrain, LL. D., Prof. Math. and Nat. Phil. Rutg. 1810–13, Prof. Math. and Nat. Phil. 1813–25, Prof. Math. Univ. Penn. 1827–34. *1843
*Joseph Hopkinson, Univ. Penn. 1786, LL. D. and N. Jers. 1818 and Harv. 1831, Judge U. S. Dist. Ct. Penn. *1842
Samuel Nichols, (Rev.), Yale 1811, A. M.
Andrew Thomson, (Rev.), S. T. D.

4

## 1819.

*Thomas Church Brownell, (Rev.), Union 1804, S. T. D. and Union 1819, LL. D. elsewhere, Bishop P. E. Ch. Conn. 1819–65. *1865
*Philander Chase, (Rev.), Dart. 1796, S. T. D. Prof. Ken. Theol. Sem., Prest. Ken. Coll., Bishop P. E. Ch. Ohio 1819–52. *1852
John Philip, (Rev.), S. T. D. and N. Jers. 1820.

3

# 1820.

William Forrest, A. M.

# 1821.

*Thaddeus Fiske, (Rev.), Harv. 1785 and A. M. Harv., S. T. D. *1855
*Washington Irving, A. M., LL. D. 1829 and Harv. 1832, J. C. D. Ox. 1831, Memb. of several learned Societies, Secy. U. S. Leg. Lond., U. S. Min. to Spain 1842–46. *1859
Daniel McDonald, (Rev.), Genev., S. T. D.
3

# 1822.

*William Lowndes, LL. D., Repr. in Congress, U. S. Sen.
*Thomas Lyell, (Rev.), A. M. Brown 1803, S. T. D. *1848
Alexis P. Proal, (Rev.), A. M.
John Reed, (Rev.), Union 1805 and A. M. Union, S. T. D.
*Stephen N. Rowan, (Rev.), Union 1804 and A. M. Union, S. T. D. *1835
5

# 1823.

John Carroll, A. M.
Abraham N. Halsey, A. M.
*Chauncey Lee, (Rev.), Yale 1784 and A. M. Yale, S. T. D. *1842
*Edward Livingston, N. Jers. 1781 and A. M. N. Jers., LL. D. and Transyl. 1824 and Harv. 1834, Trustee 1793–1806, Repr. in Congr. 1794–1801 and 1823–9, U. S. Dist.-Atty. N. Y. 1801–3, Mayor N. Y. C. 1801–3, Secy. St. U. S. 1831–3, U. S. Min. to France 1833–5. *1836
*John Stark Ravenscroft, (Rev.), S. T. D., Bishop P. E. Ch. N. Car. 1823–30. *1830
*Nathan Sanford, LL. D., U. S. Dist.-Atty. N. Y. 1803–16, Memb. N. Y. Assemb. 1811 and Speaker of the same, N. Y. Sen., U. S. Sen. 1816–22 and 1825–31, Memb. N. Y. Constit. Conven. 1821, Chancell. N. Y. 1823–5. *1838
John Savage, Union 1799, LL. D. and Union 1829, Ch.-Justice Sup. Ct. N. Y.
Samuel Seabury, (Rev.), A. M., S. T. D. 1837, Prof. Bibl. Learn. and Interp. Script. Gen. Theol. Sem. P. E. Ch.
*Ambrose Spencer, Harv. 1783, LL. D. and Univ. Penn. 1819 and Harv. 1821, Memb. N. Y. Assemb. 1793–5, N. Y. Sen. 1795–1802, Atty.-Gen. N. Y. 1802–4, Judge Sup. Ct. N. Y. 1804–19 and Ch.-Just. of the same 1819–23, Repr. in Congr. *1848
9

# 1824.

*Langdon Cheves, LL. D., Repr. in Congr. and Speaker, Supr. Judge S. Car., Prest. U. S. Bank, Ch. Commr. U. S. under Treaty of Ghent. *1857
*James Fenimore Cooper, A. M. *1851
*Thomas Addis Emmet, Trin. Coll. Dub., LL. D., Atty.-Gen. N. Y. *1827
*Ernest L. Hazelius, (Rev.), S. T. D. and Union 1824. *1853
Levi Silliman Ives, (Rev.) A. M., S. T. D. 1831, Bishop P. E. Ch. N. Car. 1831–53.

*James Kirke Paulding, A. M., Nav. Off. N. Y., Secy. U. S. Navy 1837–41. *1860
*Daniel Webster, Dart. 1801 and A. M. Dart. and Harv. 1804, LL. D. and N. Jers. 1818 and Dart. 1824 and Harv. 1824, Memb. of several learned Soc., Repr. in Congr. 1813–17 and 1823–25, Memb. Mass. Constit. Conven. 1820, U. S. Sen. 1826–41 and 1845–50, Secy. St. U. S. 1841–43 and 1850–52. *1852

7

## 1825.

*John Caldwell Calhoun, Yale 1804, LL. D. and Hamilt. 1821 and Yale 1822, Memb. S. C. Leg., Repr. in Congr. 1811–17, Secy. War U. S. 1817–24, Vice-Prest. U. S. 1825–32, U. S. Sen. 1832–43 and 1845–50, Secy. St. U. S. 1844–45. *1850
*Stephen Elliott, Yale 1791, LL. D. and Yale 1819 and Harv. 1822, Memb. S. C. Leg., Prof. Nat. Hist. and Bot. S. C. Med. Coll. *1830
Henri L. P. F. Péneveyre, (Rev.), S. T. D.
*Joel Roberts Poinsett, LL.D., Repr. in Congr. 1821–27, U. S. Min. to Mex. 1828–30, Secy. War U. S. 1837–41. *1851
William Shelton, A. M.

5

## 1826.

*William Wirt Phillips, (Rev.), Union 1813, S. T. D., Trustee N. Jers. Coll., Prest. Board For. Miss. Presbyt. Ch. *1865

## 1827.

*Jasper Adams, (Rev.), Brown 1815 and A. M. Brown and Yale 1819, S. T. D., Tutor Brown 1818–19, Prof. Math. and Nat. Phil. Brown 1819–24, Prest. Genev. Coll. 1827, Prest. Charleston S. C. Coll. and Prof. Mor. Phil., Prof. Eth. Milit. Acad. U. S. *1841
William Rollinson Whittingham, (Rev.), A. M., S. T. D. 1837, Bishop P. E. Ch. Maryland 1840–.

2

## 1828.

*Asa Eaton, (Rev.), Harv. 1803 and A. M. Harv. and Brown 1818, S. T. D. *1858
Charles Taylor Catlin, Yale 1822, A. M. and Yale.
William Buell Sprague, (Rev.), Yale 1815 and A. M. Yale 1819, S. T. D. and Harv. 1848.

3

## 1829.

Antoine Verren, (Rev.), A. M., Prof. French Lang. and Lit. 1828–39.

## 1830.

William C. Heyward, A. B.
*James Marsh, (Rev.), Dart. 1817 and A. M. Dart., S. T. D. and Amh. 1833, Tutor Dart. 1818–20, Prof. Lang. Hamp. Syd. Coll., Prest. and Prof. Mor. Phil. and Met. Univ. Verm. *1842
*Frederic Christian Schaeffer, (Rev.), A. M. N. Jers. 1818,

S. T. D., Prof. Germ. Lang. and Lit. 1830–31. *1831
William D. Snodgrass, (Rev.), Wash. Coll. Penn., A. M. N. Jers. 1822, S. T. D.
*William Murray Stone, (Rev.), S. T. D., Bishop P. E. Ch. Maryl. 1830–38. *1838

5

## 1831.

Eli Baldwin, (Rev.), S. T. D.
James Ryan, A. M.
James Shea, A. M.
Thomas W. Swords, A. B.
George Upfold, (Rev.), Union 1814, M. D. Coll. Phys. and Surg. N. Y. 1816., S. T. D., Bishop P. Epis. Ch. Ind. 1849–.

5

## 1832.

Francis Lister Hawks, (Rev.), Univ. N. Car., A. M. Yale 1818, S. T. D.

## 1833.

*Charles Burroughs, (Rev.), Harv. 1806 and A. M. Harv. and Dart. 1811, S. T. D. *1851
*George Washington Doane, (Rev.), Union 1818, S. T. D., LL. D. elsewhere, Prof. Trin. Coll. 1824–28, Bishop P. E. Ch. N. Jers. 1832–59. *1859
*James Emott, A. M. Union 1800, LL. D. *1850
*James Hervey Otey, (Rev.), S. T. D., Bishop P. E. Ch. Tenn. 1834–63. *1863
John H. Pinder, (Rev.), S. T. D., Principal of Codrington Coll. Isl. Barbad.
*David Prentice, Yale 1812, A. M. and Yale, LL. D. Union 1839, Prof. Greek and Lat. Lang. Genev. Coll. *1857

6

## 1834.

Orange Clark, (Rev.), A. M.
Thomas Winthrop Coit, (Rev.), Yale 1821 and A. M. Yale 1831, S. T. D., LL. D. Trin. 1853, Prest. Trans. Univ., Prof. Eccl. Hist. Trin. Coll.
Don Thomas Gener, LL. D., Prest. Cortes of Spain.
Robert J. Harvey, A. M.
William A. Muhlenberg, (Rev.), S. T. D.
William Sherwood, (Rev.), A. M.

6

## 1835.

Benjamin Clark Cutler, (Rev.), Brown 1822 and A. M. Brown, S. T. D.
Manuel Fetter, A. B., A. M. 1842.
*William Gaston, N. Jers. 1796 and A. M. N. Jers., LL. D. and Univ. Penn. 1819 and Harv. 1826 and Univ. N. Y. C. 1834 and N. Jers. 1835, N. Car. Sen., Judge Sup. Ct. N. Car., Repr. in Congr. *1844
James N. Reynolds, A. M.

4

## 1836.

Benjamin Hale, (Rev.), Bowd. 1818 and A. M. Bowd. and Dart. 1827, S. T. D., M. D. Dart. 1827, Prof. Chem. and Min. and Med. Juris. Dart. 1827–35, President Genev. Coll.
Benjamin Luckock, (Rev.), A. M.

*Jacob Sutherland, Yale 1807, LL. D., Judge Sup. Ct. N. Y. *1845

3

## 1837.

John Bethune, (Rev.), S. T. D.
William Cullen Bryant, A. M. and Will. 1819, LL. D. Union 1853.
*John Duer, LL. D., Memb. N. Y. Constit. Conven. 1821, Trustee 1823–30, Just. Supr. Ct. N. Y. C. 1849–57 and Ch.-Just. of same 1857–8. *1858
*George Griffin, Yale 1797, LL. D. *1860
Fitz-Greene Halleck, A. M.
Charles Fenno Hoffman, A. M.
Theodore Irving, (Rev.), A. M., LL. D. Union 1851.
Samuel Allen McCoskry, (Rev.), S. T. D., Bishop P. E. Ch. Mich. 1836–.
*Erskine Mason, (Rev.), S.T.D.
Philip Meyer, (Rev.), S. T. D.
*David B. Ogden, LL. D., Trustee 1815–49 and Chn. of Board 1843–49. *1849
Thomas H. Taylor, (Rev.), S. T. D.
Samuel A. Van Vranken, (Rev.), S. T. D.

13

## 1838.

*Isaac Boyle, (Rev.), Harv. 1813 and A. M. Harv., S. T. D. and Trin. 1838. *1850
Walter Chisholm, A. M.
*Leonidas Polk, (Rev.), S. T. D., Bishop P. E. Ch. Louis. 1838–64. *1864

3

## 1839.

Wm. M. Carmichael, (Rev.), S. T. D.
Abraham Halsey, A. M.

2

## 1840.

John Watson Adams, (Rev.), S. T. D.
Stephen Elliott, (Rev.), S. T. D., Bishop P. E. Ch. Georgia 1841–.
Abraham Bruyn Hasbrouck, Yale 1810 and A. M. Yale 1819, LL. D. and Union 1841, Repr. in Congr., Prest. Rutg. Coll.
William Hawkesworth, A. M.
*Hugh Swinton Legaré, S. C. Coll. 1814, Memb. S. C. Leg. 1824–30, Atty.-Gen. S. C. 1830–2, Chargé d'Aff. U. S. at Brussels 1832–36, Repr. in Congr. 1836–38, Atty.-Gen. U. S. 1841–43. *1843
*William Hickling Prescott, Harv. 1814 and A. M. Harv., LL. D. and Univ. N. Car. 1841 and Harv. 1843, J. C. D. Oxford 1850, Memb. of many learned societies. *1859

6

## 1841.

*Albert Gallatin, Univ. Genev. Switz. 1779, LL. D., Memb. Penn. Constit. Conven. 1789, Memb. Penn. Leg. 1790–2, Repr. in Congr. 1795–1801, Secy. Treas. U. S. 1801–13, U. S. Commr. at Ghent 1814, U. S. Min. to France 1815–23, U. S. Env. Ex. to Gr. Britain 1826–7, Prest. Council Univ. N. Y. C. 1830, Prest. N. Y. Hist. Society 1843–9. *1849
C. H. Gottsberger, A. M.
Samuel Nelson, LL. D., Just. Sup. Ct. U. S.
William M. Thompson, A. M.

4

## 1842.

Gustavus Abeel, (Rev.), Union 1823 and A. M. Union, S. T. D.
James J. Bowden, A. M.
*Charles W. Hackley, (Rev.), U. S. Mil. Acad., A. M., S. T. D. elsewhere, Prest. Jeff. Coll. Miss., Prof. Math. and Astr. 1843–57, Prof. Astr. 1857–61. *1861
Edward Y. Higbee, (Rev.), A. M., S. T. D. 1843.
George C. Schaeffer, A. M., M. D. elsewhere, Librarian 1839–47, Prof. Chem. Georget. Coll. Kent.
John H. Shepherd, A. M.

6

## 1843.

John M. Duncan, (Rev.), S. T. D.
George E. Hare, (Rev.), Union 1826, S. T. D.
Daniel Stone, A. M.

3

## 1844.

Edward E. Ford, (Rev.), S. T. D.
Joseph W. Ingraham, A. M.
Charles G. McLean, (Rev.), S. T. D.
*Ambrose S. Todd, (Rev.), A. M. Yale 1824, S. T. D. *1861
Charles E. West, A. M.

5

## 1845.

*Daniel Dewey Barnard, Will. 1818, LL. D. and Geneva and Brown 1853, Repr. in Congr., U. S. Min. at Brussels. *1861
Edward Cooper, A. M.
Charles Hewitt, A. M.
John W. McCullough, (Rev.), S. T. D.
Horatio Southgate, (Rev.), S. T. D., Bishop P. E. Ch. Constantinople 1844–.
Bird Wilson, (Rev.), S. T. D. elsewhere, LL. D., Prof. Gen. Theol. Sem. P. E. Ch.

6

## 1846.

William Bayard Blackwell, A. M.
Ezra A. Huntington, (Rev.), Union 1833, S. T. D.

2

## 1847.

William Ingraham Kip, (Rev.), Yale 1831 and A. M. Yale and Trin. 1846, S. T. D., Bishop P. E. Ch. Californ. 1853–.
Joseph Henry Price, (Rev.), Brown 1825 and A. M. Brown, S. T. D.
*John Canfield Spencer, Union 1806, LL. D. and Union 1849, Mast. in Chanc. 1811, Dist.-Atty. West. Dist. N. Y., Repr. in Congr. 1817–19, Memb. N. Y. Assemb. 1819–24 and Speaker of the same 1820, N. Y. Sen. 1824–26, Secy. St. N. Y. 1839–41, Secy. War U. S. 1841–43, Secy. Treas. U. S. 1843–44. *1855

3

## 1848.

Francis Vinton, (Rev.), U. S. Mil. Acad., A. B. Brown 1833, S. T. D.

## 1849.

George Alexander Crook, A. M.
James Stephenson, (Rev.), A. M.

2

## 1850.

William Drisler, A. M.
David X. Junkin, (Rev.), S. T. D., Prest. Wash. Coll. Va.
John B. Kerfoot, (Rev.), S. T. D., Rector St. James Coll. Md., Prest. Trin. Coll. 1864–.
Kendrick Metcalf, (Rev.), Dart. 1829, S. T. D., Prof. Greek and Lat. Lang. and Lit. Hobart.
Winfield Scott, A. M. N. Jers. 1814, LL. D. and Harv. 1861, Maj.-Gen. and Bvt. Lt.-Gen. U. S. A.
Timothy D. Williams, A. M.

6

## 1851.

Francis H. Cuming, (Rev.), S. T. D.
Martin P. Parks, (Rev.), S. T. D.
John Williams, (Rev.), S. T. D. and Union 1847, Prest. Trin. Coll. 1848–53, Asst. Bishop P. E. Ch. Conn. 1851–65 and Bishop 1865–.
Octavius Winslow, (Rev.), S. T. D.

4

## 1852.

Stephen Alexander, Union 1824 and A. M. Union, LL. D., Prof. Math. and Astr. N. Jers.
Samuel Gilman Brown, (Rev.), Dart. 1831 and A. M. Dart., S. T. D., Prof. Rhet. and Polit. Lit. Dart.
Richard Pulling Jenks, (Rev.), Harv. 1830, A. M.
William McMurray, (Rev.), S. T. D.
John Rowland, (Rev.), A. M.
John Lee Watson, (Rev.), Harv. 1815 and A. M. Harv., S. T. D.

6

## 1853.

Talbot W. Chambers, (Rev.), S. T. D.
Thomas Frederick Davis, (Rev.), S. T. D., Bishop P. E. Ch. S. C. 1853–.
Henry D. Erskine, (Rev.), A. M. elsewhere, S. T. D., Dean of Ripon, Eng.
Charles J. Quintard, M. D. elsewhere, A. M., Prof. in Medical College Memphis, Tenn.
Samuel Pratt Strong, (Rev.), S. T. D.

5

## 1854.

William R. Gordon, (Rev.), S. T. D.
Jean Romer, A. M., LL. D. elsewhere, Prof. French Lang. and Lit. Free Acad. N. Y. C.
I. Jackson Scott, (Rev.), S. T. D.
Henry Philip Tappan, (Rev.), Union 1825, S. T. D. Union 1845, LL. D., Prof. Mor. and Int. Phil. Univ. N. Y. C. 1832–38, Chancell. Univ. Mich. 1850–63, Cor. Memb. Inst. of France 1856.

4

## 1855.

John M. Macauley, (Rev.), S. T. D.
Joseph Few Smith, (Rev.), Yale 1840 and A. M. Yale, S. T. D., Prof. Sac. Lit. Aub. Theol. Sem.

2

## 1856.

John Blakely, (Rev.), S. T. D.
George Sharswood, LL. D., Ch.-Judge Dist. Ct. Penn., Prof. Law Univ. Penn.
Alfred Stubbs, (Rev.), Yale 1835 and A. M. Yale, S. T. D.

3

## 1857.

Joseph Alden, (Rev.), Union 1829 and A. M. Union and N. Jers. 1832 and Will. 1837, S. T. D. Union 1839, LL. D., Tutor N. Jers. 1830–32, Prof. Rhet. Polit. Econ. and Hist. Will. 1835–52, Prof. Metaph. and Mor. Phil. Lafay. Coll., Prest. Jeff. Coll. Penn.
Samuel Cooke, (Rev.), A. M. Yale 1847, S. T. D. and Univ. N. Y. C. 1857.
William F. Morgan, (Rev.), Union 1837 and A. M. Union, S. T. D.

3

## 1858.

Charles D. Morris, A. M. and Oxford.
Samuel Spring, (Rev.), A. B. and A. M. Yale 1821, S. T. D.
Henry Waterman, (Rev.), Brown 1831, S. T. D.
*Isaac D. Vermilyea, (Rev.), A. M. 4

## 1859.

T. De Bois Coryell, A. M.
William Armstrong Dod, (Rev.), N. Jers. 1838 and A. M. N. Jers., S. T. D., Tutor N. Jers. 1840–1, Lect. on Architect. and the Fine Arts N. Jers.
George H. Houghton, (Rev.), S. T. D.
Lot Jones, (Rev.), S. T. D.
Alexander G. Mercer, (Rev.), S. T. D.
Samuel Tyler, LL. D.

6

## 1860.

Charles P. Daly, LL. D., Just. Ct. Com. Pleas N. Y. C.
Theodore W. Dwight, Hamilton, LL. D., Prof. Law 1858–.
John W. French, (Rev.), S. T. D., Prof. Eth. U. S. Mil. Acad.
Thomas T. Guion, (Rev.), S. T. D.
Murray Hoffman, LL. D. and Union 1840, Judge Supr. Ct. N. Y.
Fordyce Mitchell Hubbard, (Rev.), Will. 1828 and A. M. Will., S. T. D. and Trin. 1860, Tutor Will. 1831–2, Prof. Lat. Lang. Univ. N. Car.
Matthew Hall McAllister, LL. D., Judge U. S. Dist. Ct. Cal.
William H. N. Stewart, (Rev.), Trin. Coll. Dub., A. M.
Charles S. Tripler, M. D. elsewhere, A. M., U. S. A.
Lewis Bartholomew Woodruff, Yale 1830 and A. M. Yale, LL. D., Judge Supr. Ct. N. Y. C.

10

## 1861.

Alexander W. Bradford, Union 1832 and A. M. Union, LL. D. and Union 1852, Corporation Atty. N. Y. C. 1843, Surrogate N. Y. C. 1848–58, Trustee 1855–.

*Abraham Lincoln, LL. D., President of the United States 1861–65. *1865

Joseph C. Passmore, (Rev.), S. T. D., Prof. Rhet. and Int. Phil. St. James Coll. Md.

S. Chipman Thrall, (Rev.), S. T. D.

Sullivan H. Weston, (Rev.), S. T. D., Trustee Med. Dept. 1860–.

5

## 1862.

Henry P. Balcom, A. M., Supt. Pub. Sch. Middlet. Conn.

Samuel Buel, (Rev.), Will. 1833 and A. M. Will., S. T. D., Tutor Ken.

George Jarvis Geer, (Rev.), Trin. 1842 and A. M. Trin., S. T. D. and Union 1862.

Benjamin Nicholas Martin, (Rev.), Yale 1837 and A. M. Yale, S. T. D., Prof. Phil. and Hist. Univ. N. Y. C.

Henry Joseph Scudder, Trin. 1846, A. M. and Trin.

John Cotton Smith, (Rev.), S. T. D.

6

## 1863.

S. Hanson Cox, (Rev.), S. T. D.

Samuel Eliot, Harv. 1839 and A. M. Harv. and Trin 1857, LL. D., Prof. Hist. and Polit. Sci. Trin., elected Prof. Anc. and Mod. Lit. 1857 and declined, President Trin. Coll. 1860–4.

Jared B. Flag, (Rev.), S. T. D.

Robert S. Howland, (Rev.), S. T. D.

Thomas Ricker Lambert, (Rev.), A. M. Brown 1845, S. T. D.

Henry B. Walbridge, (Rev.), S. T. D.

6

## 1864.

Henry Stephens Cutler, Mus. D.

Joseph G. Fox, A. M., Prof. Math. Cooper Instit. N. Y. C.

Thomas Hunter, A. M.

3

# ENUMERATION.

| | | |
|---|---|---|
| Graduates in Arts | 1911 | |
| Graduates in Medicine other than Graduates in Arts | 352 | |
| Graduates in Law other than Graduates in Arts | 155 | |
| Honorary Graduates, and Graduates of other Colleges admitted here to the same degree | 305 | |
| | —— | 2723 |

KNOWN TO BE DECEASED.

| | | |
|---|---|---|
| Graduates in Arts | 682 | |
| Graduates in Medicine, as above | 16 | |
| Graduates in Law, as above | 3 | |
| Honorary Graduates, and others, as above | 139 | |
| | —— | 840 |
| Presumed to be living | | 1883 |

# INDEX.

*h* indicates Honorary Graduates and Graduates of other Colleges who have been admitted to the same degree.
*l* " Graduates in Law, except those who have their places in the Catalogue as Graduates in Arts.
*m* " Graduates in Medicine, except those who have their places in the Catalogue as Graduates in Arts.

1860 Daniel P. *l.*
1860 George V. N. *l.*

Ball,
1814 John H.
1863 Alonzo B. *m.*

Bancroft,
1840 Charles.

Bangs,
1862 Charles W. *l.*

Banks,
1842 William G.
1860 George B. *m.*

Barclay,
1766 James.
1772 Thomas.
1796 David.

Barculoo,
1795 George.

Bard,
1768 Samuel. *h.*
1797 William.

Barker,
1824 Robert.
1827 Thomas H.
1860 Phanet C. *m.*

Barnard,
1845 Daniel D. *h.*

Barnes,
1821 William B.

Barnet,
1771 Ichabod B.

Barnum,
1804 John W.

Barron,
1861 John C. *m.*

Barrow,
1804 William. *m.*
1838 James, Jr.
1861 Thomas. *m.*

Barry,
1804 Edmund D. *h.*
1820 Edmund D., Jr.
1860 Robert P.

Bartlett,
1833 John S.

Barton,
1770 Thomas. *h.*
1864 Philip H. *m.*

Bartow,
1806 John V.
1862 Robert E.
1864 Reginald H.

Bassett,
1786 John.
1862 George P. *m.*

Baxter,
1858 Wyllys P.

Bay,
1797 William. *m.*
1798 Thomas.
1803 John.

Bayard,
1760 Samuel.
1776 Samuel.

Bayley,
1802 Joseph. *m.*
1828 William.

Beach,
1789 Abraham. *h.*
1849 Norman A.

Beadel,
1841 Daniel H.

Beardsley,
1761 John. *h.*

Beasley,
1815 Frederic. *h.*

Beck,
1813 John B.

Bedell,
1811 Gregory T.

Bedford,
1851 Henry M.
1855 Gunning S., Jr.

Beebee,
1802 Alexander M.

Beekman,
1766 Gerard.
1792 Gerard.
1834 James W.
1864 Gerard.
1864 John N.

Belden,
1846 G. Mortimer.

Bell,
1843 Samuel P.

Bellows,
1864 Henry S. *l.*

Benjamin,
1856 Eastburn.
1859 Thomas J.
1860 Richard G.
1862 William H.

Benkard,
1861 James, Jr.
1861 John P. *m.*

Bennem,
1852 John.

Bennett,
1860 William C. *m.*

Benson,
1765 Egbert.
1801 Robert.
1807 Egbert, Jr.

Berrian,
1808 William.
1809 Samuel.
1815 James W.

Best,
1798 William. *h.*

Bethune,
1837 John.

Betts,
1820 William.
1846 Beverley R.
1861 William A. *m.*

Bibby,
1805 James.
1809 Edward N.

Bidwell,
1856 Marshall S., Jr.

Binns,
1863 William C.

Birckhead,
1864 William H. *m.*

Bird,
1863 John S. *m.*
1863 Joseph. *m.*

Black,
1862 George A. *l.*

Blackwell,
1770 Robert. *h.*
1804 William D.
1846 William B. *h.*

Blake,
1847 Cornelius D.

Blakely,
1856 John. *h.*

Blanch,
1829 Thomas E.

Blatchford,
1837 Samuel.

Blauvelt,
1801 Abraham L.

Bleecker,
1791 Anthony.
1791 William.
1805 Leonard A.
1820 John B.

Bloomer,
1758 Joshua.

Bloomfield,
1861 Smith. *l.*

Blundell,
1861 William. *m.*

Blunt,
1850 Matthew M.

Boardman,
1857 William S.
1863 Daniel F.

Bodman,
1863 Lewis H. *m.*

Bogardus,
1815 Archibald R.
1860 John C. *m.*

Bogart,
1773 Cornelius.
1790 David S.

Bogert,
1801 Samuel.
1832 Horatio.

1846 Edward C.
1846 Henry A.
1852 Charles L.
1856 William P.
1861 Ryckman D. *m.*

Boggs,
1830 John B.

Bolmer,
1863 William B.

Bolton,
1801 Thomas.
1831 James.
1833 Jackson.
1847 John H.
1862 Henry C.

Bond,
1862 Daniel W. *l.*

Bonnett,
1818 Daniel.

Boorman,
1860 Robert H.

Borrowe,
1793 Samuel. *m.*

Boss,
1864 John B. *m.*

Boucher,
1771 Jonathan. *h.*

Bowden,
1772 John.
1813 James J.
1840 Samuel.
1842 James J. *h.*

Bowdoin,
1830 James.

Bowlby,
1862 William W. *m.*

Bowne,
1803 John.

Boyd,
1787 Samuel.
1797 Robert.
1806 George.
1813 William.
1823 William H.
1832 William L.
1861 William A.

Boyle,
1838 Isaac. *h.*

Boyse.
1840 Gerard S.

Bradford,
1861 Alexander W. *h.*

Brady,
1809 John.

Brashear,
1861 Basil B. *m.*

Brayton,
1861 Samuel N. *m.*

Brennan,
1862 George M. *m.*
1862 John W. *m.*

1852 Henry W.
1853 William I.
1856 Charles N.
1863 Paris G. *l.*

Clarke,
1762 Richard. *h.*
1771 Clement C.
1817 James P. F.
1823 Edward M.
1826 William A.
1863 Charles F.

Clarkson,
1774† David.
1810 David A.
1860 Howard.
1860 Walter L.
1863 Freeman.

Clement,
1856 Edward C.

Clinton,
1786 De Witt.
1793 George, Jr.
1797 George W.

Close,
1811 Ebenezer.

Clossy,
1768 Samuel. *h.*

Clowes,
1808 Timothy.

Coan,
1861 F. Munson. *m.*

Cochran,
1788 James.
1788 William. *h.*
1791 Walter L.

Cock,
1775 William.
1805 Thomas. *m.*
1805 William.

Cockcroft,
1834 James M.
1834 William.
1837 Samuel.

Cocks,
1794 William.

Codman,
1816 Richard.

Codwise,
1798 David.
1810 George.

Coffey,
1847 William S.

Coffin,
1795 John. *h.*

Coggswell,
1863 Andrew K. *l.*

Coit,
1820 Joseph H.
1834 Thomas W. *h.*

Colden,
1766 Richard N.

Coles,
1805 Benjamin U.
1864 J. Ackerman.

Collet,
1837 J. Wallace.

Collord,
1841 George W.

Conant,
1862 Abel B. *m.*

Congdon,
1854 Henry M.
1862 Charles E.

Conger,
1831 Abraham B.
1834 John.
1847 Wilhelmus B.

Connery,
1864 Thomas B. *l.*

Conolly,
1862 John T. *l.*

Conover,
1862 William A. *m.*

Conrey,
1809 Gerrit.

Constable,
1833 James.

Cook,
1848 Ralph L.

Cooke,
1857 Samuel. *h.*
1861 Nathaniel B. *l.*

Cooper,
1768 Myles. *h.*
1769 Caleb.
1805 Joab G.
1824 James F. *h.*
1838 Thomas C.
1845 Edward. *h.*
1858 Henry W.
1860 Robert. *m.*
1864. George C. *l.*

Copland,
1807 George R.
1809 Edward.

Copp,
1771 John.

Cornell,
1839 George J.
1850 J. F. Delaplaine.
1851 William T.
1858 Stephen B. M.

Cornwall,
1862 Nathaniel E., Jr.
1864 Henry B.

Coryell,
1859 T. De Bois. *h.*

Cottenet,
1845 Francis S.

Coudert,
1850 Frederick R.

Covell,
1860 Charles H. *m.*

Covert,
1811 John.

Cowdrey,
1821 Peter A.

Cowles,
1863 Edward. *m.*

Cox,
1833 Richard.
1856 Whittingham.
1863 S. Hanson. *h.*

Craft,
1821 Isaac F.
1821 William D.

Crary,
1824 Edward C.

Craven,
1829 Alfred W.

Creighton,
1770 James.
1812 William.

Croes,
1811 John. *h.*

Crolius,
1803 Thomas.

Cromwell,
1854 Charles B.

Crook,
1849 George A. *h.*
1864 Abel. *l.*

Crosby,
1802 John P.
1827 John P.
1827 William H.
1840 Edward N.

Croucher,
1863 Albert E. *m.*

Cruger,
1796 Henry, Jr.
1819 Henry N.
1823 Lewis.
1859 Gouverneur.

Cullen,
1860 Edgar M.

Cuming,
1851 Francis H. *h.*

Cumming,
1862 James R. *m.*

Cunningham,
1841 Frederick.

Currier,
1864 George W. *m.*

Curtis,
1824 William A.
1855 Benjamin L.
1858 Lewis A.
1862 John H.

Cushing,
1764 Matthew. *h.*

Cushman,
1850 Archibald F.
1859 William F.

Cutler,
1835 Benjamin C. *h.*
1864 Henry S. *h.*

Cutter,
1861 George R. *m.*

Cutting,
1758 Leonard. *h.*
1793 William.
1830 Robert L.
1856 Robert L., Jr.
1862 Walter.

Cuyler,
1762 Henry.
1763 Barent.

Cuzner,
1864 A. Thomas. *m.*

Da Costa,
1855 Charles.

Dakin,
1860 Edward S. *l.*

Daly,
1860 Charles P. *h.*

Dana,
1843 John W.
1857 Richard S.

Danker,
1864 Henry A. *m.*

Darby,
1864 Henry A. *m.*

Davidson,
1864 Edmund D.

Davies,
1818 Thomas L.
1857 Henry E., Jr.

Davis,
1798 George.
1814 Cornelius.
1853 Thomas F. *h.*
1863 Rezin P. *m.*
1864 Albert A. *m.*

Dawson,
1822 George W.

Day,
1863 Walter De F. *m.*

Dayton,
1817 Matthias O.

Deall,
1774† Samuel.

Dean,
1853 George W.
1855 William.
1861 Henry M. *m.*

De Blois,
1861 Louis G. *m.*

Decker,
1793 Cornelius.

**Emmet,**
1810 Robert.
1824 Thomas A. *h.*
1839 Richard S.

**Emory,**
1831 Robert.

**Emott,**
1833 James. *h.*
1841 James, Jr.

**Engs,**
1863 George M. *m.*

**Eno,**
1864 Henry C. *m.*

**Erskine,**
1853 Henry D. *h.*

**Evangeles,**
1836 Christodoulos L. M.

**Evans,**
1864 Lemuel E. *l.*

**Everett,**
1864 D. Darwin. *m.*

**Everson,**
1864 Duane S.

**Faesch,**
1795 John J.

**Fairfax,**
1861 Albert. *m.*

**Fairlie,**
1818 Frederick.

**Falls,**
1845 William A.

**Fanning,**
1772 Edmund. *h.*

**Fanshaw,**
1832 Daniel G. F.

**Farnsworth,**
1860 Philo J. *m.*

**Farrand,**
1863 David O. *m.*

**Farrar,**
1848 George C.

**Farrell,**
1864 Edward. *m.*

**Farrington,**
1853 William G.

**Fash,**
1836 George W.

**Fayerweather,**
1758 Samuel. *h.*

**Fearing,**
1860 George R.

**Ferguson,**
1795 John.
1823 John T.
1830 Benjamin T.
1863 George W.

**Ferris,**
1811 Charles G.
1816 Isaac.

**Fessenden,**
1837 Henry P.

**Fetter,**
1835 Manuel. *h.*

**Fettretch,**
1864 Joseph. *l.*

**Field,**
1859 Cortlandt De P.
1862 Henry M. *m.*
1863 Jacob T. *m.*
1864 Archelaus G. *m.*

**Fine,**
1805 James L.
1809 John.

**Fish,**
1827 Hamilton.
1831 P. Stuyvesant.

**Fisher,**
1794 John E.
1796 Philip.
1817 Isaac.
1821 George H.
1863 William R.

**Fiske,**
1821 Thaddeus. *h.*

**Fitch,**
1863 Samuel A. *m.*
1864 Luther P. *m.*

**Flag,**
1863 Jared B. *h.*

**Fleming,**
1791 Pierre E.
1803 Augustus.
1805 James.
1809 Alexander.

**Fletcher,**
1860 William B. *m.*

**Floy,**
1827 Michael, Jr.
1864 Henry.

**Floyd,**
1809 Alfred.

**Fogg,**
1861 Benjamin F. *m.*

**Fonda,**
1787 Nicholas.

**Forbes,**
1794 John.
1827 John M.

**Ford,**
1844 Edward E. *h.*
1860 Edward I. *m.*

**Forrest,**
1820 William. *h.*
1840 William, Jr.

**Forrester,**
1818 Peter.
1862 Peter.

**Forsyth,**
1821 William.

**Foster,**
1803 Isaac. *m.*
1841 Herman T. E.
1844 Jacob P. G.
1862 Frank P. *m.*

**Foulke,**
1823 John B.

**Fowler,**
1806 Gilbert O.
1810 Theodosius O.
1838 Isaac V.
1839 James W.
1863 De Witt C. *m.*

**Fox,**
1864 Joseph G. *h.*

**Fraligh,**
1799 Peter D.

**Francis,**
1808 Henry M.
1809 John W.
1852 John W., Jr.
1857 Samuel W.

**Franklin,**
1843 Benjamin H.
1862 Gustavus S. *m.*

**Fraser,**
1811 David H.
1862 Edward C. *l.*

**Freeke,**
1811 Richard.

**Freeman,**
1790 Jonathan.
1800 Joakam. *h.*
1849 George L.

**French,**
1860 John W. *h.*

**Frost,**
1846 William J.

**Frye,**
1842 Frederick.

**Fuller,**
1861 Winfield S. *m*
1862 Charles D.
1863 William H. *l.*

**Funk,**
1817 Seymour P.

**Furman,**
1801 John.
1864 John H. *m.*

**Gaine,**
1774† John.

**Galbraith,**
1861 Franklin B. *m.*

**Gale,**
1863 Edward D. *l.*

**Gallagher,**
1831 John B.

**Gallatin,**
1841 Albert. *h.*
1843 Albert, Jr.
1863 Frederick. *l.*

**Ganse,**
1839 Harvey D.

**Gardiner,**
1863 John L. *l.*

**Gardner,**
1825 James A. M.
1863 Eugene T. *l.*

**Garr,**
1796 Andrew S.

**Garrison,**
1810 James C.

**Gaston,**
1835 William. *h.*

**Geer,**
1862 George J. *h.*

**Geissenhainer,**
1858 Jacob A.

**Gelston,**
1833 John M.

**Gener,**
1834 Don Thomas. *h.*
1835 Benigno.

**George,**
1762 William C. *h.*

**Gerard,**
1811 James W.
1843 James W., Jr.

**Gerry,**
1857 Elbridge T.

**Gesner,**
1859 John F.

**Gibbs,**
1841 Oliver W.

**Gibert,**
1821 William N.
1824 James T.

**Gibson,**
1860 Otis W. *m.*

**Gifford,**
1809 James N.

**Gihon,**
1861 John, Jr.

**Giles,**
1764 Samuel. *h.*

**Gilfillan,**
1862 William J. *m.*

**Gilford,**
1793 Samuel, Jr.
1824 Jacob T.
1828 George.
1835 Thomas B.

**Gillespie,**
1834 William M.
1862 George W.

**Gillette,**
1863 Walter R. *m.*

Hibbard,
1861 Jerome. *m.*

Hicks,
1793 John B. *m.*
1823 John A.
1860 Joseph L. *m.*

Higbee,
1842 Edward Y. *h.*

Hill,
1807 John H.

Hillyer,
1836 Giles M.
1861 William R.

Hilman,
1832 Alexander C.

Hilton,
1814 Benjamin.

Hinton,
1852 George H.

Hitchcock,
1842 Julius S.
1861 Henry M. *m.*

Hobart,
1824 Dayton.
1824 William H.
1836 John H.

Hodges,
1850 J. Sebastian B.

Hodgkins,
1862 David W. *m.*

Hoes,
1864 William M. *l.*

Hoffman,
1760 Anthony.
1809 D. Murray.
1812 Lindley M.
1812 Ogden.
1832 Nicholas W.
1836 Edward.
1837 Charles F. *h.*
1840 Ogden, Jr.
1846 Charles B.
1851 Edward S.
1860 Murray. *h.*
1862 Burrall.

Hogan,
1811 William.
1863 Edward K. *m.*

Holahan,
1863 Francis J. *l.*

Holden,
1847 Robert.
1861 Edgar. *m.*

Holland,
1761 Henry.

Hollingsworth,
1844 Samuel.

Holmes,
1807 Philip M.
1857 Philip W.
1863 Stephen F.
1864 John C. *m.*

Holt,
1822 Edwin.
1864 Henry. *l.*

Hone,
1815 John, Jr.
1818 Henry.
1831 John P.
1838 John.
1838 Philip, Jr.

Hooper,
1864 John C. *m.*

Hopkins,
1860 Laban G.
1862 George. *m.*
1862 Laurence Y.

Hopkinson,
1818 Joseph. *h.*

Hoppin,
1860 Courtland. *m.*
1864 William W., Jr. *m.*

Horton,
1861 Elisha, Jr.
1862 Lewis S. *m.*
1862 Numon N. *m.*

Hosack,
1792 Alexander.
1823 James.
1826 Nathaniel P.

Hosmer,
1855 James R.
1864 George W. *m.*

Houghton,
1859 George H. *h.*

Howes,
1861 Reuben W., Jr.

Howland,
1863 Robert S. *h.*

Hows,
1852 John A.

Hoyt,
1828 Henry S.
1840 Lydig M.
1864 Harlow M. *l.*

Hoxie,
1839 Nathaniel B.

Hubbard,
1762 Bela. *h.*
1770 William.
1860 Fordyce M. *h.*

Hudson,
1846 William H.

Hughson,
1839 Frederick.

Humes,
1864 Hamilton B. *l.*

Hunn,
1786 Abraham.
1810 Peter F.

Hunt,
1773 Isaac. *h.*
1794 Montgomery.

Hunter,
1864 Thomas. *h.*

Huntington,
1834 Benjamin S.
1846 Ezra A. *h.*

Hurlbut,
1863 Henry A., Jr.

Hurry,
1860 Edmund A.

Hurst,
1789 William.

Hustace,
1859 E. Treadwell.

Huston,
1864 Hiram L.

Hutchinson,
1863 James. *m.*

Hutton,
1823 Mancius S.

Huyler,
1800 John.

Hyatt,
1862 Stephen B. *h.*

Hyde,
1834 William H.
1863 Edwin F. *l.*

Hyer,
1846 John G.

Hyslop,
1813 Robert.
1856 William.

Inderwick,
1808 James.

Ingersoll,
1839 Charles.
1860 William H. *l.*

Inglis,
1767 Charles. *h.*
1795 James.
1821 William

Ingraham,
1817 Daniel P.
1844 Joseph W. *h.*

Ireland,
1816 John, Jr.
1830 George, Jr.

Ironside,
1815 William.

Irving,
1794 Peter. *m.*
1798 John T.
1821 Pierre M.
1821 Washington, *h.*
1824 Pierre P.
1826 Gabriel F.
1829 John T., Jr.
1837 Theodore. *h.*
1845 George.
1848 Leslie.

Isherwood,
1817 Benjamin.

Ives,
1824 Levi S. *h.*

Izard,
1789 Henry.

Jackson,
1761 William. *h.*
1809 Samuel.
1814 Allen.
1853 Abram S.
1857 Oliver P.
1859 Charles A.
1862 William H.
1864 Frederick W.

Jaffray,
1793 Andrew. *h.*
1842 Robert, Jr.

James,
1862 William M. *m.*

Janeway,
1794 Jacob J.
1864 Edward G. *m.*

Janvrin,
1864 Joseph E. *m.*

Jarvis,
1837 Benjamin H.

Jaques,
1805 Robert.

Jaume,
1862 John A. *m.*

Jauncey,
1774 John.

Jay,
1764 John.
1794 Peter A.
1827 John C.
1836 John.
1859 William, Jr.
1863 Peter A.

Jenkins,
1804 Edward. *h.*
1833 John J.

Jenks,
1852 Richard P. *h.*
1860 John W.

Jewett,
1841 Jacob B.
1862 Dan L. *m.*

Johnson,
1761 William S. *h.*
1772 Uzal. *m.*
1788 Robert C. *h.*
1789 Samuel W. *h.*
1792 John B.
1793 John I.
1819 William L.
1820 Samuel R.
1824 George W.
1831 Bradish.
1832 William T.
1834 Samuel E.
1848 Henry W.
1851 Henry B.
1853 William A.
1862 Eldridge M. *m.*
1863 Woolsey. *m.*

Leslie,
1762 Alexander.

Lester,
1863 Elias. *m.*

Leveridge,
1835 John W. C
1840 Benjamin C.

Lewis,
1810 Horatio G.
1843 Edward Z.
1848 Theodore F.
1854 John V.
1861 Thompson B. *m.*

Lighthipe,
1863 Lewis H.

Lincoln,
1861 Abraham. *h.*

Linn,
1789 William. *h.*
1795 John B.

Linsly,
1864 William B. *m.*

Lispenard,
1761 Anthony.
1762 Leonard.

Little,
1860 James L. *m.*

Livingston,
1760 Philip.
1765 Robert R.
1775 John W.
1786 George.
1786 Philip H.
1788 Peter S. *h.*
1796 Edward P.
1799 James.
1800 Robert S.
1804 James D.
1811 Peter V. B.
1822 Anson.
1822 Carroll.
1823 Edward. *h.*
1828 Mortimer.

Lloyd,
1765 Henry.
1818 John H.

Lockwood,
1840 Levi A.
1848 John, Jr.
1863 Le Grand, Jr.
1864 William A. *m.*

Loder,
1846 Jeremiah.

Logan,
1823 Adam D.

Lomax,
1862 Jos ph D. *m.*

Lord,
1839 Daniel D.
1849 David P.

Lounsbery,
1861 Seth S. *m.*

Loutrel,
1838 Alfred M.

Low,
1812 Cornelius.
1821 Isaac.

Lowerre,
1817 William.
1819 Henry J.

Lowndes,
1822 William. *h.*
1860 Francis. *l.*

Lowther,
1774† Tristrim.

Luckock,
1836 Benjamin. *h.*

Ludlow,
1758 Carey. *h.*
1768 James.
1787 John C.
1793 Henry W.
1811 Thomas W.
1817 Edmund.
1827 Alfred.

Ludlum,
1847 William S.
1851 Nicholas F.
1862 William S. *m.*

Lummis,
1859 William.

Lupp,
1824 William H.

Lupton,
1774† Schuyler.
1788 Brandt S.
1789 William.
1791 Lancaster.

Luquer,
1852 Lea.
1858 Nicholas, Jr.

Lush,
1770 Stephen.

Lydig,
1815 Philip M.
1858 Philip M., Jr.
1860 David.

Lyell,
1822 Thomas. *h.*

Lyman,
1840 Dwight E.
1861 Henry M. *m.*

Lynch,
1775† Thomas G.
1799 James.
1836 George H.

Lyon,
1835 Charles H.
1860 Samuel K.
1863 Irving W. *m.*

Lytton,
1804 William L.

McAllister,
1854 Cutler C.
1860 Matthew H. *h.*

McCartee,
1808 Robert.

McCartin,
1863 Henry E. *m.*

McCarty,
1853 Thomas.
1857 Pierre.

Macauley,
1855 John M. *h.*

McClellan,
1864 Alfred P.

McClintock,
1859 J. Emory.

McCoskry,
1837 Samuel A. *h.*

McCue,
1845 Alexander.

McCullen,
1806 James.

McCullough,
1845 John W. *h.*

McCune,
1843 William.

McDonald,
1810 John M.
1821 Daniel. *h.*
1852 Archibald B.

McFarlan,
1827 Charles.

McFarlane,
1861 Carrington. *m.*

McGahagan,
1805 Thomas.

McGown,
1843 Henry P.

McGraw,
1863 Theodore A. *m.*

McGregor,
1810 John.

McIlvaine,
1856 Alexis E.

McIntyre,
1835 Joseph.

Mack,
1807 Daniel.

Mackaness,
1799 T. Thornton.

McKay,
1864 William M. *m.*

McKean,
1762 Robert. *h.*

McKee,
1860 James G. *m.*

McKeon,
1825 John.

McKesson,
1758 John. *h.*

Mackie,
1794 Jacob O.
1812 Peter, Jr.

McKinnon,
1800 John.

McKnight,
1798 Washington.
1808 John.
1846 Charles S.

McLane,
1864 James W. *m.*

McLaren,
1847 John S.

McLean,
1844 Charles G. *h.*
1863 Thomas M., Jr.

McLeod,
1806 Robert B. A.
1818 Alexander B.

McMullen,
1837 John.

McMurray,
1852 William. *h.*

McNary,
1851 John G.

Macneven,
1806 William J. *h.*
1831 James J.

McNulty,
1861 Albert, Jr.

Macomb,
1802 John W.
1802 Robert.

McQuesten,
1863 Rockwood.

McSweeny,
1864 Daniel E. *m.*

McVeagh,
1864 Franklin. *l.*

McVickar,
1802 Archibald.
1802 James.
1804 John.
1809 Henry.
1812 Edward.
1833 Samuel B.
1836 Henry.
1846 William A.

Maeller,
1790 Henry. *h.*

Magie,
1863 David, Jr. *m.*

Magnes,
1849 Charles A.

Main,
1828 Austin L. S.

Major,
1834 Alexander.

Malcolm,
1794 Samuel B.

Murphy,
1830 Henry C.
1854 Henry C., Jr.
1855 George J.

Murray,
1799 Alexander.
1812 John W. B.
1813 Thomas C.
1863 James.

Mursick,
1860 George A. *m.*

Muzzy,
1808 Frederick.

Myer,
1799 Philip.

Nash,
1846 Frederick.

Nathan,
1827 Jonathan.
1861 Gratz.

Nazro,
1863 Hiram H.

Neal,
1810 Ava.

Nealis,
1862 William T. *m.*

Neefus,
1854 Peter J.

Neill,
1767 Hugh. *h.*
1828 George B.

Neilson,
1817 John, Jr.
1847 John.

Nelson,
1804 Joseph.
1841 Edward D.
1841 Samuel. *h.*

Nesmith,
1860 Robert D.

Nevius,
1837 George L.

Newby,
1863 Thomas B.

Newell,
1860 William S. *l.*

Newcomb,
1840 Obadiah, Jr.

Newschafer,
1864 William H. *l.*

Newton,
1842 George L.

Nichols,
1818 Samuel. *h.*
1825 Walter.
1831 Gideon S.
1839 Edwin A.
1845 Samuel B. R.
1852 Washington R.

Nicholson,
1792 James W.
1796 Samuel.

Nicholl,
1793 John.

Nicoll,
1766 Edward.
1774 Henry.
1774 Samuel. *m.*
1775† Augustus.
1776 Matthias.
1830 Henry.
1862 Augustus W. *l.*
1863 John D. *m.*

Nitchie,
1801 John.

Norsworthy,
1826 John B.

North,
1861 Alfred. *m.*

Northrop,
1864 George J. *m.*

Norton,
1792 John L.
1793 Robert B.

Norwood,
1862 Edward M. *m.*

Nott,
1857 Henry B.

Noyes,
1861 James H. *m.*

Nutten,
1863 Wilbur F. *m.*

Oakes,
1864 George B. *m.*

O'Blenis,
1818 John.

Odell,
1811 Jackson.

O'Dowd,
1852 Charles.

Ogden,
1758 Isaac.
1758 Josiah.
1772 Nicholas.
1776 Peter.
1791 Charles.
1791 Thomas L.
1793 Abraham.
1796 Gouverneur.
1798 William.
1801 Lewis M.
1802 Isaac.
1817 Meredith.
1821 Samuel.
1823 George B.
1823 John D.
1824 Waddington.
1828 John M.
1829 Richard H.
1829 Samuel.
1829 Thomas W.
1830 Charles H.
1833 Gouverneur M.
1837 David B. *h.*
1845 David B., Jr.
1849 Aaron.
1860 Thomas L.
1862 Charles W.
1864 Henry E. *m.*

Ogilby,
1829 John D.

Ogilvie,
1767 John. *h.*
1774 George.
1793 William. *h.*
1802 William.

Olmsted,
1862 George H. *m.*

Olssen,
1846 William W.

Olyphant,
1842 Robert M.
1862 David B.

O'Mullen,
1862 William. *l.*

Onderdonk,
1771 Benjamin. *m.*
1805 Henry U.
1809 Benjamin T.
1827 Henry, Jr.
1845 Henry.
1847 Benjamin A.

O'Neil,
1862 John, Jr. *l.*

Orchard,
1862 William B. *m.*

Osborn,
1827 Laughton.

Osborne,
1853 William J.

Osgood,
1809 Walter F.

Osterhoudt,
1864 Howard.

Ostrander,
1804 Ezekiel. *m.*
1848 Peter W.
1855 George A.

O'Sullivan,
1831 John L.

Otey,
1833 James H.

Otis,
1861 Frank A.

Oudenaarde,
1775† Marinus.
1775† Peter.

Owen,
1861 William H. *l.*
1863 George H.

Packwood,
1857 Richard T.

Page,
1864 Benjamin M. *m.*

Palachè,
1835 Alexander.

Panton,
1774 George.

Paris,
1791 Daniel.

Parish,
1841 John H.
1849 Henry, Jr.

Parker,
1793 James.
1854 James C., Jr.
1864 Henry H.

Parkman,
1857 Theodore.

Parks,
1851 Martin P. *h.*

Parmele,
1762 Ebenezer. *h.*

Parmly,
1842 Wheelock H.

Passmore,
1861 Joseph C. *h.*

Paterson,
1812 Matthew C.
1822 Alexander H.

Paulding,
1824 James K. *h.*
1842 William J.

Pearsall,
1861 Andrew T. *m.*
1861 Robert W. *l.*

Pearsee,
1793 Jonathan.

Pease,
1862 Edmund M. *m.*

Peck,
1841 William L.
1846 Edward M.

Peixotto,
1816 Daniel L. M.

Pell,
1770 Philip.
1806 Ferris.
1840 George W.
1848 William C.
1852 John H.
1858 Benjamin.
1860 Robert T.
1862 Edward M.
1862 Richard V.
1863 James B.
1863 John. *l.*

Pemberton,
1849 John P.

Pendergast,
1863 Patrick. *m.*

Pendleton,
1805 Edmund H.
1813 Nathaniel G.
1814 James M.

Péneveyre,
1825 Henri L. P. F. *h.*

Robert,
1762 Daniel.
1864 Charles S. *m.*

Roberts,
1842 Oliver E.

Robertson,
1812 Jacob A.
1813 Alexander H.
1816 John J.
1823 Andrew K.
1823 Noel.
1824 Alexander.
1825 Anthony L.

Robie,
1861 John W. *m.*

Robins,
1860 Edward P.

Robinson,
1773 Beverley.
1826 Beverley, Jr.
1862 John A. *m.*
1863 Robert E.

Rockwell,
1860 Fenton. *l.*
1862 William H., Jr. *m.*

Rodman,
1842 Washington.
1850 Erskine M.

Roebuck,
1772 Peter.

Rogers,
1803 Henry F.
1804 Samuel.
1807 George P.
1812 John S.
1817 Edward N.
1817 Samuel D.
1819 George J.
1820 Archibald G.
1827 Henry.
1841 Jones.
1848 Columbus B.

Romaine,
1806 Samuel B.
1838 Benjamin, Jr.
1840 Worthington.

Romer,
1854 Jean. *h.*

Romeyn,
1795 John B.
1816 James.
1858 James W.

Roof,
1862 Frank. *m.*
1864 Stephen W. *m.*

Roorbach,
1806 Frederic.

Roosevelt,
1815 James I., Jr.
1819 James H.
1826 William H.
1842 Silas W.
1864 Van Ness. *l.*

Root,
1841 George M.
1864 Russell H.

Ross,
1795 William.
1795 William M. *m.*
1804 David M.
1808 Henry H.
1843 John H.

Routh,
1849 S. D.

Rowan,
1822 Stephen N. *h.*

Rowland,
1852 John. *h.*

Rudd,
1861 Erastus B.

Rugg,
1862 George S. *m.*

Ruggles,
1832 Henry J.
1847 James F.

Rumsey,
1819 James S.

Rushmore,
1864 Merwin. *l.*

Russel,
1814 Theophilus.
1832 William C.

Russell,
1861 Henry E. *l.*
1861 William H., Jr.
1864 Allen S. *m.*

Rutgers,
1766 Henry.

Ryan,
1831 James. *h.*
1862 James E. *l.*

Ryerson,
1860 John G. *m.*

Sabine,
1859 William T.
1861 Thomas T.

Sackett,
1818 Clarence D.
1823 Grenville A.

Saltonstall,
1796 Winthrop. *m.*

Samson,
1860 Charles M. *m.*

Sands,
1795 Henry.
1798 Lewis.
1815 Robert C.
1825 Ferdinand.
1827 Edwin.
1827 Robert M.
1850 Joseph.
1860 Walter S. *l.*
1863 Philip J.

Sandford,
1863 George W. *l.*

Sanford,
1823 Nathan. *h.*
1864 Elliot. *l.*

Sanger,
1864 Adolph L. *l.*

Satterlee,
1863 Henry Y.
1863 Walter.

Satterthwaite,
1860 James S.

Savage,
1823 John. *h.*

Sayre,
1774 James. *h.*

Sayres,
1808 Gilbert H.
1854 William J.

Schaeffer,
1830 Frederic C. *h.*
1842 George C. *h.*

Schaffer,
1864 John Le G. *l.*

Schenck,
1801 Henry.
1860 John C. *l.*
1864 John P., Jr. *m.*

Schieffelin,
1801 Henry H.
1819 Richard L.
1855 George R.

Schermerhorn,
1793 John S.
1806 Cornelius.
1824 Daniel C.
1825 John J.
1827 John.
1829 Peter A.
1833 Bruce.
1840 William C.
1861 Harry A.
1863 Burr. *m.*
1863 William B.

Schmidt,
1859 Oscar E.

Schoonmaker,
1799 Jacob.

Schroeder,
1849 J. Frederick, Jr.

Schureman,
1816 John. *h.*

Schuyler,
1765 Arent.
1806 Philip.
1863 Eugene. *l.*

Scofield,
1803 Samuel. *m.*

Scoresby,
1864 William F. *m.*

Scott,
1798 William. *h.*
1850 Winfield. *h.*
1854 I. Jackson. *h.*

Scovill,
1761 James. *h.*

Scoville,
1861 Frederick. *l.*

Scudder,
1862 Henry J. *h.*

Seabury,
1761 Samuel. *h.*
1823 Samuel. *h.*
1856 William J.

Seaman,
1774 Benjamin.
1795 Benjamin.
1802 Billopp B.
1804 Robert.
1805 Edward.
1851 George A.
1864 William A. *l.*

Searle,
1771 John.

Sears,
1857 Charles E.
1862 Henry T. *m.*

Sebring,
1771 Michael. *m.*

Sedgwick,
1829 Theodore, Jr.

Seeds,
1860 O. Henry. *m.*

Seguin,
1864 Edward C. *m.*

Segur,
1860 Benjamin A. *m.*

Seney,
1815 Robert.

Seymour,
1826 Daniel.
1836 Charles.
1850 George F.
1860 Eldridge G. *m.*

Shea,
1831 James. *h.*
1837 Charles E.

Shapter,
1840 Peter, Jr.

Sharswood,
1856 George. *h.*

Shaw,
1774† Jacob.
1862 Samuel F. *m.*
1863 Abner O. *m.*
1863 Amos S., Jr. *m.*

Shelton,
1825 William. *h.*

Shepard,
1856 William F.

Shepherd,
1842 John H. *h.*

Sherman,
1803 Alpheus.

Sherwood,
1834 William. *h.*
1849 Ezra K.

Syme,
1864 William R. *l.*

Taber,
1863 James A. *l.*

Taggard,
1835 William H.
1845 John A.

Taggart,
1860 Charles J. *m.*

Tailer,
1852 Henry A.
1857 James T.

Talbot,
1857 William R.

Talcott,
1832 Frederick L.

Tallmadge,
1845 Frederick S.

Talman,
1811 John N.
1814 George F.

Tappan,
1807 Peter V. C
1854 Henry P. *h.*

Taylor,
1792 George.
1792 William.
1793 Willett, Jr. *m.*
1796 Charles.
1831 Edwin M.
1837 Thomas H. *h.*
1861 George L.
1861 Henry A. C.

Teakle,
1842 Elisha W.

Temple,
1795 James B.

Ten Broeck,
1834 Anthony.

Terrett,
1863 Charles W.

Terry,
1850 William H.

Thatcher,
1858 Thomas F.

Thayer,
1862 Foster.
1863 Stephen H., Jr.

Thibou,
1828 Lewis.

Thomas,
1800 Charles F.
1832 Philip W.
1835 Ludlow.
1837 David P.

Thompson,
1793 Thomas.
1804 John R.
1821 Junius.
1832 Jonathan, Jr.
1833 Abraham G., Jr.
1836 William.
1841 William M. *h.*
1854 Gardiner.
1856 David G., Jr.
1863 Thomas. *m.*
1864 Edward W. *m.*

Thoms,
1860 William F. *m.*

Thomson,
1803 Samuel W.
1818 Andrew. *h.*
1842 David, Jr.
1843 John.
1846 James.

Thorn,
1852 Eugene.
1852 William E.

Thrall,
1861 S. Chipman. *h.*

Thurman,
1835 John R.
1864 William. *m.*

Thurston,
1851 A. Henry.

Tibbals,
1864 Elbert P. *m.*

Tibbitts,
1853 Washington I.

Tichenor,
1801 Gabriel.

Tiebout,
1821 John, Jr.

Tillary,
1800 Matthew.
1802 James.

Tillinghast,
1806 John L.

Timpson,
1856 John W.

Titus,
1823 James H.

Todd,
1844 Ambrose S. *h.*
1864 John R. *m*

Tomes,
1831 Francis, Jr.

Tompkins,
1795 Daniel D.

Tooker,
1859 Gabriel M.

Toppan,
1861 Robert N. *l.*

Totten,
1858 Gilbert T.

Tourtelotte,
1863 Jacob F. *m.*

Townsend,
1759 Epenetus.
1810 Jacob.
1812 Peter S.
1820 John R.
1832 Frederick.
1832 Russell N.
1841 John J.
1847 Israel L.

Tracy,
1860 Frederick A.
1863 Lewis A. *m.*

Travers,
1838 William R.

Travis,
1847 Robert, Jr.
1850 Edward F.

Treadwell,
1758 Daniel. *h.*
1761 Agur. *h.*

Trenor,
1852 Eustace.
1852 John, Jr.
1859 Thomas F.

Trevett,
1835 Russell.

Tripler,
1860 Charles S. *h.*

Trippe,
1854 J. Condit.

Troup,
1766 John.
1766 John, Jr.
1774 Robert.

Tryon,
1774 William. *h.*
1862 Amazias W. *m.*

Tucker,
1769 Robert. *m.*
1822 Thomas W.
1829 Robert.
1837 John I.
1852 Richard H.
1861 John A.
1863 Robert S.

Tuckerman,
1863 Ernest. *l.*

Turk,
1796 William.

Turnbull,
1809 William.
1861 Stephen H.

Turner,
1821 William.
1855 Herbert B.
1861 Joseph M.

Tuttle,
1857 Daniel S.

Tyler,
1767 John. *h.*
1859 Samuel. *h.*

Tyng,
1846 Alexander G.
1862 Charles R.
1863 Morris A. *l.*

Udall,
1772 Richard. *m.*

Ulshoeffer,
1856 William G.

Upfold,
1831 George. *h.*

Ustick,
1794 Thomas.

Valentine,
1864 Albert E.

Vallejo,
1864 Platon. *m.*

Van Amringe,
1815 Henry H.
1860 John H.

Van Buren,
1807 Cornelius.
1829 John D.
1863 Frank R.

Van Boskerck,
1864 Richard T. *l.*

Van Buskirk,
1796 Lawrence.

Van Cleef,
1837 George S.

Van Cortlandt,
1758 Philip.
1807 James.
1864 Augustus. *m.*

Vanderbilt,
1837 John, Jr.

Vanderhoof,
1864 Frederick D. *m.*

Vanderpoel,
1862 John A.

Vanderveer,
1816 Adrian.

Vandervoort,
1828 John L.

Vandewater,
1814 Ferdinand.

Van Duzer,
1853 Archibald S.

Van Hook,
1797 Isaac A.

Van Horne,
1791 Frederic.
1793 Cornelius A.

Van Kleeck,
1828 Robert B.
1859 Robert B., Jr.
1863 Frederick B.

Van Mater,
1808 Daniel.

Van Ness,
1789 John P.
1797 William.

Van Pelt,
1799 Peter I.

**Willis,**
1862 Francis.
1862 William H., Jr.
1864 William S. *m.*

**Wilson,**
1800 George.
1800 Peter.
1818 Abraham D.
1822 Samuel F.
1825 Peter.
1825 William.
1826 Harris.
1835 William H.
1836 James W.
1845 Bird. *h.*
1860 Philip L. *l.*
1861 Benjamin F. *m.*
1862 Merritt H. *m.*
1863 Benjamin. *m.*

**Winans,**
1840 Joseph W.

**Windsor,**
1834 Lloyd.

**Winslow,**
1761 Edward. *h.*
1857 William B.
1864 Miron, Jr. *l.*

**Winston,**
1863 Gustavus S. *m.*

**Winter,**
1801 Gabriel.
1827 William.

**Winterton,**
1772 William. *m.*

**Winthrop,**
1812 Egerton L.
1827 Grenville T.
1860 Egerton L.
1864 Buchanan. *l.*

**Wood,**
1851 J. Walter.

**Woodhull,**
1791 Jesse.

**Woodruff,**
1860 Lewis B. *h.*
1861 Charles H. *l.*
1863 Lockwood De F. *m.*

**Woods,**
1791 James.

**Woodward,**
1798 Elias B.

**Worster,**
1863 Willard P.

**Worth,**
1829 Fanning S.

**Wotherspoon,**
1837 Alexander S.

**Wright,**
1799 David.
1851 David A.
1864 Samuel P. *l.*

**Wyatt,**
1809 William E.

**Wyckoff,**
1840 Van Brunt.
1862 Albert. *l.*

**Wynkoop,**
1819 Richard.

**Yale,**
1862 Leroy M.

**Yates,**
1787 John W.

**Youle,**
1793 Joseph. *m.*

**Zabriskie,**
1828 Martin R.
1835 Christian, Jr.
1854 Jeremiah L.

# CATALOGUE

OF THE

# GOVERNORS, TRUSTEES, AND OFFICERS,

AND OF THE

# ALUMNI AND OTHER GRADUATES,

OF

# COLUMBIA COLLEGE

(ORIGINALLY KING'S COLLEGE),

IN THE

# CITY OF NEW YORK,

FROM

# 1754 TO 1870.

NEW YORK:
D. VAN NOSTRAND, 23 MURRAY STREET AND 27 WARREN STREET.

M DCCC LXXI.

# CONTENTS.

# ABBREVIATIONS.

| | | | |
|---|---|---|---|
| ACT. | Actuary. | ED. | Editor. |
| ARCH. | Architect. | ENG. | Engineer. |
| ART. | Artist. | F. | Farmer. |
| AU. | Author. | M. | Merchant. |
| B. | Banker. | PUB. | Publisher. |
| BR. | Broker. | REV. | Reverend. |
| CHEM. | Chemist. | T. | Teacher. |
| C. L. | Counsellor at Law. | | |

A star (*) prefixed to a name denotes that the individual is deceased. In every case in which the year of the decease is known, it is indicated at the right.

# ADDITIONS.

PAGE

62, 1824.—Prefix a star to the name of Benjamin Drake. aet. 66. *1871.

70, 1838.—Prefix a star to the name of Philip Hone, Jr. *1870.

73, 1845.—Prefix a star to the name of George T. Elliot, Jr. aet. 44. *1871.

74, 1846.—After the name of *R. S. Carden Abbott, add aet. 27. *1854.

74, 1846.—Prefix a star to the name of John G. Hyer. *1868.

# EXPLANATORY NOTICE.

THE present catalogue of the Alumni and other graduates of Columbia College is the seventh which has been published since the re-organization of the College under its present title in 1787. The earlier of these publications were not issued periodically. With the fifth, published in 1865, there was commenced a series designed to be continued triennially. In this, also, the attempt was for the first time made to indicate the professions or occupations of the graduates, and to present a record of the honors, academic, civic, or military, which have been conferred upon them. Such an attempt, in the absence of any written record regularly kept at the College or elsewhere of matters of this nature, could not but be, to a certain extent, unsuccessful; and accordingly in the issuing of the catalogue of 1865 no credit was claimed for that publication on the score of perfection or completeness. The publication was avowedly made, in the form adopted, quite as much in the hope of eliciting, by means of the interest it might excite, additional information in regard to the personal history of the graduates, as of giving a permanent form to the information already obtained. This hope has not been wholly disappointed. A number of the Alumni of the College have kindly contributed important additions to the knowledge which had been previously gathered in regard to members of many of the earlier classes; and in consequence of this valuable assistance, the present edition of the catalogue, though still imperfect, will be found to exhibit a sensible improvement on those which have gone before.

Copies of this catalogue will be sent, as in 1865 and in 1868, to all the living Alumni whose residences are known. Those who may not receive it may be assured that the omission is owing only to want of information as to their proper addresses. They will be promptly supplied, on application, by post or otherwise, to the President, at the College.

Notwithstanding the considerable success which has attended the efforts made to supply the deficiencies of former publications, the imperfections which will doubtless be detected in the present one can hardly fail to be numerous. This prefatory note cannot, therefore, be better concluded than by once more repeating the request earnestly made on former occasions, of every graduate into whose hands the catalogue should fall, that he would communicate to the President, or to Professor Van Amringe, at the College, any information which may serve to improve it in future editions; completing first his own record, should he find it deficient, and adding any important facts within his knowledge, which the catalogue does not contain, in regard to any other graduate or graduates.

# GOVERNORS

OF

# KING'S COLLEGE,

## NEW YORK,

## AS APPOINTED BY ROYAL CHARTER,

## OCTOBER 31, A. D. 1754.

---

THE most Reverend Father in God, THOMAS, Lord Archbishop of Canterbury; and the most Reverend the Lord Archbishop of Canterbury for the time being, *ex officio.*

The Right Honorable DUNK, Earl of Halifax, First Lord Commissioner for Trade and Plantations; and the First Lord Commissioner for Trade and Plantations for the time being, *ex officio.*

The Governor of the Province, *ex officio.*

The eldest Councillor of the Province, *ex officio.*

The Judges of the Supreme Court of Judicature of the Province, *ex officio.*

The Secretary of the Province, *ex officio.*

The Attorney-General of the Province, *ex officio.*

The Speaker of the General Assembly of the Province, *ex officio.*

The Treasurer of the Province, *ex officio.*

The Mayor of the City of New York, *ex officio.*

The Rector of Trinity Church in the City of New York, *ex officio.*

The Senior Minister of the Reformed Protestant Dutch Church in the City of New York, *ex officio.*

The Minister of the Ancient Lutheran Church in the City of New York, *ex officio.*

The Minister of the French Church in the City of New York, *ex officio.*
The Minister of the Presbyterian Congregation in the City of New York, *ex officio.*
The President of the College, *ex officio.*

[The names of those who, at various times, attended meetings of the Governors, by virtue of their office as above, are :

JOHN CHAMBERS, Second Justice of the Supreme Court of the Province.
WILLIAM KEMPE, Attorney-General of the Province.
ABRAHAM DE PEYSTER, Treasurer of the Province.
EDWARD HOLLAND, Mayor of the City of New York.
HENRY BARCLAY, Rector of Trinity Church, New York.
JOANNES RITZEMA, Senior Minister of the Reformed Protestant Dutch Church, New York.
JOHN ALBERT WEYGAND, Minister of the Ancient Lutheran Church, New York.
JOANNES CARLE, Minister of the French Church, New York.
SAMUEL JOHNSON, President of the College.
JOHN CRUGER, Jr., Mayor of the City of New York.
DANIEL HORSMANDEN, Third Justice of the Supreme Court of the Province.
JOHN TABOR KEMPE, Attorney-General of the Province.
BENJAMIN PRATT, Chief-Justice of the Supreme Court of the Province.
MYLES COOPER, President of the College.
SAMUEL AUCHMUTY, Rector of Trinity Church, New York.
JOHN CRUGER, Speaker of the General Assembly of the Province.
The Archbishop of Canterbury (by proxy).]

ARCHIBALD KENNEDY.................................Declined to qualify.

JOSEPH MURRAY..........................Deceased Between July, 1756, and May, 1757

JOSIAH MARTIN..........................Removed from the Province Between March, 1761, and Oct., 1764

PAUL RICHARD..........................Deceased Between July, 1756, and March, 1759

HENRY CRUGER..........................Retired Subsequently to 1780

WILLIAM WALTON..........................Deceased Between May, 1768, and March, 1770

JOHN WATTS..........................Retired Subsequently to 1780

HENRY BEEKMAN..........................Resigned 1770

PHILIP VERPLANCK..........................Resigned 1770

FREDERICK PHILIPSE..........................Retired Subsequently to 1780

| | | |
|---|---|---|
| | | Deceased |
| JOSEPH ROBINSON | Between May, 1755, and March, | 1759 |
| | | Retired |
| JOHN CRUGER | Subsequently to | 1770 |
| | | Retired |
| OLIVER DE LANCEY | Subsequently to | 1780 |
| | | Deceased |
| JAMES LIVINGSTON | | 1763 |
| | | Deceased |
| BENJAMIN NICOLL | Between Feb., 1760, and April, | 1763 |
| WILLIAM LIVINGSTON | Declined to qualify. | |
| | | Retired |
| JOSEPH READE | Subsequently to | 1770 |
| | | Retired |
| NATHANIEL MARSTON | Subsequently to | 1780 |
| | | Deceased |
| JOSEPH HAYNES | Between March, 1758, and Jan., | 1762 |
| | | Retired |
| JOHN LIVINGSTON | Subsequently to | 1780 |
| | | Deceased |
| ABRAHAM LODGE | Between June, 1760, and Jan., | 1762 |
| | | Retired |
| DAVID CLARKSON | Subsequently to | 1780 |
| | | Retired |
| LEONARD LISPENARD | Subsequently to | 1780 |
| | | Retired |
| JAMES DE LANCEY, Jr. | Subsequently to | 1780 |

Appointed subsequently, by virtue of the power vested in the Governors by the Charter :

| Appointed | | | |
|---|---|---|---|
| | | | Resigned |
| 1759 | SAMUEL AUCHMUTY | Having become Rector of Trinity Church, | 1764 |
| | | | Resigned |
| 1759 | GABRIEL LUDLOW | | 1770 |
| 1761 | EDWARD ANTILL | Did not qualify or serve. | |
| | | | Deceased |
| 1762 | JOHN CHAMBERS | Between Nov., 1762, and Oct., | 1764 |
| | | | Retired |
| 1762 | HENRY CUYLER | Subsequently to | 1770 |
| | | | Retired |
| 1762 | JAMES DUANE | Subsequently to | 1780 |
| | | | Retired |
| 1762 | WILLIAM ALEXANDER, Earl of Stirling | Subsequently to | 1776 |
| | | | Retired |
| 1763 | CHARLES WARD APTHORPE | Subsequently to | 1780 |
| | | | Resigned |
| 1764 | BEVERLEY ROBINSON | | 1770 |
| | | | Deceased |
| 1764 | JOHN PROVOOST | Between Aug., 1767, and March | 1770 |
| | | | Retired |
| 1764 | THOMAS JONES | Subsequently to | 1780 |
| | | | Retired |
| 1764 | ARCHIBALD KENNEDY | Subsequently to | 1780 |

| Appointed | | | Retired |
|---|---|---|---|
| 1770 | Roger Morris | Subsequently to | 1780 |
| | | | Deceased |
| 1770 | John Ogilvie, S. T. D | | 1774 |
| | | | Retired |
| 1770 | Samuel Verplanck | Subsequently to | 1780 |
| | | | Retired |
| 1770 | Goldsborough Banyar | Subsequently to | 1780 |
| | | | Retired |
| 1770 | William Walton | Subsequently to | 1780 |
| | | | Retired |
| | Charles Inglis, S. T. D | Subsequently to | 1780 |
| | | | Retired |
| | Henry White | Subsequently to | 1780 |
| | | | Retired |
| | Peter Middleton, M.D | Subsequently to | 1780 |
| | | | Retired |
| | Jacob Walton | Subsequently to | 1780 |
| | | | Retired |
| | John Harris Cruger | Subsequently to | 1780 |
| | | | Retired |
| | John Maunsell | Subsequently to | 1780 |

## REGENTS OF THE UNIVERSITY,

To whom the Government of the College, under the name of Columbia College, was committed by an Act of the Legislature of the State of New York, passed May 1,

### A. D. 1784:

The Governor of the State for the time being, *ex officio*.
The Lieutenant-Governor " "
The President of the Senate " "
The Speaker of the House of Assembly for the time being, *ex officio*.
The Mayor of the City of New York " "
The Mayor of the City of Albany " "
The Attorney-General " "
The President and Professors of the College " "
The Secretary of State " "

Brockholst Livingston,
Robert Harpur,
Walter Livingston,
Christopher Yates,
Anthony Hoffman,
Cornelius Humphrey,
Lewis Morris,
Philip Pell, Jr.,
Matthew Clarkson,
Rutgers Van Brunt,
James Townsend,
Thomas Lawrence,
Henry Wisner,
John Haring,
Christopher Tappan,
James Clinton,

Christopher P. Yates,
James Livingston,
Abraham Bancker,
John C. Dongan,
Ezra L'Hommedieu,
Caleb Smith,
John Williams,
John M'Crea.

And the following, added to the above-named, by an Act of the Legislature, passed November 26, 1784:

John Jay, LL. D.,
Samuel Provoost, S. T. D.,
John H. Livingston, S. T. D.,
John Rogers, S. T. D.,
John Mason, S. T. D.,
John Gano,
John Daniel Gross, S. T. D.,
Johann Christoff Kunze, S. T. D.,
Joseph Delaplaine,
Gershom Seixas,
Alexander Hamilton, LL. D.,
John Lawrence,
John Rutherfurd,
Morgan Lewis,
Leonard Lispenard,
John Cochran, M. D.,
Charles McKnight, M. D.,
Thomas Jones, M. D.,
Malachi Treat, M. D.,
Nicholas Romayne, M. D.,
Peter W. Yates,
Matthew Visscher,
Hunlock Woodruff, M. D.
George I. L. Dole,
John Vanderbilt,
Thomas Romaine,
Samuel Buel,
Gilbert Livingston,
Nathan Kerr,
Ebenezer Lockwood,
John Lloyd,
Herman Garrison,
Ebenezer Russell.

## TRUSTEES OF COLUMBIA COLLEGE.

The following, appointed by an Act of the Legislature of the State of New York, April 13, 1787, reviving the original Charter with amendments:

|  | | |
|---|---|---|
| James Duane | Resigned | 1795 |
| Samuel Provoost, S. T. D | Resigned | 1801 |
| John H. Livingston, S. T. D | Retired | 1810 |
| Richard Varick | Resigned | 1816 |
| Alexander Hamilton, LL. D. | Deceased | 1804 |
| John Mason, S. T. D | Resigned | 1788 |
| James Wilson | Retired | 1788 |

|  | |
|---|---|
| JOHN GANO* | Retired 1788 |
| BROCKHOLST LIVINGSTON, LL. D. | Deceased 1823 |
| ROBERT HARPUR | Resigned 1795 |
| JOHN DANIEL GROSS, S. T. D. | Resigned 1787 |
| JOHANN CHRISTOFF KUNZE, S. T. D. | Resigned 1792 |
| WALTER LIVINGSTON | Deceased 1797 |
| LEWIS A. SCOTT | Deceased 1798 |
| JOSEPH DELAPLAINE | Declined 1787 |
| LEONARD LISPENARD | Deceased 1790 |
| ABRAHAM BEACH, S. T. D. | Retired 1813 |
| JOHN LAWRENCE | Deceased 1810 |
| JOHN RUTHERFURD† | Retired 1787 |
| MORGAN LEWIS | Resigned 1804 |
| JOHN COCHRAN, M. D. | Resigned 1794 |
| GERSHOM SEIXAS | Resigned 1815 |
| CHARLES McKNIGHT, M. D. | Resigned 1787 |
| THOMAS JONES, M. D | Deceased 1798 |
| MALACHI TREAT, M. D | Deceased 1795 |
| SAMUEL BARD, M. D | Resigned 1804 |
| NICHOLAS ROMAYNE, M. D. | Resigned 1793 |
| BENJAMIN KISSAM, M. D. | Deceased 1803 |
| EBENEZER CROSBY, M. D. | Deceased 1788 |

And the following, subsequently chosen by virtue of the Act of April 13, 1787, empowering the Trustees then created to fill vacancies:

| Appointed | Name | |
|---|---|---|
| 1788 | WILLIAM SAMUEL JOHNSON, LL. D. | Resigned 1800 |
| 1788 | RICHARD HARISON, LL. D. | Deceased 1829 |

* This name does not appear on the list of Trustees after March 15, 1788.

† This name does not appear on the list of Trustees after May 20, 1787.

| Appointed | Name | | |
|---|---|---|---|
| 1789 | John Watts | Resigned | 1816 |
| 1790 | William Moore, M. D | Deceased | 1824 |
| 1793 | Edward Livingston | Retired | 1806 |
| 1793 | John McKnight, S. T. D | Resigned | 1795 |
| 1794 | John Cosine | Deceased | 1798 |
| 1795 | Cornelius I. Bogert | Resigned | 1823 |
| 1795 | John M. Mason, S. T. D | Resigned | 1821 |
| 1795 | Samuel Nicoll, M. D | Deceased | 1796 |
| 1795 | Edward Dunscomb | Deceased | 1814 |
| 1796 | George C. Anthon, M. D | Resigned | 1815 |
| 1797 | Philip Livingston | Resigned | 1806 |
| 1799 | John Charlton, M. D | Deceased | 1806 |
| 1799 | John N. Abeel, S. T. D | Deceased | 1812 |
| 1799 | James Tillary, M. D | Deceased | 1818 |
| 1801 | Charles H. Wharton, S. T. D | Resigned | 1801 |
| 1801 | John H. Hobart, S. T. D | Deceased | 1830 |
| 1802 | Benjamin Moore, S. T. D | Resigned | 1813 |
| 1804 | Egbert Benson, LL. D | Resigned | 1815 |
| 1804 | Johann C. Kunze, S. T. D | Deceased | 1807 |
| 1805 | Gouverneur Morris | Deceased | 1816 |
| 1805 | Jacob Radcliffe | Resigned | 1817 |
| 1806 | Samuel Miller, S. T. D | Retired | 1813 |
| 1806 | Rufus King, LL. D | Resigned | 1824 |
| 1807 | Nicholas Evertson | Deceased | 1807 |
| 1808 | Oliver Wolcott | Retired | 1816 |
| 1809 | John B. Romeyn, S. T. D | Deceased | 1825 |
| 1811 | William Harris, S. T. D | Deceased | 1829 |
| 1811 | Robert Troup, LL. D | Resigned | 1817 |

| Appointed | | |
|---|---|---|
| 1812 | Peter A. Jay | Resigned 1817 |
| 1813 | Clement C. Moore, LL. D | Resigned 1857 |
| 1813 | Charles Wilkes | Resigned 1824 |
| 1815 | David B. Ogden, LL. D. | Deceased 1849 |
| 1815 | William Johnson, LL. D | Resigned 1842 |
| 1815 | John Wells | Deceased 1823 |
| 1816 | Thomas Y. How, S. T. D | Retired 1818 |
| 1816 | William Henderson | Resigned 1823 |
| 1816 | Edward W. Laight | Resigned 1851 |
| 1816 | John R. Murray | Resigned 1835 |
| 1816 | Wright Post, M. D | Resigned 1828 |
| 1817 | Beverley Robinson | Resigned 1854 |
| 1817 | Thomas L. Ogden | Deceased 1844 |
| 1817 | Nicholas Fish | Resigned 1833 |
| 1817 | James Renwick | Retired 1820 |
| 1818 | Samuel F. Jarvis, S. T. D | Retired 1820 |
| 1818 | John T. Irving | Deceased 1838 |
| 1820. | David S. Jones, LL. D | Deceased 1848 |
| 1821 | Gulian C. Verplanck | Resigned 1826 |
| 1822 | Pascal N. Strong | Deceased 1825 |
| 1823 | James Kent, LL. D. | Resigned 1823 |
| 1823 | Peter A. Jay, LL. D | Deceased 1843 |
| 1823 | John Duer | Resigned 1830 |
| 1824 | Benjamin T. Onderdonk, S. T. D | Resigned 1853 |
| 1824 | Lynde Catlin | Deceased 1833 |
| 1824 | Jonathan M. Wainwright, S. T. D | Resigned 1830 |
| 1824 | Philip Hone | Deceased 1851 |
| 1824 | John Watts, M. D | Deceased 1831 |

| Appointed | Name | |
|---|---|---|
| 1825 | CHARLES KING | Resigned 1838 |
| 1825 | JAMES M. MATTHEWS, S. T. D. | Resigned 1830 |
| 1826 | SAMUEL BOYD | Resigned 1835 |
| 1828 | WILLIAM CREIGHTON, S. T. D. | Resigned 1840 |
| 1830 | GARDINER SPRING, S. T. D. | |
| 1830 | JAMES CAMPBELL | Deceased 1848 |
| 1830 | WILLIAM D. SNODGRASS, S. T. D. | Resigned 1833 |
| 1830 | JOHN L. LAWRENCE | Deceased 1849 |
| 1830 | WILLIAM A. DUER, LL. D. | Resigned 1842 |
| 1830 | JOHN FERGUSON | Deceased 1832 |
| 1831 | EDWARD R. JONES | Resigned 1838 |
| 1832 | WILLIAM BERRIAN, S. T. D. | Deceased 1862 |
| 1833 | OGDEN HOFFMAN | Deceased 1856 |
| 1833 | THOMAS W. LUDLOW | Resigned 1836 |
| 1834 | SAMUEL WARD | Deceased 1838 |
| 1836 | SAMUEL B. RUGGLES, LL. D. | |
| 1836 | JOHN KNOX, S. T. D. | Deceased 1858 |
| 1837 | THOMAS L. WELLS | Resigned 1859 |
| 1838 | WILLIAM R. WILLIAMS, S. T. D. | Resigned 1848 |
| 1838 | WILLIAM H. HARISON | Deceased 1860 |
| 1838 | JOHN B. BECK, M. D. | Deceased 1851 |
| 1840 | HAMILTON FISH | Resigned 1849 |
| 1840 | WILLIAM BARD | Deceased 1853 |
| 1842 | WILLIAM BETTS, LL. D. | |
| 1842 | NATHANIEL F. MOORE, LL. D. | Resigned 1851 |
| 1843 | BENJAMIN I. HAIGHT, S. T. D. | |
| 1845 | GERRIT G. VAN WAGENEN | Deceased 1858 |
| 1848 | JOHN L. MASON | Resigned 1853 |

| Appointed | | |
|---|---|---|
| 1848 | William H. Hobart, M. D. | Resigned 1855 |
| 1849 | Edward Jones | Deceased 1869 |
| 1849 | Robert Ray | |
| 1849 | Gouverneur M. Ogden | |
| 1849 | Charles King, LL. D. | Deceased 1867 |
| 1851 | Hamilton Fish, LL. D. | |
| 1851 | Henry James Anderson, M. D., LL. D. | |
| 1851 | Gerard W. Morris | Resigned 1855 |
| 1851 | George H. Fisher, S. T. D. | Resigned 1855 |
| 1853 | George T. Strong | |
| 1853 | Jonathan M. Wainwright, S. T. D., J. C. D. | Deceased 1854 |
| 1853 | Edward L. Beadle, M. D. | |
| 1854 | George F. Allen | Deceased 1863 |
| 1854 | Horatio Potter, S. T. D., LL. D., D. C. L. | |
| 1855 | Alexander W. Bradford, LL. D. | Deceased 1867 |
| 1855 | Mancius S. Hutton, S. T. D. | |
| 1856 | Martin Zabriskie | Resigned 1869 |
| 1856 | John Torrey, M. D., LL. D. | |
| 1858 | Thomas De Witt, S. T. D. | |
| 1858 | Lewis M. Rutherfurd | |
| 1859 | John Jacob Astor, Jr. | Resigned 1869 |
| 1859 | John C. Jay, M. D. | |
| 1860 | William C. Schermerhorn | |
| 1862 | Morgan Dix, S. T. D. | |
| 1864 | Frederick A. P. Barnard, S. T. D., LL. D. | |
| 1867 | Samuel Blatchford, LL. D. | |
| 1868 | Stephen P. Nash | |
| 1870 | Charles R. Swords | |

## COMMITTEE OF THE TRUSTEES ON THE SCHOOL OF MINES.

### 1870.

WILLIAM BETTS, LL. D., Chairman,
GEORGE T. STRONG,
STEPHEN P. NASH,
LEWIS M. RUTHERFURD,
FREDERICK A. P. BARNARD, S,T.D., LL,D.,
HAMILTON FISH, LL. D.,
JOHN TORREY, M.D., LL. D.

#### ASSOCIATE MEMBERS.

CORNELIUS R. AGNEW, M. D.,
GEORGE C. ANTHON,
SAMUEL W. BRIDGHAM,
LEWIS L. DELAFIELD,
FRANKLIN H. DELANO,
WILLIAM E. DODGE, Jr.,
JACOB P. G. FOSTER,
NATHANIEL P. HOSACK,
MORRIS K. JESUP,
GOUVERNEUR KEMBLE,
ROBERT L. KENNEDY,
EDWARD G. LUDLOW,
Baron ROBERT OSTENSACKEN,
ROBERT P. PARROTT,
HOWARD POTTER,
TEMPLE PRIME,
PERCY R. PYNE,
JAMES N. RENWICK,
OTIS D. SWAN,
LUCIUS TUCKERMAN,
GEORGE C. WARD.

## TRUSTEES OF THE MEDICAL DEPARTMENT.

### 1860.

| | Deceased |
|---|---|
| JOHN C. CHEESMAN, M. D | 1862 |
| EDWARD G. LUDLOW, M. D | |
| JOSEPH DELAFIELD | |
| FLOYD SMITH | |
| RICHARD M. BLATCHFORD | |
| EDWARD DELAFIELD, M. D. | |
| JOHN P. CROSBY | |
| GURDON BUCK, M. D | |
| LUTHER BRADISH | Deceased 1863 |
| JAMES W. BEEKMAN | |

| | |
|---|---|
| DANIEL D. LORD | |
| BENJAMIN R. WINTHROP | |
| EDWARD L. BEADLE, M. D. | |
| WICKHAM HOFFMAN | Resigned 1867 |
| ISAAC WOOD, M. D. | Resigned 1868 |
| GEORGE W. WRIGHT | |
| FREDERICK A. CONKLING | |
| CHARLES HENSCHEL, M. D. | |
| WASHINGTON MURRAY | Resigned 1868 |
| HENRY CHAUNCEY, Jr. | Resigned 1869 |
| SULLIVAN H. WESTON, S. T. D. | |
| WILLIAM BETTS, LL. D. | |
| JOHN JACOB ASTOR, Jr. | Resigned 1863 |
| GEORGE TALBOT OLYPHANT | |
| JOHN TORREY, M. D., LL. D. | |

SINCE APPOINTED.

| | |
|---|---|
| 1863 BENJAMIN OGDEN, M. D. | Resigned 1867 |
| 1863 CAMBRIDGE LIVINGSTON | |
| 1864 JARED LINSLY, M. D. | |
| 1867 JOHN J. CRANE, M. D. | |
| 1869 ELLSWORTH ELLIOT | |
| 1869 ROBERT G. REMSEN | |
| 1869 JAMES L. BANKS, M. D. | |
| 1869 GEORGE H. GILLESPIE | |

# CHAIRMEN

## OF THE BOARD OF GOVERNORS UNDER THE ROYAL CHARTER.

The Governor of the Province, or person next in rank, or Senior Governor.

## OF THE BOARD OF REGENTS, 1784-1787.

The Chancellor of the University, or Vice-Chancellor, or Senior Regent.

## OF THE BOARD OF TRUSTEES.

| Appointed | Name | |
|---|---|---|
| 1787 | JAMES DUANE | Resigned 1795 |
| 1795 | SAMUEL PROVOOST, S. T. D | Resigned 1801 |
| 1801 | JOHN H. LIVINGSTON, S. T. D | Resigned 1810 |
| 1810 | RICHARD VARICK | Resigned 1816 |
| 1816 | BROCKHOLST LIVINGSTON, LL. D | Deceased 1823 |
| 1823 | RICHARD HARISON, LL. D | Resigned 1823 |
| 1823 | WILLIAM MOORE, M. D | Deceased 1824 |
| 1824 | NICHOLAS FISH | Resigned 1832 |
| 1832 | PETER A. JAY, LL. D | Deceased 1843 |
| 1843 | DAVID B. OGDEN, LL. D | Deceased 1849 |
| 1849 | EDWARD W. LAIGHT | Resigned 1850 |
| 1850 | BEVERLEY ROBINSON | Resigned 1854 |
| 1854 | JOHN KNOX, S. T. D | Resigned 1854 |
| 1858 | GARDINER SPRING, S. T. D | Resigned 1859 |
| 1859 | HAMILTON FISH, LL. D | |

# CLERKS

## OF THE BOARD OF GOVERNORS.

LAMBERT MOORE.

## OF THE BOARD OF REGENTS, 1784-1787.

ROBERT HARPUR.

## OF THE BOARD OF TRUSTEES.

| Appointed | Name | Resigned |
|---|---|---|
| 1787 | ROBERT HARPUR | 1795 |
| 1795 | ABRAHAM BEACH, S. T. D | 1811 |
| 1811 | WILLIAM HARRIS, S. T. D | 1811 |
| 1811 | JOHN B. ROMEYN, S. T. D | 1815 |
| 1815 | CLEMENT C. MOORE, LL. D | 1850 |
| 1850 | WILLIAM BETTS, LL. D | |

# TREASURERS OF THE COLLEGE.

| | | |
|---|---|---|
| 1775 | LEONARD LISPENARD | Resigned 1784 |
| 1784 | BROCKHOLST LIVINGSTON, LL. D | Deceased 1823 |
| 1823 | NICHOLAS FISH | Resigned 1823 |
| 1824 | WILLIAM JOHNSON, LL. D | Resigned 1833 |
| 1833 | JOHN L. LAWRENCE | Deceased 1849 |
| 1849 | GERRIT G. VAN WAGENEN | Deceased 1858 |
| 1858 | GOUVERNEUR M. OGDEN | |

# PRESIDENTS OF THE COLLEGE

## UNDER THE ROYAL CHARTER.

| | | |
|---|---|---|
| 1754 | SAMUEL JOHNSON, S. T. D | Resigned 1763 |
| 1763 | MYLES COOPER, LL. D | Retired 1775 |
| 1775 | BENJAMIN MOORE, A. M. (*pro tempore*, in the absence of the President) | Resigned 1776 |

# PRESIDENTS OF THE COLLEGE

### UNDER THE NEW CHARTER.

| Appointed | | |
|---|---|---|
| 1787 | WILLIAM SAMUEL JOHNSON, LL. D. | Resigned 1800 |
| 1801 | CHARLES H. WHARTON, S. T. D. | Resigned 1801 |
| 1801 | BENJAMIN MOORE, S. T. D. | Resigned 1811 |
| 1811 | WILLIAM HARRIS, S. T. D. | Deceased 1829 |
| 1829 | WILLIAM ALEXANDER DUER, LL. D. | Resigned 1842 |
| 1842 | NATHANIEL F. MOORE, LL. D. | Resigned 1849 |
| 1849 | CHARLES KING, LL. D. | Resigned 1864 |
| 1864 | FREDERICK A. P. BARNARD, S. T. D., LL. D. | |

# PROVOST.

| | | |
|---|---|---|
| 1811 | JOHN M. MASON, S. T. D. | Resigned 1816 |

# FACULTY OF ARTS.

President Johnson was, at first, sole Instructor.

### PROFESSORS OF MATHEMATICS AND NATURAL PHILOSOPHY.

| | | |
|---|---|---|
| 1757 | Daniel Treadwell, A. M. | Deceased 1760 |
| 1761 | Robert Harpur, A. M. | Transferred 1765 |
| 1799 | John Kemp, LL. D. | Deceased 1812 |
| 1813 | Robert Adrain, LL. D. | Transferred 1820 |

### PROFESSORS OF MORAL PHILOSOPHY.

1762 Myles Cooper, A. M. ........ Promoted 1763

1787 John Daniel Gross, S. T. D. ........ Resigned 1795

In 1795, Logic was added to the Department.

1795 John McKnight, S. T. D. ........ Retired 1799

In 1799, Rhetoric and Belles Lettres were added.

1801 John Bowden, S. T. D. ........ Deceased 1817

1817 John McVickar, S. T. D. ........ Transferred 1857

In 1818, Intellectual Philosophy and Political Economy were added.

## PROFESSORS OF MATHEMATICS.

| Appointed | | Resigned |
|---|---|---|
| 1765 | Robert Harpur, A. M. | 1767 |
| | | Transferred |
| 1786 | John Kemp, LL. D. | 1799 |
| | | Transferred |
| 1857 | Charles Davies, LL D. | 1859 |
| | | Promoted |
| 1857 | William G. Peck, A. M. (Adjunct) | 1859 |
| 1863 | John H. Van Amringe, A. M. (Adjunct) | |

## PROFESSORS OF NATURAL PHILOSOPHY.

| | | Retired |
|---|---|---|
| 1765 | Samuel Clossy, M. D. | 1776 |

In 1785, Astronomy was added to the Department.

| | | Resigned |
|---|---|---|
| 1785 | Samuel Bard, M. D. | 1786 |

## PROFESSOR OF NATURAL LAW.

| | | Retired |
|---|---|---|
| 1773 | John Vardill, A. M. | 1776 |

In 1775, History and Languages were added to the Department.

## PROFESSORS OF THE FRENCH LANGUAGE.

| | | Deceased |
|---|---|---|
| 1784 | John P. Tetard | 1787 |
| | | Retired |
| 1792 | Villette De Marcellin | 1799 |

In 1828, the Department was revived under the style of the Department of the French Language and Literature.

| | | Resigned |
|---|---|---|
| 1828 | Antoine Verren, A. M. | 1839 |
| | | Retired |
| 1839 | Felix G. Berteau, LL. B. | 1856 |

This Professorship was abolished in 1866.

## PROFESSORS OF THE GREEK AND LATIN LANGUAGES.

| | | Resigned |
|---|---|---|
| 1784 | William Cochran, A. M. | 1789 |
| | | Resigned |
| 1789 | Peter Wilson, A. M. | 1792 |
| | | Resigned |
| 1792 | Elijah D. Rattoone, S. T. D. | 1797 |

In 1794, Grecian and Roman Antiquities were added to the Department.

| | | Resigned |
|---|---|---|
| 1797 | Peter Wilson, LL. D. | 1820 |
| | | Promoted |
| 1817 | Nathaniel F. Moore, A. M. (Adjunct) | 1820 |
| | | Resigned |
| 1820 | Nathaniel F. Moore, LL. D. | 1835 |
| | | Promoted |
| 1820 | Charles Anthon, A. B. (Adjunct) | 1830 |

| Appointed | | Transferred |
|---|---|---|
| 1830 | Charles Anthon, LL. D. (Jay) | 1857 |
| | | Resigned |
| 1837 | Robert G. Vermilye, A. M. (Adjunct) | 1843 |
| | | Promoted |
| 1845 | Henry Drisler, Jr., A. M (Adjunct) | 1857 |

## PROFESSOR OF RHETORIC AND LOGIC.

| | | Resigned |
|---|---|---|
| 1784 | Benjamin Moore, A. M. | 1787 |

## PROFESSORS OF THE ORIENTAL LANGUAGES.

| | | Resigned |
|---|---|---|
| 1784 | Johann C. Kunze, S. T. D | 1787 |
| | | Retired |
| 1792 | Johann C. Kunze, S. T. D | 1799 |

## PROFESSORS OF THE GERMAN LANGUAGE.

| | | Resigned |
|---|---|---|
| 1784 | John Daniel Gross, S. T. D | 1795 |

In 1830, the Department was revived, under the style of the Department of the German Language and Literature.

| | | Deceased |
|---|---|---|
| 1830 | Frederick C. Schaeffer, S. T. D | 1831 |
| | | Resigned |
| 1832 | William Ernenputsch | 1832 |
| | | Resigned |
| 1843 | John Louis Tellkampf, J. U. D. (Gebhard) | 1847 |
| 1847 | Henry I. Schmidt, S. T. D. (Gebhard) | |

## PROFESSORS OF GEOGRAPHY.

| | | Resigned |
|---|---|---|
| 1784 | John D. Gross, S. T. D. | 1795 |
| | | Transferred |
| 1795 | John Kemp, LL. D. | 1799 |

## PROFESSOR OF NATURAL HISTORY.

| | | Resigned |
|---|---|---|
| 1785 | Henry Moyes, LL. D. | 1786 |

## PROFESSOR OF NATURAL HISTORY, CHEMISTRY, AGRICULTURE, AND THE OTHER ARTS DEPENDING THEREON.

| | | Retired |
|---|---|---|
| 1792 | Samuel L. Mitchill, M. D., LL. D. | 1801 |

## PROFESSORS OF LAW.

| | | Resigned |
|---|---|---|
| 1793 | James Kent, A. M. | 1798 |
| | | Deceased |
| 1823 | James Kent, LL. D. | 1847 |
| | | Resigned |
| 1848 | William Betts, LL. D. | 1854 |

## PROFESSOR OF RHETORIC AND BELLES-LETTRES.

Appointed — Retired

1795 John Bisset, A. M. .......... 1799

## PROFESSORS OF CHEMISTRY.

1802 James S. Stringham, M. D .......... Transferred 1810

1813 John Griscom .......... Retired 1820

1857 Charles A. Joy, Ph. D ..........

## PROFESSORS OF MATHEMATICS AND ASTRONOMY.

1820 Robert Adrain, LL. D .......... Resigned 1825

1825 Henry James Anderson, M. D., LL. D., resigned 1843 .......... Emeritus 1866

1843 Charles W. Hackley, S. T. D .......... Transferred 1857

1861 William Guy Peck, LL. D ..........

## PROFESSORS OF NATURAL AND EXPERIMENTAL PHILOSOPHY AND CHEMISTRY.

1820 James Renwick, LL. D. Emeritus, 1853 .......... Deceased 1863

1854 Richard S. McCulloh .......... Transferred 1857

## PROFESSORS OF THE ITALIAN LANGUAGE AND LITERATURE.

1826 Lorenzo Da Ponte .......... Deceased 1837

1839 E. Felix Foresti, LL. B .......... Resigned 1856

## PROFESSOR OF THE HEBREW LANGUAGE AND LITERATURE.

1830 Samuel H. Turner, S. T. D .......... Deceased 1861

## PROFESSOR OF THE SPANISH LANGUAGE AND LITERATURE.

1830 Mariano Velazquez de la Cadeña, LL. B .......... Deceased 1860

## PROFESSOR OF ELEMENTARY CHEMISTRY.

1832 William H. Ellet, M. D .......... Retired 1833

## PROFESSOR OF ELOCUTION.

1844 John W. S. Hows .......... Retired 1857

### PROFESSOR OF THE EVIDENCES OF NATURAL AND REVEALED RELIGION.

Appointed — Deceased

1857 John McVickar, S. T. D. Emeritus, 1864........................ 1868

### JAY PROFESSORS OF THE GREEK LANGUAGE AND LITERATURE.

Deceased

1857 Charles Anthon, LL. D........................................ 1867

1867 Henry Drisler, LL. D........................................

### PROFESSORS OF THE LATIN LANGUAGE AND LITERATURE.

Transferred

1857 Henry Drisler, LL. D........................................ 1867

1868 Charles Short, LL. D........................................

### PROFESSOR OF ASTRONOMY.

Deceased

1857 Charles W. Hackley, S. T. D.................................... 1861

### PROFESSORS OF MECHANICS AND PHYSICS.

Expelled

1857 Richard S. McCulloh, A. M.*.................................. 1863

1863 Ogden N. Rood, A. M.........................................

### PROFESSOR OF HISTORY AND POLITICAL SCIENCE.

Transferred

1857 Francis Lieber, LL. D........................................ 1865

### PROFESSOR OF MORAL AND INTELLECTUAL PHILOSOPHY AND LITERATURE.

1857 Charles Murray Nairne, L. H. D.................................

History and Political Economy were added in 1865.

### PROFESSOR OF HIGHER MATHEMATICS.

Emeritus

1859 Charles Davies, LL. D........................................ 1865

### PROFESSOR OF PURE MATHEMATICS.

Transferred

1859 William Guy Peck, LL. D....................................... 1861

* Expelled October 15, 1863, for having abandoned his post and joined the Rebels.

## TUTORS.

| Appointed | | |
|---|---|---|
| 1755 | William Johnson, A. M. | Resigned 1755 |
| 1756 | Leonard Cutting | Resigned 1763 |
| 1757 | Daniel Treadwell, A. M. | Deceased 1760 |
| 1762 | Myles Cooper, A. M | Retired 1763 |
| 1765 | Samuel Clossy, M. D. | Retired 1776 |
| 1773 | John Vardill, A. M. | Retired 1776 |
| 1785 | John Kemp. | Promoted 1786 |
| 1831 | Abraham B. Conger, A. B. | Retired 1833 |
| 1831 | John L. O'Sullivan, A. B. | Retired 1833 |
| 1835 | Robert G. Vermilye, A. M. | Promoted 1837 |
| 1843 | Henry Drisler, Jr., A. M. | Promoted 1845 |
| 1859 | J. Emory McClintock, A. B. | Resigned 1860 |
| 1860 | J. Howard Van Amringe, A. M. | Promoted 1863 |
| 1864 | Duane S. Everson, A. M. | Resigned 1868 |
| 1865 | Eugene Lawrence, A. M. | Resigned 1868 |
| 1868 | Augustus C. Merriam, A. M. | |
| 1868 | Wendell Lamoroux, A. M. | Retired 1869 |
| 1869 | Theodore F. C. Demarest, A. M. | Resigned 1870 |
| 1870 | John D. Quackenbos, A. B. | |

## LECTURERS.

| | | |
|---|---|---|
| 1830 | William H. Ellet, M. D. (Elementary Chemistry) | Promoted 1832 |
| 1869 | William A. McVickar, S. T. D. (Evidences of Religion) | |

## LIBRARIANS.

The duties of Librarian were discharged by one of the Professors until 1837.

| | | |
|---|---|---|
| 1837 | Nathaniel F. Moore, LL. D. | Resigned 1839 |
| 1839 | George C. Schaeffer, A. M., M. D. | Resigned 1847 |

| Appointed | | Deceased |
|---|---|---|
| 1847 | LEFROY RAVENHILL, A. M., M. D. | 1851 |
| 1849 | STEPHEN R. WEEKS (Assistant) | |
| | | Resigned |
| 1851 | WILLIAM ALFRED JONES, A. M. | 1865 |
| 1865 | BEVERLEY R. BETTS, A. M. | |

### CHAPLAIN.

The President discharged the duties of this office till 1857.

1857 CORNELIUS R. DUFFIE, S. T. D.

### HEAD MASTERS OF THE GRAMMAR SCHOOL.

| | | |
|---|---|---|
| 1763 | MATTHEW CUSHING, A. M. | Retired |
| | ALEXANDER LESLIE, A. M. | Retired |
| 1784 | WILLIAM COCHRAN, A. M. | Retired |
| 1829 | JOHN D. OGILBY, A. B. | Resigned 1830 |
| 1830 | CHARLES ANTHON, LL. D. (Rector) | Retired 1864 |

## FACULTY OF MEDICINE.*

### PROFESSORS OF ANATOMY.

| | | |
|---|---|---|
| 1767 | SAMUEL CLOSSY, M. D. | Retired 1776 |
| 1785 | CHARLES MCKNIGHT, M. D. | Deceased 1792 |
| 1792 | RICHARD BAILEY, M. D. | Transferred 1793 |
| 1793 | WRIGHT POST, M. D. | Retired 1813 |
| 1860 | ROBERT WATTS, M. D. | Deceased 1867 |
| 1867 | HENRY B. SANDS, M. D. | |

### PROFESSOR OF PATHOLOGY AND PHYSIOLOGY.

| | | |
|---|---|---|
| 1767 | PETER MIDDLETON, M. D. | Retired 1776 |

* There was no Faculty of Medicine from 1813 to 1860. In this latter year it was revived by the adoption of the College of Physicians and Surgeons as the Medical Department of the College.

## PROFESSORS OF SURGERY.

| Appointed | | Retired |
|---|---|---|
| 1767 | John Jones, M. D | 1776 |
| | | Deceased |
| 1785 | Charles McKnight, M. D | 1792 |
| | | Transferred |
| 1792 | Wright Post, M. D | 1793 |
| | | Deceased |
| 1793 | Richard Bailey, M. D | 1811 |
| | | Retired |
| 1811 | Valentine Mott, M. D | 1813 |
| | | Deceased |
| 1860 | Alexander H. Stevens, M. D., LL. D. (Emeritus) | 1869 |
| | | Transferred |
| 1860 | Willard Parker, M. D | 1870 |
| | | Promoted |
| 1860 | Thomas M. Markoe, M. D. (Adjunct) | 1870 |
| 1870 | Thomas M. Markoe, M. D | |

## PROFESSORS OF CHEMISTRY AND MATERIA MEDICA.

| | | Retired |
|---|---|---|
| 1767 | James Smith, M. D | 1770 |
| | | Retired |
| 1770 | Peter Middleton, M. D | 1776 |

## PROFESSORS OF THE THEORY AND PRACTICE OF MEDICINE.

| | | Retired |
|---|---|---|
| 1767 | Samuel Bard, M. D | 1776 |
| | | Transferred |
| 1795 | William Hamersley, M. D | 1808 |

## PROFESSORS OF MIDWIFERY.

| | | Deceased |
|---|---|---|
| 1767 | John V. B. Tennent, M. D | 1770 |
| | | Retired |
| 1770 | Samuel Bard, M. D | 1776 |
| | | Deceased |
| 1785 | Ebenezer Crosby, M. D | 1788 |
| | | Resigned |
| 1792 | John R. B. Rogers, M. D | 1808 |
| | | Retired |
| 1808 | Walter C. Buchanan, M. D | 1813 |
| 1860 | Edward Delafield, M. D. (Emeritus) | |

## PROFESSORS OF CHEMISTRY.

| | | Resigned |
|---|---|---|
| 1784 | Samuel Bard, M. D | 1785 |
| | | Resigned |
| 1785 | Henry Moyes, LL. D | 1786 |

| Appointed | | Resigned |
|---|---|---|
| 1786 | Samuel Bard, M. D | 1787 |
| | | Resigned |
| 1792 | Samuel Nicoll, M. D | 1794 |
| | | Resigned |
| 1810 | James S. Stringham | 1813 |
| 1860 | John Torrey, M. D., LL. D. (Emeritus) | |
| 1860 | Samuel St. John, M. D | |

Medical Jurisprudence was added to the Department in 1870.

## PROFESSORS OF THE INSTITUTES OF MEDICINE.

| | | Resigned |
|---|---|---|
| 1785 | Benjamin Kissam, M. D | 1792 |
| | | Transferred |
| 1792 | William Hamersley, M. D | 1795 |
| | | Retired |
| 1808 | John C. Osborn, M. D | 1813 |

## PROFESSORS OF THE PRACTICE OF MEDICINE.

| | | Resigned |
|---|---|---|
| 1785 | Nicholas Romayne, M. D | 1787 |
| | | Resigned |
| 1792 | Samuel Nicoll, M. D | 1794 |
| | | Resigned |
| 1794 | Edward Stevens, M. D | 1795 |
| | | Retired |
| 1808 | William Hamersley, M. D | 1813 |

## DEAN OF THE MEDICAL FACULTY.

| | | Resigned |
|---|---|---|
| 1792 | Samuel Bard, M. D | 1804 |
| 1860 | Edward Delafield, M. D. (President) | |

## PROFESSORS OF MATERIA MEDICA.

| | | Deceased |
|---|---|---|
| 1792 | William P. Smith, M. D | 1795 |
| | | Resigned |
| 1796 | David Hosack, M. D., LL. D | 1811 |
| | | Retired |
| 1811 | John C. Osborn, M. D | 1813 |
| | | Deceased |
| 1860 | Joseph M. Smith, M. D | 1866 |

In 1860, Clinical Medicine belonged to the Department.

## PROFESSORS OF BOTANY.

| Appointed | | Resigned |
|---|---|---|
| 1792 | Richard S. Kissam, M. D. | 1793 |
| | | Resigned |
| 1793 | Samuel L. Mitchill, M. D., LL. D. | 1795 |
| | | Resigned |
| 1795 | David Hosack, M. D., LL. D. | 1811 |
| 1860 | John Torrey, M. D., LL. D. (Emeritus) | |

## PROFESSORS OF OBSTETRICS, DISEASES OF WOMEN AND CHILDREN, AND MEDICAL JURISPRUDENCE.

| | | Deceased |
|---|---|---|
| 1860 | Chandler R. Gilman, M. D. | 1865 |
| | | Promoted |
| 1863 | T. Gailliard Thomas, M. D. (Adjunct) | 1865 |
| 1865 | T. Gailliard Thomas, M. D. | |

In 1868, Medical Jurisprudence was assigned to another Department.

## PROFESSOR OF PATHOLOGY AND PRACTICAL MEDICINE.

1860 Alonzo Clark, M. D., LL. D.

## PROFESSOR OF PHYSIOLOGY AND MICROSCOPIC ANATOMY.

1860 John C. Dalton, Jr., M. D.

In 1870, the title of this chair was changed to that of "Physiology and Hygiene."

## PROFESSOR OF MILITARY SURGERY AND HYGIENE.

| | | Emeritus. |
|---|---|---|
| 1862 | William Detmold, M. D. | 1865 |

In 1866, the title of this chair was changed to that of "Clinical and Military Surgery."

## PROFESSOR OF CLINICAL MEDICINE.

1866 John T. Metcalfe, M. D.

## CLINICAL PROFESSOR OF VENEREAL DISEASES.

1867 Freeman J. Bumstead, M. D.

## PROFESSOR OF MATERIA MEDICA, THERAPEUTICS, AND MEDICAL JURISPRUDENCE.

1868 James W. McLane, M. D.

In 1870, Medical Jurisprudence was assigned to another Department.

## CLINICAL PROFESSOR OF DISEASES OF THE EYE AND EAR.

Appointed

1869 Cornelius R. Agnew, M. D.......................................

## CLINICAL PROFESSOR OF DISEASES OF THE SKIN.

1869 William H. Draper, M. D.......................................

## CLINICAL PROFESSOR OF THE DISEASES OF CHILDREN.

1869 Abraham Jacobi, M. D.......................................

## PROFESSOR OF CLINICAL SURGERY.

1870 Willard Parker, M. D.......................................

## DEMONSTRATORS OF ANATOMY.

| Appointed | Name | Retired |
|---|---|---|
| 1860 | Henry B. Sands, M. D. | 1867 |
| 1867 | Samuel B. Ward, M. D. | 1868 |
| 1868 | Erskine Mason, M. D. | 1870 |
| 1870 | Thomas T. Sabine, M. D. | |

## CURATORS OF THE MUSEUM.

| Appointed | Name | Retired |
|---|---|---|
| 1860 | Henry B. Sands, M. D. | 1867 |
| 1867 | Samuel B. Ward, M. D. | 1869 |
| 1869 | Henry C. Eno, M. D. | 1870 |
| 1870 | Christopher M. Bell, M. D. | |

## LECTURERS.

| Appointed | Name | Retired |
|---|---|---|
| 1791 | Nicholas Romayne, M. D. | 1792 |
| 1794 | William P. Smith, M. D. | 1795 |
| 1860 | Watts C. Livingston, M. D. | 1860 |
| 1860 | Freeman J. Bumstead, M. D. | 1861 |
| 1860 | George T. Elliott, M. D. | 1861 |
| 1860 | Edward W. Lambert, M. D. | 1861 |

| Appointed | | Retired. |
|---|---|---|
| 1860 | David S. Conant, M. D. | 1861 |
| 1860 | Charles K. Briddon, M. D | 1861 |
| 1860 | A. Hermance Smith, M. D. | 1862 |
| 1860 | Foster Swift, M. D | 1863 |
| 1861 | William C. Livingson, M. D | 1863 |
| 1861 | William H. Church, M. D | 1862 |
| 1861 | C. Van Allen Anderson, M. D. | 1862 |
| 1866 | Henry B. Sands, M. D. (Adjunct) | 1867 |
| 1866 | Freeman J. Bumstead, M. D | 1867 |
| 1867 | James W. McLane, M. D | 1868 |
| 1867 | D. Tilden Brown, M. D | 1868 |
| 1867 | Cornelius R. Agnew, M. D | 1869 |
| 1867 | Fessenden N. Otis, M. D | |
| 1867 | William H. Draper, M. D | 1869 |
| 1868 | James L. Little, M. D | |
| 1868 | Edward B. Dalton, M. D | 1870 |
| 1868 | Francis Delafield, M. D | 1869 |
| 1868 | George G. Wheelock, M. D | |
| 1869 | Edward C. Seguin, M. D | |
| 1870 | A. Brayton Ball, M. D | |
| 1870 | Thomas T. Sabine, M. D. (Adjunct) | |

## FACULTY OF LAW.

### PROFESSOR OF MUNICIPAL LAW.

1858 Theodore W. Dwight, LL. D.

The office of "Warden of the Law School" was added to this chair in 1864.

### PROFESSOR OF MEDICAL JURISPRUDENCE.

1860 John Ordronaux, LL. B., M. D.

### PROFESSOR OF POLITICAL SCIENCE.

Appointed
1860 Francis Lieber, LL. D.........................................

The title of this chair was changed, in 1865, to that of "Constitutional History and Public Law."

### PROFESSOR OF THE ETHICS OF JURISPRUDENCE.

1860 Charles Murray Nairne, L. H. D.................................

### LECTURERS.

Retired
1860 Marshall S. Bidwell, LL. D...................................
1860 Alexander W. Bradford, LL. D............................... 1867
1860 Charles P. Daly, LL. D...........................................
1860 William M. Evarts, LL. D......................................... 1868
1860 William Curtis Noyes, LL. D.................................. 1864
1863 Eugene Lawrence, A. M........................................... 1865
1863 Aaron J. Vanderpoel...............................................

## FACULTY OF THE SCHOOL OF MINES.

### PROFESSOR OF MINERALOGY AND METALLURGY.

1864 Thomas Egleston, Jr., A. M., E. M..............................

### PROFESSOR OF MINING ENGINEERING.

1864 Francis L. Vinton, E. M.........................................

In 1870, the title of this chair was changed to that of "Civil and Mining Engineering."

### PROFESSOR OF ANALYTICAL AND APPLIED CHEMISTRY.

1864 Charles F. Chandler, Ph. D....................................

### PROFESSOR OF GENERAL CHEMISTRY.

1865 Charles A. Joy, Ph. D............................................

### PROFESSOR OF MECHANICS AND THEIR APPLICATIONS.

1865 William G. Peck, LL. D..........................................

## PROFESSOR OF MATHEMATICS.

Appointed

1865 John H. Van Amringe, A. M. ....................................

## PROFESSOR OF PHYSICS.

1865 Ogden N. Rood, A. M ....................................

## PROFESSOR OF GEOLOGY AND PALEONTOLOGY.

1866 John S. Newberry, M. D., LL. D ....................................

## INSTRUCTOR IN GERMAN.

1870 Frederick Stengel ....................................

## INSTRUCTOR IN FRENCH.

1870 Jules E. Loiseau ....................................

# SENATUS ACADEMICUS,

# 1870.

## TRUSTEES.

| NAMES. | RESIDENCES. |
|---|---|
| HAMILTON FISH, LL. D., CHAIRMAN OF THE BOARD | 251 East 17th Street. |
| GARDINER SPRING, S. T. D., LL. D | 6 East 37th " |
| SAMUEL B. RUGGLES, LL. D | 24 Union Square. |
| WILLIAM BETTS, LL. D., CLERK | 122 East 30th Street. |
| BENJAMIN I. HAIGHT, S. T. D | 56 West 26th " |
| ROBERT RAY | 363 West 28th Street. |
| GOUVERNEUR M. OGDEN, TREASURER | 84 West 11th " |
| HENRY J. ANDERSON, M. D., LL. D | 53 West 36th " |
| EDWARD L. BEADLE, M. D | Poughkeepsie. |
| GEORGE T. STRONG | 113 East 21st Street. |
| MANCIUS S. HUTTON, S. T. D | 115 Ninth " |
| HORATIO POTTER, S. T. D., LL. D., D. C. L | 38 East 22d Street. |
| JOHN TORREY, M. D., LL. D | Columbia College. |
| LEWIS M. RUTHERFURD | 175 Second Avenue. |
| THOMAS DE WITT, S. T. D | 123 Ninth Street. |
| JOHN C. JAY, M. D | Rye. |
| WILLIAM C. SCHERMERHORN | 49 West 23d Street. |
| MORGAN DIX, S. T. D | 50 Varick " |
| FREDERICK A. P. BARNARD, S. T. D., LL. D | Columbia College. |
| SAMUEL BLATCHFORD, LL. D | 12 West 22d Street. |
| STEPHEN P. NASH | 11 West 19th Street. |
| CHARLES R. SWORDS | 156 Broadway. |

## TRUSTEES OF THE MEDICAL DEPARTMENT.

## OFFICERS OF INSTRUCTION AND GOVERNMENT.

| NAMES. | RESIDENCES. |
|---|---|
| FREDERICK A. P. BARNARD, S. T. D., LL. D. | Columbia College. |
| President. | |
| EDWARD DELAFIELD, M. D. | 2 East 17th Street. |
| President of the Medical Department, and Emeritus Professor of Obstetrics. | |
| HENRY J. ANDERSON, M. D., LL. D. | 53 West 36th " |
| Emeritus Professor of Mathematics and Astronomy. | |
| HENRY DRISLER, LL. D. | 226 East 10th " |
| Jay Professor of the Greek Language and Literature. | |
| HENRY I. SCHMIDT, S. T. D. | 126 West 43d " |
| Gebhard Professor of the German Language and Literature. | |
| CHARLES A. JOY, Ph. D. | Columbia College. |
| Professor of Chemistry. | |
| FRANCIS LIEBER, LL. D. | 48 East 34th Street. |
| Professor of Constitutional History and Public Law. | |
| CHARLES DAVIES, LL. D. | Fishkill Landing. |
| Emeritus Professor of Higher Mathematics. | |
| WILLIAM G. PECK, LL. D. | 206 West 42d Street. |
| Professor of Mathematics and Astronomy, in the Faculty of Arts, and of Mechanics and their Applications, in the Faculty of Mines. | |
| CHARLES M. NAIRNE, L. H. D. | 163 West 34th Street. |
| Professor of Moral and Intellectual Philosophy and Literature. | |
| THEODORE W. DWIGHT, LL. D. | 37 Lafayette Place. |
| Professor of Municipal Law, and Warden of the Law School. | |
| JOHN ORDRONAUX, LL. B., M. D. | 174 West 23d Street. |
| Professor of Medical Jurisprudence. | |

NAMES. RESIDENCES.

JOHN H. VAN AMRINGE, A M.......................228 West 38th Street.

Adjunct Professor of Mathematics, and Professor of Mathematics in the School of Mines.

JOHN TORREY, M. D., LL. D....... ..................Columbia College.

Emeritus Professor of Chemistry and Botany.

WILLARD PARKER, M. D.............................37 East 12th Street.

Professor of Clinical Surgery.

ALONZO CLARK, M. D., LL. D.........................30 East 21st "

Professor of Pathology and Practical Medicine.

JOHN C. DALTON, Jr., M. D..........................99 Madison Avenue.

Professor of Physiology and Hygiene.

SAMUEL St. JOHN, M. D.............................Ashland House.

Professor of Chemistry and Medical Jurisprudence.

THOMAS M. MARKOE, M. D.........................4 East 17th Street.

Professor of Surgery.

WILLIAM DETMOLD, M. D..........................103 Ninth "

Emeritus Professor of Clinical and Military Surgery.

OGDEN N. ROOD, A. M...................... .......341 East 15th "

Professor of Mechanics and Physics.

T. GAILLIARD THOMAS, M. D........ ..............86 Fifth Avenue.

Professor of Obstetrics and the Diseases of Women and Children.

THOMAS EGLESTON, Jr., A. M., E. M................10 Fifth Avenue.

Professor of Mineralogy and Metallurgy.

FRANCIS L. VINTON, E. M..........................806 Broadway.

Professor of Mining Engineering.

CHARLES F. CHANDLER, Ph. D.....................74 East 49th Street.

Professor of Analytical and Applied Chemistry, and Dean of the Faculty of Mines.

JOHN S. NEWBERRY, M. D., LL. D..... ............Columbia College.

Professor of Geology and Palæontology.

| NAMES. | RESIDENCES. |
|---|---|
| JOHN T. METCALFE, M. D.<br>Professor of Clinical Medicine. | 34 East 14th Street. |
| HENRY B. SANDS, M. D.<br>Professor of Anatomy. | 64 East 12th Street. |
| FREEMAN J. BUMSTEAD, M. D.<br>Clinical Professor of Venereal Diseases. | 162 West 23d Street. |
| CHARLES SHORT, LL. D.<br>Professor of the Latin Language and Literature. | 33 West 33d Street. |
| JAMES W. McLANE, M. D.<br>Professor of Materia Medica and Therapeutics. | 51 West 38th Street. |
| CORNELIUS R. AGNEW, M. D.<br>Clinical Professor of Diseases of the Eye and Ear. | 19 East 39th Street. |
| WILLIAM H. DRAPER, M. D.<br>Clinical Professor of Diseases of the Skin. | 37 East 12th Street. |
| ABRAHAM JACOBI, M. D.<br>Clinical Professor of Diseases of Children. | 110 West 34th Street. |

## ASSISTANTS AND OTHER OFFICERS.

| | |
|---|---|
| CORNELIUS R. DUFFIE, S. T. D.<br>Chaplain. | 233 Lexington Av. |
| WILLIAM A. McVICKAR, S. T. D.<br>Lecturer on the Evidences of Religion. | 40 West 38th Street. |
| BEVERLEY R. BETTS, A. M.<br>Librarian. | 122 East 30th Street. |
| STEPHEN R. WEEKS<br>Assistant Librarian. | Columbia College. |
| AUGUSTUS C. MERRIAM, A. M.<br>Tutor in Greek and Latin. | 33 West 33d Street. |

| NAMES. | RESIDENCES. |
|---|---|
| JOHN D. QUACKENBOS, A. B.<br>Tutor in Rhetoric and History. | 331 West 28th Street. |
| FREDERIC STENGEL<br>Instructor in German. | 51 East 20th Street. |
| JULES E. LOISEAU<br>Instructor in French. | 204 West 17th Street. |
| ALEXIS A. JULIEN, A. M.<br>Assistant in Analytical Chemistry. | 129 East 23d Street. |
| PAUL SCHWEITZER, PH. D.<br>Assistant in Analytical Chemistry. | 232 East 50th Street. |
| WILLIAM H. CHANDLER<br>Assistant in Analytical Chemistry. | 137 East 21st Street. |
| JOHN HENRY CASWELL, A. M.<br>Assistant in Mineralogy. | 370 Fifth Avenue. |
| WILLIAM B. POTTER, A. M., E. M.<br>Assistant in Geology. | 38 East 22d Street. |
| THOMAS M. BLOSSOM, A. M., E. M.<br>Assistant in Assaying. | 203 2d Avenue. |
| ALBERT FOLKE, C. E.<br>Assistant in Drawing. | 329 East 19th Street. |
| HENRY NEWTON, A. B., E. M.<br>Assistant in Mineralogy. | 26 West 21st Street. |
| DOUGLASS A. JOY.<br>Assistant in General Chemistry. | Columbia College. |
| FESSENDEN N. OTIS, M. D.<br>Lecturer on Diseases of the Genito-Urinary Organs. | 108 West 34th Street. |
| JAMES L. LITTLE, M. D.<br>Lecturer on Operative Surgery and Surgical Dressings. | 266 West 42d Street. |
| GEORGE G. WHEELOCK, M. D.<br>Lecturer on Physical Diagnosis. | 46 West 31st Street. |

| NAMES. | RESIDENCES. |
|---|---|
| EDWARD C. SEGUIN, M. D.<br>Lecturer on Diseases of the Nervous System. | 58 West 26th Street. |
| A. BRAYTON BALL, M. D.<br>Lecturer on Diseases of the Kidneys. | 36 West 10th Street. |
| THOMAS T. SABINE, M. D.<br>Demonstrator of Anatomy, and Adjunct Lecturer on Anatomy. | 46 West 23d Street. |
| JOHN G. CURTIS, M. D.<br>Assistant Demonstrator of Anatomy. | 27 Washington Pl. |
| CHRISTOPHER M. BELL, M. D.<br>Curator of the Museum of the Medical College. | 276 Fifth Avenue. |
| FRANCIS DELAFIELD, M. D.<br>Clinical Assistant for the Medical Clinique. | 1 East 17th Street. |
| W. DEFOREST DAY, M. D.<br>Clinical Assistant for the Medical Clinique. | 56 East 34th Street. |
| WOOLSEY JOHNSON, M. D.<br>Clinical Assistant for the Medical Clinique. | 220 West 43d Street. |
| JOHN T. KENNEDY, M. D.<br>Clinical Assistant for the Surgical Clinique. | 122 East 10th Street. |
| GERARDUS H. WYNKOOP, M. D.<br>Clinical Assistant for the Surgical Clinique. | 43 East 12th Street. |
| JAMES L. BROWN, M. D.<br>Assistant to the Professor of Obstetrics. | 217 West 12th Street. |
| WILLIAM PISTOR, E. M.<br>Secretary to the President. | 946 Second Avenue. |
| EDWARD C. H. DAY<br>Librarian and Registrar of the School of Mines. | Mt. Vernon. |
| EDWARD T. BOAG<br>Clerk of the School of Medicine. | School of Medicine. |

# GRADUATES IN ARTS.

## 1758.

*Joshua Bloomer, (Rev.), A. M., S. T. D. 1790. aet. 55. *1790
*Isaac Ogden, (C. L.), Judge Supr. Ct. Canada.
*Samuel Provoost, (Rev.), A. M., S. T. D. Univ. Penn. 1786, Regent Univ. N. Y. S. 1784–87, Trustee 1787–1801 and Chairman of the Board 1795–1801, Bishop P. E. Ch. N. Y. 1787–1815. *1815
*Joseph Reade, (C. L.), Master in Chanc. N. J.
*Rudolph Ritzema, Lt.-Col. H. B. M. Army.
*Philip Van Cortlandt, A. M., Lt.-Col. 4th Regt. N. Y. Vols. 1776, Lt.-Gov. N. Y. 1777–95.
*Samuel Verplanck, A. M. 1763, Gov. King's Coll. 1770.

7

## 1759.

*Epenetus Townsend, (Rev.), A. M. *1779
*William Hanna, (Rev.), A. M. 1765 and Yale 1768.

2

## 1760.

*Samuel Bayard, A. M.
*Anthony Hoffman, A. M., Regent Univ. N.Y. S. 1784–87.
*Philip Livingston, A. M., Trustee 1797–1806.
*John Marston, A. M.
*Robert Watts, A. M.
*Isaac Wilkins, (Rev.), A.M., S. T. D. 1811, Memb. of the Gen. Assemb. of N. Y. 1772–75. aet. 89. *1830

6

## 1761.

*Henry Holland, (C. L.), A. M., Mast. in Chancery N.Y.
*Anthony Lispenard. aet. 64. *1806
*Henry Van Dyck, (Rev.), A. M. aet. 60. *1804

3

## 1762.

*Edward Antill, A. M.
*Henry Cuyler, A. M.
*William Cornelius George, and Yale 1762.
*John Grinnell.
*Alexander Leslie, (T.), A. M., Master Gram. Sch. King's Coll.
*Leonard Lispenard, Regent Univ. N. Y. S. 1784–87, Trustee 1787–90. *1790
*William Benjamin Nicoll Maverick.
*Daniel Robert, (C. L.), H. B. M. Atty.-Gen. for St. Christopher's.

8

## 1763.

*Barent Cuyler, A. M.
*Abraham De Peyster, A. M.

2

## 1764.

*Richard Harison, (C. L.), A. M., D. C. L. Univ. Oxford, Del. to Fed. Constit. Conv. 1787, U. S. Dist. Atty. N. Y., Recorder N. Y. C., Trustee 1788–1829 and Chairman of the Board 1823. *1829

*John Jay, (C. L.), A. M., LL. D. Harv. 1790 and Brown 1794, Del. to Congr. 1774, 1775, Memb. Prov. Conv. N. Y. 1776, Ch.-Just. N. Y. 1777, Prest. National Congr. 1778, Min. Plenipo. to Spain 1779, U. S. Peace Commr. 1781–83, U. S. Sec. For. Aff. 1784, Del. to Congr. 1784, Regent Univ. N. Y. S. 1784–90, Del. to Fed. Constit. Conv. 1787, Del. to N. Y. Constit. Conv. 1788, Ch.-Just. U. S. 1789–94, U. S. Envoy Ex. to Gt. Britain 1794, Governor N. Y. 1795–1801. aet. 84. *1829

2

## 1765.

*Egbert Benson, (C. L.), A. M., LL. D. Union 1799 and Harv. 1808 and Dart. 1811, Memb. Prov. Conv. N. Y. 1776, Del. to Continent. Congr. 1784–88, Regent Univ. N. Y. S. 1787–1802, Repr. in Congr. 1789–92, 1813, Trustee 1804–14, Atty. Gen. N. Y., Judge Sup. Ct. N. Y., Ch.-Judge U. S. Circuit Ct. N. Y. *1833

*Richard Grant.

*Robert R. Livingston, (C. L.), A. M. and N. Jers., Recorder N. Y. C. 1773, Del. to Continent. Congr. 1775–77, 1779–81, Memb. N. Y. Constit. Conv. 1777, Chanc. N. Y. 1777–1801, U. S. Secy. For. Aff. 1781–83, Regent Univ. N. Y. S. 1784–87, Del. to Fed. Constit. Conv. 1787, U. S. Minister Plen. to France 1801–4. aet. 66. *1813

*Henry Lloyd, A. M. 1769. aet. 82. *1825

*Arent Schuyler.

5

## 1766.

*James Barclay, A. M.

*Gerard Beekman, A. M.

*Richard Nicholls Colden, Surv. of Customs, N. Y. *1777

*Richard D'Olier.

*Edward Nicoll, A. M.

*John Ray, A. M. 1773.

*Henry Rutgers, Capt. U. S. A. 1776, Memb. Assemb. N. Y., Regent Univ. N. Y. S. 1802–26. aet. 85. *1830

*John Troup, A. M. aet. 70. *1817

*John Troup, Jr., A. M.

*John Vardill, (Rev.), A. M., Tutor, Prof. Nat. Law Hist. and Lang. 1773–76.

*John Watts, A. M., Memb. Assemb. N. Y. 1788–89 and Speaker of the same 1791–2–3, Judge Westchester Co. N. Y., Recorder N. Y. City. *1794

11

## 1767.

*William Laight, A. M.

*Peter Van Schaack, 1768, (C. L.), A. M. 1773, LL. D. 1826, Commr. for revising Colonial Statutes N. Y. 1773. *1832

2

## 1768.

*Charles Doughty, A. M., M. B. 1772.
*James Ludlow, A. M.
*Benjamin Moore, (Rev.), A. M., S. T. D. 1789, President *pro tem.* 1775–76, Prof. Rhet. and Logic 1784–87, Regent Univ. N. Y. S. 1787–1802, President 1801–11, Trustee 1802–13, Bishop P. E. Ch. N. Y. 1801–16. *1816
*Gouverneur Morris, (C. L.), A. M., Memb. Prov. Conv. N. Y. 1775, Del. to Continent. Congr. 1777, Asst. Supt. Finance 1781–85, Del. to Fed. Constit. Conv. 1787, U. S. Min. to France 1792–94, U. S. Sen. 1800–3, Trustee 1805–16, Canal Commissioner of N. Y. 1810–15. aet. 65. *1816
*John Stevens, (Eng.) A. M. *1838
*Gulian Verplanck, Speaker House Assemb. N. Y., Regent Univ. N. Y. S. 1790–1800. 6

## 1769.

*Caleb Cooper, A. M. 1771.

## 1770.

*James Creighton, A. M.
*John Doughty, (Rev.)
*Jonathan Graham, and Yale 1770.
*Richard Harris, A. M.
*William Hubbard, A. M.
*Stephen Lush, A. M., N. Y. Sen. 1801–2.
*Philip Pell, A. M., Regent Univ. N. Y. S. 1784–87. 7

## 1771.

*Ichabod Best Barnet, A. M.
*Clement Cooke Clarke, A. M.
*John Copp, (T.), A. M., 1st Lt. 1st Reg. N. Y. Vols. 1776.
*Henry De Wint, A. M.
*Thomas Knox.
*John Searle, A. M. 6

## 1772.

*Thomas Barclay, Maj. H. B. M. Army 1777, Speaker Assembly Nova Scotia, Adj. Gen. Nova Scotia, British Commr. under "Jay's Treaty" and under Treaty of Ghent. *1830
*John Bowden, (Rev.), A. M., S. T. D. 1796, Prof. Mor. Phil. Bell. Lett. and Logic 1801–17. *1817
*John King.
*Nicholas Ogden.
*Peter Roebuck, A. M.
*Andrew Skeene. 6

## 1773.

*Cornelius Bogert, Lt. N. Y. Ind. Forces 1776.
*Frederick Philipse, Capt. Dragoons, British Army. *1785
*Nathaniel Philipse.
*Beverley Robinson, Lt.-Col. H. B. M. Army. *1816
*Thomas Shreve, (Rev.) aet. 64. *1816

## 1774.

*Isaac Abrahams.
*Robert Nicholls Auchmuty. *1813
*William Chandler. *1784

*Edward Dunscomb, Maj. U. S. Rev. Army, Trustee 1795–1814, Sheriff N. Y. C. 1810–11. *1814
*Nicholas Heyliger.
*John Jauncey.
*Henry Nicoll.
*George Ogilvie, (Rev.) *1797
*John Rapelje.
*Benjamin Seaman.
*Edward Stevens, M. D. elsewhere, Prof. Pract. of Med. 1794–5.
*Robert Troup, (C. L.), LL. D. elsewhere, Maj. U. S. A., Judge U. S. Dist. Ct. N.Y., Trustee 1811–17. aet. 75. *1832

12

## 1775.

*William Amory.
*Richard Auchmuty, Surgeon H. B. M. Army. *1782
*Samuel Auchmuty, G. C. B., Adj. Gen. 52d Regt. H. B. M. Army, Gov. of Isle of Thanet 1802, Brig. Gen. Commg. British Forces at Capture of Montevideo, 1806, Maj. Gen. Commg. at Madras, Lt.-Gen. in command at capture of Java, Gen. Commanding the Forces in Ireland in 1822. aet. 64. *1822
*William Cock, A. M. 1790.
*Joseph Griswold.
*John William Livingston, Lt. "N. Y. Independ. Forces" 1776.
*Jacobus Remsen.

7

## 1776.

*Samuel Bayard.
*James Devereux.
*Peter Kissam.
*Matthias Nicoll.
*Peter Ogden.
*Marinus Willett.

6

---

On the 6th of April, 1776, the College buildings were taken for military purposes. The College did not fully resume its functions till the close of the war, and no degrees were conferred till 1786. The following candidates had been admitted, but did not complete their course on account of the disturbed state of public affairs:

## In 1774.†

*Thomas Atwood.
*John Brickell.
*David Clarkson.
*Samuel Deall.
*James De Peyster.
*John Gaine. aet. 26. *1787
*Alexander Hamilton, A. M. 1788 and Harv. 1792, LL.D. Dart. 1790 and N. Jers. 1791 and Harv. 1792 and Rutgers 1792, Capt. U. S. A. 1776, Lt.-Col. staff of Washington 1777, Memb. Congr. 1782, Regent Univ. N. Y. S. 1784–87, N. Y. Leg. 1786, Del. to U. S. Constit. Conven. 1787, Secy. Treasury U. S. 1789–95, Maj.-Gen. U. S. A. 1798, Trustee 1787–1804. aet. 47. *1804
*Tristrim Lowther.
*Schuyler Lupton.
*Edward Cornwallis Moncrieff.
*Daniel Moore.
*Paul Randall.
*Nicholas Romeyn.
*Jacob Shaw.
*Horatio Smith.
*James Stiles.
*John Whitaker.

## In 1775.†

*Edward Kerin.
*Benjamin Kissam, M. D. elsewhere, Prof. Instit. of Med. 1785–92, Trustee 1787–1803. aet. 44. *1803
*Thomas Groesbeck Lynch.
*Thomas Lambert Moore, (Rev.), A. M. 1790. *1799
*Jacob Morris.
*Augustus Nicoll.
*Marinus Oudenaarde.
*Peter Oudenaarde.

## In 1777.†

*James Delancy Walton, Admiral H. B. M. Navy. *1834
*William Walton. *1806

## 1786.

*John Bassett, and Yale 1786, (Rev.), A. M., S. T. D. Will. 1804. *1824
*De Witt Clinton, (C. L.), A. M., LL. D. 1826 and Ohio Univ. 1825, N. Y. Assemb. 1797, N. Y. Sen. 1798–1802, 1805–1811, Memb. Constit. Conv. N. Y. 1801, U. S. Sen. 1802–4, Mayor N. Y. C. 1803–7, 1809–10, 1811–15, Regent Univ. N. Y. S. 1808–25, Lt.-Gov. N. Y. 1811–13, N. Y. Canal Commr. 1816–24, Gov. N. Y. 1817–21, 1825–28. aet. 59. *1828
*Abraham Hun, A. M.
*George Livingston.
*Philip H. Livingston, A. M.
*Samuel Smith, Jr., A. M.
*Peter Steddiford, (Rev.), A. M. *1826
*Francis Sylvester, (C. L.), A. M.

8

## 1787.

*Samuel Boyd, (C. L.), Trustee 1826–35.
*Nicholas Fonda.
*John C. Ludlow, (C. L.), A. M. 1793.
*Henry Cruger Van Schaack.
*John W. Yates, (B.)

5

## 1788.

*James Cochran, (C. L.), A. M., Repr. in Congr. 1797–99, Regent Univ. N. Y. S. 1796–1820. *1818
*John Eccles, (F.)
*William Hurst, 1789.
*Peter Schuyler Livingston, and Yale and N. Jers. 1788 and Harv. 1790, A. M. *1807
*Brandt Schuyler Lupton, (Rev.) *1790
*Daniel Crommelin Verplanck, (C. L.), A. M. 1788, uJdge Dutchess Co. N. Y.

6

## 1789.

*John T. Bainbridge.
*James Chatham Duane, (C. L.)
*Henry Izard.
*William Lupton, Jr.
*John Mitchell Mason, (Rev.), A. M. N. Jers. 1794, S. T. D. Univ. Penn. 1804, Trustee 1795–1821, Provost 1811–16, Prest. Dickin. Coll. Penn. 1821–24. aet. 60. *1829
*Matthew Mesier.
*Peter Mesier, (C. L.)
*John Remsen, (C. L.)
*John P. Van Ness, A. M. 1845, Repr. in Congr.

9

## 1790.

*David Schuyler Bogart, and N. Jers. 1791, (Rev.) *1839
*Marmaduke Earle, (Rev.) aet. 63. *1832
*Jonathan Freeman, (Rev.), A. M. 1800 and N. Jers. 1809. *1822
*George Graham, U. S. Asst. Secy. State 1801–25.
*John Graham.
*Frederick Halsey.
*Samuel Jones, Jr., 1793 and Yale 1790, (C. L.), LL. D. 1826 and Union 1841, Memb. N. Y. Assemb. 1812-14, Recorder N. Y. C. 1823, Chancellor N. Y. S. 1826–28, Ch.-Just. Sup. Ct. N. Y. 1828–47 and Justice of same 1847–49. aet. 83. *1853

7

## 1791.

*Peter Anderson, A. M. 1795, M. D. 1795.
*Anthony Bleecker, (C. L.), A. M. 1797, Examiner in Chancery. *1827
*William Bleecker, (C. L.)
*William Temple Broome, A. M. 1797.
*Walter L. Cochran.
*Pierre Edward Fleming, A. M. 1797.
*William Hendell, Jr., (Rev.), S. T. D. 1828.
*Cave Jones, (Rev.), A. M., S. T. D. elsewhere. aet. 59. *1829
*Isaac Knevils.
*John Knevils.
*Lancaster Lupton.
*John W. Mulligan, (C. L.), A. M. 1834, Surrogate N. Y. C. 1810, Clerk N. Y. Co. 1813–15, U. S. Consul at Athens, Greece, 1848. *1864
*Charles L. Ogden, (M.)
*Thomas Ludlow Ogden, (C. L.), Trustee 1817–44. *1844
*Daniel Paris, (C. L.), N. Y. Sen. 1810–13.
*George Rapelje, (C. L.)
*Frederic Van Horne, (Rev.), A. M. 1795.
*William Beekman Verplanck.
*Nathan H. White, (C. L.), A. M. 1795.
*Jesse Woodhull, Jr.
*James Woods, (C. L.), A. M. 1804.

21

## 1792.

*Gerard Beekman.
*Cornelius Brower.
*Alexander Hosack, M. D. 1797.
*John B. Johnson, (Rev.) *1803
*James Witter Nicholson.
*John L. Norton.
*Jotham Post, Jr., A. M., M. D. 1793.
*Alexander Proudfit, (Rev.), A. M. Union 1792, S. T. D. Middleb. Coll. 1811 and Williams 1812. aet. 75. *1844
*Jacob Sickles.
*Samuel Smith.
*George Taylor, (M.)
*William Taylor, (M.)

12

## 1793.

*John Brower.
*George Clinton, Jr., (C. L.), Repr. in Congr.
*William Cutting, (C. L.), Sheriff N. Y. C. 1807–8.
*Cornelius Decker, Jr., (M.)
*George I. Eacker, (C. L.), A. M. 1797.
*Samuel Gilford, Jr., (M.)
*Charles D. Goold, (M.), A. M. 1797.

*Robert Heaton, Jr., A. M. 1797, U. S. A.
*John I. Johnson.
*Edward W. Laight, (C. L.), Memb. N.Y. Assemb. 1816, Trustee 1816–51 and Chairman 1849–50.
*Henry William Ludlow, (F.)
*Henry Masterson, (C. L.)
*Philip Milledoler, (Rev.), A. M. 1797, S. T. D. Univ. Penn., Prof. Theol. and Prest. Rutg. Coll. 1825–35. *1852
*John Nicholl, A. M. 1797.
*Robert B. Norton, (C. L.)
*Abraham Ogden, (M.)
*James Parker, (M.), Memb. N. J. Leg., Boundary Commr. N. J. 1807, 1827, 1833, Pres. Elector N. J. 1824, U. S. Collector Perth Amboy N.J. 1829–33, Repr. in Congr. 1833–37, Memb. of the Constit. Conv. N. J. 1844. aet. 92. *1868
*Jonathan Pearsee, Jr., (C. L.)
*Valentine H. Peters, (M.)
*John S. Schermerhorn, (M.)
*Gilbert Smith, M. D. elsewhere.
*Thomas R. Smith, (M.)
*James S. Stringham, A. M. 1797, M. D. Univ. Edinb. 1799, Prof. Chem. 1802–13, Prof. Med. Juris. Coll. Phys. and Surg. N. Y. 1813–17. *1817
*Thomas Thompson.
*Cornelius Augustus Van Horne, (M.)
*Elias Brevoort Woodward, (C. L.), Judge N. Y. Territory.

26

## 1794.

*William Cocks.
*John E. Fisher, (M.)
*John Forbes.
*Levi P. Graham, (C. L.)
*Montgomery Hunt, (C. L.), Repr. in Congr.
*Jacob J. Janeway, (Rev.), A. M., S. T. D. elsewhere, Prof. Rutg. Coll. *1858
*Peter Augustus Jay, (C. L.), A. M. and Yale 1798, LL. D. 1835 and Harv. 1831, Trustee 1812–17 and 1823–43 and Chairman 1832, Memb. N. Y. Assemb. 1816, Recorder N. Y. C. 1819–20, Memb. N. Y. Constit. Conv., Prest. N. Y. Hist. Soc. *1843
*Cyrus King, (C. L.), Repr. in Congr.
*Leffert Lefferts, Jr., (C. L.), Judge Ct. Com. Pleas Kings Co. N. Y.
*Jacob Ogden Mackie, (M.)
*Samuel B. Malcolm, (C. L.)
*Gilbert Milligan, M. D. elsewhere.
*John B. Stringham, M. D. elsewhere.
*Peter G. Stuyvesant, (C. L.), Prest. N. Y. Hist. Soc. *1847
*Thomas Ustick, (C. L.)

15

## 1795.

*George Barculoo, (Rev.), S. T. D. Rutg. Coll. 1834.
*Philip Duryee, (Rev.), S. T. D. Rutg. Coll. 1834. *1850
*Bernard Elliot.
*John J. Faesch.
*John Ferguson, (C. L.), Mayor N. Y. C. 1815, U. S. Naval Off. N. Y., Trustee 1830–32. *1832
*Thomas Herring, (M.), A. M.
*James Inglis, (Rev.), S. T. D. Coll. N. Jers. 1811. *1820
*Nicholas Jones, (Rev.)

*Adolph C. Lent, A.M., M.D. 1798.
*John Blair Linn, (Rev.), A. M., S. T. D. Univ. Penn. *1804
*Silvanus Miller, (C. L.), N. Y. Assemb., Surrogate N. Y. C. 1801–7, 1811–21, Examiner in Chanc. *1861
*John H. Meier, (Rev.), A.M. 1804. aet. 32. *1806
*John Morrison.
*Alexander Phœnix, (Rev.) *1863
*Sidney Phœnix.
*Thomas Phœnix, (C. L.), Dist. Atty. N. Y. C.
*Robert Remsen.
*John Brodhead Romeyn, (Rev.), A. M. Union 1797, S. T. D. N. Jers. 1809, Trustee 1809–25 and Clerk 1811–15, Trustee Coll. N. Jers. 1809–25. *1825
*William Ross,(C.L.),Speaker N. Y. Assemb.
*Henry Sands, (C. L ), A. M.
*Benjamin Seaman, (C. L.)
*James Bowdoine Temple,† Capt. H. B. M. Army.
*Daniel D. Tompkins, (C.L.), N. Y. Assemb. 1801, Memb. N. Y. Constit. Conv. 1801, Repr. in Congr. 1805–7, Just. Supr. Ct. N. Y. 1804, Gov. N. Y. 1807–17, V.-Pres. U. S. 1817–25, Prest. Constit. Conv. N. Y. 1821. *1825
*Pierre C. Van Wyck, (C.L.), Dist. Atty. N. Y. C., Rec. N. Y. C.
*Effingham Warner, (Rev.)
*Rensselaer Westerlo, (C.L.)

26

## 1796.

*David Barclay.
*Henry Cruger, Jr.
*Philip Fisher.
*Andrew S. Garr, (C. L.) *1859
*David S. Jones,(C.L.), LL.D. Allegh. Coll. Penn., Corporation Counsel N. Y. C. 1813–16, Trustee 1820–48, Trustee Gen. Theol. Sem. P. E. Ch. 1822–48, Judge Queens Co. N. Y. 1840–1. *1848
*Edward P. Livingston, (C. L.), N. Y. Sen. 1809–12, Lt.-Gov. N. Y. 1831–33, Regent Univ. N. Y. S.
*Samuel Nicholson.
*Gouverneur Ogden.
*William Rattoone.
*Josiah Shippey, Jr., (M.)
*Charles Taylor, (M.)
*William Turk, M. D. elsewhere U. S. N.
*Lawrence Van Buskirk.
*Adrian C. Van Slyck.
*John Watts.

15

## 1797.

*William Bard, (Br.), Trustee 1840–53. *1853
*Robert Boyd, (C. L.)
*Archibald Bruce,M.D. Edinburgh, Prof. Mineralogy in N. Y. City.
George W. Clinton, Repr. in Congr.
*Henry C. Kunze.
*Abraham R. Lawrence, (M.), U. S. Naval Off. N. Y.
*William Le Conte.
*Isaac A. Van Hook, (Rev.), A. M. 1803.
*William P. Van Ness, (C. L.), Judge U. S. Circuit Ct. S. Dist. N. Y.

9

## 1798.

*Joseph Bainbridge.
*Thomas Bay.

† Known subsequently as James Bowdoine.

*George Brinckerhoff, (C.L.), A. M.
*Jacob V. Brower, A. M., M. D. 1802.
*Rudolph Bunner, (C. L.), Repr. in Congr.
*David Codwise, (C. L.), LL. D. Lafay. Coll. Penn. 1855, Mast. in Chanc. *1864
*George Davis, A. M.
*Charles Graham, (C. L.)
*John T. Irving, (C.L.), Trustee 1818–38, Judge Supr. Ct. N. Y. *1838
*Philip L. Jones.
*William B. Keese, (C. L.)
Washington McKnight, (Rev.), A. M. 1804.
*Clement C. Moore, A. M., LL. D. 1829, Trustee 1813–57 and Clerk 1815–50, Prof. Hebrew and Greek Lit. Gen. Theol. Sem. P. E. Ch. N. Y. 1821–50, and Prof. Emeritus 1850–63. *1863
*Samuel Moore, M. D. elsewhere.
*William Ogden, (M.)
*William Rhinelander, (M.), A. M. 1804.
Lewis Sands.
James Walsh.

18

## 1799.

*John Christie, (Rev.)
*Peter Ditmarse Froeligh, (Rev.) aet. 45. *1827
*Lewis Le Conte.
*James Livingston.
*James Lynch, (C. L.), Just. Mar. Ct. N. Y. C.
*Thomas Thornton Mackaness, A. M.
*James R. Manley, A. M., M. D. 1803, Prest. N. Y. S. Med. Soc. 1825–26. aet. 69. *1851
Alexander Murray.
*Philip F. Mayer, (Rev.), S. T. D. 1837.
*Stephen Price.
*Samuel Riker, Jr., (C. L.) aet. 32. *1811
*Jacob Schoonmaker, (Rev.), A. M., S. T. D. Dickin. Coll. Penn. 1831. aet. 75. *1852
*Arthur J. Stansbury, (C. L.)
Peter I. Van Pelt, (Rev.), A. M. 1803.
*Abraham Varick, Jr., (C. L)
*John Vredenburgh Varick, (M.)
Arthur M. Walter, A. M.
David Wright.

18

## 1800.

John J. De Peyster.
*Samuel Halstead, (M.)
*Philip Hamilton.
Samuel Harris, (C. L.)
John Henry.
John Huyler, A. M.
*Robert Swift Livingston (C. L.) *1867
John McKinnon, A. M.
*Nicholas J. Quackenbos, M. D. 1802, A. M.
Thomas W. Rathbone.
*Sampson Simson, (C. L.)
*Charles Floyd Thomas.
*Matthew Tillary, M. D. elsewhere.
John Y. Ward.
*George Wilson, (C.L.), A.M.
*Peter Wilson, (C. L.), A. M. *1826

16

## 1801.

*John Anthon, (C. L.), LL. D. 1861. *1863
Robert Benson, Jr., (M.)
*Abraham L. Blauvelt.
*Samuel Bogert.
*Thomas Bolton, (C.L.), Mast. in Chanc.

*John Furman.
*John Gosman, (Rev.), S. T. D. elsewhere. *1865
*John Nitchie, (C. L.), Col. U. S. A. 1814. *1838
*Lewis Morris Ogden.
*Henry Schenck.
*Henry H. Schieffelin, (M.) aet. 83. *1865
*Gabriel Tichenor.
*Gulian Crommelin Verplanck, A. M. 1821, LL. D. 1835 and Amh. 1834 and Hob. 1835, N. Y. Assemb. 1820, Prof. Ev. Christian. Gen. Theol. Sem. P. E. Ch. 1821–24, Repr. in Congr. 1825–33, N. Y. Sen., Trustee 1821–6, Regent Univ. N. Y. S. 1826–70, Pres. Commr. Emigr. N. Y. 1846–70. aet. 84. *1870
*Samuel Armstrong Walsh, M. D. Coll. Phys. and Surg. N. Y. 1811.
*Gabriel Winter, (C. L.) *1862

15

## 1802.

*Alexander M. Beebe.
*John Player Crosby, and Yale 1802 and N. Jers. 1802. *1806
*John Delafield, (M.)
*William Gardner.
*George W. Gosman.
*Francis L. Harison, (C. L.)
*James Jones.
*Henry Laight, (C. L.)
*Leffert Lefferts, (C. L.), Judge Kings Co. N. Y.
*Robert Macomb, (C. L.), A. M.
*John W. Macomb.
Nathaniel F. Moore, A. M., LL. D. 1825, Adj. Prof. Greek and Lat. Lang. 1817–20 and Prof. 1820–35, Librarian 1837–9, President 1842–9, Trustee 1842–51.
*Archibald McVickar, (C. L.)
*James McVickar, (M.) *1836
Isaac Ogden, (M.)
*William Ogilvie.
*Henry Bate Priest.
*Billopp B. Seaman.
*James Tillary, M. D. elsewhere.
*Hubert Van Wagenen.

20

## 1803.

George H. Atkinson.
John Bay.
John Bowne.
Thomas Crolius.
*Augustus Fleming.
*Edward R. Jones, (M.), Trustee 1831–38.
Gouverneur Kemble, (M.), Repr. in Congr., Memb., N. Y. S. Constit. Conven. 1846.
Peter Kemble.
Edward Kemeys.
*John L. Lawrence, (C. L.), N. Y. Assemb. 1816–17, Memb. Constit. Conv. N.Y. 1821, N. Y. Sen. 1848–50, Trustee 1830–49, Treasurer 1833–49, Compt. N. Y. C. *1849
*John Le Conte, M. D. elsewhere.
*George C. Quackenbos, M.D. elsewhere. *1858
*William Remsen, (C. L.)
*Henry F. Rogers, (M.)
*Alpheus Sherman, (C. L.), N. Y. Assemb. 1826–29, N. Y. Sen. 1830–34. *1866
*John Cox Stevens.
Samuel W. Thomson.
Robert Watts.

18

## 1804.

*Samuel Akerly, A. M.

*John W. Barnum.
*William D. Blackwell, (C. L.)
*George Bryar.
Elisha Camp, (C. L.), Capt. U. S. V. 1812, Assist. U. S. Dist. Atty. N. Dist. N. Y.
*Cornelius T. Demarest, (Rev.), A. M. 1813.
*Jeremiah I. Drake, A. M.
*William Edgar.
*William Gracie, and N. Jers. 1804.
*John T. B. Graham.
*Henry B. Hagerman.
Alexander Hamilton, Col. N. Y. M. 1812, U. S. Consul at Havanna, U. S. Boundary Commr.
*Richard N. Harison.
*James D. Livingston.
*William L. Lytton, A. M., M. D. 1807.
Thomas McGahagan, 1805.
*John McVickar, (Rev.), A.M. 1818, S. T. D. 1825, Prof. Moral and Int. Phil., Rhetoric, Belle-Lett. and Pol. Econ. 1817–57, Prof. Ev. Nat. and Rev. Relig. 1857–64 and Emeritus 1864–68. aet. 82. *1868
*Edward Manley.
*John Mitchell.
*Joseph Nelson, A. M., 1808, LL. D. Rutg. Coll. 1825, Prof. Languages Rutger's Coll. aet. 47. *1830
*William M. Price.
*Philip Rhinelander.
*Samuel Rogers. *1869
*David M. Ross, A. M.
*Robert Seaman.
*John I. Sickles, A. M.
*Thomas D. Smith.
*Charles Stewart.
*John R. Thompson, (Rev.), A. M.
*James Talcott Watson, and Yale 1804 and N. Jers. 1804.
*John Watts. Jr., M. D. Edinburgh 1809, Prof. Pract. of Physic Rutg. Coll. N. J., Pres. Coll. Phys. and Surg. N. Y. 1826–31, Trustee 1824–31. *1831

31

## 1805.

Peter Allaire, (M.)
*James Bibby.
*Leonard A. Bleecker.
*William Cock.
*Benjamin U. Coles.
*Joab G. Cooper, (Rev.), A. M.)
*James L. Fine.
*James Fleming.
*Alexander Gunn, (Rev.), A. M. and N. Jers. 1805, S. T. D. Allegh. Coll. Penn. *1829
*Richard Hatfield, Jr.
James A. Hamilton, (C. L.), LL. D. Hamilton, U. S. Dist. Atty. N. Y.
Robert Jaques, A. M.
Thomas Lefferts.
*Henry Ustick Onderdonk, (Rev.), A. M., M. D. 1810, S. T. D. 1827, Bishop P. E. Ch. Penn. 1827–58. *1858
*Edmund H. Pendleton, (C. L.), Judge Dutchess Co. N. Y., Repr. in Congr. 1831–33.
Abraham Purdy, A. M. 1810.
*Edward Seaman.
John T. Smith.
*Robert I. Watts.

19

## 1806.

*John V. Bartow, (Rev.), A. M.
*George Boyd, (Rev.), S. T. D. elsewhere. *1850
*John Chrystie.

*John Peter De Wint. aet. 84. *1870
William E. Dunscomb, (C. L.)
*Gilbert O. Fowler, (C. L.)
*Jonathan B. Gosman, (Rev.)
*James McCullen.
*Robert B. Anæas McLeod (Rev.)
*Cornelius Miller, (C. L.)
*David Moore, (Rev.), S. T. D. elsewhere. *1856
*Samuel W. Moore, M. D. 1810. aet. 68. *1854
*Ferris Pell, (C. L.)
*David Quackinbush, M. D. elsewhere.
*Samuel B. Romaine, (C. L.), N. Y. Assemb. 1816-19, 1819-22 and Speaker 1822.
*Frederic Roorbach, (C. L.)
*Cornelius Schermerhorn, (C. L.)
*Philip Schuyler, U. S. Consul at Liverpool, N. Y. Assemb. *1865
John A. Smith, (C. L.)
*John L. Tillinghast, (C. L.)

20

## 1807.

*Egbert Benson, Jr. *1866
John L. Bronk, (C.L.), Judge Greene Co. N. Y.
John H. Brouwer.
*William E. Burrell, M. D. Coll. Phys. and Surg. N. Y. 1811.
*George R. Copland. aet. 17. *1808
Henry S. Dodge, A. M.
Robert Gosman.
John H. Hill, (Rev.), A. M. 1845, S. T. D. elsewhere, LL. D. 1868, Missionary in Greece.
Philip M. Holmes.
Daniel Mack.
*Peter T. Marselis, (C. L.)
*William H. Maxwell, (C. L.), A. M. 1827.
*Simeon Remsen. *1815
*James Renwick, A. M., LL. D. 1829, Instructor in Nat. and Exper. Phil. and Chem. 1813, Trustee 1817-20, Prof. Nat. and Exper. Phil. and Chem. 1820-53, and Prof. Emeritus 1853-63. *1863
*George Paxton Rogers. *1870
Dirck B. Stockholm.
Peter V. C. Tappan.
Cornelius Van Buren.
James Van Cortlandt.
Theodore V. W. Varick, A. M.
*Philip G. Van Wyck. aet. 84. *1870
*Charles A. Williamson.

21

## 1808.

*William Atkinson, (M.)
*William Berrian, (Rev.), S. T. D. 1828, Rector Trinity Parish N. Y. C. 1830-62, Trustee 1832-62. *1862
*Lionel Brown.
*Timothy Clowes, LL. D. elsewhere. aet. 60. *1847
*Henry M. Francis, A. M., M. D. elsewhere.
*James Inderwick, M. D. elsewhere, U. S. N.
*Robert McCartee, (Rev.), A. M., S. T. D. 1831. *1865
John McKnight, (Rev.)
Hugh Maxwell, (C. L.), A. M. 1816, Dist. Atty. N. Y. C. 1819-29, U. S. Collector Port of N. Y.
Frederick Muzzy, (C. L.)
John W. Phillips, (T.)
*Edward Post, M. D. Edinburgh.
William C. Rhinelander.
*Henry Howard Ross, (C.L.), A. M. Univ. Vt. 1813, Repr. in Congr. 1825-27, Memb. and Prest. N. Y. Electoral Coll. 1848, Judge Essex Co. N. Y. 1847-48. aet. 72. *1862

*Gilbert H. Sayres, (Rev.), S. T. D. 1863. aet. 80. *1867
James A. Stevens.
*William Stuart, (M.)
*Daniel Van Mater.
*Henry Vethake, A. M., LL. D. 1836, Instr. in Math. and Geog. 1813, Prof. Math. and Nat. Phil. Rutg. Coll. 1813–17 and in Coll. N. Jers. 1817–21 and in Dickinson Coll. 1821–29 and in Univ. N. Y. C. 1832–35, Prest. Washington Coll. Va. 1835–36, Prof. Maths. Univ. Penn. 1836–54 and Provost and Prof. Moral and Int. Phil. Univ. Penn. 1854–59. *1866
Peter D. Vroom, Jr., (C. L.), A. M. 1812, LL. D. 1837 and N. Jers. 1850, N. Jers. Legis. 1826–29, Gov. and Chancellor N. Jers. 1829–36, Repr. in Congr. 1838–40, Memb. N. Jers. State Constit. Conven. 1844, U. S. Envoy Ex. and Min. Plen. to Prussia 1853–57.
*Henry Watts.
John Watts, Jr.

22

## 1809.

*Thomas S. Aspinwall.
*Samuel Berrian. *1818
Edward N. Bibby, M. D. elsewhere.
John Brady, (Rev.), A. M.
*John Cadle, A. M., M. D. Coll. Phys. and Surg. N. Y. 1822, Surg. U. S. Navy.
*Gerrit Conrey.
*Edward Copland, Mayor Brooklyn. aet. 63. *1859
*Cornelius Roosevelt Duffie, (Rev.), A. M. 1813. *1827
Thomas Duggan.
*John Fine, (C. L.), A. M., LL. D. Hamilt. Coll. 1850, Treasurer St. Lawrence Co. N. Y. 1821–33 and Judge 1824–39, 1844–47, Repr. in Congr. 1839–41, N. Y. Sen. 1848–50. aet. 74. *1867
*Alexander Fleming. aet. 77. *1867
Alfred C. Floyd.
*John Wakefield Francis, A. M., M. D. Coll. Phys. and Surg. N. Y. 1809, LL. D. 1860 and Trin. Coll. 1850, Prof. Obstet. and Med. Jurisp. Rutg. Med. Coll. N. Y., Prof. Mat. Med. Coll. Phys. and Surg. N. Y. 1813–16 and Prof. Obstet. 1820–26, Trustee Coll. Phys. and Surg. 1814–26, Prest. N. Y. Acad. Med. 1848. aet. 72. *1861
James N. Gifford, (M.)
Henry Green.
John C. Hamilton, (C. L.)
David Murray Hoffman, (C. L.), LL. D. 1860 and Union 1840, Judge Supr. Ct. N. Y.
Samuel Jackson.
*Ravaud Kearny, (Rev.), A. M.
*Jackson Kemper, (Rev.), S. T. D. 1829, LL. D. elsewhere, Missy. Bishop P. E. Ch. of the North West 1835–52, Bishop Wisconsin 1852–70. aet. 81. *1870
*Henry McVickar, (M.)
*Benjamin Tredwell Onderdonk, (Rev.), A. M. 1816, S.T.D. 1826, Trustee 1824–53, Prof. Eccles. Pol. Gen. Theol. Sem. P. E. Ch. N. Y. 1826, Bishop P. E. Ch. N. Y. 1830–61. *1861
Walter F. Osgood, A. M.
*Robert J. Renwick.
James Stryker, (C. L.), A. M. 1813, Judge Buffalo, N. Y.
William Turnbull.
*William Edward Wyatt, (Rev.), A. M. 1816, S. T. D. elsewhere.

27

## 1810.

*John Agnew.
*Andrew Anderson, M. D. Coll. Phys. and Surg. N. Y. 1813.
*Francis Child, A. M. 1816.
*David A. Clarkson, (M.)
*George Codwise.
William De Peyster.
Israel D. Disosway, (F.)
*Jacob Dyckman, A. M., M. D. Coll. Phys. and Surg N. Y. 1813.
Robert Emmet, (C. L.), Just. Supr. Ct. N. Y. C.
*Theodosius O. Fowler.
*James C. Garrison, A. M. 1816, M. D. elsewhere, U. S. Navy.
Joseph Greenleaf, (C. L.)
*Peter F. Hunn, (C. L.)
*Charles J. Kip.
*Horatio G. Lewis.
*John McLain McDonald, (C. L.) *1863
*John McGregor, (T.)
*Benjamin Moore, (M.)
*George W. Morton, (C. L.), U. S. Commissioner N. Y. C.
John L. Morton, (F.)
*Ava Neal, (Rev.), A. M. *1839
*Waldron B. Post, (M.)
John Slidell, (C. L.), U. S. Dist. Atty. for La. 1829–33, U. S. Min. to Mexico 1845 and to Central America 1853, Repr. in Congr. and U. S. Sen.
*Francis B. Stevens. *1811
*Richard Stevens, M. D. elsewhere. *1828
*James Stoughton, (C. L.), A. M. *1819
*Pascal N. Strong, (Rev.), A. M. N. Jers. 1818, S. T. D. elsewhere, Trustee 1822–25 *1825
*Jacob Townsend, (C L.)
*Charles Watts, (C. L.), Judge Dist. Ct. New Orleans. *1850

29

## 1811.

*Gregory T. Bedell, (Rev.), A. M. 1816, S. T. D. elsewhere. *1834
John Brown, (Rev.), A. M. 1815, S. T. D. elsewhere.
John Campbell.
Ebenezer Close, A. M. 1815.
*John Covert, Jr., (Rev.)
*George Douglass.
Jacobus Dyckman.
*Charles G. Ferris, A.M. 1816, Repr. in Congr. 1834–36, 1841–3.
*David H. Fraser, A.M. 1815, M. D. Coll. Phys. and Surg. N. Y. 1818. *1818
Richard Freeke, (C. L.)
James Watson Gerard, (C. L.), A. M. 1816, LL. D. 1863.
Benjamin Haight, A.M. 1816.
*William H. Harison, (C. L.), Trustee 1838–1860. *1860
*William Henry Hart, (Rev.), A. M. 1828.
William Hogan, Repr. in Congr.
*Peter V. B. Livingston, U. S. Min. to Cent. America.
Thomas William Ludlow, Trustee 1833–6.
Jackson Odell, (F.)
*George B. Purdy, M. D. Coll. Phys. and Surg. N. Y. 1816. aet. 70. *1865
Charles Rapelje, A. M. 1820.
*John R. Rhinelander, M. D. Coll. Phys. and Surg. N. Y. 1824, Prof. Anat. Coll. Phys. and Surg. 1834–9 and Trustee of same 1840–48. aet. 66. *1857
*John B. Stevenson, 1816, A. M. 1816, M. D. Coll. Phys. and Surg. N. Y. 1816. aet. 68. *1863

John N. Talman, A. M. 1815.
George J. Watts.
24

## 1812.

Albert Ammerman, (Rev.)
*Matthias Bruen, Jr., (Rev.), A. M.
John A. Burtis.
*William Creighton, (Rev.) S. T. D. 1830, elected Bishop P. E. Ch. N. Y. and declined, Prest. Gen. Conven. P. E. Ch. U. S., Trustee 1828–40. *1865
James F. De Peyster, Capt. U. S. A. 1814.
*Alexander Duer, (C. L.) *1819
*Richard Duryee, Jr., (M.)
*Lindley Murray Hoffman, (M.) *1861
*Ogden Hoffman, (C. L.), Midshipman U. S. N. 1814, Memb. N. Y. Assemb 1826–28, Repr. in Congr., Dist. Atty. N. Y. C., Atty.-Gen. N. Y., Trustee 1833–56. *1856
*Benjamin R. Kissam, M. D. Coll. Phys. and Surg. N. Y. 1819.
Augustine N. Lawrence, (B.)
*Philip K. Lawrence, A. M. 1818.
*Cornelius F. Low, (C. L.) *1849
*Peter Mackie, Jr.
*Edward McVickar. *1866
*John W. B. Murray, A. M., M. D. elsewhere. *1818
*Matthew Charles Paterson, (C. L.), A. M. 1819, Dist. Atty. N. Y. C.
*Jacob A. Robertson, (M.), A. M. 1818.
*John Smyth Rogers, and Harv. 1827, M. D. Coll. Phys. and Surg. N. Y. 1821, and Bowd. 1825, Prof. Chem. and Nat. Sci. Trinity, Prof. Mat. Med. N. Y. Coll. of Pharmacy. aet. 57. *1851
*John A. Sidell, (C. L.)
John Swartwout.
*Peter S. Townsend, A. M. 1816, M. D. Coll. Phys. and Surg. N. Y. 1816. aet. 54. *1849
*Egerton L. Winthrop, M.D. Coll. Phys. and Surg. N. Y. 1817. *1834
23

## 1813.

*Henry Anthon, (Rev.), A. M., S. T. D. 1832. *1861
*William Bailey.
*John Brodhead Beck, A. M. 1818 and Union 1816 and N. Jers. 1818, M. D. Coll. Phys. and Surg. N.Y. 1817, Prof. Mat. Med. Coll. Phys. and Surg. 1826–51, Trustee 1838–51. *1851
*James J. Bowden, (Rev.)
*William Boyd.
*George W. Bruen, (M.), A. M.
*Richard F. Cadle, (Rev.), A. M.
Thomas L. Davies.
*Robert Hyslop, (M.)
William Kemble, (M.)
*Thomas C. Mitchell, A. M.
*Nicholas Morris, Jr., A. M.
Thomas C. Murray, A. M. 1818.
*Nathaniel Greene Pendleton, Repr. in Congr. *1861
Robert Ray, (C. L.), A. M. 1817, Trustee 1849–.
*Alexander H. Robertson, A. M.
*Hugh Smith, (Rev.), A. M., S. T. D. 1838. *1849
*John Varick. 18

## 1814.

John H. Ball.

*James Brooks, (M.) aet. 74. *1868
*Cornelius Davis.
*William H. Heyer.
Benjamin Hilton.
*Allen Jackson, A. M. 1821.
Henry R. Judah.
*James Murison Pendleton, A. M. 1819, M. D. Coll. Phys. and Surg. N. Y. 1818. aet. 33. *1832
*Theophilus Russel.
George F. Talman, (C. L.), Corporation Counsel N. Y. C. 1838-9.
*Ferdinand Vandewater.

11

## 1815.

*Charles Anthon, LL.D.1831, Adj.-Prof. Greek and Latin Lang. 1820-30, Jay Prof. Greek and Latin Lang. 1830-57 and Rect. Gram. School 1830-64, Jay Prof. Greek Lang. and Lit. 1857-67. aet. 70. *1867
*James W. Berrian.
*Archibald R. Bogardus.
Robert G. L. De Peyster, (M.)
*Archibald Gracie, Jr., (M.) *1865
*William S. Heyer, (Rev.), A. M.
*John Hone, Jr., (M.)
*William Ironside.
*John Q. Jones, (C. L.)
*Leonard William Kip, (C. L.), A. M. 1820. aet. 67. *1863
Philip Mesier Lydig, (M.)
*John L. Mason, (C. L.), A. M., Judge Supr. Ct. N. Y., Trustee 1848-53.
*Francis Morton.
*Frederic William Rhinelander, (M.)
James John Roosevelt, Jr., (C.L.), N. Y. Assemb. 1835, 1840, Repr. in Congr. 1841-43, Judge Supr. Ct. N. Y.
*Robert Charles Sands, (Au.), A. M. *1832
*Robert Seney, (Rev.), A. M. 1828.
*Henry Hamlin Van Amringe, (Rev.), A. M. aet. 66. *1862
*James S. Watkins, M. D. Coll. Phys. and Surg. N.Y. 1817. *1817

19

## 1816.

*Abel T. Anderson, (C. L.), A. M. *1864
*John D. Campbell, (C. L.), A. M. 1820. *1852
*Richard Codman, (M.) *1847
Frederic De Peyster, Jr., (C. L.), A. M., LL. D. 1867, Milit. Secy. to Gov. Clinton 1825-8, Master in Chancery for 17 years, Prest. N. Y. Historical Society.
*Maurice William Dwight, (Rev.), A. M. 1820, S. T. D. elsewhere. *1860
*James Wallis Eastburn, (Rev.), A. M. *1819
Isaac Ferris, (Rev.), A. M., S. T. D. Union 1833, LL. D. 1853, Chancell. Univ. N. Y. C. 1852-70, and Emeritus Chancellor 1870-.
John Ireland, Jr., (F.)
*John Edgar Mowatt, (M.)
*Daniel Levi Medora Peixotto, A. M. 1823, M. D. Coll. Phys. and Surg. N. Y. 1819, Prof. Theory and Pract. Med. Willoughby Med. Coll. aet. 43. *1843
*Samuel G. Raymond, (C.L.), A.M., Memb. N.Y. Assemb. *1850
John J. Robertson, (Rev.), S. T. D. elsewhere.
*James Romeyn, (Rev.), S. T. D. 1838, elected Prof. of Rhet. Rutg. Coll. and declined.

*John M. Smith, (Rev.), A.M., Prof. in Wesl. Univ. Conn. *1832
*Samuel L. Steer,(F.),Speaker Lower House of Louisiana.
*Thomas M. Strong, (Rev.), A. M. 1820, S. T. D. elsewhere. *1861
*Adrian Vanderveer, A. M., M.D. Coll. Phys. and Surg. N. Y. 1818. *1857

17

## 1817.

*John M. Cannon, (C. L.) *1835
James P. F. Clarke, (Rev.)
*Matthias O. Dayton, (C L.)
Manton Eastburn, (Rev.), A. M., S. T. D. 1835, Bishop P. E. Ch. Mass. 1842-.
*Isaac Fisher, (Rev.), A. M. *1839
*Seymour P. Funk, (Rev.), A. M. 1821. *1828
*Samuel L. Gouverneur, U.S. Postmr. N. Y. C. 1821–25, N. Y. Assemb. 1825. *1865
*John Grigg, (Rev.), A. M. aet. 72. *1868
Daniel Phœnix Ingraham, (C. L.), LL.D. 1860, Just. Supr. Ct. N. Y.
*Benjamin Isherwood, A. M., M. D. Coll. Phys. and Surg. N. Y. 1820. *1832
William Lowerre, (C. L ), A. M.
Edmund Ludlow.
*William Minturn.
*John Neilson, Jr., A. M., M. D. Coll. Phys. and Surg. N. Y. 1821. *1857
Meredith Ogden, (M.)
*Richard Ray, A. M. *1839
*Edward N. Rogers, A. M.
*Samuel D. Rogers, (M.) *1850

18

## 1818.

Henry James Anderson, A.M., M. D. Coll. Phys. and Surg. N. Y. 1824, LL. D. 1850, Prof. of Math. and Astr. 1825–43, Emeritus 1866–, Trustee 1851–.
Daniel Bonnett.
*Richard Varick Dey, (Rev.), A. M. and Yale 1823. *1837
*Frederick Fairlie, (C. L.)
*Peter Forrester, A.M. Rutg., M. D. Coll. Phys. and Surg. N. Y. 1822. *1837
Robert Gracie, and Harv. 1818, (M.), A. M. and Yale 1825.
*Henry Hone, (M.), N. Y. Assemb. 1834.
Richard F. Kemble, (C. L.)
William Beach Lawrence, (C. L.), A. M. 1823, and Yale 1826, LL. D. Brown Univ. 1869, U. S. Chargé d' Aff. London 1827–29, Lt.-Governor of R. I., Trustee Coll. Phys. and Surg. 1837–55.
James Lenox, A. M. and N. Jers. 1821, Trustee N. J. 1823–57.
*John H. Lloyd.
*Alexander B. McLeod.
*Gerard W. Morris, (C. L.), Trustee 1851–5. *1865
*John O'Blenis.
George D. Post, (C. L.)
*Clarence D. Sackett, (C. L.)
*William Staley, A. M.
*Abraham D. Wilson, A. M., M. D. Coll. Phys. and Surg. N. Y. 1821.

18

## 1819.

*Henry N. Cruger, (C. L.), A. M. 1823.
*Gabriel Poillon Disosway, (M.), A. M. and Wesl. 1833, Member N. Y. Assembly 1849. aet. 70. *1868

*Peter Dykers, M. D. Coll. Phys. and Surg. N.Y. 1823. *1845
*Andrew Hamersley, M. D. Coll. Phys. and Surg. N. Y. 1823, Fellow Coll. Phys. and Surg.
*Edward P. Heyer, (M.)
*Walter E. Hyer, (M.) *1845
*William Lupton Johnson, (Rev.), A. M., S. T. D. Allegheny Coll. Penn. aet. 70. *1870
*Charles Jones. *1854
George Jones.
*Henry James Lowerre, (C. L.), A. M. *1830
George J. Rogers, (M.)
*James H. Roosevelt, (C.L.), A. M. *1863
James S. Rumsey, M. D. Coll. Phys. and Surg. N. Y. 1824.
Richard L. Schieffelin, (C.L.), A. M.
*John L. Suckley, A.M. 1823, M. D. Coll. Phys. and Surg. N. Y. 1823. *1836
*Samuel Verplanck, (C. L.), A. M.
Thomas L. Wells, (C. L.), Trustee 1837–59.
*Marinus Willett, Jr., M. D. Coll. Phys. and Surg. N. Y. 1823, Trustee Coll. Phys. and Surg. 1827–40. *1840
*Richard Wynkoop, (Rev.), A. M.

19

## 1820.

William Betts, (C. L.), A.M., LL D. 1850, Trustee 1842– and Clerk 1850–, Prof. of Law 1848–54.
*John B. Bleecker, (M.) *1831
*Joseph H. Coit, (Rev.), S. T. D. 1855. *1866
Cornelius Ryerrs Disosway, (C.L.), A. M. Wesl. 1838.
*James Johnstone, (C. L.) *1854
Samuel Roosevelt Johnson, (Rev.), A. M., S. T. D. 1848, Prof. System. Divinity and Dogmatic Theol. Gen. Theolog. Sem. P. E. Ch., Emeritus 1869–.
Henry Lawrence, (M.)
*Philip Edward Milledoler, (Rev.), M. D. Coll. Phys. and Surg. N. Y. 1824, A. M. Rutg. 1827, N. Y. Assemb. 1832. *1850
*John F. Mitchell, (C. L.), A. M.
William Mitchell, (C. L.), A. M., LL. D. 1863, Master in Chancery N. Y. 1840–43, Just. Supr. Ct. N. Y. State 1850–58.
Archibald G. Rogers, (C. L.)
Rutsen Suckley, (C. L.)
*John R. Townsend, (C. L.) *1846

13

## 1821.

*William B. Barnes, (B.)
*Peter A. Cowdrey, (C. L.), A. M., N. Y. Assemb. 1836. *1852
*Isaac F. Craft, (M.)
William D. Craft, (C. L.)
George H. Fisher, (Rev.), S. T. D. elsewhere, Trustee 1851–55.
*William Forsyth. *1851
William N. Gibert, (C. L.)
Frederic Philipse Gouverneur,† (C. L.)
William P. Hawes, (C. L.), A. M.
*William Inglis, (C.L.), Judge Ct. Common Pleas N. Y. 1839–44. *1863
Pierre M. Irving, (C. L.)
*Thomas Kermit.

† Known subsequently as Frederic Philipse

*Elisha S. King, (C. L.), A. M. 1826.
*Isaac Low, A. M.
Stephen H. Meeker, (Rev.), A. M.
William Henry Munn, (C.L.), A. M.
Samuel Ogden, (M.)
Edwin Post, (M.)
*Henry A. V. Post.
George Shrady.
*John C. Slack, (T.)
*Charles E. Stagg, (M.)
Peter Stagg, (C. L.)
*Junius Thompson, A. M. 1825, M. D. Coll. Phys. and Surg. N. Y. 1825. aet. 31. *1831
*John Tiebout, Jr., A. M., M. D. Coll. Phys. and Surg. N. Y. 1825.
*William Turner, A. M., M. D. elsewhere. *1858
*Gerrit G. Van Wagenen, (C. L.), Trustee 1845–58, and Treasurer 1849–58. *1858
*John H. Waddell, A. M.
Henry John Whitehouse, (Rev.), A. M., S. T. D. 1865 and Oxford Univ. Eng. 1867, LL. D. Cambr. Univ. Eng. 1867, Bishop P. E. Ch. Ill. 1851–.
George Wilkes, M. D. Coll. Phys. and Surg. N. Y. 1824.
30

## 1822.

George Abeel, (M.)
*George W. Dawson, (M.)
*Peter F. Dustan, (C. L.)
*John M. Glover, A. M. Yale 1825, M. D. Coll. Phys. and Surg. N. Y. 1826. *1832
*Josiah Dwight Harris, A. M., M. D. Coll. Phys. and Surg. N. Y. 1826, Asst. Surg. U. S. A. 1833. *1833
*Edwin Holt, 1826.
Henry Philip Jones, (C. L.)
*Theodore F. King, M. D. Coll. Phys. and Surg. N.Y. 1827. aet. 63. *1868
N. Gouverneur Kortright, (C. L.)
Anson Livingston, (C. L.)
*Carroll Livingston, (C. L.) *1867
Edward N. Mead, (Rev.), A. M. 1833, S. T. D. 1861, Secy. Trustees Gen. Theo. Sem.
Adrian H. Müller, (M.)
*Alexander H. Paterson, (M.)
Alfred C. Post, M. D. Coll. Phys. and Surg. N. Y. 1827, Prof. Ophthal. Anat. and Surg. Castleton Med. Coll., Prof. Surg. Univ. N. Y. C., Prest. N. Y. Acad. Med. 1868.
*John Lloyd Stephens, (C. L.), A. M. 1827, U. S. Special Embassador to Central America 1839, Del. to N. Y. S. Constit. Conven. 1846. *1852
*Thomas William Tucker, (C. L.), A. M. 1826. *1864
Alfred Wagstaff, M. D. Coll. Phys. and Surgeons N. Y. 1826.
*Alfred Augustus Weeks, (C. L.), A. M. 1826. *1847
*Hamilton Wilkes, (F.) *1852
Edward M. Willett, (C. L.), A. M.
William R. Williams, (Rev.), A. M. 1835, S. T. D. 1837, Trustee 1838–48.
*Samuel F. Wilson, (C. L.) *1870
23

## 1823.

*Christopher Allen.
Horatio Allen, (Eng.)
*Edward Anthon, (C. L.) *1830
William H. Boyd, A. M., M. D. Coll. Phys. and Surg. N. Y. 1826.

Edward M. Clarke, (C. L.)
Lewis Cruger, (C. L.)
*Edmund B. Elmendorf, (C. L.) *1846
*John T. Ferguson, A. M., M. D. elsewhere.
*John Brain Foulke, A. M. and Yale 1827.
*Adolphus N. Gouverneur, (C. L.)
*Edmund Dorr Griffin, (Rev.), A. M. *1830
William F. Havemeyer, (M.), Mayor N. Y. C.
*William D. Henderson, (C. L.), A. M.
*Henry Augustus Heyer, (M.)
*John A. Hicks, (Rev.), A. M. 1830, S. T. D. Univ. Vt. 1847. *1869
*James Hosack.
Mancius Smedes Hutton, (Rev.), S. T. D. 1841, Trustee 1855–.
*William L. Keese, (Rev.), A. M.
*Jonathan Lawrence, (C.L.) *1833
William A. Lawrence, (M.)
*Adam David Logan, (C.L.) aet. 66. *1869
*George B. Ogden, (B.)
John D. Ogden, M. D. elsewhere.
Smith Pyne, (Rev.), S. T. D. elsewhere.
*Andrew K. Robertson.
*Noel Robertson, (Rev.), A. M.
*Grenville A. Sackett, (C. L.)
Charles J. Smith, (C. L.)
James H. Titus, (M.), A. M., Memb. N. Y. Assemb.

29

# 1824.

Benjamin Aycrigg, (Eng.), A. M. 1839, Chief Engineer Penn.
*Robert Barker.
*Alexander M. Burrill, (C. L.) aet. 62. *1869
*Edward C. Crary, (M.)
*William A. Curtis, (Rev.), A. M. 1838. *1864
Benjamin Drake, A. M., M. D. Coll. Phys. and Surg. N. Y. 1828, Prest. N.Y. Co. Med. Soc.
William Duer, (C. L.), Repr. in Congr. 1849–51, U. S. Consul at Valparaiso.
*William H. Ellet, M. D. elsewhere, Lect. on Element. Chem. 1830–32, Prof. Element. Chem. 1832–33, Prof. Chem. Mineral. and Geol. S. C. Coll. 1835–48. *1859
*James T. Giber , A. M., M. D. elsewhere. *.868
*Jacob Townsend Gilford, M. D. Coll. Phys. and Surg. Geneva. aet. 64. *1869
*Timothy R. Green, (C. L.), A. M. 1834. *18[illegible]0
*John K. Hardenbrook, A.M., M. D. elsewhere.
*Dayton Hobart, (C. L.), A. M. *1870
*William Henry Hobart, A. M., M. D. Coll. Phys. and Surg. N. Y. 1829, Trustee 1848–55. *1857
Pierre Paris Irving, (Rev.)
*George W. Johnson, (F.) *1856
William H. Lupp, (C. L.), A. M.
*Elias Joseph Marsh, A. M., M. D. Coll. Phys. and Surg. N. Y. 1828, Prest. N. J. Med. Soc. aet. 45. *1850
Hamilton Morton, A.M. 1834, M. D. Rutg. Med. Coll N. Y.
*Waddington Ogden, (M.)
*Henry Perkins, A. M., M. D. elsewhere.
*Alexander Robertson, A. M., M. D. elsewhere.
Daniel C. Schermerhorn. 23

## 1825.

*George P. Cammann, M. D. elsewhere. aet. 59. *1863
*James A. M. Gardner, A. M., M. D. Coll. Phys. and Surg. N. Y. 1829.
*Nathaniel Marius Graves, (M.)
Robert William Harris, (Rev.), A. M., S. T. D. 1849.
*Jacob Harsen, Jr., A. M. 1829, M. D. Coll. Phys. and Surg. N. Y. 1829, Prest. North. Dispens. N. Y. aet. 55. *1863
*William E. Laight. *1859
Alexander S. Leonard, (Rev.), A.M. 1847, S. T. D. 1859.
John McKeon, (C. L.), A. M. 1831, N. Y. Assemb. 1831, Repr. in Congr. 1835–37, 1841–43, Dist. Atty. N. Y. C. 1845–51, U. S. Dist. Atty. N. Y. 1853.
*Isaac T. Minard, (C. L.), Surrogate Otsego Co. N. Y.
Edward E. Mitchell, (M.)
*Walter Nichols. aet. 21. *1825
*William Peshine.
William Phyfe.
*Anthony Lispenard Robertson, (C. L.), Asst. Vice-Chancellor N. Y. S. 1846–48, Surrogate N. Y. C. 1848, Justice Superior Ct. N. Y. 1860–65 and Ch.-Just. of same 1865–68, Memb. Constit. Conven. N. Y. 1867. aet. 60. *1868
*Ferdinand Sands, (M.)
John J. Schermerhorn, (M.)
John Fletcher Smith.
*Wessell S. Smith, (C. L.), N. Y. Assemb. *1860
Oliver S. Strong, (M.)
*Peter Wilson, (C. L.)
William Wilson, M. D. Coll. Phys. and Surg. N. Y. 1829.

1

## 1826.

Charles E. Anderson, (Br.), Secy. U. S. Legation Paris 1836–39 and Chargé d'Aff. 1837.
*William A. Clarke, M. D. elsewhere.
John Marshall Guion, (Rev.), S. T. D. 1865.
John W. Hamersley, (C. L.), A. M.
Nathaniel Pendleton Hosack, and Harv. 1826, (M.)
*Gabriel F. Irving.
*Robert Kelly, Jr., Regent Univ. N. Y. S. 1856–57.
Francis M. Kip, (Rev.), S. T. D. 1857.
John N. McLeod, (Rev.), A. M. 1833, S. T. D. elsewhere.
*Joshua S. Marsh.
*Thomas H. Merry, Jr.
*William Henry Milnor, M.D. Coll. Phys. and Surg. N. Y. 1832. aet. 60. *1862
Thomas R. Minturn, (M.)
Henry Morris, (C. L.)
Richard Lewis Morris, M. D. Coll. Phys. and Surg. N. Y. 1830, Health Commr. N. Y. C. 1848–52 and Health Off. 1852–54.
*John B. Norsworthy.
Hewlett R. Peters, (Rev.), S. T. D. elsewhere.
*Daniel Phœnix Riker, (C. L.) aet. 61. *1868
Beverley Robinson, Jr., (C. L.)
William H. Roosevelt.
*Daniel Seymour.
Abraham A. Slover, Jr.
Thomas Swords, Jr., 1831, Brig-Gen. U. S. A.
*Gerrit Hubert Van Wagenen, Jr.
Harris Wilson, (C. L.)

25

## 1827.

Jonathan Trumbull Backus, (Rev.), A. M., S. T. D. Union 1847.
Jacob Sperry Baker, (M.)
William Sperry Baker, M. D. Coll. Phys. and Surg. N. Y. 1831.
Thomas Hazard Barker, (B.), U. S. Consul at Antwerp 1836.
Henry Neilson Brush.
John P. Crosby, (C.L.), Trust. Med. Dept. 1860–.
William Henry Crosby, (C.L.), Prof. Greek and Latin Lang. Rutg. Coll. 1841–9, Acting Prof. Lat. Lang. and Lit. 1859–60.
Henry Augustus Du Bois, M.D. Coll. Phys. and Surg. N. Y. 1830, LL. D. Yale 1864, Memb. Conn. Acad. Arts and Sciences, Memb. Geolog. Soc. France.
Edward Dunscomb, (M.)
*Edward Bristed Eastburn. *1830
Hamilton Fish, (C.L.), A.M., LL. D. 1850, Trustee 1840– and Chn. Board 1859–, Repr. in Congr. 1843–5, Lt.-Gov. N. Y. 1847–9, Gov. N. Y. 1849–51, U. S. Sen. 1851–7, Secy. State U. S. 1869–.
*Michael Floy, Jr., A. M. *1837
John Murray Forbes, (Rev.), A. M., S. T. D. 1847, Tutor Trin. Coll. 1830, Dean Gen. Theol. Sem. P. E. Ch. 1869–.
*John Henry Hobart Haws, (C. L.), Repr. in Congr. 1851–3. *1858
*William C. Heyward, 1830, (F.) *1863
John Clarkson Jay, M. D. Coll. Phys. and Surg. N.Y. 1831, Trustee 1859–.
Joshua Jones, (C. L.)
*Abraham Beakley Labagh, (F.)
*Alfred Ludlow. *1831
Charles McFarlan, N. J. Sen. 1846.
Henry J. Morton, (Rev.), A. M., S. T. D. Univ. Penn. 1844, Trustee Univ. Penn.
*Jonathan Nathan, (C. L.), Master in Chanc. N. Y. 1840–5. *1863
Henry Onderdonk, Jr., (T.), A. M. 1833.
Laughton Osborn, (Au.)
*Samuel Penny, Jr., (Rev.) *1853
*Minturn Post, M. D. Univ. Penn. 1832. aet. 61. *1869
*James M. Quin, 1830, M. D. Rutg. Med. Coll. N. Y., A. M. 1833. aet. 62. *1868
Charles Rhind, Jr., (M.)
*Henry Rogers, Jr., (C. L.) *1840
*Edwin Sands. *1828
*Robert Mott Sands, (C. L.) *1833
John Schermerhorn, (Br.)
*Theodore A. Swords, (C. L.) aet. 33. *1841
Joseph C. Wallace, (F.)
*William Winter, (C. L.)
*Grenville Temple Winthrop, and Harv. 1827 and Bowd. 1827, (C. L.), A. M., Memb. Mass. Leg. 1840. *1852

36

## 1828.

*William Bayley, (Art.) *1857
*Edmund D. Barry, Jr.
*Jonas Butler, (C. L.) *1858
*George Catlin, (C. L.), Dist. Atty. Richmond Co. N. Y.
Thomas W. Chrystie, (Rev.)
Thomas T. Devan, (Rev.), A. M., M. D. Coll. Phys. and Surg. N. Y. 1831, Missionary in China 1848, Chaplain U. S. A. 1862.
Cornelius Dubois, Jr., (M.)

Edmund Embury, (Rev.), A. M. 1833.
George Gilford.
Robert Goelet.
Alexander N. Gunn, A. M. Rutg. 1832, M. D. Coll. Phys. and Surg. N.Y. 1833.
Benjamin I. Haight, (Rev.), A. M., S. T. D. 1846, LL.D. Hobart 1870, Trustee 1843 –, Prof. Past. Theol. and Pulp. Eloq. Gen. Theol. Sem. P. E. Ch., Asst. Minister Trinity Parish N. Y. C. 1847–.
Henry S. Hoyt.
*Mortimer Livingston, (M.) *1857
*Austin L. S. Main, M. D. Coll. Phys. and Surg. N. Y. 1832. aet. 58. *1867
*John A. Morrill, (C. L.)
George B. Neill.
*John M Ogden. *1836
Joel B. Post, (M.)
Barzillai Slosson, (C.L.), Dist. Atty. Ontario Co. N. Y.
Samuel Sidney St. John, (T.), A. M. 1834.
Lewis Thibou, (Rev.)
John Ledyard Vandervoort, A.M., M.D. Coll. Phys. and Surg. N. Y. 1832.
Robert Boyd Van Kleeck, (Rev.), A. M. and Trin., S. T. D. Trin. 1847, Instr. 1830–1.
William Wheeler Van Wagenen, (C. L.), A. M. 1834.
Alexander Robertson Walsh, (M.)
*William Walton, (Rev.), A.M. 1836, S. T. D. 1852, Inst. in Hebrew Gen. Theol. Sem. P. E. Ch., and Prof. Hebrew and Greek Lang. 1869. aet. 59. *1869
*Richard Whiley, Jr., (C. L.)
Martin Ryerson Zabriskie,† (C. L.), Trustee 1856–. 29

† Known, since 1864, as Martin Zborowski.

## 1829.

*George Featherstone Allen, (Eng.), Trustee 1854–63. *1863
*Theodore A. Bailey, (M.)
Thomas E. Blanch, (C. L.), Dist. Atty. Rockland Co. N. Y.
*James Augustus Carter, M. D. Coll. Phys. and Surg. N. Y. 1832.
Alfred W. Craven, (Eng.), Ch. Eng. Croton. Aq. Dept. N. Y. C.
Robert James Dillon, (C.L.), Counsel to Corp. N. Y. C. 1853–6.
*Benjamin S. Downing, M.D. Coll. Phys. and Surg. N. Y. 1832. aet. 24. *1834
William Edgar.
*James Heyward, M. D. elsewhere.
John T. Irving, Jr., (C. L.)
*Richard H. Ogden, (C. L.)
Samuel Ogden, (C. L.)
Thomas W. Ogden, (Br.)
*John D. Ogilby, A. M. 1833, Mast. Col. Coll. Gram. Sch. 1829–30, Prof. Lang. Rutg. Coll. 1832–40, Prof. Eccles. Hist. Gen. Theol. Sem. P. E. Ch. 1841–51. *1851
*Peter Augustus Schermerhorn, A. M. 1833. *1845
*Theodore Sedgwick, Jr., (C. L.), U. S. Dist. Atty. N. Y., Trustee Coll. Phys and Surg. N. Y. 1842–59. *1859
Charles R. Swords, (M.), N.Y. Assemb., Trustee 1870–.
*Robert Tucker, M. D. Coll. Phys. and Surg. N. Y. 1832. *1846
John D. Van Buren, (C. L.), N. Y. Assemb.
*Fanning S. Worth, (T.), A. M. 1835.

20

## 1830.

*John B. Boggs.
James Bowdoin, (C. L.)
Robert L. Cutting, (Br.)
John Delafield, Jr., (C. L.), A. M. 1837.
Hugh T. Dickie, (C. L.), Judge Sup. Ct. Ill.
*Benjamin T. Ferguson, (C. L.) *1836
Lewis C. Gunn, (Ed.)
*Nicholas C. Heyward. *1852
George Ireland, Jr., (C. L.)
*Edward Jones, M. D. Coll. Phys. and Surg. 1834, Trustee 1849–69. aet. 58. *1869
*John Taylor Kneeland, M.D. Coll. Phys. and Surg. N. Y. 1833. *1838
Henry Ledyard, (C.L.), Secy. U. S. Legation at Paris 1839–42, and Chargé d'Aff. 1842–44, Mayor Detroit, Mich. 1855, Mich. Sen. 1857.
*Benjamin Franklin Miller, (C. L.) *1837
Henry C. Murphy, (C. L.), Mayor Brooklyn N. Y., Repr. in Congr. 1843–45, Memb. N. Y. Constit. Conven. 1846, 1867, U. S. Min. at the Hague, N. Y. Sen. 1864–.
Henry Nicoll, (C. L.), LL.D. 1870, Repr. in Congr., Memb. N. Y. Constit. Conven. 1846.
Charles H. Ogden, (M.)
William Steele, (M.), M. D. Coll. Phys. and Surg. N. Y. 1833.
William D. Waddington, (C. L.)
George William Wright, (C. L.)

## 1831.

James Bolton, A. M. 1835, M.D. Coll. Phys. and Surg. N. Y. 1836.
*Peter Schermerhorn Chauncey, (Rev.), A.M. 1836, S. T. D. Trin. Coll. 1848, Trustee Trin. Coll. *1866
*James Chrystie, Jr.
Abraham B. Conger, A. M., Tutor 1831–3, N. Y. Sen., Prest. N. Y. S. Agricult. Soc., Memb. N. Y. S. Constit. Conv. 1867.
William E. Eigenbrodt, (Rev.), A. M. 1835, S. T. D. 1855, Prof. Past. Theol. Gen. Theol. Sem. P. E. Ch.
*Robert Emory, (Rev.), A.M., S. T. D. 1846, Prof. Anc. Lang. Dickin. Coll. 1834–9, and Prest. Dickin. 1842–8. *1848
*Petrus Stuyvesant Fish, A. M. *1834
*John B. Gallagher, (Rev.) *1849
John P. Hone.
Bradish Johnson, (M.)
Charles R. King, M. D. Univ. Penn. 1834.
*James Joseph Macneven. *1832
James McCready Morgan.
Gideon S. Nichols, (F.)
*John L. O'Sullivan, A. M., Tutor 1831–3, U. S. Min. Portugal, Regent Univ. N. Y. S. 1846–55.
John Punnett, A. M., M. D. elsewhere.
*John B. Purroy, (C. L.), A. M., Consul for Venezuela N. Y. *1859
*Richard W. Redfield, A. M. 1838. *1846
Edwin M. Taylor, (Eng.), State Eng. Virginia.
Francis Tomes, Jr., (Br.)
Robert G. Vermilye, (Rev.), A. M. 1836, S. T. D. 1851,

Tutor 1835-7, Ad. Prof. Greek and Lat. Lang. 1837 –43, Prof. Christ. Theol. in Theol. Inst. Conn.
*Lloyd Saxbury Waddell. *1832
Samuel Ward, Jr., (Br.), A. M. 1835.
*Robert Watts, Jr., A. M., M.D. Coll. Phys and Surg. N. Y. 1835, Prof. Anat. and Physiol. Coll. Phys. and Surg. 1843–48, Prof. Anat. 1848–67. *1867

24

## 1832.

Henry T. Anthony, (M.)
Walter T. Avery, (M.)
Horatio Bogert, (C. L.), A. M. 1836.
William L. Boyd, (M.), A. M.
George Carvill, Jr., (M.)
*John Chrystie, (M.) *1856
*Henry S. Dodge, (C. L.), A. M. *1855
*Daniel G. F. Fanshaw. *1833
James Heard, Jr., (M.), A.M. 1836.
Alexander C. Hillman, (Rev.)
*Nicholas W. Hoffman, (M.) *1843
Aaron Jarvis, A. M., M. D. Coll. Phys. and Surg. N.Y. 1835. aet. 45. *1859
*William Templeton Johnson, (C. L.), A. M. *1869
Philip Livingston Jones, M. D. Coll. Phys. and Surg. N. Y. 1835.
*John J. C. Kane, (C. L.) *1854
Frederick W. Miller, (Rev.)
Stephen Reed, Jr., (C. L.), A. M.
*Thomas A. Richmond, (C. L.), A. M. *1859
William Channing Russel, (C. L.), A. M., Prof. Antioch Coll. Ohio, Prof. Cornell Univ. N. Y. 1867–.
Henry J. Ruggles, (C. L.)
Erasmus P. Smith, (C. L.)
John E. Stillwell, M. D. Coll. Phys. and Surg. N. Y. 1836.
Frederick L. Talcott, (M.)
Philip W. Thomas, (C. L.)
Jonathan Thompson, Jr., (M.), A. M. 1836.
Frederick Townsend, (C. L.)
*Russell N. Townsend, (C. L.) *1837
William S. Verplanck.

28

## 1833.

*Stephen D. Allen, M. D. elsewhere. *1840
*James Barrow, Jr., (C. L.) *1868
*John S. Bartlett, Jr., (Ed.)
*Jackson Bolton, M. D. elsewhere.
James Constable, (C. L.)
*Richard Cox, (Rev.), A. M.
John F. Delaplaine, Jr., (C. L.), Attaché at Madrid 1852, and at Vienna, Secy. U. S. Legation Vienna 1869–.
*Pierre Cortlandt DePeyster, (M.) *1854
*John M. Gelston.
Charles Hall, (M.), A. M. 1838.
John Jay Jenkins, (C. L.)
*Philip Kearny, Jr., Major U. S. A. 1847, Brig.-Gen. U. S. V. 1861, and Maj.-Gen. 1862. aet 47. *1862
*Francis P. Lee, (Rev.), A. M. *1847
*Samuel Bard McVickar. *1837
*James W. Metcalf, M. D. elsewhere. *1856
Gouverneur Morris Ogden, (C. L.), Trustee 1849– and Treasurer 1858–.
Henry B. Renwick, (Eng.), Examr. U. S. Pat. Off.

William Rhinelander Renwick, (M.)
*Bruce Schermerhorn. *1862
Edward Slosson, (C. L.)
John G. Smedberg, (F.)
*Robert Spencer, (C. L.)
Abraham Gardiner Thompson, Jr., A. M., M. D. Coll. Phys. and Surg. N.Y. 1837, N. Y. Assemb. 1845 and 1857.
James A. Williams, (Rev.), A. M., S. T. D. 1863.

24

## 1834.

William M. Allen, (C. L.), A. M.
James William Beekman, (C. L.), A. M. 1838, N. Y. Assemb. 1848, N. Y. Senate 1849-51, Trustee Med. Dept. 1860-.
Edward Bryar, (F.), A. M. 1838.
William Bryan Casey, M. D. elsewhere.
James Michael Cockcroft, (M.)
William Cockcroft, M. D. Coll. Phys. and Surg. N.Y. 1838.
*John Conger, A. M., M. D. Coll. Phys. and Surg. N.Y. 1838.
*Isaac C. Delaplaine, (C. L.), A. M., Repr. in Congr. aet. 48. *1866
William Demarest, (Rev.), A. M.
William Dennis, (Rev.)
*William Dodge, (C. L.), A. M., N. Y. Assemb. *1858
*William Mitchell Gillespie, (Eng.), A. M., LL.D. 1859, and Univ. Nashville 1857, Prof. Civ. Eng. Union Coll. 1845-68. aet. 52. *1868
John S. Heard, A. M., M. D. Coll. Phys. and Surg. N.Y. 1837.
Henry Heyward, A. M. 1838.
Benjamin S. Huntington, (Rev.), A. M. 1839.
William Henry Hyde, (M.)
Samuel Evan Johnson, (C.L.), A. M., Judge Kings Co. N. Y.
William Gracie King.
Alexander Major, (M.)
Richard E. Mount, Jr., (C.L.), A. M.
*Philip Rhinelander.
Robert S. Swords, (C. L.), Lt. Col. N. J. Vols.
Anthony Ten Broeck, (Rev.), A. M., S. T. D. 1867, Rector Burlington Coll.
Lloyd Windsor, (Rev.), A.M.

24

## 1835.

*Jedediah Blakeney Auld, (C. L.), A. M. aet. 51. *1866
Romaine Dillon, (C.L.), Secy. U. S. Legation Brazil.
Evert A. Duyckinck, (Au.), A. M.
Benigno Gener, (C. L.)
Thomas Buchanan Gilford, (C. L.)
Andrew Stelle Hamersley, (C. L.), A. M. 1839.
Orlando Harriman, Jr., (Rev.), A. M.
William Heard, (M.)
*Joshua E. Jones. *1839
*Charles C. Lee.
John W. C. Leveridge, (C.L.), A. M. 1839.
Charles Ha rison Lyon, (M.), A. M.
*Joseph McIntyre.
Charles D. Mead, (C. L.), A. M. 1839.
William Mulligan, A. M.
*Al xander Palachè, (M.)

George Quartus Pomeroy, (C. L.)
John H. Riker, (C. L.)
William H. Taggard, (C. L.)
Ludlow Thomas, (Br.)
*John Richard Thurman, Repr. in Congr. 1849–51. *1854
*Russell Trevett, (Rev.), A. M., S.T.D. 1855, Prof. Anc. Lang. St. James, Md. *1865
William H. Wilson, (T.), A.M.
Christian Zabriskie, Jr., (M.) 24

## 1836.

Newbold Edgar.
Christodoulos L. M. Evangeles, (T.)
*George William Fash, (Rev.), A. M. 1840.
John Graham, (C. L.)
Giles Mumford Hillyer, (C. L.), A. M.
John Henry Hobart, (Rev.), S. T. D. 1856.
Edward Hoffman, (C. L.)
John Jay, (C. L.), A. M., U. S. Min. Plen. to Austria 1869–.
William Alfred Jones, (Au.), A. M., Librarian 1851–65.
*Edward Huger Laight, (M.) *1853
James Phillips Lake.
George Harrison Lynch, (C. L.)
*Henry McVickar, (Rev.)
Daniel McLaren Quackinbush, (Rev.)
James Renwick, Jr., (Arch.), A. M.
Charles Maison Seymour, (Rev.), A. M.
William Thompson.
*Henry Ward, Jr., A. M.
George Gilfert Waters, (C. L.), A. M.
Harvey Augustus Weed, (C. L.), A. M.
*James Willis Wilson, (C.L.), A. M. aet. 53. *1868
21

## 1837.

*Charles Aldis, (Rev.), A.M. *1857
Samuel Blatchford, (C. L.), LL. D. 1867, Judge U. S. Circ. Ct. N. Y. 1867–, Trustee 1867–.
Nathaniel W. Chittenden, (C. L.), A. M.
John William Clark, (Rev.)
Samuel Cockcroft.
*J. Wallace Collet, A. M. 1841.
*Stephen Douglass, (Rev.), A. M. *1857
*Henry P. Fessenden, (C.L.) *1867
Anthony Halsey, (B.), A. M.
*Benjamin Holmes Jarvis, (C. L.)
William Henry Leggett, (T.)
John McMullen, Jr., (T.), A. M.
*Charles D. March.
*William J. Masterton, (M.)
George L. Nevius, (M.)
*Charles Edward Shea, (C. L.), A. M.
Jesse Ames Spencer, (Rev.), A. M. and Trin. 1854, S. T. D. 1852, Prof. Lat. and Orient Lang. Burlington Coll. 1850–51, Prof. Greek Lang. and Lit. Coll. City of N. Y. 1869–.
*David Provoost Thomas, (C. L.)
John Ireland Tucker, (Rev.), S. T. D. 1858.
*George Stayley Van Cleef, (Rev.)
John Vanderbilt, Jr., (C.L.), N. Y. Sen., Judge Kings Co. N. Y.
*Samuel H. Whitlock, (C.L.) *1856
*Alexander Somerville Wotherspoon, M.D. Coll. Phys. and Surg. N. Y. 1841, Asst. Surg. U. S. A. 1843–54. *1854
23

## 1838.

*Frederic Anthon, (C. L.) *1868
Edward Anthony, (M.)
Mancer M. Backus, (M.), A. M. Geneva 1841.
*Thomas Colden Cooper, Capt. U. S. V. *1864
Richard H. Douglass.
*Isaac V. Fowler, (C. L.), A. M. 1842, U. S. Postmr. N. Y. C. aet. 52. *1869
John Hone, (C. L.)
Philip Hone, Jr.
Benjamin T. Kissam, (C.L.), A. M. 1851.
John Mason Knox, (C. L.), A. M.
*Jeremiah Larocque, (C. L.) aet. 46 *1868
Alfred Mersan Loutrel, (Rev.)
*William Brinckerhoff Moffat, A. M., M.D. Coll. Phys. and Surg. N. Y. 1842.
*Benjamin Romaine, Jr., (C. L.) *1841
William Edward Snowden, (Rev.)
Charles Spear, (Br.)
George Templeton Strong, (C. L.), Trustee 1853–, Treas. U. S. San. Comm.
William R. Travers, (Br.)
Henry Hall Ward, (B.), A.M.
*Francis Marion Ward, A.M. *1847

20

## 1839.

Charles Edward Anthon, A.M. 1853, Prof. Coll. City of N. Y.
George Christian Anthon, Prof. Greek Univ. N. Y. C.
John Jacob Astor, Jr., Trustee 1859–69, Col. U. S. Vols. 1861–2 and Bvt. Brig. Gen. 1866.
Allen H. Brown, (Rev.)
*James C. Roosevelt Brown. *1864
John Ebenezer Burrill, Jr., (C. L.), A. M., 1843, Memb. N.Y.S. Constit. Conv. 1867.
Frederic Augustus Cairns.
*Arthur Carey, (Rev.), A. M. *1864
John Carey, Jr., (Eng.), A.M.
*George James Cornell, (C.L.), A. M., Memb. N.Y. Assemb.
Henry Drisler, Jr., A. M., LL.D. 1864, Tutor 1843–45, Adj. Prof. Greek and Lat. Lang. 1845–57, Prof. Lat. Lang. and Lit. 1857–67, Acting President 1867, Jay-Prof. Greek Lang. and Lit. 1867–.
Richard Stockton Emmet, (C. L.)
James Walker Fowler, (C.L.), A. M.
Harvey D. Ganse, (Rev.), A. M. 1844.
Nathaniel Blossom Hoxie, (C. L.), A. M.
Frederick Hughson, (C. L.)
Charles Ingersoll, (C.L.), LL. B. Harv. 1841.
Daniel DeForest Lord, (C.L.), Trustee Med. Dep. 1860–.
Joseph Rich Mann, (Rev.), A.M. 1844, S. T. D. N. Jers. 1862.
Edwin Augustus Nicholls, (Rev.)
*John Pirnie, Jr., (C. L.), A. M.
*Peter B. Pirnie, A. M.
George Warner Quackenbos, (T.), A. M.
Edward Sabine Renwick, (M.), A. M.
James William Walsh, (M.)

25

## 1840.

Charles Bancroft, (Rev.), A. M., S. T. D. 1861.

Samuel Bowden, (Rev.), A. M.
Gerard Smith Boyse.
Charles Bûlow Bucknor, (C. L.), A. M.
*James Farley Clark, (C. L.), A. M.
*Edward Nicoll Crosby. *1865
William Forrest, Jr., (Rev.), A. M.
James George Graham, (C. L.), A. M., N. Y. Assemb.
Ogden Hoffman, Jr., (C. L.), LL. B. Harv. 1842, Judge U. S. Dist. Ct. California.
*Lydig Monson Hoyt. aet. 48. *1868
*Alfred George Jones, (C. L.), A. M., LL. B. Harv. 1842. aet. 47. *1868
Robert Lenox Kennedy, A. M.
Edward Henry Lawrance, (F.)
Benjamin Chase Leveridge, (C. L.), A. M. 1844.
Levi Arnold Lockwood, (C. L.), A. M.
Dwight Edwards Lyman, (Rev.)
John Mitchell Mason, (C.L.), A. M.
Thomas C. Meyer, (Eng.)
Alonzo Castle Monson, (C.L.), A. M., Judge Sup. Ct. California.
Obadiah Newcomb, Jr.
William Nicoll.
George W. Pell, A. M. 1852.
Jotham Post, M. D. Coll. Phys. and Surg. N. Y. 1845.
Ellis Potter, Jr., (C. L.)
Worthington Romaine, (C.L.), A. M.
William Colford Schermerhorn, (C.L.), A.M., Trustee 1860–.
*Peter Shapter, Jr., A. M.
Peter Remsen Strong, (C.L.), A. M.
Owen Sweeny, A. M., M. D. Coll. Phys. and Surg. N. Y. 1845.
Van Brunt Wyckoff, A. M. 1844, M. D. Coll. Phys. and Surg. N. Y. 1845.
Joseph Webb Winans, (C.L.), A. M. 31

## 1841.

*Daniel Henry Beadel.
*Edward Lewis Chichester, M. D. elsewhere.
John Hicks Clark.
George Washington Collord, (T.), A. M.
*Frederick Cunningham, (C. L.)
Richard Varick De Peyster, (B.)
Thomas Bloodgood Dibblee, (C. L.), A. M.
Cornelius Roosevelt Duffie, (Rev.), A.M., S T. D. Univ. N. Y. C. 1865, Chaplain 1857–.
William Ward Duffield, (Eng.)
James Emott, Jr., (C. L.), Just. Supr. Ct. N. Y.
*Herman Ten Eyck Foster, (F.) aet. 47. *1869
Oliver Wolcott Gibbs, A. M., M. D. Coll. Phys. and Surg. N. Y. 1845, Prof. Chem. and Phys. Free Acad. N. Y. 1848–63, Prof. Chem. Harv. 1863–, Memb. U. S. San. Com., Memb. Nat. Acad. Science.
Thomas Strong Griffing, Lieut. U. S. V. 1846–8.
Jacob Boerum Jewett, (C. L.)
*William Kemble, Jr., A.M. *1845
James Hall Mason Knox, (Rev.), A. M., S. T. D. 1861.
Joseph Effingham Lawrence, (Ed.)

*Robert Le Roy, Jr., (Br.), Capt. U. S. V. aet. 41. *1865
John Hodgson Mortimer, (M.)
Israel Moses, A.M., M.D. Coll. Phys. and Surg. N.Y. 1845.
Edward Delavan Nelson, (M.), A. M.
John Harris Parish, (C. L.), LL. B. Harv. 1844.
William Lewis Peck, (Rev.), A. M. 1857.
John Rankin, Jr., (C. L.)
Jones Rogers.
George Metcalfe Root, (Eng.), A. M.
Robert G. Simpson, (C. L.)
Augustus Lyons Smith, (F.)
William Lyons Smith, (F.)
John Joseph Townsend, (C. L.), A. M.
*Robert Dorlon Van Voorhis.

31

## 1842.

Hector Craig Ames, Attaché U. S. Leg. Madrid.
*William Gould Banks, (C. L.), A. M.
*Abraham Smith Brouwer, (C. L.)
Benjamin Franklin Clark, (F.)
William Henry Ebbets, (C. L.)
Frederick Frye, (C. L.), A. M.
William Henry Harison, Jr., (Rev.), A. M.
Abram Stevens Hewitt, (M.), A. M., Secy. and Direct. Cooper Union, N. Y. C., U. S. Commr. to Univ. Exposition, Paris, 1867.
Julius Sleight Hitchcock, (M.)
Robert Jaffray, Jr., (M.)
William Seymour Kernochan, (C. L.), LL B. Harv. 1844.
*Richard Montgomery Lawrence, Jr., (M.)
Livingston Kip Miller, (C.L.), A. M. 1846.
Clement Moore, (C. L.), A.M.
*George Lucas Newton, (C. L.), A. M.
Robert Morrison Olyphant, (M.)
Wheelock Hendee Parmly, (Rev.), A. M.
William J. Paulding.
James Hunter Phinney.
Edward Elmer Potter, Brig.-Gen. U. S. Vols.
*Zebedee Ring, Jr., (C. L.)
Oliver Everett Roberts, (M.), A. M.
Washington Rodman, (Rev.)
*Silas Weir Roosevelt, (C. L.) aet. 47. *1870
David Reid Stanford, (M.)
John Baker Stevens, (C. L.)
*William Pinckney Stewart, (C. L.), A. M. 1848. *1870
*John Sym, (Rev.) *1845
Elisha William Teakle.
David Thomson, Jr., (M.), A. M.

30

## 1843.

*Benjamin Nibbs Aymar, (M.)
Samuel P. Bell, (C. L.)
Thomas C. T. Buckley, (C. L.), A. M.
William Edgar Bunker, (M.)
*John White Dana, M. D. Coll. Phys. and Surg. N.Y. 1846.
*William Cecil Duncan, (Rev.), A. M., S.T.D. 1857. *1864
Benjamin H. Franklin, (M.)
*Albert Gallatin, Jr., (C. L.), A. M. aet. 35. *1859
James Watson Gerard, Jr., (C. L.), A. M.
*William Beach Lawrence, Jr., (C. L.), A. M. 1845. *1870
Edward Zechariah Lewis, (Rev.)

William McCune, (F.)
Henry Post McGowan, (C.L.)
*Robert K. Moffet.
William R. Morgan, (B.)
John Christian Philip, M. D. Coll. Phys. and Surg. N. Y. 1847.
George Payn Quackenbos, (T.), A. M., LL. D. Wesl. Univ. Conn. 1868.
Charles Reynolds, (Rev.), A. M., S. T. D. elsewhere.
John Henry Ross, M. D. Coll. Phys. and Surg. N.Y. 1847.
Matson Meier Smith, (Rev.), A. M., S. T. D. 1863.
John B. Stevens, (C. L.)
*John Thomson, M. D. Coll. Phys. and Surg. N. Y. 1847. aet. 31. *1856
Cornelius Van Vorst, Jr., (C. L.) 23

## 1844.

Clement W. Al Burtis, (F.)
*John Babcock Arden, M. D. Coll. Phys. and Surg. N. Y. 1848. *1851
Robert Bayard Campbell, (C. L.)
Jacob Post Giraud Foster, (C. L.)
Samuel Hollingsworth, (Rev.), A. M., S. T. D. 1868.
Nicholas Bergasse Labau, (C. L.), N. Y. Sen. 1867–69, N. Y. Assemb. 1869–.
Charles William Lawrence.
Edward McGee, (Rev.)
William Bowne Minturn, M.D. Coll. Phys. and Surg. N. Y. 1848.
William Taylor Moore.
*Peter Martin Pirnie.
Edward Henry Swan, (C.L.), LL. B. Harv. 1847.
Otto William Erasmus Van Tuyl, M. D. Coll. Phys. and Surg. N. Y. 1847.
Charles Whipple Whiley, M. D. Coll. Phys. and Surg. N. Y. 1848.
14

## 1845.

*John Knickerbocker Adams,
James Anderson.
*Francis S. Cottenet. *1848
John Drake, (C. L.), A. M. 1851.
George Barnard Draper, (Rev.), A. M., S. T. D. 1868.
George T. Elliot, Jr., A. M. 1849, M. D. Univ. N. Y. C. 1861, Prof. Obstet. Diseases Wom. and Childr. Bellev. Med. Coll. N. Y. C.
John James Elmendorf, (Rev.), A. M., S. T. D. 1866, Instr. in Maths. 1848, Prof. Phil. and Belles-Lettres Racine Coll. 1868.
William Alexander Falls, (B.)
George Irving.
George A. Jones, (C. L.)
Samuel Thomas Jones, (C. L.), Just. Sup. Ct. N. Y.
John Wheeler Leavitt, Jr.
Alexander McCue, (C. L.)
Charles Armand Minton.
*Samuel B. Romaine Nichols.
*David B. Ogden, Jr. *1865
Henry Onderdonk, Prof. Chem. St. Timothy's Hall., Md.
*Lefroy Ravenhill, A.M. 1849, M. D. Coll. Phys. and Surg. N.Y. 1849, Librarian 1847–51. aet. 26. *1851
Aaron B. Reid, (M.)
Stephen K. Stanton.
*John A. Taggard. *1865
Frederick Samuel Tallmadge, (C. L.), A. M. 1849.
Pierre Marston Van Wyck.
*Henry P. Wainwright. *1845
24

## 1846.

*R. S. Carden Abbott, A. M.
G. Mortimer Belden, (F.), A. M. 1850.
Beverley Robinson Betts, (Rev.), A. M., Librarian 1865-.
Edward C. Bogert, (M.)
Henry A. Bogert, (C. L.), A. M.
Arthur Bronson, Jr.
Elias G. Brown, (C. L.), A. M.
William J. Frost, (Rev.), A. M.
William B. Harison, (C. L.)
Charles B. Hoffman, (B.)
*William H. Hudson.
John G. Hyer, (C. L.)
*William M. Johnston, (M.)
John Grenville Kane, (C. L.), A. M.
Edwin M. Kellogg, M.D. elsewhere.
John L. Lefferts, (C. L.)
Jeremiah Loder, (C. L.), A. M., LL. B. Yale 1848.
Charles Scott McKnight.
William Augustus McVickar, (Rev.), A. M. 1850, S. T. D, 1870, Lect. on Ev. of Religion 1869-.
*Frederick Nash, A.M., M.D. Coll. Phys. and Surg. N.Y. 1850. aet. 34. *1861
William Whittingham Olssen, (Rev.), A. M. 1850.
Edward M. Peck, (Rev.), A. M. and Trinity Coll. 1852.
James Thompson, (C. L.), A. M.
Alexander G. Tyng.

24

## 1847.

*Cornelius Duffie Blake, (C. L.), A. M.
John H. Bolton, (M.)
Henry Pearsall Campbell, (M.), A. M.
John Winthrop Chanler, (C. L.), N. Y. Assemb. 1858-9, Repr. in Congr.
William Samuel Coffey, (Rev.), A. M.
Wilhelmus Bogart Conger, (M.)
Carroll Dunham, M. D. Coll. Phys. and Surg. N. Y. 1850.
John Whetten Ehninger, (Art.)
Robert Holden, (Rev.), A.M., Prof. Burlington Coll. N. Jers. 1849-51.
*Arthur M. Jones. *1850
John Stearns Lane, (M.), A. M.
Isaac Lawrence, (C. L.), A. M.
William Simmons Ludlum, (Rev.), A. M., M. D. 1862.
John James McLaren, (B.)
Clarence Green Mitchell, (C. L.), A. M.
*Timothy G. Mitchell, A. M., Prof. Burl. Coll. N. Jers. 1849-57. *1857
John Moneypenny, Jr., M. D. Coll. Phys. and Surg. N. Y. 1850, Surg. 123d N. Y. S. Vols.
John Wells Moore, (Rev.), A. M. 1860.
John Neilson, (M.)
*Benjamin Augustus Onderdonk.
Frederic W. Rhinelander, (M.)
Joseph Kanick Riggs, (B.)
James Francis Ruggles, (C. L.)
Archibald M. Stone, (Rev.)
Israel Leander Townsend, (Rev.), A. M.
*Robert Travis, Jr., (Rev.), A. M. *1866
Francis Van Rensselaer, (F.)

Tompkins Westervelt, (C. L.) 28

## 1848.

Theodorus Bailey Bronson, (C. L.), A. M.
Horace W. Carpenter, (C.L.)
Ralph L. Cook, (M.)
Lyman Denison Demaray, (M.)
Richard Mead De Mille, (C. L.), A. M.
Morgan Dix, (Rev.), A. M., S.T.D. 1862, Rector Trinity Parish N. Y. 1862–, Trustee 1862–.
George Clinton Farrar, (M.), A. M.
Joseph Wesley Harper, Jr., (Pub.), A. M.
P. Leslie Irving, (C. L.)
*Henry Whitlock Johnson, (C. L.) *1863
Levi M. Kellogg.
Cornelius Low King, Capt. and Bvt. Maj. and Lt.-Col. U. S. A.
George Morford Klots, (M.)
Edward Leavenworth.
Theodore Frelinghuysen Lewis, (M.), A. M.
John Lockwood, Jr., (T.)
*Lewis Morris, Jr.
Peter Wilson Ostrander, (C. L.), A. M.
William Cruger Pell, (C. L.)
Columbus B. Rogers, (C.L.)
*Thomas P. St. John.
Otis Dwight Swan, (B.), LL. B. Harv. 1850.
Isaac Van Winkle, (C. L.), (A. M.)
Benjamin Clark Wetmore, (C. L.)
*Joseph Moss White, (M.) 25

## 1849.

Cornelius Rea Agnew, M. D. Coll. Phys. and Surg. N. Y. 1852, Memb. U. S. San. Com. 1860–67, Prof. Diseases of the Eye and Ear 1869–.
William Edmond Armitage, (Rev.), A.M., S. T. D. 1866, Asst. Bishop P. E. Ch. Wis. 1867–70 and Bishop 1870–.
William Astor.
*Edward Courtlandt Babcock, (Rev.) *1867
Norman Adams Beach, Prof. Coll. City N. Y.
*Charles Hinckley Brown.
Churchill John Cambreling, (C. L.), Major U. S. V.
*Baldwin Dix, (C. L.)
George Lloyd Freeman, M.D. elsewhere.
Henry De Costa Hanners.
William Abel Hardenbrook, (T.)
John Vernor Henry, (M.), A. M.
William Henry Herriman.
Lewis Ashhurst Kemper, (Rev.), B.D. elsewhere, S.T. D. 1868, Prof. Bibl. Interp. Nashota Theol. Sem. P. E. Ch. Wis.
*William Morrow Knox, A.M. 1855, M. D. Coll. Phys. and Surg. N. Y. 1854, Asst. Surg. U. S. V. *1862
Joseph Larocque, (C. L.)
David Porter Lord, (M.)
Charles A. Magnes, Jr.
*Ebenezer Bowman Miner, M. D. elsewhere. *1869
Daniel Morrelle, (Rev.), (T.), A. M. 1855.
Aaron Ogden, (C. L.), A. M.
Henry Parish, Jr., (M.)
John Prince Pemberton, M.D. 1864.
*George C. Pollen. aet. 39. *1867
Charles E. Rhinelander.
Saumarez Dobreé Routh, (M.)

John Frederick Schroeder, Jr., (Rev.)
Ezra Kellogg Sherwood.
John Shrady, Jr., A. M. 1858, M. D. 1861, Surg. U. S. V. 1862–64.
John Drake Skidmore, (C. L.), A. M.
*Prosper M. Wetmore, Jr., (M.)
John Jay White, (C. L.)

32

## 1850.

John Martin Gabriel Aims, M. D. elsewhere.
Mathew M. Blunt, Major U. S. A.
George G. Byron, (M.)
Malcolm Campbell, (C. L.)
Galen Augustus Carter, (Br.)
James Stark Clark, (Rev.), A. M.
Frederic R. Coudert, (C. L.)
John Ferris Delaplaine Cornell, (Rev.)
Archibald FalconerCushman, (C. L.), LL. B. Harv. 1852.
Edwin Wakeman Edwards, (M.)
Thomas Ludlow Harison, (F.)
John Sebastian Bach Hodges, (Rev.), A. M.
Walter R. T. Jones, (M.)
Adolphe Le Moyne, Jr., (B.)
Frederick L. Purroy.
Erskine M. Rodman, (Rev.), A. M.
Joseph Sands, (Arch.)
George Franklin Seymour, (Rev.), A. M., Prof. Eccles. Hist. Gen. Theol. Sem. P. E. Ch. N. Y.
Charles Augustus Silliman, (M.), A. M., LL. B. 1860.
John Esten Cooke Smedes, (Rev.), A. M.
William Hazard Terry.
*Edward Forbes Travis, (C. L.) *1867
Evan Thomas Walker, (M.)

23

## 1851.

John H. Anthon, (C. L.), A. M., N. Y. Assemb., Asst. Dist. Atty. N. Y. C., Prof. Med. Jurisp. N. Y. Coll. Med.
Henry M. Bedford, M. D. elsewhere.
Stewart H. Brown, (B.)
Charles Arms Cook, (Br.), A. M.
*William T. Cornell.
John De Ruyter, Jr., (M.)
James De Koven, (Rev.), S. T. D. elsewhere, Prest. Racine Coll. Wis.
Legh R. Dickinson, (Rev.), A. M.
William H. Draper, A. M., M. D. Coll. Phys. and Surg. N. Y. 1855, Asst. to Prof. Surgery, Prof. Diseases of the Skin 1869–.
Edward S. Hoffman, M. D. Coll. Phys. and Surg. N. Y. 1855, Surgeon U. S. V.
Henry B. Johnson.
Nicholas F. Ludlum, (Rev.)
John G. McNary, (T.)
George A. Seaman.
William R. Smith.
*A. Henry Thurston, A. M., M. D. elsewhere, Surgeon U. S. V. *1865
Charles H. Ward, (B.), A. M. 1864.
William G. Ward, (B.), Col. U. S. V.
Merritt H. Wellman, (Rev.), A. M.
J. Walter Wood, (Br.), A. M.
David Augustus Wright.

21

## 1852.

*John Bennem, Jr., (Rev.) *1853
Charles Ludlow Bogert, (Arch.), A. M.
James Livingston Brown, M. D. Univ. N. Y. C. 1856, A. M. 1868.
Henry W. Clark, (C. L.), A. M.
*John Wakefield Francis, Jr., M. D. elsewhere. *1855
John W. Harper, (Pub.), A. M.
George H. Hinton, A. M.
John Augustine Hows, (Art.), A. M.
Ansel N. Kellog, (Ed.)
Lea Luquer, (Rev.), A. M.
*Archibald Bleecker McDonald, Jr., (Arch.), A. M. *1866
Samuel L. Mitchill, Jr., (M.), A. M.
James Morris, (C. L.), LL.B. Harv. 1854.
Charles De Gray Mount, A. M.
Washington R. Nichols, (C. L.)
Charles O'Dowd.
John H. Pell, (C. L.), A. M., U. S. V.
George C. Pennell, (Rev.), A. M.
*Robert Ray, Jr., A.M., M. D. Coll. Phys. and Surg. N. Y. 1856. aet. 28. *1860
James Renwick Smedberg, (Eng.), A. M.
Richard F. Stevens.
Henry A. Tailer, (C. L.), A. M.
Eugene Thorn, Capt. U. S. V.
William E. Thorn, (C. L.)
Eustace Trenor, A. M., M. D. Coll. Phys. and Surg. N. Y. 1856, Surg. N. Y. S. Vols.
*John Trenor, Jr., A.M., M.D. Coll. Phys. and Surg. N. Y. 1856, Surg. U. S. V. 1863-65, Bvt. Lt.-Col. U. S. V. *1867
Richard H. Tucker, (C.L.) 27

## 1853.

*Cornelius Van Alen Anderson, A. M., M.D. Coll. Phys. and Surg. N. Y. 1857. *1862
William Irving Clark, (M.)
George Washington Dean, (Rev.), A. M. 1861, Tutor 1854, Prof. Gr. and Lat. Lang. Racine Coll. Wis.
Joseph Smith Dodge, Jr., A.M., M.D. Coll. Phys. and Surg. N. Y. 1856, Tutor 1854, Prof. Dental Coll. N. Y. C.
*Daniel Embury, Jr., (M.), A. M. aet. 34. *1869
*William Emerson, Jr., (C.L.), A. M., LL. B. Harv. 1856. *1864
William George Farrington, (Rev.), A. M.
Isaac J. Greenwood, Jr., (Chem.), A. M. 1857.
Albert Ward Hale, (Eng.), A. M. 1862, E. M.
Abraham S. Jackson, (C. L.), A. M.
William Allen Johnson, (Rev.), A. M. 1857.
John A. Kernochan, (M.)
Delancy W. Knevels, (M.), A. M. 1857.
*Edward William Laight, Jr., (M.) aet. 33. *1867
Thomas McCarty, (C. L.), A. M.
William J. Osborne, (C. L.)
*St. Clair Smith, (C. L.) *1869
*Washington Irving Tibbitts. *1853
*Archibald Somerville Van Duzer, (C. L.), A. M. aet. 36. *1870
19

## 1854.

George Washington Bacon,

(Rev.), (T.), A. M., LL. B. 1862, M. D. 1865.
Cullen L. Carter, (F.)
Henry M. Congdon, (Arch.)
*Charles B. Cromwell, (C.L.)
*Francis A. De Wint, (C. L.), A. M. 1860. *1866
Elias G. Drake, Jr., (C. L.), A. M.
Leicester K. Ely, (B.)
Carleton Moses Herrick, (C. L.), A. M., LL. B. 1860.
Edward Kirkland, (Br.), U. S. Vols.
George C. Kissam, M.D. Coll. Phys. and Surg. N. Y. 1857.
John V. Lewis, (Rev.), A. M.
Cutler C. McAllister, (C. L.), A. M.
Elias J. Marsh, M. D. Coll. Phys. and Surg. N.Y. 1858, Asst. Surg. U. S. A. 1861–, Med. Direct. U. S. V.
*Henry C. Marvin, (C. L.), A. M. *1865
James S. Merriam, (C. L.)
*Charles Edwards Morgan, M. D. Coll. Phys. and Surg. N. Y. 1857. *1867
*Orlando H. Morris, (C. L.), Col. U. S. Vols. *1864
Henry C. Murphy, Jr., (C.L.), A. M. 1860.
Peter J. Neefus, (F.)
*James Cortlandt Parker, Jr., (C. L.), A. M., Lieut. U. S. Vols. *1862
Charles S. Pomeroy, (Rev.), A. M.
*George V. Pomeroy, Jr., (M.), A. M. *1867
William J. Sayres, (C. L.), A. M. 1862.
Reginald Hebèr Smith, (C.L.), A. M., LL. B. 1866.
Benjamin Strong, (F.)
Gardiner Thompson, (B.)
John Condit Trippe, (M.)
Marvin R. Vincent, (Rev.), A. M., S. T. D. Union 1868, Prof. Lat. Troy Univ.
Stewart L. Woodford, (C.L.), A. M. 1866 and Yale 1866, LL. D. Trin. 1870, Asst. Atty. U. S. South Dist. N. Y. 1861, Col. and Brev. Brig.-Gen. U. S. Vols., Lieut.-Gov. N. Y. 1867–9.
Jeremiah L. Zabriskie, (C.L.) 29

## 1855.

Gunning S. Bedford, Jr., (C. L.), A. M., LL. B. Harv. 1859, Asst. Dist. Atty. N. Y. C., City Judge N. Y. C. 1869–.
Edward Cammann, (C.L.), A. M.
Benjamin L. Curtis, (M.), A. M.
Charles Da Costa, (C. L.), A. M.
William Dean, (C. L.), A. M.
Lewis L. Delafield, (C. L.), A. M.
*Philip A. Embury, (M.), A. M.
Edward O. Harmon, (M.)
James R. Hosmer, (C. L.), Capt. U. S. V.
Walter Knight, M. D. elsewhere.
Charles E. Miller, A. M.
David Burgess Miller, A. M., M.D. Coll. Phys. and Surg. N. Y. 1858.
George J. Murphy, A. M. 1860.
George Augustus Ostrander, A. M., M. D. Coll. Phys. and Surg. N. Y. 1858.
William A. Perry, (Eng.), A. M.
George R. Schieffelin, (C.L.), A. M.
Oscar Smedberg, (C.L.), A.M.
Herbert B. Turner, (C. L.), A. M.
John G. Wendel. 19

## 1856.

William Warren Ayres, (M.), A. M.
Edwin S. Babcock, (C. L.), A.M., Lieut.-Col. U. S. V.
Charles A. Bacon, A. M. 1863, M. D. elsewhere.
Albert H. Baldwin, (Art.), A. M.
Eastburn Benjamin, (Rev.), A. M.
Marshall Spring Bidwell, Jr., A. M. 1868.
William Pell Bogert, (F.)
Abbot Brown, (Rev.), A. M. 1863.
Henry J. Cammann, (M.), A. M. 1863.
Charles N. Clark, (B.), A. M., U. S. V.
Edward C. Clement, A. M. 1860.
Whittingham Cox, A.M. 1860, Lt. 4th U. S. Inf
Robert Livingston Cutting, Jr., (C. L.), A. M., LL. B. Harv. 1859, U. S. V.
Maturin L. Delafield, (M.), A. M.
Walter Gregory.
Francis Hendricks, (M.), A. M. 1861.
*William R. Hyslop, (C. L.), A. M., Capt. U. S. V. aet. 31. *1868
Ambrose C. Kingsland, Jr., (M.), A. M. 1861.
George L. Kingsland, (M.), A. M. 1861.
Leonard William Kip, Jr., (Rev.), A. M.
Peter I. Labagh, (C. L.), A. M.
Thomas Townsend Lawrence, (C.L.), LL.B. Harv. 1862.
David B. Lee.
*Hermon F. Lee. *1864
Alexis Emerson McIlvaine, (M.)
Joseph Meeks, (C. L.), A. M., LL. B. Harv. 1858.
Robert B. Minturn, Jr., (M.)
Richard C. Moore, Jr.
Mandeville Mower, A. M.
James G. Osborne, (C. L.), A. M.
G. Wendell Prime, (Rev.)
William Jones Seabury, (Rev.), A. M.
William F. Shepard, (C.L.)
Alexander M. Stanton, (Br.), A. M.
Russel Stebbins, Jr., (M.)
*Thomas Suffern, Jr. *1857
Charles C. Suydam, (Br.), A.M., Lt.-Col. U. S. V.
David G. Thompson, Jr., (Br.), A. M. 1860.
John W. Timpson, (C. L.), A. M.
William Gracie Ulshoeffer, (C. L.), Capt. U. S. V.
*William T. Van Riper, (C. L.), A. M.
*John Francis Walton, (C. L.), A. M.
James Weeks, (M.)
Elbert M. Willett, (C. L.), A. M.
Howell L. Williams, Jr., (M.), A. M. 45

## 1857.

William S. Boardman, (Rev.), A. M.
*Morgan L. S. Brower, A.M. *1864
Richard S. Dana, A. M.
Henry Eugene Davies, Jr., (C. L.), A. M., Maj.-Gen. U. S. V., Pub. Admin. N. Y. C.
Samuel W. Francis, A. M., M. D. elsewhere.
Elbridge Thomas Gerry, (C. L.), A. M., Memb. N. Y. S. Constit. Conv. 1867.
George G. Haven, A. M.

James B. Herrick, A. M.
Philip W. Holmes, (C. L.), A. M.
Oliver Phelps Jackson, A. M.
William Hamett Martin, A.M., M. D. 1861.
Erskine Mason, A. M., M. D. 1860, Asst. Dem. Anat. 1861–66, Dem. Anat. 1866–.
*W. Carey Massett, A. M., Lt.-Col. U. S. V. aet. 23. *1862
Mytton Maury, (Rev.), A. M.
Pierre McCarty, A. M.
*Henry B. Nott. *1859
Richard T. Packwood, A. M.
*Theodore Parkman, (Chem.), A. M., Ph. D. Univ. Göttingen 1860, U. S. V. aet 27. *1862
Goold H. Redmond.
Charles E. Sears, (C.L.), A.M.
James H. Slipper, A. M.
William Renwick Smedberg, A. M., Capt. and Bvt. Maj. and Lt.-Col. U. S. A.
Edgar Pinckney Smith, A.M.
James T. Tailer, (M.), A. M.
William R. Talbot, A. M.
Daniel S. Tuttle, (Rev.), A.M., S. T. D. 1867, Bishop P. E. Ch. Montana 1867–.
William B. Winslow, A. M.

27

## 1858.

Wyllys P. Baxter, (C. L.), A. M.
Henry Woodward Cooper, (C. L.), A. M., LL. B. 1860.
Stephen B. M. Cornell, A.M.
Lewis A. Curtis.
Daniel Sickles Duvall, (C. L.), LL. B. 1860.
Jacob A. Geissenhainer, A. M.
Harmon Hendricks, A. M.
Henry L. Jones, (Rev.), A.M.
Henry C. Kinney, (Rev.), A.M.
Nicholas Luquer, Jr.
*Philip Mesier Lydig, Jr., (C. L.), LL. B. 1861, Major and Bvt. Lt.-Col. and Col. U. S. V. aet. 31. *1868
*D. Ledyard Mallison.
James R. Manley, A. M.
Charles H. Marshall, Jr., (M.), A. M.
William J. Marrin, A.M. 1864.
*Benjamin Pell. *1862
A. G. Richards.
Robert K. Richards.
Henry C. Riley, (Rev.)
James W. Romeyn, A. M.
Thomas F. Thatcher.
Gilbert T. Totten, A. M., M. D. 1861, Asst. Surg. N. Y. V.
Hubert Van Wagenen.
Francis C. Wainwright, (Rev.), A. M.
John Ward, Jr., LL. B. 1860, A. M. 1864, M. D. Univ. N. Y. C. 1864, Capt. U. S. V.

25

## 1859.

Edward H. Anderson, (C.L.), A. M., N. Y. Assemb. 1866.
Richard Smith Bacon, (T.), A. M., LL. B. 1862, M. D. 1865
Thomas J. Benjamin, A. M.
John Crosby Brown, (B.), A. M.
Edward F. Browning, (M.), A. M.
Elisha S. Caldwell, (C. L.), A. M.
Frank Pharcellus Church, (Ed.), A. M.
Gouverneur Cruger, A. M.
William Floyd Cushman, A. M., M. D. 1862.
John William Duer, (C. L.), LL. B. 1861.
Cortlandt De Peyster Field, (M.), A. M.

John Frederic Gesner, A. M.
Irving Grinnell, 1862, A. M. 1862.
*E. Treadwell Hustace. *1859
William Jay, Jr., (C. L.), A. M., LL. B. 1867, Bvt. Lt.-Col. U. S. V.
Charles A. Jackson, Jr., (C. L.), A. M.
James Pierre Lacombe, A.M.
William Lummis, (B.), A.M.
J. Emory McClintock, (Act.), A. M., Tutor 1859–60.
George William Maynard, A. M. 1868, Prof. Metall. Polyt. Inst., Troy N. Y., 1867–.
James Frederic Moore, A. M., M. D. elsewhere.
Stephen Whitney Phœnix, A. M., LL. B. 1863.
William Lewis Raymond, (C. L.), A. M., U. S. Consul, Leeds, Eng., 1864–68.
*Stephen Richard Reynolds, A. M., Capt. U. S. V. aet. 26. *1864
William T. Sabine, (Rev.), A. M.
Oscar E. Schmidt, A. M.
J. Augustus Slipper, (Ed.), A. M., Maj. U. S. V.
Thomas F. Trenor, A. M., M. D. elsewhere.
Gabriel Mead Tooker, (C.L.), A. M., LL. B. 1861.
Robert Boyd Van Kleeck, Jr., (C. L.), A. M., LL. B. 1862.
William David Walker, (Rev.), A. M. 1863.
Edward N. Whitehouse, (A. M., U. S. N.
Henry Bruen Whitehouse, (M.), A. M., LL. B. elsewhere. 33

## 1860.

Robert P. Barry, 1865, Capt. U. S. A.
*Richard G. Benjamin, A. M. *1864
Clarence Stewart Brown, (B.), A. M., Major U. S. V.
*J. Lorillard Cammann, A.M. aet. 28. *1868
Howard Clarkson.
Walter Livingston Clarkson, (C. L.), A. M., LL.B. 1863.
Edgar M. Cullen, A. M., Col. U. S. V., Lt. 1st U. S. Inf.
Charles De Ruyter, (M.), A. M., LL.B. 1862, U. S. V.
Eugene Du Bois.
John Haven Emerson, A. M., M. D. 1865.
George R. Fearing, (B.), Capt. and Bvt. Major U. S. V.
Robert Goelet, Jr., (C. L.), A. M., LL. B. 1862.
Joseph Greenleaf, Jr., (Rev.), A. M.
Edward L. Greenwood, (C.L.)
Laban Gardner Hopkins, (C. L.), A. M., LL. B. 1862, LL. M. 1864.
Edmund Abdy Hurry, (C.L.), A. M., LL.B. 1862, U. S. N.
*John William Jenks, Lieut. U. S. V. *1861
Edward Renshaw Jones, (Br.)
Herbert Kettell, A. M.
*Augustus F. King, U. S. V. aet. 23. *1862
David Lydig, A. M.
Samuel Kuypers Lyon, A.M., M. D. 1866.
Thomas H. Messenger, A. M.
George Mason Miller, A. M., LL. B. 1862, Capt. U. S. V.
Augustus Newbold Morris, A. M., LL. B. 1864.
Richard Lewis Morris, Jr., A. M. 1866, Capt. and Bvt. Major U. S. A.
Robert Dillon Nesmith, A. M., M. D. Univ. N. Y. C. 1862.
Thomas Ludlow Ogden, (C.L.), A. M., LL. B. 1862.
*Robert Troup Pell, (C. L.),

A. M., LL. B. 1863, U. S.V. aet. 27. *1868
Eugene Hall Pomeroy, (C.L.), LL. B. 1862, U. S. V.
Edward P. Robins.
James S. Satterthwaite, A. M.
*John W. Southack, Jr., A.M., M.D. Bellevue Med. Coll. N. Y. 1865, Asst. Dem. Anat. Bell. Med. Coll. aet. 30. *1869
Abraham Suydam, (Eng.), A. M.
*Frederick A. Tracy, Lieut. U. S. A. aet. 23. *1863
John Howard Van Amringe, A. M., Tutor 1860–63, Adj. Prof. Maths. 1863–, and Prof. Maths. School of Mines 1865–.
George Waddington, (C. L.), LL. B. 1862.
William Fitzhugh Whitehouse, (C. L.), A.M., LL.B. elsewhere.
Pierre Washington Wildey, (C. L.), A. M. and Yale 1865, LL. B. 1863.
Egerton L. Winthrop, A. M. 40

# 1861.

James Benkard, Jr., A. M., Capt. U. S. V.
William Alexander Boyd, (C. L.), A. M., Lieut. U. S. V.
George Herbert Carey, (C.L.), A. M., LL. B. 1863.
William Halsted Caswell, (M.), A. M.
Henry Dudley, A. M.
John Gihon, Jr., (M.), A. M.
Langdon Greenwood, (C.L.), A. M.
Charles Coolidge Haight, (Arch.), A. M., Capt. U. S. V.
Edward Haight, Jr., A. M., Capt. U. S. A.
William Richards Hillyer, (M.), A. M., Capt. U. S. V.
Elisha Horton, Jr., (C. L.), A. M.
Reuben Wing Howes, Jr., (Rev.), A. M.
Walter Bowne Lawrence, (Br.), A. M.
Albert McNulty, Jr., (C. L.), A. M., LL. B. 1864, U. S V.
Edward Mitchell, (C. L.), A. M., LL. B. 1865.
Gratz Nathan, (C. L.), A. M., Asst. Corporation Atty. N. Y. C.
Frank Alleyne Otis, (C. L.), A. M., LL. B. 1864.
*Richard Cornelius Ray, Lieut. U. S. V. *1863
*William Alexander Rice, (C.L.), A. M., U.S.V. aet. 24. *1866
Erastus Barnes Rudd, (C.L.), A. M., LL. B. 1863.
William Henry Russell, Jr., A. M., Capt. U. S. V.
Thomas Taunton Sabine, A. M., M. D. 1864, Asst. Dem. Anat. 1866–.
*Henry Augustus Schermerhorn, (C. L.), A.M., LL. B. 1867. aet. 29. *1869
Thomas Henry Sill, (Rev.), A. M.
George Lansing Taylor, (Rev.), A. M.
Henry A. Coit Taylor, (M.), A. M.
John Ayscough Tucker, (M.), A. M., U. S. V.
Stephen Hague Turnbull, (C. L.), A. M.
Joseph Mason Turner, A. M.
*William Mansfield Van Wagenen, (Rev.), A. M. aet. 21. *1866
Luis Puertas Walton, A. M.
Isaac Johnson Ward, (C. L.), A. M.
Samuel Baldwin Ward, A.M., M. D. Georgetown Med. Coll., Asst. Surg. U. S. V.,

Curator Coll. Museum 1868–69, Prof. Anat. Woman's Med. Coll. N. Y. C. 1869–.
Edward Walter West, (C.L.), LL. B. Univ. N. Y. C. 1861, A. M., Col. U. S. V.
Frederick Cope Whitehouse, (Rev.), A. M.
Albert Beach Whitney, A.M., M. D. Univ. N. Y. C. 1863.

36

## 1862.

Edward Rob r Atwill, (Rev.), A. M.
*Francis Babcock, (Br.), A. M. aet. 24. *1866
*Robert Erskine Bartow, A. M. *1867
William Harbert Benjamin, (F.), A. M.
Henry Carrington Bolton, A. M. 1866.
John Thomas Burr.
Robert Bage Canfield, (C.L.)
Leslie Chase, (Br.)
*John Lawrence Churchill, A. M., Lieut. U. S. A. *1868
*Charles Ernest Congdon, aet. 21. *1862
Nathaniel Elsworth Cornwall, Jr., (T.), A. M. and Harv. 1868.
John Halsey Curtis, A. M.
Walter Cutting, Maj. U. S. V.
Henry Ammi Dows, (Rev.), A. M. 1869.
James Gore King Duer, (B.)
Peter Forrester, (M.)
Charles Dudley Fuller, A. M., U. S. V.
*George Wolfe Gillespie, (Eng.), A. M. aet. 28. *1870
Louis Haight, A. M.
William Augustus Ogden Hegeman, (C. L.), LL. B. 1864, LL. M. 1865, A. M.
Burrall Hoffman, (C. L.), LL. B. 1864, LL. M. 1865, A. M.
Lawrence Yvonnet Hopkins, A. M., U. S. V.
William Henry Jackson, A.M.
Charles Sigourney Knox, A. M., Act. Prof. Mor. and Int. Phil. 1869–70.
William Elliott Laight, (C.L.)
William Gerard Lathrop, Jr., (C.L.), LL. B. Harv. 1864, A. M.
George Anderson Lawrence, (M.), A. M.
William Henry Martin, (M.)
*Henry Howard Marvin, Lt.-Col. U. S. Eng. 1862–3. *1863
Cornelius Berrian Mitchell, (M.), A. M., U. S. V.
John Fulton Berrian Mitchell, (M.), A. M., Capt. U. S. V.
Charles Walton Ogden, (M.), LL. B. 1864, A. M.
*David Burr Olyphant. *1864
*Edward Mesnard Pell. *1863
*Richard Varick Pell, M. D. Bellevue Med. Coll., A. M. aet. 23. *1866
*Gerardus Post, (C.L.), LL.B. 1864. aet. 22. *1864
Russell Harper Root, (C.L.), LL. B. 1864.
Charles Ames Spencer, (T.), A. M.
Foster Thayer, M.D. Bellevue Med. Coll. N.Y. 1866, A. M. 1866, U. S. N.
Charles Rockland Tyng, (M.), A. M.
*John A. Vanderpoel, (C.L.), LL. B. 1865, A. M. aet. 24. *1866
*Francis Willis, (M.), A. M. aet. 31. *1870
William Henry Willis, Jr., (M.), A. M.
Leroy Milton Yale, M. D. Bellevue Med. Coll., A. M.

44

## 1863.

James Herman Aldrich, (M.), A. M.
Fanning Cobham Tucker Beck.
William Cornell Binns, A. M.
Daniel Frederick Boardman, (C. L.), LL. B. 1866.
William Brevoort Bolmer, (C. L.), LL. B. 1865, A. M. 1868.
Melville Brown.
Thomas Tileston Bryce, A.M.
Charles Frederick Clarke, A. M., M. D. 1866.
Freeman Clarkson, (C. L.), LL. B. 1865, A. M.
William Peshine Douglass.
Clifford Faitoute Eagle, (Br.), A. M., Lieut. U. S. A.
George Wilson Ferguson, (Rev.), A. M.
William Redwood Fisher, A. M., M. D. 1867.
Randall Cook Hall, (Rev.), A. M., Inst. in Hebrew Gen. Theol. Sem. P. E. Ch. 1869–.
Richard Mentor Henry, (C. L.), A. M.
Stephen Ferris Holmes, (Rev.), A. M.
Henry Augustus Hurlbut, Jr., A. M.
Peter Augustus Jay, (Rev.), A. M.
Emile Henry Lacombe, (C. L.), LL. B. 1865.
William Scott Leggat.
Lewis Henry Lighthipe, (Rev.), A. M.
Le Grand Lockwood, Jr., (Br.)
Thomas Morwood McLean, Jr.
James Allen Macdonald, A. M., U. S. V.
Rockwood McQuesten, (Rev.), A. M.
William Matthews Martin, (C.L.), LL. B. 1865, A.M.
Dan Marvin, Jr., A.M., Asst. Prof. Grk. and Lat. Lang. Racine Coll. Wis. 1868–.
William Anderson Mitchell.
Stuyvesant Fish Morris, M. D. 1867.
James Murray, (Rev.), A. M.
Hiram Hunt Nazro, A. M.
Thomas Bellamy Newby, (Rev.), A. M.
George Henry Owen, (C.L.), A. M.
*James Brinckerhoff Pell. aet 28. *1870
George Decatur Pond.
Robert Emmet Robinson, (C. L.), LL. B. 1865.
Philip Justice Sands.
Henry Yates Satterlee, (Rev.)
Walter Satterlee, (Art.)
William Barnewall Schermerhorn.
Rutherfurd Stuyvesant.
Charles William Terrett, A.M.
Stephen Howard Thayer, Jr., (C. L.), LL. B. 1865, A. M.
Robert Schuyler Tucker, A. M.
Frank Roe Van Buren, A.M.
Frederick Brinsmade Van Kleeck, (Rev.), A. M.
Egbert Ward.
Sylvester Ward.
Ellsworth Westervelt.
Willard Parker Wooster, A. M., M. D. 1867.

50

## 1864.

John Magnus Adams, (Eng.), A. M., E. M. 1867.
David Wylie Alexander, (C. L.), LL. B. 1866, A. M.
William Gardiner Appleton.
Reginald Heber Bartow.
Gerard Beekman, (C. L.), A. M., LL. B. 1867.

John Neilson Beekman, A.M., M. D. 1868.
Walston Hill Browne, (Br.), A. M.
Thomas Baird Browning, (C. L.), LL. B. 1866, A. M.
Charles Stedman Bull, A. M., M. D. 1868.
John Frederick Butterworth, (Rev.), A. M.
William Henry Butterworth, (C. L.), LL.B. 1866, A.M.
Jonathan Ackerman Coles, A. M., M. D. 1868.
Henry Bedinger Cornwall, (Eng.), A. M., E. M. 1869.
Edmund Dewees Davidson, A. M.
Theodore Frelinghuysen Cornell Demarest, (C. L.), A. M., LL. B. 1868, Tutor 1869–70.
Matthew Brinckerhoff Du Bois, A. M., M. D. 1868.
Duane Shuler Everson, (T.), A. M., Tutor 1864–68.
*Henry Floy, LL. B. 1866. aet. 23. *1866
William Newton Goddard, A. M.
Thomas Hays Harmer, (Eng.), A. M.
Hiram Lyman Huston, A.M.
Frederick Wendell Jackson, (Br.)
Charles Henry Kaufman.
Jonas Butler Kissam, (Br.)
Joseph Bayley Lawrence, (C. L.), LL. B. 1866, A. M.
Isidor Mayer.
Alfred Perry McClellan.
William Meikleham, 1868.
John Brainard Morgan, (Rev.), A. M.
William Franklin Mott, (Br.)
Howard Osterhoudt, (C. L.), LL. B. 1866, A. M.
Henry Hills Parker, (C. L.), LL. B. 1866, A. M.
Charles Burroughs Rice, 1865, (C.L.), A. M., LL.B. 1867.
Frederick William Stevens, (C. L ), A. M.
*Arthur Pemberton Sturges. aet. 24. *1866
Albert Edward Valentine, A. M., M. D. elsewhere.
Isidor Walz, (Chem.), Ph. D. Heidelberg 1867.
Marinus Willett, Jr. 38

## 1865.

Henry Beadel, Jr., 1869, (C. L.), LL. B. 1870.
Henry Rutgers Beekman, (C. L.), LL. B. 1867, A. M.
Edward Stelle Brownson, (Eng.), A. M., E. M. 1869.
Douglas William Burnham, A. M.
Archibald Murray Campbell, A. M.
Thomas Cooper Campbell, (C. L.), A. M.
John Henry Caswell, Asst. in Mineral. 1870–.
Jonathan Odell Fowler, Jr., A. M.
Charles King Gracie, (Eng.), A. M., E. M. 1868.
James Hooker Hamersley, (C. L.), LL. B. 1867, A. M.
John Moore Heffernan, (Rev.), A. M.
*Julian James, A. M., Lieut. U. S. V. aet. 26. *1870
Frederic Rhinelander Jones, A. M.
George Goelet Kip, (C. L.), LL. B. 1867, A. M.
William Gilman Low, (C.L.), LL. B. 1867, A. M.
Henry Richard McElligott, A. M.
William Neilson McVickar, (Rev.), A. M., U. S. V.
Randolph Brant Martine, A. M.
James Fontaine Maury, A. M.

George Webster Peck, A.M., U. S. V.
James Lyman Price, A. M., LL. B. 1868.
Frederick Prime, Jr., Prof. Metall. Lafay. Coll. 1870–.
Arthur Bernard Ross, A. M.
Roderick Burt Seymour, A. M., U. S. V.
Lenox Smith, A. M., E. M. 1868, U. S. V,
John Edwin Swezey, (C. L.), LL. B. 1867, A. M.
Seymour Van Nostrand, A.M.
Abraham Van Santvoord, (C. L.), LL. B. 1867, A. M.
Edward Henry Van Winkle, A. M.
Isaac Van Winkle, (Rev.), A. M. Prof. Maths. and Nat. Phil. St. Stephen's Coll. Annandale 1869–.
William Bogert Walker, A. M.
Willard Parker Ward, (Eng.)
James Lee Wells, A. M.
John Visscher Wheeler, A. M.
Francis French Wilson, (T.), U. S. V., A. M. 35

## 1866.

Marshall Pepoon Bell,† (C.L.), LL. B. 1868.
Louis Edward Binsse.
Thomas Monahan Blossom, (Eng.), A. M., E. M. 1869.
Clarence Brainerd.
James Manning Bruce, A. M.
*Nathan Robins Carter. *1866
Julian Tappan Davies, (C. L.), LL. B. 1868.
Augustus Floyd Delafield.
Moses Downs Getty.
Edward Clark Houghton, (Rev.), A. M.
William Augustus Hooker, (Eng.), A. M., E. M. 1869.
Daniel Lord, Jr., (C. L.), LL. B. 1868, A. M.
Theodore Holmes McNamee.
Edward Ward Malloy.
Augustus Chapman Merriam, A. M., Tutor 1869–.
Frank Ames Mullany.
Edward Holland Nicoll, (C. L.), LL. B. 1868, A. M.
Willard Parker, Jr., M. D. 1870.
William Bleecker Potter, (Eng.), E. M. 1869.
William Edwin Smalley, (C. L.), LL. B. 1868.
George Putnam Smith, (C. L.), LL. B. 1868.
Stephen Dover Stephens, Jr., (C. L.), A. M., LL. B. 1868.
Horace Stetson, (C. L.), LL. B. 1869.
Augustus Talbot.
Richmond Talbot.
William Jameson Thomson, (Rev.)
Henry Crosswell Tuttle, (C. L.), LL. B. 1868.
Martin Van Buren.
James Moore Wayne.
Henry Augustus Whiting, (Eng.), A. M., E. M. 1869.
John Fritz Wissman.
Graham Youngs. 32

## 1867.

Joseph Halsey Anderson, A. M.
James Baker, Jr., (C. L.), A. M.
Henry Anthony Waldburg Barclay.
Walton Peckham Bell, (C.L.), LL. B. 1869, A. M.
Samuel Appleton Blatchford, (C. L.), A. M.
Jacques Arnold Bernheimer, A. M.

† Known subsequently as Marshall Bell.

Charles Henry Burtis, (C.L.), LL. B. 1869, A. M.
Henry Cohn, A. M.
Theodore Hedges Conger, 1870.
John Alexander Denniston, Jr., (Rev.), A. M.
George Gosman Dewitt, Jr., (C. L.), LL. B. 1869, A. M.
George Duyckinck, A. M.
Edgar Fawcett, A. M.
Nicholas Fish, (C. L.), LL. B. Harv. 1869.
Antoine Lentilhon Foster.
Giraud Graham.
Clarence Melville Hyde, (C. L.), LL. B. 1869, A. M.
William Halsey Ingersoll, (C. L.), LL. B. 1869, A. M.
George Barent Johnson, A.M.
John Alsop King.
*Hobart Lewis. aet. 23. *1870
Henry Demarest Lloyd, A.M.
James McNamee, (C. L.), A. M.
Cadwalader Evans Ogden, (C. L.), LL. B. 1869.
Henry Evelyn Pierrepont, Jr., A. M.
Hector Craig Fitz Randolph, A. M.
Julius Sachs.
Henry Schneeberger, A. M.
Aaron Ernest Vanderpoel, (C.L.), LL. B. 1869, A. M.
Rudolph August Witthaus, Jr., A. M.
James Henry Work, (C. L.), LL. B. 1869, A. M.

31

## 1868.

Isaac Adler.
John William Schmidt Arnold.
Henry Denison Babcock.
William Preston Beck.
James Michael Brady, (C.L.), LL. B. 1870.
Benjamin Howell Campbell, (T.)
Walter Ewing Colton.
Frederic De Peyster Foster.
Talmadge Woodward Foster.
Andrew Jackson Gilhooly, (C. L.), LL. B. 1870.
Elmslie Morven Gillett.
Joseph Bayley Halsey.
John Archibald Macdonald.
Edward Schermerhorn Mead.
William Mitchell, Jr.
John McLean Nash, (C. L.), LL. B. 1870.
Duane Livingston Peabody, (C.L.), LL. B. 1870.
John Duncan Quackenbos, Tutor 1870–.
George Lockhart Rives.
George Nicholas Sanders, Jr., (C. L.), LL. B. 1870.
Arthur Sloan.
William James Milligan Sloane.
John Steward, Jr.
James Prescott Swain, Jr.
Horace Holden Thayer.
Stephen Whittingham Williams.
Lucius Kellogg Wilmerding.

27

## 1869.

Charles Augustus Adams.
Hal Allaire.
Willard Bartlett, (C.L.), LL. B. Univ. City N. Y. 1868.
Evelyn Bartow.
Robert Lenox Belknap.
Jacob Bininger.
Thomas Newby Cuthbert.
William Bayard Cutting.
Henry Drisler, Jr.
William Alexander Duer.
Hamilton Fish, Jr.
William Dudley Foulke, (C. L.)
William Montague Geer.
Edward John Hallock.

George Webster Heasley.
William Berrian Hooper.
*Robert Henry Hunt. aet 21. *1870
William Iselin.
Henry Madison Jones.
Shipley Jones.
John Henry Livingston.
David B. Ogden.
John Owen.
Charles Augustus Peabody, Jr.
George Plato Pierce.
Samuel Augustus Purdy, Jr.
William Macnevin Purdy.
Horace Nelson Seaver, Jr.
Frank Norseworthy Shepard.
John Adams Smedberg.
Edward Bayard Smith.
David Stewart, Jr.
Henry Cady Sturges.
Edward Tillou.
Edward Francis Weeks.
Thenford Woodhull. 36

## 1870.

Felix Adler.
Walden Pell Anderson.
Isaac Baker Barrett.
Richard Berrian.
Towson Caldwell.
Lewis Buffett Carll.
John Cropper.
George Hicks Dibblee.
Thomas Charles Edward Ecclesine, (C. L.)
William Fanning, Jr.
Charles Meredith Garth.
William Erwin Gilhooly.
Henry Waterman Holden.
Arthur Ingraham.
Edmond Kelly.
Franklin Butler Lord.
Seth Low.
John Bartow Montell.
Robert Stratton Morison.
Isidor Pierce Oberndorfer.
Walter Ogden.
George Livingston Peabody.
Spencer Summerfield Roche.
David Alvah Rowe.
George Starr Scofield, Jr.
Robert Norsworthy Shepard.
Deming Beadle Smith.
Frank Dodge Sturges.
William Naylor Webbe.
Dennistoun Wood. 30

# GRADUATES IN MEDICINE,

EXCEPT THOSE PREVIOUSLY NAMED AS GRADUATES IN ARTS.

## 1769.

*Samuel Kissam.
*Robert Tucker.

2

## 1771.

*Benjamin Onderdonk. aet. 21. *1772
*Michael Sebring.

2

## 1772.

*John Augustus Graham, Yale 1768 and A. M. Yale.
*Uzal Johnson.
*James Muirson.
*Richard Udall, Trustee Coll. Phys. and Surg. N.Y. 1807–11.
*William Winterton.

5

## 1773.

*Jabez Doty.

## 1774.

*Samuel Nicoll, Prof. Pract. of Med. and of Chem. 1792–94.

## 1793.

*Samuel Borrowe, Trustee Coll. Phys. and Surg. N. Y. 1820–28.
*John Bowne Hicks.
*Willett Taylor, Jr.
*Joseph Youle.

4

## 1794.

*David G. Abeel.
*Peter Irving.
*Henry Mead.

3

## 1795.

*William Morey Ross.
*Timothy Fletcher Wetmore.

2

## 1796.

*Alexander Anderson. aet. 95. *1870
*Winthrop Saltonstall, Yale 1793. *1802

2

## 1797.

*William Bay.

## 1802.

*Joseph Bailey, Trustee Coll. Phys. and Surg. N. Y. 1820-37.
Richard L. Walker.

2

## 1803.

Isaac Foster.
Samuel Scofeld.

2

## 1804.

William Barrow.
Ezekiel Ostrander.
Daniel D. Walters.

3

## 1805.

*Thomas Cock, Prof. Anat. and Physiol. Rutg. Coll. N. Jers., V.-Prest. Coll. Phys. and Surg. N. Y. 1827-55 and Prest. 1855-58. aet. 87. *1869
*Benjamin Kissam. aet. 50. *1831

2

## 1806.

*Valentine Mott, LL.D. elsewhere, Prof. Surg. 1811-13, Prof. Surg. Coll. Phys. and Surg. N. Y. 1813-26 and in Rutg. Med. Coll. N.Y. 1826-30, Prof. Surg. and Relative Anat. Univ. N. Y. C. 1830-65, Prest. N.Y. Acad. Med. aet. 79. *1865

## 1807.

Alire R. Delisle.

## 1810.

Robert Morrell.

## 1860.

Thomas Henry Allen.
Galusha Birchard Balch.
George Burr Banks.
Phanet Coe Barker.
William Comstock Bennett, Yale 1858, Surg. 5th Conn. Vols.
John Caruthers Bogardus, Asst. Surg. 102d N. Y. S. Vols.
Samuel White Briggs, Asst. Surg. U. S. N. aet. 26. *1861
Orlo Myron Bump.
Charles Carrington.
Seth Lyman Chase.
Robert Cooper.
*Charles Henry Covell, A. A. Surg. U. S. N.
Juan Bautista Ponce DeLeon.
Frank Wadsworth Doolittle, Surg. 5th N. Y. S. Vols.
Philo Judson Farnsworth, and Univ. Verm.
William Baldwin Fletcher.
Edward Irving Ford, A. B. elsewhere.
Otis W. Gibson.
Walter James Hadden.
Joseph Lawrence Hicks, Surg. 1st, N. Y. S. Vols.
Courtland Hoppin, A.B. elsewhere.
David Kennedy.
Daniel Avery Langworthy.
William Whipple Leavitt, Asst. Surg. U. S. N.
James Lawrence Little.
James Gifford McKee, A. A., Surg. U. S. A.
Thomas Knowlton Marcy.
David Matthews, Surg. 143d N. Y. S. Vols.

Barnet Wisner Morse, Asst. Surg. 27th N. Y. S. V.
Archibald Finn Mudie, Asst. Surg. U. S. V.
George Andrew Mursick, Asst. Surg. U. S. V.
William Sheldon Clark Perkins.
Howard Pinckney, A.M. elsewhere, Surg. U. S. V.
Oren Day Pomeroy.
James Henry Pooley, Jr., Asst. Surg. U. S. A.
Peter Prius.
John George Ryerson, A. M. elsewhere.
Charles Mase Samson.
Orin Henry Seeds.
Benjamin Avery Segur.
Elbridge Gilbert Seymour, Asst. Surg. 94th N. Y. S. V.
Dwight Delavan Stebbins, A. B. elsewhere.
George Miller Sternberg, Asst. Surg. U. S. A.
William Harrison Studley, A. M. elsewhere.
George Edwin Summers, N. Jers. 1857 and A. M. N. Jers.
Charles James Taggart.
William Faulds Thoms.
Julius Vaughan.
Edmund Carlyle Ver Meulen, Asst. Surg. U. S. N.
Joel Addington Warren.
Augustus Purdy Williams, Surg. U. S. V.

51

# 1861.

George Badger, A. A. Surg. U. S. A.
William Badger, A. A. Surg. U. S. A.
John Conner Barron, Asst. Surg. 69th N. Y. S. V.
*Thomas Barrow. aet. 23. *1861
John Philip Benkard.
William Alexander Betts.
William Blundell.
Ryckman D. Bogert, Asst. Surg. 6th N. Y. Art.
Basil Brown Brashear.
Samuel Nelson Brayton, Asst. Surg. U. S. N.
Asahel Norton Brockway, Hamilt. Coll. 1857, A. A. Surg. U. S. V.
William McQueen Bryce, Asst. Surg. 144th N.Y.S.V.
Edmund Shackelford Carew.
George William Carleton, William's 1858.
William Henry Carmalt, Asst. to Prof. Physiol. 1862–.
Charles Carter, Surg. U. S. A.
Matthew Chalmers, Yale 1858 and A. M. Yale, Asst. Surg. U. S. N.
John Francis Hamlin Chipman.
George Rogers Cutter, Surg. 127th N. Y. V.
F. Munson Coan.
Henry Munson Dean, Asst. Surg. U. S. V.
Louis George De Blois.
Daniel McComb Devendorf.
John Abbott Douglass, Jr., Bowdoin Coll. 1854, Surg. 11th Mass. V.
Albert Fairfax.
Benjamin Franklin Fogg.
Winfield Scott Fuller, Surg. 78th N. Y. S. V.
Franklin Benjamin Galbraith.
Josiah H. Goddard.
James Grange.
Theodore E. Hamilton.
Jerome Hibbard.
Henry M. Hitchcock.
Edgar Holden, N. Jers. 1859, Asst. Surg. U. S. N.
John T. Kennedy, A. A. Surg. U. S. A.
Charles John Kipp, Surg. U. S. V.
Thompson Bailey Lewis.

Seth Stephen Lounsbery, Surg. N. Y. S. V.
Henry Munson Lyman, William's 1858, A. A. Surg. U. S. A.
Carrington McFarlane, Surg. 115th N. Y. S. V.
Edward Gardner Marshall, Asst. Surg. 124th N. Y. S. V.
B. Ellis Martin, Asst. Surg. 5th N. Y. S. V.
Theodore Millspaugh.
Richard H. Moore.
Alfred North.
James H. Noyes.
Andrew T. Pearsall.
William B. Pierce.
Henry Sylvanus Plympton.
Alfred Edgar Martindale Purdy.
Charles H. Reynolds.
Charles Douglas Rigby.
John W. Robie.
Heber Smith, Asst. Surg. U. S. N.
Normand Smith, Yale 1858.
Norman Leslie Snow.
Frederick Dennis Sturges, A. A. Surg. U. S. A.
Charles Henry Suydam, Asst. Surg. 27th N. J. V.
Norman Leslie Swan, A. B. elsewhere.
Garrett W. Veeder Van Voast, Union 1857 and A. M. Union, A. A. Surg. U. S. A.
Maus Rosa Vedder.
Edwin Fletcher Ward.
Robert Watts, Jr., Surg. 133d N. Y. S. V.
William Lamont Wheeler, Asst. Surg. U. S. N.
John Phillips Payson White, A. B. elsewhere, Surg. 10th N. Y. S. V.
Charles M. Wight, Asst. Surg. 26th N. Y. S. V.
Benjamin Franklin Wilson.

67

# 1862.

George Pierce Andrews.
Cyrus Ebenezer Baker.
George Page Bassett.
William Whitfield Bowlby, Surg. 3d N. J. Cav.
George Marsden Brennan.
John Weston Brennan.
Sidney Rogers Burnap, Surg. N. Y. S. V.
Garabed Caloosdian.
John Ely Carey.
Thomas Knowlton Chandler.
*Abel Blood Conant, Surg. 3d Kent. V., Lect. on Physiol. Univ. Vermont. aet. 28. *1864
William Conover, N. Jers. 1859.
*Henry White Cooke. aet. 26. *1863
James Russell Cumming, Asst. Surg. 12th Conn. V.
Rem Lefferts Disbrow.
Barnard Douglass Eastman.
William Eddy.
Henry Marlyn Field, Harv. 1859.
Frank Pierce Foster, A. A. Surg. U. S. A.
Gustavus Scott Franklin.
William James Gilfillan.
William Henry Harlin.
Solomon E. Hasbrouck.
Jonathan Havens.
Andrew H. Hershey.
George Hopkins, A. A. Surg. U. S. A.
Lewis Slocomb Horton.
Numon N. Horton, Surg. 47th U. S. Coll. Inf.
John Andrew Jaume.
William Malcolm James.
Dan Lee Jewett, Asst. Surg. 20th Conn. V.
Eldridge Monroe Johnson.
Joseph Dodson Lomax.
Frederick Wentworth Mercer.
William Thomas Nealis, St. Joseph's Coll. Ohio, 1858,

and A.M. St. Joseph's, Surg. 69th N. Y. S. V.
Edward Monroe Norwood, Surg. 4th E. Tenn. V.
*George Herschel Olmsted, A. A. Surg. U. S. A. *1863
William Browne Orchard.
Edmund Morris Pease.
George Porter.
William Chardavoyne Pryer.
Nathaniel B. Reber.
Jasper Godsvenor Reynolds.
John A. Robinson, Asst. Surg. 38th N. Y. S. V.
William H. Rockwell, Jr.
Frank H. Roof.
George Schuyler Rugg, Asst. N. Y. S. V., Surg.-in-Chief. 2d and 3d Brigades Art. Reserves, Army of the Potomac.
Henry Thatcher Sears.
Samuel Francis Shaw.
Franklin Staples.
Thomas Hunt Stilwell.
John L. Swift.
Amazias Walter Tryon, Asst. Surg. 100th N. Y. V.
Edwin Morrison Ward, N. Jers. 1859.
Richard Halsted Ward, William's 1858, A. A. Surg. U. S. A.
James H. Wheeler.
Merrit H. Wilson. 57

## 1863.

William Bruce Almon.
Wendell Abraham Anderson, Surg. 3d Maryland Vol. Inf.
Alonzo Brayton Ball, Yale 1860.
John Sterling Bird.
Joseph Bird, N. Jers. 1860.
Lewis Henry Bodman.
Wesley M. Carpenter.
George Augustus Christie, and Royal Coll. Surg. Edinburgh 1864.
Edward Cowles.
Albert E. Croucher.
Rezin Pollard Davis.
Walter De Forest Day, William's 1859.
Francis Delafield, Yale 1860.
Samuel Demarest, Jr.
*George Clinton Dewey, William's 1860, and A. M. Will. aet. 23. *1864
John Elderkin, Yale 1852 and A.M. Yale, Asst. Surg. 10th U. S. Col. Inf.
George M. Engs, Yale 1860.
David Osburn Farrand.
Jacob T. Field, A. B. elsewhere.
Samuel A. Fitch, A. B. elsewhere, Asst. Surg. N. Y. S. V.
De Witt C. Fowler.
Walter Roberts Gillette, Mad. Univ. 1861.
Frank West Goodall.
Wait Robbins Griswold, Yale 1844.
Charles Everett Hall, N. Jers. 1860.
Frank Granger Hasbrouck.
John Cornelius Hasbrouck.
David Webb Hodgkins, A. A. Surg. U. S. A.
Edward Kelly Hogan, Asst. Surg. U. S. V., Bvt. Maj. U. S. V. 1865.
James Hutchinson.
Woolsey Johnson, N. Jers. 1860 and A. M. N. Jers.
Charles S. Kittredge.
William Lee, Lect. on Physical and Micr. Anat. National Med. Coll. Washington, D.C.
Elias Lester, Med. Director U. S. V.
Irving Whitall Lyon, and Univ. Vt., Dem. Anat. Berkshire Med. Coll. 1862, A. A. Surg. U. S. A.

Henry Emmet McCartin.
Theodore A. McGraw.
David Magie, Jr., N. Jer. 1859.
George Van Rensselaer Merrill, Surg. 6th U. S. Col. Inf.
Martin Alexander Miller.
Lucius Mills, A.B. elsewhere.
Sherman Morse.
*John D. Nicoll. *1863
Wilbur Fisk Nutten.
Patrick Pendergast, Asst. Surg. 107th N. Y. S. V.
Charles Leander Pierce.
Peter Van Schaack Pruyn, A. B. elsewhere, Asst. Surg. N. Y. S. V.
Burr Schermerhorn, Asst. Surg. 108th N. Y. Vols.
Abner Orimel Shaw, Surg. 20th Maine V.
Amos Shaw, Jr., Asst. Surg. 41st N. Y. S. V.
Andrew Jackson Smith.
Joseph George Smith.
Thomas Thompson, Asst. Surg. N. Y. S. V.
Jacob Francis Tourtelotte.
Lewis Arnold Tracy.
Samuel D. Wadsworth.
De Witt Webb.
Walter Henry Wentworth.
Lewis Westfall.
Benjamin Wilson.
Gustavus S. Winston.
Lockwood DeForest Woodruff, Free Acad. N. Y. C.

62

## 1864.

Samson American.
Theophilus H. Andress.
George W. Baker, Union 1861, A. A. Surg. U. S. A.
Philip H. Barton, A. A. Surg. U. S. N.
William Hunter Birckhead.
John Bedell Boss.
Richard B. Brown, Yale 1860, Asst. Surg. U. S. V., Bvt. Major U. S. V. 1865.
George J. Bucknall, A. B. elsewhere.
J. Otis Burt, Harv. 1858, Asst. Surg. U. S. N.
Adolphe Carit.
Francis P. Casey.
Samuel F. Chapin.
Albert T. Chapman.
Charles De Cockerille.
George W. Currier.
A. Thomas Cuzner.
*Henry A. Danker, Asst. Surg. U. S. N. *1864
Henry A. Darby.
Albert Austin Davis.
*Henry J. Devlin. aet. 25. *1864
Dwight Dudley.
George H. Dunbar.
Francis D. Edgerton, and elsewhere, Wesleyan Univ. 1861.
Henry Clay Eno, Yale 1860.
D. Darwin Everett.
Edward Farrell.
Archelaus G. Field, and Starling Med. Coll. Ohio 1854.
Luther P. Fitch, Beloit Coll. and A.M. Beloit, Asst. Surg. 47th U. S. Col. Inf.
John H. Furman.
Archibald McI. Gregory, A.A. Surg. U. S. N.
David L. Laight.
John C. Holmes.
William Warner Hoppin, Jr., Brown Univ. and A. M. Brown, LL. B. 1869.
John C. Hooper.
George W. Hosmer.
Edwar G. Janeway, Rutger's 1860 and A. M. Rutg.
Joseph Edward Janvrin, Asst. Surg. 15th N. H. Vols.
William H. Kinney.
Henry M. Knowles.
William Baldwin Linsly, A. A. Surg. U. S. A.

William A. Lockwood.
William M. McKay.
James W. McLane, Yale 1861.
Daniel E. McSweeny, St. Francis Xavier's Coll. 1861 and A. M. St. F. X., A.A. Surg. U. S. A.
George J. Northrop, Asst. Surg. U. S. V.
Henry Eagle Ogden, Union 1862.
Benjamin M. Page.
James L. Phillips.
Henry F. Piffard, Univ. N.Y. C. 1862.
Stephen C. Powell.
*Alfred Pryor. *1865
Charles S. Robert.
Stephen W. Roof.
Allen S. Russell, Surg. in Chief 3d Brig. Hardin's Div. 22d Army Corps.
John P. Schenck, Jr.
William F. Scoresby.
George W. Stout.
Edward Constant Seguin, Asst. Surg. U. S. V.
Charles E. Simmons.
H. Lyle Smith.
Montross L. Smith.
*William R. Stilwell. *1864
Freman Stoddard.
Edward W. Thompson, Asst. Surg. U. S. A.
William Thurman.
Elbert P. Tibbals.
John R. Todd.
Platon Vallejo.
Augustus Van Courtlandt.
Frederick D. Vanderhoof, Asst. Surg. 51st N. Y. Vet. Vols.
William P. Warren.
Lathrop P. Weaver.
George G. Wheelock, Harv. 1860.
J. Elias Whitehead, Rutgers 1844 and A. M. Rutg.
Thomas Wight.
William S. Willis, Surg. 1st N. J. Cav. 77

## 1865.

Andrew Anderson.
Calvin Anderson.
Harvey Napoleon Austin, and elsewhere.
James E. Barbour.
George Lewis Beers, Yale 1860 and A. M. Yale.
Christopher M. Bell.
Timothy Bigelow.
Henry Edward Bissett, A. A. Surg. U. S. A.
Edward Bleecker.
Sylvester S. Bogert.
Theodore Dwight Bradford, A. B. elsewhere.
John Boyd Campbell.
Dexter Selwyn Clark, Beloit Coll. 1860, Asst. Surg. 25th Ill. Vols. 1863–4 and Surg. 1864.
Lucian Dean Clark.
Charles A. Conover.
Thomas Vaughn Crandall, A. A. Surg. U. S. A.
Clarence E. De Wolfe.
James A. De Wolfe, Brown Univ. and A. M. Brown.
Richard Dey.
Andrew J. Disbrow.
Alvan Dodge.
Frank O. Earle.
Daniel H. Fairweather.
Levi Farrow.
Edwin B. Flagg, A. M. elsewhere.
Horace S. Fuller, A. M. elsewhere.
Charles F. George.
John Francis Gignoux, A. M. elsewhere.
William Chalk Gouinlock.
John R. Greenleaf, Jr.
Edward D. Griffin.
Thomas Haigh, A. A. Surg. U. S. A. 1864.

William Henry Hoag.
Stephen E. De Witt Hoornbeck.
David Post Jackson.
John Clarkson Jay, Jr.
Parley H. Johnson.
Edgar K. Kelley.
Daniel W. Kissam.
James F. Laughlin.
John B. Learned.
John Lawrence Lee.
Thomas W. Lowerree, Jr.
John Gilman McAllaster, A. A. Surg. U. S. A.
John C. Minor.
Alfred Mitchell, A. M. elsewhere.
Lawrence O. Morgan.
Martin Luther Overton.
Joseph Otis Pinneo.
John A. Purney.
Eli D. Sargent,
Peter Laurence Schenck, A. B. elsewhere.
Tennis Schenck, A. B. elsewhere.
Octavius Barrell Shreve, A. B. elsewhere.
Elijah Herman Smith.
James Welch Smith.
Albert Leroy W. Stephenson.
William George Stevenson.
Alexander Stewart, A. B. elsewhere.
Jay Stephen Stone.
David L. Stricklin.
James Buckley Tweedle.
Nelson S. Westcott.
Alvord E. Winchell, A.B. elsewhere.
Russell Withers.
George Powell Wright.

66

## 1866.

Lewis Applegate.
David Penfield Austin.
Edward Woodbridge Avery.
James McMillan Ayer, A. B. elsewhere.
Silas Cook Baldwin.
George Miller Beard, Yale 1862 and A. M. Yale.
William Graham Bryson.
Lafayette Bugbee.
George Owen Burgess.
George Cary.
Thomas Edwards Clark.
John Wordsworth Clemesha.
William S. Combs, A.M. elsewhere.
William Augustine Conway.
Adam C. Corson.
David Magie Cory.
John Cowan.
Patrick W. Cremin.
Benjamin Frederick Dawson.
John J. De Motte.
Marcus Dodd.
John William Dooley.
Henry Dusenbury.
James Anderson Exton.
Daniel McLean Forman.
Addison Howard Foster.
David R. Francis.
Edward Frothingham.
John Pool Garrish, Jr.
Ralph Schuyler Goodwin.
Jay Levins Greene.
James Romeyn Gregory.
George Wheelock Grover.
Orrin Franklin Harris.
Samuel Harris.
George Elias Hawes, A. B. elsewhere.
Tecumseh K. Holmes.
Edward R. Hun, A. B. elsewhere.
Joseph Slater Hunt.
James B. Hunter.
Edward Carroll Huse.
Edwin Hutchinson, A. M. elsewhere, Ph. B. Yale 1860.
James C. Hutchinson.
Stephen Hyde.
Richard Douglas James.
Joseph Johnson.

Henry De Witt Joy.
Robert P. Jump, and elsewhere.
Samuel Lisle Kennedy.
James Suydam Knox, A. M. elsewhere.
Mortimer Lampson.
Archibald Lawson.
Charles E. Lee.
Thomas Le Guen.
Algernon Sidney Leonard.
Walter Lindsay.
William Henry McKelvie.
Edward Macomb, A. M. elsewhere.
Isaac Newton Mead.
John Calvin Mead.
George Le Roy Menzie.
Hubbard Winslow Mitchell.
William Morton.
John Moore.
George Washington Newcomb.
Henry D. Nicoll, A. B. elsewhere.
Joseph O'Dwyer.
John Wright Ostrander.
Edwin Phillips, and elsewhere.
Charles Talbot Poore.
Francisco Repetto.
William G. Ridout.
Charles Roth.
Samuel Fowler Rouse.
Dayton Wykoff Searle.
Thomas Skelding.
David Augustine Smith.
Samuel St. John Smith.
Whitmer Snively.
Richmond Joseph Southworth.
Richard Henry Stone.
Joseph Stubbs.
James Madison Study, and elsewhere.
Ralph Partridge Thatcher.
Walter Ure.
James D. Van Der Veer.
Henry Clay Van Gieson.
Cornelius Van Riper.
Frederick Judd Van Wagner.
Henry Freeman Walker, A.M. elsewhere.
Charles Washburn.
Peter Wheeler.
Samuel Whitall.
Henry Simmons White, LL. B. 1870.
James Wright Wilson.
Joseph Sands Winston.
Augustus Wohlfarth.
Alfred H. Woodill.
Joel Williston Wright.
Gerardus Willis Wynkoop.
George Ludlow Yost.
Charles Young, A. M. elsewhere.
William Henry Young.

103

## 1867.

Thomas R. Almon.
Theodore F. Alverson.
John W. Baldwin.
Oglevie D. Ball.
Frederick S. Barclay.
Willis J. Beach.
Herbert C. Belden.
Charles M. Billings, A. M. elsewhere.
James A. Blanchard.
Francis V. Brush.
Albert H. Buck, Yale 1864.
Charles C. Buckley.
Charles A. Carle.
Frank Carter.
Philo W. Clark.
James D. Clyde.
James E. Cooper.
Frederick S. Creelman.
Samuel Decker.
John O'Fallon Delany.
Laban Dennis.
Charles M. Des Brisay.
Stephen M. Disbrow.
Francis Du Bois, Jr., A. B. elsewhere.
Morton W. Easton, Yale 1863.

Jonathan Edwards, Jr., Yale 1863.
Frederick W. Elberg, A. M. elsewhere.
William S. Ely, A. B. elsewhere.
Bache McEvers Emmet.
Edward S. Eveleth.
Charles W. Ferguson.
David F. Fetter, and Phila. Coll. Med. 1853.
James N. Fitch, A. B. elsewhere.
Edward T. Fuller.
Burns Gilman, and Bowd. Med. Coll.
Zeeb Gilman, Jr.
Frederick Gilnack.
Harry Gove.
Henry Gray.
Emile Gruening.
Martin Hagan, and Starling Med. Coll.
John D. Hall, A. B. elsewhere.
Henry E. Handerson, A. M. elsewhere.
Daniel De W. Harrington.
Audley Haslett, A. M elsewhere.
Henry Henderson, A.M. elsewhere.
Edward J. Hogan.
George F. Hollick.
Charles H. Horton.
Erasmus Darwin Hudson, Jr. A. B. elsewhere.
Stephen J. Hutchinson.
Thomas L. Janeway, A. M. elsewhere.
Samuel Johnson.
Henry I. Jordan, A. B. elsewhere.
John J. Keator.
John J. Ketchum.
William A. Kissam.
Eustis F. Langdon, A. B. elsewhere.
William M. Lyttleton.
William C. McFarland.
Theodore Dwight Martin.
David H. Muir.
George W. Murdock.
John H. Murfee.
Henry E. Owen, Yale 1864.
William H. Palmer, A. B. elsewhere.
James F. Peyton.
Edward R. Post, A. M. elsewhere.
William H. B. Pratt, Yale 1864.
Albert R. Randol.
Ira Remsen.
Nathan S. Roberts.
George W. Robinson, A. M. elsewhere.
John W. Robinson.
Charles F. Rodenstein, A. M. elsewhere.
Albert S. Rogers.
Eugene B. Sanborn.
Charles R. Sanderson, and Cleveland Med. Coll.
ThomasEdwardSatterthwaite, Yale 1864.
Thomas Sidney Scales, A. B. elsewhere.
Warren Schoonover, A. B. elsewhere.
Alonzo De Loos Smith.
Josiah P. Sugg.
Thomas Terrill, Jr.
Henry C. Turner.
James Vanderpool, A.B. elsewhere.
Nicholas Berdan Van Houten.
James Van Derveer Van Nest.
Richard C. Van Wyck.
William A. M. Wainwright, A. B. elsewhere.
Eli Warner.
George Wells, Jr.
John Winslow, and Bellevue Med. Coll. N. Y. C.
Silas O. Witherbee. 94

# 1868.

Frederick Mixer Aitken.
Philip Edward Arcularius, A. M. elsewhere.
William Augustus Avery.
Joseph Ritner Benjamin, A. M. elsewhere.
John Ferguson Black, A. B. elsewhere.
Thomas Sheldon Bond, A.M. • and M. D. elsewhere.
Calvin F. Bonney.
George Henry Bosley, and elsewhere.
Benjamin Mills Briggs, M. S. elsewhere.
John Anthon Callender.
William Jessup Chandler.
Henry Waldburg Coleman.
William Albert Corwin.
Samuel Pierce Craig.
Cnarles Culver.
Byron Cummings.
Henry Nehemiah Dodge.
John Luther Duryee, A. M. elsewhere.
Henry O. Ely, A. B. elsewhere.
David Combs English.
George Emory Foster, A. M. elsewhere.
Edward Frankel.
Gustav Frauenstein.
Samuel Horace Frazer.
Charles D. T. Gibson, A. B. elsewhere.
Theodore Giddings.
James Glynn Gregory, A. B. elsewhere.
William Edward Griffiths.
Albert E. Ham, A. B. elsewhere.
Frederick Fanning Harral, A. M. elsewhere.
George Fuller Hawley.
Frederick Porteous Henry.
Neil Jamieson Hepburn, A.M. elsewhere.
Joseph Bassette Holland, A. M. elsewhere.
Charles Taylor Jewett.
Herschel Vespasian Johnson, Jr.
Adoniram Brown Judson, A. M. and M. D. elsewhere.
John Marshall Kellogg.
Warren Kemble.
Thomas H. Kenan.
Frederick Kidder.
Edwin A. Kilbourne.
Charles Laight.
A. J. Lanterman.
Charles Henry Leonard, A.B. elsewhere.
Charles Edward Lockwood, A. B. elsewhere.
James E. M. Lordly.
John Tarleton Luck.
Robert Louis Lusby.
David Valentine Lynch.
Frederick Dey Marshall.
Frederick D. R. Marshall.
James Joseph McCarty.
Daniel McEwan, Jr.
Robert James McGay.
John Hector McKay.
John Abner Mead, A. M. elsewhere.
Morris Henry Miesse.
Henry James Miller.
John Nolan.
Aggeus Outerbridge.
Julius L. Parke, A. M. elsewhere.
Charles B. Parkhurst.
Howard Whited Phillips.
James Oakley Pingry.
John Joseph Prendergast, A. M. elsewhere.
Monroe T. Pultz.
Robert Morgan Rea.
Philippe Ricord.
Frank Warren Rockwell, A. B. elsewhere.
Charles S. Rodman.
William Chambers Rogers.
William H. Ross, Jr.
Wallace Edgar Sabin.

Norton Jerome Sands.
Edward William Schauffler.
Walter Keeler Scofield.
John Sharp, A. B. elsewhere.
Charles Stuart Sheldon, A.M. and M. D. elsewhere.
George Henry Sherman.
Daniel MacMartin Stimson, A. M. elsewhere.
Stephen Van Wickle Stout.
Henry Tunstall Strong, A. B. elsewhere.
Benjamin Ralph Swan.
Robert William Taylor.
Charles Henry Thompson.
Samuel William Torrey, A. B. elsewhere.
Roger Sherman Tracy.
Thomas Hall Tripler.
John Bennett Tyler, A. B. elsewhere.
Jerome Walker.
Leslie Dodd Ward.
John William Warth, Jr., A. M. elsewhere.
Francis Henry Weismann.
Frank Wilmarth, A. M. elsewhere.
Theodore Frelinghuysen Wolfe.
John Frank Young.

## 1869.

Amos Wilson Abbott.
George Henry Aiken.
Clinton Atkinson.
Charles Howell Bailey, and elsewhere.
George Henry Balleray.
George Wilson Bell.
Henry M. Bishop.
James Augustus Blake, A. B. and M. D. elsewhere.
Hector Seager Bowen.
Edward Bennett Bronson, A. B. elsewhere.
Lawton Stickney Brooks.
Lucius Duncan Bulkley, A. B. elsewhere.
Richard Winthrop Bull.
Edward Worthington Burnett.
Craft Coast Carroll.
William Hanford Cartter, and elsewhere.
Charles Hoag Case.
Curtis Chapman.
James Francis Chapman.
Sherman Hartwell Chapman, A. B. elsewhere.
Nelson Henry Claflin.
John Ralph Coffman, and elsewhere.
Gustavus Pierrepont Davis, A. B. elsewhere.
Francis E. Doughty, and elsewhere.
John Edwards.
Nathaniel Bright Emerson, A. M. elsewhere.
Julius Fehr.
Ira William Fletcher.
Seth Burnham Foster.
Alonzo Freeman.
Charles Lindol French.
Omer Tousey Gillett, A. B. elsewhere.
William Joseph Haine.
97 George Adelbert Hathaway.
Russel Thayer Hayes, and elsewhere.
George Benedict Hickok, A. M. elsewhere.
Augustus Villery Hill, A. B. elsewhere.
Urban Gillespie Hitchcock, A. B. elsewhere.
William Mulligan Hodges.
Charles Barnes Huffman.
John Hurdsfield.
Andrew Jackson Jessup.
John Henry Korff.
Isadore Perrin Latour, A. B. elsewhere.
John Howard Lever.
Newton Adams Lindley.
James Cook Linsly, A. M. elsewhere.

Justin Martin.
Forster Jonas Maynard.
Joseph Williams McCall, and elsewhere.
John Cameron McDougall.
John McGuirk.
Thomas Joseph McLoughlin.
Malcolm McLean.
Henry McManus, A. M. elsewhere.
Augustus Aloysius Moloney.
Jesse Lee Morrill.
Eugene Bernard Murtha, A. M. elsewhere.
James Robert Nelson.
Ashel Griswold Nettleton.
Stephen Pierson.
Thomas Jefferson Pitner, B. S. elsewhere.
William Mecklenburgh Polk.
Joseph Henry Raymond, A. B. elsewhere.
John Joseph Reid.
Benjamin Clapp Riggs, A. B. elsewhere.
Orville Forrest Rogers.
Leavitt Sanderson.
William Darwin Schuyler.
Jefferson Scoonover.
Xenophon Christmas Scott, A. M. and M. D. elsewhere.
Alexander Grant Sinclair.
Charles Elihu Slocum.
Horatio Nelson Spencer, Jr., A. B. elsewhere.
Louis D. Sproat.
Ralph Edward Starkweather, A. M. elsewhere.
Charles Sackett Starr, A. B. elsewhere.
Darwin Adelbert Stewart.
Charles Stokes, Jr.
Louis Stoskopf, A. M. elsewhere.
Erastus Perry Swasey.
David Thompson.
Charles Alonzo Todd.
William Sheridan Todd, A.M. elsewhere.
Edward Torrey.
Thomas Trenaman.
William Henry Vail, A. M. elsewhere.
John Van Harlengen.
George Wackerhagen.
Charles Edwards Willard.
William Bull Wright.
Samuel Monell Zabriskie.

92

## 1870.

J. Freeman Atwood.
Daniel S. Ayers, Jr.
Lewis Balch.
Arthur A. Barrows, A. B. elsewhere.
John A. Bevan.
John M. Bigelow, A. M. elsewhere.
Eugene P. Boise, A. B. and M. D. elsewhere.
George P. Bradley.
William Brand.
Eugene W. Brooks.
James Y. Bryce.
Harvey S. Calderwood.
Stewart Church.
Staats V. D. Clark.
Leartus Connor, A. M. elsewhere.
Frederic C. Curtis, A. M. elsewhere.
John G. Curtis, A. M. elsewhere.
Nathaniel P. Dandridge, A.B. elsewhere.
Henry C. Day.
William J. Duffield.
Herbert M. Eddy, A. M. and M. D. elsewhere.
Charles Enfield.
Edwin Evans.
James D. Featherstonhaugh, Jr., A. B. elsewhere.
Charles O. Files, A. B. elsewhere.
Charles A. Foster.
Bernhard Grunhut, A.B. elsewhere.

George M. Haines.
William E. Hall.
Allan McL. Hamilton.
D. Brainerd Hunt, A. M. elsewhere.
Walter Judson, A. M. elsewhere.
Eugene Kingman.
Hugh S. Kinmonth.
George M. Lefferts, A. M. elsewhere.
Albert H. Little.
Samuel O. Loughridge, and elsewhere.
William Markham.
George Martin.
Frederic R. Marvin.
Robert Mason.
Charles McBurney, Jr., A.M. elsewhere.
John V. Morgan.
Samuel H. Morris.
Albert J. Murdock.
Henry T. Pierce, A. B. elsewhere.
Milton G. Planck, A. B. elsewhere.
Frederic Powers.
Robert Prentiss.
Robert A. Quin.
William H. T. Reynolds, A.M. elsewhere.
Joseph S. Ripley.
Francis E. Ross, and elsewhere.
John D. Rushmore.
Francis F. Sanders, A. B. elsewhere.
Francis A. Stanley.
Samuel B. St. John, A. M. elsewhere.
George M. Swain.
Robert E. Thompson.
Clayton W. Townsend.
David Clark Van Deursen.
William H. Vermilye.
George H. Whaley.
Francis A. Wheeler.
Howard Whiting.
Charles T. Whybrow.
John P. Wilson. 67

# GRADUATES IN LAW,

EXCEPT THOSE PREVIOUSLY NAMED AS GRADUATES IN ARTS.

## 1860.

Daniel Pratt Baldwin, Med. Univ.
George Van Nest Baldwin, A. M. Rutg. Coll.
Robert Henry Boorman.
BradburyChandlerChetwood, Burlingt. Coll.
Edward Salstonstall Dakin, Ham. Coll.
*Van Buren Dutton. aet. 31. *1865
*William Sprague Ely. *1862
Harry Allen Grant, Ham. Coll. 1858, A.M. Hamil. and Yale 1861.
Robert Chadwick Hutchings, N. Jers. N. Y. Assemb. 1861–3, Surrogate N. Y. C. 1870–.
William Henry Ingersoll.
*Isaac Henry Kirby, Univ. N. Y. C. *1862
Charles McLean Knox, Major U. S. V.
Francis Lewis Lowndes.
*William Creighton Meade, A. M. St. James' Coll. 1857, U. S. V. aet. 23. *1863
William Stevens Newell.
Julius Harris Ranney, Free Acad. N. Y. C.
Fenton Rockwell.
Walter Seabury Sands, Free Acad. N. Y. C.
John Cornell Schenck.
Samuel Farland Simpson.
Theodore Murray Squires.
Philip Lee Wilson, Lieut. U. S. V. 22

## 1861.

Smith Bloomfield, A.M. Free Acad. N. Y. C.
Miles Standish Bromley.
Herman Washington Bruen.
Nathaniel Barto Cooke, Yale 1859.
Cornelius Jay Du Bois, Capt. U. S. V.
Jas. McLaren Breed Dwight, Yale 1846 and A. M. Yale.
Sidney Stewart Henop.
Benjamin Franklin Lee, Jr., Will. 1858.
Robert Morris, Yale 1858.
Seth Miller Murdock, Harv. 1858 and A. M. Harv.
William Henry Owen, A. M. Bowd., Capt. U. S. V.
Robert Willets Pearsall.
Temple Prime.
Henry Everett Russell, N. Jers. 1859 and A. M. N. Jers.
Frederick Scoville, Univ. N. Y. C., Lieut. U. S. V.
Robert Noxon Toppan, Harv. 1858 and A. M. Harv.
*Prescott Hall Ward. aet. 29. *1870
James Raymond Weeks, Lafayette Coll.

Charles Hornblower Woodruff, Yale 1858. 19

## 1862.

Charles Wesley Bangs.
George Alexander Black, Free Acad. N. Y. C.
Daniel Webster Bond.
*Edward Carrington, Jr., Yale 1859, Lieut. U. S. V. *1865
John Townsend Conolly, Lt. U. S. V.
William Miller Denman, Free Acad N. Y. C.
Frederic James De Peyster, Free Acad. N. Y. C., LL.M. 1864.
Robert Thomas Brown Easton, Free Acad. N. Y. C.
Edward Clarence Fraser.
Charles Henry Hatch, Yale 1859.
Stephen Burdett Hyatt, Free Acad. N. Y. C.
Sidmon Thorne Keese, Yale 1860.
Edgar Ketchum, Jr., Free Acad. N. Y. C.
Bruce Moffatt.
Augustus White Nicoll, Univ. N. Y. C.
William O'Mullen.
John O'Neil, Jr.
George Percy.
James Edward Ryan.
John Bailey Storm, LL. M. 1864.
John Simpson Walker.
Henry Kirke White, Sci. B. Free Acad. N. Y. C.
Albert Wyckoff, Lieut. U. S. V. 23

## 1863.

James Bruen Andrews, Yale 1861.
John Campbell Broderick.
Willett Bronson, William's 1861.
William Campbell.
George Chalmers, Yale 1861.
Paris Garner Clark, Jr.
Andrew Kirkpatrick Cogswell, Rutgers.
Richard William Ely, Univ. N. Y. C.
William Henry Fuller, Yale 1861.
Edward Douglas Gale.
Frederick Gallatin, Univ. N. Y. C.
John Lyon Gardiner.
Eugene Terry Gardner.
Francis Joseph Holahan, St. John's.
Edwin Francis Hyde, Free Acad. N. Y. C.
Peter Duncan Kenny.
Francis Edward Kernochan, Yale 1861.
Carleton White Miller.
John Pell.
Charles Osborne Phelps.
George Dwight Phelps, Jr., Yale 1860.
William Walter Phelps, Yale 1860.
William Rounds Potter.
Josiah Collins Pumpelly, Rutger's.
George Washington Sandford.
Eugene Schuyler, Ph. D. Yale 1861.
Jacob Shrady, Univ. N. Y. C.
Archibald Walker Spier, Free Acad. N. Y. C.
James Steers, Free Acad. N. Y. C.
James Ayers Taber.
Ernest Tuckerman.
Morris Ashhurst Tyng, (Rev.), Will. 1861, Prof. Bibl. Lit. Gambier Theol. Sem. 1870.
George Edmondson Walker.
Josiah Otis Ward.

Edmund Wetmore, Harv. 1860. 35

## 1864.

Richard Armstrong.
William Philip Arnold.
Henry Sandford Bellows.
Henry Brodhead, Yale 1859.
Eldred Absalom Carley, Free Acad. N. Y. C.
Thomas Bernard Connery, St. John's.
George Campbell Cooper, Free Acad. N. Y. C.
Abel Crook, Will. 1862, LL. M. 1865.
Hiram Robert Dixon.
Jeremiah Donovan.
John Esler Eckerson.
Washington White Ellsworth.
Lemuel Edward Evans.
Joseph Fettretch.
Jacob Alfred Gross, LL. M. 1865.
Frank Harris, Christian Bros. Mri., LL. M. 1865.
Andrew Josephus Hennion.
William Myers Hoes, Will. 1861.
Henry Holt, Yale 1862.
Harlow Mather Hoyt, Free Acad. N. Y. C.
Hamilton Bailey Humes.
Charles Nichols Judson, Yale 1862.
William Platt Ketcham, Yale 1862.
Arthur Malachi Lee, Free Acad. N. Y. C.
Franklin McVeagh, Yale 1862.
Joseph Augustus Marsh.
Luther Ainsworth Milbank.
Horatio Woodhull Mills.
Israel Minor, Jr., Yale 1862.
Charles Hoskins Mundy.
William Henry Newschafer, Free Acad. N. Y. C.
Henry Delafield Phelps, Trin. Coll.
Albert Alfred Reuwee.
James Richards, N. Jers. 1858, LL. M. 1865.
Van Ness Roosevelt.
Merwin Rushmore.
Elliot Sanford, Amh. 1861.
Adolph Lewis Sanger, Free Acad. N.Y.C., LL. M. 1865.
John Le Grand Schaffer.
William Arnet Seaman.
Thomas Buckman Shoemaker.
William Shrady.
William Vanderbilt Simpson.
William Edwin Slocum, B. S. Free Acad. N. Y. C.
Jacob Philip Solomon.
Frederick William Stevens, Yale 1858.
John Stout.
Sidney Harrison Stuart, Jr., B. S. Free Acad. N. Y. C.
Frederick Swarts, LL. M. 1865.
William Robert Syme, Univ. N. Y. C.
Richard Terheun Van Boskerck, Free Acad. N. Y. C.
Julius Sylvester Walsh, St. Joseph's.
Frederick Augustus Ward, Yale 1862.
Robert Kelley Weeks, Yale 1862.
William Leggett Whiting.
Miron Winslow, Jr.
Buchanan Winthrop, Yale 1862.
Samuel Purdy Wright.
58

## 1865.

Edmund Bragdon Barnum.
William Nelson Bedelle.
George Alvin Bevins.
Edward Griffiths Black.
Andrew Benton Chalmers.
Gasheree De Witt Clock.

Thomas Cochran, Jr., Univ. N. Y. C.
Lewis Osborn Corbet.
Adrian Voorhees Cortelyou, Yale.
Ten Broeck Crawford.
James Geddes Day.
Hugh Duffy.
William Henry Field, Union Coll.
Henry Edward Fitzsimons, St. Francis Xavier Coll.
Henry Rankin Freeland, N. Jers.
Charles Miles Gilman, Yale.
Edmund Banks Graham.
Richard Henry Greene, Yale.
Richard Booth Greenwood, Jr.
Isaac Hollister Hall, Hamilt. Coll.
George Scovill Hamlin, Yale.
Thornton Mills Hinkle, Yale.
George Hoffman, Yale.
Samuel Huntington, Yale.
Cortlandt Irving.
Luther Manard Jones, Yale.
Joseph Frederick Kernochan, Yale.
George Keyser.
Robert Blair Keyser, Free Acad. N. Y. C.
George Pliny Kingsley.
Joseph Koch, Free Acad. N. Y. C.
Mordecai Lewis.
Francis Ferdinand Marbury, Jr.
William Lewis Matson, Yale.
Charles Frederick Mawbey.
Theodore Florence Henry Mayer.
James Slade Millard, Yale.
William Stewart Ross Ogilby.
James Augustus Olwell, A. M. St. John's Coll.
Charles Godfrey Patterson.
Charles Alfred Post.
Henry Foster Ranney.
Thomas Robinson, M.D. elsewhere.
Louis Ruttkay, Union.
Peter John Sause.
Charles Carroll Smith.
Gerrit Smith Stanton.
Henry Brewster Stanton, Jr.
George Washington Stephens. Free Acad. N. Y. C.
David Dean Terry, Free Acad. N. Y. C.
John Julius Thomasson.
Isaac Van Alst.
Singleton Van Buren.
Elias Williams Van Voorhis, Jr.
Hamilton Wallis, Yale.
Townsend Wandell, Free Acad. N. Y. C.
Almar Preston Webster.
Charles Howland Wesson, Yale. 58

## 1866.

John Johnson Allen, Univ. Vermont.
Edward Sandford Atwater, N. Jers.
Edwin Bergh, Jr.
Frederick Henry Betts, Yale.
Thomas Bracken, A. M. St. John's Coll.
Ebenezer Buckingham Convers, A. M. Yale.
John Thomas Cornell.
Albert Crane, Tuft's Coll.
Charles Henry Douglas, Beloit Coll.
William Oliver Embury.
Lewis C. Goebel, Coll. City N. Y.
Charles Auguste Lambert Goldey.
James John Gray.
Daniel Judson Holden, Yale.
William Allen Hoyt.
Ephraim Arnold Jacob, Coll. City N. Y.
John Watts Kearny.

Samuel Lawrence, Jr.
Alfred James McCullough.
Alexander Taggart McGill, N. Jers.
Henry Major, Jr., Georgetown Coll.
Frederick Halsey Man, Coll. City N. Y.
Nicholas Murray, A. B. William's.
William Chauncey Prall.
L. Bradford Prince.
Jarrett Thomas Richards.
Edward Ross Robinson.
William Henry Rooney.
Washington Sackmann.
Henry J. Schenck.
Murray Colgate Shoemaker, Yale.
Nathaniel Ferdinand Smith.
William Washington Smith.
Edward Fay Stilwell.
Samuel John Storrs, Amherst.
Charles Phelps Taft, Yale 1864, and A. M. Yale, J. U. D. Heidelberg, 1867.
Frederick Thompson.
Alfred Wagstaff, Jr.
Benjamin Robert Winthrop, Jr. 39

## 1867.

Wilbur Russell Bacon, Yale.
Charles Henry Baldwin.
Truman Hamilton Baldwin, Coll. City N. Y.
James Bell, Jr.
William Johnson Binney, Amherst.
Eugene Samuel Blois.
Edward Payson Brewster, N. Jers.
John Edward Brooks, Yale.
John Lovett Brower, A. M. Coll. City N. Y.
Edward Sears Clinch, B. S. Coll. City N. Y.
Edwin Walter Coggeshall.
Theodore Pease Cook.
Frank Hull Cowdrey.
Samuel Oakley Crawford.
William Bedlow Crosby, Coll. City N. Y.
N. Gano Dunn.
Clarence Uriah Embury.
Thomas Rawdon Fisher.
William Hubbell Fisher, Hamilt. Coll.
Horace Webster Fowler, Yale.
William Edgar Glover.
James Sandford Greves, Hamilt. Coll.
William Fearing Hall.
Henry Bailey Hathaway.
William Herring.
Archibald Hopkins, William's.
Isaac Samuel Isaacs, Univ. N. Y. C.
Charles Swift Joslyn, and Yale.
William Lampson, Yale.
John Thomas Lockman.
Edwin McCahill, Georget. Coll. D. C.
John Alfred Mack.
John Hobart McMurdy.
Thomas Martin Moore.
Philip Murphy.
Daniel Weir Northrup.
David Robinson Nutter, Dartmouth.
Sidney Oaksmith.
Daniel Parish, Jr.
Phœnix Remsen.
Joseph Swift Richards, M. S. Norwich Univ. Vt.
Zabdiel Sidney Sampson, Amherst.
Lorenzo S. B. Sawyer, Hamilton.
William Andrew Senger.
Morris Woodruff Seymour.
Charles Christmas Shelton.
Eugene Carroll Skinner.
Charles Edward Smith, Renss. Polytech. Inst. N.Y.
Charles Henry Smith, Jr., B. S. Coll. City N. Y.

Freling H. Smith, Union.
Isaac Spencer Smith.
John William Sterling, Yale.
William Edwin Stiger.
John Hervey Stitt, Coll. City N. Y.
Frederick Wilmot Sturges.
Frank Thompson, Union.
Charles Harmer Trafford.
Henry Edwin Tremain, Coll. City N. Y.
John Hamilton Turner, A. M. Coll. City N. Y.
Augustus Gifford Vanderpoel.
Philip Livingston Van Rensselaer, A. M. N. Jers.
George West Van Siclen, M. S. Coll. City N. Y.
Edmund Augustus Ward.
Francis H. Weeks, William's.
James Keappoch Hamilton Willcox, Univ. N. Y. C.
William Henry Williams, Brown Univ.
William Clitus Witter, Yale.

## 1868.

Osmin W. Atkins, Wesleyan Univ.
Emile Beneville, Coll. City N. Y. and A. M. Coll. C. N. Y.
William Warwick Bliss, Brown Univ.
Morris Mumford Budlong, Yale.
George Noyes Burt, Union Coll.
Albertson Case, Harv. Univ.
Newton Henry Chittenden.
Simeon Baldwin Chittenden, Jr., Yale.
Elihu Church.
George Clinton.
Henry Kiersted Coddington, M. S. Coll. City N. Y.
Edmund Coffin, Jr., Yale.
Arthur Douglas Collins.
Edward Donaldson Cowman, Hobart Coll.
Henry Sprong Davis, Hobart Coll.
Charles Willoughby Dayton.
John Ambrose Deady, Amherst, Coll.
Frederick Nevins Dodge, Ya e.
Franklin Woodward Earl.
Wilberforce Freeman, Coll. New Jersey.
Michael Emanuel Goodhart.
Dar iel Edward Hervey.
William Monefeldt Howland, Harv. and A. M. Harv.
Walter Langdon Kane.
John Vincent Kernan, Seton Hall. Coll.
James King Lawrence, Brown Univ.
Theodore Akerly Lord, Yale.
James A. McCreery, Mt. St. Mary's Coll.
67 George Souter McKay.
Payson Merrill, Yale.
Ormond Tucker Middleton.
Fordham Morris, Trin. Coll.
Henry Lewis Morris.
Max Moses.
David Judson Newland, Middleb. Coll.
William Greenly Nicoll, Yale.
William Franklin North.
Robert Hunter Patton.
George Jones Peet, Kenyon Coll.
Thomas Bond Raynolds.
Henry Hutchinson Reid.
Thomas Rogers, Union Coll.
Henry Andrew Root.
Edward Whelan Searing.
Thomas Parish Sherman.
Frank Sherman Smith.
Asa Adams Spear, Amherst Coll.
Samuel Hempstead Valentine, Amherst Coll.
Thomas Sedgwick Van Valkenburgh, Yale.

John Waring Weed.
John Brandagee Wood, Yale. 51

## 1869.

William Henry Andrews.
James Knox Averill.
Charles Wyllys Betts, Yale.
James Lord Bishop, Amherst Coll.
Henry Herrick Bond.
Charles Goodrich Coe, Yale.
Duane Conant, Hamilt. Coll.
Thomas Duncan Cottman, Mt. St. Mary's Coll.
Robert Emmett Cowart.
George Hubert Cowell, Yale.
James Ambrose Deering, Manhattan Coll.
John J. Du Bois, Yale.
Patrick Gavan Duffy.
Frank J. Dupignac.
George Ozro Emerson, Rochester Univ.
Charles Emmett.
John Barnard Fairbank, Amherst Coll.
Louis Fellows, Coll. City N. Y.
Francis Forbes, Rochester Univ.
Louis William Frost.
George Griswold Greene.
Edward Graham Haight.
George Henry Hansen.
Thomas Hedge, Jr., Yale.
John Homer Hildreth.
Pierre Van Buren Hoes.
George Chandler Holt, Yale.
William Warner Hoppin, Jr., Brown and A. M. Brown, M. D. 1864.
George Landon Ingraham.
Henry Whitman Kennedy.
Henry Thomas Lee, Lafayette Coll.
Hamilton Wright Mabie, William's Coll.
William Hector McAllister.
John Thomas McDonough.
Dennis McMahon, Jr., Manhattan Coll.
Charles Anson Maltby.
George Manierre, Yale.
Francis Elston Marsh, Coll. N. Jers.
Abram John Miller.
James Appleton Morgan, Racine Coll.
James Edward Morrison, Coll. City N. Y.
William Pitt Mudgett, Bowdoine Coll.
George Francis Murray, Georgetown Coll.
Henry Loomis Nelson, William's Coll.
Courtlandt Palmer, Jr.
Richard Wayne Parker, Coll. N. Jers.
Charles Ewing Patterson.
Walter Pell.
Caleb Purdy.
Rudolph Frederick Rabe.
Theodore Ritter.
Charles Roberts, Coll. City N. Y.
Charles Hall Rockwell.
Francis Markoe Scott, Coll. City N. Y.
William Henry Secor.
George Preston Sheldon, Yale.
Frederick Isaac Small, Yale.
Charles Edward Souther, Harvard Univ.
Calvert Spensley.
Ernest Gordon Stedman, Yale.
Francis Lynde Stetson, William's Coll.
Solomon Thayer Streeter, Amherst Coll.
Charles Avery Tracy.
Charles Edward Tracy, Coll. City N. Y.
Edgar Abel Turrill, Yale.
Waldemar Jonas Tuska.

Philip Van Rensselaer Van Wyck.

Frank Ward Wessels.

Charles Warren West, William's Coll.

George Peabody Wetmore, Yale.

Ezekiel Webster Whipple, Dartmouth Coll.

William Wilson.

Edward Marshall Wright, Yale. 72

## 1870.

George Augustus Adee.

Edward Knapp Anderton.

Lemuel Hastings Arnold, Jr.

Theodore Aub.

George Augustus Baker, Jr., Coll. City N. Y.

Edward Wells Bell, Yale.

Alfred Douglas Brush.

Peter Vincent Burtsell.

Charles Kinsey Cannon, Yale.

Samuel Cardwell, Jr.

Timothy Pitkin Chapman, Yale.

Henry Abel Chittenden, Jr., Yale.

John Chorlton.

Edgar Bradford Clark.

John Henry Clayton.

Stacy B. Collins, Jr.

Le Baron Bradford Colt, Yale.

John Christopher Connor, Jr.

William Edgar Conover.

Gilbert Holmes Crawford, Coll. City N. Y.

Charles Edward Crowell.

Albert Delafield, B. S. Coll. City N. Y.

Leo Charles Dessar.

Francis Charles Devlin, St. Francis Xavier's Coll.

George Gillespie Dickson, Keny. Coll.

William Palmer Dixon, Yale.

John Holmes Prentiss Dodge.

Charles Arthur Doten.

George Williams Ellis, Middlebury Coll.

George Washington Flaacke.

William Riley Foster, J. D. Heidelberg.

J. Henry Fowler, Jr.

Robert Ludlow Fowler.

Joseph Warren Greene, Yale.

Augustus Fraugott Gurlitz.

Lovell Hall, Yale.

Frederick Robert Halsey, Harv. Union.

George Henry Hart.

Walter Howe, B. S. Coll. City N. Y.

William Reed Jerome, Hamilt. Coll.

Charles Dunn Jones.

Clarence Delafolie Jones.

Samuel Kalish.

James Knox, A. M. Coll. City N. Y.

Samuel Spahr Laws.

Thomas Alphonso McGlade, Jr.

Robert Bach McMaster, B.S. Coll. City N. Y.

William Fleming McRae.

John Calvin Paulison, Coll. N. Jers.

Henry Wilson Payne, Yale.

Paul Pelletier, A. M. St. Louis.

Samuel Edmund Perry.

William Franklin Pitschke, B. S. Coll. City N. Y.

James M. Poulsen, Coll. N. Jers.

Arthur Rickards Robertson.

Roderick Robertson.

Kaufman Simon.

Orrin Skinner.

William Brown Slocum.

Nathaniel Phillips Smith Thomas, Yale.

William Knapp Thorn, Jr.

Thomas Birdsall Van Boskerck.
Albert Warren Wells.
Henry Simmons White, M.D. 1866.
James Henry Wood, Yale.

65

# GRADUATES IN MINING ENGINEERING,

EXCEPT THOSE PREVIOUSLY NAMED AS GRADUATES IN ARTS.

E. M.

## 1868.

George Strong Baxter, A. B. Will. 1865.
Samuel Willard Bridgham.
Francis Gordon Brown.
James Pettigrew Carson.
Albert Huntington Chester.
John Adams Church.
George Hampton Coursen.
George Jarvis Geer, Jr.
George Byron Hanna, A. B. Coll. N. J.
Archibald MacMartin, A. M. Coll. N. J.
Edward Stewart Moffatt, A. M. Coll. N. J., Adj. Prof. Mining and Metall. Lafayette Coll. 1869–.
Charles Slason Plat
Kenneth Robertson.
William Allen Smith.
William Wey Tuttle.
William Henry Van Arsdale, A. M. Coll. N. Y. C.
David Van Lennep.
Moses Dillon Wheeler, A. B. Harv. Univ. 18

## 1869.

Frederick Buckman.
Alonzo Clarence Campbell.
Roland Duer Irving, A. M. 1870, Prof. of Geology, Mining, and Metallurgy Univ. of Wis.
Lionel Robert Nettre.
Henry Newton, A. M. Coll. N. Y. C.
George Howland Parsons.
William Pistor.
John Cooper Randolph, A. M. N. Jers.
Albert P. Schack.
Henry Maynard Smith.
Frederic Stallknecht.

11

## 1870.

Augustus Porter Barnard.
Ogden Haight.
John Augustus Knapp. A. M. Coll. N. Y. C.
Stuart Lindsley.
Frederick Augustus Schermerhorn.
Richard Henry Terhune.
Theodore Francis Van Wagenen.
Elwyn Waller, A. M. Harv.

8

# HONORARY GRADUATES,

AND

## GRADUATES OF OTHER COLLEGES

WHO HAVE BEEN ADMITTED IN COLUMBIA COLLEGE TO THE SAME DEGREE.

## 1758.

*Daniel Isaac Brown, (C. L.), N. Jers. 1753, A. M. and N. Jers., Prothonotary Bergen Co. N. J. 1776, Major H. B. M. Army 1780.

*Samuel Brown, Yale 1749, A. M and Yale. *1778

*Isaac Browne, (Rev.), Yale 1729, A. M. and Yale. *1786

*Thomas Bradbury Chandler, (Rev.), Yale 1745, A. M. and Yale and Oxford 1753, S. T. D. 1767 and Oxford 1766. *1790

*Leonard Cutting, (Rev.), Cambridge, A. M., Tutor 1756–63. aet. 69. *1794

*Samuel Fayerweather, (Rev.), Harv. 1743, A. M. and Yale 1753 and Oxford 1756 and Cambridge. *1781

*Carey Ludlow, (C.L.), A. M., Mast. in Chanc. N. Y. 1776, Surrogate N. Y. C. 1782.

*John McKesson, N. Jers. 1753, (C.L.), A. M. and N. Jers.

David Matthews, N. Jers. 1754, (C. L.), A.M., Alderman N. Y. C. 1776.

Josiah Ogden, A. B. and N. Jers. 1756.

*Cyrus Punderson, Yale 1755, A. M. and Yale. *1789

*Ebenezer Punderson, Yale 1755, A. M. and Yale. *1809

*Daniel Treadwell, Harv. 1754, A.M. and Harv., Fellow and Prof. Math. and Nat. Phil. 1757–60. *1760

*Timothy Wetmore, (T.), A. M. 14

## 1761.

*John Beardsley, (Rev.), A. B., A. M. 1768.

*William Jackson, A.M. and Yale 1763 and N. Jers. 1771 and Univ. Utrecht. *1813

*William Samuel Johnson, Yale 1744, A. M. and Yale and Harv. 1747, J.C. D. Ox. 1766, LL. D. Yale 1788, Del. to Coll. Congr. 1765, Judge Supr. Ct. Conn., 1772, Del. to Congr. 1774, Memb. Council Conn. 1780, Repr. in Congr. 1784–7, Memb. U.S. Constit. Conven. 1787, President 1787–1800, U. S. Sen. 1788. *1819

*Samuel Andrew Peters, (Rev.), Yale 1757, A.M. and Yale, LL. D. elsewhere. *1826

*Samuel Seabury, (Rev.),

Yale 1748, A. M. and Yale S. T. D. Ox. 1777, Bishop P. E. Ch. Conn. 1784-96. *1796
*James Scovill, (Rev.), Yale 1757, A. M. and Yale. *1808
*Agur Treadwell, (Rev.), A. B. and Yale 1760, A. M. Yale. *1763
*Edward Winslow, (Rev.), Harv. 1736, A. M. and Harv. *1784

8

## 1762.

*Samuel Andrews, (Rev.), Yale 1759, A. M. *1818
*Richard Clarke, (Rev.), A.B. and Yale 1762, A. M. 1766, and Yale. *1824
*Robert Harpur, Glasgow, A.M., Prof. Math. and Nat. Phil. 1761-7, Regent Univ. N. Y S. and Clerk of Board 1784-7, Trustee and Clerk of Board 1787-95, Secy. St. N. Y.
*Bela Hubbard, (Rev.), Yale 1758, A.M. and Yale, S. T.D. Yale 1804. *1812
*Robert McKean, (Rev.), Phila. Coll., A. M.
*Ebenezer Parmele, Yale 1758, A. M. and Yale. *1802

6

## 1764.

*Matthew Cushing, Harv. 1739, A. M. and Harv., Librarian Harv. *1779
*Samuel Giles, A.B., Instr. in Maths. King's Coll.

2

## 1765.

*Jeremiah Leaming, (Rev.), Yale 1745, A. M. and Yale S. T. D. 1789. *1804

## 1767.

*Samuel Auchmuty, (Rev.), A. B. Harv. 1745 and A. M. Harv. 1746, S.T.D. and Oxford 1766. *1777
*Ephraim Avery, (Rev.), Yale 1761, A. M. *1776
*George Glentworth, M. D. Edinb., A. M.
*Charles Inglis, (Rev.), A.M., S. T. D. elsewhere, Bishop P. E. Ch. Nov. Scot., Governor King's Coll. aet. 82. *1816
*Hugh Neill, A. M.
*John Ogilvie, (Rev.), Yale 1748, A.M. and Yale, S.T.D. 1770 and Aberd., Gov. King's Coll. 1770-4. *1774
*John Tyler, (Rev.), A. B., A. M. 1769. *1823

7

## 1768.

*Samuel Bard, M. D. and Edinb. 1765, LL.D. N.Jers. 1815, Prof. Theor. and Pract. Med. 1767-76 and of Midw. 1770-6, Prof. Chem. 1784-5, 1786-7, Dean Med. Fac. 1792-1804. *1821
*Samuel Clossy, M. D. and Trin. Coll. Dub., Prof. Anat. 1767-76.
*Myles Cooper, (Rev.), Oxford, LL.D. and Ox., Prof. Mor. Phil. 1762-3, President 1763-75. *1785
*John Jones, M. D. and Rheims, Prof. Surg. 1767-76. *1791
*Peter Middleton, M. D. and St. And., Prof. Path. and Physiol. 1767-76 and Mat. Med. and Chem. 1770-6, Governor King's Coll.

5

## 1769.

*Ebenezer Kneeland, (Rev.), Yale 1761, A. M. *1777

## 1770.

*Thomas Barton (Rev.), A.M.
*Robert Blackwell, (Rev.), A. B. and N. Jers. 1768. A. M. N. Jers., S. T. D. N. Jers. and Univ. Penn. 1788.

2

## 1771.

*Jonathan Boucher, (Rev.), A. M.

## 1772.

*Edmund Fanning, Yale 1757, A. M. and Yale and Harv. 1764, J. C. D. Oxford, 1774, LL. D. Yale 1803 and Dart. 1803, Surveyor Genl. Prov. N. Y. 1776, Lt.-Gov. Nov. Scot., Gov. Prince Edw. Isl. *1818

## 1773.

*Isaac Hunt, Phila., A. M.
*Joseph Lamson, (Rev.), Yale 1741, A.M. and Yale. *1773
*John Marshall, (Rev.), A.M.
*Harry Monroe, (Rev.), A.M.
*John Stuart, (Rev.), A. M.

5

## 1774.

*Luke Babcock, Yale 1755, A. M. and Yale. *1777
*George Panton, (Rev.), Aberd., A. M.
*James Sayre, (Rev.), Phila. Coll. A. M. aet. 53. *1798
*William Tryon, LL. D., Governor of the Province of New York. *1788

4

## 1787.

*James Hardie, A. B., A. M. 1790.

## 1788.

*Robert Annan, (Rev.), A.M.
*William Cochran, (Rev.), Trin. Coll. Dub., A. M., Prof. Greek and Lat. Lang. 1784–9.
*Robert Charles Johnson, Yale 1783, A. M. and Yale. *1806
*Samuel Latham Mitchill, M. D. Univ. Edinb. 1786, A. M., LL. D. elsewhere, Memb. N.Y. Assemb. 1790–2 and 1797-9, Prof. Bot. 1792–5 and Prof. Nat. Hist. Chem. and Agricult. 1792–1801, Repr. in Congr. 1801–3 and 1810–12, U. S. Sen. 1804–10, elected Prof. Chem. Coll. Phys. and Surg. N. Y. 1807 and declined, Prof. Nat. Hist. Coll. Phys. and Surg. N. Y. 1808–20 and Prof. Bot. and Mat. Med. 1820–6, Vice-Prest. Rutg. Med. Coll. N.Y. 1826–30. *1831
*John W. Watkins, A. M.

5

## 1789.

*Roger Alden, Yale 1773, A. M. and Yale. *1836
*Abraham Beach, (Rev.), Yale 1757, S. T. D., Trus-

tee 1787–1813 and Clerk 1795–1811. *1828
*John Daniel Gross, (Rev.), S. T. D., Regent Univ. N.Y. S. 1784–7, Trustee 1787–92, Prof. Germ. Lang. and Geogr. 1784–95, and Prof. Mor. Phil. 1787–95.
*Jacob Rutsen Hardenbergh, (Rev.), A. M. N. Jers. 1770, S. T. D., Prest. Rutg. Coll. *1790
*Samuel William Johnson, Yale 1779, A.M. and Yale. *1846
*William Linn, (Rev.), N. Jers. 1772, S. T. D., Regent Univ. N. Y. S. 1787–1808. *1808
6

## 1790.

*Henry Maeller, (Rev.), A.M.
*James Proudfit, (Rev.), A.M.
2

## 1793.

*Ebenezer Dibble, (Rev.), Yale 1734, S. T. D. *1799
*Andrew Jaffray, (Rev.), S. T. D.
*William Ogilvie, LL. D., Prof. Human. Univ. Aberd.
3

## 1794.

*Richard Channing Moore, (Rev.), A. M., S.T.D. Dart. 1805, Bishop P. E. Ch. Va. 1814–41. aet. 79. *1841

## 1795.

John Campbell, A. M.
*John Coffin, Dart. 1791, A.M. and Dart. and N. Jers. 1795 and Yale 1798. *1852
2

## 1797.

*James Kent, Yale, 1781 and A. M. Yale, LL. D. and Harv. 1810 and Dart. 1819. N. Y. Leg. 1790–94 and 1796, Prof. Law 1793–98 and 1823–47, Mast. in Chanc. N. Y. C. 1793, Recorder N. Y. C. 1797, Judge Sup. Ct. N. Y. 1798–1814 and Ch. Just. N. Y. 1804–14, Regent Univ. N. Y. S. 1800–17, Chanc. N.Y. 1814–23, Trustee 1823. aet. 85. *1847
*Samuel Andrew Law, (Rev.), Yale 1792, A. M. and Yale and N. Jers. 1797. *1845
2

## 1798.

William Best (Rev.), A. M.
William Scott, (Rev.), A. M.
Andrew Smith, A. M.
Robert G. Wetmore, (Rev.), A. M. 4

## 1802.

William Duke, (Rev.), A. M.
*James Kemp, (Rev.), S. T. D., Bishop P. E. Ch. Maryland 1814–27. *1827
2

## 1804.

*Edmund D. Barry, (Rev.), A. M.
Edward Jenkins, (Rev.), S.T. D. and Brown Univ. 1803.
Jacob Larzelere, (Rev.), A.M.
*Peter Stryker, (Rev.), A.M. *1847
4

## 1805.

Clement Meriam, (Rev.), A. M.

## 1806.

*William James Macneven, M. D. and Univ. Vienna 1783, Prof. Mat.Med. Rutg. Med. Coll. N. Y. *1841

## 1809.

Abraham Bronson, (Rev.), A. M.

## 1811.

*John Croes, (Rev.), A. M. N. Jers. 1797, S. T. D., Bishop P. E. Ch. N. Jers. 1815-32. *1832
James Hall, (Rev.), S. T. D.
*William Harris, (Rev.),Harv. 1786 and A.M.Harv.,S.T.D. and Harv. 1811, President 1811-29, Trustee 1811-29 and Clerk 1811. *1829
3

## 1815.

*Frederic Beasley, (Rev.), N. Jers. 1797 and A. M. N. Jers., S. T. D. and Univ. Penn. 1815, Tutor N. Jers. 1798-1800, Provost Univ. Penn. 1815. *1845

## 1816.

*John Schureman, (Rev.), Rutg. Coll. 1795 and A.M. Rutg. and N. Jers. 1801, S. T. D., Prof. Eccles. Hist. and Past. Theol. in Theol. Sem. N. Brunsw. N. J. *1818

## 1818.

*Robert Adrain, LL.D., Prof. Math. and Nat. Phil. Rutg. 1810-13, Prof. Math. and Nat. Phil. 1813-25, Prof. Math. Univ. Penn. 1827-34. *1843
*Joseph Hopkinson, Univ. Penn. 1786, LL. D. and N. Jers. 1818 and Harv. 1831, Judge U. S. Dist. Ct. Penn. *1842
Samuel Nichols, (Rev.), Yale 1811, A. M.
Andrew Thomson, (Rev.), S. T. D.
4

## 1819.

*Thomas Church Brownell, (Rev.), Union 1804, S.T.D. and Union 1819, LL. D. elsewhere, Bishop P.E. Ch. Conn. 1819-65, Prest. Trin. Coll. 1824-31. *1865
*Philander Chase, (Rev.), Dart. 1796, S. T. D., Prest. Ken. Theol. Sem., Prest. Ken. Coll., Bishop P.E. Ch. Ohio 1819-52. aet. 76. *1852
John Philip, (Rev.), S. T. D. and N. Jers. 1820.
3

## 1820.

William Forrest, A. M.

## 1821.

*Thaddeus Fiske, (Rev.),

Harv. 1785 and A. M. Harv., S. T. D. *1855

*Washington Irving, A. M., LL.D.1829 and Harv. 1832, J. C. D. Ox. 1831, Memb. of several learned Societies. Regent Univ. N.Y. S. 1835–42, Secy. U. S. Leg. Lond., U. S. Min. to Spain, 1842–46. aet. 76. *1859

Daniel McDonald, (Rev.), S. T. D. 3

## 1822.

*William Lowndes, LL. D., Repr. in Congress, U. S. Sen.

*Thomas Lyell, (Rev.), A. M. Brown 1803, S. T. D. *1848

*Alexis P. Proal (Rev.), A.M.

John Reed, (Rev.), Union 1805 and A. M. Union, S. T. D.

*Stephen N. Rowan (Rev.), Union 1804 and A. M. Union, S. T. D. *1835

John Walsh, A. M.

6

## 1823.

John Carroll, A. M.

Abraham N. Halsey, A. M.

*Chauncey Lee, (Rev.), Yale 1784 and A. M. Yale, S. T. D. *1842

*Edward Livingston, N. Jers. 1781 and A. M. N. Jers., LL. D. and Transyl. 1824 and Harv. 1834, Trustee 1793–1806, Repr. in Congr. 1794–1801 and 1823–9, U. S. Dist.-Atty. N. Y. 1801–3, Mayor N. Y. C. 1801–3, Secy. St. U. S. 1831–3. U.S. Min. to France 1833–5. *1836

*John Stark Ravenscroft, (Rev.), S. T. D. Bishop P. E. Ch. N. Car. 1823–30. *1830

*Nathan Sandford, LL.D.,U. S. Dist.-Atty. N. Y. 1803–16, Memb. N. Y. Assemb. 1811 and Speaker of the same, N. Y. Sen., U. S. Sen. 1816–22 and 1825–31, Memb. N. Y. Constit. Conven. 1821, Chancell. N. Y. 1823–25. *1838

*John Savage, Union 1799 LL. D. and Union 1829, Ch. Justice Sup. Ct. N. Y.

Samuel Seabury, (Rev.), A. M., S. T. D. 1837, Prof. Bibl. Learn. and Interp. Script. Gen. Theol. Sem. P. E. Ch.

*Ambrose Spencer, Harv. 1783, LL. D. and Univ. Penn. 1819 and Harv. 1821, Memb. N.Y. Assemb. 1793–5, N. Y. Sen. 1795–1802, Atty.-Gen. N. Y. 1802–4, Regent Univ. N.Y.S. 1805–17, Judge Sup. Ct. N. Y. 1804–19 and Ch.-Just. of the same 1819–23, Repr. in Congr. *1848

9

## 1824.

*Langdon Cheves, LL. D., Repr. in Congr. and Speaker, Supr. Judge S. Car., Prest. U. S. Bank, Ch. Commr. U.S. under Treaty of Ghent. *1857

William A. Clark, (Rev.), A. M.

*James Fenimore Cooper, A. M. *1851

*Thomas Addis Emmet,Trin. Coll. Dub. LL. D., Atty.-Gen. N. Y. *1827

*Ernest Lewis Hazelius, (Rev.), S. T. D. and Union 1824. *1853

*Levi Silliman Ives, (Rev.), Hamilton Coll., A. M., S.T.

D. 1831, Bishop P. E. Ch. N. Car. 1831–53. aet. 70. *1867
*James Kirke Paulding, A. M., Nav. Off. N. Y., Secy. U. S. Navy 1837–41. *1860
*Daniel Webster, Dart. 1801 and A. M. Dart. and Harv. 1804, LL. D. and N. Jers. 1818 and Dart. 1824 and Harv. 1824, Memb. of several learned Soc., Repr. in Congr. 1813–17 and 1823–25, Memb. Mass. Constit. Conven. 1820, U. S. Sen. 1826–41 and 1845–50, Secy. St. U.S. 1841–43 and 1850–52. *1852

8

## 1825.

*John Caldwell Calhoun, Yale 1804, LL. D. and Hamilt. 1821 and Yale 1822, Memb. S. C. Leg., Rep. in Congr. 1811–17, Secy. War U. S. 1817–24, Vice-Prest. U. S. 1825–32, U S. Sen. 1832–43 and 1845–50, Secy. St. U. S. 1844–45. *1850
*Stephen Elliot, Yale 1791, LL. D. and Yale 1819 and Harv. 1822, Memb. S. C. Leg., Prof. Nat. Hist. and Bot. S. C. Med. Coll. *1830
Henri L. P. F. Peneveyre, (Rev.), S. T. D.
*Joel Roberts Poinsett, LL. D., Repr. in Congr. 1821–27, U.S. Min. to Mex. 1828–30, Secy. War U. S. 1837–41. *1851
William Shelton, A. M.

5

## 1826.

*William Wirt Phillips, (Rev.), Union 1813, S. T. D., Trustee N. Jers. Coll., Prest. Board For. Miss. Presbyt. Ch. *1865

## 1827.

*Jasper Adams, (Rev.), Brown 1815 and A. M. Brown and Yale 1819, S. T. D., Tutor Brown 1818–19, Prof. Math. and Nat. Phil. Brown 1819–24, Prest. Genev. Coll. 1827, Prest. Charleston S. C. Coll. and Prof. Mor. Phil., Prof. Eth. Milit. Acad. U. S. *1841
William Rollinson Whittingham, (Rev.), A. M., S.T.D. 1837, Prof. in Gen. Theol. Sem. P. E. Ch. N.Y., Bishop P. E. Ch. Maryland 1840–.

2

## 1828.

*Asa Eaton, (Rev.), Harv. 1803 and A. M. Harv. and Brown 1818, S. T. D. *1858
*Charles Taylor Catlin, Yale 1822, A. M. and Yale. aet. 67. *1870
William Buell Sprague, (Rev.), Yale 1815 and A. M. Yale 1819, S. T. D. and Harv. 1848.

3

## 1829.

Antoine Verren, (Rev.), A.M. Prof. French Lang. and Lit. 1828–39.

## 1830.

*James Marsh, (Rev.), Dart. 1817 and A.M. Dart. S. T.D. and Amh. 1833, Tutor Dart. 1818–20, Prof. Lang. Hamp. Syd. Coll. Prest. and Prof. Mor. Phil. and Met. Univ. Vt. *1842
*Frederic Christian Schaeffer,

(Rev.), A. M. N. Jers. 1818, S. T. D., Prof. Germ. Lang. and Lit. 1830–31. *1831
*William D. Snodgrass, (Rev.), Wash. Coll. Penn., A. M. N. Jers. 1822, S. T. D.
*William Murray Stone, (Rev.), S. T. D., Bishop P. E. Ch. Md. 1830–38. *1838

4

## 1831.

*Eli Baldwin, (Rev.), S.T.D. *1839
*James Ryan, A. M.
James Shea, A. M.
George Upfold, (Rev.), Union 1814, M.D. Coll. Phys. and Surg. N. Y. 1816, S. T. D., LL. D. elsewhere, Bishop P. E. Ch. Ind. 1849.

4

## 1832.

* Francis Lister Hawks, (Rev.), Univ. N. Car. 1815, A. M. Yale 1818, S. T. D., LL. D. elsewhere. *1866

## 1833.

*Charles Burroughs, (Rev.), Harv. 1806, and A.M. Harv. and Dart. 1811, S. T. D. *1851
*George Washington Doane, (Rev.), Union 1818, S. T. D. and Trin. 1833, LL. D. elsewhere, Prof. Rhet. and Orat. Trin. Coll. 1824–28, Prest. Burlington Coll. N. J., Bishop P. E. Ch. N. Jers. 1832–59. *1859
*James Emott, A. M., Union 1800, LL. D. *1850
*James Hervey Otey, (Rev.), S. T. D., Bishop P. E. Ch. Tenn. 1834–63. *1863
John H. Pinder (Rev.), S. T. D., Principal of Codrington Coll. Isl. Barbad.
*David Prentice, Yale 1812, A. M. and Yale, LL. D. Union 1839, Prof. Greek and Lat. Lang. Genev. Coll. *1857

6

## 1834.

Orange Clark, (Rev.), A. M.
Thomas Winthrop Coit, (Rev.), Yale 1821 and A.M. Yale 1831, S. T. D., LL.D. Trin. 1853, Prest. Trans. Univ., Prof. Eccl. Hist. Trin. Coll.
Don Thomas Gener, LL. D., Prest. Cortes of Spain.
Robert J. Harvey, A. M.
William Augustus Muhlenberg, (Rev.), S. T. D.
William Sherwood, (Rev.), A. M.

6

## 1835.

*Benjamin Clark Cutler, (Rev.), Brown 1822 and A. M. Brown, S. T. D. *1863
Manuel Fetter, A. B., A. M. 1842, Prof. Greek Lang. and Lit. Univ. N. Carolina.
* William Gaston, N. Jers. 1796 and A. M. N. Jers., LL. D., and Univ. Penn. 1819 and Harv. 1826 and Univ. N. Y. C. 1834 and N. Jers. 1835, N. Car., Sen., Judge Sup. Ct. N. Car., Repr. in Congr. *1844
James Neilson Reynolds, A. M.

4

## 1836.

* Benjamin Hale (Rev.),

Bowd. 1818 and A. M. Bowd. and Dart. 1827, M. D. Dart. 1827, S. T. D. Prof. Chem. and Min. and Med. Juris. Dart. 1827–35, President Genev. Coll. aet. 66. *1863
Benjamin Luckock, (Rev.), A. M.
*Jacob Sutherland, Yale 1807, LL. D., Judge Sup. Ct. N. Y. *1845

3

# 1837.

John Bethune (Rev.), S.T.D.
William Cullen Bryant, A.M. and Will. 1819, LL. D. Union 1853.
*John Duer, LL. D., Memb. N. Y. Constit. Conven. 1821, Trustee 1823-30, Just. Supr. Ct. N. Y. C. 1849–57 and Ch.-Just. same 1857–8. *1858
*George Griffin, Yale 1797, LL. D. *1860
*Fitz-Greene Halleck, A. M. *1867
*Charles Fenno Hoffman, A. M.
Theodore Irving, (Rev.), A. M., LL. D., Union 1851, Prof. Belles-Lettr. Geneva Coll. 1837.
Samuel Allen McCoskry, (Rev.), Dickin. Coll. 1823 and A. M. Dickinson, S. T. D., D. C. L. Univ. Oxf., Bishop P. E. Ch. Mich. 1836–.
*Erskine Mason (Rev.), Dickins. Coll. Penn. 1823 and A. M. Dickin., S. T. D.
*David B. Ogden, LL. D., Trustee 1815–49 and Chn. of Board 1843–49. *1849
*Thomas House Taylor, (Rev.), S. T. D. *1867
*Samuel A. Van Vranken, (Rev.), S. T. D.

12

# 1838.

*Isaac Boyle, (Rev.), Harv. 1813 and A. M. Harv., S. T. D. and Trin. 1838. *1850
Walter Chisholm, A. M.
*Leonidas Polk (Rev.), U. S. Mil. Acad. 1829, S. T. D., Bishop P. E. Ch. Ark. 1838–41, and Bishop of Louisania 1841–64. aet. 58. *1864

3

# 1839.

Wm. M. Carmichael (Rev.), S. T. D.
Abraham Halsey, A. M.

2

# 1840.

John Watson Adams (Rev.), S. T. D.
*Stephen Elliott, (Rev.), Harv. 1824 and A. M. Harv., S. T. D., and Trin. 1840, Bishop P. E. Ch. Georgia 1841–66. *1866
Abraham Bruyn Hasbrouck, Yale 1810 and A. M. Yale 1819, LL. D. and Union 1841, Repr. in Congr., Prest Rutg. Coll.
William Hawkesworth, A.M., Prof. Lang. S. Car. Coll. 1840.
*Hugh Swinton Legaré, (C.L.) S. C. Coll. 1814, LL. D., Memb. S. C. Leg. 1824–30, Atty.-Gen. S. C. 1830–2, Chargé d'Aff. U. S. at Brussels 1832–36, Repr. in Congr. 1836–38, Atty.-Gen. U. S. 1841–43. *1843
*William Hickling Prescott, Harv. 1814 and A.M. Harv., LL. D. and Univ. N. Car.

1841 and Harv. 1843, J. C. D. Oxford 1850, Memb. of many learned societies. *1859
6

## 1841.

*Albert Gallatin, Univ. Genev. Switz. 1779, LL. D., Memb. Penn. Constit. Conven. 1789, Memb Penn. Leg. 1790–2, Repr. in Congr. 1795–1801, Secy. Treas. U. S. 1801–13, U. S. Commr. at Ghent 1814, U. S. Min. to France, 1815–23, U. S. Env. Ex. to Gr. Britain 1826–7, Prest. Council Univ. N.Y.C. 1830, Prest. N. Y. Hist. Society 1843–9. *1849
C. H. Gottsberger, A. M.
Samuel Nelson, LL. D., Just. Sup. Ct. U. S.
William M. Thompson, A. M.
4

## 1842.

Gustavus Abeel, (Rev.), Union 1823 and A. M. Union S. T. D.
James J. Bowden, A. B.
*Charles W. Hackley, (Rev.), U. S. Mil. Acad. 1829, A.M., S.T.D. elsewhere, A.A.Prof. Maths. U.S. Mil. Acad. 1829–31, 1832–33, Prof. Maths. Univ. N.Y.C. 1833–39, Prest. Jeff. Coll. Miss. 1839, Prof. Math. and Astr. 1843–57, Prof. Astr. 1857–61. *1861
Edward Y. Higbee, (Rev.), A. M., S. T. D. 1843.
George C. Schaeffer, A. M., M. D. elsewhere, Librarian 1839–47, Professor Chem. Georget. Coll. Kent.
John H. Shepherd, A. M.
6

## 1843.

John M. Duncan, (Rev.), S. T. D.
George E. Hare, (Rev.), Union 1826, S. T. D.
Daniel Stone, A.M., Prof. Anc. Lang. West. Univ. Penn. 1843. 3

## 1844.

Edward E. Ford, (Rev.), S. T. D.
Joseph W. Ingraham, A. M.
Charles G. McLean, (Rev.), S. T. D.
*Ambrose Seymour Todd, (Rev.), A. M. Yale 1824, S. T. D. *1861
Charles E. West, A. M. Princ. Rutg. Female Instit. N. Y. C. 1844. 5

## 1845.

*Daniel Dewey Barnard, Will. 1818, LL. D. and Geneva and Brown, 1853, Repr. in Congr., U. S. Min. at Brussels. *1861
Edward Cooper, A. M.
Charles Hewitt, A. M.
John W. McCullough, (Rev.), S. T. D.
Horatio Southgate, (Rev.). Bowd. 1832 and A.M. Bowd., S. T.D. and Trin. Coll. 1846, Bishop P. E. Ch. Constantinople 1844–.
*Bird Wilson, (Rev.), S. T. D. elsewhere, LL.D., Prof. Gen. Theol. Sem. P. E. Ch. 6

## 1846.

William Bayard Blackwell, A. M.

Ezra A. Huntington, (Rev.), Union 1833, S. T. D.

2

## 1847.

William Ingraham Kip, (Rev.), Yale 1831 and A.M. Yale and Trin. 1846, S. T. D., Bishop P. E. Ch. Californ. 1853–.

Joseph Henry Price (Rev.), Brown 1825 and A. M. Brown, S. T. D.

*John Canfield Spencer, Union 1806, LL. D. and Union 1849, Mast. inChanc. 1811, Dist. Atty. West. Dist. N. Y., Repr. in Congr. 1817–19, Memb. N. Y. Assemb. 1819–24 and Speaker of the same 1820, N. Y. Sen. 1824–26, Secy. St. N. Y. 1839–41, Secy. War U. S. 1841–43, Secy. Treas. U. S. 1843–44, Regent Univ. N. Y. S. 1840–44. *1855

3

## 1848.

Francis Vinton, (Rev.), U. S. Mil. Acad. 1830, A. B. Brown Univ. 1833, S. T. D., LL. D. Will. Coll. 1869, elected Bishop P. E. Ch. Indiana 1847 and declined, Prof. Divin. Gen. Theol. Sem. P. E. Ch. N.Y. 1869–.

## 1849.

George Alexander Crook, A.M

James Stephenson, (Rev.), A. M.

Horace Webster, U. S. Mil- Acad. 1818, A. M. N. Jers. 1823, LL. D. and Keny. Coll. 1842, M. D. Univ. Penn. 1850, Asst. Prof. Math. U. S. Mil. Acad. 1818–25, Prof. Math. Geneva Coll. 1825–48, Prest. Coll City N. Y. 1848–69.

3

## 1850.

*William Drisler, A. M. *1870

David X. Junkin, (Rev.), S. T. D., Prof. Belles Lettr. and Eng. Lit. Lafay. Coll. 1837–42, Prest. Wash. Coll. Va.

John Barrett Kerfoot, (Rev.), S. T. D., Rector St. James Coll. Md., Prest. Trin. Coll. 1864–65, Bishop P. E. Ch. Pittsburg 1865–.

Kendrick Metcalf, (Rev.), Dart. 1829. S. T. D., Prof. Greek and Lat. Lang. and Lit. Hobart.

*Winfield Scott, A. M. N. Jers. 1814, LL. D. and Harv. 1861, Maj.-Gen. and Bvt.-Lt.-Gen. U.S.A. aet. 80. *1866

Timothy D. Williams, A. M.

6

## 1851.

Francis H. Cuming, (Rev.), S. T. D.

*Martin P. Parks, (Rev.), S. T. D.

John Williams, (Rev.), S.T.D. and Union 1847, LL. D. Hobart 1870, Prest. Trin. Coll. 1848–53, Asst. Bishop P. E. Ch. Conn. 1851–65 and Bishop 1865–.

Octavius Winslow, (Rev.), S. T. D.

4

## 1852.

Stephen Alexander, Union 1824 and A. M. Union, LL. D., Prof. Math. and Astr. N. Jers.

Samuel Gilman Brown, (Rev.), Dart. 1831 and A. M. Dart., S. T. D., Prof. Rhet. and Polit. Lit. Dart. 1840–63 and Prof. Int. Phil. and Pol. Econ. 1863–66 and Prest. 1866–68, Prest. Ham. Coll. 1868–.

William B. Franklin, U. S. Mil. Acad. 1843, A. M., Prof. Nat. Phil. Free Acad. N. Y. C., Maj.-Gen. U.S.V.

Richard Pulling Jenks, Harv. 1830, A. M.

William McMurray, (Rev.), A. M. Trin. 1846, S. T. D.

John Rowland, (Rev.), A.M.

John Lee Watson, (Rev.), Harv. 1815 and A.M. Harv., S. T. D. 7

## 1853.

Talbot W. Chambers, (Rev.), S. T. D.

Thomas Frederick Davis, (Rev.), S. T. D.. Bishop P. E. Ch. S. C. 1853–.

Henry D. Erskine, (Rev.), A. M. elsewhere, S.T.D., Dean of Ripon, Eng.

Charles Todd Quintard, (Rev.), M. D. elsewhere, A. M., S. T. D. 1866, Prof. in Medical College, Memphis, Tenn., Bishop P. E. Ch. Tenn. 1865–.

Charles Rogers, (Rev.), LL. D., Fellow Scottish Soc. of Antiquarians, Prof. Eng. Lang. and Lit. Univ. Penn.

Samuel Pratt Strong, (Rev.), S. T. D. 6

## 1854.

William R. Gordon, (Rev.), S. T. D.

Jean Romer, A. M., LL. D. elsewhere, Prof. French Lang. and Lit. Free Acad. N. Y. C.

I. Jackson Scott, (Rev.), S. T. D.

Henry Philip Tappan, (Rev.), Union 1825, S. T. D. Union 1845, LL.D., Prof. Mor. and Int. Phil. Univ. N. Y. C. 1832–38, Chancell. Univ. Mich. 1850–63, Cor. Memb. Inst. of France 1856.

4

## 1855.

John M. Macauley, (Rev.), S. T. D.

Joseph Few Smith,† (Rev.), Yale 1840 and A. M. Yale, S. T.D., Prof. Sac. Lit. Aub. Theol. Sem.

2

## 1856.

John Blakely, (Rev.), S. T. D.

George Sharswood, LL. D., Ch.-Judge Dist. Ct. Penn., Prof. Instit. of Law Univ. Penn., Judge Sup. Ct. Penn. 1867–.

Richard Somers Smith, U. S. Mil. Acad. 1834, A.M., Prof. Maths., Eng. and Drawing, Brooklyn Polyt. Inst. 1855–59, Director Cooper Union N. Y. C. 1859–61, Major U. S. A. 1861–63, Prest. Girard Coll. Penn. 1863–.

† Known subsequently as Joseph Fewsmith.

Alfred Stubbs, (Rev.), Yale 1835, and A. M. Yale S. T. D.

4

## 1857.

Joseph Alden, (Rev.), Union 1829 and A. M. Union and N. Jers. 1832 and Will. 1837, S. T. D. Union 1839, LL.D., Tutor N. Jers. 1830–32, Prof. Rhet. Polit. Econ. and Hist. Will. 1835–52, Prof. Metaph. and Mor. Phil. Lafay. Coll., Prest. Jeff. Coll. Penn.

Alfred Baury Beach, (Rev.), Trin. Coll. 1841 and A. M. Trin., S. T. D.

Samuel Cooke, (Rev.), A. M. Yale 1847, S. T. D. and Univ. N. Y. C. 1857.

William Ferdinand Morgan, (Rev.), Union 1837 and A. M. Union and Trin., S. T. D. and Trin. 1849.

4

## 1858.

Charles D. Morris, A. M. and Oxford.

Samuel Spring, (Rev.), A. B. and A. M. Yale 1821, S. T. D.

Henry Waterman, (Rev.), Brown 1831, S. T. D.

*Isaac Dyckman Vermilye, (Rev.), A.M.

4

## 1859.

Thomas De Boice Coryell, Univ. Wis., A. M.

William Armstrong Dod, (Rev.), N. Jers 1838 and A. M. N. Jers. S. T. D., Tutor N. Jers. 1840–1, Lect. on Architect. and the Fine Arts N. Jers.

George H. Houghton, (Rev.), S. T. D., Instr. in Hebr. Gen. Theol. Sem. P. E. Ch. N. Y.

*Lot Jones, (Rev.), Bowd. 1821 and A. M. Bowd., S. T. D. *1865

Alexander G. Mercer, (Rev.), S. T. D.

Samuel Tyler, LL. D.

6

## 1860.

Charles P. Daly, LL. D., Just. Ct. Com. Pleas N. Y. C., Memb. N. Y. S. Constit. Conv. 1867.

Theodore W. Dwight, Hamilton and A. M. Hamilt., LL. D. and Rutg. Coll. 1859, Tutor Hamilt. 1842–46, Prof. Law Hist. Civ. Pol. and Pol. Econ. Hamilt. 1846–58, Prof. Munic. Law 1858–, and Warden Law Sch. 1864–, Memb. N. Y. Constit. Conv. 1867.

John W. French, (Rev.), Trin. 1832 and A. M. Trin., S. T. D., Prof. Ethics U. S. Mil. Acad.

Thomas Tompkins Guion, (Rev.), Trin. 1847, S. T. D.

Fordyce Mitchell Hubbard, (Rev.), Will. 1828 and A. M. Will., S. T. D. and Trin. 1860, Tutor Will. 1831–2, Prof. Lat. Lang. Univ. N. Car.

*Matthew Hall McAllister, LL. D., Judge U. S. Dist. Ct. Cal. *1865

William H. N. Stewart, (Rev,), Trin. Coll. Dub., A. M., LL D. Lafayette 1868.

Charles S. Tripler, M. D. Coll. Phys. and Surg. N. Y. 1827, A. M., Asst. Surg. U. S. A. 1830-38 and Surg. 1838-, Maj. and Bvt. Col. U. S. A.

Lewis Bartholomew Woodruff, Yale 1830 and A. M. Yale, LL D., Judge Supr. Ct. N. Y. C., Judge U. S. Circ. Ct. 1870-.

9

# 1861.

*Alexander Warfield Bradford, Union 1832 and A. M. Union, LL. D. and Union 1852, Corporation Atty. N. Y. C. 1843, Surrogate N .Y. C. 1848-58, Trustee 1855-67 aet. 52. *1867

Charles H. Hall, (Rev.), Yale 1862, S. T. D. and Hobart 1862.

*Abraham Lincoln, LL. D., President of the United States 1861-65. *1865

*Joseph C. Passmore, (Rev.), S. T. D., Prof. Rhet. Int. Phil. and Pol. Econ. St. James Coll. Md.

S. Chipman Thrall, (Rev.), S. T. D.

Sullivan H. Weston, (Rev.), S. T. D., Trustee Med. Dept. 1860-.

6

# 1862.

Henry P. Balcom, A. M. Supt. Pub. Sch. Middlet., Conn.

Samuel Buel, (Rev.), Will. 1833 and A. M. Will., S. T. D., Tutor Ken.

George Jarvis Geer, (Rev.), Trin. 1842 and A. M. Trin., S. T. D. and Union 1862.

Benjamin Nicholas Martin, (Rev.), Yale 1837 and A. M. Yale, S. T. D., Prof. Phil. and Hist. Univ. N. Y. C.

Henry Joel Scudder, Trin. 1846, A. M. and Trin.

John Cotton Smith, (Rev.), Bowd. 1847 and A. M. Bowd., S. T. D.

6

# 1863.

Samuel Hanson Cox, (Rev.), Univ. N. Y. C., A. M. Trin. 1852, S. T. D.

Samuel Eliot, Harv. 1839 and A.M. Harv. and Trin. 1857, LL.D., Prof. Hist. and Polit. Sci. Trin., elected Prof. Anc. and Mod. Lit. 1857 and declined, President Trin. Coll. 1860-4.

Jared B. Flagg, (Rev.), S. T. D.

Robert S. Howland, (Rev.), S. T. D.

Thomas Ricker Lambert, (Rev.), A. M. Brown 1845 and Trin. 1852, S. T. D.

Henry B. Walbridge, (Rev.), S. T. D.

6

# 1864.

Henry Stephens Cutler, Mus. D.

Joseph G. Fox, C. E. elsewhere, A. M., Prof. Math. Cooper Inst. N. Y. C.

Thomas Hunter, A. M.

3

# 1865.

Samuel Ely, (Rev.), S. T. D.

Richard Graham Hutton, (Rev.), A. M.

Andrew Johnson, LL.D., Vice-President of the United States 1865 and President 1865–69.
McWalter B. Noyes (Rev.), A. M.
Samuel S. Shedden, (Rev.), S. T. D.
James Tuttle Smith, (Rev.), A.M., Hosp. Chapl. U. S. A. 1862–65.
William H. Walter, Mus. D.
George D. Waters, (Rev.), S. T. D.
John Freeman Young, (Rev.), S. T. D., Bishop P. E. Ch. Florida 1867–.

9

## 1866.

Abner Jackson, (Rev.), Trin. Coll. 1837 and A. M. Trin., S. T. D. Trin. 1858, LL.D., Tutor Trin. 1837–38, and Libr. 1837–49, Adj. Prof. Greek and Lat. Lang. Trin. 1838-40, Lect. in Chem. and Nat. Sci. Trin. 1840–51 and Prof. Ethics and Metaphys. 1840–58, Prest. and Prof. Ev. Christ. Hobart Coll. Prest. Trin. Coll. 1867–.
Charles P. Kirkland, LL. D., Judge Sup. Court N. Y.
James Mulchahey, (Rev.), Trin. 1842 and A. M. Trin. S. T. D.

3

## 1867.

Samuel B. Bostwick, (Rev.), S. T. D.
William Croswell Doane, (Rev.), S. T. D., Bishop P. E. Ch. Albany 1868–.
Ferdinand Cartwright Ewer, (Rev.), Harv. 1848 and A. M. Harv. 1868, S. T. D.
Channing Moore Williams, (Rev.), S. T. D., Bishop P. E. Ch. China 1866–.

4

## 1868.

Philander Kinney Cady, (Rev.), S. T. D.
Benjamin Wistar Morris, (Rev.), S. T. D. Bishop P. E. Ch. Oregon and Washington 1868–.
Charles Franklin Robertson, (Rev.), Yale 1859, S. T. D. Bishop P. E. Ch. Missouri 1868–.

3

## 1869.

Charles Breck, (Rev.), S. T. D.
Theodore Augustus Eaton, (Rev.), S. T. D.
Asa Bird Gardner, (Rev.), Dart. 18—, A.M. and Dartmouth.
Thomas Williams Hughes, (Rev.), S.T.D., Prest. Univ. East Tenn.
William Quintard Ketchum, (Rev.), S. T. D.
Benson J. Lossing, A. M.
John Carpenter Smith, (Rev.), S. T. D.

7

## 1870.

Samuel Brazer Babcock, (Rev.), S. T. D.
George Marlow Everhart, (Rev.), S. T. D.

2

## ENUMERATION.

| | | |
|---|---|---|
| Graduates in Arts | 2109 | |
| Graduates in Medicine other than Graduates in Arts | 868 | |
| Graduates in Law other than Graduates in Arts | 487 | |
| Graduates in Mining other than Graduates in Arts | 37 | |
| Honorary Graduates, and Graduates of other Colleges admitted here to the same degree | 333 | |
| | —— | 3834 |

### KNOWN TO BE DECEASED.

| | | |
|---|---|---|
| Graduates in Arts | 910 | |
| Graduates in Medicine, as above | 38 | |
| Graduates in Law, as above | 6 | |
| Honorary Graduates, and others, as above | 159 | |
| | —— | 1113 |
| Presumed to be living | | 2721 |

# ROLL OF ALUMNI

WHO SERVED IN THE

# ARMY OR NAVY OF THE UNITED STATES, 1861-1865.

## 1826.

Thomas Swords, Jr.,
Brig.-General U. S. A.

## 1828.

Thomas T. Devan,
Hospital Chaplain U. S. A., 1862.

## 1833.

*Philip Kearny, Jr.,
Brig.-General U. S. Vols., May 17, 1861; Major-General, July 4, 1862. Killed at the battle of Chantilly, Va., Sept. 1, 1862.

## 1834.

Robert S. Swords,
Lieut.-Colonel 13th N. Jersey Vols.

## 1838.

*Thomas Colden Cooper,
Captain U. S. Vols. Killed at the battle of the "Wilderness," 1864.

## 1839.

John Jacob Astor, Jr.,
Colonel U. S. Vols., and Volunteer A. D. C. on staff of Maj.-General McClellan, Nov., 1861–July, 1862. Resigned July, 1862. Brevet Brig.-General U. S. Vols., 1866, for meritorious services on the Peninsula.

## 1841.

*Robert Le Roy, Jr.,
Captain U. S. Vols., A. A. G. on staff of Gen. McCook. Died of chronic diarrhœa, March 5, 1865.

## 1842.

Edward Elmer Potter,
Captain U. S. Vols. and C. S. on staff of Gen. J. G. Foster, Dec., 1861; Brig.-General, Chief of Staff to Gen. Foster, Jan., 1863; Brevet Major-General, June, 1865. Resigned, July, 1865.

## 1847.

John Moneypenny, Jr.,
Surgeon 123d N. Y. S. Vols.

## 1848.

Cornelius Low King,
1st Lieutenant 14th U. S. Infantry, May, 1861; Captain 30th U. S. Infantry; Brevet Major and Lieut.-Colonel U. S. A., for the battles of the "Wilderness" and "Spottsylvania." Still in service.

## 1849.

Churchill John Cambreling,
Private 7th Regt. N. Y. S. M., April, 1861; Lieutenant 5th N. Y. S. Vols; Captain, Sept., 1861; Major —— Regt. N. Y. S. Vols., 1862. Resigned 1862, in consequence of sickness contracted in the field.

*William Morrow Knox,
Asst.-Surgeon 78th Penn. Vols. Died April 28, 1862, from fracture of the skull.

John Shrady, Jr.,
Acting Asst.-Surgeon U. S. A., May 4, 1862; Surgeon 2d East Tenn. Inf., Oct. 18, 1862. Mustered out Oct. 8, 1864.

## 1850.

Matthew M. Blunt,
Major U. S. A.

## 1851.

Edward S. Hoffman,
Surgeon 90th N. Y. S. Vols.

*A. Henry Thurston,
Surgeon 12th Regt. N. Y. S. M., April, 1861; Brigade Surgeon U. S. Vols., Sept., 1861; Medical Director U. S. Vols. Died in 1865, while in service.

William G. Ward,
Lieut.-Colonel 12th Regt. N. Y. S. M., April 21, 1861-July, 1861; Colonel, May, 1862. Taken prisoner at Harper's Ferry, Va., Sept. 15, 1862.

## 1852.

John H. Pell.

Eugene Thorn,
Corporal 71st Regt. N. Y. S. M., April 20, 1861-May, 1861; 2d Lieutenant, May, 1861-July 30, 1861; 1st Lieutenant, May 28, 1862-July, 1862; Captain, July, 1862-Sep. 2, 1862.

Eustace Trenor,
Surgeon N. Y. S. Vols.

*John Trenor, Jr.,
Asst.-Surgeon 2d N. Y. Vol. Cavalry; Asst.-Surgeon U. S. V., March 11, 1863; Surgeon, Oct., 1863-Dec., 1863. Died at sea, July 7, 1867.

## 1854.

Edward Kirkland,
Sergeant 71st Regt. N. Y. S. M., April 20, 1861-July 30, 1861; Sergeant-Major, May 28, 1862-Sept. 2, 1862, June, 1863-Aug., 1863.

Elias J. Marsh,
Asst.-Surg. U. S. A., 1861-; Medical Director U. S. V.

*Orlando H. Morris,
Major 66th N. Y. Vols., 1861; Colonel. Killed in battle, 1864.

*James Cortlandt Parker,
2d Lieut. 4th N. Y. Battery, 1861-June 4, 1862. Died of typhoid fever at Bottom's Bridge, Va., June 4, 1862.

Stewart L. Woodford,
Lieut.-Colonel 127th N. Y. Vols., Aug., 1862; Chief of Staff, Dept. of the South, Feb., 1865; Colonel 103d U. S. C. T., Feb., 1865; Bvt. Brig.-General U. S. V. 1865; and assigned to duty as Brig.-General. Resigned in 1866.

## 1855.

James R. Hosmer,
Private 8th Md. Vols., Aug., 1862; Capt. and A. Q. M. on Maj.-Gen. Sheridan's Staff, May-Dec., 1864.

## 1856.

Edwin S. Babcock,
Captain 2d N. J. Vols., April, 1861–July, 1861; Lieut.-Colonel 27th N. J. Vols, 1861–62; Captain 9th Regt. U.S. Colored Troops, 1862–May, 1865. Resigned May, 1865.

Charles A. Bacon,
In service U. S. San. Comm., May–July, 1862.

Charles N. Clark,
— Regt. Iowa Vols.

Whittingham Cox,
Private 7th Regt. N.Y.S.M., May, 1862; 2d Lieutenant 14th U. S. Infantry; 1st Lieutenant. Still in service.

Robert Livingston Cutting.

William R. Hyslop,
Captain 32d N. Y. Vols.

Charles C. Suydam,
1st Lieutenant 5th N. Y. Cavalry, Oct. 31, 1861–March 6, 1862; Captain and A.A.G., March 6, 1862–Aug. 20, 1862; Lieut.-Colonel and A. A.G. 4th Army Corps, Aug. 20, 1862–Aug. 10, 1863, and A. A. G. Cavalry Corps, "Army of the Potomac," Sept. 16, 1863–Jan. 8, 1864; Lieut.-Colonel 3d N. J. Cavalry, Jan. 16, 1864–Nov. 15, 1864. Resigned Nov. 15, 1864, on account of illness.

William Gracie Ulshoeffer,
Private 7th Regt. N.Y.S.M., April 19, 1861–June, 1861; 1st Lieutenant and Adjutant 36th N. Y. Vols., June 1861–Dec. 4, 1861; Captain, Dec. 4, 1861–Sept. 10, 1862; Captain and A. A. A.G. Deven's Brigade, 3d Div. 6th Army Corps, Sept. 10, 1862–Oct., 1862; Captain and A. D. C. to Brig.-General John Newton, Oct., 1862–July 15, 1863. Mustered out July 15, 1863.

## 1857.

Henry Eugene Davies, Jr.,
Captain 5th N. Y. Vols., April 20, 1861; Major 2d N. Y. Cavalry, July, 1861; Lieut.-Colonel, Dec. 6, 1862; Colonel, June 16, 1863; Brig.-General U.S. Vols., Sept. 17, 1863; Bvt. Major-General, Oct. 2, 1864; Major-General, April 6, 1865. Resigned Feb. 1, 1866.

*W. Carey Massett,
Captain 61st N.Y. Vols., Aug., 1861; Major, 1861; Lieut.-Colonel. Killed at the battle of Fair Oaks, Va., May 31, 1862.

*Theodore Parkman,
Color-Bearer 45th Mass. Vols., Sept. 26, 1862–Dec. 16, 1862. Killed at the battle of Whitehall, N. C., Dec. 16, 1862.

William Renwick Smedberg,
1st Lieutenant 14th U. S. Infantry, May 14, 1861; Captain, Oct. 25, 1861; Bvt. Major U.S.A., July 2, 1863; Bvt. Lieut.-Colonel May 5, 1864. Still in service.

## 1858.

*Philip Mesier Lydig,
Volunteer A D. C. to Gen. Parke, Jan. 8, 1862; Capt. U.S.V. and A. D. C. to Gen. Burnside, April, 1862; Major and Adj.-General 9th Army Corps; Bvt. Lieut.-Colonel and Colonel U. S. V. Resigned April 24, 1865.

Gilbert T. Totten,
Asst. Surgeon 32d N.Y.S.V.

John Ward, Jr.,
Captain U.S.V.

## 1859.

William Jay, Jr.,
Brevet Lieut.-Colonel U.S.V.

*Stephen Richard Reynolds,
2d Lieutenant 99th N.Y.S.V., Dec. 16, 1861; 1st Lieutenant and Adjutant, Oct. 1, 1862; Captain U.S.V. and A.A.G. on Staff of General Wistar, June 23, 1863. Mortally wounded at the battle of Cold Harbor, Va., June 3, 1864, and died July 30, 1864.

J. Augustus Slipper,
Major U.S.V.

## 1860.

Robert P. Barry,
Captain 16th U. S. Infantry.

Clarence Stewart Brown,
Major U.S.V.

Edgar M. Cullen,
2d Lieutenant 1st U. S. Infantry, March 24, 1862; 1st Lieutenant, Sept. 20, 1863; Colonel 96th N. Y. S. V. Dec. 24, 1862–April 6, 1865.

Charles De Ruyter,
Private 7th Regt. N.Y.S.M., April, 1861–July, 1861, May, 1862–Aug. 1862.

John Haven Emerson.

George R. Fearing,
Volunteer A. D. C. on Staff of Gen. Burnside, Nov. 22, 1861; Captain U. S. V. and Additional A. D.C. April 4, 1862. Resigned Feb. 1, 1864. Brevet Major U. S. V., March 13, 1865.

Edmund Abdy Hurry,
Captain's Clerk to Commander Homer G. Blake, U.S.N., June, 1863–Nov., 1864.

*John William Jenks,
1st Lieutenant, Serrell's Engineer Regt. Died in 1861, of disease contracted in camp.

*Augustus F. King,
Private 7th Regt. N.Y.S.M., April 21, 1861–July, 1861. Died Aug. 11, 1862, of typhoid fever.

George Mason Miller,
Private 7th Regt. N.Y.S.M., May, 1862; Captain U.S.V. and A. A. G. on Staff of Gen. Meagher, July, 1862. Resigned Dec., 1862.

Richard Lewis Morris, Jr.,
Private 7th Regt. N.Y.S.M., April, 21, 1861; 1st Lieutenant 18th U. S. Infantry, — 1861; Captain; Brevet Major U. S. A. Still in service.

*Robert Troup Pell,
Private 7th Regt. N.Y.S.M., May, 1862–July 1862. Died April 18, 1868.

Eugene Hall Pomeroy,
Private 7th Regt. N.Y.S.M., April, 1861–July, 1861, May 1862–Aug., 1862, May, 1863–July, 1863.

*Frederick A. Tracy,
2d Lieutenant 12th U. S. Infantry, Oct. 26, 1861; 1st Lieutenant, Sep. 16, 1862. Died of typhoid fever, June 3, 1863.

## 1861.

James Benkard, Jr.,
Private 7th Regt. N.Y.S M., April 21, 1861; Captain U.S.V., on staff of Gen. King, 1861. Resigned 1864.

William Alexander Boyd,
Private 71st Regt. N.Y.S.M., April 20, 1861; Lieutenant and Adjutant 62d N.Y.S.V. Resigned 1862.

Edward Haight, Jr.,
Lieutenant 16th U.S. Infantry; Captain and A. D.C. on staff of Gen. Pope, 1862.

Charles Coolidge Haight,
Private 7th Regt. N.Y.S.M., May, 1862; Lieutenant and Adjutant 31st N.Y.S.V., 1863; Captain 39th N.Y.S.V. Resigned 1864.

William Richards Hillyer,
Private 2d N. Jers M., April 25, 1861; 1st Lieutenant 7th N. Jers. V., Oct. 2, 1861; Captain July 21, 1862. Discharged for disability resulting from exposure, Sept. 15, 1864.

Edward Mitchell,
Relief Agent U. S. Sanitary Commission, 1862–1864.

*Richard Cornelius Ray,
Lieutenant U.S.V., and A.D.C. on Staff of General Schuyler Hamilton, 1862. Died Feb. 5, 1863, of sickness contracted by exposure.

*William Alexander Rice,
Private 9th Regt. N.Y.S.M., April 21, 1861; Lieutenant, 1862. Resigned 1862. Died Oct. 9, 1866.

William Henry Russell, Jr.,
Lieutenant U.S.V., and A.D.C. to Gen. Vielé; Captain, and A.D.C. to Gen. Hooker. Resigned 1864.

John Ayscough Tucker,
Private 7th Regt. N.Y.S.M., April, 1861–July, 1861; May, 1862–Aug., 1862.

Samuel Baldwin Ward,
Acting Medical Cadet U. S. V., Sept. 12, 1862; Acting Asst.-Surgeon, July 18, 1864; Asst.-Surgeon, April 20, 1865. Mustered out Oct. 7, 1865.

Edward Walter West,
Private 7th Regt. N.Y.S.M., April 19, 1861; 2d Lieut. 4th R. I. Inf., Oct. 30, 1861; A.D.C. to Brig.-Gen. Casey, Nov. 1, 1861; 1st Lieut. 4th R. I. Inf., Nov. 8, 1861; appointed Capt. 2d R. I. Inf., Jan. 1, 1863, and declined; A.D.C. to Gen. Hooker, April 28, 1863, and to Gen. Heintzleman, May 30, and Judge Adv. Dept. of Washington, April; Lt.-Col. 33d N. J. V., Aug. 31, 1863, and declined; Private 14th Inf. U. S. A, Aug. 29, 1863, and Sergeant; 2d Lieut. 1st Artillery U. S. A., Oct. 3, 1863. Resigned, April 8, 1864.

## 1862.

*John Lawrence Churchill,
Private 7th Regt. N.Y.S.M., May, 1862–Aug., 1862; May, 1863–July, 1863; Lieut. U. S. A. Died at Jackson, Miss., Oct. 14, 1868.

Walter Cutting,
Captain U.S.V., June, 1862; Major, Dec., 1863; A. D. C. on Gen. Augur's staff.

Charles Dudley Fuller,
Private 22d Regt. N.Y.S.M.

George Wolfe Gillespie,
In U. S. service as Civil Engineer for three years.

Laurence Yvonnet Hopkins.

William Henry Jackson,
Private 7th Regt. N.Y.S.M., May, 1863–July, 1863.

*Henry Howard Marvin,
In the U. S. Engineer Corps, with the rank of Lieut.-Colonel, Aug, 1862–Aug., 1863. Died at Louisville, Aug. 25, 1863, of typhoid fever.

Cornelius Berrian Mitchell.

John Fulton Berrian Mitchell,
Captain 2d N. Y. Cavalry.

Foster Thayer,
U. S. Navy.

## 1863.

Daniel Frederick Boardman,
Private 7th Regt. N.Y.S.M.

Clifford Faitoute Eagle,
Private 22d Regt. N.Y.S.M., May–Sept., 1862; 1st Lieut. 1st U.S. Colored Troops, June, 1863, and Capt., May, 1864. Resigned, April, 1864.

Emile Henry Lacombe,
Private 7th Regt. N.Y.S.M., May, 1862–Aug., 1862; May, 1863–July, 1863.

Le Grand Lockwood, Jr.,
Private 22d N.Y.S.M.

James Allen Macdonald.

Stuyvesant Fish Morris,
Private 7th Regt. N.Y S.M., May, 1862–Aug., 1862; May, 1863–July, 1863.

James Brinckerhoff Pell,
Private 7th Regt. N.Y.S.M., May, 1862–Aug., 1862.

William Barnewall Schermerhorn,
Private 7th Regt. N.Y.S.M., May, 1862–Aug., 1862; May, 1863–July, 1863.

Charles William Terrett,
Private 7th Regt. N.Y.S.M., May, 1862–Aug., 1862; May, 1863–July, 1863.

Egbert Ward.

## 1864.

William Gardiner Appleton,
Private 22d Regt. N.Y.S.M.

*Henry Floy,
Private 71st Regt. N.Y.S.M., April, 30, 1861–July 30, 1861. Died July 17, 1866.

Alfred Perry McClellan.

Albert Edward Valentine,
Private 7th Regt. N.Y.S.M.

Marinus Willett, Jr.,
Private 71st Regt. N.Y.S.M., April, 20, 1861–July 30, 1861.

## 1865.

John Mcore Heffernan,
Private 22d Regt. N.Y.S.M., June-Sept., 1863.

*Julian James,
Lieutenant U.S.V., and A.D.C. on staff of Major-General Warren. Died.

William Neilson McVickar,
Private 22d N.Y.S.M.

George Webster Peck,
Private 22d Regt. N.Y.S.M., June-Sept. 1863.

Roderick Burt Seymour,
Private 22d Regt. N.Y.S.M., June, 1863-Sept., 1863; —— Regt. N.J. V., June, 1864-Sept., 1864.

Lenox Smith,
Private 71st Regt. N Y.S.M., April, 20, 1861-July 30, 1861.

Francis French Wilson,
Private 22d Regt. N.Y.S.M., June, 1863-Sept., 1863; —— Regt N.J. Vols., June 1864-Sept., 1864.

# INDEX OF OFFICERS.

# INDEX OF GRADUATES.

*h* indicates Honorary Graduates and Graduates of other Colleges who have been admitted to the same degree.
*l* indicates Graduates in Law, except those who have their places in the Catalogue as Graduates in Arts.
*m* indicates Graduates in Medicine, except those who have their places in the Catalogue as Graduates in Arts.
*m. e.* indicates Graduates in *Mining Engineering*, except those who have their places in the Catalogue as Graduates in Arts.

**Abbott,**
1846 R. S. Carden.
1869 Amos W. *m.*

**Abeel,**
1794 David G. *m.*
1822 George.
1842 Gustavus. *h.*

**Abrahams,**
1774 Isaac.

**Adams,**
1827 Jasper. *h.*
1840 John W. *h.*
1845 John K.
1864 John M.
1869 Charles A.

**Adee,**
1870 George A. *l.*

**Adler,**
1868 Isaac.
1870 Felix.

**Adrain,**
1818 Robert. *h.*

**Agnew,**
1810 John.
1849 Cornelius R.

**Aiken,**
1869 George H. *m.*

**Aims,**
1850 John M. G.

**Aitken,**
1868 Frederick M. *m.*

**Akerly,**
1804 Samuel.

**Al Burtis,**
1844 Clement W.

**Alden,**
1789 Roger. *h.*
1857 Joseph. *h.*

**Aldis,**
1837 Charles.

**Aldrich,**
1863 James H.

**Alexander,**
1852 Stephen. *h.*
1864 David W.

**Allaire,**
1805 Peter.
1869 Hal.

**Allen,**
1823, Christopher.
1823 Horatio.
1829 George F.
1833 Stephen D.
1834 William M.
1860 Thomas H. *m.*
1866 John J. *l.*

**Almon,**
1863 William B. *m.*
1867 Thomas R. *m.*

**Alverson,**
1867 Theodore F. *m.*

**American,**
1864 Samson. *m.*

**Ames,**
1842 Hector C.

**Ammerman,**
1812 Albert.

**Amory,**
1775 William.

**Anderson,**
1791 Peter.
1796 Alexander. *m.*
1810 Andrew.
1816 Abel T.
1818 Henry J.
1826 Charles E.
1845 James.
1853 Cornelius V. A.
1859 Edward H.
1863 Wendell A. *m.*
1865 Andrew. *m.*
1865 Calvin. *m.*
1867 Joseph H.
1870 Walden P.

**Anderton,**
1870 Edward K. *l.*

**Andress,**
1864 Theophilus H. *m.*

**Andrews,**
1762 Samuel. *h.*
1862 George P. *m.*
1863 James B. *l.*
1869 William H. *l.*

**Annan,**
1788 Robert. *h.*

**Anthon,**
1801 John.
1813 Henry.
1815 Charles.
1823 Edward.
1838 Frederic.
1839 Charles E.
1839 George C.
1851 John H.

**Anthony,**
1832 Henry T.
1838 Edward.

**Antill,**
1762 Edward.

**Applegate,**
1866 Lewis. *m.*

**Appleton.**
1864 William G.

**Arcularius,**
1868 Philip E. *m.*

**Arden,**
1844 John B.

**Armitage,**
1849 William E.

**Armstrong,**
1864 Richard. *l.*

**Arnold,**
1864 William P. *l.*
1868 John W. S.
1870 Lemuel H., Jr. *l.*

**Aspinwall,**
1809 Thomas S.

**Astor,**
1839 John J., Jr.
1849 William.

**Atkins,**
1868 Osmin W. *l.*

**Atkinson,**
1803 George H.
1808 William.
1869 Clinton. *m.*

**Atwater,**
1866 Edward S. *l.*

**Atwill,**
1862 Edward R.

**Atwood,**
1774† Thomas.
1870 J. Freeman. *m.*

Aub,
1870 Theodore. *l.*

Auchmuty,
1767 Samuel. *h.*
1774 Robert N.
1775 Richard.
1775 Samuel.

Auld,
1835 Jedediah B.

Austin,
1865 Harvey N. *m.*
1866 David P. *m.*

Averill,
1869 James K. *l.*

Avery,
1767 Ephraim. *h.*
1832 Walter T.
1866 Edward W. *m.*
1868 William A. *m.*

Aycrigg,
1824 Benjamin.

Ayer,
1866 James M. *m.*

Ayers,
1870 Daniel S., Jr. *m.*

Aymar,
1843 Benjamin N.

Ayres,
1856 William W.

Babcock,
1774 Lucas. *h.*
1849 Edward C.
1856 Edwin S.
1862 Francis.
1868 Henry D.
1870 Samuel B. *h.*

Backus,
1827 J. Trumbull.
1838 Mancer M.

Bacon,
1854 George W.
1856 Charles A.
1859 Richard S.
1867 Wilbur R. *l.*

Badger,
1861 George. *m.*
1861 William. *m.*

Bailey,
1802 Joseph. *m.*
1813 William.
1829 Theodore A.
1869 Charles H. *m.*

Bainbridge,
1789 John T.
1798 Joseph.

Baker,
1827 Jacob S.
1827 William S.
1862 Cyrus E. *m.*
1864 George W. *m.*
1867 James, Jr.
1870 George A., Jr., *l.*

Balch,
1860 Galnsha B. *m.*
1870 Lewis. *m.*

Balcom,
1862 Henry P. *h.*

Baldwin,
1831 Eli. *h.*
1856 Albert H.
1860 Daniel P. *l.*
1860 George V. N. *l.*
1866 Silas C. *m.*
1867 Charles H. *l.*
1867 John W. *m.*
1867 Truman H. *l.*

Ball,
1814 John H.
1863 Alonzo B. *m.*
1867 Oglevie D. *m.*

Balleray,
1869 George H. *m.*

Bancroft,
1840 Charles.

Bangs,
1862 Charles W. *l.*

Banks,
1842 William G.
1860 George B. *m.*

Barbour,
1865 James E. *m.*

Barclay,
1766 James.
1772 Thomas.
1796 David.
1867 Frederick S. *m.*
1867 Henry A. W.

Barculoo,
1795 George.

Bard,
1768 Samuel. *h.*
1797 William.

Barker,
1824 Robert.
1827 Thomas H.
1860 Phanet C. *m.*

Barnard,
1845 Daniel D. *h.*
1870 Augustus P. *m. e.*

Barnes,
1821 William B.

Barnet,
1771 Ichabod B.

Barnum,
1804 John W.
1865 Edmund B. *l.*

Barrett,
1870 Isaac B.

Barron,
1861 John C. *m.*

Barrow,
1804 William. *m.*
1833 James, Jr.
1861 Thomas. *m.*

Barrows,
1870 Arthur A. *m.*

Barry,
1804 Edmund D. *h.*
1820 Edmund D., Jr.
1860 Robert P.

Bartlett,
1833 John S.
1869 Willard.

Barton,
1770 Thomas. *h.*
1864 Philip H. *m.*

Bartow,
1806 John V.
1862 Robert E.
1864 Reginald H.
1869 Evelyn.

Bassett,
1786 John.
1862 George P. *m.*

Baxter,
1858 Wyllys P.
1868 George S. *m. e.*

Bay,
1797 William. *m.*
1798 Thomas.
1803 John.

Bayard,
1760 Samuel.
1776 Samuel.

Bayley,
1802 Joseph. *m.*
1828 William.

Beach,
1789 Abraham. *h.*
1849 Norman A.
1857 Alfred B. *h.*
1867 Willis J. *m.*

Beadel,
1841 Daniel H.
1865 Henry, Jr.

Beard,
1866 George M. *m.*

Beardsley,
1761 John. *h.*

Beasley,
1815 Frederick. *h.*

Beck,
1813 John B.
1863 Fanning C. T.
1868 William P.

Bedell,
1811 Gregory T.

Bedelle,
1865 George A. *l.*

Bedford,
1851 Henry M.
1855 Gunning S., Jr.

Beebee,
1802 Alexander M.

Beekman,
1766 Gerard.
1792 Gerard.
1834 James W.
1864 Gerard.
1864 John N.
1865 Henry R.

Beers,
1865 George L. *m.*

Belden,
1846 G. Mortimer.
1867 Herbert C. *m.*

Belknap,
1869 Robert L.

Bell,
1843 Samuel P.
1865 Christopher M. *m.*
1866 Marshall P.
1867 James, Jr. *l.*
1867 Walton P.
1869 George W. *m.*
1870 Edward W. *l.*

Bellows,
1864 Henry S. *l.*

Beneville,
1868 Emile. *l.*

Benjamin,
1856 Eastburn,
1859 Thomas J.
1860 Richard G.
1862 William H.
1868 Joseph R. *m.*

Benkard,
1861 James, Jr.
1861 John P. *m.*

Bennem,
1852 John.

Bennett,
1860 William C. *m.*

Benson,
1765 Egbert.
1801 Robert, Jr.
1807 Egbert, Jr.

Bergh,
1866 Edwin W. *l.*

Bernheimer,
1867 Jacques A.

Berrian,
1808 William.
1809 Samuel.
1815 James W.
1870 Richard.

Best,
1798 William. *h.*

Bethune,
1837 John.

Betts,
1820 William.
1846 Beverley R.

**Browne,**
1758 Isaac. *h.*
1864 Walston H.

**Brownell,**
1819 Thomas C. *h.*

**Browning,**
1859 Edward F.
1864 Thomas B.

**Brownson,**
1865 Edward S.

**Bruce,**
1797 Archibald.
1866 James M.

**Bruckman,**
1869 Frederick. *m. e.*

**Bruen,**
1812 Matthias, Jr.
1813 George W.
1861 Herman W. *l.*

**Brush,**
1827 Henry N.
1867 Francis V. *m.*
1870 Alfred D. *l.*

**Bryant,**
1837 William C. *h.*

**Bryar,**
1804 George.
1834 Edward.

**Bryce,**
1861 William McQ. *m.*
1863 Thomas T.
1870 James Y. *m.*

**Bryson,**
1866 William G. *m.*

**Buck,**
1867 Albert H. *m.*

**Buckley,**
1843 Thomas C. T.
1867 Charles C. *m.*

**Bucknall,**
1864 George J. *m.*

**Bucknor,**
1840 Charles B.

**Budlong,**
1868 Morris M. *l.*

**Buel,**
1862 Samuel. *h.*

**Bugbee,**
1866 Lafayette. *m.*

**Bulkley,**
1869 Lucius D. *m.*

**Bull,**
1864 Charles S.
1869 Richard W. *m.*

**Bump,**
1860 Orlo M. *m.*

**Bunker,**
1843 William E.

**Bunner,**
1798 Rudolph.

**Burgess,**
1866 George O. *m.*

**Burnap,**
1862 Sidney R. *m.*

**Burnett,**
1869 Edward W. *m.*

**Burnham,**
1865 Douglas W.

**Burr,**
1862 John T.

**Burrell,**
1807 William E.

**Burrill,**
1824 Alexander M.
1839 John E., Jr.

**Burroughs,**
1833 Charles. *h.*

**Burt,**
1864 J. Otis. *m.*
1868 George N. *l.*

**Burtis,**
1812 John A.
1867 Charles H.

**Burtsell,**
1870 Peter V. *l.*

**Butler,**
1828 Jonas.

**Butterworth.**
1864 John F.
1864 William H.

**Byron,**
1850 George G.

**Cadle,**
1809 John.
1813 Richard F.

**Cady,**
1868 Philander K. *h.*

**Cairns,**
1839 Frederick A.

**Calderwood,**
1870 Harvey S. *m.*

**Caldwell,**
1859 Elisha S.
1870 Towson.

**Calhoun,**
1825 John C. *h.*

**Callender,**
1868 John A. *m.*

**Caloosdian,**
1862 Garabed. *m.*

**Cambreling,**
1849 Churchill J.

**Cammann,**
1825 George P.
1855 Edward.
1856 Henry J.
1860 J. Lorrillard.

**Camp,**
1804 Elisha.

**Campbell,**
1795 John. *h.*
1811 John.
1816 John D.
1844 Robert B.
1847 Henry P.
1850 Malcolm.
1863 William. *l.*
1865 Archibald M
1865 John B. *m.*
1865 Thomas C.
1868 Benjamin H.
1869 Alonzo C. *m. e.*

**Canfield,**
1862 Robert B.

**Cannon,**
1817 John M.
1870 Charles K. *l.*

**Cardwell,**
1870 Samuel, Jr. *l.*

**Carew,**
1861 Edmund S. *m.*

**Carey,**
1839 Arthur.
1839 John, Jr.
1861 George H.
1862 John E. *m.*
1865 George. *m.*

**Carit,**
1864 Adolphe. *m.*

**Carle,**
1867 Charles A. *m.*

**Carleton,**
1861 George W. *m.*

**Carley,**
1864 Eldred A. *m.*

**Carll,**
1870 Lewis B.

**Carmalt,**
1861 William H. *m.*

**Carmichael,**
1839 William M. *h.*

**Carpenter,**
1848 Horace W.
1863 Wesley M. *m.*

**Carrington,**
1860 Charles. *m.*
1862 Edward. *l.*

**Carroll,**
1823 John. *h.*
1869 Craft C. *m.*

**Carson,**
1868 James P. *m. e.*

**Carter,**
1829 James A.
1850 Galen A.
1854 Cullen L.
1861 Charles. *m.*
1866 Nathan R.
1867 Frank. *m.*

**Cartter,**
1869 William H. *m.*

**Carvill,**
1832 George, Jr.

**Case,**
1868 Albertson. *l.*
1869 Charles H. *m.*

**Casey,**
1834 William B.
1864 Francis P. *m.*

**Caswell,**
1861 William H.
1865 John H.

**Catlin,**
1828 George.
1828 Charles T. *h.*

**Chalmers,**
1861 Matthew. *m.*
1863 George. *l.*
1865 Andrew B. *l.*

**Chambers,**
1853 Talbot W. *h.*

**Chandler,**
1758 Thomas B. *h.*
1774 William.
1862 Thomas K. *m.*
1868 William J. *m.*

**Chanler,**
1847 John W.

**Chapin,**
1864 Samuel F. *m.*

**Chapman,**
1864 Albert T. *m.*
1869 Curtis. *m.*
1869 James F. *m.*
1869 Sherman H. *m.*
1870 Timothy P. *l.*

**Chase,**
1819 Philander. *h.*
1860 Seth L. *m.*
1862 Leslie.

**Chauncey,**
1831 Peter S.

**Chester,**
1868 Albert H. *m. e.*

**Cheves,**
1824 Langdon. *h.*

**Chetwood,**
1860 Bradbury C. *l.*

**Chichester,**
1841 Edward L.

**Child,**
1810 Francis.

**Chipman,**
1861 John F. H. *m.*

**Cowles,**
1863 Edward. *m.*

**Cowman,**
1868 Edward D. *l.*

**Cox,**
1833 Richard.
1856 Whittingham.
1863 Samuel H. *h.*

**Craft,**
1821 Isaac F.
1821 William D.

**Craig,**
1868 Samuel P. *m.*

**Crandall,**
1865 Thomas V. *m.*

**Crane,**
1866 Albert. *l.*

**Crary,**
1824 Edward C.

**Craven,**
1829 Alfred W.

**Crawford,**
1865 Ten Broeck. *l.*
1867 Samuel D. *l.*
1870 Gilbert H. *l.*

**Creelman,**
1867 Frederick S. *m.*

**Creighton,**
1770 James.
1812 William.

**Cremin,**
1866 Patrick W. *m.*

**Croes,**
1811 John. *h.*

**Crolius,**
1803 Thomas.

**Cromwell,**
1854 Charles B.

**Crook,**
1849 George A. *h.*
1864 Abel. *l.*

**Cropper,**
1870 John.

**Crosby,**
1802 John P.
1827 John P.
1827 William H.
1840 Edward N.
1867 William B. *l.*

**Croucher,**
1863 Albert E. *m.*

**Crowell,**
1870 Charles E. *l.*

**Cruger,**
1796 Henry, Jr.
1819 Henry N.
1823 Lewis.
1859 Gouverneur.

**Cullen,**
1860 Edgar M.

**Culver,**
1868 Charles. *m.*

**Cuming,**
1851 Francis H. *h.*

**Cumming,**
1862 James R. *m.*

**Cummings,**
1868 Byron. *m.*

**Cunningham,**
1841 Frederick.

**Currier,**
1864 George W. *m.*

**Curtis,**
1824 William A.
1855 Benjamin L.
1858 Lewis A.
1862 John H.
1870 Frederic C. *m.*
1870 John G. *m.*

**Cushing,**
1764 Matthew. *h.*

**Cushman,**
1850 Archibald F.
1859 William F.

**Cuthbert,**
1869 Thomas N.

**Cutler,**
1835 Benjamin C. *h.*
1864 Henry S. *h.*

**Cutter,**
1861 George R. *m.*

**Cutting,**
1758 Leonard. *h.*
1793 William.
1830 Robert L.
1856 Robert L., Jr.
1862 Walter.
1869 William B.

**Cuyler,**
1762 Henry.
1763 Barent.

**Cuzner,**
1864 A. Thomas. *m.*

**Da Costa,**
1855 Charles.

**Dakin,**
1860 Edward S. *l.*

**Daly,**
1860 Charles P. *h.*

**Dana,**
1843 John W.
1857 Richard S.

**Dandridge,**
1870 Nathaniel P. *m.*

**Danker,**
1864 Henry A. *m.*

**Darby,**
1864 Henry A. *m.*

**Davidson,**
1864 Edmund D.

**Davies,**
1813 Thomas L.
1857 Henry E., Jr.
1866 Julian T.

**Davis,**
1798 George.
1814 Cornelius.
1853 Thomas F. *h.*
1863 Rezin P. *m.*
1864 Albert A. *m.*
1868 Henry S. *l.*
1869 Gustavus P. *m.*

**Dawson,**
1822 George W.
1866 Benjamin T. *m.*

**Day,**
1863 Walter De F. *m.*
1865 James G. *l.*
1870 Henry C. *m.*

**Dayton,**
1817 Matthias O.
1868 Charles W. *l.*

**Deady,**
1868 John A. *l.*

**Deall.**
1774† Samuel.

**Dean,**
1853 George W.
1855 William.
1861 Henry M. *m.*

**De Blois,**
1861 Louis G. *m.*

**Decker,**
1793 Cornelius.
1867 Samuel. *m.*

**Deering,**
1869 James A. *l.*

**De Koven,**
1851 James.

**Delafield,**
1802 John.
1830 John, Jr.
1855 Lewis.
1856 Maturin L.
1863 Francis. *m.*
1866 Augustus F.
1870 Albert. *l.*

**Delaney,**
1867 John O. F. *m.*

**Delaplaine,**
1833 John F., Jr.
1834 Isaac C.

**De Leon,**
1860 Juan B. P. *m.*

**Delile,**
1807 Alire R. *m.*

**Demaray,**
1848 Lyman D.

**Demarest,**
1804 Cornelius T.
1834 William.
1863 Samuel. *m.*
1864 Theodore F. C.

**De Mille,**
1848 Richard M.

**De Motte,**
1866 John J. *m.*

**Denman,**
1862 William M. *l.*

**Dennis,**
1834 William.
1866 Laban. *m.*

**Denniston,**
1867 John A.

**De Peyster,**
1763 Abraham.
1774† James.
1800 John J.
1810 William.
1812 James F.
1815 Robert G. L.
1816 Frederic, Jr.
1833 Pierre C.
1841 Richard V.
1862 Frederic J. *l.*

**De Ruyter,**
1851 John, Jr.
1860 Charles.

**Des Brisay,**
1867 Charles M. *m.*

**Dessar,**
1870 Leo C. *l.*

**Devan,**
1828 Thomas T.

**Devendorf,**
1861 David McC. *m.*

**Devereux,**
1776 James.

**Devlin,**
1864 Henry J. *m.*
1870 Francis C. *l.*

**Dewey,**
1863 George C. *m.*

**De Wint,**
1771 Henry.
1806 John P.
1854 Francis A.

**De Witt,**
1867 George G., Jr.

**De Wolfe,**
1865 Clarence E. *m.*
1865 James A. *m.*

**Dey,**
1818 Richard V.
1865 Richard. *m.*

**Emmet,**
1810 Robert.
1824 Thomas A. *h.*
1839 Richard S.
1867 Bache McE. *m.*

**Emmett,**
1869 Charles. *l.*

**Emory,**
1831 Robert.

**Emott,**
1833 James. *h.*
1841 James, Jr.

**Enfield,**
1870 Charles. *m.*

**English,**
1868 David C. *m.*

**Engs,**
1863 George M. *m.*

**Eno,**
1864 Henry C. *m.*

**Erskine,**
1853 Henry D. *h.*

**Evangeles,**
1836 Christodoulos L. M.

**Evans,**
1864 Lemuel E. *l.*
1870 Edwin. *m.*

**Eveleth,**
1866 Edward S. *m.*

**Everett,**
1864 D. Darwin. *m.*

**Everhart,**
1870 George M. *h.*

**Everson,**
1864 Duane S.

**Ewer,**
1867 Ferdinand C. *h.*

**Exton,**
1866 James A. *m.*

**Faesch,**
1795 John J.

**Fairbank,**
1869 John B. *l.*

**Fairfax,**
1861 Albert. *m.*

**Fairlie,**
1818 Frederick.

**Fairweather,**
1865 Daniel H. *m.*

**Falls,**
1845 William A.

**Fanning,**
1772 Edmund. *h.*
1870 William, Jr.

**Fanshaw,**
1832 Daniel G. F.

**Farnsworth,**
1860 Philo J. *m.*

**Farrand,**
1863 David O. *m.*

**Farrar,**
1848 George C.

**Farrell,**
1864 Edward. *m.*

**Farrington,**
1853 William G.

**Farrow,**
1865 Levi. *m.*

**Fash,**
1836 George W.

**Fayerweather,**
1758 Samuel. *h.*

**Fawcett,**
1867 Edgar.

**Fearing,**
1860 George R.

**Featherstonhaugh,**
1870 James D. *m.*

**Fehr,**
1869 Julius. *m.*

**Fellows,**
1869 Louis. *l.*

**Ferguson,**
1795 John.
1823 John T.
1830 Benjamin T.
1863 George W.
1867 Charles W. *m.*

**Ferris,**
1811 Charles G.
1816 Isaac.

**Fessenden,**
1837 Henry P.

**Fetter,**
1835 Manuel. *h.*
1867 David F. *m.*

**Fettretch,**
1864 Joseph. *l.*

**Field,**
1859 Cortlandt De P.
1862 Henry M. *m.*
1863 Jacob T. *m.*
1864 Archelaus G. *m.*
1865 William H. *l.*

**Files,**
1870 Charles O. *m.*

**Fine,**
1805 James L.
1809 John.

**Fish,**
1827 Hamilton.
1831 P. Stuyvesant.
1867 Nicholas.
1869 Hamilton, Jr.

**Fisher,**
1794 John E.
1796 Philip.
1817 Isaac.
1821 George H.
1863 William R.
1867 Thomas R. *l.*
1867 William H. *l.*

**Fiske,**
1821 Thaddeus. *h.*

**Fitch,**
1863 Samuel A. *m.*
1864 Luther P. *m.*
1867 James N. *m.*

**Fitzsimons,**
1865 Henry E. *l.*

**Flaacke,**
1870 George W. *l.*

**Flagg,**
1863 Jared B. *h.*
1865 Edwin B. *m.*

**Fleming,**
1791 Pierre E.
1803 Augustus.
1805 James.
1809 Alexander.

**Fletcher,**
1860 William B. *m.*
1869 Ira W. *m.*

**Floy,**
1827 Michael, Jr.
1864 Henry.

**Floyd,**
1809 Alfred.

**Fogg,**
1861 Benjamin F. *m.*

**Fonda,**
1787 Nicholas.

**Forbes,**
1794 John.
1827 John M.
1869 Francis. *l.*

**Ford,**
1844 Edward E. *h.*
1860 Edward I. *m.*

**Forman,**
1866 Daniel M. *m.*

**Forrest,**
1820 William. *h.*
1840 William, Jr.

**Forrester,**
1818 Peter.
1862 Peter.

**Forsyth,**
1821 William.

**Foster,**
1803 Isaac. *m.*
1841 Herman T. E.
1844 Jacob P. G.
1862 Frank P. *m.*
1866 Addison H. *m.*
1867 Antoine L.
1868 Frederic De P.
1868 George E. *m.*
1868 Talmadge W.
1869 Seth B. *m.*
1870 Charles A. *m.*
1870 William R. *l.*

**Foulke,**
1823 John B.
1869 William D.

**Fowler,**
1806 Gilbert O.
1810 Theodosius O.
1838 Isaac V.
1839 James W.
1863 De Witt C. *m.*
1865 Jonathan O., Jr.
1867 Horace W. *l.*
1870 J. Henry, Jr. *l.*
1870 Robert L. *l.*

**Fox,**
1864 Joseph G. *h.*

**Francis,**
1808 Henry M.
1809 John W.
1852 John W., Jr.
1857 Samuel W.

**Frankel,**
1868 Edward. *m.*

**Franklin,**
1843 Benjamin H.
1852 William B. *h.*
1862 Gustavus S. *m.*

**Fraser,**
1811 David H.
1862 Edward C. *l.*

**Frauenstein,**
1868 Gustav. *m.*

**Frazer,**
1868 Samuel H. *m.*

**Freeke,**
1811 Richard.

**Freeland,**
1865 Henry E. *l.*

**Freeman,**
1790 Jonathan.
1849 George L.
1868 Wilberforce. *l.*
1869 Alonzo. *m.*

**French,**
1860 John W. *h.*
1869 Charles L. *m.*

**Froeligh,**
1799 Peter D.

**Frost,**
1846 William J.
1869 Louis W. *l.*

Hadden,
1860 Walter J. *m.*

Hagan,
1867 Martin. *m.*

Hagerman,
1804 Henry B.

Haigh,
1865 Thomas. *m.*

Haight,
1811 Benjamin.
1828 Benjamin I.
1861 Charles C.
1861 Edward, Jr.
1862 Louis.
1864 David L. *m.*
1869 Edward G. *l.*
1870 Ogden. *m. e.*

Haine,
1869 William J. *m.*

Haines,
1870 George M. *m.*

Hale,
1836 Benjamin. *h.*
1853 Albert W.

Hall,
1811 James. *h.*
1833 Charles.
1861 Charles H. *h.*
1863 Charles E. *m.*
1863 Randall C.
1865 Isaac H. *l.*
1867 John D. *m.*
1867 William F. *l.*
1870 Lovell. *l.*
1870 William E. *m.*

Halleck,
1837 Fitz-Greene. *h.*

Hallock,
1869 Edward J.

Halsey,
1790 Frederick.
1823 Abraham N. *h.*
1837 Anthony.
1839 Abraham. *h.*
1868 Joseph B.
1870 Frederick R. *l.*

Halstead,
1800 Samuel.

Ham,
1868 Albert E. *m.*

Hamilton,
1774† Alexander.
1800 Philip.
1804 Alexander.
1805 James A.
1809 John C.
1861 Theodore E. *m.*
1870 Allan McL. *m.*

Hamersley,
1819 Andrew.
1826 John W.
1835 Andrew S.
1865 James H.

Hamlin,
1865 George S. *l.*

Handerson,
1867 Henry E. *m.*

Hanna,
1759 William.
1868 George B. *m. e.*

Hanners,
1849 Henry De C.

Hansen,
1869 George H. *l.*

Hardenbrook,
1824 John K.
1849 William A.

Hardenburgh,
1789 James R. *h.*

Hardie,
1787 James. *h.*

Hare,
1843 George E. *h.*

Harison,
1764 Richard.
1802 Francis L.
1804 Richard N.
1811 William H., Jr.
1842 William H.
1846 William B.
1850 Thomas L.

Harlin,
1862 William H. *m.*

Harmer,
1864 Thomas H.

Harmon,
1855 Edward O.

Harper,
1848 Joseph W., Jr.
1852 John W.

Harpur,
1762 Robert. *h.*

Harral,
1868 Frederick F. *m.*

Harriman,
1835 Orlando, Jr.

Harrington,
1867 Daniel DeW. *m.*

Harris,
1770 Richard.
1800 Samuel.
1811 William.
1822 Josiah D.
1825 Robert W.
1864 Frank. *l.*
1866 Orrin F. *m.*
1866 Samuel. *m.*

Harsen,
1825 Jacob.

Hart,
1811 William H.
1870 George H. *l.*

Harvey,
1834 Robert J. *h.*

Hasbrouck,
1834 Abraham B. *h.*
1862 Solomon E. *m.*
1863 Frank G. *m.*
1863 John C. *m.*

Haslett,
1867 Audley. *m.*

Hatch,
1862 Charles H. *l.*

Hatfield,
1805 Richard, Jr.

Hathaway,
1867 Henry B. *l.*
1869 George A. *m.*

Havemeyer,
1823 William F.

Haven,
1857 George G.

Havens,
1862 Jonathan. *m.*

Hawes,
1821 William P.
1866 George E. *m.*

Hawkesworth,
1860 William. *h.*

Hawks,
1832 Francis L. *h.*

Hawley,
1868 George F. *m.*

Haws,
1827 John H. H.

Hayes,
1869 Russel T. *m.*

Hazelius,
1824 Ernest L. *h.*

Heard,
1832 James, Jr.
1834 John S.
1835 William.

Heasley,
1869 George W.

Heaton,
1793 Robert, Jr.

Hedge,
1869 Thomas, Jr. *l.*

Heffernan,
1865 John M.

Hegeman,
1862 William A. O.

Hendell,
1791 William, Jr.

Henderson,
1823 William D.
1867 Henry. *m.*

Hendricks,
1856 Francis.
1858 Harmon.

Hennion,
1864 Andrew J. *l.*

Henop,
1861 Sidney S. *l.*

Henry,
1800 John.
1849 John V.
1863 Richard M.
1868 Frederick P. *m.*

Hepburn,
1868 Neil J. *m.*

Herrick,
1854 Carleton M.
1857 James B.

Herriman,
1849 William H.

Herring,
1795 Thomas.

Hershey.
1862 Andrew H. *m.*
1867 William. *l.*

Hervey,
1868 Daniel E. *l.*

Hewitt,
1842 Abram S.
1845 Charles. *h.*

Heyer,
1814 William H.
1815 William S.
1819 Edward P.
1823 Henry A.

Heyliger,
1774 Nicholas.

Heyward,
1827 William C.
1829 James.
1830 Nicholas C.
1834 Henry.

Hibbard,
1861 Jerome. *m.*

Hickok,
1869 George B. *m.*

Hicks,
1793 John B. *m.*
1823 John A.
1860 Joseph L. *m.*

Higbee,
1842 Edward Y. *h.*

Hildreth,
1869 John H. *l.*

Hill,
1807 John H.
1869 Augustus V. *m.*

Hillman,
1832 Alexander C.

1862 William H.
1864 Frederick W.
1865 David P. *m.*
1866 Abner. *h.*

## Jacob,
1866 Ephraim A. *l.*

## Jaffray,
1793 Andrew. *h.*
1842 Robert, Jr.

## James,
1862 William M. *m.*
1865 Julian.
1865 Richard D. *m.*

## Janeway,
1794 Jacob J.
1864 Edward G. *m.*
1867 Thomas L. *m.*

## Janvrin,
1864 Joseph E. *m.*

## Jarvis,
1837 Benjamin H.

## Jaques,
1805 Robert.

## Jaume,
1862 John A. *m.*

## Jauncey,
1774 John.

## Jay,
1764 John.
1794 Peter A.
1827 John C.
1836 John.
1859 William, Jr.
1863 Peter A.
1865 John C., Jr. *m.*

## Jenkins,
1804 Edward. *h.*
1833 John J.

## Jenks,
1852 Richard P. *h.*
1860 John W.

## Jerome,
1870 William R. *l.*

## Jessup,
1869 Andrew J. *m.*

## Jewett,
1841 Jacob B.
1862 Dan L. *m.*
1868 Charles T. *m.*

## Johnson,
1761 William S. *h.*
1772 Uzal. *m.*
1788 Robert C. *h.*
1789 Samuel W. *h.*
1792 John B.
1793 John I.
1819 William L.
1820 Samuel R.
1824 George W.
1831 Bradish.
1832 William T.
1834 Samuel E.
1848 Henry W.
1851 Henry B.
1853 William A.
1862 Eldridge M. *m.*
1863 Woolsey. *m.*
1865 Andrew. *h.*
1865 Parley H. *m.*
1866 Joseph. *m.*
1867 George B.
1867 Samuel. *m.*
1868 Herschel V., Jr. *m.*

## Johnston,
1846 William M.

## Johnstone,
1820 James.

## Jones,
1768 John. *h.*
1790 Samuel, Jr.
1791 Cave.
1795 Nicholas.
1796 David S.
1798 Philip L.
1802 James.
1803 Edward R.
1815 John Q.
1819 Charles.
1819 George.
1822 Henry P.
1827 Joshua.
1830 Edward.
1832 Philip L.
1835 Joshua E.
1836 William A.
1840 Alfred G.
1845 George A.
1845 Samuel T.
1847 Arthur M.
1850 Walter R. T.
1858 Henry L.
1859 Lot. *h.*
1860 Edward R.
1865 Frederick R.
1865 Luther M. *l.*
1869 Henry M.
1869 Shipley.
1870 Charles D. *l.*
1870 Clarence D. *l.*

## Jordan,
1867 Henry I. *m.*

## Joslyn,
1867 Charles S. *l.*

## Joy,
1866 Henry D. W. *m.*

## Judah,
1814 Henry R.

## Judson,
1864 Charles N. *l.*
1868 Adoniram B. *m.*
1870 Walter. *m.*

## Jump,
1866 Robert P. *m.*

## Junkin,
1850 David X. *h.*

## Kalish,
1870 Samuel. *l.*

## Kane,
1832 John J. C.
1846 John G.
1868 Walter L. *l.*

## Kaufman,
1864 Charles H.

## Kearny,
1809 Ravaud.
1833 Philip, Jr.
1866 John W. *l.*

## Keator,
1867 John J. *m.*

## Keese,
1798 William B.
1823 William L.
1862 Sidmon T. *l.*

## Kellogg,
1846 Edwin M.
1848 Levi M.
1852 Ansel N.
1868 John M. *m.*

## Kelley,
1865 Edgar K. *m.*

## Kelly,
1826 Robert.
1870 Edmond.

## Kemble,
1803 Gouverneur.
1803 Peter.
1813 William.
1818 Richard F.
1841 William, Jr.
1868 Warren. *m.*

## Kemeys,
1803 Edward.

## Kemp,
1802 James. *h.*

## Kemper,
1809 Jackson.
1849 Lewis A.

## Kenan,
1868 Thomas H. *m.*

## Kennedy,
1840 Robert L.
1860 David. *m.*
1861 John T. *m.*
1866 Samuel L. *m.*
1869 Henry W. *l.*

## Kenny,
1863 Peter D. *m.*

## Kent,
1797 James. *h.*

## Kerfoot,
1850 John B. *h.*

## Kerin,
1775† Edward.

## Kermit,
1821 Thomas.

## Kernan,
1868 John V. *l.*

## Kernochan,
1842 William S.
1853 John A.
1863 Francis E. *l.*
1865 Joseph F. *l.*

## Ketcham,
1864 William P. L.

## Ketchum,
1862 Edgar, Jr. *l.*
1867 John J. *m.*
1869 William Q. *h.*

## Kettell,
1860 Herbert.

## Keyser,
1865 George. *l.*
1865 Robert B. *l.*

## Kidder,
1868 Frederick. *m.*

## Kilbourne,
1868 Edwin A. *m.*

## King,
1772 John.
1794 Cyrus.
1821 Elisha S.
1822 Theodore F.
1831 Charles R.
1834 William G.
1848 Cornelius L.
1860 Augustus F.
1867 John A.

## Kingman,
1870 Eugene. *m.*

## Kingsland,
1856 Ambrose C., Jr.
1856 George L.

## Kingsley,
1865 George P. *l.*

## Kinmonth,
1870 Hugh S. *m.*

## Kinney,
1858 Henry C.
1864 William H. *m.*

## Kip,
1810 Charles J.
1815 Leonard W.
1826 Francis M.
1847 William I. *h.*
1866 Leonard W., Jr.
1867 George G.

## Kipp,
1861 Charles J. *m.*

## Kirby,
1860 Isaac H. *l.*

## Kirkland,
1854 Edward.
1866 Charles P. *h.*

## Kissam,
1769 Samuel. *m.*
1775† Benjamin.
1776 Peter.
1805 Benjamin. *m.*
1812 Benjamin R.
1838 Benjamin T.
1854 George C.
1864 Jonas B.
1865 Daniel W. *m.*
1867 William A. *m.*

Kittredge,
1863 Charles S. *m.*

Klots,
1848 George M

Knapp,
1870 John A. *m. e.*

Kneeland,
1769 Ebenezer. *h.*
1830 John T.

Knevels,
1853 Delancy W.

Knevils,
1781 John.
1791 Isaac.

Knight,
1855 Walter.

Knowles,
1864 Henry M. *m.*

Knox,
1771 Thomas.
1838 John M.
1841 James H. M.
1849 William M.
1860 Charles McL. *l.*
1862 Charles S.
1866 James S. *m.*
1870 James. *l.*

Koch,
1865 Joseph. *l.*

Korff,
1869 John H. *m.*

Kortright,
1822 N. Gouverneur.

Kunze,
1797 Henry.

Labagh,
1827 Abraham B.
1856 Peter I.

Labau,
1844 N. Bergasse.

Lacombe,
1859 James P.
1863 Emile H.

Laight,
1767 William.
1793 Edward W.
1802 Henry.
1825 William E.
1836 Edward H.
1853 Edward W.
1862 William E.
1868 Charles. *m.*

Lake,
1836 James P.

Lambert,
1863 Thomas R. *h.*

Lampson,
1867 William. *l.*

Lamson,
1773 Joseph. *h.*

Lane,
1847 John S.

Langdon,
1867 Eustis F. *m.*

Langworthy,
1860 Daniel A. *m.*

Lanterman,
1868 A. J. *m.*

Larocque,
1838 Jeremiah.
1849 Joseph.

Larzelere,
1804 Jacob. *h.*

Lathrop,
1862 William G.

Latour,
1869 Isaac P *m*

Laughlin,
1865 James F *m.*

Law,
1797 Samuel A *h.*

Lawrance,
1840 Edward H.

Lawrence,
1797 Abraham R
1803 John L.
1812 Augustine N.
1812 Philip K.
1818 William B.
1820 Henry.
1823 Jonathan.
1823 William A.
1841 Joseph E.
1842 Richard M., Jr.
1843 William B., Jr.
1844 Charles W.
1847 Isaac.
1856 Thomas T.
1861 Walter B.
1862 George A.
1864 Joseph B.
1866 Samuel, Jr. *l.*
1868 James K. *l.*

Laws,
1870 Samuel S. *l.*

Leaming,
1765 Jeremiah.

Learned,
1865 John B. *m.*

Leavenworth,
1848 Edward.

Leavitt,
1845 John W.
1860 William W. *m.*

Le Conte,
1797 William.
1799 Lewis.
1803 John.

Ledyard,
1830 Henry.

Lee,
1823 Chauncey. *h.*
1833 Francis P.
1835 Charles C.
1856 David B.
1856 Hermon F.
1861 Benjamin F. *l.*
1863 William. *m.*
1864 Arthur M. *l.*
1865 John L. *m.*
1866 Charles E. *m.*
1869 Henry T. *l.*

Lefferts,
1794 Leffert.
1802 Leffert.
1805 Thomas.
1846 John L.
1870 George M. *m.*

Legaré,
1840 Hugh S. *h.*

Leggat,
1863 William S.

Leggett,
1837 William H.

Le Moyne,
1850 Adolphe, Jr.

Lenox,
1818 James.

Lent,
1795 Adolph C.

Leonard,
1825 Alexander S.
1866 Algernon S. *m.*
1868 Charles H. *m.*

Le Roy,
1841 Robert, Jr.

Leslie,
1762 Alexander.

Lester,
1863 Elias. *m.*

Lever,
1869 John H. *m.*

Leveridge,
1835 John W. C.
1840 Benjamin C.

Lewis,
1810 Horatio G.
1843 Edward Z.
1848 Theodore F.
1854 John V.
1861 Thompson B. *m.*
1865 Mordecai. *l.*
1867 Hobart.

Lighthipe,
1863 Lewis H.

Lincoln,
1861 Abraham, *h.*

Lindley,
1869 Newton A. *m.*

Lindsay,
1866 Walter. *m*

Lindsley,
1870 Stuart. *m. e.*

Linn,
1789 William *h.*
1795 John B.

Linsly,
1864 William B. *m.*
1869 James C. *m.*

Lispenard,
1761 Anthony.
1762 Leonard.

Little,
1860 James L. *m.*
1870 Albert H. *m.*

Livingston,
1760 Philip.
1765 Robert R.
1775 John W.
1786 George.
1786 Philip H.
1788 Peter S.
1796 Edward P
1799 James.
1800 Robert S.
1804 James D
1811 Peter V. B.
1822 Anson.
1822 Carroll.
1823 Edward. *h.*
1828 Mortimer.
1869 John H.

Lloyd,
1765 Henry.
1818 John H.
1867 Henry D.

Lockwood,
1840 Levi A.
1848 John, Jr.
1863 Le Grand, Jr.
1864 William A. *m.*
1867 John T. *l.*
1868 Charles E. *m.*

Loder,
1846 Jeremiah.

Logan,
1823 Adam D.

Lomax,
1862 Joseph D. *m.*

Lord,
1839 Daniel D.
1849 David P.
1867 Daniel, Jr.
1868 Theodore A. *l.*
1870 Franklin B.

Lordly,
1868 James E. M. *m.*

Lossing,
1869 Benson J. *h.*

Loughridge,
1870 Samuel O. *m.*

Lounsbery,
1861 Seth S. *m.*

**Loutrel,**
1838 Alfred M.

**Low,**
1812 Cornelius F.
1821 Isaac.
1865 William G.
1870 Seth.

**Lowerre,**
1817 William.
1819 Henry J.

**Lowerree,**
1865 Thomas W., Jr. *m.*

**Lowndes,**
1822 William. *h.*
1860 Francis. *l.*

**Lowther,**
1774† Tristrim.

**Luck,**
1868 John T. *m.*

**Luckock,**
1836 Benjamin. *h.*

**Ludlow,**
1758 Carey. *h.*
1768 James.
1787 John C.
1793 Henry W.
1811 Thomas W.
1817 Edmund.
1827 Alfred.

**Ludlum,**
1847 William S.
1851 Nicholas F.

**Lummis,**
1859 William.

**Lupp,**
1824 William H.

**Lupton,**
1774† Schuyler.
1788 Brandt S.
1789 William.
1791 Lancaster.

**Luquer,**
1852 Lea.
1858 Nicholas, Jr.

**Lusby,**
1868 Robert L. *m.*

**Lush,**
1770 Stephen.

**Lydig,**
1815 Philip M.
1858 Philip M., Jr.
1860 David.

**Lyell,**
1822 Thomas. *h.*

**Lyman,**
1840 Dwight E.
1861 Henry M. *m.*

**Lynch,**
1775† Thomas G.
1799 James.
1836 George H.
1868 David V. *m.*

**Lyon,**
1835 Charles H.
1860 Samuel K.
1863 Irving W. *m.*

**Lyttleton,**
1864 William M. *m.*

**Lytton,**
1804 William L.

**Mabie,**
1869 Hamilton W. *l.*

**McBurney,**
1870 Charles, Jr. *m.*

**McAllaster,**
1865 John G. *m.*

**McAllister,**
1854 Cutler C.
1860 Matthew H. *h.*
1869 William H. *l.*

**McCahill,**
1867 Edwin. *l.*

**McCall,**
1869 Joseph W. *m.*

**McCartee,**
1808 Robert.

**McCartin,**
1863 Henry E. *m.*

**McCarty,**
1853 Thomas.
1857 Pierre.
1868 James J. *m.*

**Macauley,**
1855 John M. *h.*

**McClellan,**
1864 Alfred P.

**McClintock,**
1859 J. Emory.

**McCoskry,**
1837 Samuel A. *h.*

**McCreery,**
1868 James A. *l.*

**McCue,**
1845 Alexander.

**McCullen,**
1806 James.

**McCullough,**
1845 John W. *h.*
1866 Alfred J. *l.*

**McCune,**
1843 William.

**McDonald,**
1810 John M.
1821 Daniel. *h.*
1852 Archibald B.

**Macdonald,**
1863 James A.
1868 John A.

**McDonough,**
1869 John T. *l.*

**McDougall,**
1869 John C. *m.*

**McElligott,**
1865 Henry R.

**McEwen,**
1868 Daniel, Jr. *m.*

**McFarlan,**
1827 Charles.

**McFarland,**
1867 William C. *m.*

**McFarlane,**
1861 Carrington. *m.*

**McGahagan,**
1804 Thomas.

**McGay,**
1868 Robert J. *m.*

**McGill,**
1866 Alexander T. *l.*

**McGlade,**
1870 Thomas A., Jr. *l.*

**McGown,**
1843 Henry P.

**McGraw,**
1863 Theodore A. *m.*

**McGregor,**
1810 John.

**McGuirk,**
1869 John. *m.*

**McIlvaine,**
1856 Alexis E.

**McIntyre,**
1835 Joseph.

**Mack,**
1807 Daniel.
1867 John A. *l.*

**Mackaness,**
1799 Thomas T.

**McKay,**
1864 William M. *m.*
1868 George S. *l.*
1868 John H. *m.*

**McKean,**
1762 Robert. *h.*

**McKee,**
1860 James G. *m.*

**McKelvie,**
1866 William H. *m.*

**McKeon,**
1825 John.

**McKesson,**
1758 John. *h.*

**Mackie,**
1794 Jacob O.
1812 Peter, Jr.

**McKinnon,**
1800 John.

**McKnight,**
1798 Washington.
1808 John.
1846 Charles S.

**McLane,**
1864 James W. *m.*

**McLaren,**
1847 John J.

**McLean,**
1844 Charles G. *h.*
1863 Thomas M., Jr.
1869 Malcolm. *m.*

**McLeod,**
1806 Robert B. A.
1818 Alexander B.
1826 John N.

**McLoughlin,**
1869 Thomas J. *m.*

**McMahon,**
1869 Dennis, Jr., *l.*

**McManus,**
1869 Henry. *m.*

**McMartin,**
1868 Archibald, *m. e.*

**McMaster,**
1870 Robert B. *l.*

**McMullen,**
1837 John, Jr.

**McMurdy,**
1867 John H. *l.*

**McMurray,**
1852 William. *h.*

**McNamee,**
1866 Theodore H.
1867 James.

**McNary,**
1851 John G.

**Macneven,**
1806 William J. *h.*
1831 James J.

**McNulty,**
1861 Albert, Jr.

**Macomb,**
1802 John W.
1802 Robert.
1866 Edward. *m.*

**McQuesten,**
1863 Rockwood.

**McRae,**
1870 William F. *l.*

**McSweeny,**
1864 Daniel E. *m.*

**Montell,**
1870 John B.

**Morgan,**
1831 James M.
1843 William R.
1854 Charles E.
1857 William F. *h.*
1864 John B.
1865 Lawrence O. *m.*
1869 James A. *l.*
1870 John V. *m.*

**Moore,**
1768 Benjamin.
1774† Daniel.
1775† Thomas L.
1794 Richard C. *h.*
1798 Clement C.
1798 Samuel.
1802 Nathaniel F.
1806 David.
1806 Samuel W.
1810 Benjamin.
1842 Clement.
1844 William T.
1847 John W.
1856 Richard C., Jr.
1859 James F.
1861 Richard H. *m.*
1866 John. *m.*
1867 Thomas M. *l.*

**Morison,**
1870 Robert S.

**Morrell,**
1810 Robert. *m.*

**Morrelle,**
1849 Daniel.

**Morrill,**
1828 John A.
1869 Jesse L. *l.*

**Morris,**
1768 Governeur.
1775† Jacob.
1813 Nicholas, Jr.
1818 Gerard W.
1826 Henry.
1826 Richard L.
1848 Lewis.
1852 James.
1854 Orlando H.
1858 Charles D. *h.*
1860 Augustus N.
1860 Richard L.
1861 Robert. *l.*
1863 Stuyvesant F.
1868 Benjamin W. *h.*
1868 Fordham. *l.*
1868 Henry L. *l.*
1870 Samuel H. *m.*

**Morrison,**
1795 John.
1869 James E. *l.*

**Morse,**
1860 Barnett W. *m.*
1863 Sherman. *m.*

**Mortimer,**
1841 John H.

**Morton,**
1810 George W.
1810 John L.
1815 Francis.
1824 Hamilton.
1827 Henry J.

**Moses,**
1841 Israel.
1868 Max. *l.*

**Mott,**
1806 Valentine. *m.*
1864 William F.

**Mount,**
1834 Richard E., Jr.
1852 Charles De G.

**Mowatt,**
1816 John E.

**Mower,**
1856 Mandeville.

**Mudgett,**
1869 William P. *l.*

**Mudie,**
1860 Archibald F. *m.*

**Muhlenberg,**
1834 William A. *h.*

**Muir,**
1867 David H. *m.*

**Muirson,**
1772 James *m.*

**Mulchahey,**
1866 James. *h.*

**Mullany,**
1866 Frank A.

**Muller,**
1822 Adrian H.

**Mulligan,**
1791 John W.
1835 William.

**Mundy,**
1864 Charles H. *l.*

**Munn,**
1821 William H.

**Murdock,**
1861 Seth M. *l.*
1867 George W. *m.*
1870 Albert J. *m.*

**Murfee,**
1867 John H. *m.*

**Murphy,**
1830 Henry C.
1854 Henry C., Jr.
1855 George J.
1867 Philip. *l.*

**Murray,**
1799 Alexander.
1812 John W. B.
1813 Thomas C.
1863 James.
1866 Nicholas. *l.*
1869 George F. *l.*

**Mursick,**
1860 George A. *m.*

**Murtha,**
1869 Eugene B. *m.*

**Muzzy,**
1808 Frederick.

**Nash,**
1846 Frederick.
1868 John M.

**Nathan,**
1827 Jonathan.
1861 Gratz.

**Nazro,**
1863 Hiram H.

**Neal,**
1810 Ava.

**Nealis,**
1862 William T. *m.*

**Neefus,**
1854 Peter J.

**Neill,**
1767 Hugh. *h.*
1828 George B.

**Neilson,**
1817 John, Jr.
1847 John.

**Nelson,**
1804 Joseph.
1841 Edward D.
1841 Samuel. *h.*
1869 Henry L. *l.*
1869 James R. *m.*

**Nesmith,**
1860 Robert D.

**Nettleton,**
1869 Asbel G. *m.*

**Nettre,**
1869 Lionel R. *m. e.*

**Nevius,**
1837 George L.

**Newby,**
1863 Thomas B.

**Newell,**
1860 William S. *l.*

**Newcomb,**
1840 Obadiah, Jr.
1864 George W. *m.*

**Newland,**
1868 David J. *l.*

**Newschafer,**
1864 William H. *l.*

**Newton,**
1842 George L.
1869 Henry. *m. e.*

**Nichols,**
1818 Samuel. *h.*
1825 Walter.
1831 Gideon S.
1839 Edwin A.
1845 Samuel B. R.
1852 Washington R.

**Nicholson,**
1792 James W.
1796 Samuel.

**Nicholl,**
1793 John.

**Nicoll,**
1766 Edward.
1774 Henry.
1774 Samuel. *m.*
1775† Augustus.
1776 Matthias.
1830 Henry.
1862 Augustus W. *l.*
1863 John D. *m.*
1866 Edward H.
1866 Henry D. *m.*
1868 William G. *l.*

**Nitchie,**
1801 John.

**Nolan,**
1868 John. *m.*

**Norsworthy,**
1826 John B.

**North,**
1861 Alfred. *m.*
1868 William F. *l.*

**Northrop,**
1864 George J. *m.*

**Northrup,**
1867 Daniel W. *l.*

**Norton,**
1792 John L.
1793 Robert B.

**Norwood,**
1862 Edward M. *m.*

**Nott,**
1857 Henry P.

**Noyes,**
1861 James H. *m.*
1865 McWalter B. *h.*

**Nutten,**
1863 Wilbur F. *m.*

**Nutter,**
1867 David R. *l.*

**Oakes,**
1864 George B. *m.*

**Oaksmith,**
1867 Sidney. *l.*

**Oberndorfer,**
1870 Isidor P.

**O'Blenis,**
1818 John.

**Odell,**
1811 Jackson.

**O'Dowd,**
1852 Charles.

**O'Dwyer,**
1866 Joseph. *m.*

Pierrepont,
1867 Henry E., Jr.

Pierson,
1869 Stephen. *m.*

Piffard,
1864 Henry G. *m.*

Pinckney,
1860 Howard. *m.*

Pinder,
1833 John H. *h.*

Pingry,
1868 James O. *m.*

Pinneo,
1865 Joseph O. *m.*

Pirnie,
1839 John, Jr.
1839 Peter B.
1844 Peter M.

Pistor,
1869 William. *m. e.*

Pitner,
1869 Thomas J. *m.*

Pitschke,
1870 William F. *l.*

Planck,
1870 Milton G. *m.*

Platt,
1868 Charles S. *m. e.*

Plympton,
1861 Henry S. *m.*

Poinsett,
1825 Joel R. *h.*

Polk,
1838 Leonidas. *h.*
1869 William M. *m.*

Pollen,
1849 George C.

Pomeroy,
1835 George Q.
1854 Charles S.
1854 George Q., Jr.
1860 Eugene H.
1860 Oren D. *m.*

Pond,
1863 George D.

Pooley,
1860 James H. *m.*

Poore,
1866 Charles T. *m.*

Porter,
1862 George. *m.*

Post,
1792 Jotham, Jr.
1808 Edward.
1810 Waldron B.
1818 George D.
1821 Edwin.
1821 Henry A. V.
1822 Alfred C.
1827 Minturn.
1828 Joel B.
1840 Jotham.
1862 Gerardus.
1865 Charles A. *l.*
1867 Edward R. *m.*

Potter,
1840 Ellis, Jr.
1842 Edward F.
1863 William R. *l.*
1866 William B.

Poulsen,
1870 James M. *l.*

Powell,
1864 Stephen C. *m.*

Powers,
1870 Frederic. *m.*

Prall,
1866 William C. *l.*

Pratt,
1867 William H. B. *m.*

Prendergast,
1868 John J. *m.*

Prentice,
1833 David. *h.*

Prentiss,
1870 Robert. *m.*

Prescott,
1840 William H. *h.*

Price,
1799 Stephen.
1804 William M.
1847 Joseph H. *h.*
1865 James L.

Priest,
1802 Henry B.

Prime,
1856 G. Wendell.
1861 Temple. *l.*
1865 Frederick, Jr.

Prince,
1866 L. Bradford. *l.*

Prius,
1860 Peter. *m.*

Proal,
1822 Alexis P. *h.*

Proudfit,
1790 James. *h.*
1792 Alexander.

Provoost,
1758 Samuel.

Pruyn,
1863 Henry V. S. *m.*

Pryer,
1862 William C. *m.*

Pryor,
1864 Alfred. *m.*

Pultz,
1868 Monroe T. *m.*

Pumpelly,
1863 Josiah C. *l.*

Punderson,
1758 Ebenezer. *h.*
1758 Cyrus. *h.*

Punnett,
1831 John.

Purdy,
1805 Abraham.
1811 George B.
1861 Alfred E. M. *m.*
1869 Caleb. *l.*
1869 Samuel A., Jr.
1869 William M.

Purney,
1865 John A. *m.*

Purroy,
1831 John B.
1850 Frederick L.

Pyne,
1823 Smith.

Quackenbos,
1800 Nicholas J.
1803 George C.
1839 George W.
1843 George P.
1868 John D.

Quackinbush,
1806 David.
1836 Daniel McL.

Quin,
1827 James M.
1870 Robert A. *m.*

Quintard,
1853 Charles T. *h.*

Rabe,
1869 Rudolph F. *l.*

Randall,
1774† Paul.

Randol,
1867 Albert R. *m.*

Randolph,
1867 Hector C. F.
1869 John C. *m. e.*

Rankin,
1841 John.

Ranney,
1860 Julius H. *l.*
1865 Henry F. *l.*

Rapelje,
1774 John.
1791 George.
1811 Charles.

Rathbone,
1800 Thomas W.

Rattoone,
1796 William.

Ravenhill,
1845 Lefroy.

Ravenscroft,
1823 John S. *h.*

Ray,
1766 John.
1813 Robert.
1817 Richard.
1852 Robert, Jr.
1861 Richard C.

Raymond,
1816 Samuel G.
1859 William L.
1869 Joseph H. *m.*

Raynolds,
1868 Thomas B. *l.*

Rea,
1868 Robert M. *m.*

Reade,
1758 Joseph.

Reber,
1862 Nathaniel B. *m.*

Redfield,
1831 Richard W.

Redmond,
1857 Goold H.

Reed,
1822 John. *h.*
1832 Stephen, Jr.

Reid,
1845 Aaron B.
1868 Henry H. *l.*
1869 John J. *m.*

Remsen,
1775 Jacobus.
1789 John.
1795 Robert.
1803 William.
1807 Simeon.
1867 Ira. *m.*
1867 Phœnix. *l.*

Renwick,
1807 James.
1809 Robert J.
1833 Henry B.
1833 William R.
1836 James, Jr.
1839 Edward S.

Repetto,
1866 Francisco. *m.*

Reuwee,
1864 Albert A. *l.*

Reynolds,
1835 James N. *h.*
1843 Charles.
1859 Stephen R.
1861 Charles H. *m.*
1862 Jasper G. *m.*
1870 William H. T. *m.*

Rhind,
1827 Charles, Jr.

Sayre,
1774 James. *h.*

Sayres,
1808 Gilbert H.
1854 William J.

Scales,
1867 Thomas S. *m.*

Schack,
1869 Albert P. *m. e.*

Schaeffer,
1830 Frederic C. *h.*
1842 George C. *h.*

Schaffer,
1864 John Le G. *l.*

Schauffler,
1868 Edward W. *m.*

Schenck,
1801 Henry.
1860 John C. *l.*
1864 John P., Jr. *m.*
1865 Peter L. *m.*
1865 Tennis. *m.*
1866 Henry J. *l.*

Schermerhorn,
1793 John S.
1806 Cornelius.
1824 Daniel C.
1825 John J.
1827 John.
1829 Peter A.
1833 Bruce.
1840 William C.
1861 Harry A.
1863 Burr. *m.*
1863 William B.
1870 Frederick A. *m. e.*

Schieffelin,
1801 Henry H.
1819 Richard L.
1855 George R.

Schmidt,
1859 Oscar E.

Schneeberger,
1867 Henry.

Schoonmaker,
1799 Jacob.

Schoonover,
1867 Warren. *m.*

Schroeder,
1849 John F., Jr.

Schureman,
1816 John. *h.*

Schuyler,
1765 Arent.
1806 Philip.
1863 Eugene. *l.*
1869 William D. *m.*

Scofield,
1803 Samuel. *m.*
1868 Walter K. *m.*
1870 George S., Jr.

Scoonover,
1869 Jefferson. *m.*

Scoresby,
1864 William F. *m.*

Scott,
1798 William. *h.*
1850 Winfield. *h.*
1854 I. Jackson. *h.*
1869 Francis M. *l.*
1869 Xenophon C. *m.*

Scovill,
1761 James. *h.*

Scoville,
1861 Frederick. *l.*

Scudder,
1862 Henry J. *h.*

Seabury,
1761 Samuel. *h.*
1823 Samuel. *h.*
1856 William J.

Seaman,
1774 Benjamin.
1795 Benjamin.
1802 Billopp B.
1804 Robert.
1805 Edward.
1851 George A.
1864 William A. *l.*

Searing,
1868 Edward W. *l.*

Searle,
1771 John.
1866 Dayton W. *m.*

Sears,
1857 Charles E,
1862 Henry T. *m.*

Seaver,
1869 Horace N., Jr.

Sebring,
1771 Michael. *m.*

Secor,
1869 William H. *l.*

Sedgwick,
1829 Theodore, Jr.

Seeds,
1860 Orin H. *m.*

Seguin,
1864 Edward C. *m.*

Segur,
1860 Benjamin A. *m.*

Seney,
1815 Robert.

Senger,
1867 William A. *l.*

Seymour,
1826 Daniel.
1836 Charles M.
1850 George F.
1860 Elbridge G. *m.*
1865 Roderick B.
1867 Morris W. *l.*

Shapter,
1840 Peter, Jr.

Sharp,
1868 John. *m.*

Sharswood,
1856 George. *h.*

Shaw,
1774† Jacob.
1862 Samuel F. *m.*
1863 Abner O. *m.*
1863 Amos S., Jr. *m.*

Shea,
1831 James. *h.*
1837 Charles E.

Shedden,
1865 Samuel S. *h.*

Sheldon,
1868 Charles S. *m.*
1869 George P. *l.*

Shelton,
1825 William. *h.*
1867 Charles C. *l.*

Shepard,
1856 William F.
1869 Frank N.
1870 Robert N.

Shepherd,
1842 John H. *h.*

Sherman,
1803 Alpheus.
1868 George H. *m.*
1868 Thomas P. *l.*

Sherwood,
1834 William. *h.*
1849 Ezra K.

Shippey,
1796 Josiah, Jr.

Shoemaker,
1864 Thomas B. *l.*
1866 Murray C. *l.*

Shrady,
1821 George.
1849 John, Jr.
1863 Jacob. *l.*
1864 William. *l.*

Shreve,
1773 Thomas.
1865 Octavius B. *m.*

Sickles,
1792 Jacob.
1804 John J.

Sidell,
1812 John A.

Sill,
1861 Thomas H.

Silliman,
1850 Charles A.

Simmons,
1864 Charles E. *m.*

Simpson,
1841 Robert G.
1860 Samuel F. *l.*
1864 William V. *l.*

Simson,
1800 Sampson.

Simon,
1870 Kaufman. *l.*

Sinclair,
1869 Alexander G. *m.*

Skeene,
1772 Andrew.

Skelding,
1866 Thomas. *m.*

Skidmore,
1849 John D.

Skinner,
1867 Eugene C. *l.*
1870 Orrin. *l.*

Slack,
1821 John C.

Slidell,
1810 John.

Slipper,
1857 James H.
1859 J. Augustus.

Sloan,
1868 Arthur.

Sloane,
1868 William J. M.

Slocum,
1864 William E. *l.*
1869 Charles E. *m.*
1870 William B. *l.*

Slosson,
1828 Barzillai.
1833 Edward.

Slover,
1826 Abraham A., Jr.

Small,
1869 Frederick I. *l.*

Smalley,
1866 William E.

Smedberg,
1833 John G.
1852 James R.
1855 Oscar.
1857 William R.
1869 John A.

Smedes,
1850 John E. C.

Smith,
1774† Horatio.
1786 Samuel.
1792 Samuel.
1793 Gilbert.
1793 Thomas R.

Summers,
1860 George F. *m.*

Sutherland,
1836 Jacob. *h.*

Suydam,
1856 Charles C.
1860 Abraham.
1861 Charles H. *m.*

Swain,
1868 James P., Jr.
1870 George M. *m.*

Swan,
1844 Edward H.
1848 Otis D.
1861 Norman L. *m.*
1868 Benjamin R. *m.*

Swarts,
1864 Frederick. *l.*

Swartwout,
1812 John.

Swasey,
1869 Erastus P. *m.*

Sweeny,
1840 Owen.

Sweezey,
1865 John E.

Swift,
1862 John I. *m.*

Swords,
1826 Thomas, Jr.
1827 Theodore A.
1829 Charles R.
1834 Robert S.

Sylvester,
1786 Francis.

Sym,
1842 John.

Syme,
1864 William R. *l.*

Taber,
1863 James A. *l.*

Taft,
1866 Charles P. *l.*

Taggard,
1835 William H.
1845 John A.

Taggart,
1860 Charles J. *m.*

Tailer,
1852 Henry A.
1857 James T.

Talbot,
1857 William R.
1866 Augustus.
1866 Richmond.

Talcott,
1832 Frederick L.

Tallmadge,
1845 Frederick S.

Talman,
1811 John N.
1814 George F.

Tappan,
1807 Peter V. C.
1854 Henry P. *h.*

Taylor,
1792 George.
1792 William.
1793 Willett, Jr. *m.*
1796 Charles.
1831 Edwin M.
1837 Thomas H. *h.*
1861 George L.
1861 Henry A. C.
1868 Robert W. *m.*

Teakle,
1842 Elisha W.

Temple,
1795 James B.

Ten Broeck,
1834 Anthony.

Terhune,
1870 Richard H. *m. e.*

Terrett,
1863 Charles W.

Terrill,
1867 Thomas, Jr. *m.*

Terry,
1850 William H.
1865 David D. *l.*

Thatcher,
1858 Thomas F.
1866 Ralph P. *m.*

Thayer,
1862 Foster.
1863 Stephen H., Jr.
1868 Horace H.

Thibou,
1828 Lewis.

Thomas,
1800 Charles F.
1832 Philip W.
1835 Ludlow.
1837 David P.
1870 Nathaniel P. S. *l.*

Thomasson,
1865 John J. *l.*

Thompson,
1793 Thomas.
1804 John R.
1821 Junius.
1832 Jonathan, Jr.
1833 Abraham G., Jr.
1836 William.
1841 William M. *h.*
1854 Gardiner.
1856 David G., Jr.
1863 Thomas. *m.*
1864 Edward W. *m.*
1866 Frederick. *l.*
1867 Frank. *l.*
1868 Charles H. *m.*
1869 David. *m.*
1870 Robert E. *m.*

Thoms,
1860 William F. *m.*

Thomson,
1803 Samuel W.
1818 Andrew. *h.*
1842 David, Jr.
1843 John.
1846 James.
1866 William J.

Thorn,
1852 Eugene.
1852 William E.
1870 William K., Jr. *l.*

Thrall,
1861 S. Chipman. *h.*

Thurman,
1835 John R.
1864 William. *m.*

Thurston,
1851 A. Henry.

Tibbals,
1864 Elbert P. *m.*

Tibbitts,
1853 Washington I.

Tichenor,
1801 Gabriel.

Tiebout,
1821 John, Jr.

Tillary,
1800 Matthew.
1802 James.

Tillinghast,
1806 John L.

Tillou,
1869 Edward.

Timpson,
1856 John W.

Titus,
1823 James H.

Todd,
1844 Andrew S. *h.*
1864 John R. *m.*
1869 Charles A. *m.*
1869 William S. *m.*

Tomes,
1831 Francis, Jr.

Tompkins,
1795 Daniel D.

Tooker,
1859 Gabriel M.

Toppan,
1861 Robert N. *l.*

Torrey,
1868 Samuel W. *m.*
1869 Edward. *m.*

Totten,
1858 Gilbert T.

Tourtelotte,
1863 Jacob F. *m.*

Townsend,
1759 Epenetus.
1810 Jacob.
1812 Peter S.
1820 John R.
1832 Frederick.
1832 Russell N.
1841 John J.
1847 Israel L.
1870 Clayton W. *m.*

Tracy,
1860 Frederick A.
1863 Lewis A. *m.*
1868 Roger S. *m.*
1869 Charles A. *l.*
1869 Charles E. *l.*

Trafford,
1867 Charles H. *l.*

Travers,
1838 William R.

Travis,
1847 Robert, Jr.
1850 Edward F.

Treadwell,
1758 Daniel. *h.*
1761 Agur. *h.*

Tremain,
1867 Henry E. *l.*

Trenaman,
1869 Thomas. *m.*

Trenor,
1852 Eustace.
1852 John, Jr.
1859 Thomas F.

Trevett,
1835 Russell.

Tripler,
1860 Charles S. *h.*
1868 Thomas H. *m.*

Trippe,
1854 John C.

Troup,
1766 John.
1766 John, Jr.
1774 Robert.

Tryon,
1774 William. *h.*
1862 Amazias W. *m.*

Tucker,
1769 Robert. *m.*
1822 Thomas W.
1829 Robert.
1837 John I.
1852 Richard H.
1861 John A.
1863 Robert S.

Tuckerman,
1863 Ernest L.

Wallace,
1827 Joseph C.

Waller,
1870 Elwyn. *m. e.*

Wallis,
1865 Hamilton. *l.*

Walsh,
1798 James.
1801 Samuel A.
1822 John. *h.*
1828 Alexander R.
1839 James W.
1864 Julius S. *l.*

Walter,
1799 Arthur M.
1865 William H. *h.*

Walters,
1804 Daniel D. *m.*

Walton,
1777† James De L.
1777† William.
1828 William.
1861 Louis P.

Walz,
1864 Isidor.

Wandell,
1865 Townsend. *l.*

Ward,
1800 John Y.
1831 Samuel, Jr.
1836 Henry, Jr.
1838 Henry H.
1838 Francis M.
1851 Charles H.
1851 William G.
1858 John, Jr.
1861 Edwin F. *m.*
1861 Isaac J.
1861 Prescott H. *l.*
1861 Samuel B.
1861 Edward M. *m.*
1862 Richard H. *m.*
1863 Josiah O. *l.*
1864 Frederick A. *l.*
1865 Willard P.
1867 Edmund A. *l.*
1868 Leslie D. *m.*

Warner,
1795 Effingham.
1867 Eli. *m.*

Warren,
1860 Joel A. *m.*
1864 William. P. *m.*

Warth,
1868 John W. *m.*

Washburn,
1866 Charles. *m.*

Waterman,
1858 Henry. *h.*

Waters,
1836 George G.
1865 George D. *h.*

Watkins,
1788 John W. *h.*
1815 James S.

Watson,
1804 James T.
1852 John L.

Watts,
1760 Robert.
1766 John.
1796 John.
1803 Robert, Jr.
1804 John, Jr.
1805 Robert I.
1808 Henry.
1808 John, Jr.
1810 Charles.
1811 George J.
1831 Robert, Jr.
1861 Robert, Jr. *m.*

Wayne,
1866 James M.

Weaver,
1864 Lathrop P. *m.*

Webb,
1863 De Witt. *m.*

Webbe,
1870 William N.

Webster,
1824 Daniel. *h.*
1849 Horace. *h.*
1865 Almar P. *l.*

Weed,
1836 Harvey A.
1868 John W. *l.*

Weeks,
1822 Alfred A.
1856 James.
1861 James R. *l.*
1864 Robert K. *l.*
1867 Francis H. *l.*
1869 Edward F.

Weisman,
1868 Francis H. *m.*

Wellman,
1851 Merritt H.

Wells,
1819 Thomas L.
1865 James L.
1867 George, Jr. *m.*
1870 Albert W. *l.*

Wendel,
1855 John G.

Wentworth,
1863 Walter H. *m.*

Wessels,
1869 Frank W. *l.*

Wesson,
1865 Charles H. *l.*

West,
1844 Charles E. *h.*
1861 Edward W.
1869 Charles W. *l.*

Westcott,
1865 Nelson S. *m.*

Westerlo,
1795 Rensselaer.

Westervelt,
1863 Ellsworth.

Westfall,
1863 Lewis. m.

Weston,
1861 Sullivan H. *h.*

Wetmore,
1758 Timothy. *h.*
1795 Timothy F. *m.*
1798 Robert G. *h.*
1848 Benjamin C.
1849 Prosper M., Jr.
1863 Edmund. *l.*
1869 George P. *l.*

Whaley,
1870 George H. *m.*

Wheeler,
1861 William L. *m.*
1862 James H. *m.*
1865 John V.
1866 Peter. *m.*
1868 Moses D. *m. e.*
1870 Francis A. *m.*

Wheelock,
1864 George G. *m.*

Whiley,
1828 Richard, Jr.
1844 Charles W.

Whipple,
1869 Ezekiel W. *l.*

Whitaker,
1774† John.

Whitall,
1866 Samuel. *m.*

White,
1791 Nathan.
1848 Joseph M.
1849 John J.
1861 John P P. *m.*
1862 Henry K *l.*
1866 Henry S. *m.*
1870 Henry S. *l.*

Whitehead,
1864 J. Elias. *m.*

Whitehouse,
1821 Henry J.
1859 Edward N.
1859 Henry B.
1860 William F.
1861 Frederick C.

Whiting,
1864 William L. *l.*
1866 Henry A.
1870 Howard. *m.*

Whitlock,
1837 Samuel H.

Whitney,
1861 Albert B.

Whittingham,
1827 William R. *h.*

Whybrow,
1870 Charles T. *m.*

Wight,
1861 Charles M. *m.*
1864 Thomas. *m.*

Wildey,
1860 Pierre W.

Wilkes,
1821 George.
1822 Hamilton.

Wilkins,
1760 Isaac.

Willard,
1869 Charles E. *m.*

Willcox,
1867 James K. H. *l.*

Willett,
1776 Marinus.
1819 Marinus, Jr.
1822 Edward M.
1856 Elbert M.
1864 Marinus, Jr.

Williams,
1822 William R.
1833 James A.
1850 Timothy D. *h.*
1851 John. *h.*
1856 Howell L., Jr.
1860 Augustus P. *m.*
1867 Channing M. *h.*
1867 William H. *l.*
1868 Stephen W.

Williamson,
1807 Charles A.

Willis,
1862 Francis.
1862 William H., Jr.
1864 William S. *m.*

Wilmarth,
1868 Frank. *m.*

Wilmerding,
1868 Lucius K.

Wilson,
1800 George.
1800 Peter.
1818 Abraham D.
1822 Samuel F.
1825 Peter.
1825 William.
1826 Harris.
1835 William H.
1836 James W.
1845 Bird. *h.*
1860 Philip L. *l.*
1861 Benjamin F. *m.*
1862 Merritt H. *m.*
1863 Benjamin. *m.*
1865 Francis F.
1866 James W. *m.*
1869 William. *l.*
1870 John P. *m.*

Winans,
1840 James W.

# CATALOGUE

OF THE

# GOVERNORS, TRUSTEES, AND OFFICERS,

AND OF THE

## ALUMNI AND OTHER GRADUATES,

OF

# COLUMBIA COLLEGE

(ORIGINALLY KING'S COLLEGE),

IN THE

# CITY OF NEW YORK,

FROM

## 1754 TO 1876.

PRINTED FOR THE COLLEGE.

1876.

Macgowan & Slippei, Printers, 30 Beekman Street, N. Y.

# CONTENTS.

# ABBREVIATIONS.

| | | | |
|---|---|---|---|
| ACT. | Actuary. | ED. | Editor. |
| ARCH. | Architect. | ENG. | Engineer. |
| ART. | Artist. | F. | Farmer. |
| AU. | Author. | M. | Merchant. |
| B. | Banker. | PUB. | Publisher. |
| BR. | Broker. | PR. | Printer. |
| CHEM. | Chemist. | REV. | Reverend. |
| C. L. | Counsellor at Law. | T. | Teacher. |

A star (*) prefixed to a name denotes that the individual is deceased. In every case in which the year of the decease is known, it is indicated at the right.

# EXPLANATORY NOTICE.

THE present catalogue of the Alumni and other graduates of Columbia College is the eighth which has been published since the re-organization of the College under its present title in 1787. The earlier of these publications were not issued periodically. With the fifth, published in 1865, there was commenced a series designed to be continued triennially. (One triennium, 1870–73, has been, however, allowed to pass without the issuing of a catalogue.) In this, also, the attempt was for the first time made to indicate the professions or occupations of the graduates, and to present a record of the honors, of whatever kind, which have been conferred upon them. Such an attempt, in the absence of any written record regularly kept at the College or elsewhere of matters of this nature, could not but be, to a certain extent, unsuccessful; and accordingly in the issuing of the catalogue of 1865 no credit was claimed for that publication on the score of perfection or completeness. The publication was avowedly made, in the form adopted, quite as much in the hope of eliciting, by means of the interest it might excite, additional information in regard to the personal history of the graduates, as of giving a permanent form to the information already obtained. This hope has not been wholly disappointed. A number of the Alumni of the College have kindly contributed important additions to the knowledge which had been previously gathered in regard to members of many of the earlier classes: and in consequence of this valuable assistance, the present edition of the catalogue, though still imperfect, will be found to exhibit a sensible improvement on those which have gone before.

Copies of this catalogue will be sent, as in 1865, in 1868 and in 1871, to all the living Alumni whose residences are known. Those who may not receive it may be assured that the omission is owing only to want of information as to their proper addresses. They will be promptly supplied, on application, by post or otherwise, to the President, at the College.

Notwithstanding the considerable success which has attended the efforts made to supply the deficiencies of former publications, the imperfections which will doubtless be detected in the present one can hardly fail to be numerous. This prefatory note cannot, therefore, be better concluded than by once more repeating the request earnestly made on former occasions, of every graduate into whose hands the catalogue should fall, that he would communicate to the President, or to Professor Van Amringe, at the College, any information which may serve to improve it in future editions; completing first his own record, should he find it deficient, and adding any important facts within his knowledge, which the catalogue does not contain, in regard to any other graduate or graduates.

Columbia College, July 4, 1876.

# GOVERNORS
OF
# KING'S COLLEGE,
## NEW YORK,
### AS APPOINTED BY ROYAL CHARTER,
## OCTOBER 31, A. D. 1754.

The most Reverend Father in God, Thomas, Lord Archbishop of Canterbury; and the most Reverend the Lord Archbishop of Canterbury for the time being, *ex officio.*

The Right Honorable Dunk, Earl of Halifax, First Lord Commissioner for Trade and Plantations; and the First Lord Commissioner for Trade and Plantations for the time being, *ex officio.*

The Governor of the Province, *ex officio.*

The eldest Councillor of the Province, *ex officio.*

The Judges of the Supreme Court of Judicature of the Province, *ex officio.*

The Secretary of the Province, *ex officio.*

The Attorney-General of the Province, *ex officio.*

The Speaker of the General Assembly of the Province, *ex officio.*

The Treasurer of the Province, *ex officio.*

The Mayor of the City of New York, *ex officio.*

The Rector of Trinity Church in the City of New York, *ex officio.*

The Senior Minister of the Reformed Protestant Dutch Church in the City of New York, *ex officio.*

The Minister of the Ancient Lutheran Church in the City of New York, *ex officio.*

The Minister of the French Church in the City of New York, *ex officio.*

The Minister of the Presbyterian Congregation in the City of New York, *ex officio.*

The President of the College, *ex officio.*

[The names of those who, at various times, attended meetings of the Governors, by virtue of their office as above are:

JOHN CHAMBERS, Second Justice of the Supreme Court of the Province.
WILLIAM KEMPE, Attorney-General of the Province.
ABRAHAM DE PEYSTER, Treasurer of the Province.
EDWARD HOLLAND, Mayor of the City of New York.
HENRY BARCLAY, Rector of Trinity Church, New York.
JOANNES RITZEMA, Senior Minister of the Reformed Protestant Dutch Church, New York.
JOHN ALBERT WEYGAND, Minister of the Ancient Lutheran Church, New York.
JOANNES CARLE, Minister of the French Church, New York.
SAMUEL JOHNSON, President of the College.
JOHN CRUGER, JR., Mayor of the City of New York.
DANIEL HORSMANDEN, Third Justice of the Supreme Court of the Province.
JOHN TABOR KEMPE, Attorney-General of the Province.
BENJAMIN PRATT, Chief-Justice of the Supreme Court of the Province.
MYLES COOPER, President of the College.
SAMUEL AUCHMUTY, Rector of Trinity Church, New York.
JOHN CRUGER, Speaker of the General Assembly of the Province.
The Archbishop of Canterbury (by proxy).]

ARCHIBALD KENNEDY..............................Declined to qualify.

JOSEPH MURRAY.............Deceased Between July, 1756, and May, 1757

JOSIAH MARTIN.............Removed from the Province Between March, 1761, and Oct., 1764

PAUL RICHARD.............Deceased Between July, 1756, and March, 1759

HENRY CRUGER.............Retired Subsequently to 1780

WILLIAM WALTON.............Deceased Between May, 1768, and March, 1770

JOHN WATTS.............Retired Subsequently to 1780

HENRY BEEKMAN.............Resigned 1770

PHILIP VERPLANCK.............Resigned 1770

FREDERICK PHILIPSE.............Retired Subsequently to 1780

JOSEPH ROBINSON.............Deceased Between May, 1755, and March, 1759

JOHN CRUGER.............Retired Subsequently to 1770

OLIVER DE LANCEY.............Retired Subsequently to 1780

|  | |  |
|---|---|---|
| James Livingston | | Deceased 1763 |
| Benjamin Nicoll | Between Feb., 1760, and April | Deceased 1763 |
| William Livingston | Declined to qualify | |
| Joseph Reade | Subsequently to | Retired 1770 |
| Nathaniel Marston | Subsequently to | Retired 1780 |
| Joseph Haynes | Between March, 1758, and Jan., | Deceased 1762 |
| John Livingston | Subsequently to | Retired 1780 |
| Abraham Lodge | Between June, 1760, and Jan., | Deceased 1762 |
| David Clarkson | Subsequently to | Retired 1780 |
| Leonard Lispenard | Subsequently to | Retired 1780 |
| James De Lancey, Jr. | Subsequently to | Retired 1780 |

Appointed subsequently, by virtue of the power vested in the Governors by the Charter:

| Appointed | Name | | Resigned / Retired / Deceased |
|---|---|---|---|
| 1759 | Samuel Auchmuty | Having become Rector of Trinity Church, | Resigned 1764 |
| 1759 | Gabriel Ludlow | | Resigned 1770 |
| 1761 | Edward Antill | Did not qualify or serve | |
| 1762 | John Chambers | Between Nov., 1762, and Oct., | Deceased 1764 |
| 1762 | Henry Cuyler | Subsequently to | Retired 1770 |
| 1762 | James Duane | Subsequently to | Retired 1780 |
| 1762 | William Alexander, Earl of Stirling | Subsequently to | Retired 1776 |
| 1763 | Charles Ward Apthorpe | Subsequently to | Retired 1780 |
| 1764 | Beverley Robinson | | Resigned 1770 |
| 1764 | John Provoost | Between Aug., 1767, and March | Deceased 1770 |
| 1764 | Thomas Jones | Subsequently to | Retired 1780 |
| 1764 | Archibald Kennedy | Subsequently to | Retired 1780 |
| 1770 | Roger Morris | Subsequently to | Retired 1780 |
| 1770 | John Ogilvie, S. T. D. | | Deceased 1774 |
| 1770 | Samuel Verplanck | Subsequently to | Retired 1780 |

| Appointed | | | Retired |
|---|---|---|---|
| 1770 | Goldsborough Banyar | Subsequently to | 1780 |
| 1770 | William Walton | Subsequently to | 1780 |
| | Charles Inglis, S. T. D | Subsequently to | 1780 |
| | Henry White | Subsequently to | 1780 |
| | Peter Middleton, M.D. | Subsequently to | 1780 |
| | Jacob Walton | Subsequently to | 1780 |
| | John Harris Cruger | Subsequently to | 1780 |
| | John Maunsell | Subsequently to | 1780 |

## REGENTS OF THE UNIVERSITY,

To whom the Government of the College, under the name of Columbia College, was committed by an Act of the Legislature of the State of New York, passed May 1,

## A. D. 1784:

The Governor of the State for the time being, *ex officio.*
The Lieutenant-Governor " "
The President of the Senate " "
The Speaker of the House of Assembly for the time being, *ex officio.*
The Mayor of the City of New York " "
The Mayor of the City of Albany " "
The Attorney-General " "
The President and Professors of the College " "
The Secretary of State " "

Brockholst Livingston,
Robert Harpur,
Walter Livingston,
Christopher Yates,
Anthony Hoffman,
Cornelius Humphrey,
Lewis Morris,
Philip Pell, Jr.,
Christopher P. Yates,
James Livingston,
Matthew Clarkson,
Rutgers Van Brunt,
James Townsend,
Thomas Lawrence,
Henry Wisner,
John Haring,
Christopher Tappan,
James Clinton,
Ezra L'Hommedieu,
Caleb Smith,

Abraham Bancker,
John C. Dongan,
John Williams,
John M'Crea.

And the following, added to the above-named by an Act of the Legislature, passed November 26, 1784:

John Jay, LL. D.,
Samuel Provoost, S. T. D.,
John H. Livingston, S. T. D.,
John Rogers, S. T. D.,
John Mason, S. T. D.,
John Gano,
John Daniel Gross, S. T D.,
Johann Christoff Kunze, S. T. D.,
Joseph Delaplaine,
Gershom Seixas,
Alexander Hamilton, LL. D.,
John Lawrence,
John Rutherfurd,
Morgan Lewis,
Leonard Lispenard.
John Cochran, M. D.,
Charles McKnight, M. D.,
Thomas Jones, M. D.,
Malachi Treat, M. D.,
Nicholas Romayne, M. D.,
Peter W. Yates,
Matthew Visscher,
Hunlock Woodruff, M. D.
George I. L. Dole,
John Vanderbilt,
Thomas Romaine.
Samuel Buel,
Gilbert Livingston,
Nathan Kerr,
Ebenezer Lockwood,
John Lloyd,
Herman Garrison,
Ebenezer Russell.

## TRUSTEES OF COLUMBIA COLLEGE.

The following, appointed by an Act of the Legislature of the State of New York, April 13, 1787, reviving the original charter with amendments:

| | |
|---|---|
| James Duane | Resigned 1795 |
| Samuel Provoost, S. T. D | Resigned 1801 |
| John H. Livingston, S. T. D | Retired 1810 |
| Richard Varick | Resigned 1816 |
| Alexander Hamilton, LL. D | Deceased 1804 |
| John Mason, S. T. D | Resigned 1788 |
| James Wilson | Retired 1788 |

|  | |  |
|---|---|---|
| John Gano* | Retired | 1788 |
| Brockholst Livingston, LL. D | Deceased | 1823 |
| Robert Harpur | Resigned | 1795 |
| John Daniel Gross, S. T. D | Resigned | 1787 |
| Johann Christoff Kunze, S. T. D. | Resigned | 1792 |
| Walter Livingston | Deceased | 1797 |
| Lewis A. Scott | Deceased | 1798 |
| Joseph Delaplaine | Declined | 1787 |
| Leonard Lispenard | Deceased | 1790 |
| Abraham Beach, S. T. D | Retired | 1813 |
| John Lawrence | Deceased | 1810 |
| John Rutherfurd† | Retired | 1787 |
| Morgan Lewis | Resigned | 1804 |
| John Cochran, M. D | Resigned | 1794 |
| Gershom Seixas | Resigned | 1815 |
| Charles McKnight, M. D | Resigned | 1787 |
| Thomas Jones, M. D | Deceased | 1798 |
| Malachi Treat, M. D. | Deceased | 1795 |
| Samuel Bard, M. D. | Resigned | 1804 |
| Nicholas Romayne, M. D | Resigned | 1793 |
| Benjamin Kissam, M. D. | Deceased | 1803 |
| Ebenezer Crosby, M. D | Deceased | 1788 |

And the following, subsequently chosen by virtue of the Act of April 13, 1787, empowering the Trustees then created to fill vacancies:

| Appointed | Name | | Year |
|---|---|---|---|
| 1788 | William Samuel Johnson, LL. D. | Resigned | 1800 |
| 1788 | Richard Harison, LL. D. | Deceased | 1829 |

* This name does not appear in the list of Trustees after March 15, 1788.

† This name does not appear on the list of Trustees after May 20, 1787.

|  |  | | |
|---|---|---|---|
| 1789 | John Watts | Resigned | 1816 |
| 1790 | William Moore, M. D | Deceased | 1824 |
| 1793 | Edward Livingston | Retired | 1806 |
| 1793 | John McKnight, S. T. D | Resigned | 1795 |
| 1794 | John Cosine | Deceased | 1798 |
| 1795 | Cornelius I. Bogert | Resigned | 1823 |
| 1795 | John M. Mason, S. T. D | Resigned | 1821 |
| 1795 | Samuel Nicoll, M. D | Deceased | 1796 |
| 1795 | Edward Dunscomb | Deceased | 1814 |
| 1796 | George C. Anthon, M. D | Resigned | 1815 |
| 1797 | Philip Livingston | Resigned | 1806 |
| 1799 | John Charlton, M. D | Deceased | 1806 |
| 1799 | John N. Abeel, S. T. D | Deceased | 1812 |
| 1799 | James Tillary, M. D | Deceased | 1818 |
| 1801 | Charles H. Wharton, S. T. D | Resigned | 1801 |
| 1801 | John H. Hobart, S. T. D | Deceased | 1830 |
| 1802 | Benjamin Moore, S. T. D | Resigned | 1813 |
| 1804 | Egbert Benson, LL. D | Resigned | 1815 |
| 1804 | Johann C. Kunze, S. T. D | Deceased | 1807 |
| 1805 | Gouverneur Morris | Deceased | 1816 |
| 1805 | Jacob Radcliffe | Resigned | 1817 |
| 1806 | Samuel Miller, S. T. D | Retired | 1813 |
| 1806 | Rufus King, LL. D | Resigned | 1824 |
| 1807 | Nicholas Evertson | Deceased | 1807 |
| 1808 | Oliver Wolcott | Retired | 1816 |
| 1809 | John B. Romeyn, S. T. D | Deceased | 1825 |
| 1811 | William Harris, S. T. D | Deceased | 1829 |
| 1811 | Robert Troup, LL. D | Resigned | 1817 |

| Appointed | | |
|---|---|---|
| 1812 | Peter A. Jay | Resigned 1817 |
| 1813 | Clement C. Moore, LL. D. | Resigned 1857 |
| 1813 | Charles Wilkes | Resigned 1824 |
| 1815 | David B. Ogden, LL. D. | Deceased 1849 |
| 1815 | William Johnson, LL. D. | Resigned 1842 |
| 1815 | John Wells | Deceased 1823 |
| 1816 | Thomas Y. How, S. T. D. | Retired 1818 |
| 1816 | William Henderson | Resigned 1823 |
| 1816 | Edward W. Laight | Resigned 1851 |
| 1816 | John R. Murray | Resigned 1835 |
| 1816 | Wright Post, M. D. | Resigned 1828 |
| 1817 | Beverley Robinson | Resigned 1854 |
| 1817 | Thomas L. Ogden | Deceased 1844 |
| 1817 | Nicholas Fish | Resigned 1833 |
| 1817 | James Renwick | Retired 1820 |
| 1818 | Samuel F. Jarvis, S. T. D | Retired 1820 |
| 1818 | John T. Irving | Deceased 1838 |
| 1820 | David S. Jones, LL. D | Deceased 1848 |
| 1821 | Gulian C. Verplanck | Resigned 1826 |
| 1822 | Pascal N. Strong | Deceased 1825 |
| 1823 | James Kent, LL. D | Resigned 1823 |
| 1823 | Peter A. Jay, LL. D. | Deceased 1843 |
| 1823 | John Duer | Resigned 1830 |
| 1824 | Benjamin T. Onderdonk, S. T. D. | Resigned 1853 |
| 1824 | Lynde Catlin | Deceased 1833 |
| 1825 | Jonathan M. Wainwright, S. T D | Resigned 1830 |
| 1824 | Philip Hone | Deceased 1851 |
| 1824 | John Watts, M. D. | Deceased 1831 |

| Appointed | Name | |
|---|---|---|
| 1825 | CHARLES KING | Resigned 1838 |
| 1825 | JAMES M. MATTHEWS, S. T. D. | Resigned 1830 |
| 1826 | SAMUEL BOYD | Resigned 1835 |
| 1828 | WILLIAM CREIGHTON, S. T. D. | Resigned 1840 |
| 1830 | GARDINER SPRING, S. T. D. | Deceased 1873 |
| 1830 | JAMES CAMPBELL | Deceased 1848 |
| 1830 | WILLIAM D. SNODGRASS, S. T. D | Resigned 1833 |
| 1830 | JOHN L. LAWRENCE | Deceased 1849 |
| 1830 | WILLIAM A. DUER, LL. D | Resigned 1842 |
| 1830 | JOHN FERGUSON | Deceased 1832 |
| 1831 | EDWARD R. JONES | Resigned 1838 |
| 1832 | WILLIAM BERRIAN, S. T. D. | Deceased 1862 |
| 1833 | OGDEN HOFFMAN | Deceased 1856 |
| 1833 | THOMAS W. LUDLOW | Resigned 1836 |
| 1834 | SAMUEL WARD | Deceased 1838 |
| 1836 | SAMUEL B. RUGGLES, LL. D. | |
| 1836 | JOHN KNOX, S. T. D. | Deceased 1858 |
| 1837 | THOMAS L. WELLS | Resigned 1859 |
| 1838 | WILLIAM R. WILLIAMS, S. T. D. | Resigned 1848 |
| 1838 | WILLIAM H. HARISON | Deceased 1860 |
| 1838 | JOHN B. BECK, M. D. | Deceased 1851 |
| 1840 | HAMILTON FISH | Resigned 1849 |
| 1840 | WILLIAM BARD | Deceased 1853 |
| 1842 | WILLIAM BETTS, LL. D. | |
| 1842 | NATHANIEL F. MOORE, LL. D. | Resigned 1851 |
| 1843 | BENJAMIN I. HAIGHT, S. T. D., LL. D. | |
| 1845 | GERRIT G. VAN WAGENEN | Deceased 1858 |
| 1848 | JOHN L. MASON | Resigned 1853 |

| Appointed | | |
|---|---|---|
| 1848 | William H. Hobart, M. D. | Resigned 1855 |
| 1849 | Edward Jones | Deceased 1869 |
| 1849 | Robert Ray | |
| 1849 | Gouverneur M. Ogden | |
| 1849 | Charles King, LL. D. | Deceased 1867 |
| 1851 | Hamilton Fish, LL. D. | |
| 1851 | Henry James Anderson, M. D., LL. D. | Deceased 1875 |
| 1851 | Gerard W. Morris | Resigned 1855 |
| 1851 | George H. Fisher, S. T. D. | Resigned 1855 |
| 1853 | George T. Strong | Deceased 1875 |
| 1853 | Jonathan M. Wainwright, S. T. D., J. C. D. | Deceased 1854 |
| 1853 | Edward L. Beadle, M. D. | |
| 1854 | George F. Allen | Deceased 1863 |
| 1854 | Horatio Potter, S. T. D., LL. D., D. C. L. | |
| 1855 | Alexander W. Bradford, LL. D. | Deceased 1867 |
| 1855 | Mancius S. Hutton, S. T. D. | |
| 1856 | Martin Zabriskie | Resigned 1869 |
| 1856 | John Torrey, M. D., LL. D. | Deceased 1873 |
| 1858 | Thomas De Witt, S. T. D. | Retired 1874 |
| 1858 | Lewis M. Rutherfurd | |
| 1859 | John Jacob Astor, Jr. | Resigned 1869 |
| 1859 | John C. Jay, M. D. | |
| 1860 | William C. Schermerhorn | |
| 1862 | Morgan Dix, S. T. D. | |
| 1864 | Frederick A. P. Barnard, S. T. D., LL. D., L. H. D. | |
| 1867 | Samuel Blatchford, LL. D. | |
| 1868 | Stephen P. Nash | |
| 1870 | Charles R. Swords | |
| 1872 | Anthony Halsey | |

| Appointed | |
|---|---|
| 1873 | Joseph W. Harper, Jr. |
| 1874 | Cornelius R. Agnew, M. D. |
| 1874 | Evert A. Duyckinck |
| 1875 | James W. Beekman |
| 1876 | Aaron Ernest Vanderpoel |
| 1876 | Charles A. Silliman |

## TRUSTEES OF THE MEDICAL DEPARTMENT.

### 1860.

|  | |
|---|---|
| John C. Cheesman, M. D. | Deceased 1862 |
| Edward G. Ludlow, M D. | |
| Joseph Delafield | Retired 1871 |
| Floyd Smith | Deceased 1874 |
| Richard M. Blatchford | Deceased 1871 |
| Edward Delafield, M. D. | Deceased 1875 |
| John P. Crosby | |
| Gurdon Buck, M. D. | |
| Luther Bradish | Deceased 1863 |
| James W. Beekman | |
| Daniel D. Lord | |
| Benjamin R. Winthrop | |
| Edward L. Beadle, M. D. | |
| Wickham Hoffman | Resigned 1867 |
| Isaac Wood, M. D. | Resigned 1868 |
| George W. Wright | Retired 1872 |
| Frederick A. Conkling | |
| Charles Henschel, M. D. | Retired 1872 |
| Washington Murray | Resigned 1868 |

| | |
|---|---|
| HENRY CHAUNCEY, Jr. | Resigned 1869 |
| SULLIVAN H. WESTON, S. T. D. | |
| WILLIAM BETTS, LL. D. | |
| JOHN JACOB ASTOR, Jr. | Resigned 1863 |
| GEORGE TALBOT OLYPHANT | Deceased 1873 |
| JOHN TORREY, M. D., LL. D. | Deceased 1873 |

### *SINCE APPOINTED.*

| | | |
|---|---|---|
| 1863 | BENJAMIN OGDEN, M. D. | Resigned 1867 |
| 1863 | CAMBRIDGE LIVINGSTON | |
| 1864 | JARED LINSLY, M. D. | |
| 1867 | JOHN J. CRANE, M. D. | |
| 1869 | ELLSWORTH ELLIOT, M. D. | |
| 1869 | ROBERT G. REMSEN | |
| 1869 | JAMES L. BANKS, M. D. | |
| 1869 | GEORGE D. H. GILLESPIE | Retired 1874 |
| 1872 | EDWARD PARKER, M. D. | |
| 1872 | EDWARD H. LUDLOW | |
| 1872 | EDWARD DELAFIELD, Jr. | |
| 1872 | CHARLES C. GOODHUE | Retired 1874 |
| 1873 | JOHN G. ADAMS, M. D. | |
| 1874 | JOHN SHERWOOD | |
| 1875 | FREDERICK A. P. BARNARD, S. T. D., LL. D., L. H. D. | |
| 1875 | SAMUEL T. HUBBARD, M. D. | |
| 1876 | ALFRED S. PURDY, M. D., President Alumni Association, *ex officio* | |
| 1876 | ALONZO CLARK, President of the School, *ex officio* | |
| 1876 | THOMAS F. COCK, M. D. | |

# CHAIRMEN

### *OF THE BOARD OF GOVERNORS UNDER THE ROYAL CHARTER.*

The Governor of the Province, or person next in rank, or Senior Governor.

### *OF THE BOARD OF REGENTS, 1784–1787.*

The Chancellor of the University, or Vice-Chancellor, or Senior Regent.

### *OF THE BOARD OF TRUSTEES.*

| Appointed | Name | |
|---|---|---|
| 1787 | JAMES DUANE | Resigned 1795 |
| 1795 | SAMUEL PROVOOST, S. T. D. | Resigned 1801 |
| 1801 | JOHN H. LIVINGSTON, S. T. D. | Resigned 1810 |
| 1810 | RICHARD VARICK | Resigned 1816 |
| 1816 | BROCKHOLST LIVINGSTON, LL. D. | Deceased 1823 |
| 1823 | RICHARD HARISON, LL. D. | Resigned 1823 |
| 1823 | WILLIAM MOORE, M. D. | Deceased 1824 |
| 1824 | NICHOLAS FISH | Resigned 1832 |
| 1832 | PETER A. JAY, LL. D. | Deceased 1843 |
| 1843 | DAVID B. OGDEN, LL. D. | Deceased 1849 |
| 1849 | EDWARD W. LAIGHT | Resigned 1850 |
| 1850 | BEVERLEY ROBINSON | Resigned 1854 |
| 1854 | JOHN KNOX, S. T. D. | Resigned 1854 |
| 1858 | GARDINER SPRING, S. T. D. | Resigned 1859 |
| 1859 | HAMILTON FISH, LL. D. | |

# CLERKS

## *OF THE BOARD OF GOVERNORS.*

LAMBERT MOORE.

## *OF THE BOARD OF REGENTS, 1784-1787.*

ROBERT HARPUR.

## *OF THE BOARD OF TRUSTEES.*

| Appointed | | Resigned |
|---|---|---|
| 1787 | ROBERT HARPUR | 1795 |
| | | Resigned |
| 1795 | ABRAHAM BEACH, S. T. D. | 1811 |
| | | Resigned |
| 1811 | WILLIAM HARRIS, S. T. D. | 1811 |
| | | Resigned |
| 1811 | JOHN B. ROMEYN, S. T. D. | 1815 |
| | | Resigned |
| 1815 | CLEMENT C. MOORE, LL. D. | 1850 |
| | | Resigned |
| 1850 | WILLIAM BETTS, LL. D. | 1874 |
| 1874 | ANTHONY HALSEY | |

# TREASURERS OF THE COLLEGE.

| | | Resigned |
|---|---|---|
| 1775 | LEONARD LISPENARD | 1784 |
| | | Deceased |
| 1784 | BROCKHOLST LIVINGSTON, LL. D. | 1823 |
| | | Resigned |
| 1823 | NICHOLAS FISH | 1823 |
| | | Resigned |
| 1824 | WILLIAM JOHNSON, LL. D. | 1833 |
| | | Deceased |
| 1833 | JOHN L. LAWRENCE | 1849 |
| | | Deceased |
| 1849 | GERRIT G. VAN WAGENEN | 1858 |
| 1858 | GOUVERNEUR M. OGDEN | |

# PRESIDENTS OF THE COLLEGE

## *UNDER THE ROYAL CHARTER.*

| | | Resigned |
|---|---|---|
| 1754 | SAMUEL JOHNSON, S. T. D. | 1763 |
| | | Retired |
| 1763 | MYLES COOPER, LL. D. | 1775 |
| | | Resigned |
| 1775 | BENJAMIN MOORE, A. M. (*pro tempore,* in the absence of the President) | 1776 |

## PRESIDENTS OF THE COLLEGE

### *UNDER THE NEW CHARTER.*

| Appointed | | |
|---|---|---|
| 1787 | WILLIAM SAMUEL JOHNSON, LL. D. | Resigned 1800 |
| 1801 | CHARLES H. WHARTON, S. T. D. | Resigned 1801 |
| 1801 | BENJAMIN MOORE, S. T. D. | Resigned 1811 |
| 1811 | WILLIAM HARRIS, S. T. D. | Deceased 1829 |
| 1829 | WILLIAM ALEXANDER DUER, LL. D. | Resigned 1842 |
| 1842 | NATHANIEL F. MOORE, LL. D. | Resigned 1849 |
| 1849 | CHARLES KING, LL. D. | Resigned 1864 |
| 1864 | FREDERICK A. P. BARNARD, S. T. D., LL. D. | |

## PROVOST.

| | | |
|---|---|---|
| 1811 | JOHN M. MASON, S. T. D. | Resigned 1816 |

## FACULTY OF ARTS.

President JOHNSON was at first sole Instructor.

### *PROFESSORS OF MATHEMATICS AND NATURAL PHILOSOPHY.*

| | | |
|---|---|---|
| 1757 | DANIEL TREADWELL, A. M. | Deceased 1760 |
| 1861 | ROBERT HARPUR, A. M. | Transferred 1765 |
| 1799 | JOHN KEMP, LL. D. | Deceased 1812 |
| 1813 | ROBERT ADRAIN, LL. D. | Transferred 1820 |

### *PROFESSORS OF MORAL PHILOSOPHY.*

| | | |
|---|---|---|
| 1762 | MYLES COOPER, A. M. | Promoted 1763 |
| 1787 | JOHN DANIEL GROSS, S. T. D. | Resigned 1795 |

In 1795, Logic was added to the Department.

| | | |
|---|---|---|
| 1795 | JOHN McKNIGHT, S. T. D. | Retired 1799 |

In 1799, Rhetoric and Belles-Lettres were added.

| Appointed | | Deceased |
|---|---|---|
| 1801 | John Bowden, S. T. D. | 1817 |
| | | Transferred |
| 1817 | John McVickar, S. T. D. | 1857 |

In 1818, Intellectual Philosophy and Political Economy were added.

### PROFESSORS OF MATHEMATICS.

| | | Resigned |
|---|---|---|
| 1765 | Robert Harpur, A. M. | 1767 |
| | | Transferred |
| 1786 | John Kemp, LL. D. | 1799 |
| | | Transferred |
| 1857 | Charles Davies, LL. D. | 1859 |
| | | Promoted |
| 1857 | William G. Peck, A. M. (Adjunct) | 1859 |
| | | Promoted |
| 1863 | J. Howard Van Amringe, A. M. (Adjunct) | 1873 |
| 1873 | J. Howard Van Amringe, A. M. | |

### PROFESSORS OF NATURAL PHILOSOPHY.

| | | Retired |
|---|---|---|
| 1765 | Samuel Clossy, M. D. | 1776 |

In 1785, Astronomy was added to the Department.

| | | Resigned |
|---|---|---|
| 1785 | Samuel Bard, M. D. | 1786 |

### PROFESSOR OF NATURAL LAW.

| | | Retired |
|---|---|---|
| 1773 | John Vardill, A. M. | 1776 |

In 1775, History and Languages were added to the Department.

### PROFESSORS OF THE FRENCH LANGUAGE.

| | | Deceased |
|---|---|---|
| 1784 | John P. Tetard | 1787 |
| | | Retired |
| 1792 | Villette De Marcellin | 1799 |

In 1828, the Department was revived under the style of the Department of the French Language and Literature.

| | | Resigned |
|---|---|---|
| 1828 | Antoine Verren, A. M. | 1839 |
| | | Retired |
| 1839 | Felix G. Berteau, LL. B. | 1856 |

This Professorship was abolished in 1866.

### PROFESSORS OF THE GREEK AND LATIN LANGUAGES.

| | | Resigned |
|---|---|---|
| 1784 | William Cochran, A. M. | 1789 |
| | | Resigned |
| 1789 | Peter Wilson, A. M. | 1792 |

| Appointed | | |
|---|---|---|
| 1792 | Elijah D. Rattoone, S. T. D | Resigned 1797 |

In 1794, Grecian and Roman Antiquities were added to the Department.

| | | |
|---|---|---|
| 1797 | Peter Wilson, LL. D | Resigned 1820 |
| 1817 | Nathaniel F. Moore, A. M. (Adjunct) | Promoted 1820 |
| 1820 | Nathaniel F. Moore, LL. D | Resigned 1835 |
| 1820 | Charles Anthon, A. B. (Adjunct) | Promoted 1830 |
| 1830 | Charles Anthon, LL. D. (Jay) | Transferred 1857 |
| 1837 | Robert G. Vermilye, A. M. (Adjunct) | Resigned 1843 |
| 1845 | Henry Drisler, Jr., A. M. (Adjunct) | Promoted 1857 |

### *PROFESSOR OF RHETORIC AND LOGIC.*

| | | |
|---|---|---|
| 1784 | Benjamin Moore, A. M | Resigned 1787 |

### *PROFESSORS OF THE ORIENTAL LANGUAGES.*

| | | |
|---|---|---|
| 1784 | Johann C Kunze, S. T. D | Resigned 1787 |
| 1792 | Johann C. Kunze, S. T. D | Retired 1799 |

### *PROFESSORS OF THE GERMAN LANGUAGE.*

| | | |
|---|---|---|
| 1784 | John Daniel Gross, S. T. D | Resigned 1795 |

In 1830, the Department was revived, under the style of the Department of the German Language and Literature.

| | | |
|---|---|---|
| 1830 | Frederick C. Schaeffer, S. T. D | Deceased 1831 |
| 1832 | William Ernenputsch | Resigned 1832 |
| 1843 | John Louis Tellkampf, J. U. D. (Gebhard) | Resigned 1847 |
| 1847 | Henry I. Schmidt, S. T. D. (Gebhard) | |

### *PROFESSORS OF GEOGRAPHY.*

| | | |
|---|---|---|
| 1784 | John D. Gross, S. T. D | Resigned 1795 |
| 1795 | John Kemp, LL. D | Transferred 1799 |

### *PROFESSOR OF NATURAL HISTORY.*

| | | |
|---|---|---|
| 1785 | Henry Moyes, LL. D | Resigned 1786 |

### *PROFESSOR OF NATURAL HISTORY, CHEMISTRY, AGRICULTURE, AND THE OTHER ARTS DEPENDING THEREON.*

| Appointed | | Retired |
|---|---|---|
| 1792 | SAMUEL L. MITCHILL, M. D., LL. D. | 1801 |

### *PROFESSORS OF LAW.*

| | | |
|---|---|---|
| 1793 | JAMES KENT, A. M. | Resigned 1798 |
| 1823 | JAMES KENT, LL. D. | Deceased 1847 |
| 1848 | WILLIAM BETTS, LL. D. | Resigned 1854 |

### *PROFESSOR OF RHETORIC AND BELLES-LETTRES.*

| | | |
|---|---|---|
| 1795 | JOHN BISSET, A. M. | Retired 1799 |

### *PROFESSORS OF CHEMISTRY.*

| | | |
|---|---|---|
| 1802 | JAMES S. STRINGHAM, M. D. | Transferred 1810 |
| 1813 | JOHN GRISCOM | Retired 1820 |
| 1857 | CHARLES A. JOY, Ph. D. | |

### *PROFESSORS OF MATHEMATICS AND ASTRONOMY.*

| | | |
|---|---|---|
| 1820 | ROBERT ADRAIN, LL. D. | Resigned 1825 |
| 1825 | HENRY JAMES ANDERSON, M. D., LL. D. Resigned, 1843. Emeritus, 1866 | Deceased 1875 |
| 1843 | CHARLES W. HACKLEY, S. T. D. | Transferred 1857 |
| 1861 | WILLIAM GUY PECK, LL. D. | |

In 1865, Mechanics was added to the Department.

### *PROFESSORS OF NATURAL AND EXPERIMENTAL PHILOSOPHY AND CHEMISTRY.*

| | | |
|---|---|---|
| 1820 | JAMES RENWICK, LL. D. Emeritus, 1853 | Deceased 1863 |
| 1854 | RICHARD S. MCCULLOH | Transferred 1857 |

### *PROFESSORS OF THE ITALIAN LANGUAGE AND LITERATURE.*

| | | |
|---|---|---|
| 1826 | LORENZO DA PONTE | Deceased 1837 |
| 1839 | E. FELIX FORESTI, LL. B. | Resigned 1856 |

### *PROFESSOR OF THE HEBREW LANGUAGE AND LITERATURE.*

| | | |
|---|---|---|
| 1830 | SAMUEL H. TURNER, S. T. D. | Deceased 1861 |

### *PROFESSOR OF THE SPANISH LANGUAGE AND LITERATURE.*

Appointed — Deceased

1830 Mariano Velazquez de la Cadeña, LL. B. .................... 1860

### *PROFESSOR OF ELEMENTARY CHEMISTRY.*

Retired

1832 William H. Ellet, M. D. .................... 1833

### *PROFESSOR OF ELOCUTION.*

Retired

1844 John W. S. Hows .................... 1857

### *PROFESSOR OF THE EVIDENCES OF NATURAL AND REVEALED RELIGION.*

Deceased

1857 John McVickar, S. T. D. Emeritus, 1864.................... 1868

### *JAY PROFESSORS OF THE GREEK LANGUAGE AND LITERATURE.*

Deceased

1857 Charles Anthon, LL. D .................... 1867

1867 Henry Drisler, LL. D. ....................

### *PROFESSORS OF THE LATIN LANGUAGE AND LITERATURE.*

Transferred

1857 Henry Drisler, LL. D .................... 1867

1868 Charles Short, LL. D. ....................

### *PROFESSOR OF ASTRONOMY.*

Deceased

1857 Charles W. Hackley, S. T. D .................... 1861

### *PROFESSORS OF MECHANICS AND PHYSICS.*

Expelled

1857 Richard S. McCulloh, A. M.* .................... 1863

1863 Ogden N. Rood, A. M ....................

In 1865, Mechanics was transferred to the Department of Mathematics and Astronomy.

### *PROFESSORS OF HISTORY AND POLITICAL SCIENCE.*

Transferred

1857 Francis Lieber, LL. D .................... 1865

In 1876, this Professorship was succeeded by one entitled the Professorship of History, Political Science, and International Law.

1876 John W. Burgess, A. M ....................

---

*Expelled October 15, 1863, for having abandoned his post and joined the Rebels.

### *PROFESSOR OF MORAL AND INTELLECTUAL PHILOSOPHY AND LITERATURE.*

Appointed
1857 CHARLES MURRAY NAIRNE, L. H. D.

History and Political Economy were added in 1865.

### *PROFESSOR OF HIGHER MATHEMATICS.*

1859 CHARLES DAVIES, LL. D. — Emeritus 1865

### *PROFESSOR OF PURE MATHEMATICS.*

1859 WILLIAM GUY PECK, LL. D. — Transferred 1861

### *TUTORS.*

1755 WILLIAM JOHNSON, A. M. — Resigned 1755
1756 LEONARD CUTTING — Resigned 1763
1757 DANIEL TREADWELL, A. M. — Deceased 1760
1762 MYLES COOPER, A. M. — Retired 1763
1765 SAMUEL CLOSSY, M. D. — Retired 1776
1773 JOHN VARDILL, A. M. — Retired 1776
1785 JOHN KEMP — Promoted 1786
1831 ABRAHAM B. CONGER, A. B. — Retired 1833
1831 JOHN L. O'SULLIVAN, A. B. — Retired 1833
1835 ROBERT G. VERMILYE, A. M. — Promoted 1837
1843 HENRY DRISLER, Jr., A. M. — Promoted 1845
1859 J. EMORY MCCLINTOCK, A. B. — Resigned 1860
1860 J. HOWARD VAN AMRINGE, A. M — Promoted 1863
1864 DUANE S. EVERSON, A. M. — Resigned 1868
1865 EUGENE LAWRENCE, A. M. — Resigned 1868
1868 AUGUSTUS C. MERRIAM, A. M.
1868 WENDELL LAMOROUX, A. M. — Retired 1869
1869 THEODORE F. C. DEMAREST, A. M. — Resigned 1870
1870 JOHN D. QUACKENBOS, A. M., M. D.

| Appointed | | Resigned |
|---|---|---|
| 1873 | LEONARD WALDO, B. S., (assistant) | 1875 |
| 1875 | WILLIAM H. INGERSOLL, A. M., LL. B., (assistant) | |
| 1875 | MAGNUS C. IHLSENG, E. M., (assistant) | |

### *LECTURERS.*

| | | |
|---|---|---|
| 1830 | WILLIAM H. ELLET, M. D. (Elementary Chemistry) | Promoted 1832 |
| 1869 | WILLIAM A. McVICKAR, S. T. D. (Evidences of Religion) | Retired 1871 |

### *LIBRARIANS.*

The duties of Librarian were discharged by one of the Professors until 1837.

| | | |
|---|---|---|
| 1837 | NATHANIEL F. MOORE, LL. D | Resigned 1839 |
| 1839 | GEORGE C. SCHAEFFER, A. M., M. D | Resigned 1847 |
| 1847 | LEFROY RAVENHILL, A. M., M. D | Deceased 1851 |
| 1849 | STEPHEN R. WEEKS (Assistant) | |
| 1851 | WILLIAM ALFRED JONES, A. M | Resigned 1865 |
| 1865 | BEVERLEY R. BETTS, A. M | |

### *CHAPLAIN.*

The President discharged the duties of this office till 1857.

| | | |
|---|---|---|
| 1857 | CORNELIUS R. DUFFIE, S. T. D | |

### *HEAD MASTERS OF THE GRAMMAR SCHOOL.*

| | | |
|---|---|---|
| 1763 | MATTHEW CUSHING, A. M | Retired |
| | ALEXANDER LESLIE, A. M | Retired |
| 1784 | WILLIAM COCHRAN, A. M | Retired |
| 1829 | JOHN D. OGILBY, A. B | Resigned 1830 |
| 1830 | CHARLES ANTHON, LL. D. (Rector) | Retired 1864 |

# FACULTY OF MEDICINE.*

## *PROFESSORS OF ANATOMY.*

| Appointed | | |
|---|---|---|
| 1767 | Samuel Clossy, M. D. | Retired 1776 |
| 1785 | Charles McKnight, M. D. | Deceased 1792 |
| 1792 | Richard Bailey, M. D. | Transferred 1793 |
| 1793 | Wright Post, M. D. | Retired 1813 |
| 1860 | Robert Watts, M. D. | Deceased 1867 |
| 1867 | Henry B. Sands, M. D. | |
| 1871 | Thomas T. Sabine, M. D. (adjunct) | |

## *PROFESSOR OF PATHOLOGY AND PHYSIOLOGY.*

| | | |
|---|---|---|
| 1767 | Peter Middleton, M. D. | Retired 1776 |

## *PROFESSORS OF SURGERY.*

| | | |
|---|---|---|
| 1767 | John Jones, M. D. | Retired 1776 |
| 1785 | Charles McKnight, M. D. | Deceased 1792 |
| 1792 | Wright Post, M. D. | Transferred 1793 |
| 1793 | Richard Bailey, M. D. | Deceased 1811 |
| 1811 | Valentine Mott, M. D. | Retired 1813 |
| 1860 | Alexander H. Stevens, M. D., LL. D. (Emeritus) | Deceased 1869 |
| 1860 | Willard Parker, M. D. | Transferred 1870 |
| 1860 | Thomas M. Markoe, M. D. (adjunct) | Promoted 1870 |
| 1870 | Thomas M. Markoe, M. D. | |

## *PROFESSORS OF CHEMISTRY AND MATERIA MEDICA.*

| | | |
|---|---|---|
| 1767 | James Smith, M. D. | Retired 1770 |
| 1770 | Peter Middleton, M. D. | Retired 1776 |

* There was no Faculty of Medicine from 1813 to 1860. In this latter year it was revived by the adoption of the College of Physicians and Surgeons as the Medical Department of the College.

### *PROFESSORS OF THE THEORY AND PRACTICE OF MEDICINE.*

| Appointed | | Retired |
|---|---|---|
| 1767 | SAMUEL BARD, M. D. | 1776 |
| | | Transferred |
| 1795 | WILLIAM HAMERSLEY, M. D. | 1808 |

### *PROFESSORS OF MIDWIFERY.*

| | | |
|---|---|---|
| | | Deceased |
| 1767 | JOHN V. B. TENNENT, M. D. | 1770 |
| | | Retired |
| 1770 | SAMUEL BARD, M. D. | 1776 |
| | | Deceased |
| 1785 | EBENEZER CROSBY, M. D. | 1788 |
| | | Resigned |
| 1792 | JOHN R. B. ROGERS, M. D. | 1808 |
| | | Retired |
| 1808 | WALTER C. BUCHANAN, M. D. | 1813 |
| | | Deceased |
| 1860 | EDWARD DELAFIELD, M. D. (Emeritus) | 1875 |

### *PROFESSORS OF CHEMISTRY.*

| | | |
|---|---|---|
| | | Resigned |
| 1784 | SAMUEL BARD, M. D. | 1785 |
| | | Resigned |
| 1785 | HENRY MOYES, LL. D. | 1786 |
| | | Resigned |
| 1786 | SAMUEL BARD, M. D. | 1787 |
| | | Resigned |
| 1792 | SAMUEL NICOLL, M. D. | 1794 |
| | | Resigned |
| 1810 | JAMES S. STRINGHAM | 1813 |
| | | Deceased |
| 1860 | JOHN TORREY, M. D., LL. D. (Emeritus) | 1873 |
| 1860 | SAMUEL ST. JOHN, M. D. | |

Medical Jurisprudence was added to the Department in 1870.

| | | |
|---|---|---|
| 1872 | CHARLES F. CHANDLER, Ph. D., M. D., LL. D. (Adjunct) | |

### *PROFESSORS OF THE INSTITUTES OF MEDICINE.*

| | | |
|---|---|---|
| | | Resigned |
| 1785 | BENJAMIN KISSAM, M. D. | 1792 |
| | | Transferred |
| 1792 | WILLIAM HAMERSLEY, M. D. | 1795 |
| | | Retired |
| 1808 | JOHN C. OSBORN, M. D. | 1813 |

### *PROFESSORS OF THE PRACTICE OF MEDICINE.*

| | | |
|---|---|---|
| | | Resigned |
| 1785 | NICHOLAS ROMAYNE, M. D. | 1787 |
| | | Resigned |
| 1792 | SAMUEL NICOLL, M. D. | 1794 |

| Appointed | | Resigned |
|---|---|---|
| 1794 | EDWARD STEVENS, M. D. | 1795 |
| | | Retired |
| 1808 | WILLIAM HAMERSLEY, M. D. | 1813 |

### DEAN OF THE MEDICAL FACULTY.

| | | Resigned |
|---|---|---|
| 1792 | SAMUEL BARD, M. D. | 1804 |
| | | Deceased |
| 1860 | EDWARD DELAFIELD, M. D. (President) | 1875 |
| 1875 | ALONZO CLARK, M. D. (President) | |

### PROFESSORS OF MATERIA MEDICA.

| | | Deceased |
|---|---|---|
| 1792 | WILLIAM P. SMITH, M. D. | 1795 |
| | | Resigned |
| 1796 | DAVID HOSACK, M. D., LL. D. | 1811 |
| | | Retired |
| 1811 | JOHN C. OSBORN, M. D. | 1813 |
| | | Deceased |
| 1860 | JOSEPH M. SMITH, M. D. | 1866 |

In 1860 Clinical Medicine belonged to the Department.

### PROFESSORS OF BOTANY.

| | | Resigned |
|---|---|---|
| 1792 | RICHARD S. KISSAM, M. D. | 1793 |
| | | Resigned |
| 1793 | SAMUEL L. MITCHILL, M. D., LL. D. | 1795 |
| | | Resigned |
| 1795 | DAVID HOSACK, M. D., LL. D. | 1811 |
| | | Deceased |
| 1860 | JOHN TORREY, M. D., LL. D. (Emeritus) | 1873 |

### PROFESSORS OF OBSTETRICS, DISEASES OF WOMEN AND CHILDREN, AND MEDICAL JURISPRUDENCE.

| | | Deceased |
|---|---|---|
| 1860 | CHANDLER R. GILMAN, M. D. | 1865 |
| | | Promoted |
| 1863 | T. GAILLIARD THOMAS, M. D. (Adjunct) | 1865 |
| 1865 | T. GAILLIARD THOMAS, M. D. | |

In 1868 Medical Jurisprudence was assigned to another Department.

| | | |
|---|---|---|
| 1872 | JAMES W. McLANE, M. D. (Adjunct) | |

### PROFESSOR OF PATHOLOGY AND PRACTICAL MEDICINE.

| | | |
|---|---|---|
| 1860 | ALONZO CLARK, M. D., LL. D. | |

### *PROFESSOR OF PHYSIOLOGY AND MICROSCOPIC ANATOMY.*

Appointed

1860 John C. Dalton, Jr., M. D.........................................

In 1870 the title of this chair was changed to that of "Physiology and Hygiene."

### *PROFESSOR OF MILITARY SURGERY AND HYGIENE.*

Emeritus

1862 William Detmold, M. D.......................................... 1865

In 1866 the title of this chair was changed to that of "Clinical and Military Surgery."

### *PROFESSOR OF CLINICAL MEDICINE.*

Emeritus

1866 John T. Metcalfe, M. D.......................................... 1874

### *CLINICAL PROFESSORS OF VENEREAL DISEASES.*

Retired

1867 Freeman J. Bumstead, M. D.......................................... 1872

1872 Fessenden N. Otis, M. D..........................................

### *PROFESSORS OF MATERIA MEDICA, THERAPEUTICS, AND MEDICAL JURISPRUDENCE.*

Transferred

1868 James W. McLane, M. D.......................................... 1872

In 1870 Medical Jurisprudence was assigned to another Department.

1873 Edward Curtis, M. D..........................................

### *CLINICAL PROFESSOR OF DISEASES OF THE EYE AND EAR.*

1869 Cornelius R. Agnew, M. D..........................................

### *CLINICAL PROFESSOR OF DISEASES OF THE SKIN.*

1869 William H. Draper, M. D..........................................

### *CLINICAL PROFESSOR OF THE DISEASES OF CHILDREN.*

1869 Abraham Jacobi, M. D..........................................

### *PROFESSOR OF CLINICAL SURGERY.*

1870 Willard Parker, M. D..........................................

### *CLINICAL PROFESSOR OF DISEASES OF THE MIND AND NERVOUS SYSTEM.*

1874 Edward C. Seguin, M. D..........................................

## DEMONSTRATORS OF ANATOMY.

| Appointed | | Retired |
|---|---|---|
| 1860 | Henry B. Sands, M. D. | 1867 |
| 1867 | Samuel B. Ward, M. D. | 1868 |
| 1868 | Erskine Mason, M. D. | 1870 |
| 1870 | Thomas T. Sabine, M. D. | 1871 |
| 1871 | John G. Curtis, M. D. | 1875 |
| 1875 | Charles McBurney, M. D. | |

## CURATORS OF THE MUSEUM.

| | | |
|---|---|---|
| 1860 | Henry B. Sands, M. D. | 1867 |
| 1867 | Samuel B. Ward, M. D. | 1869 |
| 1869 | Henry C. Eno, M. D. | 1870 |
| 1870 | Christopher M. Bell, M. D. | 1872 |
| 1872 | George B. Fowler, M. D. | |

## LECTURERS.

| | | |
|---|---|---|
| 1791 | Nicholas Romayne, M. D. | 1792 |
| 1794 | William P. Smith, M. D. | 1795 |
| 1860 | Watts C. Livingston, M. D. | 1860 |
| 1860 | Freeman J. Bumstead, M. D. | 1861 |
| 1860 | George T. Elliott, M. D. | 1861 |
| 1860 | Edward W. Lambert, M. D. | 1861 |
| 1860 | David S. Conant, M. D. | 1861 |
| 1860 | Charles K. Briddon, M. D. | 1861 |
| 1860 | A. Hermance Smith, M. D. | 1862 |
| 1860 | Foster Swift, M. D. | 1863 |
| 1861 | William C. Livingston, M. D. | 1863 |
| 1861 | William H. Church, M. D. | 1862 |
| 1861 | C. Van Allen Anderson, M. D. | 1862 |
| 1866 | Henry B. Sands, M. D. (Adjunct) | 1867 |
| 1866 | Freeman J. Bumstead, M. D. | 1867 |

| Appointed | | Retired |
|---|---|---|
| 1867 | JAMES W. MCLANE, M. D. | 1868 |
| 1867 | D. TILDEN BROWN, M. D. | 1868 |
| 1867 | CORNELIUS R. AGNEW, M. D. | 1869 |
| 1867 | FESSENDEN N. OTIS, M. D. | 1873 |
| 1867 | WILLIAM H. DRAPER, M. D. | 1870 |
| 1868 | JAMES L. LITTLE, M. D. | |
| 1868 | EDWARD B. DALTON, M. D. | 1870 |
| 1868 | FRANCIS DELAFIELD, M. D. | 1875 |
| 1868 | GEORGE G. WHEELOCK, M. D. | |
| 1869 | EDWARD C. SEGUIN, M. D. | 1878 |
| 1870 | A. BRAYTON BALL, M. D. | |
| 1870 | THOMAS T. SABINE, M. D. (Adjunct) | 1872 |
| 1870 | WOOLSEY JOHNSON, M. D. | 1871 |
| 1871 | EDWARD CURTIS, M. D. | 1873 |
| 1873 | ROBERT F. WEIR, M. D. | |
| 1873 | JOHN G. CURTIS, M. D. | 1875 |
| 1875 | FRANK E. BECKWITH, M. D. | |
| 1875 | MATTHEW D. MANN, M. D. | |

# FACULTY OF LAW.

### *PROFESSORS OF MUNICIPAL LAW.*

1858 THEODORE W. DWIGHT, LL. D.

The office of "Warden of the Law School" was added to this chair in 1864.

1874 GEORGE CHASE, LL. B. (assistant)

### *PROFESSOR OF MEDICAL JURISPRUDENCE.*

1860 JOHN ORDRONAUX, LL. B., M. D.

### *PROFESSOR OF POLITICAL SCIENCE.*

| | | Deceased |
|---|---|---|
| 1860 | FRANCIS LIEBER, LL. D | 1872 |

The title of this chair was changed, in 1865, to that of "Constitutional History and Public Law," which chair, in 1876, was succeeded by one entitled the chair of "History, Political Science, and International Law."

Appointed

1876 JOHN W. BURGESS, A. M. ....................................

*PROFESSOR OF THE ETHICS OF JURISPRUDENCE.*

1860 CHARLES MURRAY NAIRNE, L. H. D. ....................................

*LECTURERS.*

| Appointed | Name | Retired |
|---|---|---|
| 1860 | MARSHALL S. BIDWELL, LL. D. | 1872 |
| 1860 | ALEXANDER W. BRADFORD, LL. D | 1867 |
| 1860 | CHARLES P. DALY, LL. D. | 1875 |
| 1860 | WILLIAM M. EVARTS, LL. D. | 1868 |
| 1860 | WILLIAM CURTIS NOYES, LL. D | 1864 |
| 1863 | EUGENE LAWRENCE | 1865 |
| 1863 | AARON J. VANDERPOEL | 1866 |
| 1872 | GEORGE H. YEAMAN | |
| 1872 | E. MULFORD | 1873 |
| 1873 | CHARLES F. MACLEAN | 1874 |
| 1875 | JOHN W. BURGESS | 1876 |

## FACULTY OF THE SCHOOL OF MINES.

*PROFESSOR OF MINERALOGY AND METALLURGY.*

1864 THOMAS EGLESTON, Jr., A. M., E. M. ....................................

*PROFESSOR OF MINING ENGINEERING.*

1864 FRANCIS L. VINTON, E. M. ....................................

In 1870, the title of this chair was changed to that of "Civil and Mining Engineering."

*PROFESSOR OF ANALYTICAL AND APPLIED CHEMISTRY.*

1864 CHARLES F. CHANDLER, Ph. D. ....................................

*PROFESSOR OF GENERAL CHEMISTRY.*

1865 CHARLES A. JOY, Ph. D ....................................

### *PROFESSOR OF MECHANICS AND THEIR APPLICATIONS.*

| Appointed | | Retired |
|---|---|---|
| 1865 | WILLIAM G. PECK, LL. D. | |

### *PROFESSOR OF MATHEMATICS.*

| | | |
|---|---|---|
| 1865 | J. HOWARD VAN AMRINGE, A. M. | |

### *PROFESSOR OF PHYSICS.*

| | | |
|---|---|---|
| 1865 | OGDEN N. ROOD, A. M. | |

### *PROFESSOR OF GEOLOGY AND PALÆONTOLOGY.*

| | | |
|---|---|---|
| 1866 | JOHN S. NEWBERRY, M. D., LL. D | |

### *INSTRUCTORS IN GERMAN.*

| | | Retired |
|---|---|---|
| 1869 | HENRY COHN, A. B. | 1870 |
| 1870 | FREDERICK STENGEL | |

### *INSTRUCTORS IN FRENCH.*

| | | |
|---|---|---|
| 1869 | GEORGES LEROUX | 1870 |
| 1870 | JULES E. LOISEAU | |

### *ASSISTANTS.*

| | | |
|---|---|---|
| 1864 | JULIUS MAIER, Ph. D. | 1865 |
| 1864 | WILLIAM A. POTTER | 1865 |
| 1864 | ALBERT H. CHESTER | 1869 |
| 1864 | HENRY B. CORNWALL | 1866 |
| 1865 | MILOS KROLIKOWSKI, C. E | 1866 |
| 1865 | ALEXIS A. JULIEN, A. M. | |
| 1865 | EDWARD W. ROOT, A. B. | 1868 |
| 1866 | FRITZ RINTELEN | 1867 |
| 1866 | JOSEPH J. CASEY, A. B. | 1867 |
| 1866 | PAUL SCHWEITZER | 1872 |
| 1866 | EDWARD E. C. H. DAY | 1869 |
| 1866 | JULES MABRÜ | 1869 |

| Appointed | | Retired |
|---|---|---|
| 1867 | Albert Folké, C. E | 1871 |
| 1867 | George B. Hanna, A. B. | 1868 |
| 1868 | Henry B. Cornwall, A. M., E. M. | 1870 |
| 1868 | William H. Chandler | 1871 |
| 1868 | George S. Baxter, A. M., E. M. | 1869 |
| 1868 | John H. Caswell, A. B | 1871 |
| 1869 | Frederick Prime, Jr., A. M. | 1870 |
| 1869 | Alonzo C. Campbell, E. M. | 1870 |
| 1869 | William B. Potter, A. M., E. M. | 1871 |
| 1870 | Thomas M. Blossom, A. M., E. M. | 1872 |
| 1870 | Henry Newton, A. B., E. M. | 1875 |
| 1870 | Douglas A. Joy | 1871 |
| 1871 | Elwyn Waller, A. M., E. M., Ph. D. | |
| 1871 | Pierre De P. Ricketts, E. M. | |
| 1871 | William Pistor, E. M. | |
| 1871 | Edward J. Hallock, A. M | |
| 1872 | Henry C. Bolton, A. M., Ph. D. | |
| 1873 | Charles A. Colton, E. M. | |
| 1873 | Leonard Waldo, B. S. | 1875 |
| 1873 | John Krom Rees, A. M., E. M | |
| 1873 | William H. Ingersoll, A. M., LL. B., E. M | |
| 1874 | John H. Caswell, A. B | |
| 1874 | Gracie S. Roberts, E. M. | |
| 1875 | James S. C. Wells, Ph. B. | |
| 1875 | Malvern W. Iles, Ph. B. | |
| 1875 | I. C. Russell | |

# SENATUS ACADEMICUS,

# 1876.

## TRUSTEES.

## TRUSTEES OF THE MEDICAL DEPARTMENT.

|  |  |
|---|---|
| EDWARD G. LUDLOW, M. D. | 49 East 23d Street. |
| JOHN P. CROSBY | 31 West 17th Street. |
| GURDON BUCK, M. D. | 121 Tenth Street. |
| JAMES W. BEEKMAN | 5 East 34th Street. |
| DANIEL D. LORD | 45 West 19th Street. |
| BENJAMIN R. WINTHROP | 134 Second Avenue. |
| EDWARD L. BEADLE, M. D. | Poughkeepsie. |
| FREDERICK A. CONKLING | 27 East 10th Street. |
| SULLIVAN H. WESTON, S. T. D. | 3 East 45th Street. |
| WILLIAM BETTS, LL. D. | 122 East 30th Street. |
| CAMBRIDGE LIVINGSTON | 44 West 22d Street. |
| JARED LINSLY, M. D. | 22 Lafayette Place. |
| JOHN J. CRANE, M. D. | 31 West 21st Street. |
| ROBERT G. REMSEN | 5 Wall Street. |
| ELLSWORTH ELIOT, M. D. | 48 West 36th Street. |
| JAMES L. BANKS, M. D. | 57 Fifth Avenue. |
| EDWARD DELAFIELD | 46 East 44th Street. |
| WILLARD PARKER, M. D. | 41 East 12th Street. |
| JOHN G. ADAMS, M. D. | 12 Fifth Avenue. |
| JOHN SHERWOOD | 18 West 32d Street. |
| FREDERICK A. P. BARNARD, S.T.D., LL.D., L.H.D. | College Green. |
| SAMUEL T. HUBBARD, M. D. | 27 West 9th Street. |
| ALFRED A. PURDY, M. D. | 15 West 43d Street. |
| THOMAS F. COCK, M. D. | 233 Madison Avenue. |

## OFFICERS OF INSTRUCTION AND GOVERNMENT.

| NAMES. | RESIDENCES. |
|---|---|
| FREDERICK A. P. BARNARD, S.T. D., LL. D., L. H. D., President. | Columbia College. |
| ALONZO CLARK, M. D. President of the Medical Department, and Professor of Pathology and Practical Medicine. | 23 East 21st Street. |
| HENRY DRISLER, LL. D. Jay Professor of the Greek Language and Literature. | 48 West 46th Street. |
| HENRY I. SCHMIDT, S. T. D. Gebhard Professor of the German Language and Literature. | 126 West 43d Street. |
| CHARLES A. JOY, Ph. D. Professor of Chemistry. | 117 East 70th Street. |
| CHARLES DAVIES, LL. D. Emeritus Professor of Higher Mathematics. | Fishkill Landing. |
| WILLIAM G. PECK, LL. D. Professor of Mathematics and Astronomy, in the Faculty of Arts, and of Mechanics and their applications, in the Faculty of Mines. | Greenwich, Conn. |
| CHARLES M. NAIRNE, L. H. D. Professor of Moral and Intellectual Philosophy and Literature. | 163 West 34th Street. |
| THEODORE W. DWIGHT, LL. D. Professor of Municipal Law, and Warden of the Law School. | 8 Great Jones Street. |
| JOHN ORDRONAUX, LL. B., M. D. Professor of Medical Jurisprudence. | 8 Great Jones Street. |
| J. HOWARD VAN AMRINGE, A. M. Professor of Mathematics in the Faculty of Arts and in the School of Mines, Secretary of the Faculty of Arts. | 165 West 46th Street. |
| WILLARD PARKER, M. D. Professor of Clinical Surgery. | 37 East 12th Street. |

NAMES. RESIDENCES.

JOHN C. DALTON, M. D. .......... 41 West 28th Street.

Professor of Physiology and Hygiene.

SAMUEL St. JOHN, M. D. .......... Ashland House.

Professor of Chemistry and Medical Jurisprudence.

THOMAS M. MARKOE, M. D. .......... 4 East 17th Street.

Professor of Surgery.

WILLIAM DETMOLD, M. D. .......... 103 Ninth Street.

Emeritus Professor of Clinical and Military Surgery.

OGDEN N. ROOD, A. M. .......... 341 East 15th Street.

Professor of Mechanics and Physics.

T. GAILLIARD THOMAS, M. D. .......... 86 Fifth Avenue.

Professor of Obstetrics and the Diseases of Women and Children.

THOMAS EGLESTON, Jr., A. M., E. M. .......... 10 Fifth Avenue.

Professor of Mineralogy and Metallurgy.

FRANCIS L. VINTON, E. M. .......... 806 Broadway.

Professor of Mining Engineering.

CHARLES F. CHANDLER, Ph. D. .......... 51 East 54th Street.

Professor of Analytical and Applied Chemistry, Dean of the Faculty of Mines, and Adjunct Professor of Chemistry and Medical Jurisprudence, School of Medicine.

JOHN S. NEWBERRY, M. D., LL. D .......... Columbia College.

Professor of Geology and Palæontology.

JOHN T. METCALFE, M. D. .......... 18 West 30th Street.

Emeritus Professor of Clinical Medicine.

HENRY B. SANDS, M. D. .......... 35 West 33d Street.

Professor of Anatomy.

CHARLES SHORT, LL. D .......... 24 West 60th Street.

Professor of the Latin Language and Literature.

JOHN W. BURGESS, A. M. .......... Columbia College.

Professor of History, Political Science, and International Law.

NAMES. RESIDENCES.

JAMES W. McLANE, M. D ........................51 West 38th Street.
Adjunct Professor of Obstetrics and the Diseases of Women and Children.

CORNELIUS R. AGNEW, M. D......................19 East 39th Street.
Clinical Professor of Diseases of the Eye and Ear.

WILLIAM H. DRAPER, M. D.... ................ ..4 East 37th Street.
Clinical Professor of Diseases of the Skin.

ABRAHAM JACOBI, M. D.......................... 110 West 34th Street.
Clinical Professor of Diseases of Children.

THOMAS T. SABINE, M. D....... ...............46 West 23d Street.
Adjunct Professor of Anatomy.

EDWARD CURTIS, M. D.... ... ..................27 Washington Place.
Professor of Materia Medica and Therapeutics.

FESSENDEN N. OTIS, M. D.... ... ...... ......108 West 34th Street.
Clinical Professor of Venereal Diseases.

EDWARD C. SEGUIN, M. D..................... 17 East 21st Street.
Clinical Professor of Diseases of the Mind and Nervous System.

## ASSISTANTS AND OTHER OFFICERS.

CORNELIUS R. DUFFIE, S. T. D.... ............. 233 Lexington Ave.
Chaplain.

BEVERLEY R. BETTS, A. M............. . ......122 East 30th Street.
Librarian.

STEPHEN R. WEEKS............................Columbia College.
Assistant Librarian.

AUGUSTUS C. MERRIAM, A. M...................Columbia College.
Tutor in Greek and Latin.

JOHN D. QUACKENBOS, A. B........ ..........331 West 28th Street.
Tutor in Rhetoric and History.

| NAMES. | RESIDENCES. |
|---|---|
| FREDERIC STENGEL<br>Instructor in German. | 122 Waverley Place. |
| JULES E. LOISEAU<br>Instructor in French. | 23 East 33d Street. |
| ALEXIS A. JULIEN, A. M.<br>Assistant in Analytical Chemistry. | Columbia College. |
| JOHN HENRY CASWELL, A. M.<br>Assistant in Mineralogy. | 370 Fifth Avenue. |
| I. C. RUSSELL<br>Assistant in Geology. | Plainfield, N. J. |
| ELWYN WALLER, A. M., E. M., Ph. D.<br>Assistant in Analytical Chemistry. | 33 West 15th Street. |
| FREDERICK A. CAIRNS, A. M.<br>Assistant in Analytical Chemistry. | 40 Grove Street. |
| WILLIAM PISTOR, E. M.<br>Assistant in Drawing. | 413 West 21st Street. |
| PIERRE DEPEYSTER RICKETTS, E. M.<br>Assistant in Assaying. | 50 West 50th Street. |
| HENRY CARRINGTON BOLTON, A. M., Ph. D.<br>Assistant in Analytical Chemistry. | 49 West 51st Street. |
| CHARLES ADAMS COLTON, E. M.<br>Assistant in Mineralogy. | 748 Fifth Street. |
| EDWARD JOHN HALLOCK, A. M.<br>Assistant in General Chemistry. | 115 East 56th Street. |
| JOHN KROM REES, A. M., E. M.<br>Assistant in Mathematics. | 303 East 17th Street. |
| WILLIAM HALSEY INGERSOLL, A.M., LL. B., E. M.<br>Assistant in the Astronomical Observatory. | 105 East 21st Street. |

| NAMES. | RESIDENCES. |
|---|---|
| GRACIE S. ROBERTS, E. M.<br>Assistant in Civil and Mining Engineering. | 88 Union Av., Brooklyn. |
| MAGNUS C. IHLSENG, E. M.<br>Assistant in Physics. | Columbia College. |
| JAMES S. C. WELLS, Ph. B<br>Assistant in Analytical Chemistry. | Hackensack, N. J. |
| MALVERN W. ILES, Ph. B.<br>Assistant in Analytical Chemistry. | Columbia College. |
| GEORGE H. YEAMAN, A. M.<br>Lecturer on Constitutional Law. | 339 East 15th Street. |
| FRANCIS DELAFIELD, M. D.<br>Adjunct Lecturer on Pathology and Practical Medicine. | 12 East 32d Street. |
| JOHN G. CURTIS, M. D.<br>Adjunct Lecturer on Physiology and Hygiene. | 35 West 33d Street. |
| GEORGE M. LEFFERTS, M. D.<br>Clinical Lecturer on Laryngoscopy and Diseases of the Throat. | 333 West 22d Street. |
| CHARLES McBURNEY, M. D.<br>Demonstrator of Anatomy. | 46 East 30th Street. |
| CHARLES KELSEY, M. D.<br>Assistant Demonstrator of Anatomy. | 23d St., cor. 4th Ave. |
| JAMES L. LITTLE, M. D.<br>Lecturer on Operative Surgery and Surgical Dressing. | 266 West 42d Street. |
| GEORGE G. WHEELOCK, M. D.<br>Lecturer on Physical Diagnosis. | 11 West 37th Street. |
| A. BRAYTON BALL, M. D.<br>Lecturer on Diseases of the Kidneys. | 38 West 36th Street. |
| ROBERT F. WEIR, M. D.<br>Lecturer on Diseases of the Genito-Urinary Organs. | 19 East 32d Street. |

| NAMES. | RESIDENCES. |
|---|---|
| FRANK E. BECKWITH, M. D. | Lexington Ave. cor. 51st Street. |
| Lecturer on Diseases of Children. | |
| MATTHEW D. MANN, M. D. | 8 West 45th Street. |
| Lecturer on the Microscope as an Aid to Diagnosis. | |

## CLINICAL ASSISTANTS IN SCHOOL OF MEDICINE.

James L. Little, M. D.
John T. Kennedy, M. D.
Henry F. Walker, M. D.
Charles S. Ward, M. D.
Robert W. Taylor, M. D.
W. De Forest Day, M. D.
Woolsey Johnson, M. D.
Oren D. Pomeroy, M. D.
A. Brayton Ball, M. D.
Albert H. Buck, M. D.
Lucius D. Bulkley, M. D.
Thomas E. Satterthwaite, M. D.
Thomas A. McBride, M. D.
Frank P. Kinnicutt, M. D.
Isaac Adler, M. D.
Samuel B. St. John, M. D.
Robert F. Weir, M. D.
David Webster, M. D.
W. H. Vermilye, M. D.
George G. Wheelock, M. D.

| | |
|---|---|
| STEPHEN R. WEEKS | Columbia College. |
| Janitor and Assistant Librarian. | |
| PETER V. LE ROY | Columbia College. |
| Curator of the Herbarium. | |
| GEORGE B. FOWLER, M. D. | 143 West 45th Street. |
| Curator of Museum, School of Medicine. | |
| JOHN F. MEYER | Columbia College. |
| Librarian and Registrar, School of Mines. | |
| CHARLES A. CUSHMAN | 419 West 19th Street. |
| Secretary to the President. | |
| EDWARD T. BOAG | 23d St., cor 3d Ave. |
| Clerk of School of Medicine. | |

FELIX CURTIS........ .......... ... ........ ....8 Great Jones Street.

**Janitor School of Law.**

CHARLES RICHTER........ .......... ..........Columbia College.

**Janitor School of Mines.**

ANDREW LOUGHLIN... ............ ...... .....23d Street and 4th Ave.

**Janitor School of Medicine.**

BENNO KUNKE......................... ..........Columbia College.

**Engineer, School of Mines.**

# GRADUATES IN ARTS.

## 1758.

*Joshua Bloomer, (Rev.), A. M., S. T. D. 1790. aet. 55. *1790
*Isaac Ogden, (C. L.), Judge Supr. Ct. Canada.
*Samuel Provoost, (Rev.), A. M., S. T. D. Univ. Penn. 1786, Regent Univ. N. Y. S. 1784–87, Trustee 1787–1801 and Chairman of the Board 1795–1801, Bishop P. E. Ch. N. Y. 1787–1815. *1815
*Joseph Reade, (C. L.), Master in Chanc. N. J.
*Rudolph Ritzema, Lt.-Col. H. B. M. Army.
*Philip Van Cortlandt, A. M., Lt.-Col. 4th Regt. N. Y. Vols. 1776, Lt.-Gov. N. Y. 1777–95.
*Samuel Verplanck, A. M. 1763, Gov. King's Coll. 1770.

7

## 1759.

*Epenetus Townsend, (Rev.), A. M. *1779
*William Hanna, (Rev.), A. M. 1765 and Yale 1768.

2

## 1760.

*Samuel Bayard, A. M.
*Anthony Hoffman, A. M., Regent Univ. N. Y. S. 1784–87.
*Philip Livingston, A. M., Trustee 1797–1806.
*John Marston, A. M.
*Robert Watts, A. M.
*Isaac Wilkins, (Rev.), A. M., S. T. D. 1811, Memb. of the Gen. Assemb. of N. Y. 1772–75. aet. 89. *1830

6

## 1761.

*Henry Holland, (C. L.), A. M., Mast. in Chancery N. Y.
*Anthony Lispenard. aet. 64. *1806
*Henry Van Dyck, (Rev.), A. M. aet. 60. *1804

3

## 1762.

*Edward Antill, A. M.
*Henry Cuyler, A. M.
*William Cornelius George, and Yale 1762.
*John Grinnell.
*Alexander Leslie, (T.), A. M., Master Gram. Sch. King's Coll.
*Leonard Lispenard, Regent Univ. N. Y. S. 1784–87, Trustee 1787–90. *1790
*William Benjamin Nicoll Maverick.
*Daniel Robert, (C. L.), H. B. M. Atty.-Gen. for St. Christopher's.

8

## 1763.

*Barent Cuyler, A. M.
*Abraham De Peyster, A. M.

2

## 1764.

*Richard Harison, (C. L.), A. M., D. C. L. Univ. Oxford, Del. to Fed. Constit. Conv. 1787, U. S. Dist. Atty. N. Y., Recorder N. Y. C., Trustee 1788–1829 and Chairman of the Board 1823. *1829

*John Jay, (C. L.), A. M., LL. D. Harv. 1790 and Brown 1794, Del. to Cong. 1774, 1775, Memb. Prov. Conv. N. Y. 1776, Ch.-Just. N. Y. 1777, Prest. National Congr. 1778, Min. Plenipo. to Spain 1779, U. S. Peace Commr. 1781–83, U. S. Sec. For. Aff. 1784, Del. to Cong. 1784, Regent Univ. N. Y. S. 1784–90, Del. to Fed. Constit. Conv. 1787, Del. to N. Y. Constit. Conv. 1788, Ch.-Just. U. S. 1789-94, U. S. Envoy Ex. to Gt. Britain 1794, Governor N. Y. 1795–1801. aet. 84. *1829

2

## 1765.

*Egbert Benson, (C. L.), A. M., LL. D. Union 1779 and Harv. 1808 and Dart. 1811, Memb. Prov. Conv. N. Y. 1776, Del. to Continent. Congr. 1784–88 Regent Univ. N. Y. S. 1787–1802, Repr. in Congr. 1789–92, 1813, Trustee 1804–14, Atty. Gen. N. Y., Judge Sup. Ct. N. Y., Ch.-Judge U. S. Circuit Ct. N. Y. *1833

*Richard Grant.

*Robert R. Livingston, (C. L.), A. M. and N. Jers., Recorder N. Y. C. 1773, Del to Continent. Congr. 1775–77, 1779–81, Memb. N. Y. Constit. Conv. 1777, Chanc. N. Y. 1777–1801, U. S. Secy. For. Aff. 1781–83, Regent Univ. N. Y. S. 1784–87, Del. to Fed. Constit. Conv. 1787, U. S. Minister Plen. to France 1801–4. aet. 66. *1813

*Henry Lloyd, A. M. 1769. aet. 82. *1825

*Arent Scuyler.

5

## 1766.

*James Barclay, A. M.

*Gerard Beekman, A. M.

*Richard Nicholls Colden, Surv. of Customs, N. Y. *1777

*Richard D'Olier.

*Edward Nicoll, A. M.

*John Ray, A. M. 1773.

*Henry Rutgers, Capt. U. S. A. 1776, Memb. Assemb. N. Y., Regent Univ. N. Y. S. 1802–26. aet. 85. *1830

*John Troup, A. M. aet. 70. 1817

*John Troup, Jr., A. M.

*John Vardill, (Rev.), A. M., Tutor, Prof. Nat. Law Hist. and Lang. 1773–76.

*John Watts, A. M., Memb. Assemb. N. Y. 1788–89 and Speaker of the same 1791–2–3, Judge Westchester Co. N. Y., Recorder N. Y. City. *1794

11

## 1767.

*William Laight, A. M.

*Peter Van Schaack, 1768, (C. L.), A. M. 1773, LL. D. 1826, Commr. for revising Colonial Statutes N. Y. 1773. *1832

2

## 1768.

*Charles Doughty, A. M., M. B. 1772.
*James Ludlow, A. M.
*Benjamin Moore, (Rev.), A. M., S. T. D. 1789, President *pro tem.* 1775–76, Prof. Rhet. and Logic 1784–87, Regent Univ. N. Y. S. 1787–1802, President 1801–11, Trustee 1802–13, Bishop P. E. Ch. N. Y. 1801–16. *1816
*Gouverneur Morris, (C. L.), A. M., Memb. Prov. Conv. N. Y. 1775, Del. to Continent. Congr. 1777, Asst. Supt. Finance 1781–85, Del. to Fed. Constit. Conv. 1787, U. S. Min. to France, 1792–94, U. S. Sen. 1800–3, Trustee 1805–16, Canal Commissioner of N. Y. 1810–15. aet. 65. *1816
*John Stevens, (Eng.) A. M. *1838
*Gulian Verplanck, Speaker House Assemb., N. Y., Regent Univ. N. Y. S. 1790–1800.

6

## 1769.

*Caleb Cooper, A. M. 1771.

## 1770.

*James Creighton, A. M.
*John Doughty, (Rev.)
*Jonathan Graham, and Yale 1770.
*Richard Harris, A. M.
*William Hubbard, A. M.
*Stephen Lush, A. M., N. Y. Sen. 1801–2.
*John Rutgers Marshall, (Rev.), A. M.
*Philip Pell, A. M., Regent Univ. N. Y. S. 1784–87.

8

## 1771.

*Ichabod Best Barnet, A. M.
*Clement Cooke Clarke, A. M.
*John Copp, (T.), A. M., 1st Lt. 1st Reg. N. Y. Vols. 1776.
*Henry DeWint, A. M.
*Thomas Knox.
*John Searle, A. M.

6

## 1772.

*Thomas Barclay, Maj. H. B. M. Army 1777, Speaker Assembly Nova Scotia, Adj. Gen. Nova Scotia, British Commr. under "Jay's Treaty" and under Treaty of Ghent. *1830
*John Bowden, (Rev.), A. M., S. T. D. 1796, Prof. Mor. Phil. Bell. Lett. and Logic 1801–17. *1817
*John King.
*Nicholas Ogden.
*Peter Roebuck, A. M.
*Andrew Skeene.

6

## 1773.

*Cornelius Bogert, Lt. N. Y. Ind. Forces 1776.
*Frederick Philipse, Capt. Dragoons, British Army. *1785
*Nathaniel Philipse.
*Beverley Robinson, Lt.-Col. H. B. M. Army. *1816
*Thomas Shreve, (Rev.) aet. 64. *1816

## 1774.

*Isaac Abrahams.
*Robert Nicholls Auchmuty. *1813
*William Chandler. *1784

*Edward Dunscomb, Maj. U. S. Rev. Army, Trustee 1795–1814, Sheriff N. Y. C. 1810–11. *1814
*Nicholas Heyliger.
*John Jauncey.
*Henry Nicoll.
*George Ogilvie, (Rev.) *1797
*John Rapelje.
*Benjamin Seaman.
*Edward Stevens, M. D. elsewhere, Prof. Pract. of Med. 1794–5.
*Robert Troup (C. L.), LL. D. elsewhere, Maj. U. S. A., Judge U. S. Dist. Ct. N. Y., Trustee 1811–17. aet. 75. *1832

12

## 1775.

*William Amory.
*Richard Auchmuty, Surgeon H. B. M. Army. *1782
*Samuel Auchmuty, G. C. B., Adj. Gen. 52d Regt. H. B. M. Army, Gov. of Isle of Thanet 1802, Brig. Gen. Commg. British Forces at Capture of Montevideo, 1806, Maj. Gen. Commg. at Madras, Lt.-Gen. in command at capture of Java, Gen. Commanding the Forces in Ireland in 1822. aet. 64.* 1822
*William Cock, A. M. 1790.
*Joseph Griswold.
*John William Livingston, Lt. "N. Y. Independ. Forces" 1776.
*Jacobus Remsen.

7

## 1776.

*Samuel Bayard.
*James Devereux.
*Peter Kissam.
*Matthias Nicholl, (M.) *1827
*Peter Ogden.
*Marinus Willett.

6

---

On the 6th of April, 1776, the College buildings were taken for military purposes. The College did not fully resume its functions till the close of the war, and no degrees were conferred till 1786. The following candidates had been admitted, but did not complete their course on account of the disturbed state of public affairs :

## In 1774.†

*Thomas Atwood.
*John Brickell.
*David Clarkson.
*Samuel Deall.
*James De Peyster.
*John Gaine. aet. 26. *1787
*Alexander Hamilton, A. M. 1788 and Harv. 1792, LL. D. Dart. 1790 and N. Jers. 1791 and Harv. 1792 and Rutgers 1792, Capt. U. S. A. 1776, Lt.-Col. staff of Washington 1777, Memb. Congr. 1782, Regent Univ. N. Y. S. 1784–87, N. Y. Leg. 1786, Del. to U. S. Constit. Conven. 1787, Secy. Treasury U. S. 1789–95, Maj.-Gen. U. S. A. 1798, Trustee 1787, 1804. aet. 47. *1804
*Tristrim Lowther.
*Schuyler Lupton.
*Edward Cornwallis Moncrieff.
*Daniel Moore.
*Paul Randall.
*Nicholas Romeyn.
*Jacob Shaw.
*Horatio Smith.
*James Stiles.
*John Whitaker.

## In 1775.†

*Edward Kerin.
*Benjamin Kissam, M. D. elsewhere, Prof. Instit. of Med. 1785–92, Trustee 1787–1803. aet. 44. *1803
*Thomas Groesbeck Lynch.
*Thomas Lambert Moore, (Rev.), A. M. 1790. *1799
*Jacob Morris.
*Augustus Nicoll.
*Marinus Oudenaarde.
*Peter Oudenaarde.

## In 1777.†

*James Delancy Walton, Admiral H. B. M. Navy. *1834
*William Walton. *1806

## 1786.

*John Bassett, and Yale 1786, (Rev.), A. M., S. T. D. Will. 1804. *1824
*De Witt Clinton, (C. L.), A. M., LL. D. 1826 and Ohio Univ. 1825, N. Y. Assemb. 1797, N. Y. Sen. 1798–1802, 1805–1811, Memb. Constit. Conv. N. Y. 1801, U. S. Sen. 1802–4, Mayor N. Y. C. 1803–7, 1809–10, 1811–15, Regent Univ. N. Y. S. 1808–25, Lt.-Gov. N. Y. 1811–13, N. Y. Canal Commr. 1816–24, Gov. N. Y. 1817–21, 1825–28. aet. 59. *1828
*Abraham Hun, A. M.
*George Livingston.
*Philip H. Livingston, A. M.
*Samuel Smith, Jr., A. M.
*Peter Steddiford, (Rev.), A. M. *1826
*Francis Sylvester, (C. L.), A. M.

8

## 1787.

*Samuel Boyd, (C. L.), Trustee 1826–35.
*Nicholas Fonda.
*John C. Ludlow, (C. L.), A. M. 1793.
*Henry Cruger Van Schaack.
*John W. Yates, (B.)

5

## 1788.

*James Cochran, (C. L.), A. M., Repr. in Congr. 1797–99, Regent Univ. N. Y. S. 1796–1820. *1848
*John Eccles, (F.)
*William Hurst, 1789.
*Peter Schuyler Livingston, and Yale and N. Jers. 1788 and Harv. 1790, A. M. *1807
*Brandt Schuyler Lupton, (Rev.) *1790
*Daniel Crommelin Verplanck, (C. L.), A. M. 1788, Judge Dutchess Co. N. Y.

6

## 1789.

*John T. Bainbridge.
*James Chatham Duane, (C. L.)
*Henry Izard.
*William Lupton, Jr.
*John Mitchell Mason, (Rev.), A. M. N. Jers. 1794, S. T. D. Univ. Penn. 1804, Trustee 1795–1821, Provost 1811–16, Prest. Dickin. Coll. Penn. 1821–24 aet. 60. *1829
*Matthew Mesier.
*Peter Mesier, (C. L.)
*John Remsen, (C. L.)
*John P. Van Ness, A. M. 1845, Repr. in Congr.

9

## 1790.

*David Schuyler Bogart, and N. Jers. 1791, (Rev.) *1839
*Marmaduke Earle, (Rev.) aet. 63. *1832
*Jonathan Freeman, (Rev.), A. M. 1800 and N. Jers. 1809. *1822
*George Graham, U. S. Asst. Secy. State 1801–25.
*John Graham.
*Frederick Halsey.
*Samuel Jones, Jr., 1793 and Yale 1790, (C. L.), LL. D. 1826 and Union 1841, Memb. N. Y. Assemb. 1812–14, Recorder N. Y. C. 1823, Chancellor N. Y. S. 1826–28, Ch.-Just. Sup. Ct. N. Y. 1828–47 and Justice of same 1847–49. aet. 83. *1853
7

## 1791.

*Peter Anderson, A. M. 1795, M. D. 1795.
*Anthony Bleecker, (C. L.), A. M. 1797, Examiner in Chancery. *1827
*William Bleecker, (C. L.)
*William Temple Broome, A. M. 1797.
*Walter L. Cochran.
*Pierre Edward Fleming, A. M. 1797.
*William Hendell, Jr., (Rev.), S. T. D. 1828.
*Cave Jones, (Rev.), A. M., S. T. D. elsewhere. aet. 59. *1829
*Isaac Knevils.
*John Knevils.
*Lancaster Lupton.
*John W. Mulligan, (C. L.), A. M. 1834, Surrogate N. Y. C. 1810, Clerk N. Y. Co. 1813–15, U. S. Consul at Athens, Greece, 1848. *1864
*Charles L. Ogden, (M.)
*Thomas Ludlow Ogden, (C. L.), Trustee 1817–44. *1844
*Daniel Paris, (C. L.), N. Y. Sen. 1810–13.
*George Rapelje, (C. L.)
*Frederic Van Horne, (Rev.), A. M. 1795.
*William Beekman Verplanck.
*Nathan H. White, (C. L.), A. M. 1795.
*Jesse Woodhull, Jr.
*James Woods, (C. L.), A. M. 1804.
21

## 1792.

*Gerard Beekman.
*Cornelius Brower.
*Alexander Hosack, M. D. 1797.
*John B. Johnson, (Rev.) *1803
*James Witter Nicholson.
*John L. Norton.
*Jotham Post, Jr., A. M., M. D. 1793.
*Alexander Proudfit, (Rev.), A. M. Union 1792, S. T. D. Middleb. Coll. 1811 and Williams 1812. aet. 75. *1844
*Jacob Sickles.
*Samuel Smith.
*George Taylor, (M.)
*William Taylor, (M.)
12

## 1793.

*John Brower.
*George Clinton, Jr., (C. L.), Repr. in Congr.
*William Cutting, (C. L.), Sheriff N. Y. C. 1807–8.
*Cornelius Decker, Jr., (M.)
*George I. Eacker, (C. L.), A. M. 1797.
*Samuel Gilford, Jr., (M.)
*Charles D. Goold, (M.), A. M. 1797.

Robert Heaton, Jr., A. M. 1797, U. S. A.
*John I. Johnson.
*Edward W. Laight, (C. L.), Memb. N. Y. Assemb. 1816, Trustee 1816–51 and Chairman 1849–50.
*Henry William Ludlow, (F.)
*Henry Masterson, (C. L.)
*Philip Milledoler, (Rev.), A. M. 1797, S. T. D. Univ. Penn., Prof. Theol. and Prest. Rutg. Coll. 1825–35. *1852
*John Nicholl, A. M. 1797.
*Robert B. Norton, (C. L.)
*Abraham Ogden, (M.)
*James Parker, (M.), Memb. N. J. Leg., Boundary Commr. N. J. 1807, 1827, 1833, Pres. Elector N. J. 1824, U. S. Collector Perth Amboy N. J. 1829–33, Repr. in Congr. 1833–37, Memb. of the Constit. Con. N. J. 1844. aet. 92. *1868
*Jonathan Pearsee, Jr., (C. L.)
*Valentine H. Peters, (M.)
*John S. Schermerhorn, (M.)
*Gilbert Smith, M. D. elsewhere.
*Thomas R. Smith, (M.)
*James S. Stringham, A. M. 1797, M. D. Univ. Edinb. 1799, Prof. Chem. 1802–13, Prof. Med. Juris. Coll. Phys. and Surg. N. Y. 1813–17. *1817
*Thomas Thompson.
*Cornelius Augustus Van Horne, (M.)
*Elias Brevoort Woodward, (C. L.), Judge N. Y. Territory.

26

## 1794.

*William Cocks.
*John E. Fisher, (M.)
*John Forbes, Libr. N. Y. Soc. Lib. 1794–1824, Commr. for improving and laying out city of N. Y. 1808–1824. *1824
*Levi P. Graham, (C. L.)
*Montgomery Hunt. aet. 60. *1837
*Jacob J. Janeway, (Rev.), A. M., S. T. D. elsewhere, Prof. Rutg. Coll. *1858
*Peter Augustus Jay, (C. L.), A. M. and Yale 1798, LL. D. 1835 and Harv. 1831, Trustee 1812–17 and 1823–43 and Chairman 1832, Memb. N. Y. Assemb. 1816, Recorder N. Y. C. 1819–20, Memb. N. Y. Constit. Conv., Prest. N. Y. Hist. Soc. *1843
*Cyrus King, (C. L.), Repr. in Congr.
*Leffert Lefferts, Jr., (C. L.), Judge Ct. Com. Pleas Kings Co. N. Y.
*Jacob Ogden Mackie, (M.)
*Samuel B. Malcolm, (C. L.)
*Gilbert Milligan, M. D. elsewhere.
*John B. Stringham, M. D. elsewhere.
*Peter G. Stuyvesant, (C. L.), Prest. N. Y. Hist. Soc. *1847
*Thomas Ustick, (C. L.)

15

## 1795.

*George Barculoo, (Rev.), S. T. D. Rutg. Coll. 1834.
*Philip Duryee, (Rev.), S. T. D. Rutg. Coll. 1834. *1850
*Bernard Elliot.
*John J. Faesch.
*John Ferguson, (C. L.), Mayor N. Y. C. 1815, U. S. Naval Off. N. Y., Trustee 1830–32. *1832
*Thomas Herring, (M.), A. M.

*James Inglis, (Rev.), S. T. D. Coll. N. Jers. 1811. *1820
*Nicholas Jones, (Rev.)
*Adolph C. Lent, A. M., M. D., 1798.
*John Blair Linn, (Rev.), A. M., S. T. D. Univ. Penn. *1804
*Silvanus Miller, (C. L.), N. Y. Assemb., Surrogate N. Y. C. 1801–7, 1811–21, Examiner in Chanc. *1861
*John H. Meier, (Rev.), A. M. 1804. aet. 32. *1806
*John Morrison.
*Alexander Phœnix, (Rev.) aet. 86. *1863
*Sidney Phœnix. aet. 24. *1804
*Thomas Phœnix, (C. L.), Dist. Atty. N. Y. C.
*Robert Remsen.
*John Brodhead Romeyn, (Rev.), A. M. Union 1797, S. T. D. N. Jers. 1809, Trustee 1809–25 and Clerk 1811–15, Trustee Coll. N. Jers. 1809–25. *1825
*William Ross, (C. L.), Speaker N. Y. Assemb.
*Henry Sands, (C. L.), A. M.
*Benjamin Seaman, C. L.)
*James Bowdoine Temple,† Capt. H. B. M. Army.
*Daniel D. Tompkins, (C. L.), N. Y. Assemb. 1701, Memb. N. Y. Constit. Conv. 1801, Repr. in Congr. 1805–7, Just. Supr. Ct. N. Y. 1804, Gov. N. Y. 1807–17, V.-Pres. U. S. 1817–25, Prest. Constit. Con. N. Y. 1821. *1825
*Pierre C. Van Wyck, (C. L.), Dist. Atty. N. Y. C., Rec. N. Y. C.
*Effingham Warner, (Rev.)
*Rensselaer Westerlo, C. L.)

26

† Known subsequently as James Bowdoine.

## 1796.

*David Barclay.
*Henry Cruger, Jr.
*Philip Fisher.
*Andrew S. Garr, (C. L.) *1859
*David S. Jones, (C. L.) LL. D. Alleg. Coll. Penn., Corporation Counsel N. Y. C. 1813–16, Trustee 1820–48, Trustee Gen. Theol. Sem. P. E. Ch. 1822–48, Judge Queens Co. N. Y. 1840–1. *1848
*Edward P. Livingston, (C. L.), N. Y. Sen. 1809–12, Lt.-Gov. N. Y. 1831–33, Regent Univ. N. Y. S.
*Samuel Nicholson.
*Gouverneur Ogden.
*William Rattoone.
*Josiah Shippey, Jr., (M.)
*Charles Taylor, (M.)
*William Turk, M. D. elsewhere, U. S. N.
*Lawrence Van Buskirk.
*Adrian C. Van Slyck.
*John Watts.

15

## 1797.

*William Bard, (Br.), Trustee 1840–53. *1853
*Robert Boyd, (C. L.)
*Archibald Bruce, M. D. Edinburg, Prof. Mineralogy in New York City.
George W. Clinton, Repr. in Congr.
*Henry C. Kunze.
*Abraham R. Lawrence, (M.), U. S. Naval Off. N. Y.
*William Le Conte.
*Isaac A. Van Hook, (Rev.), A. M. 1803.
*William P. Van Ness, (C. L.), Judge U. S. Circuit Ct. S. Dist. N. Y.

9

## 1798.

*Joseph Bainbridge.
*Thomas Bay.
*George Brinckerhoff, (C.L.), A. M.
*Jacob V. Brower, A. M., M. D. 1802.
*Rudolph Bunner, (C. L.), Repr. in Congr.
*David Codwise, (C. L.), LL. D. Lafay. Coll. Penn. 1855, Mast. in Chanc. *1864
*George Davis, A. M.
*Charles Graham, (C. L.)
*John T. Irving, (C.L.), Trustee 1818–38, Judge Supr. Ct. N. Y. *1838
*Philip L. Jones.
*William B. Keese, (C. L.)
*Washington McKnight, (Rev.), A. M. 1804.
*Clement C. Moore, A. M., LL. D. 1829, Trustee 1813–57 and Clerk 1815–50, Prof. Hebrew and Greek Lit. Gen. Theol. Sem. P. E. Ch. N. Y. 1821–50, and Prof. Emeritus 1850–63. *1863
*Samuel Moore, M. D. elsewhere.
William Ogden, (M.)
William Rhinelander, (M.), A. M. 1804.
Lewis Sands.
James Walsh.

18

## 1799.

*John Christie, (Rev.)
*Peter Ditmarse Froeligh, (Rev.) aet. 45. *1827
*Lewis LeConte.
*James Livingston.
*James Lynch, (C. L.), Just. Mar. Ct. N. Y. C.
*Thomas Thornton Mackaness, A. M.
*James R. Manley, A. M., M. D. 1803, Prest. N. Y. S. Med. Soc. 1825–26. aet. 69. *1851
Alexander Murray.
*Philip F. Mayer, (Rev.), S. T. D. 1837.
*Stephen Price.
*Samuel Riker, Jr., (C. L.) aet. 32. *1811
*Jacob Schoonmaker, (Rev.), A. M., S. T. D. Dickin. Coll. Penn. 1831. aet. 75. *1852
*Arthur J. Stansbury, (C. L.)
*Peter I. Van Pelt, (Rev.), A. M. 1803.
*Abraham Varick, Jr., (C. L.)
*John Vredenburgh Varick, (M.)
*Arthur M. Walter, A. M.
*David Wright.

18

## 1800.

*John J. De Peyster.
*Samuel Halstead, (M.)
*Philip Hamilton.
Samuel Harris, (C. L.)
John Henry.
John Huyler, A. M.
*Robert Swift Livingston (C. L.) *1867
John McKinnon, A. M.
*Nicholas J. Quackenbos, M. D. 1802, A. M. *1847
Thomas W. Rathbone.
*Sampson Simson, (C. L.)
*Charles Floyd Thomas.
*Matthew Tillary, M. D. elsewhere.
*John Y. Ward.
*George Wilson, (C.L.), A.M.
*Peter Wilson, (C. L.), A. M. *1826

16

## 1801.

*John Anthon, (C.L.), LL.D. 1861. *1863
*Robert Benson, Jr., (M.) *1872

*Abraham L. Blauvelt.
*Samuel Bogert.
*Thomas Bolton, (C.L.), Mast. in Chanc.
*John Furman.
*John Gosman, (Rev.), S. T. D. elsewhere. *1865
*John Nitchie, (C. L.), Col. U. S. A. 1814. *1838
*Lewis Morris Ogden.
*Henry Schenck.
*Henry H. Schieffelin, (M.) aet. 83. *1865
*Gabriel Tichenor.
*Gulian Crommelin Verplanck, A. M. 1821, LL. D. 1835 and Amh. 1834 and Hob. 1835, N. Y. Assemb. 1820, Prof. Ev. Christian. Gen. Theol. Sem. P. E. Ch. 1821–24, Repr. in Congr. 1825–33, N. Y. Sen., Trustee 1821–6, Regent Univ. N. Y. S. 1826–70, Pres. Commr. Emigr. N. Y. 1846–70. aet. 84. *1870
*Samuel Armstrong Walsh, M. D. Coll. Phys. and Surg. N. Y. 1811.
*Gabriel Winter, (C. L.) *1862
15

## 1802.

*Alexander M. Beebe.
*John Player Crosby, and Yale 1802 and N. Jers. 1802. *1806
*John Delafield, (M.)
*William Gardner.
*George W. Gosman.
*Francis L. Harison, (C. L.)
*James Jones.
*Henry Laight, (C. L.)
*Leffert Lefferts, (C. L.), Judge Kings Co. N. Y.
*Robert Macomb, (C. L.), A. M.
*John W. Macomb.
*Nathaniel F. Moore, A. M., L.L. D. 1825, Adj. Prof. Greek and Lat. Lang. 1817–20 and Prof. 1820–35, Librarian 1837–9, President 1842–9, Trustee 1842–51. aet. 90. *1872
*Archibald McVickar, (C.L.)
*James McVickar, (M.) *1836
*Isaac Ogden, (M.)
*William Ogilvie.
*Henry Bate Priest.
*Billopp B. Seaman.
*James Tillary, M. D. elsewhere.
Hubert Van Wagenen.
20

## 1803.

George H. Atkinson.
John Bay.
John Bowne.
*Thomas Crolius.
*Augustus Fleming.
*Edward R. Jones, (M.), Trustee 1831–38.
*Gouverneur Kemble, (M.), Repr. in Congr., Memb., N. Y. S. Constit. Conven. 1846. aet. 90. *1875
*Peter Kemble.
Edward Kemeys.
*John L. Lawrence, (C. L.), N. Y. Assemb. 1816–17, Memb. Constit. Conv. N.Y. 1821, N. Y. Sen. 1848–50, Trustee 1830–49, Treasurer 1833–49, Compt. N. Y. C. *1849
*John Le Conte, M. D. elsewhere.
*George C. Quackenbos, M.D. elsewhere. *1858
*William Remsen, (C. L.)
*Henry F. Rogers, (M.)
*Alpheus Sherman, (C. L.), N. Y. Assemb. 1826–29, N. Y. Sen. 1830–34. *1866
*John Cox Stevens.
Samuel W. Thomson.
*Robert Watts.
18

## 1804.

*Samuel Akerly, A. M.
*John W. Barnum.
*William D. Blackwell, (C. L.)
*George Bryar.
Elisha Camp, (C. L.), Capt. U. S. V. 1812, Assist. U. S. Dist. Atty. N. Dist. N. Y.
*Cornelius T. Demarest, (Rev.), A. M. 1813.
*Jeremiah I. Drake, A. M.
*William Edgar.
*William Gracie and N. Jers. 1804.
*John T. B. Graham.
*Henry B. Hagerman.
*Alexander Hamilton, Col. N. Y. M. 1812, U. S. Consul at Havana, U. S. Boundary Commr. *1875
*Richard N. Harison.
*James D. Livingston.
*William L. Lytton, A. M., M. D. 1807.
Thomas McGahagan, 1805.
*John McVickar, (Rev.), A.M. 1818, S. T. D. 1825, Prof. Moral and Int. Phil. Rhetoric, Belle-Lett. and Pol. Econ. 1817–57, Prof. Ev. Nat. and Rev. Relig. 1857–64 and Emeritus 1864–68. aet. 82. *1868
*Edward Manley.
*John Mitchell.
*Joseph Nelson, A. M. 1808, LL. D. Rutg. Coll. 1825, Prof. Languages Rutger's Coll. aet. 47. *1830
*William M. Price.
*Philip Rhinelander.
*Samuel Rogers. *1869
*David M. Ross, A. M.
*Robert Seaman.
*John I. Sickles, A. M.
*Thomas D. Smith.
*Charles Stewart.
*John R. Thompson, (Rev.), A. M.
*James Talcott Watson, and Yale 1804 and N. Jers. 1804.
*John Watts, Jr., M. D. Edinburgh 1809, Prof. Pract. of Physic Rutg. Coll. N. J., Pres. Coll. Phys. and Surg. N. Y. 1826–31, Trustee 1824–31. *1831

31

## 1805.

Peter Allaire, (M.)
*James Bibby.
*Leonard A. Bleecker.
*William Cock.
*Benjamin U. Coles.
*Joab G. Cooper, (Rev.), A. M.)
*James L. Fine.
*James Fleming.
*Alexander Gunn, (Rev.), A. M. and N. Jers. 1805, S. T. D. Allegh. Coll. Penn. *1829
*Richard Hatfield, Jr.
James A. Hamilton, (C. L.), LL. D. Hamilton, U. S. Dist. Atty. N. Y.
Robert Jaques, A. M.
Thomas Lefferts.
*Henry Ustick Onderdonk, (Rev.), A. M., M. D. 1810, S. T. D. 1827, Bishop P. E. Ch. Penn. 1827–45. *1858
*Edmund H. Pendleton, (C. L.), Judge Dutchess Co. N. Y., Repr. in Congr. 1831–33.
Abraham Purdy, A. M. 1810.
*Edward Seaman.
John T. Smith.
*Robert I. Watts.

19

## 1806.

*John V. Bartow, (Rev.), A. M.

*George Boyd, (Rev.), S. T. D. elsewhere. *1850
*John Chrystie.
*John Peter De Wint. aet. 84. *1870
*William Elsworth Dunscomb, (C. L.) aet. 85. *1874
*Gilbert O. Fowler, (C. L.)
*Jonathan B. Gosman, (Rev.)
*James McCullen.
*Robert B. Anæas McLeod (Rev.)
*Cornelius Miller, (C. L.)
*David Moore, (Rev.), S. T. D. elsewhere. *1856
*Samuel W. Moore, M. D. 1810. aet. 68. *1864
*Ferris Pell, (C. L.)
*David Quackinbush, M. D. elsewhere.
*Samuel B. Romaine, (C. L.), N. Y. Assemb. 1816–19, 1819–22 and Speaker 1822.
*Frederic Roorbach, (C. L.)
*Cornelius Schermerhorn, (C. L.)
*Philip Schuyler, U. S. Consul at Liverpool, N. Y. Assemb. *1865
John A. Smith, (C. L.)
*John L. Tillinghast, (C. L.)

20

## 1807.

*Egbert Benson, Jr. *1866
John L. Bronk, (C. L.), Judge Greene Co. N. Y.
*John H. Brouwer.
*William E. Burrell, M. D. Coll. Phys. and Surg. N. Y. 1811.
*George R. Copland. aet. 17. *1808
Henry S. Dodge, A. M.
Robert Gosman.
John H. Hill, (Rev.), A. M. 1845, S. T. D. elsewhere, LL. D. 1868, Missionary in Greece.
Philip M. Holmes.
Daniel Mack.
*Peter T. Marselis, (C. L.)
*William H. Maxwell, (C. L.), A. M. 1827.
*Simeon Remsen. *1815
*James Renwick, A. M., LL. D. 1829, Instructor in Nat. and Exper. Phil. and Chem. 1813, Trustee 1817–20, Prof. Nat. and Exper. Phil. and Chem. 1820–53, and Prof. Emeritus 1853–63. *1863
*George Paxton Rogers. *1870
Dirck B. Stockholm.
Peter V. C. Tappan.
Cornelius Van Buren.
*James Van Cortlandt.
Theodore V. W. Varick, A. M.
*Philip G. Van Wyck. aet. 84. *1870
*Charles A. Williamson.

21

## 1808.

*William Atkinson, (M.)
*William Berrian, (Rev.), S. T. D. 1828, Rector Trinity Parish N. Y. C. 1830–62, Trustee 1832–62. *1862
*Lionel Brown.
*Timothy Clowes, LL. D. elsewhere. aet. 60. *1847
*Henry M. Francis, A. M., M. D. elsewhere.
*James Inderwick, M. D. elsewhere, U. S. N.
*Robert McCartee, (Rev.), A. M., S. T. D. 1831. *1865
*John McKnight, (Rev.)
*Hugh Maxwell, (C. L.), A. M. 1816, Dist. Atty. N. Y. C. 1819–29, U. S. Collector Port of N. Y. aet. 86. *1873
Frederick Muzzy, (C. L.)
John W. Phillips, (T.)
*Edward Post, M. D. Edinburgh.
William C. Rhinelander.
*Henry Howard Ross, (C. L.),

A. M. Univ. Vt. 1813, Repr. in Congr. 1825–27, Memb. and Prest. N. Y. Electoral Coll. 1848, Judge Essex Co. N. Y. 1847–48. aet. 72. *1862
*Gilbert H. Sayres, (Rev.,) S. T. D., 1863. aet. 80. *1867
*James Alexander Stevens. aet. 84. *1873
*William Stuart, (M.)
*Daniel Van Mater.
*Henry Vethake, A. M., LL. D. 1836, Instr. in Math. and Geog. 1813, Prof. Math. and Nat. Phil. Rutg. Coll. 1813–1817 and in Coll. N. Jers. 1817–21 and in Dickinson Coll. 1821–29 and in Univ. N. Y. C. 1832–35, Prest. Washington Coll. Va. 1835–36, Prof. Maths. Univ. Penn. 1836–54, and Provost and Prof. Moral and Int. Phil. Univ. Penn. 1854–59. *1866
*Peter D. Vroom, Jr., (C. L.), A.M. 1812, LL.D. 1837 and N. Jers. 1850, N. Jers. Legis. 1826–29, Gov. and Chancellor N. Jers. 1829–36, Repr. in Congr. 1838–40, Memb. N. Jers. State Constit. Conven. 1844, U. S. Envoy Ex. and Min. Plen. to Prussia, 1853–57. aet. 82. *1873
*Henry Watts.
*John Watts, Jr.

22

## 1809.

*Thomas S. Aspinwall.
*Samuel Berrian. *1818
*Edward N. Bibby, M.D. elsewhere.
John Brady, (Rev.), A. M.
*John Cadle, A. M., M. D. Coll. Phys. and Surg. N. Y. 1822, Surg. U. S. Navy.
*Gerrit Conrey.
*Edward Copland, Mayor Brooklyn. aet. 63. *1859
*Cornelius Roosevelt Duffie, (Rev.), A. M. 1813. *1827
Thomas Duggan.
*John Fine, (C. L.), A. M., LL. D. Hamilt. Coll. 1850, Treas'r St. Lawrence Co. N. Y. 1821–33 and Judge 1824–39, 1844–47, Repr. in Cong. 1839–41, N. Y. Sen. 1848–50. aet. 74. *1867
*Alexander Fleming. aet. 77. *1867
Alfred C. Floyd.
*John Wakefield Francis, A. M., M. D. Coll. Phys. and Surg. N. Y. 1809, LL. D. 1860 and Trin. Coll. 1850, Prof. Obstet. and Med. Jurisp. Rut. Med. Coll. N. Y., Prof. Mat. Med. Coll. Phys. and Surg. N. Y. 1813–16 and Prof. Obstet. 1820–26, Trustee Coll. Phys. and Surg. 1814–26, Prest. N. Y. Acad. Med. 1848. aet. 72. *1861
*James N. Gifford, (M.) aet. 81. *1873
Henry Green.
John C. Hamilton (C. L.)
David Murray Hoffman, (C. L.) LL.D. 1860 and Union 1840, Judge Supr. Ct. N.Y.
Samuel Jackson.
*Ravaud Kearny, (Rev.) A.M.
*Jackson Kemper, (Rev.), S. T. D. 1829, LL. D. elsewhere, Missy. Bishop P. E. Ch. of the North West 1835–54, Bishop Wisconsin 1854–70. aet. 81. *1870
*Henry McVickar, (M.)
*Benjamin Tredwell Onderdonk, (Rev.), A. M. 1816, S.T.D. 1826, Trustee 1824–53, Prof. Eccles. Pol. Gen. Theol. Sem. P. E. Ch. N.Y. 1826, Bishop P. E. Ch. N. Y. 1830–61. *1861

*Walter F. Osgood, A. M.
*Robert J. Renwick.
James Stryker, (C. L.), A. M. 1813, Judge Buffalo, N. Y.
William Turnbull.
*William Edward Wyatt, (Rev.), A. M. 1816, S. T. D. elsewhere. 27

## 1810.

*John Agnew.
*Andrew Anderson, M. D. Coll. Phys. and Surg. N. Y. 1813.
*Francis Child, A. M. 1816.
*David A. Clarkson, (M.)
*George Codwise.
*William De Peyster.
*Israel D. Disosway (F.)
*Jacob Dyckman, A. M., M.D. Coll. Phys. and Surg. N.Y. 1813.
*Robert Emmet, (C. L.), Just. Supreme Ct. N. Y. C. *1873
*Theodosius O. Fowler.
*James C. Garrison, A. M. 1816, M. D. elsewhere, U. S. Navy.
*Joseph Greenleaf, (C. L.) *1871
*Peter F. Hunn, (C. L.)
*Charles J. Kipp.
*Horatio G. Lewis.
*John McLain McDonald, (C. L.) *1863
*John McGregor, (T.)
*Benjamin Moore, (M.)
*George W. Morton, (C. L.), U. S. Commissioner N.Y.C.
*John L. Morton (F.) *1871
*Ava Neal, (Rev.), A. M. *1839
*Waldron B. Post, (M.) *1874
*John Slidell, (C. L.), U. S. Dist. Atty. for La. 1829–33, U. S. Min. to Mexico 1845 and to Central America 1853, Repr. in Congr. and U. S. Sen. *1871
*Francis B. Stevens. *1811
*Richard Stevens, M. D. elsewhere. *1828
*James Stoughton, (C. L.), A. M. *1819
*Pascal N. Strong (Rev.), A. M. N. Jers. 1818, S. T. D. elsewhere, Trustee 1822–25. *1825
*Jacob Townsend, (C. L.)
*Charles Watts, (C. L.), Judge Dist. Ct. New Orleans. *1850
29

## 1811.

*Gregory T. Bedell, (Rev.), A. M. 1816, S. T. D. elsewhere. *1834
John Brown, (Rev.), A. M. 1815, S. T. D. elsewhere.
John Campbell.
Ebenezer Close, A. M. 1815.
*John Covert, Jr., (Rev.)
*George Douglass.
Jacobus Dyckman, (C. L.)
*Charles G. Ferris, A. M. 1816, Repr. in Congr. 1834–36, 1841–3.
*David H. Fraser, A. M. 1815, M. D. Coll. Phys. and Surg. N. Y. 1818. *1818
Richard Freeke, (C. L.)
*James Watson Gerard, (C. L.), A. M. 1816, LL. D. 1863. aet. 86. *1874
*Benjamin Haight, A. M. 1816.
*William H. Harison, (C. L.), Trustee 1838–1860. *1860
*William Henry Hart, (Rev.), A. M. 1828.
William Hogan, Repr. in Congr.
*Peter V. B. Livingston, U. S. Min. to Cent. America.
Thomas William Ludlow, Trustee 1833–6.
Jackson Odell, (F.)

*George B. Purdy, M. D. Coll. Phys. and Surg. N. Y. 1816. aet. 70. *1865
Charles Rapelje, A. M. 1820.
*John R. Rhinelander, M. D. Coll. Phys. and Surg. N. Y. 1824, Prof. Anat. Coll. Phys. and Surg. 1834–9 and Trustee of same 1840–48. aet. 66. *1857
*John B. Stevenson, 1816, A. M. 1816, M. D. Coll. Phys. and Surg. N. Y. 1816. aet. 63. *1868.
*John N. Tallman, A.M. 1815.
George J. Watts.

24

## 1812.

Albert Ammerman, (Rev.)
*Matthias Bruen, Jr., (Rev.), A. M.
John A. Burtis.
*William Creighton, (Rev.), S. T. D. 1830, elected Bishop P. E. Ch. N. Y. and declined, Prest. Gen. Conven. P. E. Ch. U. S., Trustee 1828–40. *1865
*James F. De Peyster, Capt. U. S. A. 1814. aet. 80. *1874.
*Alexander Duer, (C. L.) *1819
*Richard Duryee, Jr., (M.)
*Lindley Murray Hoffman, (M.) *1861
*Ogden Hoffman, (C. L.), Midshipman U. S. N. 1814, Memb. N. Y. Assemb. 1826–28, Repr. in Congr., Dist. Atty. N. Y. C., Atty.-Gen. N. Y., Trustee 1833–56. *1856
*Benjamin R. Kissam, M. D. Coll. Phys, and Surg. N. Y. 1819.
*Augustine N. Lawrence, (B.)
*Philip K. Lawrence, A. M. 1818.
*Cornelius F. Low, (C. L.) *1849
*Peter Mackie, Jr.
*Edward McVickar. *1866
*John W. B. Murray, A. M., M. D. elsewhere. *1818
*Matthew Charles Paterson, (C. L.), A. M. 1819, Dist. Atty. N. Y. C.
*Jacob A. Robertson, (M.), A. M. 1818.
*John Smyth Rogers, and Harv. 1827, M. D. Coll. Phys. and Surg. N. Y. 1821 and Bowd. 1825, Prof. Chem. and Nat. Sci. Trinity, Prof. Mat. Med. N. Y. Coll. of Pharmacy. aet. 57. *1851
*John A. Sidell, (C. L.)
*John SwartPout.
*Peter S. Townsend, A. M. 1816, M. D. Coll. Phys. and Surg. N. Y. 1816. aet. 54. *1849
*Egerton L. Winthrop, M. D. Coll. Phys. and Surg. N. Y. 1817. *1834

23

## 1813.

*Henry Anthon, (Rev.), A. M., S. T. D., 1832. *1861
*William Bailey.
*John Brodhead Beck, A. M. 1818 and Union 1816 and N. Jers. 1818, M. D. Coll. Phys. and Surg. N. Y. 1817, Prof. Mat. Med. Coll. Phys. and Surg. 1826–51, Trustee 1838–51. *1861
*James J. Bowden, (Rev.)
*William Boyd.
*George W. Bruen, (M.), A. M.
*Richard F. Cadle, (Rev.), A. M.
Thomas L. Davies.
*Robert Hyslop, (M.)
William Kemble, (M.)
*Thomas C. Mitchell, A. M.

*Nicholas Morris, Jr., A. M.
Thomas C. Murray, A. M. 1818.
*Nathaniel Greene Pendleton, Repr. in Congr. *1861
Robert Ray, (C. L.), A. M. 1817, Trustee 1849–.
*Alexander H. Robertson, A. M.
*Hugh Smith, (Rev.), A. M., S. T. D. 1838. *1849
*John Varick.

18

## 1814.

John H. Ball.
*James Brooks, (M.) aet. 74. *1868
*Cornelius Davis.
*William H. Heyer.
Benjamin Hilton.
*Allen Jackson, A. M. 1821.
Henry R. Judah.
*James Murison Pendleton, A. M. 1819, M. D. Coll. Phys. and Surg. N. Y. 1818. aet. 33. *1832
*Theophilus Russel.
George F. Talman, (C. L.), Corporation Counsel N. Y. C. 1838–9.
*Ferdinand Vandewater.

11

## 1815.

*Charles Anthon, LL. D. 1831, Adj.-Prof. Greek and Latin Lang. 1820–30, Jay Prof. Greek and Latin Lang. 1830–57 and Rect. Gram. School 1830–64, Jay Prof. Greek Lang. and Lit. 1857–67. aet. 70. *1867
*James W. Berrian.
*Archibald R. Bogardus.
*Robert G. L. De Peyster, (M.) *1873
*Archibald Gracie, Jr., (M.) *1865
*William S. Heyer, (Rev.), A. M.
*John Hone, Jr., (M.) *1829
*William Ironside.
*John Q. Jones, (C. L.)
*Leonard William Kip, (C. L.), A. M. 1820. aet. 67. *1863
*Philip Mesier Lydig, (M.) aet. 77. *1872
*John L. Mason, (C. L.), A. M., Judge Supr. Ct. N. Y., Trustee 1848–53.
*Francis Morton.
*Frederic William Rhinelander, (M.)
*James John Roosevelt, Jr., (C. L.), N. Y. Assemb. 1835, 1840, Repr. in Congr. 1841–43, Judge Supr. Ct. N. Y. aet. 79. *1875
*Robert Charles Sands, (Au.), A. M. *1832
*Robert Seney, (Rev.), A. M. 1828.
*Henry Hamlin Van Amringe, (Rev.), A. M. aet. 66. *1862
*James S. Watkins, M. D. Coll. Phys. and Surg. N. Y. 1817. *1817

19

## 1816.

*Abel T. Anderson, (C. L.), A. M. *1862
*John D. Campbell, (C. L.), A. M. 1820. *1852
*Richard Codman, (M.) *1847
Frederic De Peyster, Jr., (C. L.), A. M., LL. D. 1867, Milit. Secy. to Gov. Clinton 1825–8, Master in Chancery for 17 years, Prest. N. Y. Historical Society.
*Maurice William Dwight, (Rev.), A. M. 1820, S. T. D. elsewhere. *1860
*James Wallis Eastburn, (Rev.), A. M. aet. 22. *1819

*Isaac Ferris, (Rev.), A. M., S. T. D. Union 1833, LL. D. 1853, Chancell. Univ. N. Y. C. 1852–70, and Emeritus Chancellor 1870–73. aet. 74. *1873

John Ireland, Jr., (F.)

*John Edgar Mowatt, (M.)

*Daniel Levi Medora Peixotto, A. M. 1823, M. D. Coll. Phys. and Surg. N. Y. 1819, Prof. Theory and Pract. Med. Willoughby Med. Coll. aet. 43. *1843

*Samuel G. Raymond, (C. L.), A. M., Memb. N. Y. Assemb. *1850

John J. Robertson, (Rev.), S. T. D. elsewhere.

*James Romeyn, (Rev.), S. T. D. 1838, elected Prof. of Rhet. Rutg. Coll. and declined.

*John M. Smith, (Rev.), A.M., Prof. in Wesl. Univ. Conn. *1832

*Samuel L. Steer, (F.), Speaker Lower House of Louisiana.

*Thomas M. Strong, (Rev.), A. M. 1820, S. T. D. elsewhere. *1861

*Adrian Vanderveer, A. M., M. D. Coll. Phys. and Surg. N. Y. 1818. *1857

17

# 1817.

*John M. Cannon, (C. L.) *1835

James P. F. Clarke, (Rev.)

*Matthias O. Dayton, (C. L.)

*Manton Eastburn, (Rev.), A. M., S. T. D. 1835, Bishop P. E. Ch. Mass. 1842–72. aet. 71. *1872

*Isaac Fisher, (Rev.), A. M. *1839

*Seymour P. Funk, (Rev.), A. M. 1821. *1828

*Samuel L. Gouverneur, U. S. Postmr. N. Y. C. 1821–25, N. Y. Assemb. 1825. *1865

*John Grigg, (Rev.), A. M. aet. 72. *1868

Daniel Phœnix Ingraham, (C. L.), LL.D. 1860, Just. Supr. Ct. N. Y.

*Benjamin Isherwood, A. M., M. D. Coll. Phys. and Surg. N. Y. 1820. *1832

William Lowerre, (C. L.), A. M.

Edmund Ludlow.

*William Minturn.

*John Neilson, Jr., A. M., M. D. Coll. Phys. and Surg. N. Y. 1821. *1857

*Meredith Ogden, (M.)

*Richard Ray, A. M. *1839

*Edward N. Rogers, A. M.

*Samuel D. Rogers, (M.) *1850

18

# 1818.

*Henry James Anderson, A. M., M. D. Coll. Phys. and Surg. N. Y. 1824, LL. D. 1850, Prof. of Math. and Astr. 1825–43, Emeritus 1866–75, Trustee 1851–75. aet. 77. *1875

*Daniel Bonnett. aet. 74. *1871

*Richard Varick Dey, (Rev.), A. M. and Yale 1823. *1837

*Frederick Fairlie, (C. L.)

*Peter Forrester, A.M. Rutg., M. D. Coll. Phys. and Surg. N. Y. 1822. *1837

Robert Gracie, and Harv. 1818, (M.), A. M. and Yale 1825.

*Henry Hone, (M.), N. Y. Assemb. 1834. *18[illegible]6

*Richard F. Kemble, (C. L.)

William Beach Lawrence, (C. L.), A. M. 1823, and Yale 1826, LL. D. Brown Univ. 1869, U. S. Chargé d' Aff. London 1827–29, Lt.-Governor of R. I., Trustee Coll. Phys. and Surg. 1837–55.

James Lenox, A. M. and N. Jers. 1821, LL. D. 1875, Trustee N. J. 1823–57.
*John H. Lloyd.
*Alexander B. McLeod.
*Gerard W. Morris, (C. L.), Trustee 1851–5. *1865
*John O'Blenis.
*George D. Post, (C. L.) *1869
*Clarence D. Sackett, (C. L.)
*William Staley, A. M.
*Abraham D. Wilson, A. M., M. D. Coll. Phys. and Surg. N. Y. 1821.

18

## 1819.

*Henry N. Cruger, (C. L.), A. M. 1823.
*Gabriel Poillon Disosway, (M.), A. M. and Wesl. 1833, Member N. Y. Assembly 1849. aet. 70. *1868
*Peter Dykers, M. D. Coll. Phys. and Surg. N. Y. 1823. *1845
*Andrew Hamersley, M. D. Coll. Phys. and Surg. N. Y. 1823, Fellow Coll. Phys. and Surg.
*Edward P. Heyer, (M.)
*Walter E. Hyer, (M.) *1845
*William Lupton Johnson, (Rev.), A. M., S. T. D. Allegheny Coll. Penn. aet. 70. *1870
*Charles Jones. *1854
George Jones.
*Henry James Lowerre, (C. L.), A. M. *1830
*George J. Rogers, (M.)
*James H. Roosevelt, (C. L.), A. M. *1863
*James S. Rumsey, M.D. Coll. Phys. and Surg. N. Y. 1824. aet. 73. *1872
Richard L. Schieffelin, (C. L.), A. M.
*John L. Suckley, A.M. 1823, M. D. Coll. Phys. and Surg. N. Y. 1823. *1836
*Samuel Verplanck, (C. L.), A. M.
Thomas L. Wells, (C. L.), Trustee 1837–59.
*Marinus Willett, Jr., M. D. Coll. Phys. and Surg. N. Y. 1823, Trustee Coll. Phys. and Surg. 1827–40. *1840
*Richard Wynkoop, (Rev.), A. M.

19

## 1820.

William Betts, (C. L.), A. M., LL. D. 1850, Trustee 1842– and Clerk 1850–74, Prof. of Law 1848–54.
*John B. Bleecker, (M.) *1831
*Joseph H. Coit, (Rev.), S. T. D. 1855. *1866
Cornelius Ryerrs Disosway, (C. L.), A. M. Wesl. 1838.
*James Johnstone, (C. L.) *1854
*Samuel Roosevelt Johnson, (Rev.), A. M., S. T. D. 1848, Prof. System. Divinity and Dogmatic Theol. Gen. Theolog. Sem. P. E. Ch., Emeritus 1869–73. *1873
Henry Lawrence, (M.)
*Philip Edward Milledoler, (Rev.), M. D. Coll. Phys. and Surg. N. Y. 1824, A. M. Rutg. 1827, N. Y. Assemb. 1832. *1850
John F. Mitchell, (C. L.), A. M.
William Mitchell, (C. L.), A. M., LL. D. 1863, Master in Chancery N. Y. 1840–43, Just. Supr. Ct. N. Y. State 1850–58.
Archibald G. Rogers, (C. L.)
*Rutsen Suckley, (C. L.) aet. 75. *1875
*John R. Townsend, (C. L.) *1846

13

## 1821.

*William B. Barnes, (B.)
*Peter A. Cowdrey, (C. L.), A. M., N. Y. Assemb. 1836. *1852
*Isaac F. Craft, (M.)
William D. Craft, (C. L.)
*George H. Fisher, (Rev.), S. T. D. elsewhere, Trustee 1851–55. aet. 69. *1872
*William Forsyth. *1851
*William N. Gibert, (C. L.)
*Frederic Philipse Gouverneur,† (C. L.) aet. 71. *1874
*William P. Hawes, (C. L.), A. M.
*William Inglis, (C.L.), Judge Ct. Common Pleas N. Y. 1839–44. *1863
*Pierre Munroe Irving, (C.L), *1876
*Thomas Kermit.
*Elisha S. King, (C. L.), A. M. 1826.
*Isaac Low, A. M.
*Stephen H. Meeker, (Rev.), A. M. aet. 77. *1876
William Henry Munn, (C.L.), A. M.
Samuel Ogden, (M.)
Edwin Post, (M.)
*Henry A. V. Post, (C. L.)
George Shrady.
*John C. Slack, (T.)
*Charles E. Stagg, (M.)
*Peter Stagg, (C. L.)
*Junius Thompson, A. M 1825, M. D. Coll Phys. and Surg. N. Y. 1825. aet. 31. *1831
*John Tiebout, Jr., A. M., M.D. Coll. Phys. and Surg. N. Y. 1825.
*William Turner, A.M., M.D. elsewhere. *1858
*Gerrit G. Van Wagenen, (C. L.), Trustee 1845–58, and Treasurer 1849–58. *1858
*John H. Waddell, A. M.

†Known subsequently as Frederic Philipse.

*Henry John Whitehouse, (Rev.), A. M., S. T. D. 1865 and Oxford Univ. Eng. 1867, LL. D. Cambr. Univ. Eng. 1867, Bishop P. E. Ch. Ill. 1851–74 aet. 71. *1874
George Wilkes, M. D. Coll. Phys. and Surg. N. Y. 1824

30

## 1822.

George Abeel, (M.)
*George W. Dawson, (M.)
*Peter F. Dustan, (C. L.)
*John M. Glover, A. M. Yale 1825, M. D. Coll. Phys. and Surg. N. Y. 1826. *1832
*Josiah Dwight Harris, A. M., M. D. Coll. Phys. and Surg. N. Y. 1826, Asst. Surg. U. S. A. 1833. *1833
*Edwin Holt, 1826.
Henry Philip Jones, (C. L.)
*Theodore F. King, M. D. Coll. Phys. and Surg. N. Y. 1827. aet. 63. *1868
Nicholas Gouverneur Kortright, (C. L.) aet. 69. *1874
*Anson Livingston, (C. L.) aet. 67. *1873
*Carroll Livingston, (M.) *1867
Edward N. Mead, (Rev.), A. M 1833, S. T. D. 1861, Secy. Trustees Gen. Theo. Sem.
Adrian H. Müller, (M.), Prest. Roosevelt Hosp. N. Y. C.
*Alexander H. Paterson, (M.)
Alfred C. Post, M. D. Coll. Phys. and Surg. N. Y. 1827, LL. D. Univ. N. Y. City 1872, Prof. Ophthal. Anat. and Surg. Castleton Med. Coll., Prof. Surg. Univ. N. Y. C., Prest. N. Y. Acad. Med. 1868.
*John Lloyd Stephens, (C. L.), A. M. 1827, U. S. Special Embassador to

Central America 1839, Del. to N. Y. S. Constit. Conven. 1846. *1852
*Thomas William Tucker, (C. L.), A. M. 1826, Memb. N. Y. Assemb. *1854
Alfred Wagstaff, M. D. Coll. Phys. and Surgeons N. Y. 1826.
*Alfred Augustus Weeks, (C. L.), A. M. 1826. *1847
*Hamilton Wilkes, (F.) *1852
Edward M. Willett, (C. L.), A. M.
William R. Williams, (Rev.), A. M. 1835, S. T. D. 1837, Trustee 1838–48.
*Samuel F. Wilson, (C. L.) *1870

23

## 1823.

*Christopher Allen.
Horatio Allen, (Eng.)
*Edward Anthon, (C. L.) *1830
William H. Boyd, A. M., M. D. Coll. Phys. and Surg. N. Y. 1826.
Edward M. Clarke, (C. L.)
Lewis Cruger, (C. L.)
*Edmund B. Elmendorf, (C L.) *1846
*John T. Ferguson, A. M., M. D. elsewhere.
*John Brain Foulke, A. M. and Yale 1827.
*Adolphus N. Gouverneur, (C. L.)
*Edmund Dorr Griffin, (Rev.), A. M. *1830
*William Frederick Havemeyer, (M.), Mayor N.Y. C. aet. 71. *1871
*William D. Henderson, (C. L.), A. M.
*Henry Augustus Heyer, (M.)
*John A. Hicks, (Rev.), A. M. 1830, S. T. D. Univ. Vt. 1847. *1869
*James Hosack.
Mancius Smedes Hutton, (Rev.), S. T. D. 1841, Trustee 1855–.
*William L. Keese, (Rev.), A. M.
*Jonathan Lawrence, (C.L.) *1833
*William A. Lawrence, (M.)
*Adam David Logan, (C. L.) aet. 66. *1869
*George B. Ogden, (B.)
John D. Ogden, M. D. elsewhere.
*Smith Pyne, (Rev.), S. T. D. elsewhere. aet. 73. *1875
*Andrew K. Robertson.
*Noel Robertson, (Rev.), A. M.
*Grenville A. Sackett, (C. L.)
*Charles J. Smith, (C. L.) aet. 73. *1876
James H. Titus, (M.), A. M., Memb. N. Y. Assemb.

29

## 1824.

Benjamin Aycrigg, (Eng.), A.M. 1839, Chief Engineer Penn.
*Robert Barker.
*Alexander M. Burrill, (C.L.) aet. 62. *1869
*Edward C. Crary, (M.)
*William A. Curtis, (Rev.), A. M. 1838. *1864
*Benjamin Drake, A. M., M. D. Coll. Phys. and Surg. N.Y. 1828, Prest. N.Y. Co. Med. Soc. aet. 66. *1871
William Duer, (C. L.), Repr. in Congr. 1849–51, U. S. Consul at Valparaiso.
*William H. Ellet, M.D. elsewhere, Lect. on Element. Chem. 1830–32, Prof. Element. Chem. 1832–33, Prof. Chem. Mineral. and Geol. S. C. Coll. 1835–48. *1859
*James T. Gibert, A. M., M. D. elsewhere. *1868

*Jacob Townsend Gilford, M. D. Coll. Phys. and Surg. Geneva. aet. 64. *1869
*Timothy R. Green, (C. L.), A. M. 1834. *1840
*John K. Hardenbrook, A.M., M. D. elsewhere.
*Dayton Hobart, (C. L.), A. M. *1870
*William Henry Hobart, A. M, M. D. Coll. Phys. and Surg. N. Y. 1829, Trustee 1848–55. *1857
Pierre Paris Irving, (Rev.)
*George W. Johnson, (F.) *1856
*William Henry Lupp, (C. L.), A. M. *1874
*Elias Joseph Marsh, A. M., M. D. Coll. Phys. and Surg. N. Y. 1828, Prest. N. J. Med. Soc. aet. 45. *1850
Hamilton Morton, A. M. 1834, M. D. Rutg. Med. Coll. N. Y.
*Waddington Ogden, (M.)
*Henry Perkins, A. M., M. D. elsewhere.
*Alexander Robertson, A. M., M. D. elsewhere.
Daniel C. Schermerhorn.
John McKeon, (C. L.), A. M. 1831, N. Y. Assemb. 1831, Repr. in Congr. 1835–37, 1841–43, Dist. Atty. N. Y. C. 1845–51, U. S. Dist. Atty. N. Y. 1853.
*Isaac T. Minard, (C. L.), Surrogate Otsego Co. N. Y.
Edward E. Mitchell, (M.)
*Walter Nichols. aet. 21. *1825
*William Peshine.
William Phyfe.
*Anthony Lispenard Robertson, (C. L.), Asst. Vice-Chancellor N. Y. S. 1846–48, Surrogate N. Y. C. 1848, Justice Superior Ct. N. Y. 1860–65 and Ch.-Just. of same 1865–68, Memb. Constit. Conven. N. Y. 1867. aet. 60. *1868
*Ferdinand Sands, (M.)
John J. Schermerhorn, (M.)
John Fletcher Smith.
*Wessell S. Smith, (C. L.), N. Y. Assemb. *1860
*Oliver S. Strong, (M.) aet. 68. *1874
*Peter Wilson, (C. L.)
*William Wilson, M. D. Coll. Phys. and Surg. N. Y. 1829. aet. 66. *1872

23 21

## 1825.

*George P. Cammann, M. D. elsewhere aet. 59. *1863
*James A. M. Gardner, A. M., M. D. Coll. Phys. and Surg. N. Y. 1829.
*Nathaniel Marius Graves, (M.)
Robert William Harris, (Rev.), A. M., S. T. D. 1849.
*Jacob Harsen, Jr., A. M. 1829, M. D. Coll. Phys. and Surg. N. Y. 1829, Prest. North. Dispens. N. Y. aet. 55. *1863
*William E. Laight. *1859
Alexander S. Leonard, (Rev.), A. M. 1847, S. T. D. 1859.

## 1826.

Charles E. Anderson, (Br.), Secy. U. S. Legation Paris 1836–39 and Chargé d'Aff. 1837.
*William A. Clarke, M. D. elsewhere.
John Marshall Guion, (Rev.), S. T. D. 1865.
John W. Hamersley, (C. L.), A. M.
Nathaniel Pendleton Hosack, and Harv. 1826, (M.)
*Gabriel F. Irving.
*Robert Kelly, Jr., Regent Univ. N. Y. S. 1856–57.

Francis M. Kip, (Rev.), S. T. D. 1857.
*John Neil McLeod, (Rev.), A. M. 1833, S. T. D. elsewhere. aet. 68. *1874
*Joshua S. Marsh.
*Thomas H. Merry, Jr.
*William Henry Milnor, M.D. Coll. Phys. and Surg. N. Y. 1832. aet. 60. *1862
*Thomas R. Minturn, (M.) *1871
*Henry Morris, (C. L.) aet. 54. *1854
Richard Lewis Morris, M. D. Coll. Phys. and Surg. N. Y. 1830, Health Commr. N. Y. C. 1848–52 and Health Off. 1852–54.
*John B. Norsworthy.
Hewlett R. Peters, (Rev.), S. T. D. elsewhere.
*Daniel Phœnix Riker, (C. L.) aet. 61. *1868
*Beverley Robinson, Jr., (C. L.) aet. 69. *1876
William H. Roosevelt.
*Daniel Seymour.
Abraham A. Slover, Jr.
Thomas Swords, Jr., 1831, Brig.-Gen. U. S. A.
*Gerrit Hubert Van Wagenen, Jr.
*Harris Wilson, (C. L.) *1874
25

## 1827.

Jonathan Trumbull Backus, (Rev.), A.M., S.T.D. Union 1847.
Jacob Sperry Baker, (M.)
William Sperry Baker, M. D. Coll. Phys. and Surg. N. Y. 1831.
Thomas Hazard Barker, (B.), U. S. Consul at Antwerp 1836.
*Henry Neilson Brush. *1873
John P. Crosby, (C. L.), Trust. Med. Dept. 1860–.
William Henry Crosby, (C.L.), Prof. Greek and Latin Lang. Rutg. Coll. 1841–9, Acting Prof. Lat. Lang. and Lit. 1859–60.
Henry Augustus Du Bois, M. D. Coll. Phys. and Surg. N. Y. 1830, LL. D. Yale 1864, Memb. Conn. Acad. Arts and Sciences, Memb. Geolog. Soc. France.
Edward Dunscomb, (M.)
*Edward Bristed Eastburn. *1830
Hamilton Fish, (C. L.), A. M., LL. D. 1850 and Harv. Univ. 1871, Trustee 1840– and Chn. Board 1859–, Repr. in Congr. 1843–5, Lt.-Gov. N. Y. 1847–9, Gov. N. Y. 1849–51, U. S. Sen. 1851–7, Secy. State U. S. 1869–, Memb. Joint High Commn. to arrange "Treaty of Washington" with Great Britain 1871.
*Michael Floy, Jr., A. M. *1837
John Murray Forbes, (Rev.), A. M., S. T. D. 1847, Tutor Trin. Coll. 1830, Dean Gen. Theol. Sem. P. E. Ch. 1869.
*John Henry Hobart Haws, (C. L.), Repr. in Congr. 1851–3. *1858
*William C. Heyward, 1830, (F.) *1863
John Clarkson Jay, M. D. Coll. Phys. and Surg. N. Y. 1831, Trustee 1859–.
Joshua Jones, (C. L.)
*Abraham Beakley Labagh, (F.)
*Alfred Ludlow. *1831
*Charles McFarlan, N. J. Sen. 1846. *1873
Henry J. Morton, (Rev.), A. M., S. T. D. Univ. Penn. 1844, Trustee Univ. Penn.
*Jonathan Nathan, (C. L.),

Master in Chanc. N. Y. 1840–5. *1683
Henry Onderdonk, Jr., (T.), A. M. 1833.
Laughton Osborn, (Au.)
*Samuel Penny, Jr., (Rev.) *1853
*Minturn Post, M. D. Univ. Penn. 1832. aet. 61. *1869
*James M. Quin, 1830, M. D. Rutg. Med. Coll. N. Y., A. M. 1833. aet. 62. *1868
Charles Rhind, Jr., (M.)
*Henry Rogers, Jr., (C. L.) *1840
*Edwin Sands. *1828
*Robert Mott, (C. L.) *1833
John Schermerhorn, (Br.)
*Theodore A. Swords, (C.L.) aet. 33. *1841
Joseph C. Wallace, (F.)
William Winter, (C. L.)
*Grenville Temple Winthrop, and Harv. 1827 and Bowd. 1827, (C. L.), A. M., Memb. Mass. Leg. 1840. *1852
36

## 1828.

*William Bayley, (Art.) *1857
*Edmund D. Barry, Jr.
*Jonas Butler, (C. L.) *1858
*George Catlin, (C. L.), Dist. Atty. Richmond Co. N. Y.
Thomas W. Chrystie, (Rev.)
Thomas T. Devan, (Rev.), A. M., M. D. Coll. Phys. and Surg. N. Y. 1831, Missionary in China 1848, Chaplain U. S. A. 1862.
Cornelius Dubois, Jr., (M.)
Edmund Embury, (Rev.), A. M. 1833.
George Gilford.
Robert Goelet.
*Alexander N. Gunn, A. M. Rutg. 1832, M. D. Coll. Phys. and Surg. N. Y. 1833. aet. 61. *1871
Benjamin I. Haight, (Rev.), A. M., S. T. D. 1846, LL.D. Hobart 1870, Trustee 1843 –, Prof. Past. Theol. and Pulp. Eloq. Gen. Theol. Sem. P. E. Ch., Asst. Minister Trinity Parish N. Y. C. 1847–, elected Bishop P. E. Ch. Mass. 1872 and declined.
Henry S. Hoyt.
*Mortimer Livingston, (M.) *1857
*Austin L. S. Main, M. D. Coll. Phys. and Surg. N.Y. 1832. aet. 58. *1867
*John A. Morrill, (C. L.)
George B. Neill.
*John M. Ogden *1836
Joel B. Post, (M.)
*Barzillai Slosson, (C.L.), Dist. Atty Ontario Co. N. Y. *1874
Samuel Sidney St. John, (T.), A. M. 1834.
Lewis Thibou, (Rev.)
John Ledyard Vandervoort, A.M., M.D. Coll. Phys. and Surg. N. Y. 1832.
Robert Boyd Van Kleeck, (Rev.), A. M. and Trin., S. T. D. Trin. 1847, Instr. 1830–1.
*William Wheeler Van Wagenen, (C. L.), A. M. 1834.
Alexander Robertson Walsh, (M.)
*William Walton, (Rev.), A. M. 1836, S. T. D. 1852, Inst. in Hebrew Gen. Theol. Sem. P. E. Ch., and Prof. Hebrew and Greek Lang. 1869. aet. 59. *1869
*Richard Whiley, Jr., (C.L.)
Martin Ryerson Zabriskie,† (C. L.), Trustee 1856–69, 1871–2.
29

## 1829.

*George Featherstone Allen, (Eng.), Trustee 1854–63. *1863

†Known, since 1864, as Martin Zborowski.

*Theodore A. Bailey, (M.)
Thomas E. Blanch, (C. L.), Dist. Atty. Rockland Co. N. Y.
*James Augustus Carter, M. D. Coll. Phys. and Surg. N. Y. 1832.
Alfred W. Craven, (Eng.), Ch. Eng. Croton. Aq. Dept. N. Y. C.
*Robert James Dillon, (C.L.), Counsel to Corp. N. Y. C. 1853–6. aet. 63. *1872
*Benjamin S. Downing, M.D. Coll. Phys. and Surg. N.Y. 1832. aet. 24. *1834
William Edgar.
*James Heyward, M. D. elsewhere.
John T. Irving, Jr., (C. L.)
*Richard H. Ogden, (C. L.)
Samuel Ogden, (C. L.)
Thomas W. Ogden, (Br.)
*John D. Ogilby, A.M. 1833, Mast. Col. Coll. Gram. Sch. 1829–30, Prof. Lang. Rutg. Coll. 1832–40, Prof. Eccles. Hist. Gen. Theol. Sem. P. E. Ch. 1841–51. *1851
*Peter Augustus Schermerhorn, A. M. 1833. *1845
*Theodore Sedgwick, Jr., (C. L.), U. S. Dist. Atty. N.Y., Trustee Coll. Phys. and Surg. N. Y. 1842–59. *1859
Charles R. Swords, (M.), N.Y. Assemb., Trustee 1870–.
*Robert Tucker, M. D. Coll. Phys. and Surg. N. Y. 1832. *1846
John D. Van Buren, (C. L.), N. Y. Assemb.
*Fanning S. Worth, (T.), A. M. 1835.

20

## 1830.

*John B. Boggs.
James Bowdoin, (C. L.)
Robert L. Cutting, (Br.)
John Delafield, Jr., (C. L), A. M. 1837.
Hugh T. Dickie, (C. L.), Judge Sup. Ct. Ill.
*Benjamin T. Ferguson, (C. L.) *1836
Lewis C. Gunn, (Ed.)
*Nicholas C. Heyward. *1852
*George Ireland, Jr., (C. L.) aet. 61. *1873
*Edward Jones, M. D. Coll. Phys. and Surg. 1834, Trustee 1849–69. aet. 58. *1869
*John Taylor Kneeland, M.D. Coll. Phys. and Surg. N.Y. 1833. *1838
Henry Ledyard, (C.L.), Secy. U. S. Legation at Paris 1839–42, and Chargé d'Aff. 1842–44, Mayor Detroit, Mich. 1855, Mich. Sen. 1857.
*Benjamin Franklin Miller, (C. L.) *1837
Henry C. Murphy, (C. L.), Mayor Brooklyn, N. Y., Repr. in Congr. 1843–45, Memb. N. Y. Constit. Conven. 1846, 1867, U. S. Min. at the Hague, N. Y. Sen.
Henry Nicoll, (C. L.), LL.D. 1870, Repr. in Congr., Memb. N. Y. Constit. Conven. 1846.
*Charles H Ogden, (M.) aet. 62. *1874
William Steele, (M.), M. D. Coll. Phys. and Surg. N.Y. 1833.
William D. Waddington, (C. L.)
*George William Wright, (C. L.) *1873

19

## 1831.

James Bolton, A. M. 1835, M. D. Coll. Phys. and Surg. N. Y. 1836.

*Peter Schermerhorn Chauncey, (Rev.), A.M. 1836, S. T. D. Trin. Coll. 1848, Trustee Trin. Coll. *1866
*James Chrystie, Jr.
Abraham B. Conger, A. M., Tutor 1831–3, N. Y. Sen., Prest. N. Y. S. Agricult. Soc., Memb. N. Y. S. Constit. Conv. 1867.
William E. Eigenbrodt, (Rev.), A. M. 1835, S. T. D. 1855, Prof. Past. Theol. Gen. Theol. Sem. P. E. Ch.
*Robert Emory, (Rev.), A.M., S. T. D. 1846, Prof. Anc. Lang. Dickin. Coll. 1834–9, and Prest. Dickin. 1842–8. *1848
*Petrus Stuyvesant Fish, A. M. *1834
*John B. Gallagher, (Rev.) *1849
*John P. Hone.
Bradish Johnson, (M.)
Charles R. King, M.D. Univ. Penn. 1834.
*James Joseph Macneven. *1832
James McCready Morgan.
Gideon S. Nichols, (F.)
John L. O'Sullivan, A. M., Tutor 1821–3, U. S. Min. Portugal, Regent Univ. N. Y. S. 1846–55.
John Punnett, A. M., M. D. elsewhere.
*John B. Purroy, (C. L.), A. M., Consul for Venezuela N. Y. *1859
*Richard W. Redfield, A. M. 1838. *1846
Edwin M. Taylor, (Eng.), State Eng. Virginia
Francis Tomes, Jr., (Br.)
Robert G. Vermilye, (Rev.), A. M. 1836, S. T. D. 1851, Tutor 1835–7, Ad. Prof. Greek and Lat. Lang. 1837–43, Prof. Christ. Theol. in Theol. Inst. Conn.
*Lloyd Saxbury Waddell. *1832
Samuel Ward, Jr., (Br.), A. M. 1835.
*Robert Watts, Jr., A. M., M. D. Coll. Phys. and Surg. N.Y. 1835, Prof. Anat. and Physiol. Coll. Phys. and Surg. 1843–48, Prof. Anat. 1848–67. *1867

/24

## 1832.

Henry T. Anthony, (M.)
Walter T. Avery, (M.)
Horatio Bogert, (C. L.), A. M. 1836.
William L. Boyd, (M.), A.M.
George Carvill, Jr., (M.)
*John Chrystie, (M.) *1856
*Henry S. Dodge, (C. L.), A. M. *1855
*Daniel G. F. Fanshaw. *1833
James Heard, Jr., (M.), A.M. 1836.
*Alexander C. Hillman, (Rev.) *1875
*Nicholas W. Hoffman, (M.) *1843
Aaron Jarvis, A. M., M. D. Coll. Phys. and Surg. N.Y. 1835. aet. 45. *1859
*William Templeton Johnson, (C. L.), A. M. *1869
Philip Livingston Jones, M. D. Coll. Phys. and Surg. N. Y. 1835.
*John J. C. Kane, (C. L.) *1854
Frederick W. Miller, (Rev.)
Stephen Reed, Jr., (C. L.), A. M.
*Thomas A. Richmond, (C. L.), A. M. *1859
William Channing Russel, C.) L.), A., M.LL.D. 1875, Prof. Antioch Coll. Ohio, Prof. Cornell Univ. N. Y. 1867–, Vice-Prest. Cornell and Univ.
Henry J. Ruggles, (C. L.)
Erasmus P. Smith, (C. L.)
John E. Stillwell, M. D. Coll. Phys. and Surg. N. Y. 1836.

Frederick L. Talcott, (M.) *1872
*Philip W. Thomas, (C. L.)
*Jonathan Thompson, Jr., (M.), A. M. 1836. aet. 59. *1872
Frederick Townsend, (C. L.)
*Russell N. Townsend, (C. L.) *1837
William S. Verplanck.

28

## 1833.

*Stephen D. Allen, M. D. elsewhere. *1840
*James Barrow, Jr., (C. L.) *1868
*John S. Bartlett, Jr., (Ed.)
*Jackson Bolton, M. D. elsewhere.
James Constable, (C. L.)
*Richard Cox, (Rev.), A. M.
John F. Delaplaine, Jr., (C. L.), Attaché at Madrid 1852, and at Vienna, Secy. U. S. Legation Vienna 1869–.
*Pierre Cortlandt DePeyster, (M.) *1854
*John M. Gelston.
Charles Hall, (M.), A. M. 1838.
John Jay Jenkins, (C. L.)
*Philip Kearny, Jr., Major U. S. A. 1847, Brig.-Gen. U. S. V. 1861, and Maj.-Gen. 1862. aet. 47. *1862
*Francis P. Lee, (Rev.), A. M. *1847
*Samuel Bard McVickar. *1837
*James W. Metcalf, M. D. elsewhere. *1856
Gouverneur Morris Ogden, (C. L.), Trustee 1849–, and Treasurer 1858–.
Henry B. Renwick, (Eng.), Examr. U. S. Pat. Off.
William Rhinelander Renwick, (M.)
*Bruce Schermerhorn. *1862
*Edward Slosson, (C. L.) *1871
*John G. Smedberg, (F.) aet. 57 *1873
*Robert Spencer, (C. L.)
Abraham Gardiner Thompson, Jr., A. M., M. D. Coll. Phys. and Surg. N.Y. 1837, N. Y. Assemb. 1845 and 1857.
James A. Williams, (Rev.), A. M., S. T. D. 1863.

24

## 1834.

William M. Allen, (C. L.), A. M.
James William Beekman, (C. L.), A. M. 1838, N. Y. Assemb. 1848, N. Y. Senate 1849–51, Trustee Med. Dept. 1860–, Trustee 1875–.
Edward Bryar, (F.), A. M. 1838.
William Bryan Casey, M. D. elsewhere.
James Michael Cockcroft, (M.)
William Cockcroft, M. D. Coll. Phys. and Surg. N. Y. 1838.
*John Conger, A. M., M. D. Coll. Phys. and Surg. N. Y. 1838.
*Isaac C. Delaplaine, (C. L.), A. M., Repr. in Congr. aet 48. *1866
*William Demarest, (Rev.), A. M. *1874
William Dennis, (Rev.)
*William Dodge, (C. L.), A. M., N. Y. Assemb. *1858
*William Mitchell Gillespie, (Eng.), A. M., LL. D. 1859, and Univ. Nashville 1857, Prof. Civ. Eng. Union Coll. 1845–68. aet. 52. *1868
John S. Heard, A. M., M. D. Coll. Phys. and Surg. N. Y. 1837.
Henry Heyward, A. M. 1838.

Benjamin S. Huntington, (Rev.), A. M. 1839.
William Henry Hyde, (M.)
*Samuel Evan Johnson, (C.L.), A. M., Judge Kings Co. N. Y.
William Gracie King.
Alexander Major, (M.)
Richard E. Mount, Jr., (C. L.), A. M.
*Philip Rhinelander.
Robert S. Swords, (C. L.), Lt.-Col. N. J. Vols.
Anthony Ten Broeck, (Rev.), A. M., S. T. D. 1867, Rector Burlington Coll.
Lloyd Windsor, (Rev.), A. M.
24

## 1835.

*Jedediah Blakeney Auld, (C. L.), A. M. aet. 51. *1866
Romaine Dillon, (C. L.), Secy. U. S. Legation Brazil.
Evert A. Duyckinck, (Au.), A. M., Trustee 1874–.
Benigno Gener, (C. L.)
Thomas Buchanan Gilford, (C. L.)
Andrew Stelle Hamersley, (C. L.), A. M. 1839.
Orlando Harriman, Jr., (Rev.), A. M.
William Heard, (M.)
*Joshua E. Jones. *1839
*Charles C. Lee.
John W. C. Leveridge, (C. L.), A. M. 1839.
Charles Harrison Lyon, (M.), A. M.
*Joseph McIntyre.
Charles D. Mead, (C. L.), A. M. 1839.
William Mulligan, A. M.
*Alexander Palachè, (M.)
George Quartus Pomeroy, (C. L.)
John H. Riker, (C. L.)
William H. Taggard, (C. L.)
Ludlow Thomas, (Br.)
*John Richard Thurman, Repr. in Congr. 1849–51. *1854
*Russell Trevett, (Rev.), A. M., S. T. D. 1855, and Coll. St. James 1857, Prof. Anc. Lang. St. James, Md. and St. Anne's, Md. *1865
William H. Wilson, (T.), A. M.
Christian Zabriskie, Jr., (M) 24

## 1836.

*Newbold Edgar.
Christodoulos L. M. Evangeles, (T.)
*George William Fash, (Rev.), A. M. 1840
John Graham, (C. L.)
*Giles Mumford Hillyer, (C. L.) A. M. *1871
John Henry Hobart, (Rev.), S. T. D. 1856.
Edward Hoffman, (C. L.)
John Jay, (C.L.), A. M., U. S. Min. Plen. to Austria 1869–75.
William Alfred Jones, (Au)., A. M., Librarian 1851–65.
*Edward Huger Laight, (M.) *1853
James Phillips Lake.
George Harrison Lynch, (C. L.)
*Henry McVickar, (Rev.)
Daniel McLaren Quackinbush, (Rev.)
James Renwick, Jr., (Arch.), A. M.
Charles Maison Seymour, (Rev.), A. M.
William Thompson.
*Henry Ward, Jr., A. M.
*George Gilfert Waters, (C. L.), A. M. aet. 56. *1875
*Harvey Augustus Weed, (C. L.), A. M. *1872

*James Willis Wilson, (C.L.), A. M. aet. 53. *1868

21

## 1837.

*Charles Aldis, (Rev.), A. M. *1857
Samuel Blatchford, (C. L.), L.L. D. 1867, Judge U. S. Circ. Ct. N. Y. 1867–, Trustee 1867–.
Nathaniel W. Chittenden, (C. L.), A. M.
John William Clark, (Rev.)
Samuel Cockcroft.
*J. Wallace Collet, A. M. 1841.
*Stephen Douglass, (Rev.), A. M. *1857
*Henry P. Fessenden, (C. L.) *1867
Anthony Halsey, (B.), A. M., Trustee 1872–, and Clerk of Board 1874–.
*Benjamin Holmes Jarvis, (C. L.)
William Henry Leggett, (T.)
John McMullen, Jr., (T.), A. M.
*Charles D. March.
*William J. Masterton, (M.)
*George L. Nevius, (M.) aet. 55. *1873
*Charles Edward Shea, (C. L.), A. M.
Jesse Ames Spencer, (Rev.), A. M. and Trin. 1854, S. T. D. 1852, Prof. Lat. and Orient Lang. Burlington Coll. 1850–51, Prof. Greek Lang. and Lit. Coll. City of N. Y. 1869–.
*David Provost Thomas, (C. L.)
John Ireland Tucker, (Rev.), S. T. D. 1858.
*George Stayley Van Cleef, (Rev.)
John Vanderbilt, Jr., (C. L.), N. Y. Sen., Judge Kings Co. N. Y.
*Samuel H. Whitlock, (C. L.) *1856
*Alexander Somerville Wotherspoon, M. D. Coll. Phys. and Surg. N. Y. 1841, Asst. Surg. U. S. A. 1843–54. *1854

23

## 1838.

*Frederic Anthon, (C. L.) *1868
Edward Anthony, (M.)
Mancer M. Backus, (M.), A. M. Geneva 1841.
*Thomas Colden Cooper, Capt. U. S. V. *1864
Richard H. Douglass.
*Isaac V. Fowler, (C. L.), A. M. 1842, U. S. Postm. N. Y. C. aet. 52. *1869
John Hone, (C. L.)
*Philip Hone, Jr. *1870
Benjamin T. Kissam, (C. L.), A. M. 1851.
John Mason Knox, (C. L.), A. M.
*Jeremiah Larocque, (C. L.) aet. 46. *1868
Alfred Mersan Loutrel, (Rev.)
*William Brinckerhoff Moffat, A.M., M.D. Coll. Phys. and Surg. N. Y. 1842.
*Benjamin Romaine, Jr., (C. L.) *1841
*William Edward Snowden, (Rev.)
*Charles Spear, (Br.) *1871
*George Templeton Strong, (C. L.), Trustee 1853–75, Treas. U. S. San. Comm. *1875
William R. Travers, (Br.)
*Henry Hall Ward, (B.), A. M. aet. 52. *1872
*Francis Marion Ward, A.M. *1847

20

## 1839.

Charles Edward Anthon, A. M. 1853, LL.D. Univ. City

N. Y. 1866, Prof. Hist. and Belle Lettr. N. Y. Free Acad. 1852, Prof. Coll. City of N. Y.
George Christian Anthon, (T.), Prof. Greek Univ. N. Y. C.
John Jacob Astor, Jr., Trustee 1859–69, Col. U. S. Vols. 1861–2 and Bvt. Brig.-Gen. 1866.
Allen H. Brown, (Rev.)
*James C. Roosevelt Brown. *1864
John Ebenezer Burrill, Jr., (C. L.), A.M., 1843, Memb. N.Y.S. Constit. Conv. 1867.
Frederick Augustus Cairns, (Chem.), A. M. 1873.
*Arthur Carey, (Rev.), A.M. *1864
John Carey, Jr., (Eng.), A.M.
*George James Cornell, (C.L.), A.M., Memb. N.Y. Assemb.
Henry Drisler, Jr., A. M., LL.D. 1864, Tutor 1843–45, Adj. Prof. Greek and Lat. Lang. 1845–57, Prof. Lat. Lang. and Lit. 1857–67, Acting President 1867, Jay-Prof. Greek Lang. and Lit. 1867–.
Richard Stockton Emmet, (C. L.)
James Walker Fowler, (C.L.), A. M.
Harvey D. Ganse, (Rev.), A. M. 1844, S.T.D. elsewhere.
Nathaniel Blossom Hoxie, (C. L.), A. M.
Frederick Hughson, (C. L.)
Charles Ingersoll, (C.L.), LL. B. Harv. 1841.
Daniel DeForest Lord, (C.L.), Trustee Med. Dep. 1860–.
Joseph Rich Mann, (Rev.), A. M. 1844, S.T.D. N. Jers. 1862.
Edwin Augustus Nicholls, (Rev.)
*John Pirnie, Jr., (C. L.), A. M.
*Peter B. Pirnie, A. M.
George Warner Quackenbos, (T.), A. M.
Edward Sabine Renwick, (M.), A. M.
James William Walsh, (M.)

25

# 1840.

Charles Bancroft, (Rev.), A. M., S. T. D. 1861.
Samuel Bowden, (Rev.), A. M.
Gerard Smith Boyse.
Charles Bülow Bucknor, (C. L.), A. M.
*Anthony Post Campbell.
*James Farley Clark, (C.L.), A. M.
*Edward Nicoll Crosby. *1865
William Forrest, Jr., (Rev.), A. M.
James George Graham, (C. L.), A. M., N. Y. Assemb.
Ogden Hoffman, Jr., (C. L.), LL. B. Harv. 1842, Judge U. S. Dist. Ct. California.
*Lydig Monson Hoyt. aet. 48. *1868
*Alfred George Jones, (C. L.), A. M., LL. B. Harv. 1842. aet. 47. *1868
Robert Lenox Kennedy, A. M.
Edward Henry Lawrance, (F.)
Benjamin Chase Leveridge, (C. L.), A. M. 1844.
Levi Arnold Lockwood, (C. L.), A. M.
Dwight Edwards Lyman, (Rev.)
John Mitchell Mason, (C.L.), A. M.
Thomas C. Meyer, (Eng.)

Alonzo Castle Monson, (C.L.), A.M., Judge Sup. Ct. California.
Obadiah Newcomb, Jr.
William Nicoll.
George W. Pell, A. M. 1852.
Jotham Post, M. D. Coll. Phys. and Surg. N.Y. 1845.
Ellis Potter, Jr., (C. L.)
Worthington Romaine, (C. L.), A. M.
William Colford Schermerhorn, (C.L.), A.M., Trustee 1860–.
*Peter Shapter, Jr., A. M.
Peter Remsen Strong, (C.L.), A. M.
Owen Sweeny, A. M., M. D. Coll. Phys. and Surg. N.Y. 1845.
Van Brunt Wyckoff, A. M. 1844, M.D. Coll. Phys. and Surg. N. Y. 1845.
Joseph Webb Winans, (C.L.), A. M. 32

## 1841.

*Daniel Henry Beadel.
*Edward Lewis Chichester, M. D. elsewhere.
John Hicks Clark.
George Washington Collord, (T.), A. M.
*Frederick Cunningham, (C. L.)
*Richard Varick De Peyster, (B.) aet. 54. *1874
Thomas Bloodgood Dibblee, (C. L.), A. M.
Cornelius Roosevelt Duffie, (Rev.), A.M., S.T.D. Univ. N. Y. C. 1865, Chaplain 1857–.
William Ward Duffield, (Eng.)
James Emott, Jr., (C. L.), Just. Supr. Ct. N. Y.
*Herman Ten Eyck Foster, (F.) aet. 47. *1869
Oliver Wolcott Gibbs, A.M., M.D. Coll. Phys. and Surg. N. Y. 1845, L.L D. 1873, Prof. Chem. and Phys. Free Acad. N. Y. 1848–63, Prof. Chem. Harv. 1863–, Memb. U. S. San. Com., Memb. Nat. Acad. Science.
Thomas Strong Griffing, Lieut. U. S. V. 1846–8.
Jacob Boerum Jewett, (C.L.)
*William Kemble, Jr., A.M. *1845
*James Hall Mason Knox, (Rev.), A. M., S. T. D. 1861.
Joseph Effingham Lawrence, (Ed.)
*Robert Le Roy, Jr., (Br.), Capt. U. S. V. aet. 41. *1865
John Hodgson Mortimer, (M.)
*Israel Moses, A. M., M. D. Coll. Phys. and Surg. N. Y. 1845. *1871
Edward Delavan Nelson, (M.), A. M.
John Harris Parish, (C. L.), LL. B. Harv. 1844.
William Lewis Peck, (Rev.), A. M. 1857.
John Rankin, Jr., (C. L.)
Jones Rogers.
George Metcalfe Root, (Eng.), A. M.
Robert G. Simpson, (C. L.)
Augustus Lyons Smith, (F.)
William Lyons Smith, (F.)
John Joseph Townsend, (C. L.), A. M.
*Robert Dorlon Van Voorhis. 31

## 1842.

Hector Craig Ames, Attaché U. S. Leg. Madrid.
*William Gould Banks, (C. L.), A. M.

*Abraham Smith Brouwer, (C. L.)
Benjamin Franklin Clark, (F.)
William Henry Ebbets, (C. L.)
Frederick Frye, (C. L.), A. M.
William Henry Harison, Jr., (Rev.), A. M.
Abram Stevens Hewitt, (M.), A. M., Secy. and Direct. Cooper Union, N. Y. C., U. S. Commr. to Univ. Exposition, Paris, 1867, Repr. in Congr. 1875–.
Julius Sleight Hitchcock, (M.)
Robert Jaffray, Jr., (M.)
William Seymour Kernochan, (C. L.), LL. B. Harv. 1844.
*Richard Montgomery Lawrence, Jr., (M.)
Livingston Kip Miller, (C. L.), A. M. 1846.
Clement Moore, (C. L.), A. M.
*George Lucas Newton, (C. L.), A. M.
Robert Morrison Olyphant, (M.)
Wheelock Hendee Parmly, (Rev.), A. M.
William J. Paulding.
James Hunter Phinney.
Edward Elmer Potter, Brig.-Gen. U. S. Vols.
*Zebedee Ring, Jr., (C. L.)
Oliver Everett Roberts, (M.), A. M.
Washington Rodman, (Rev.)
*Silas Weir Roosevelt, (C. L.) aet. 47. *1870
David Reid Stanford, (M.)
John Baker Stevens, (C. L.)
*William Pinckney Stewart, (C. L.), A. M. 1848. *1870
*John Sym. *1845
Elisha William Teakle.
David Thomson, Jr., (M.), A. M.

30

## 1843.

*Benjamin Nibbs Aymar, (M.)
Samuel P. Bell, (C. L.)
*Thomas C. T. Buckley, (C. L.), A. M. *1873
*William Edgar Bunker, (M.) aet. 52 *1874
*John White Dana, M. D. Coll. Phys. and Surg. N. Y. 1846.
*William Cecil Duncan, (Rev.), A. M., S. T.D. 1857. *1864
Benjamin H. Franklin, (M.)
*Albert Gallatin, Jr., (C. L.), A. M. aet. 35 *1859
James Watson Gerard, Jr., (C. L.), A. M., N. Y. Sen.
*William Beach Lawrence, Jr., (C. L.), A. M. 1845. *1870
Edward Zechariah Lewis, (Rev.)
William McCune, (F.)
Henry Post McGowan, (C.L.)
*Robert K. Moffet.
William R. Morgan, (B.)
John Christian Philip, M. D. Coll. Phys. and Surg. N. Y. 1847.
George Payn Quackenbos, (T.), A. M., LL. D. Wesl. Univ. Conn. 1868.
Charles Reynolds, (Rev.), A. M., S. T. D. elsewhere.
John Henry Ross, M. D. Coll. Phys. and Surg. N. Y. 1847.
Matson Meier Smith, (Rev.), A. M., S. T. D. 1863.
John B. Stevens, (C. L.)
*John Thomson, M. D. Coll. Phys. and Surg. N. Y. 1847. aet. 31. *1871
Cornelius Van Vorst, Jr., (C. L.)

23

## 1844.

Clement W. Al Burtis, (F.)
*John Babcock Arden, M. D. Coll. Phys and Surg. N. Y. 1848. *1851

Robert Bayard Campbell, (C. L.)
Jacob Post Giraud Foster, (C. L.)
Samuel Hollingsworth, (Rev.), A. M., S. T. D. 1868.
*Nicholas Bergasse Labau, (C. L.), N. Y. Sen. 1867–69, N. Y. Assemb. 1869–71. aet. 53. *1874
Charles William Lawrence.
Edward McGee, (Rev.)
William Bowne Minturn, M. D. Coll. Phys and Surg. N. Y. 1848.
William Taylor Moore.
*Peter Martin Pirnie.
Edward Henry Swan, (C. L.), LL. B. Harv. 1847.
Otto William Erasmus Van Tuyl, M. D. Coll. Phys. and Surg. N. Y. 1847.
*Charles Whipple Whiley, M. D. Coll. Phys. and Surg. N. Y. 1848. *1874
14

## 1845.

*John Knickerbocker Adams.
James Anderson.
*Francis S. Cottenet. *1848
John Drake, (C. L.), A. M. 1851.
George Barnard Draper, (Rev.), A. M., S. T. D. 1868.
*George T. Elliot, Jr., A. M. 1849, M. D. Univ. N. Y. C. 1861, Prof. Obstet. Diseases Wom. and Childr. Bellev. Med. Coll. N. Y. C. aet. 44. *1871
John James Elmendorf, (Rev.), A. M., S. T. D. 1866, Instr. in Maths. 1848, Prof. Phil. and Belles-Lettres Racine Coll. 1868.
William Alexander Falls, (B.)
George Irving.
George A. Jones, (C. L.)
Samuel Thomas Jones, (C. L.), Just. Sup. Ct. N. Y.
John Wheeler Leavitt, Jr.
Alexander McCue, (C. L.)
Charles Armand Minton.
*Samuel B. Romaine Nichols.
*David B. Ogden, Jr. *1865
Henry Onderdonk, Prof. Chem. St. Timothy's Hall, Md.
*Lefroy Ravenhill, A. M. 1849, M. D. Coll. Phys. and Surg. N. Y. 1849, Librarian 1847–51. aet. 26. *1851
Aaron B. Reid, (M.)
Stephen K. Stanton.
*John A. Taggard. *1865
Frederick Samuel Tallmadge, (C. L.), A. M. 1849.
Pierre Marston Van Wyck.
*Henry P. Wainwright. *1845
24

## 1846.

*R. S. Carden Abbott, A. M. *1854.
*G. Mortimer Belden, (F.), A. M. 1850. *1873.
Beverley Robinson Betts, (Rev.), A. M., Librarian 1865–.
Edward C. Bogert, (M.)
*Henry A. Bogert, (C. L.), A. M.
Arthur Bronson, Jr.
Elias G. Brown, (C. L.), A. M.
William J. Frost, (Rev.), A. M., S. T. D. elsewhere.
William B. Harison, (C. L.)
Charles B. Hoffman, (B.)
*William H. Hudson.
*John G. Hyer, (C. L.) *1868.
*William M. Johnston, (M.)
John Grenville Kane, (C. L.), A. M.
Edwin M. Kellogg, M.D. elsewhere.

John L. Lefferts, (C. L.)
Jeremiah Loder, (C. L.), A. M., LL. B. Yale 1848.
Charles Scott McKnight.
William Augustus McVickar, (Rev.), A. M. 1850, S. T. D. 1870, Lect. on Ev. of Religion.
*Frederick Nash, A. M., M.D. Coll. Phys. and Surg. N. Y. 1850. aet. 34. *1861.
William Whittingham Olssen, (Rev.), A. M. 1850, S. T. D. 1876, Prof. Greek and Heb. Langs St. Stephen's Coll. N. Y. 1871–.
Edward M. Peck, (Rev.), A. M. and Trinity Coll. 1852.
James Thompson, (C. L.), A. M.
Alexander G. Tyng.

24

## 1847.

*Cornelius Duffie Blake, (C. L.), A. M.
John H. Bolton, (M.)
Henry Pearsall Campbell, (M.), A. M.
John Winthrop Chanler, (C. L.), A. M. 1873, N. Y. Assemb. 1858–9, Repr. in Congr.
William Samuel Coffey, (Rev.), A. M.
Wilhelmus Bogart Conger, (M.)
Carroll Dunham, M. D. Coll. Phys. and Surg. N. Y. 1850.
John Whetten Ehninger, (Art.)
Robert Holden, (Rev.), A.M., Prof. Burlington Coll. N. Jers. 1849–51.
*Arthur M. Jones. *1850.
*John Stearns Lane, (M.), A. M.
Isaac Lawrence, (C. L.), A. M.
William Simmons Ludlum, (Rev.), A. M., M. D. 1862.
John James McLaren, (B.)
Clarence Green Mitchell, (C. L.), A. M.
*Timothy G. Mitchell, A. M., Prof. Burl. Coll. N. Jers. 1849–57. *1857.
John Moneypenny, Jr., M. D Coll. Phys. and Surg. N. Y. 1850, Surg. 123d N. Y. S. Vols.
John Wells Moore, (Rev.), A. M. 1860.
John Neilson, (M.)
*Benjamin Augustus Onderdonk.
Frederic W. Rhinelander, (M.)
Joseph Kanick Riggs, (B.)
James Francis Ruggles, (C. L.)
Archibald M. Stone, (Rev.)
Israel Leander Townsend, (Rev.), A. M. and Trin. Coll.
*Robert Travis, Jr., (Rev.), A. M. *1866.
Francis Van Rensselaer, (F.)
Tompkins Westervelt, (C. L.)

28

## 1848.

Theodorus Bailey Bronson, (C. L.), A. M.
Horace W. Carpenter, (C. L.)
Ralph L. Cook, (M.)
Lyman Denison Demaray, (M.)
Richard Mead De Mille, (C. L.), A. M.
Morgan Dix, (Rev.), A. M,. S. T. D. 1862, Rector Trinity Parish N. Y. 1862–, Trustee 1862–.

George Clinton Farrar, (M.), A. M.
Joseph Wesley Harper, Jr., (Pub.), A. M., Trustee 1873–.
P. Leslie Irving, (C. L.)
*Henry Whitlock Johnson, (C. L.) *1863.
Levi M. Kellogg.
Cornelius Low King, Capt. and Bvt.-Maj. and Lt.-Col. U. S. A.
George Morford Klots, (M.)
Edward Leavenworth.
Theodore Frelinghuysen Lewis, (M.), A. M.
John Lockwood, Jr., (T.)
*Lewis Morris, Jr.
Peter Wilson Ostrander, (C. L.), A. M.
William Cruger Pell, (C. L.)
Columbus B. Rogers, (C. L.)
*Thomas P. St. John.
Otis Dwight Swan, (B.), LL. B. Harv. 1850.
Isaac Van Winkle, (C. L.), (A. M.)
Benjamin Clark Wetmore, (C. L.)
*Joseph Moss White, (M.)

25

## 1849.

Cornelius Rea Agnew, M. D. Coll. Phys. and Surg. N. Y. 1852, Memb. U. S. San. Com. 1860–67, Prof. Diseases of the Eye and Ear 1869–, Trustee 1874–.
*William Edmond Armitage, (Rev.), A. M., S. T. D. 1866, Asst. Bishop P. E. Ch. Wis. 1867–70, and Bishop 1870–73. *1873
William Astor.
*Edward Courtlandt Babcock, (Rev.) *1857.
Norman Adams Beach, Tutor Coll. City N. Y.
Charles Hinckley Brown.
Churchill John Cambreleng, (C. L.), Major U. S. V.
*Baldwin Dix, (C. L.)
George Lloyd Freeman, M.D. elsewhere.
Henry DeCosta Hanners.
William Abel Hardenbrook, (T.)
*John Vernon Henry, (M.), A. M. aet. 44. *1874.
William Henry Herriman.
Lewis Ashhurst Kemper, (Rev.), B. D. elsewhere, S. T. D. 1868, Prof. Bibl. Interp. Nashota Theol. Sem. P. E. Ch. Wis.
*William Morrow Knox, A.M. 1855, M. D. Coll. Phys. and Surg. N. Y. 1854, Asst. Surg. U. S. V. *1862
Joseph Larocque, (C. L.)
David Porter Lord, (M.)
Charles A. Magnes, Jr.
*Ebenezer Bowman Miner, M. D. elsewhere. *1869
Daniel Morrelle, (Rev.), (T.), A. M. 1855.
Aaron Ogden, (C. L.), A. M.
Henry Parish, Jr., (M.)
John Prince Pemberton, M. D. 1864.
*George C. Pollen. aet. 39. *1867.
Charles E. Rhinelander.
Saumarez Dobreé Routh, (M.)
John Frederick Schroeder, Jr., (Rev.)
Ezra Kellogg Sherwood.
John Shrady, Jr., A. M. 1858, M. D. 1861, Surg. U. S. V. 1862–64.
John Drake Skidmore, (C. L.), A. M.
*Prosper Montgomery Wetmore, Jr., (M.)
John Jay White, (C. L.)

32

## 1850.

John Martin Gabriel Aims, M. D. elsewhere.

Mathew M. Blunt, Major U. S. A.

George G. Byron, (M.)

Malcolm Campbell, (C. L.)

Galen Augustus Carter, (Br.)

James Starr Clark, (Rev.), A. M., S. T. D. 1872.

Frederic R. Coudert, (C. L.)

John Ferris Delaplaine Cornell, (Rev.)

Archibald Falconer Cushman, (C. L.), LL. B. Harv. 1852.

Edwin Wakeman Edwards, (M.)

Thomas Ludlow Harison, (F.)

John Sebastian Bach Hodges, (Rev.), A. M., S. T. D. Racine Coll. Wis.

Walter R. T. Jones, (M.)

*Adolphe Le Moyne, Jr., (B.) aet. 44. *1874

Frederick L. Purroy.

Erskine M. Rodman, (Rev.), A. M.

Joseph Sands, (Arch.)

George Franklin Seymour, (Rev.), A. M., S. T. D. Racine Coll. Wis., Elec. Bishop Ill. P. E. Ch., Prof. Eccles. Hist. Gen. Theol. Sem. P. E. Ch. N. Y.

Charles Augustus Silliman, (M.), A. M., LL. B. 1860, Trustee 1876–.

John Esten Cooke Smedes, (Rev.), A. M.

William Hazard Terry.

*Edward Forbes Travis, (C. L.) *1867

Evan Thomas Walker, (M.)

23

## 1851.

*John H. Anthon, (C. L.), A. M., N. Y. Assemb., Asst. Dist. Atty. N. Y. C., Prof. Med. Jurisp. N. Y. Coll. Med. aet. 42. *1874

Henry M. Bedford, M. D. elsewhere.

Stewart H. Brown, (B.)

Charles Arms Cook, (Br.), A. M.

*William T. Cornell.

John De Ruyter, Jr., (M.)

James De Koven, (Rev.), S. T. D. elsewhere, Prest. Racine Coll. Wis., Elected Bishop P. E. Ch. Ill.

Legh R. Dickinson, (Rev.), A. M.

William H. Draper, A. M., M. D. Coll. Phys. and Surg. N. Y. 1855, Asst. to Prof. Surgery, Prof. Diseases of the Skin 1869–.

Edward S. Hoffman, M. D. Coll. Phys. and Surg. N. Y. 1855, Surgeon U. S. V.

Henry B. Johnson.

Nicholas F. Ludlum, (Rev.)

John G. McNary, (T.)

George A. Seaman.

William R. Smith.

*A. Henry Thurston, A. M., M. D. elsewhere, Surgeon U. S. V. *1865

Charles H. Ward, (B.), A. M. 1864.

William G. Ward, (B.), Col. U. S. V.

Merritt H. Wellman, (Rev.), A. M.

J. Walter Wood, (Br.), A. M.

David Augustus Wright.

21

# 1852.

*John Bennem, Jr., (Rev.) *1853
*Charles Ludlow Bogert, (Arch.), A. M. *1874
*James Livingston Brown, M. D. Univ. N. Y. C. 1856, A. M. 1868. *1874
Henry W. Clark, (C. L.), A. M.
*John Wakefield Francis, Jr., M. D. elsewhere. *1855
John W. Harper, (Pub.), A. M.
George H. Hinton, A. M.
*John Augustine Hows, (Art.), A. M. *1874
Ansel N. Kellog, (Ed.)
Lea Luquer, (Rev.), A. M.
*Archibald Bleecker McDonald, Jr., (Arch.), A. M. *1866
Samuel L. Mitchill, Jr., (M.), A. M.
James Morris, (C. L.), LL. B. Harv. 1854.
*Charles De Gray Mount, A. M. *1872
Washington R. Nichols, (C. L.)
Charles O'Dowd.
John H. Pell, (C. L.), A. M., U. S. V.
George C. Pennell, (Rev.), A. M.
*Robert Ray, Jr., A. M., M. D. Coll. Phys. and Surg. N. Y. 1856. aet. 28. *1860
James Renwick Smedberg. (Eng.), A. M.
Richard F. Stevens.
Henry A. Tailer, (C. L.), A. M.
Eugene Thorn, Capt. U. S. V.
William E. Thorn, (C. L.)
Eustace Trenor, A. M., M. D. Coll. Phys. and Surg. N. Y. 1856, Surg. N. Y. S. Vols.
*John Trenor, Jr., A.M., M.D. Coll. Phys. and Surg. N. Y. 1856, Surg. U. S. V. 1863–65, Bvt. Lt.-Col. U. S. V. *1867
Richard H. Tucker, (C. L.) 27

# 1853.

*Cornelius Van Alen Anderson, A. M., M. D. Coll. Phys. and Surg. N. Y. 1857. *1862
William Irving Clark, (M.)
George Washington Dean, (Rev.), A. M. 1861, Instr. 1854, Prof. Gr. and Lat. Lang. Racine Coll. Wis.
Joseph Smith Dodge, Jr., A.M., M. D. Coll. Phys and Surg. N. Y. 1856, Instr. 1854, Prof. Dental Coll. N. Y. C.
*Daniel Embury, Jr., (M.), A. M. aet. 34. *1869
*William Emerson, Jr., (C. L.), A. M., LL. B. Harv. 1856. *1864
William George Farrington, (Rev.), A. M.. Secy. Trustees Gen. Theol. Sem. P. E. Ch. 1868–.
Isaac J. Greenwood, Jr., (Chem.), A. M. 1857.
Albert Ward Hale, (Eng.), A. M. 1862, E. M. 1872.
Abraham S. Jackson, (C. L.), A. M.
William Allen Johnson, (Rev.), A. M. 1857.
John A. Kernochan, (M.)
*Delancy W. Knevels, (M.), A. M. aet. 38. *187
*Edward William Laight, Jr., (M.) aet. 33. *1867
Thomas McCarty, (C. L.), A. M.
William J. Osborne, (C. L.)
*St. Clair Smith, (C. L.) *1869
*Washington Irving Tibbitts. *1853
*Archibald Somerville VanDuzer, (C. L.), A. M. aet. 36. *1870
19

## 1854.

*George Washington Bacon, (Rev.), (T.), A. M., LL. B. 1862, M. D. 1865. *1874
Cullen L. Carter, (F.)
Henry M. Congdon, (Arch.)
*Charles B. Cromwell, (C.L.)
*Francis A. De Wint, (C. L.), A. M. 1860. *1866
Elias G. Drake, Jr., (C. L.), A. M.
Leicester K. Ely, (B.)
Carleton Moses Herrick, (C. L.), A. M., LL.B. 1860.
Edward Kirkland, (Br.), U. S. Vol.
George C. Kissam, M.D. Coll. Phys. and Surg. N. Y. 1857.
John V. Lewis, (Rev.), A. M.
Cutler C. McAllister, (C. L.), A. M.
Elias J. Marsh, M. D. Coll. Phys. and Surg. N.Y. 1858, Asst. Surg. U. S. A. 1861–, Med. Direct. U. S. V.
*Henry C. Marvin, (C. L.), A. M. *1865
James S. Merriam, (C. L.)
*Charles Edwards Morgan, M. D. Coll. Phys. and Surg. N. Y. 1857. *1867
*Orlando H. Morris, (C. L.), Col. U. S. Vols. *1864
Henry C. Murphy, Jr., (C. L.), A. M. 1860.
Peter J. Neefus, (F.)
*James Cortlandt Parker, Jr., (C. L.), A. M., Lieut. U. S. Vols. *1862
Charles S. Pomeroy, (Rev.), A. M.
*George V. Pomeroy, Jr., (M.), A. M. *1867
William J. Sayres, (C. L.), A. M. 1862.
Reginald Heber Smith, (C.L.), A. M., LL. B. 1866.
Benjamin Strong, (F.)
Gardiner Thompson, (B.)
John Condit Trippe, (M.)
Marvin R. Vincent, (Rev.), A. M., S. T. D. Union 1868, Prof. Lat. Troy Univ.
Stewart L. Woodford, (C. L.), A. M. 1866 and Yale 1866 and Trin. 1869, LL.D. Trin. 1870, Trustee Cornell Univ. 1870, Asst. Atty. U. S. South. Dist. N. Y. 1861, Col. and Brev. Brig.-Gen. U. S. Vols., Lieut.-Gov. N. Y. 1867–9, Prest. N. Y. Electoral Coll. 1872, Repr. in Congr. 1874.
Jeremiah L. Zabriskie, (C.L.)

29

## 1855.

Gunning S. Bedford, Jr., (C. L.), A. M., LL. B. Harv. 1859, Asst. Dist. Atty. N. Y. C., City Judge N. Y. C. 1869.
Edward Cammann, (C. L.), A. M.
Benjamin L. Curtis, (M.), A. M.
Charles Da Costa, (C. L.), A. M.
William Dean, (C. L.), A. M.
Lewis L. Delafield, (C. L.), A. M.
*Philip A. Embury, (M.), A. M.
Edward O. Harmon, (M.)
James R. Hosmer, (C. L.), Capt. U. S. V.
Walter Knight, M. D. elsewhere.
Charles E. Miller, A. M.
David Burgess Miller, A. M., M. D. Coll. Phys. and Surg. N. Y. 1858.
George J. Murphy, A. M. 1860.

George Augustus Ostrander, A. M., M. D. Coll. Phys. and Surg. N. Y. 1858.
William A. Perry, (Eng.), A. M.
George R. Schieffelin, (C. L.), A. M.
Oscar Smedberg, (C.L.), A.M.
Herbert B. Turner, (C. L.), A. M.
John G. Wendel.

19

## 1856.

William Warren Ayres, (M.), A. M.
Edwin S. Babcock, (C. L.), A. M., Lieut.-Col. U. S. V.
Charles A. Bacon, A. M. 1863, M. D. elsewhere.
Albert H. Baldwin, (Art.), A. M.
*Eastburn Benjamin, (Rev.), A. M. aet. 38. *1874
Marshall Spring Bidwell, Jr. A. M. 1868.
William Pell Bogert, (F.)
Abbot Brown, (Rev.), A. M. 1863.
Henry J. Cammann, (M.), A. M. 1863.
Charles N. Clark, (B.), A. M., U. S. V.
Edward C. Clement, A. M. 1860.
Whittingham Cox, A.M. 1860, Lt. 4th U. S. Inf.
Robert Livingston Cutting, Jr., (Br.), A. M., LL. B. Harv. 1859.
Maturin L. Delafield, (M.), A. M.
Walter Gregory.
Francis Hendricks, (M.), A. M. 1861.
*William R. Hyslop, (C. L.), A. M., Capt. U. S. V. aet. 31. *1868
Ambrose C. Kingsland, Jr., (M.), A. M. 1861.
George L. Kingsland, (M.), A. M. 1861.
Leonard William Kip, Jr., (Rev.), A. M.
Peter I. Labagh, (C. L.), A. M.
Thomas Townsend Lawrence, (C. L.), LL. B. Harv. 1862.
David B. Lee.
*Hermon F. Lee. *1864
Alexis Emerson McIlvaine, (M.)
Joseph Meeks, (C. L.), A. M., LL. B. Harv. 1858.
Robert B. Minturn, Jr., (M.)
Richard C. Moore, Jr.
Mandeville Mower, A. M.
James G. Osborne, (C. L.), A. M.
G. Wendell Prime, (Rev.)
William Jones Seabury, (Rev.), A. M.
William F. Shepard, (C. L.)
Alexander M. Stanton, (Br.), A. M.
Russel Stebbins, Jr., (M.)
*Thomas Suffern, Jr. *1857
Charles C. Suydam, (Br.), A. M., Lt.-Col. U. S. V.
David G. Thompson, Jr., (Br.), A. M. 1860.
John W. Timpson, (C. L.), A. M.
William Gracie Ulshoeffer, (C. L.), Capt. U. S. V.
*William T. Van Riper, (C. L.), A. M.
*John Francis Walton, (C. L.), A. M.
James Weeks, (M.)
*Elbert M. Willett, (C. L.), A. M. *1875
Howell L. Williams, Jr., (M.), A. M.

45

## 1857.

William S. Boardman, (Rev.), A. M.
*Morgan L. S. Brower, A. M. *1864
Richard S. Dana, A. M.
Henry Eugene Davies, Jr., (C. L.), A. M., Maj.-Gen. U. S. V., Pub. Admin. N. Y. C.
Samuel W. Francis, A. M., M. D. elsewhere.
Elbridge Thomas Gerry, (C. L.), A. M., Memb. N. Y. S. Constit. Conv. 1867.
George G. Haven, (Br.), A. M.
James B. Herrick, A. M.
Philip W. Holmes, (C. L.), A. M.
Oliver Phelps Jackson, A. M.
William Hamett Martin, A.M., M. D. 1861.
Erskine Mason, A. M., M. D. 1860, Asst. Dem. Anat. 1861–66, Dem. Anat. 1866.
*W. Carey Massett, A. M., Lt.-Col. U. S. V. aet. 23. *1862
Mytton Maury, (Rev.), (T.), A. M., S. T. D. Univ. N. Y. C. 1876.
Pierre McCarty, A. M.
*Henry B. Nott. *1859
Richard T. Packwood, A. M.
*Theodore Parkman, (Chem.), A. M., Ph. D. Univ. Göttingen 1860, U. S. V. aet. 27. *1862
Goold H. Redmond, (Br.)
Charles E. Sears, (C. L.), A.M.
James H. Slipper, A. M.
William Renwick Smedberg, A. M., Capt. and Bvt.-Maj. and Lt.-Col. U. S. A.
Edgar Pinckney Smith, A.M.
*James T. Tailer, (M.), A. M. *1876
William R. Talbot, A. M.
Daniel S. Tuttle, (Rev.), A.M., S. T. D. 1867, Bishop P. E. Ch. Montana 1867–.
William B. Winslow, A. M.

27

## 1858.

*Wyllys Pomeroy Baxter, (C. L.), A. M. aet. 33. *1872
*Henry Woodward Cooper, (C. L.), A. M., LL. B. 1860. *1872
Stephen B. M. Cornell, A. M.
Lewis A. Curtis.
Daniel Sickles Duvall, (C.L.), LL. B. 1860.
Jacob A. Geissenhainer, (C. L.), A. M.
Harmon Hendricks, A. M.
Henry L. Jones, (Rev.), A. M.
Henry C. Kinney, (Rev.), A. M.
Nicholas Luquer, Jr.
*Philip Mesier Lydig, Jr., (C. L.), LL. B. 1861, Major and Bvt. Lt.-Col. and Col. U. S. V. aet. 31. *1868
*D. Ledyard Mallison.
James R. Manley, A. M.
Charles H. Marshall, Jr., (M.), A. M.
William J. Marrin, A.M. 1864.
*Benjamin Pell. *1862
A. G. Richards.
Robert K. Richards.
Henry C. Riley, (Rev.)
James W. Romeyn, A. M.
Thomas F. Thatcher.
*Gilbert T. Totten, A. M., M. D. 1861, Asst. Surg. N. Y. V. aet. 33. *1872
Hubert Van Wagenen.
*Francis C. Wainwright, (Rev.), A. M. *1874
John Ward, Jr., LL. B. 1860, A. M. 1864, M. D. Univ. N. Y. C. 1864, Capt. U. S. V.

25

## 1859.

Edward H. Anderson, (C. L.), A. M., N. Y. Assemb. 1866.
Richard Smith Bacon, (T.), A. M., LL. B. 1862, M. D. 1865.
Thomas J. Benjamin, A. M.
John Crosby Brown, (B.), A. M.
Edward F. Browning, (M.), A. M.
Elisha S. Caldwell, (C. L.), A. M.
Frank Pharcellus Church, (Ed.), A. M.
Gouverneur Cruger, A. M.
William Floyd Cushman, A. M., M. D. 1862.
John William Duer, (C. L.), LL. B. 1861.
Cortlandt De Peyster Field, (M.), A. M.
John Frederic Gesner, A. M.
Irving Grinnell, 1862, A. M. 1862.
*E. Treadwell Hustace. *1859
William Jay, Jr., (C. L.), A. M., LL. B. 1867, Bvt. Lt.-Col. U. S. V.
Charles A. Jackson. Jr., (C. L.), A. M.
James Pierre Lacombe, A. M.
William Lummis, (B.), A. M.
J. Emory McClintock, (Act.), A. M., Tutor 1859–60.
George William Maynard, A. M. 1868, Prof. Metall. Polyt. Inst. Troy N. Y. 1867.
James Frederic Moore, A. M., M. D. elsewhere.
Stephen Whitney Phœnix, A. M., LL. B. 1863.
William Lewis Raymond (C. L.), A. M., U. S. Consul, Leeds, Eng., 1864–68.
*Stephen Richard Reynolds, A. M., Capt. U. S. V. aet. 26. *1864
William T. Sabine, (Rev.), A. M.
Oscar E. Schmidt, A. M.
Joseph Augustus Slipper, (Pr.), A. M., Col. U. S. V.
Thomas F. Trenor, A. M., M. D. elsewhere.
Gabriel Mead Tooker, (C. L.), A. M., LL. B. 1861.
Robert Boyd Van Kleeck, Jr., (Rev.), A. M., LL. B. 1862.
William David Walker, (Rev.), A. M. 1863.
Edward N. Whitehouse, A. M., U. S. N.
Henry Bruen Whitehouse, (M.), A. M., LL. B. elsewhere. 33

## 1860.

Robert P. Barry, 1865, Capt. U. S. A.
*Richard G. Benjamin, A. M. *1864
*Clarence Stewart Brown, (B.), A. M., Major U. S. V. aet. 36. *1875
*J. Lorillard Cammann, A. M. aet. 28. *1868
Howard Clarkson.
Walter Livingston Clarkson, (C. L.), A. M., LL. B. 1863.
Edgar M.Cullen, (C.L.), A.M., Col. U. S. V., Lt. 1st U. S. Inf.
Charles De Ruyter, (M.), A. M., LL. B. 1862, U. S. V.
Eugene Du Bois.
John Haven Emerson, A. M., M. D. 1865.
George R. Fearing, (B.), Capt. and Bvt. Major U. S. V.
Robert Goelet, Jr., (C. L.), A. M., LL. B. 1862.
Joseph Greenleaf, Jr., (Rev.), A. M.
Edward L. Greenwood, (C.L.)
Laban Gardner Hopkins, (C. L.), A. M., LL. B. 1862, LL. M. 1864.

Edmund Abdy Hurry, (C. L.), A. M., LL. B. 1862, U. S. N.
*John William Jenks, Lieut. U. S. V. *1861
Edward Renshaw Jones, (Br.)
Herbert Kettell, A. M.
*Augustus F. King, U. S. V. aet. 23. *1862
David Lydig, A. M.
Samuel Kuypers Lyon, A. M., M. D. 1866.
Thomas H. Messenger, (M.), A. M.
George Mason Miller, (Br.), A. M., LL. B. 1862, Capt. U. S. V.
Augustus Newbold Morris, A. M., LL. B. 1864.
Richard Lewis Morris, Jr., A. M. 1866, Capt. and Bvt. Major U. S. A.
Robert Dillon Nesmith, A. M., M. D. Univ. N. Y. C. 1862.
Thomas Ludlow Ogden, (C. L.), A. M., LL. B. 1862.
*Robert Troup Pell, (C. L.), A. M., LL. B. 1863, U. S. V. aet. 27. *1868
Eugene Hall Pomeroy, (C.L.), LL. B. 1862, U. S. V.
Edward P. Robins.
James S. Satterthwaite, A. M.
*John W. Southack, Jr., A.M., M.D. Bellevue Med. Coll. N. Y. 1865, Asst. Dem. Anat. Bell. Med. Coll. aet. 30. *1869
Abraham Suydam, (Eng.), A. M.
*Frederick A. Tracy, Lieut. U. S. A. aet. 23. *1863
John Howard Van Amringe, A. M., Tutor 1860–63, Adj. Prof. Maths. 1863–73, and Prof. 1873–, Lect. Maths. School of Mines 1864–65, and Prof. 1865–.
George Waddington, (C. L.), LL. B. 1862.
William Fitzhugh Whitehouse, (C. L.), A.M., LL. B. elsewhere.
Pierre Washington Wildey, (C. L.), A. M. and Yale 1865, LL. B. 1863.
Egerton L. Winthrop, A. M. 40

# 1861.

James Benkard, Jr., A. M., Capt. U. S. V.
William Alexander Boyd, (C. L.), A. M., Lieut. U.S.V.
George Herbert Carey, (C.L.), A. M., LL. B. 1863.
William Halsted Caswell, (M.), A. M.
Henry Dudley, A. M.
John Gihon, Jr., (M.), A. M.
Langdon Greenwood, (C. L.), A. M.
Charles Coolidge Haight, (Arch.), A. M., Capt. U. S. V.
Edward Haight, Jr., A. M., Capt. U. S. A.
William Richards Hillyer, (M.), A. M., Capt. U. S. V.
Elisha Horton, Jr., (C. L.), A. M.
Rueben Wing Howes, Jr., (Rev.), A. M.
Walter Bowne Lawrence (Br.), A. M.
Albert McNulty, Jr., (C. L.), A. M., LL. B. 1864, U. S. V.
Edward Mitchell, (C. L.), A. M., LL. B. 1865.
Gratz Nathan, (C. L.), A. M., Asst. Corporation Atty. N. Y. C.
Frank Alleyne Otis, (C. L.), A. M., LL. B. 1864.
*Richard Cornelius Ray, Lieut. U. S. V. *1863
*William Alexander Rice, (C. L.), A. M., U. S. V. aet. 24. *1866

*Erastus Barnes Rudd, (C.L.), A. M., LL. B. 1863. aet. 30. *1872

William Henry Russell, Jr., A. M., Capt. U. S. V.

Thomas Taunton Sabine, A. M., M. D. 1864, Asst. Dem. Anat. 1866–70 and Dem. 1870, Adj. Lectr. Anat. 1870 and Adj. Prof. 1871–.

*Henry Augustus Schermerhorn, (C. L.), A. M., LL. B. 1867. aet. 29. *1869

Thomas Henry Sill, (Rev.), A. M.

George Lansing Taylor, (Rev.), A. M., S. T. D. Syracuse Univ. N. Y. 1876.

Henry A. Coit Taylor, (M.), A. M.

John Ayscough Tucker, (M), A. M., U. S. V.

Stephen Hague Turnbull, (C. L.), A. M.

Joseph Mason Turner, (Rev.), A. M.

*William Mansfield VanWagenen, (Rev.), A. M. aet. 24. *1866

Luis Puertas Walton, A. M., M. D. 1870.

Isaac Johnson Ward, (C. L.), A. M.

Samuel Baldwin Ward, A.M., M. D. Georgetown Med. Coll., Asst. Surg. U. S. V., Curator Coll. Museum 1868–69, Prof. Anat. Woman's Med. Coll. N. Y. C. 1869–76, Prof. Surgery Albany Med. School 1876–.

Edward Walter West, (C. L.), LL. B. Univ. N. Y. C. 1861, A. M., Col. U. S. V.

Frederick Cope Whitehouse, (Rev.), A. M.

Albert Beach Whitney, A.M, M. D. Univ. N. Y. C. 1863.



# 1862.

Edward Robert Atwill, (Rev.), A. M.

*Francis Babcock, (Br.), A. M. aet. 24. *1866

*Robert Erskine Bartow, A. M. *1867

William Harbert Benjamin, (F.), A M.

Henry Carrington Bolton, A. M. 1866, Ph. D. elsewhere, Asst. in Anal. Chem Sch. of Mines 1872–.

John Thomas Burr.

Robert Bage Canfield, (C. L.)

Leslie Chase, (Br.)

*John Lawrence Churchill, A. M., Lieut. U. S. A. *1868

*Charles Ernest Congdon. aet. 21. *1862

Nathaniel Elsworth Cornwall, Jr., (T.), (Rev.), A. M. and Harv. 1868.

John Halsey Curtis, A. M.

Walter Cutting, (M.), Maj. U. S. V.

Henry Ammi Dows, (Rev.), A. M. 1869.

James Gore King Duer, (B.)

Peter Forrester, (M.)

Charles Dudley Fuller, A.M., U. S. V.

*George Wolfe Gillespie, (Eng.), A. M. aet. 28. *1870

Louis Haight, A. M.

William Augustus Ogden Hegeman, (C. L.), LL. B. 1864, LL. M. 1865, A. M.

Burrall Hoffman, (C. L.), LL. B. 1864, LL. M. 1865, A. M.

Lawrence Yvonnet Hopkins, A. M., U. S. V.

*William Henry Jackson, A.M. aet. 28. *1872

Charles Sigourney Knox, A. M., Act. Prof. Mor. and Int. Phil. 1869–70.

William Elliott Laight, (C. L.)

William Gerard Lathrop, Jr., (C. L.), LL. B. Harv. 1864, A. M.

George Anderson Lawrence, (M.), A. M.

*William Henry Martin, (M.) aet. 31. *1872

*Henry Howard Marvin, U. S. Eng. 1862–3. *1863

Cornelius Berrian Mitchell, (M.), A. M., U. S. V.

John Fulton Berrian Mitchell, (M.), A. M., Capt. U. S. V.

Charles Walton Ogden, (M.), LL. B. 1864, A. M.

*David Burr Olyphant. *1864

*Edward Mensard Pell. *1863

*Richard Varick Pell, M. D. Bellevue Med. Coll., A. M. aet. 23. *1866

*Gerardus Post, (C.L.), LL. B. 1864. aet. 22. *1864

Russell Harper Root, (C.L.), LL.B. 1864.

Charles Ames Spencer, (T.), A. M.

Foster Thayer, M.D. Bellevue Med. Coll. N.Y. 1866, A. M. 1866, U. S. N.

Charles Rockland Tyng, (M.), A. M.

*John A. Vanderpoel, (C.L.), LL. B. 1865, A. M. aet. 24 *1866

*Francis Willis, (M.), A. M. aet. 31. *1870

William Henry Willis, Jr., (C. L.), A. M.

Leroy Milton Yale, M. D. Bellevue Med. Coll., A. M.

44

## 1863.

James Herman Aldrich, (M.), A. M.

Fanning Cobham Tucker Beck.

William Cornell Binns, A. M.

Daniel Frederick Boardman, (C. L.), LL. B. 1866.

William Brevoort Bolmer, (Rev.), LL. B. 1865, A. M. 1868.

Melville Brown, (M.)

Thomas Tileston Pryce, A.M.

Charles Frederick Clarke, A. M., M. D. 1866.

*Freeman Clarkson, (C. L.), LL. B. 1865, A. M.

William Peshine Douglass.

Clifford Faitoute Eagle, (Br.), A. M., Lieut. U. S. A.

George Wilson Ferguson, (Rev.), A. M.

William Redwood Fisher, A. M., M. D. 1867.

Randall Cook Hall, (Rev.), A. M., Inst. in Hebrew Gen. Theol. Sem. P. E. Ch. 1869–71, and Prof. Hebr. and Greek 1871–.

Richard Mentor Henry, (C. L.), A. M.

Stephen Ferris Holmes, (Rev.), A. M.

Henry Augustus Hurlbut, Jr., (Br.), A. M.

*Peter Augustus Jay, (Rev.), A. M. aet. 35. *1867

Emile Henry Lacombe, (C. L.), LL. B. 1865.

William Scott Leggat, (M.)

Lewis Henry Lighthipe, (Rev.), A. M.

Le Grand Lockwood, Jr., (Br.)

Thomas Morwood McLean, Jr.

James Allen Macdonald, A. M., U. S. V.

Rockwood McQuesten, (Rev.), A. M.

William Matthews Martin, (C. L.), LL. B. 1865, A. M.

Dan. Marvin, Jr., (Rev.), M. M., Asst. Prof. Grk. and Lat. Lang. Racine Coll. Wis. 1868.

William Anderson Mitchell.

Stuyvesant Fish Morris, M. D. 1867.
*James Murray, (Rev.), A. M. *1872
Hiram Hunt Nazro, A. M.
Thomas Aellamy Newby, (Rev.), A. M.
George Henry Owen, (C. L.), A. M.
*James Brinckerhoff Pell. aet. 28. *1870
George Decatur Pond.
Robert Emmet Robinson, (C. L.), LL. B. 1865.
Philip Justice Sands.
Henry Yates Satterlee, (Rev.)
Walter Satterlee, (Art.)
William Barnewall Schermerhorn.
Rutherfurd Stuyvesant.
*Charles William Terrett, A. M. *1872
Stephen Howard Thayer, Jr., (C. L.), LL. B. 1865, A. M.
Robert Schuyler Tucker, A. M.
Frank Roe Van Buren, A. M.
Frederick Brinsmade Van Kleeck, (Rev.), A. M.
Egbert Ward.
Sylvester Ward.
Ellsworth Westervelt.
Willard Parker Wooster, A. M., M. D. 1867.

50

# 1864.

John Magnus Adams, (Eng.), A. M., E. M. 1867.
*David Wylie Alexander, (C. L.), LL. B. 1866, A. M. aet. 30 *1872
William Gardiner Appleton.
Reginald Heber Bartow.
Gerard Beekman, (C. L.), A. M., LL. B. 1867.
John Neilson Beekman, A.M., M. D. 1868.
Walston Hill Browne, (Br.), A. M.
Thomas Baird Browning, (C. L.), LL. B. 1866, A. M.
Charles Stedman Bull, A. M., M. D. 1868.
John Frederick Butterworth, (Rev.), A. M.
William Henry Butterworth, (C.L.), LL.B. 1866, A. M.
Jonathan Ackerman Coles, A. M., M. D. 1868.
Henry Bedinger Cornwall, (Eng.), A. M., E. M. 1869, Asst. in Mineral. and Metall. Sch. of Mines 1869–73, Prof. Anal. Chem. and Mining Princeton Coll. 1873–.
Edmund Dewees Davidson, A. M.
Theodore Frelinghuysen Cornell Demarest, (C. L.), A. M., LL. B., 1858, Tutor 1869–70.
Matthew Brinckerhoff Du Bois, A. M., M. D. 1868.
Duane Shuler Everson, (T.), A. M., Tutor 1864–68.
*Henry Floy, LL. B. 1866. aet. 23. *1866
*William Newton Goddard, A. M. aet. 28. *1873
Thomas Hays Harmer, (Eng.), A. M.
Hiram Lyman Huston, A. M.
Frederick Wendell Jackson, (Br.)
Charles Henry Kaufman.
Jonas Butler Kissam, (Br.)
Joseph Bayley Lawrence, (C. L.), LL. B. 1866, A. M.
Isidor Mayer.
Alfred Perry McClellan.
William Meikleham, 1868, A. M. 1871.
John Brainard Morgan, (Rev.), A. M.
William Franklin Mott, (C. L.), LL.B. 1873.
Howard Osterhoudt, (C. L.), LL. B. 1866, A. M.

Henry Hills Parker, (C. L.), LL. B. 1866, A. M.
Charles Burroughs Rice, 1865, (C.L.), A. M., LL. B. 1867.
Frederick William Stevens, (C. L.), A. M.
*Arthur Pemberton Sturges. aet. 24. *1866
Albert Edward Valentine, A. M., M. D. elsewhere.
Isidor Walz, (Chem.), Ph. D. Heidelberg 1867.
Marinus Willett, Jr., (M.) 38

## 1865.

Henry Beadel, Jr., 1869, (C. L.), LL. B. 1870.
Henry Rutgers Beekman, (C. L.), LL. B. 1867, A. M.
Edward Stelle Brownson, (Eng.), A.M., E. M. 1869.
Douglas William Burnham, A. M.
Archibald Murray Campbell, A. M., M. D. 1873.
Thomas Cooper Campbell, (C. L.), A. M., N. Y. Assemb. 1875–6.
John Henry Caswell, Asst. in Mineral. 1870–.
Jonathan Odell Fowler, Jr., A. M.
Charles King Gracie, (Eng.), A. M., E. M. 1868.
James Hooker Hamersley, (C. L.), LL. B. 1867, A. M.
John Moore Heffernan, (Rev.), A. M.
*Julian James, A. M., Lieut. U. S. V. aet. 26. *1870
Frederic Rhinelander Jones, (M.), A. M.
George Goelet Kip, (C. L.), LL. B. 1867, A. M.
William Gilman Low, (C.L.), LL. B. 1867, A. M.
Henry Richard McElligott, (M.), A. M.
William Neilson McVickar, (Rev.), A. M., U. S. V.
Randolph Brant Martine, (C. L.), A. M.
James Fontaine Maury, A. M.
George Webster Peck, A. M., U. S. V.
James Lyman Price, A. M., LL. B. 1868.
Frederick Prime, Jr., Asst. in Assaying Sch. of Mines 1869–70, Prof. Metall. Lafay. Coll. 1870–, Asst. Geol. of Penna. 1874–.
Arthur Bernard Ross, A. M.
Roderick Burt Seymour, A. M., U. S. V.
Lenox Smith, A. M., E. M. 1868, U. S. V.
*John Edwin Swezey, (C.L.), LL. B. 1867, A. M. *1873
Seymour Van Nostrand, A.M.
Abraham Van Santvoord, (C.L.), LL. B. 1867, A. M.
Edward Henry Van Winkle, A. M.
Isaac Van Winkle, (Rev.), A. M. Prof. Maths. and Nat. Phil. St. Stephen's Coll. Annandale 1869–71.
William Bogert Walker, (Rev.), A. M.
Willard Parker Ward, (Eng.), A. M. 1871.
James Lee Wells, A. M.
John Visscher Wheeler, A. M.
Francis French Wilson, (T.), U. S. V., A. M. 35

## 1866.

Marshall Pepoon Bell,† (C.L.), LL. B. 1868.
Louis Edward Binsse.

† Known subsequently as Marshall Bell.

Thomas Monahan Blossom, (Eng.), A. M., E. M. 1869.
Clarence Brainerd.
James Manning Bruce, A. M.
*Nathan Robins Carter. *1866
Julien Tappan Davies, (C. L.), A. M., LL. B. 1868.
Augustus Floyd Delafield.
Moses Downs Getty.
Edward Clark Houghton, (Rev.), A. M.
William Augustus Hooker, (Eng.), A. M., E. M. 1869.
Daniel Lord, Jr., (C. L.), LL. B. 1868, A. M.
Theodore Holmes McNamee.
*Edward Ward Malloy. *1872
Augustus Chapman Merriam, A. M., Tutor 1869–.
Frank Ames Mullany.
Edward Holland Nicoll, (C. L.), LL. B. 1868, A. M.
Willard Parker, Jr., M. D. 1870.
William Bleecker, Potter, (Eng.), E. M. 1869, Prof. Mining and Metall. Wash. Univ. Miss.
William Edwin Smalley, (C. L.), LL. B. 1868.
George Putnam Smith, (C. L.), LL. B. 1868.
Stephen Dover Stephens, Jr., (C.L.), A. M., LL. B. 1868, N. Y. Assemb. 1874–75.
Horace Stetson, (C. L.), LL. B. 1869.
Augustus Talbot.
Richmond Talbot.
William Jameson Thomson, (Rev.)
Henry Crosswell Tuttle, (C. L.), LL. B. 1868.
Martin Van Buren.
James Moore Wayne, A. M. 1871, E. M. elsewhere.
Henry Augustus Whiting, (Eng.), A.M., E. M. 1869.
John Fritz Wissmann, (M.), A. M. 1876.
Graham Youngs. (M.) 32

## 1867.

Joseph Halsey Anderson, A. M.
James Baker, Jr., (C. L.), A. M.
Henry Anthony Waldburg Barclay, (C.L.)
Walton Peckham Bell, (C.L.), LL. B. 1869, A. M.
Samuel Appleton Blatchford, (C. L.), A. M.
Jacques Arnold Bernheimer, A. M.
Charles Henry Burtis, (C. L.), LL. B. 1869, A. M.
Henry Cohn, (T.), A. M.
Theodore Hedges Conger, 1870.
John Alexander Denniston, Jr., (Rev.), A. M.
George Gosman Dewitt, Jr., (C. L.), LL. B. 1869, A. M.
George Duyckinck, A. M.
Edgar Fawcett, (Au.), A. M.
Nicholas Fish, (C. L.), LL. B. Harv. 1869, A. M. 1871.
Antoine Lentilhon Foster.
Giraud Graham.
Clarence Melville Hyde, (C. L.), LL. B. 1869, A. M.
William Halsey Ingersoll, (C. L.), LL. B. 1869, A. M.
George Barent Johnson, A.M.
John Alsop King.
*Hobart Lewis. aet. 23. *1870
Henry Demarest Lloyd, A.M.
James McNamee, (C. L.), A. M.
Cadwalader Evans Ogden, (C. L.), LL. B. 1869.
Henry Evelyn Pierrepont, Jr., A. M.
Hector Craig Fitz Randolph, A. M.

Julius Sachs, (T.), A. M. 1871.
Henry Schneeberger, A. M.
Aaron Ernest Vanderpoel, (C. L.), LL. B. 1869, A. M., Trustee 1876–.
Rudolph August Witthaus, Jr., A. M., M. D. Univ. N. Y. C. 1875, Assoc. Prof. Chem. and Physiol. Univ. N. Y C. 1876–.
James Henry Work, (C. L.), LL. B. 1869, A. M.

31

## 1868.

Isaac Adler.
John William Schmidt Arnold, A. M., M. D. Univ. N. Y. C., Prof. Univ. Med. Coll.
Henry Denison Babcock, (M.), A. M.
William Preston Beck.
James Michael Brady, (C.L.), LL. B. 1870, A. M.
Benjamin Howell Campbell, (T.), A. M.
Walter Ewing Colton.
Frederic De Peyster Foster, (C. L.), A. M., LL. B. 1872.
Talmadge Woodward Foster, (C. L.), A. M.
Andrew Jackson Gilhooly, (C. L.), LL. B. 1870, A. M.
Elmslie Morven Gillett, (C. L.), A. M.
Joseph Bayley Halsey, A. M.
John Archibald Macdonald.
Edward Schermerhorn Mead, A. M. 1872.
William Mitchell, Jr., (C.L.), A. M., LL. B. 1871.
John McLean Nash, (C. L.), LL. B. 1870, A. M.
Duane Livingston Peabody, (C. L.), LL. B. 1870, A. M.
John Duncan Quackenbos, A. M., M. D. 1871, Tutor 1870–.
George Lockhart Rives, (C. L.), B. A. Trin. Coll. Camb. Eng. 1872, A. M. 1872, LL. B. 1873.
George Nicholas Sanders, Jr., (C. L.), LL. B. 1870, A. M.
Arthur Sloan, (Rev.), A. M.
William James Milligan Sloane, A. M.
John Steward, Jr.
James Prescott Swain, Jr., (M.), A. M.
Horace Holden Thayer, (M.)
Stephen Whittingham Williams, A. M.
Lucius Kellogg Wilmerding, (M.), A. M.

27

## 1869.

Charles Augustus Adams, (Rev.), A. M.
Hal Allaire, (F.), A. M.
Willard Bartlett, (C. L.), LL. B. Univ. City N. Y. 1868.
Evelyn Bartow, (Rev.), A. M.
Robert Lenox Belknap, and Coll. N. J. 1869, A. M.
Jacob Bininger, A. M.
Thomas Newby Cuthbert, (C. L.), LL. B. 1871, A. M.
William Bayard Cutting, (C. L.), LL. B. 1871, A. M.
Henry Drisler, Jr., (M.), A.M.
William Alexander Duer, (C. L.), LL. B. 1871, A. M.
Hamilton Fish, Jr., (C. L.), A. M., LL. B. 1873, N. Y. Assemb. 1874, 1876.
William Dudley Foulke, (C. L.), LL. B. 1871, A. M.
William Montague Geer, (C. L.), LL. B. 1871, A. M.
Edward John Hallock, (Chem.), A. M., Asst. in Chem.
*George Webster Heasly. aet. 23. *1872

William Berrian Hooper, (Rev.), A. M.
Robert Henry Hunt. aet. 21. *1870
William Iselin, (M.)
Henry Madison Jones, (C. L.), LL. B. 1873.
Shipley Jones, (Br.), A. M.
John Henry Livingston, (C. L.), LL. B. 1871.
David B. Ogden, (C. L.), LL. B. 1871.
*John Oven, (Rev.), A. M. *1875
Charles Augustus Peabody, Jr., (C. L.), LL. B. 1871, A. M., N. Y. Assemb. 1876.
George Plato Pierce.
Samuel Augustus Purdy, Jr., (C. L.), LL. B. 1871, A. M.
William Macnevin Purdy, (C. L.), LL. B. 1871, A. M.
Horace Nelson Seaver, Jr., (T.)
Frank Norsworthy Shepard, (C. L.), LL. B. 1871, A. M.
John Adams Smedberg.
Edward Bayard Smith, (Rev.), LL. B. 1871, A. M.
*David Stewart, Jr. *1874
Henry Cady Sturges, A. M.
Edward Tillou, (C. L.), LL. B. 1871, A. M.
Edward Francis Weeks, (C. L.), LL. B. 1871, A. M.
Thenford Woodhull, (C. L.), LL. B. 1871, A. M.

36

## 1870.

Felix Adler, Prof. Cornell Univ.
Walden Pell Anderson, (Arch.)
Isaac Baker Barrett, A. M.
Richard Berrian, A. M.
Towson Caldwell, A. M.
Lewis Buffett Carll, A. M.
John Cropper, (C. L.), A. M., LL. B. 1872.
*George Hicks Dibblee. *1873
William Fanning, Jr., (C.L.), LL. B.
Thomas Charles Edward Ecclesine, (C. L.), A. M., LL. B. 1871.
Charles Meredith Garth.
William Erwin Gilhooly, (C. L.), LL. B. 1873.
Henry Waterman Holden, A. M.
Arthur Ingraham, A. M.
Edmond Kelly, B. A. St. John's Coll. Camb. Eng. 1876.
Franklin Butler Lord.
Seth Low, (M.)
John Bartow Montell.
Robert Stratton Morison, A. M.
Isidor Pierce Oberndorfer, A. M., M. D. 1874.
Walter Ogden.
George Livingston Peabody, M. D. 1873, A. M.
Spencer Summerfield Roche, (Rev.), A. M.
David Alvah Rowe, (T.)
George Starr Scofield, Jr., (C. L.), LL. B. 1872, A. M. 1874.
Robert Norsworthy Shepard, (C. L.), A. M., LL. B. 1876.
Deming Beadle Smith.
Frank Dodge Sturges, (C.L.), LL. B. 1872, A. M.
William Naylor Webbe, (Rev.), A. M.
Dennistoun Wood, (C. L.), LL. B. 1872, A. M.

30

## 1871.

Robert Barbour, A. M.
Valentine Alexander Blacque.
William Haliburton Bridgham.

Frederic Bronson, (C. L.), LL. B. 1873.
Clarence Rapelje Conger, (C. L.), LL. B., 1873, A. M.
William Henry Conover.
Robert Fulton Cutting, A. M. 1875.
Denning Duer, Jr.
Moses Henry Epstein.
Stuyvesant Fish, (B.), A. M.
Frank Goddard Haughwout, (C. L.), LL. B. 1875.
Jacob Herrick Henry, (C. L.), LL. B. 1873, A. M.
Joseph Hooper, (Rev.), A.M.
Francis Hustace, A. M., M. D. 1874.
Richard Busteed Kelly, (C. L.), LL. B. 1873, A. M.
Henry Day Loder, (C. L.), LL. B. 1873, A. M.
James Brander Matthews, (C. L.) LL. B. 1873, A. M.
James Otis Morse, Jr., A. M.
Chester Clark Munroe.
Benjamin Franklin Romaine, Jr., (C. L.), LL. B. 1872.
John Watts Russell, (C. L.), LL. B. 1871, A. M.
William Henry Sage, (C. L.), LL. B. 1874, A. M.
Henry Mason Smyth, (Rev.)
Oscar Solomon Straus, (C. L.), LL. B. 1873, A. M.
Robert Swan, Jr., A. M., M. D. 1874.
Obadiah Valentine, A. M.
Joseph Fenelon Vermilye, (C. L.), A. M., LL. B. 1875.
Robert Waller, Jr., A. M.
George Whitefield Ward.
*Augustus Ward Whiton. aet. 24. *1875
George Francis Work, A. M.

31

## 1872.

*Robert Arnold, (C. L.), LL. B. 1875, A M. aet. 23. *1875
Sidney Gillespie Ashmore, A. M., Tutor in Greek and Lat. Lehigh Univ. Penn. 1873–.
Frederick Augustus Brown, (B.), A. M.
Robert Clarence Dorsett, (M.), A. M.
Clarence Cushing Edgerton, (C. L.), LL.B. 1874, A. M.
Haliburton Fales, (C. L.), LL. B. 1874, A. M.
Edward Fermor Hall, (Br.), A. M.
Robert Ray Hamilton, (C.L.), LL. B. 1874, A. M.
Schuyler Hamilton, Jr., A.M., E. M. 1876.
William Henry Haldane, (C. L.), LL. B. 1874, A. M.
William Edgar Keyes, (C.L.), LL. B. 1874, A. M.
Charles Henry Knox, (C. L.), LL. B. 1874, A. M.
John Holme Maghee, A. M., C. E. 1876.
Frederick Panet Marshall, (C. L.), A. M., LL. B. 1876.
Edmund McCaffil.
Valentine Mott.
Ludlow Ogden, (C. L.), LL.B. 1874, A. M.
Richard Ogden, A. M.
James Lawrence Onderdonk, (C. L.), LL. B. 1874, A. M.
*Augustus Coe Pirsson, (C. L.), LL. B. 1875, A. M. aet. 24. *1875
John Krom Rees, A. M., E. M. 1875, Asst. in Math. School of Mines 1873–.
*Edward Lazarus Rosenfeld. *1873
Charles Lancaster Short, (Rev.), A. M.
John Ruggles Strong, (C. L.), A. M., LL. B 1875.
Edmund Grindle Rawson Trimble, A. M.
Arthur Delano Weeks, (C.L.), LL. B. 1874, A. M.

Robert Henry Wilkinson, (Rev.), A. M.
Henry Duncan Wood, (Br.)
Henry Edgar Woodward, (C. L.), LL. B. 1874, A. M.

29

## 1873.

José Aymar, A. M.
Ira Leo Bamberger, (C. L.), LL. B. 1875.
Emilio Ysidoro Del Pino, (C. L.), LL. B. 1875, A. M.
Otis Field, 1874, (T.)
William Seton Gordon.
Frederick Remsen Hutton, A. M., E. M. 1876, C. E. 1876.
Percy Hamilton McMahon, (C. L.), LL. B. 1875, A. M.
Henry Rutgers Marshall, (Arch.), A. M.
Cassimir DeRham Moore, (C. L.), LL. B. 1875, A. M.
Alexander Bethmann Simonds, (C.L.), LL. B. 1875.
Alonzo Wybrants Smith, (C. L.), A. M., LL. B. 1876.
Gilbert MacMaster Speir, Jr., (C. L.), LL. B. 1875, A. M.
Louis St. Amant, A. M.
Silas Moore Stilwell, Jr., (C. L.), LL. B. 1875, A. M.
Lefferts Strebeigh, (C. L.), LL. B. 1875, A. M.
Sutherland Tenney, (C. L ), LL. B. 1875, A. M.
David Thomson, (C. L.), LL. B. 1875, A. M.
Daniel Babbit Vermilye, (C. L.), LL. B. 1875, A. M.
James Montaudevert Waterbury, Jr., (M.), A. M.
Bache McEvers Whitlock, (C. L.), LL. B. 1875, A. M.
George Norman Williamson.

21

## 1874.

Spencer Aldrich, (C. L.), LL. B. 1876.
Walter Scott Allerton.
Charles Ramsey Buckley.
George Forrest Butterworth, (C. L.), LL. B. 1876.
Timothy Matlack Cheesman.
Robert Clifford Cornell, (C. L.), LL. B. 1876.
Frank Drisler, (T.)
John Hone Foster.
Pierre Pascal Harrower.
Selden T. Scranton Henry, (C. L.), LL. B. 1876.
Frederic William Hinrichs, (C. L.), LL. B. 1875.
Jay Humphreys.
William Warner Johnson, (Pub.)
George Kennedy.
George Christian Kobbé, (C. L.), LL. B. 1876.
Albert Jared Loder, (C. L.), LL. B. 1876.
Alfred Mayer.
Edward Sumner Rapallo, (C. L.), LL. B. 1876.
Sylvanus Albert Reed.
Benjamin Aymar Sands, (C. L.), LL. B. 1876.
Henry Townsend Scudder.
Frank Dunlap Shaw.
Frank Storrs, (C. L.), LL. B. 1876.
Thomas Dewitt Thompson.

24

## 1875.

William James Adams.
William Babcock.
Thomas Cumming Bach.
Homer Kirtland Flanagan Blake.
Harry Innes Bodley, Jr.
John Aaron Browning.
William Edward Conroy.

Henry Churchill De Mille.
Howard Gallup.
Evan Philip George, Jr.
Alister Greene.
Randolph Hurry.
William Duncan McKim.
Thomas Samuel Ormiston.
Edward Willard Price.
John Henry Purdy.
Edward Delavan Perry.
Samuel Cady Root.
George Sherman.
Edward Lyman Short.
Chalmers Wood.

21

## 1876.

Harold Arrowsmith.
Richard Theodore Bang.
Henry Whitney Bates.
David Calman.
Herman Drisler.
Philip Henry Dugro.
Richard Theodore Ely.
Aymar Embury.
Jaspar Tillerous Goodwin.
Gaspar Griswold.
John Edmund Hindon Hyde.
Louis Oliver Ivey.
Wilmot Johnson, Jr.
Townsend Jones, Jr.
Edwin Clark Kent.
Robert Armstrong Livingston.
Theodore Frelinghuysen Lozier.
Benjamin Franklin Mayer.
Cornelius Wortendyke Morrow.
Frederick Oakes.
Edward Washington Page.
Edward Pratt.
Louis Christian Raegener.
Egbert Guernsey Rankin.
James Armstrong Renwick.
Nathaniel Pendleton Schenck.
Eugene Seligman.
George Washington Seligman.
Isaac Newton Seligman.
Du Bois Smith.
Irvin Auchincloss Sprague.
William Cleveland Thayer.
Montgomery Hunt Throop, Jr.
Robert Townsend.
William Edward Verplanck.
William Francis Augustus Von Sachs.
Leighton Williams.

37

# GRADUATES IN MEDICINE.

## 1769.

*Samuel Kissam.
*Robert Tucker.

2

## 1771.

*Benjamin Onderdonk. aet. 21. *1772
*Michael Sebring.

2

## 1772.

*John Augustus Graham, A. B. Yale 1768 and A. M. Yale.
*Uzal Johnson.
*James Muirson.
*Richard Udall, Trustee Coll. Phys. and Surg. N. Y. 1807–11.
*William Winterton.

5

## 1773.

*Jabez Doty.

## 1774.

*Samuel Nicoll, Prof. Pract. of Med. and of Chem. 1792–94.

## 1793.

*Samuel Borrowe, Trustee Coll. Phys. and Surg. N. Y. 1820–28.
*John Bowne Hicks.
*Willett Taylor, Jr.
*Joseph Youle.

4

## 1794.

*David G. Abeel.
*Peter Irving.
*Henry Mead.

3

## 1795.

*William Morey Ross.
*Timothy Fletcher Wetmore.

2

## 1796.

*Alexander Anderson. aet. 95. *1870
*Winthrop Saltonstall, A. B. Yale 1793. *1802

2

## 1797.

*William Bay.

## 1802.

*Joseph Bailey, Trustee Coll. Phys. and Surg. N.Y. 1820–37.
Richard L. Walker.
2

## 1803.

Isaac Foster.
Samuel Scofield.
2

## 1804.

William Barrow.
Ezekiel Ostrander.
Daniel D. Walters.
3

## 1805.

*Thomas Cock, Prof. Anat. and Physiol. Rutg. Coll. N. Jers., V.-Prest. Coll. Phys. and Surg. N. Y. 1827–55 and Prest. 1855–58 aet. 87. *1869
*Benjamin Kissam. aet. 50. *1831
2

## 1806.

*Valentine Mott, LL.D. elsewhere, Prof. Surg. 1811–13, Prof. Surg. Coll. Phys. and Surg. N.Y. 1813–26 and in Rutg. Med. Coll. N.Y. 1826–30, Prof. Surg. and Relative Anat. Univ. N. Y. C. 1830–65, Prest. N.Y. Acad. Med. aet. 79. *1865

## 1807.

Alire R. Delisle.

## 1810.

Robert Morrell.

## 1860.

Thomas Henry Allen.
Birchard Galusha Balch.
George Burr Banks.
Phanet Coe Barker.
William Comstock Bennett, A. B. Yale 1858, Surg. 5th Conn. Vols.
John Caruthers Bogardus, Asst. Surg. 102d N. Y. S. Vols.
Samuel White Briggs, Asst. Surg. U. S. N. aet. 26. *1861
Orlo Myron Bump.
Charles Carrington.
Seth Lyman Chase.
Robert Cooper.
*Charles Henry Covell, A. A. Surg. U. S. N. aet. 26. *1861
Juan Bautista Ponce DeLeon.
Frank Wadsworth Doolittle, Surg. 5th N. Y. S. Vols.
Philo Judson Farnsworth, M. D. Univ. Verm.
William Baldwin Fletcher.
Edward Irving Ford, A. B. elsewhere.
Otis Willard Gibson.
Walter James Hadden.
Joseph Lawrence Hicks, Surg. 1st N. Y. S. Vols.
Courtland Hoppin, A.B. elsewhere.
David Kennedy.
Daniel Avery Langworthy.
William Whipple Leavitt, Asst. Surg. U. S. N.
James Lawrence Little.
Orrin Porter McDonald.
James Gifford McKee, A. A., Surg. U. S. A.
Thomas Knowlton Marcy.

Erskine Mason, A. B. 1857, Asst. Dem. Anat. 1861–66, and Dem. Anat. 1866–70.
David Matthews, Surg. 143d N. Y. S. Vols.
Barnet Wisner Morse, Asst. Surg. 27th N. Y. S. V.
Archibald Finn Mudie, Asst. Surg. U. S. V.
George Andrew Mursick, Asst. Surg. U. S. V.
William Sheldon Clark Perkins.
Howard Pinckney, A.M. elsewhere, Surg. U. S. V.
Oren Day Pomeroy.
James Henry Pooley, Jr., Asst. Surg. U. S. A.
Peter Prius
John George Ryerson, A. M. elsewhere.
Charles Mase Samson.
Orin Henry Seeds.
Benjamin Avery Segur.
Elbridge Gilbert Seymour, Asst. Surg. 94th N.Y. S. V.
Dwight Delavan Stebbins, A. B. elsewhere.
George Miller Sternberg, Asst. Surg. U. S. A.
William Harrison Studley, A. M. elsewhere.
George Edwin Summers, A.B. N. Jers. 1857, A. M. N. Jers.
Charles James Taggart.
William Faulds Thoms.
Julius Vaughan.
Edmund Carlyle Ver Meulen, Asst. Surg. U. S. N.
Joel Addington Warren.
Augustus Purdy Williams, Surg. U. S V.

53

## 1861.

George Badger, A. A. Surg. U. S. A.
William Badger, A. A. Surg. U. S. A.
John Conner Barron, Asst. Surg. 69th N. Y. S. V.
*Thomas Barrow. aet. 23. *1861
John Philip Benkard.
William Alexander Betts.
William Blundell.
Ryckman D. Bogert, Asst. Surg. 6th N. Y. Art.
Basil Brown Brashear.
Samuel Nelson Brayton, Asst. Surg. U. S. N.
Asahel Norton Brockway, A. B. Hamil. Coll. 1857, A. A. Surg. U. S. V.
William McQueen Bryce, Asst. Surg. 144th N.Y.S.V.
Edmund Shackelford Carew.
George William Carleton, A. B. William's 1858.
William Henry Carmalt.
Charles Carter, Surg. U.S.A.
Matthew Chalmers, A. B. Yale 1858 and A.M. Yale, Asst. Surg. U. S. N.
John Francis Hamlin Chipman.
F. Munson Coan.
George Rogers Cutter, Surg. 127th N. Y. V.
Henry Munson Dean, Asst. Surg. U. S. V.
Louis George De Alois.
Daniel McComb Devendorf.
John Abbott Douglass, Jr., A. B. Bowdoin Coll. 1854, Surg. 11th Mass. V.
Albert Fairfax.
Benjamin Franklin Fogg.
Winfield Scott Fuller, Surg. 78th N. Y. S. V.
Franklin Benjamin Galbraith.
Josiah H. Goddard.
James Grange.
Thomas E. Hamilton.
Jerome Hibbard.
Henry W. Hitchcock.

Edgar Holden, A.B. N. Jers. 1859, Asst. Surg. U. S. N.
John Thomas Kennedy, A.A. Surg. U. S. A.
Charles John Kipp, Surg. U. S. V.
Thompson Bailey Lewis.
Seth Stephen Lounsbery, Surg. N. Y. S. V.
Henry Munson Lyman, A. B. William's 1858, A. A. Surg. U. S. A.
Carrington McFarlane, Surg. 115th N. Y. S. V.
Edward Gardner Marshall, Asst. Surg. 124th N. Y. S. V.
B. Ellis Martin, Asst. Surg. 5th N. Y. S. V.
William Hammett Martin, A. B. 1857 and A.M. 1860.
Theodore Millspaugh.
Richard H. Moore.
Alfred North, A. B. Brown Univ. 1858.
James H. Noyes.
Andrew T. Pearsall.
William B. Pierce.
*Henry Sylvanus Plympton, M. D. Harv. 1860. *1863
Alfred Edgar Martindale Purdy.
Charles H. Reynolds.
Charles Douglas Rigby.
John Wilson Robie.
John Shrady, Jr., A. B. 1849 and A. M. 1852, Surg. U. S. V. 1862–4.
Heber Smith, Asst. Surg. U. S. N.
Normand Smith, A. B. Yale 1858.
Norman Leslie Snow.
Frederick Dennis Sturges, A. A. Surg. U. S. A.
Charles Henry Suydam, Asst. Surg. 27th N. J. V.
Norman Leslie Swan, A. B. elsewhere.
Gilbert T. Totten, A. B. 1858.
Garrett W. Veeder Van Voast, A.B. Union 1857 and A.M. Union, A. A. Surg. U. S. A.
Maus Rosa Vedder.
Edwin Fletcher Ward.
Robert Watts, Jr., Surg. 133d N. Y. S. V.
William Lamont Wheeler, Asst. Surg. U. S. N.
John Phillips Payson White, A. B. elsewhere, Surg. 10th N. Y. S. V.
Charles M. Wight, Asst. Surg. 26th N. Y. S. V.
Benjamin Franklin Wilson. 70

## 1862.

George Pierce Andrews.
Cyrus Ebenezer Baker.
George Page Bassett.
William Whitfield Bowlby, Surg. 3d N. J. Cav.
George Marsden Brennan.
John Weston Brennan.
Sidney Rogers Burnap, Surg. N. Y. S. V.
Garabed Caloosdian.
John Ely Carey.
Thomas Knowlton Chandler.
*Abel Blood Conant, Surg. 3d Kent. V., Lect. on Physiol. Univ. Vermont. aet. 28 *1864
William Conover, A. B. N. Jers. 1859.
*Henry White Cooke. aet. 26. *1863
James Russell Cumming, Asst. Surg. 12th Conn. V.
William Floyd Cushman, A. B. 1859.
Rem Lefferts Disbrow.
Barnard Douglass Eastman.
William Eddy.
Henry Marlyn Field, A. B. Harv. 1859.

Frank Pierce Foster, A. A. Surg. U S. A.
Gustavus Scott Franklin.
William James Gilfillan.
William Henry Harlin.
Solomon E. Hasbrouck.
Jonathan Havens.
Andrew H. Hershey.
George Hopkins, A. A. Surg. U. S. A.
Lewis Slocomb Horton.
Numon N. Horton, Surg. 47th U. S. Col. Inf.
William Malcolm James.
John Andrew Jaume.
Dan Lee Jewett, Asst. Surg. 20th Conn. V.
Eldridge Monroe Johnson.
Joseph Dodson Lomax.
William Simmons Ludlum, A. B. 1847 and A. M. 1850.
Frederick Wentworth Mercer.
William Thomas Nealis, A. B. St. Joseph's Coll. Ohio 1858, and A. M. St. Joseph's, Surg. 69th N. Y. S. V.
Edward Monroe Norwood, Surg. 4th E. Tenn. V.
*George Herschel Olmsted, A. A. Surg. U. S. A. *1863
William Browne Orchard.
Edmund Morris Pease.
George Porter.
William Chardavoyne Pryer.
Nathaniel B. Reber.
Jasper Godsvenor Reynolds.
John A. Robinson, Asst. Surg. 38th N. Y. S. V.
William H. Rockwell, Jr.
Frank H. Roof.
George Schuyler Rugg, Asst. Surg. N. Y. S. V., Surg.-in-Chief 2d and 3d Brigades Art. Reserves, Army of the Potomac.
Henry Thatcher Sears.
Samuel Francis Shaw.
Franklin Staples.
Thomas Hunt Stilwell.
John L. Swift.
Amazias Walter Tryon, Asst. Surg. 100th N. Y. V.
Edwin Morrison Ward, A. B. N. Jers. 1859.
Richard Halsted Ward, A. B. William's 1858, A.A. Surg. U. S. A.
James H. Wheeler.
Merrit H. Wilson.

59

## 1863.

William Bruce Almon.
Wendell Abraham Anderson, Surg. 3d Maryland Vol. Inf.
Alonzo Brayton Ball, A. B. Yale 1860.
John Sterling Bird.
Joseph Bird, A. B. N. Jers. 1860.
Lewis Henry Bodman.
Wesley M. Carpenter.
George Augustus Christie, M. D. Royal Coll. Surg. Edinburgh 1864.
Edward Cowles.
Albert E. Croucher.
Rezin Pollard Davis.
Walter De Forest Day, A. B. William's 1859, San. Supt. N. Y. C.
Francis Delafield, A. B. Yale 1860.
Samuel Demarest, Jr.
*George Clinton Dewey, A.B. William's 1860 and A. M. Will. aet. 23. *1864
John Elderkin, A.B. Yale 1852 and A. M. Yale, Asst. Surg. 10th U. S. Col. Inf.
George M. Engs, A. B Yale 1860.
David Osburn Farrand.
Jacob T. Field, A. B. elsewhere.

Samuel A. Fitch, A. B. elsewhere, Asst. Surg. N. Y. S. V.
De Witt C. Fowler.
Walter Roberts Gillette, A.B. Mad. Univ. 1861.
Frank West Goodall.
Wait Robbins Griswold, A.B. Yale 1844.
Charles Everett Hall, A. B. N. Jers. 1860.
Frank Granger Hasbrouck.
John Cornelius Hasbrouck.
David Webb Hodgkins, A. A. Surg. U. S. A.
Edward Kelly Hogan, Asst. Surg. U. S. V., Bvt. Maj. U. S. V. 1865.
James Hutchinson.
Woolsey Johnson, A. B. N. Jers. 1860 and A. M. N. Jers. 1863.
Charles S. Kittredge.
William Lee, Lect. on Physical and Micr. Anat. National Med. Coll. Washington, D. C.
Elias Lester, Med. Director U. S. V.
Irving Whitall Lyon, M. D. Univ. Vt., Dem. Anat. Berkshire Med. Coll. 1862, A. A. Surg. U. S. A.
Henry Emmet McCartin.
Theodore A. McGraw.
David Magie, Jr., A. B. N. Jer. 1859.
George Van Rensselaer Merrill, Surg. 6th U. S. Col. Inf.
Martin Alexander Miller.
Lucius Mills, A. B. elsewhere.
Sherman Morse.
*John D. Nicoll. *1863
Wilbur Fisk Nutten.
Patrick Pendergast, Asst. Surg. 107th N. Y. S. V.
Charles Leander Pierce.
Peter Van Schaack Pruyn, A. B. elsewhere, Asst. Surg. N. Y. S. V.
Burr Schermerhorn, Asst. Surg. 108th N. Y. Vols.
Abner Orimel Shaw, Surg. 20th Maine V.
Amos Shaw, Jr., Asst. Surg. 41st N. Y. S. V.
Andrew Jackson Smith.
Joseph George Smith.
Thomas Thompson, Asst. Surg. N. Y. S. V.
Jacob Francis Tourtelotte.
Lewis Arnold Tracy.
Samuel D. Wadsworth, A. B. elsewhere.
De Witt Webb.
Walter Henry Wentworth.
Lewis Westfall.
Benjamin Wilson.
Gustavus S. Winston.
*Lockwood DeForest Woodruff, A. B. Free Acad. N. Y. C. *1876

62

## 1864.

Samson American.
Theophilus H. Andress.
George W. Baker, A. B. Union 1861 and A. M. Union, A. A. Surg. U. S. A.
Philip Hale Barton, A. A. Surg. U. S. N.
William Hunter Birckhead.
John Bedell Boss.
Richard B. Brown, A. B. Yale 1860, Asst. Surg. U. S. V., Bvt. Major U. S. V. 1865.
George J. Bucknall, A. B. elsewhere.
J. Otis Burt, A. B. Harv. 1858, Asst. Surg. U. S. N.
Adolphe Carit.
Francis P. Casey.
Samuel Fletcher Chapin.
Albert T. Chapman.
George W. Currier.
Thomas A. Cuzner.

*Henry A. Danker, Asst. Surg. U. S. N. *1864
Henry A. Darby.
Albert Austin Davis.
Charles De Cockerille.
*Henry J. Devlin. aet. 25 *1864
Dwight Dudley.
George H. Dunbar.
Francis D. Edgerton, M. D. elsewhere, A. B. Wesleyan Univ. 1861.
Henry Clay Eno, A. B. Yale 1860.
D. Darwin Everett.
Edward Farrell.
Archelaus G. Field, M. D. Sterling Med. Coll. Ohio 1854.
Luther P. Fitch, A. B. Beloit Coll. and A. M. Beloit, Asst. Surg. 47th U. S. Col. Inf.
John H. Furman.
Archibald McI. Gregory, A. A. Surg. U. S. N.
David L. Laight.
John C. Holmes.
John C. Hooper.
William Warner Hoppin, Jr., A. B. Brown Univ. and A. M. Brown, LL. B. 1869.
George W. Hosmer.
Edgar G. Janeway, A. B. Rutgers 1860 and A. M. Rutg.
Joseph Edward Janvrin, Asst. Surg. 15th N. H. Vols.
William H. Kinney.
Henry M. Knowles.
William Baldwin Linsly, A. A. Surg. U. S. A.
William A. Lockwood.
William M. McKay.
James W. McLane, A. B. Yale 1861.
Daniel E. McSweeny, A. B. St. Francis Xavier's Coll. 1861 and A. M. St. F. X., A. A. Surg. U. S. A.
George J. Northrup, Asst. Surg. U. S. V.
George B. Oakes.
Henry Eagle Ogden, A. B. Union 1862.
Benjamin Maltby Page.
John Prince Pemberton, A. B. 1849 and A. M. 1852.
James L. Phillips.
Henry G. Piffard, A. B. Univ. N. Y. C. 1862, Prof. Univ. Med. Dept. N. Y. C.
Stephen C. Powell.
*Alfred Pryor. *1865
Charles S. Robert.
Stephen W. Roof.
Allen S. Russell, Surg.-in-Chief 3d Brig. Hardin's Div. 22d Army Corps.
Thomas Taunton Sabine, A. B. 1861 and A. M. 1863, Adj. Prof. Anat.
John P. Schenck, Jr.
William F. Scoresby.
George W. Stout.
Edward Constant Seguin, Asst. Surg. U. S. V.
Charles E. Simmons.
Henry Lyle Smith.
Montross L. Smith.
*William R. Stilwell. *1864
Freman Stoddard.
Edward W. Thompson, Asst. Surg. U. S. A.
William Thurman.
Elbert P. Tibbals.
John R. Todd.
Platon Vallejo.
Augustus Van Courtlandt.
Frederick D. Vanderhoof, Asst. Surg. 51st N. Y. Vet. Vols.
William P. Warren.
Lathrop P. Weaver.
George G. Wheelock, A. B. Harv. 1860.
J. Elias Whitehead, A. B. Rutgers 1844 and A. M. Rutg.
Thomas Wight.
William S. Willis, Surg. 1st N. J. Cav. 80

## 1865.

Andrew Anderson.
Calvin Anderson.
Harvey Napoleon Austin.
*George Washington Bacon, A. B. 1854, A. M. 1857, LL. B. 1862. *1874
Richard Smith Bacon, A. B. 1859, A. M. 1862, LL. B. 1862.
James E. Barbour.
George Lewis Beers, A. B. Yale 1860 and A. M. Yale.
Christopher M. Bell.
Timothy Bigelow.
Henry Edward Bissett, A. A. Surg. U. S. A.
Edward Bleecker.
Sylvester S. Bogert.
Theodore Dwight Bradford, A. B. elsewhere.
John Boyd Campbell.
Dexter Selwyn Clark, A. B. Beloit Coll. 1860, Asst. Surg. 25th Ill. Vols. 1863–4 and Surg. 1864.
Lucian Dean Clark.
Charles A. Conover.
Thomas Vaughn Crandall, A. A. Surg. U. S. A.
Clarence E. De Wolfe.
James A. De Wolfe, A. B. Brown Univ. and A. M. Brown.
Richard Dey.
Andrew J. Disbrow.
Alvan Dodge.
Frank O. Earle.
Daniel H. Fairweather.
Levi Farrow.
Edwin B. Flagg, A. M. elsewhere.
Horace S. Fuller, A. M. elsewhere.
Charles F. George.
John Francis Gignoux, A. M. elsewhere.
William Chalk Gouinlock.
John R. Greenleaf, Jr.
Edward D. Griffin.
Thomas Haigh, A. A. Surg. U. S. A. 1864.
William Henry Hoag.
Stephen E. De Witt Hoornbeck.
David Post Jackson.
John Clarkson Jay, Jr.
Parley H. Johnson.
Edgar K. Kelley.
Daniel W. Kissam.
James F. Laughlin.
John B. Learned.
John Lawrence Lee.
Thomas W. Lowerree, Jr.
John Gilman McAllaster, A. A. Surg. U. S. A.
John C. Minor.
Alfred Mitchell, A. M. elsewhere.
Lawrence O. Morgan.
Martin Luther Overton.
Joseph Otis Pinneo.
John A. Purney.
Eli D. Sargent.
Peter Laurence Schenck, A. B. elsewhere.
Tennis Schenck, A. B. elsewhere.
Octavius Barrell Shreve, A. B elsewhere.
Elijah Herman Smith
James Welch Smith.
Albert Leroy W. Stephenson.
William George Stevenson.
Alexander Stewart, A. B. elsewhere.
Jay Stephen Stone.
David L. Stricklin.
James Buckley Tweedle.
Nelson S. Westcott.
Alvord E. Winchell, A. M. elsewhere.
Russell Withers.
George Powell Wright.
68

## 1866.

Lewis Applegate.

David Penfield Austin.
Edward Woodbridge Avery.
James McMillan Ayer, A. B. elsewhere.
Silas Cook Baldwin.
George Miller Beard, A. B. Yale 1862 and A. M. Yale.
William Graham Bryson.
Lafayette Bugbee.
George Owen Burgess.
George Cary.
Charles Frederick Clarke, A. B. 1863 and A. M. 1866.
Thomas Edwards Clark.
John Wordsworth Clemesha.
William S. Combs, A.M. elsewhere.
William Augustine Conway.
Adam C. Corson.
David Magie Cory.
John Cowan
Patrick W. Cremin.
Benjamin Frederick Dawson.
Laban Dennis.
John J. De Motte.
Marcus Dodd.
John William Dooley.
Henry Dusenbury.
Edward Smith Eveleth.
James Anderson Exton.
Daniel McLean Forman.
Addison Howard Foster.
David R. Francis.
Edward Frothingham.
John Pool Garrish, Jr.
Ralph Schuyler Goodwin.
Jay Levins Greene.
James Romeyn Gregory.
George Wheelock Grover.
Orrin Franklin Harris.
Samuel Harris.
George Elias Hawes, A. B. elsewhere.
Tecumseh K. Holmes.
Edward R. Hun, A. B. elsewhere.
Joseph Slater Hunt.
James B. Hunter.
Edward Carroll Huse.
Edwin Hutchinson, A. M. elsewhere, Ph. B. Yale. 1860.
James C. Hutchinson.
Stephen Hyde.
Richard Douglas James.
Joseph Johnson.
Henry De Witt Joy.
Robert P. Jump, and elsewhere.
Samuel Lisle Kennedy.
James Suydam Knox, A. M. elsewhere.
Mortimer Lampson.
Archibald Lawson.
Charles E. Lee.
Thomas Le Guen.
Algernon Sidney Leonard.
Walter Lindsay.
Samuel Kuypers Lyon, A. .B 1860, A. M. 1863.
William Henry McKelvie.
Edward Macomb, A. M. elsewhere.
Isaac Newton Mead.
John Calvin Mead.
George Le Roy Menzie.
Hubbard Winslow Mitchell.
William Morton.
John Moore.
George Washington Newcomb.
Henry D. Nicoll, A. B. elsewhere.
Joseph O'Dwyer.
John Wright Ostrander.
Edwin Phillips.
Charles Talbot Poore.
Francisco Repetto.
William G. Ridout.
Charles Roth.
Samuel Fowler Rouse.
Dayton Wykoff Searle.
Thomas Skelding.
David Augustine Smith.
Samuel St. John Smith.
Whitmer Snively.
Richmond Joseph Southworth.
Richard Henry Stone.

Joseph Stubbs.
James Madison Study.
Ralph Partridge Thatcher.
Walter Ure.
James D. Van Der Veer.
Henry Clay Van Gieson.
Cornelius Van Riper.
Frederick Judd Van Wagner.
Henry Freeman Walker, A.M. elsewhere.
Charles Washburn.
Peter Wheeler.
Samuel Whitall.
Henry Simmons White, LL. B. 1870.
James Wright Wilson.
Joseph Sands Winston.
Augustus Wohlfarth.
Alfred H. Woodill.
Joel Williston Wright.
Gerardus Willis Wynkoop.
George Ludlow Yost.
Charles Young, A. M. elsewhere.
William Henry Young.

107

## 1867.

Thomas R. Almon.
Theodore F. Alverson.
John W. Baldwin.
Oglevie D. Ball.
Frederick S. Barclay.
Willis J. Beach.
Herbert C. Belden.
Charles M. Billings, A. M. elsewhere.
James A. Blanchard.
Francis V. Brush.
Albert H. Buck, A. B. Yale 1864.
Charles C. Buckley.
Charles A. Carle.
Frank Carter.
Philo W. Clark.
James D. Clyde.
James E. Cooper.
Frederick S. Creelman.
Samuel Decker.
John O'Fallon Delany.
Laban Dennis.
Charles M. Des Brisay.
Stephen M. Disbrow.
Francis Du Bois, Jr., A. B. elsewhere.
Morton W. Easton, A. B. Yale 1863.
Jonathan Edwards, Jr., A. B. Yale 1863.
Frederick W. Elberg, A. M. elsewhere.
William S. Ely, A. B. elsewhere.
Bache McEvers Emmet.
Charles W. Ferguson.
David F. Fetter.
James N. Fitch, A. B. elsewhere.
Edward T. Fuller.
Burns Gilman.
Zeeb Gilman, Jr.
Frederick Gilnack.
Harry Gove.
Henry Gray.
Emile Gruening.
Martin Hagan.
John D. Hall, A. B. elsewhere.
Henry E. Handerson, A. M. elsewhere.
Daniel De W. Harrington.
Audley Haslett, A. M. elsewhere.
Henry Henderson, A. M. elsewhere.
Edward J. Hogan.
George F. Hollick.
Charles H. Horton.
Erasmus Darwin Hudson, Jr., A. B. elsewhere.
Stephen J. Hutchinson.
Thomas L. Janeway, A. M. elsewhere.
Samuel Johnson.
Henry I. Jordan, A. B. elsewhere.
John J. Keator.
John J. Ketchum.

William A. Kissam.
Eustis F. Langdon, A. B. elsewhere.
William M. Lyttleton.
William C. McFarland.
Theodore Dwight Martin.
Stuyvesant Fish Morris, A. B. 1863.
David H. Muir.
George W. Murdock.
John H. Murfee.
Henry E. Owen, A. B. Yale 1864.
William H. Palmer, A. B. elsewhere.
James F. Peyton.
Edward R. Post, A. M. elsewhere.
William H. B. Pratt, A. B. Yale 1864.
Albert R. Randol.
Ira Remsen.
Nathan S. Roberts.
George W. Robinson, A. M. elsewhere.
John W. Robinson.
Charles F. Rodenstein, A. M. elsewhere.
Albert S. Rogers.
Eugene B. Sanborn.
Charles R. Sanderson, and Cleveland Med. Coll.
Thomas Edward Satterthwaite, Yale 1864.
Thomas Sidney Scales, A. B. elsewhere.
Warren Schoonover, A. B. elsewhere.
Alonzo De Loos Smith.
Josiah P. Sugg.
Thomas Terrill, Jr.
Henry C. Turner.
James Vanderpool, A. B. elsewhere.
Nicholas Berdan Von Houten.
James Van Derveer Van Nest.
Richard C. Van Wyck.
William A. M. Wainwright, A. B. elsewhere.
Eli Warner.
George Wells, Jr.
John Winslow, and Bellevue Med. Coll. N. Y. C.
Silas O. Witherbee.
Willard Parker Worster, A. B. 1863, A. M. 1866.

95

## 1868.

Frederick Mixer Aitken.
Philip Edward Arcularius, A. M. elsewhere.
William Augustus Avery.
John Neilson Beekman, A. B. 1864, A. M. 1867.
Joseph Ritner Benjamin, A. M. elsewhere.
John Ferguson Black, A. B. elsewhere.
Thomas Sheldon Bond, A. M. and M. D. elsewhere.
Calvin F. Bonney.
George Henry Bosley, and elsewhere.
Benjamin Mills Briggs, M. S. elsewhere.
Charles Stedman Bull, A. B. 1864, A. M. 1867.
John Anthon Callender.
William Jessup Chandler.
Henry Waldburg Coleman.
Jonathan Ackerman Coles, A. B. 1864, A. M. 1867.
William Albert Corwin.
Samuel Pierce Craig.
Charles Culver.
Byron Cummings.
Henry Nehemiah Dodge.
Matthew Brinckerhoff Du Bois, A. B. 1864, A. M. 1867.
John Luther Duryee, A. M. elsewhere.
Henry O. Ely, A. B. elsewhere.

David Combs English.
George Emory Foster, A. M. elsewhere.
Edward Frankel.
Gustav Frauenstein.
Samuel Horace Frazer.
Charles D. T. Gibson, A. B. elsewhere.
Theodore Giddings.
James Glynn Gregory, A. B. elsewhere.
William Edward Griffiths.
Albert E. Ham, A. B. elsewhere.
Frederick Fanning Harral, A. M. elsewhere.
George Fuller Hawley.
Frederick Porteous Henry.
Neil Jamieson Hepburn, A. M. elsewhere.
Joseph Bassette Holland, A. M. elsewhere.
Charles Taylor Jewett.
Herschel Vespasian Johnson, Jr.
Adoniram Brown Judson, A. M. and M. D. elsewhere.
John Marshall Kellogg.
Warren Kemble.
Thomas H. Kenan.
Frederick Kidder.
Edwin A. Kilbourne.
Charles Laight.
A. J. Lanterman.
Charles Henry Leonard, A.B. elsewhere.
Charles Edward Lockwood, A. B. elsewhere.
James E. M. Lordly.
John Tarleton Luck.
Robert Louis Lusby.
David Valentine Lynch.
Frederick Dey Marshall.
Frederick D. R. Marshall.
James Joseph McCarty.
Daniel McEwan, Jr.
Robert James McGay.
John Hector McKay.
John Abner Mead, A. M. elsewhere.
Morris Henry Miesse.
Henry James Miller.
John Nolan.
Aggeus Outerbridge.
Julius L. Parke, A. M. elsewhere.
Charles B. Parkhurst.
Howard Whited Phillips.
James Oakley Pingry.
John Joseph Prendergast, A. M. elsewhere.
Monroe T. Pultz.
Robert Morgan Rea.
Philippe Ricord.
Frank Warren Rockwell, A. B. elsewhere.
Charles S. Rodman.
William Chambers Rogers.
William H. Ross, Jr.
Wallace Edgar Sabin.
Morton Jerome Sands.
Edward William Schauffler.
Walter Keeler Scofield.
John Sharp, A. B. elsewhere.
Charles Stuart Sheldon, A. M. and M. D. elsewhere.
George Henry Sherman.
Daniel MacMartin Stimson, A. M. elsewhere.
Stephen Van Wickle Stout.
Henry Tunstall Strong, A. B. elsewhere.
Benjamin Ralph Swan.
Robert William Taylor.
Charles Henry Thompson.
Samuel William Torrey, A. B. elsewhere.
Roger Sherman Tracy.
Thomas Hall Tripler.
John Bennett Tyler, A. B. elsewhere.
Jerome Walker.
Leslie Dodd Ward.
John William Warth, Jr., A. M. elsewhere.
Francis Henry Weismann.

Frank Wilmarth, A. M. elsewhere.
Theodore Frelinghuysen Wolfe.
John Frank Young.

101

## 1869.

Amos Wilson Abbott.
George Henry Aiken.
Clinton Atkinson.
Charles Howell Bailey, and elsewhere.
George Henry Balleray.
George Wilson Bell.
Henry M. Bishop.
James Augustus Blake, A. B. and M. D. elsewhere.
Hector Seager Bowen.
Edward Bennett Bronson, A. B. elsewhere.
Lawton Stickney Brooks.
Lucius Duncan Bulkley, A. B. elsewhere.
Richard Winthrop Bull.
Edward Worthington Burnett.
Craft Coast Carroll.
William Hanford Cartter, and elsewhere.
Charles Hoag Case.
Curtis Chapman.
James Francis Chapman.
Sherman Hartwell Chapman, A. B. elsewhere.
Nelson Henry Claflin.
John Ralph Coffman, and elsewhere.
Gustavus Pierrepont Davis, A. B. elsewhere.
Francis E. Doughty, and elsewhere.
John Edwards.
Nathaniel Bright Emerson, A. M. elsewhere.
Julius Fehr.
Ira William Fletcher.
Seth Burnham Foster.
Alonzo Freeman.
Charles Lindol French.
Omer Tousey Gillett, A. B. elsewhere.
William Joseph Haine.
George Adelbert Hathaway.
Russel Thayer Hayes, and elsewhere.
George Benedict Hickok, A. M. elsewhere.
Augustus Villery Hill, A. B. elsewhere.
Urban Gillespie Hitchcock, A. B. elsewhere.
William Mulligan Hodges.
Charles Barnes Huffman.
John Hurdsfield.
Andrew Jackson Jessup.
John Henry Korff.
Isadore Perrin Latour, A. B. elsewhere.
John Howard Lever.
Newton Adams Lindley.
James Cook Linsly, A. M. elsewhere.
Justin Martin.
Forster Jonas Maynard.
Joseph Williams McCall, and elsewhere.
John Cameron McDougall.
John McGuirk.
Thomas Joseph McLoughlin.
Malcolm McLean.
Henry McManus, A. M. elsewhere.
Augustus Aloysius Moloney.
Jesse Lee Morrill.
Eugene Bernard Murtha, A. M. elsewhere.
James Robert Nelson.
Ashel Griswold Nettleton.
Stephen Pierson.
Thomas Jefferson Pitner, B. S. elsewhere.
William Mecklenburgh Polk.
Joseph Henry Raymond, A. B. elsewhere.
John Joseph Reid.

Benjamin Clapp Riggs, A. B. elsewhere.
Orville Forrest Rogers.
Leavitt Sanderson.
William Darwin Schuyler.
Jefferson Scoonover.
Xenophon Christmas Scott, A. M. and M. D. elsewhere.
Alexander Grant Sinclair.
Charles Elihu Slocum.
Horatio Nelson Spencer, Jr. A. B. elsewhere.
Louis D. Sproat.
Ralph Edward Starkweather, A. M. elsewhere.
Charles Sackett Starr, A. B. elsewhere.
Darwin Adelbert Stewart.
Charles Stokes, Jr.
Louis Stoskopf, A. M. elsewhere.
Erastus Perry Swasey.
David Thompson.
Charles Alonzo Todd.
William Sheridan Todd, A. M. elsewhere.
Edward Torrey.
Thomas Trenaman.
William Henry Vail, A. M. elsewhere.
John Van Harlengen.
George Wackerhagen.
Charles Edwards Willard.
William Bull Wright.
Samuel Monell Zabriskie.

## 1870.

J. Freeman Atwood.
Daniel S. Ayers, Jr.
Lewis Balch.
Arthur A. Barrows, A. B. elsewhere.
John A. Bevan.
John M. Bigelow, A. M. elsewhere.
Eugene P. Boise, A. B. and M. D. elsewhere.
George P. Bradley.
William Brand.
Eugene W. Brooks.
James Y. Bryce.
Harvey S. Calderwood.
Stewart Church.
Staats V. D. Clark.
Leartus Connor, A. M. elsewhere.
Frederic C. Curtis, A. M. elsewhere.
John G. Curtis, A. M. elsewhere.
Nathaniel Pendleton Dandridge, A. B. Kenyon Coll. Ohio 1866.
Henry C. Day.
William J. Duffield.
Herbert M. Eddy, A. M. and M. D. elsewhere.
Charles Enfield.
Edwin Evans.
James D. Featherstonhaugh, Jr., A. B. elsewhere.
Charles O. Files, A. B. elsewhere.
Charles A. Foster.
Bernhard Grunhut, A. B. elsewhere.
George M. Haines.
William E. Hall.
Allan McLane Hamilton.
D. Brainerd Hunt, A. M. elsewhere.
Walter Judson, A. M. elsewhere.
92 Eugene Kingman.
Hugh S. Kinmonth.
George M. Lefferts, A. M. elsewhere.
Albert H. Little.
Samuel O. Loughridge, and elsewhere.
William Markham.
George Martin.
Frederic R. Marvin.
Robert Mason.
Charles McBurney, Jr., A. M elsewhere.
John V. Morgan.

Samuel H. Morris.
Albert J. Murdock.
Willard Parker, Jr., A. B. 1866.
Henry T. Pierce, A. B. elsewhere.
Milton G. Planck, A. B. elsewhere.
Frederic Powers.
Robert Prentiss.
Robert A. Quin.
William H. T. Reynolds, A.M. elsewhere.
Joseph S. Ripley.
Francis E. Ross, and elsewhere.
John D. Rushmore.
Francis F. Sanders, A. B. elsewhere.
Francis A. Stanley.
Samuel B. St. John, A. M. elsewhere.
George M. Swain.
Robert E. Thompson.
Clayton W. Townsend.
David Clark Van Deursen.
William H. Vermilye.
Luis Puertas Walton, A. B. 1861, A. M. 1864.
George H. Whaley.
Francis A. Wheeler.
Howard Whiting.
Charles T. Whybrow.
John P. Wilson.

69

## 1871.

Caleb Huntington Atwater.
William Vestus Balch.
Frank Edwin Beckwith, and M. D. elsewhere.
Albert Clark Benedict.
George Duckworth Bleything.
James Peter Boyd, Jr., A. B. elsewhere.
Richard C. Brandeis, A. B. elsewhere.
Walter Abram Brooks.
Frederic Samuel Buckingham.
Herbert Cutler Bullard, A. M. elsewhere.
Archibald Campbell.
Charles Walter Chamberlain, A. B. elsewhere.
Edward Baron Chandler.
Clement Cleveland, A. M. elsewhere.
Henry Cochran.
Fetterman Wine Conn.
Joseph Felix Corrigan, A. M. elsewhere.
Henry M. Cox, A. B. elsewhere.
Horatio Nelson Crane, and M. D. elsewhere.
Ernest Watson Cushing, A. B. elsewhere.
Bennett Franklin Davenport, A. M. elsewhere.
James Henry Davenport, A. B. elsewhere.
William Burr Dunning, A. B. elsewhere.
Henry Thurloe Elliot.
Eustace Whipple Fisher, A. M. elsewhere.
Charles Forbes.
George Bingham Fowler.
John James Frederick.
Thomas Rushmore French.
Edwin Alonzo Goodridge, A. M. elsewhere.
John Frederic Schiller Gray.
John Price Harley.
Theodore Romeyne Hornblower.
Jacob Frank Howe.
George Huntington.
Francis Linsly Ives.
Charles Jewett, A. M. elsewhere.
Champion Hiram Judson.
Frank Parker Kinnicutt, A. B. elsewhere.
Hugo Kuenstler.
Daniel Lewis, A. B. elsewhere.

Edward Lewis Chichester Macwithey.
Philip James Maguire.
Matthew Darbyshire Mann, A. B. elsewhere.
Joseph Wilkins Marsee.
Edward Elias Mather, A. B. elsewhere.
Thomas Alexander McBride, A. B. elsewhere.
Robert Emmet McCauley.
Arthur H. McFarland, A. B. elsewhere.
Archibald Mercer, A. B. elsewhere.
Cyrus Strong Merrill.
Francis Johnston Metcalfe.
Albert Judson Minor.
William Seth Mitchell, A. M. elsewhere.
Henry Moeller.
Henry Smith Noble, A. B. elsewhere.
Edwin De Witt Nooney.
John Francis Oaks.
Jackson Brainard Pellet.
John Edwin Pope, A. B. elsewhere.
John Duncan Quackenbos, A. B. 1668, A. M. 1871.
William Rankin, Jr., A. B. elsewhere.
John Orlando Roe, and M. D. elsewhere.
Clarence Satterlee.
William John Scott.
Marsh Shaw.
Charles Simpson, A. B. elsewhere.
Henry Melville Smith.
James Wesley Smith.
George Monroe Steele, B. S. elsewhere.
Alexander Strong.
Augustus Walter Suiter.
Henry Storer Swan.
Mahlon Edwin Swartz.
William Clark Telford.
James Luther Terry, A. B. elsewhere.
Edward Livingston Trudeau.
George Alexander Van Wagenen, A. B. elsewhere.
William Barry Wallace.
Edward Turnbull Ward.
William Hilton Warn, A. B. elsewhere.
E. Jansen Westfall, A. B. elsewhere.
Charles Boaz Whitfield.
Richard Dewees Wilcox.
Simon Peter Wise.

85

## 1872.

Daniel Simmons Adams.
Lemuel Bolton Bangs.
George Warner Bartow.
Guy Carleton Bayley.
James William Belvin.
Edward Sherburne Blanchard.
Peter Anthony Edward Boetzkes.
Thomas Neylor Bradfield, D. D. S. elsewhere.
William Gunton Budington.
William Tillinghast Bull, A. B. elsewhere.
William Busse.
Norman Call, A. B. elsewhere.
Henry Caminero, A. B. elsewhere.
Pantaleon Candidus.
Thomas Augustus Carson.
Henry Skelton Carter, A. B. elsewhere.
Harvey Henderson Chase.
Dennis Church, Jr.
Franklin Chase Clark, A. B. elsewhere.
Frederick Halsey Conger.
Richard Bonnet Coutant.
Charles Livingstone Dey.
Gabriel Rafael Diaz.
Charles Russell Doane.

Coert Du Bois, A. M. elsewhere.
William Willis Durden.
Barnard Ellis.
John Edwin Ensell.
Mathias Figueira.
Martin Joseph Fleming, A. M. elsewhere.
George Clarence Gage.
James A. Gladstone.
William Guden.
George Weeks Hale, A. B. elsewhere.
Henry Prentiss Harvey, and elsewhere.
James Joseph Healy.
Joseph Solomon Heine, Jr.
Joseph Julius Henna.
Edward Karck Henschell.
Charles Hitchcock, Ph. B. elsewhere.
Wyatt Hollingsworth, and elsewhere.
Allan Clark Hutton, A. B. elsewhere.
Samuel Beach Jones.
William Rollo Kinmonth.
John Deare Kline, A. M. elsewhere.
Louis Griffin Knox.
Henry August Kornemann.
John Stanislaus Martin, A. M. elsewhere.
Martin Sims Matheny.
Alfred Walter Maynard.
William Patrick Meagher.
John Arthur Montgomery.
William Oliver Moore.
Joseph Varnum Mott.
David Hutchinson Mount, A. M. elsewhere.
Denis Dowling Mulcahy.
Thomas Joseph Naughton, A. M. elsewhere.
Alfred Emanuel Regensburger.
Joel Henry Rieger.
Charles Diedrich Van Romondt.
John Henry Seabury.
Wellington Brown Searls.
George Law Sinclair.
Andrew Bartholomew Somers.
Marcus Frederic Squier.
Samuel Dillingcourt Stillwell.
Samuel Swift, Ph. B. elsewhere.
Thomas Jackson Thompson, A. B. elsewhere.
John Ross Thomson.
Cornelius Gilman Trow, A. B. elsewhere.
Charles Prentice Uhle.
John Stagg Webb.
Henry Bentley Webster, Jr.
Carl Heinrich Achilles Weider.
Nicholas Williamson, A. B. elsewhere.
Robert Bruce Wilson.
Enoch Day Woodbridge, A. B. elsewhere.

77

## 1873.

Egbert Tilton Andrews.
Frederick William Bennett.
Hermann Berendt.
Edward John Bermingham.
Gerrit Franklin Blauvelt.
Charles Erskine Brayton.
James Albert Breakell.
Charles Henry Brockway.
Joseph Scribner Burns, A. M. elsewhere.
Charles William Burton.
William Morris Butler, A. B. elsewhere.
Maurice Thomas Calnek.
William Murdock Cameron.
Archibald Murray Campbell, A. B. 1865, and A. M. 1868.
Harrie P. Chace.
Frederic Wilcox Chapin, A. B. elsewhere.
Frederick E. Clark.

Apollos Comstock, A. B. elsewhere
Joseph Peter Couse, and M. D elsewhere.
Ernest Cleveland Coxe, A. B. elsewhere.
James Edwin Crisfield.
John Beverly Crowell, B. S. elsewhere.
William Frederick Mittendorf.
Jesse Sims Montgomery, A. B. elsewhere.
Charles Hampton Moore, A. B. elsewhere.
Henry Christian Müller.
Franklin Avery Munson.
Angel Joseph Navarro, B. M. elsewhere.
Robert Fanning Noyes.
Wallace K. Oakes, A. B. elsewhere.
Matthew Charles O'Connor, A. B. elsewhere.
James Francis O'Reilly.
George Livingston Peabody, A. B. 1870, A. M. 1873.
John Edward Perry.
David Phillips.
Andrew Martin Pierce.
Enrique Carlos Rafael.
William H. Raymenton.
Joseph Redfearn, Jr.
Charles Augustus Ring, M. D. elsewhere.
Charles Clark Rublee.
Charles Frederick Schmidt.
James Chester Shafter.
Harry Lucas Sims.
Sidney Isaac Small, M. D. elsewhere.
Daniel H. Smith.
Thomas Henry Smith.
William David Spencer.
Robert Staehlin.
Vung Piau Suvoong.
Charles Turner Torrey, A. B. elsewhere.
John Meeker Townsend.
Edmund Van Wyck.
Hamilton Berrien Walker.
William Charles Walser
Theodore Benjamin Wettling.
Marshall Whiting, A. M. elsewhere.
James Manning Winslow.
Joseph Coddington Young, Jr.
Charles Benjamin Cutter.
Charles Romeyn Dake.
Nathaniel Babcock Darling.
Silas Augustus Davenport.
Henry Ganett Voorhees De Hart.
Henry Nelson Drake.
Elmer Bertly Eddy.
Arthur Mead Edwards.
Richmond Bullock Elliott, A. M. elsewhere.
Edwin Field.
Frederic Forchheimer, A. B. elsewhere.
George Cornell Freeborn.
Richard Watson Fry, and M. D. elsewhere.
Vivian Pendleton Gaines, and M. D. elsewhere.
Frank Gow.
Edward Vaughan Granger.
Richardson Gray.
John Ford Hager.
Philander A. Harris.
George Hart.
James Augustus Hart.
Thomas Francis Healy.
William Henry Hodgman.
George Payne Holmân, Jr.
Edwin Jenkins Howe.
Henry Hughes, B. S. elsewhere.
Joseph Hill Hunt.
James Polk Jackson, and M. D. elsewhere.
John Wesley Jackson, and M. D. elsewhere.
Charles Kelsey, A. B. elsewhere.
Charles Augustus Kinch, A. B. elsewhere.

# NOTE.

On page 117, there should be added after the name of Albert Merritt (class of 1873, School of Medicine) the following:

William Frederick Mittendorf.
Jesse Sims Montgomery, A.B.
Charles Hampton Moore, A. B.
Henry Christian Müller.
Franklin Avery Munson.
Angel Joseph Navarro, B. M.
Robert Fanning Noyes.
Wallace K. Oakes, A. B.
Matthew Charles O'Connor, A. B.
James Francis O'Reilly.
George Livingston Peabody, A. B. 1870, A. M. 1873.
John Edward Perry.
David Phillips.
Andrew Martin Pierce.
Enrique Carlos Rafael.
William H. Raymenton.
Joseph Redfearn, Jr.
Charles Augustus Ring, M. D.
Charles Clark Rublee.
Charles Frederick Schmidt.
James Chester Shafter.
Harry Lucas Sims.
Sidney Isaac Small, M. D.
Daniel H. Smith.
Thomas Henry Smith.
William David Spencer.
Robert Staehlin.
Vung Piau Suvoong.
Charles Turner Torrey, A. B.
John Meeker Townsend.
Edmund Van Wyck.
Hamilton Berrien Walker.
William Charles Walser.
Theodore Benjamin Wettling.
Marshall Whiting, A. M.
James Manning Winslow.
Joseph Coddington Young, Jr.

Julius Koch.
Langdon Rives Longworth, A. B. elsewhere.
Maitland Lorenzo Mallory.
James Irving Marcley.
Francis Martin, and M. D. elsewhere.
Edward Harvey Maynard.
Thomas McCosker.
Ansil Smith McIntire.
Albert Merritt. 99

## 1874.

Robert Abbe, A. B. elsewhere.
Frank Anderson, A. B. elsewhere.
Lehman P. Ashmead, Jr., A. B. elsewhere.
James Pervine Atwood.
Walter Clinton Bannard.
Joseph W. Battershall.
Edward Perry Bowles.
Charles Washington Bray.
Henry Gaylord Buckingham.
William Ebenezer Bullard, and M. D. elsewhere.
Felix A. Campuzano.
George Francis Carey.
Eduardo Casalduc.
Isaac B. Cowen.
Newton Freeman Curtis, A. B. elsewhere.
Alfred S. Dana.
Loomis LeGrand Danforth.
George A Davie.
James Joseph Delaney.
Richard G. P. Dieffenbach.
Edward Talbot Ely, A. B. elsewhere.
George Abraham Evans.
Porter Farley, A. B. elsewhere.
Joseph Fewsmith, Jr., A. B. elsewhere.
Thomas Joseph Ingoldsby Ford.
Arthur Mott Haight.
Junius Merwin Hall.
Edward Mitchell Harding.
Henry Newton Heineman, B. S. elsewhere.
J. S. Van Rensselaer Hoff, A. B. elsewhere.
Charles Alonzo Holbrook.
William Bird Hull.
Leonard Huntress, Jr., A. B. elsewhere.
Francis Hustace, A. B. 1871, A. M. 1874.
Nicholas Conover Jobs.
Weldon W. Jones.
Charles Montgomery Kellogg.
Theodore F. Kerr, A. B. elsewhere.
David Francis King.
Charles Huntoon Knight.
Charles Henry Langdon.
Walter Elliot Lauderdale, Jr.
John Willard Lee, A. B. elsewhere.
James N. Lewis.
William May.
Burnett C. McIntyre.
George Reuken Metcalf.
Lewis Miller, A. B. elsewhere.
Charles Frederic Wm. Myers.
Alexander Frederic Newman.
Isidor Pierce Oberndorfer, A. B. 1871, A. M. 1874.
Charles O. Olmstead.
Frederic Samuel Osborn.
George Washington Papen.
George William Rachel.
Frank L. Radcliffe.
Barna E. Radeker.
John Augustus Ray.
Samuel D. Rhodes.
Arthur Hopkins Rice.
Clinton Josiah Ricker,
Robert Henry Saunders.
Thomas Rutherford Savage.
John C. Shaw.
Edwin Daniel Simpson.
Charles Peck Smith.
Charles Livingston Squire.
G. Adolphus F. Steinführer.

Gustave Mozart Stoeckel, A. B. elsewhere.
Douglas Rudd Sutherland.
Robert Swan, A. B. 1871, A. M. 1874.
James Russell Taber.
Cantine Hasbrouck Ten Eyck.
Henry Mariane Thorne.
Daniel Mountfort Tolford.
Thomas M. Trego, A. M. elsewhere.
Cornelius Van Keuren.
William Wirt Wendover.
John Blake White.
Joseph Wiener.
Cornelius Williams.
Frederic Newton Winans.
Henry Worthington.
Abraham Philip Zemansky.

84

## 1875.

Thomas Herbert Allen, B. M. elsewhere.
Joseph Longworth Anderson.
Joseph Daniel Anway.
Morgan Wilcox Ayres.
Daniel Edmund Barry.
Burnham Roswell Benner,
Albert Osborn Bogert.
Alfred Victor Brailly.
George Edwin Brown.
Stephen Smith Burt.
Gonzalo Edward Buxton.
George Edward Carpenter, A. B. elsewhere.
James Harmer Casey.
Alonzo Gidley Chadsey.
James Chasey.
Frank Avery Coates, A. B. elsewhere.
John Joseph Cochran.
Edmund DeWitt Converse, and M. D. elsewhere.
Heman Dunbar Copley.
Michael Aloysius Cremin, A. M. elsewhere.
George Henry Cummings, A. B. elsewhere.
David Bryson Delavan, A. B. elsewhere.
George Morris Dillow, A. B. elsewhere.
Francis Duffy, and M. D. elsewhere
Joseph D'Vore.
George Michael Edebohls, A. B. elsewhere.
Richard Biddle Faulkner.
Chauncey Mitchell Field, A. B. elsewhere.
Crawford Ellsworth Fritts.
Jacob Fuchs.
Eugene French Gage.
John Frederick Golding.
Frank Sargent Grant.
Edward Gray, A. B. elsewhere.
G. Harrison Gray.
Frank Bertangue Green.
Nelson Henry Griffin.
Chester Webb Harvey.
Ernesto Maximilian Hegewisch.
Samuel Hendrickson.
Benjamin Leggett Holt, A. B. elsewhere.
Erastus Eugene Holt, and M. D. elsewhere.
Harmon George Howe, and M. D. elsewhere.
Walter Lowne Hunt.
Nathaniel Gerhard Hutchison.
Edward Joseph Ill,
Henry Louis Irish.
Walter Addison Jayne.
Charles Garret Johnston.
Lionel Benedict Joseph.
William Thaddeus Keeler.
John Calvin Kendall, A. B. elsewhere.
George Luther Kent,
John Beach Knapp.
Amos Knight, and M. D. elsewhere.
Henry Krollpfeiffer.
Monroe Budd Long.

Howard Williams Longyear.
Charles Robert Knight Lordly.
William Joseph P. Mackey.
Albert Warner Mallalieu.
Luther Orrin Martin.
William Platt McLaury, A. M. elsewhere.
John DeWitt Nelson.
John Henry Nesbitt.
Harris Burnett Osborne, and M. D. elsewhere.
George Alexander Oviatt, A. B. elsewhere.
Arthur Richards Paine, A. M. elsewhere.
Edward Lasell Partridge.
Edward Henry Peaslee, A. B. elsewhere.
John Condit Pennington, A. M. elsewhere.
Jeremiah Phelan.
William Henry Powell.
John Warren Rice.
Harry Edward Richards, A. B. elsewhere.
Jacob Irving Roe.
John Alexander Rogers.
Charles Buckley Roof.
Philip Marcellus Ryan.
George Schlereth.
Arthur Raymond Simmons, A. B. elsewhere.
Edward Beardsley Skellenger.
Henry George Small.
Edward Pythian Smith.
George Atherton Spalding, A. B. elsewhere.
Gottleib Stein.
John Edwin Stillwell.
Cleveland Stuart Stillwell.
Charles Edwin Swasey.
George Brooks Swasey.
John Higgins Swasey.
James Symington, Jr.
Frederick Coolidge Talcott.
Stanley Davis Terry.
Edgar Rudolphus Troxell.
William Augustus Valentine, A. M. elsewhere.
Fernando Forrester Walker.
Newell Perry Warner.
John Erastus Weaver.
William Seward Webb.
William Henry Welch, A. B. elsewhere.
Frederick Weygandt.
William John Whelan, and M. D. elsewhere.
Thomas Hastings Wight.
Edward Payson Williams.
James Little Wilson, A. B. elsewhere.
Halsey Lathrop Wood, A. M. elsewhere.
John E. Woodruff, A. B. elsewhere.

108

## 1876.

J. Alfred Andrews.
Frank A. Beck.
Russell F. Benson, Jr.
William B. Berry, A.B. elsewhere.
Arthur S. Bird, A. B. elsewhere.
Frederick W. Bissett.
John H. Blanks, M. D. elsewhere.
Alonzo Blauvelt, B. S. elsewhere.
Thomas B. Bloomfield.
Algernon T. Bristow, A. B. elsewhere.
Augustus F. Büchler.
Francis D. Buck, Ph. D. elsewhere.
John Burnett.
Henry M. Burns.
Stephen E. Churchill.
David B. Clark.
Frank P. Clark.
Alexander S. Clarke.
H. Ashland Clay.
Seth D. Close.

John Joseph Crane, A. B. elsewhere.
Franz Dastler.
David H. Davison, B. S. elsewhere.
Le Grand N. Denslow.
Benjamin F. Dexter.
James M. Donnelly.
George W. Duryee.
Ellsworth S. Ellis.
Etienne Evetsky.
Edward B. Foote, Jr.
Alfred Friedman.
Alonzo M. Garcelon.
Henry B. Garner.
Frederic P. Griswold.
William A. Hamilton, A. B. elsewhere.
Joseph B. Harrison, M. D. elsewhere.
Joseph Healy, M.D. elsewhere.
Richard L. Hoelger.
Adams C. Hoffman.
George S. Knickerbocker, A. B. elsewhere.
Newell E. Landon.
William P. Langworthy.
Charles Ward Lewis.
D. Stanley Lyons.
Frederick A. Lyons, A.B. elsewhere.
Michael A. MacDonald.
Alfred Masters.
Abraham Mayer.
Clarence C. Miles.
Theodore D. Mills, A. B. elsewhere.
Lewis B. Minor.
William D. Morgan, A.B. elsewhere.
Frank A. Morrill.
John J. M. Neville.
Russell H. Nevins.
Henry S. Oppenheimer.
Isaac Oppenheimer, A. B. and B. S. elsewhere.
De Loyd Otis.
William L. Paddock, A. B. elsewhere.
Frank Parsons.
Myron R. C. Peck, B. S. elsewhere.
Clarence C. Perry.
Edmund L. Pettengill, A. B. elsewhere.
Eugene Philippe.
George B. Pratt.
William Radloff.
Robert G. Remsen, A.B. elsewhere.
William Rhame.
Thomas P. Ryan.
William Rynne, A. B. elsewhere.
Albert H. Smith.
E. Fayette Smith, A. M. elsewhere.
George De Forest Smith.
Jared K. Smith.
Charles F. Stillman, B.S. elsewhere.
Phillip Taylor.
Franklin Townsend, Jr., B.S. elsewhere.
Lawrence D. Trowbridge.
George E. Twiss.
Lachlan Tyler.
Spencer Van Dalsen.
S. O. Vanderpoel, Jr., A. B. elsewhere.
Jacob A. Van Houten.
Edward F. Walker.
J. Augustus Walther, B. S. elsewhere.
David B. Ward, A. B. elsewhere.
Louis Weigert.
Clarke A. West, B. S. elsewhere.
William E. Wheelock, A. B. elsewhere.
Claude Wilson, A. B. elsewhere.
Howard E. Wilson.
D. Sidney Woodworth.
William G. Wright.

93

# GRADUATES IN LAW.

LL. B.

## 1860.

Daniel Pratt Baldwin, A. B. Mad. Univ. 1856, LL. D. Mad. Univ. 1872 and Wabash Coll. Ind. 1872, Judge 25th Dist. Indiana 1870–.

George Van Nest Baldwin, A. M. Rutg. Coll.

Robert Henry Boorman.

Bradbury Chandler Chetwood, A. B. Burlingt. Coll.

*Henry Woodward Cooper, A. B. 1858, A. M. 1861. *1872

Edward Salstonstall Dakin, A. B. Ham. Coll.

*Van Buren Dutton. aet. 31. *1865

Daniel Sickles Duvall, A. B. 1858.

*William Sprague Ely. *1862

Harry Allen Grant, A.B. Ham. Coll. 1858, A.M. Hamil. and Yale 1861.

Carleton Moses Herrick, A.B. 1854, A. M. 1857.

Robert Chadwick Hutchings, A. B. Coll. N. Jers., N. Y. Assemb. 1861–3, Surrogate N. Y. C. 1870.

William Henry Ingersoll.

*Isaac Henry Kirby, A. B. Univ. N. Y. C. *1862

Charles McLean Knox, Major U. S. V.

Francis Lewis Lowndes.

*William Creighton Meade, A. M. St. James Coll. 1857, U. S. V. aet. 23. *1863

William Stevens Newell.

Julius Harris Ranney, A. B. Free Acad. N. Y. C.

Fenton Rockwell.

Walter Seabury Sands, A. B. Free Acad. N. Y. C.

John Cornell Schenck.

Charles Augustus Silliman, A. B. 1850, A. M. 1853, Trustee Col. Coll.

Samuel Farland Simpson.

Theodore Murray Squires.

John Ward, Jr., A. B. 1858, A. M. 1864, M. D. Univ. N. Y. C. 1864.

Philip Lee Wilson, Lieut. U. S. V.



## 1861.

Smith Bloomfield, A. M. Free Acad. N. Y. C.

Miles Standish Bromley.

Herman Washington Bruen.

Nathaniel Barto Cooke, A. B. Yale 1859.

Cornelius Jay Du Bois, Capt. U. S. V.

John William Duer, A.B. 1859.

Jas. McLaren Breed Dwight, A. B. Yale 1846 and A. M. Yale.

Sidney Stewart Henop.

Benjamin Franklin Lee, Jr., A. B. Will. 1858.

*Philip Mesier Lydig, Jr., A. B. 1858. aet. 31. *1868

Robert Morris, Yale 1858.

Seth Miller Murdock, A. B. Harv. 1858 and A.M. Harv.

William Henry Owen, A. M. Bowd., Capt. U. S. V.

Robert Willets Pearsall.

Temple Prime.

Henry Everett Russell, A. B. N. Jers. 1859 and A. M. N. Jers.
Frederick Scoville, A.B. Univ. N. Y. C., Lieut. U. S. V.
Gabriel Mead Tooker, A. B. 1859, A. M. 1862.
Robert Noxon Toppan, A. B. Harv. 1858 and A.M. Harv.
*Prescott Hall Ward. aet. 29. *1870
James Raymond Weeks, A.B. Lafayette Coll.
Charles Hornblower Woodruff, A. B. Yale 1858.
22

## 1862.

*George Washington Bacon, A. B. 1854, A. M. 1857, M. D. 1865. *1874
Richard Smith Bacon, A. B. 1859, A. M. 1862, M. D. 1865.
Charles Wesley Bangs.
George Alexander Black, A.B. Free Acad. N. Y. C.
Daniel Webster Bond.
*Edward Carrington, Jr.,A.B. Yale 1859, Lieut. U. S. V. *1865
John Townsend Conolly, Lt. U. S. V.
William Miller Denman, A.B. Free Acad. N. Y. C.
Frederic James De Peyster, A. B. Free Acad. N. Y. C., LL. M. 1864.
Charles De Ruyter, A. B. 1860, A. M. 1863.
Robert Thomas Brown Easton, A. B. Free Acad. N. Y. C.
Edward Clarence Fraser.
Robert Goelet, Jr., A. B. 1860, A. M. 1863.
Charles Henry Hatch, A. B. Yale 1859.
Laban Gardner Hopkins, A. B. 1860, A. M. 1863.
Edmund Abdy Hurry, A. B. 1860, A. M. 1863.
Stephen Burdett Hyatt, A.B. Free Acad. N. Y. C.
Sidmon Thorne Keese, A. B. Yale 1860.
Edgar Ketchum, Jr., A. B. Free Acad. N. Y. C.
George Mason Miller, A. B. 1860, A. M. 1863.
Bruce Moffatt.
Augustus White Nicoll, A. B. Univ. N. Y. C.
Thomas Ludlow Ogden, A. B. 1860, A. M. 1863.
William O'Mullen.
John O'Neil, Jr.
George Percy.
Eugene Hall Pomeroy, A. B. 1860.
James Edward Ryan.
John Bailey Storm, LL. M. 1864.
Robert Boyd Van Kleeck, A. B. 1859, A. M. 1862.
George Waddington, A. B. 1860.
John Simpson Walker.
Henry Kirke White, B. S. Free Acad. N. Y. C.
Albert Wyckoff, Lieut. U. S. V. 34

## 1863.

James Bruen Andrews, A. B. Yale 1861.
John Campbell Broderick.
Willett Bronson, A. B. William's 1861.
William Campbell.
George Herbert Carey, A. B. 1861, A. M. 1864.
George Chalmers, A. B. Yale 1861.
Paris Garner Clark, Jr.
Walter Livingston Clarkson, A. B. 1860, A. M. 1863.
Andrew Kirkpatrick Cogswell, A. B. Rutgers.

Richard William Ely, A. B. Univ. N. Y. C.
William Henry Fuller, A. B. Yale 1861.
Edward Douglas Gale.
Frederick Gallatin, A. B. Univ. N. Y. C.
John Lyon Gardiner.
Eugene Terry Gardner.
Francis Joseph Holahan, A. B. St. John's.
Edwin Francis Hyde, A. B. Free Acad. N. Y. C.
Peter Duncan Kenny.
Francis Edward Kernochan, A. B. Yale 1861.
Carleton White Miller.
John Pell.
*Robert Troup Pell, A. B. 1860, A. M. 1863. aet. 27. *1868.
Charles Osborne Phelps.
George Dwight Phelps, Jr., A. B. Yale 1860.
William Walter Phelps, A.B. Yale 1860.
Stephen Whitney Phœnix, A. B. 1859, A. M. 1862.
William Rounds Potter.
Josiah Collins Pumpelly, A.B. Rutger's.
*Erastus Barnes Rudd, A. B. 1861, A. M. 1864. aet. 30. *1872
George Washington Sandford.
Eugene Schuyler, Ph. D. Yale 1861.
Jacob Shrady, A. B. Univ. N. Y. C.
Archibald Walker Spier, A. B. Free Acad. N. Y. C.
James Steers, A.B. Free Acad. N. Y. C.
James Ayers Taber.
Ernest Tuckerman.
Morris Ashhurst Tyng, (Rev.), A. B. Will. 1861, Prof. Bibl. Lit. Gambier Theol. Sem. 1870.
George Edmondson Walker.
Josiah Otis Ward.
Edmund Wetmore, A. B. Harv. 1860.
Pierre Washington Wildey, A. B. 1860, A. M. 1863.

41

## 1864.

Richard Armstrong.
William Philip Arnold.
Henry Sandford Bellows.
Henry Brodhead, A. B. Yale 1859.
Eldred Absalom Carley, A.B. Free Acad. N. Y. C.
Thomas Bernard Connery, A. B. St. John's.
George Campbell Cooper, A. B. Free Acad. N. Y. C.
Abel Crook, A. B. William's 1862, LL. M. 1864.
Hiram Robert Dixon.
Jeremiah Donovan.
John Esler Eckerson.
Washington White Ellsworth.
Lemuel Edward Evans.
Joseph Fettretch.
Jacob Alfred Gross, LL. M. 1865.
Frank Harris, A. B. Christian Bros. Mri., LL. M. 1865.
Wm. Augustus Ogden Hegeman, A. B. 1862, A. M. 1865, LL. M. 1865.
Andrew Josephus Hennion.
William Myers Hoes, A. B. William's 1861.
Burrall Hoffman, A. B. 1862, A. M. 1865, LL.M. 1865.
Henry Holt, A. B. Yale 1862.
Harlow Mather Hoyt, A. B. Free Acad. N. Y. C.
Hamilton Bailey Humes.
Charles Nichols Judson, A.B. Yale 1862.
William Platt Ketcham, A.B. Yale 1862.

Arthur Malachi Lee, A. B. Free Acad. N. Y. C.
Albert McNulty, Jr., A. B. 1861, A. M. 1864.
Franklin McVeagh, A.B. Yale 1862.
Joseph Augustus Marsh.
Luther Ainsworth Milbank.
Horatio Woodhull Mills.
Israel Minor, Jr., A. B. Yale 1862.
Augustus Newbold Morris, A. B. 1860, A. M. 1863.
Charles Hoskins Mundy.
William Henry Newschafer, A.B. Free Acad. N. Y. C.
Charles Walton Ogden, A. B. 1862, A. M. 1865.
Frank Alleyne Otis, A. B. 1861, A. M. 1864.
Henry Delafield Phelps, A. B. Trin. Coll.
*Gerardus Post, A. B. 1862. aet. 22. *1864
Albert Alfred Reuwee.
James Richards, A. B. N. Jers. 1858, LL. M. 1865.
Van Ness Roosevelt.
Russell Harper Root, A. B. 1862.
Merwin Rushmore.
Elliot Sanford, A. B. Amh. 1861.
Adolph Lewis Sanger, A. B. Free Acad. N. Y. C., LL. M. 1865.
John Le Grand Schaffer.
William Arnet Seaman.
Thomas Buckman Shoemaker.
William Shrady.
William Vanderbilt Simpson.
William Edwin Slocum, B. S. Free Acad. N. Y. C.
Jacob Philip Solomon.
Frederick William Stevens, A. B. Yale 1858.
John Stout.
Sidney Harrison Stuart, Jr., B. S. Free Acad. N. Y. C.
Frederick Swarts, LL. M. 1865.
William Robert Syme, A. B. Univ. N. Y. C.
Richard Terheun Van Boskerck, A. B. Free Acad. N. Y. C.
Julius Sylvester Walsh, A. B. St. Joseph's.
Frederick Augustus Ward, A. B. Yale 1862.
Robert Kelley Weeks, A. B. Yale 1862.
William Leggett Whiting.
Miron Winslow, Jr.
Buchanan Winthrop, A. B. Yale 1862.
Samuel Purdy Wright.

66

## 1865.

Edmund Bragdon Barnum.
William Nelson Bedelle.
George Alvin Bevins.
Edward Griffiths Black.
William Brevoort Bolmer, A. B. 1863, A. M. 1868.
Andrew Benton Chalmers.
*Freeman Clarkson, A. B. 1863, A. M. 1866.
Gasheree De Witt Clock.
Thomas Cochran, Jr., A. B. Univ. N. Y. C.
Lewis Osborn Corbet.
Adrian Voorhees Cortelyou, A. B. Yale.
Ten Broeck Crawford.
James Geddes Day.
Hugh Duffy.
William Henry Field, A. B. Union Coll.
Henry Edward Fitzsimons, A. B. St. Francis Xavier Coll.
Henry Rankin Freeland, A. B. N. Jers.
Charles Miles Gilman, A. B. Yale.

Edmund Banks Graham.
Richard Henry Greene, A. B. Yale.
Richard Booth Greenwood, Jr.
Isaac Hollister Hall, A. B. Hamilt. Coll.
George Scovill Hamlin, A. B. Yale.
Thornton Mills Hinkle, A. B. Yale.
George Hoffman, A. B. Yale.
Samuel Huntington, A. B. Yale.
Cortlandt Irving.
Luther Manard Jones, A. B. Yale.
Joseph Frederick Kernochan, A. B. Yale.
George Keyser.
Robert Blair Keyser, A. B. Free Acad. N. Y. C.
George Pliny Kingsley.
Joseph Koch, A. B. Free Acad. N. Y. C.
Emile Henry Lacombe, A. B. 1863.
Mordecai Lewis.
Francis Ferdinand Marbury, Jr.
William Matthews Martin, A. B. 1863, A. M. 1866.
William Lewis Matson, A. B. Yale.
Charles Frederick Mawbey.
Theodore Florence Henry Mayer.
James Slade Millard, A. B. Yale.
Edward Mitchell, A. B. 1861, A. M. 1864.
William Stewart Ross Ogilby.
James Augustus Olwell, A. M. St. John's Coll.
Charles Godfrey Patterson.
Charles Alfred Post.
Henry Foster Ranney.
Robert Emmet Robinson, A. B. 1863.
Thomas Robinson, M. D. elsewhere.
Louis Ruttkay, A. B. Union.
Peter John Sause.
Charles Carroll Smith.
Gerrit Smith Stanton.
Henry Brewster Stanton, Jr.
George Washington Stephens, A. B. Free Acad. N. Y. C.
David Dean Terry, A. B. Free Acad. N. Y. C.
Stephen Howard Thayer, A. B. 1863, A. M. 1866.
John Julius Thomasson.
Isaac Van Alst.
Singleton Van Buren.
*John A. Vanderpoel, A. B. 1862, A. M. 1865. aet. 24. *1866
Elias Williams Van Voorhis, Jr.
Hamilton Wallis, A. B. Yale.
Townsend Wandell, A. B. Free Acad. N. Y. C.
Almar Preston Webster.
Charles Howland Wesson, Yale.

66

## 1866.

*David Wylie Alexander, A. B. 1864, A. M. 1867. aet. 30. *1872
John Johnson Allen, A. B. Univ. Vermont.
Edward Sandford Atwater, A. B. N. Jers.
Edwin Bergh, Jr.
Frederick Henry Betts, A. B. Yale.
Daniel Frederick Boardman, A. B. 1863.
Thomas Bracken, A. M. St. John's Coll.
Thomas Baird Browning, A. B. 1864, A. M. 1867.
William Henry Butterworth, A. B. 1864, A. M. 1867.
Ebenezer Buckingham Convers, A. M. Yale.
John Thomas Cornell.

Albert Crane, A. B. Tuft's Coll.
Charles Henry Douglas, A. B. Beloit Coll.
William Oliver Embury.
*Henry Floy, A. B. 1864. aet. 23. *1866
Lewis C. Goebel, A. B. Coll. City N. Y.
Charles Auguste Lambert Goldey.
Joseph Bayley Lawrence, A. B. 1864, A. M. 1867.
James John Gray.
Daniel Judson Holden, A. B. Yale.
William Allen Hoyt.
Ephraim Arnold Jacob, A. B. Coll. City N. Y.
John Watts Kearny.
Samuel Lawrence, Jr.
Alfred James McCullough.
Alexander Taggart McGill, A. B. N. Jers.
Henry Major, Jr., A. B. Georgetown Coll.
Frederick Halsey Man, A. B. Coll. City N. Y.
Nicholas Murray, A. B. William's.
Howard Osterhoudt, A. B. 1864, A. M. 1867.
Henry Hills Parker, A. B. 1864, A. M. 1867.
William Chauncey Prall.
L. Bradford Prince.
Jarrett Thomas Richards.
Edward Ross Robinson.
William Henry Rooney.
Washington Sackmann.
Henry J. Schenck.
Murray Colgate Shoemaker, A. B. Yale.
Nathaniel Ferdinand Smith.
Reginald Heber Smith, A. B. 1854, A. M. 1857.
William Washington Smith.
Edward Fay Stilwell.
Samuel John Storrs, A. B. Amherst.
Charles Phelps Taft, A. B. Yale 1864 and A. M. Yale, J. U. D. Heidelberg 1867.
Frederick Thompson.
Alfred Wagstaff, Jr.
Benjamin Robert Winthrop, Jr. 48

## 1867.

Wilbur Russell Bacon, A. B. Yale.
Charles Henry Baldwin.
Truman Hamilton Baldwin, A. B. Coll. City N. Y.
Gerard Beekman, A. B. 1864, A. M. 1867.
Henry Rutgers Beekman, A. B. 1865, A. M. 1868.
James Bell, Jr.
William Johnson Binney, A. B. Amherst.
Eugene Samuel Blois.
Edward Payson Brewster, A. B. N. Jers.
John Edward Brooks, A. B. Yale.
John Lovett Brower, A. M. Coll. City N. Y.
Edward Sears Clinch, B. S. Coll. City N. Y.
Edwin Walter Coggeshall.
Theodore Pease Cook.
Frank Hull Cowdrey.
Samuel Oakley Crawford.
William Bedlow Crosby, A. B. Coll. City N. Y.
N. Gano Dunn.
Clarence Uriah Embury.
Thomas Rawdon Fisher.
William Hubbell Fisher, A. B. Hamilt. Coll.
Horace Webster Fowler, A. B. Yale.
William Edgar Glover.
James Sandford Greves, A. B. Hamilt. Coll.
William Fearing Hall.

James Hooker Hamersley, A. B. 1865, A. M. 1868.
Henry Bailey Hathaway.
William Herring.
Archibald Hopkins, A. B. William's.
Isaac Samuel Isaacs, A. B. Univ. N. Y. C.
William Jay, Jr., A. B. 1859, A. M. 1862.
Charles Swift Joslyn, and LL. B. Yale.
George Goelet Kip, A. B. 1865, A. M. 1868.
William Lampson, A.B. Yale.
John Thomas Lockman.
William Gilman Low, A. B. 1865, A. M. 1868.
Edwin McCahill, A. B. Georget. Coll. D. C.
John Alfred Mack.
John Hobart McMurdy.
Thomas Martin Moore.
Philip Murphy.
Daniel Weir Northrup.
David Robinson Nutter, A. B. Dartmouth.
Sidney Oaksmith.
Daniel Parish, Jr.
Charles Burroughs Rice, A. B. 1864, A. M. 1867.
Phœnix Remsen.
Joseph Swift Richards, M. S. Norwich Univ. Vt.
Zabdiel Sidney Sampson, A. B. Amherst.
Lorenzo S. B. Sawyer, Hamilton.
*Henry Augustus Schermerhorn, A. B. 1861, A. M. 1864. aet. 29. *1869
William Andrew Senger.
Morris Woodruff Seymour.
Charles Christmas Shelton.
Eugene Carroll Skinner.
Charles Edward Smith, Renss. Polytech. Inst. N.Y.
Charles Henry Smith, Jr., B. S. Coll. City N. Y.
Freling H. Smith, A. B. Union.
Isaac Spencer Smith.
John William Sterling, A. B. Yale.
William Edwin Stiger.
John Hervey Stitt, A. B. Coll. City N. Y.
Frederick Wilmot Sturges.
*John Edwin Swezey, A. B. 1865, A. M. 1868. *1873
Frank Thompson, A. B. Union.
Charles Harmer Trafford.
Henry Edwin Tremain, A. B. Coll. City N. Y.
John Hamilton Turner, A. M. Coll. City N. Y.
Augustus Gifford Vanderpoel.
Philip Livingston Van Rensselaer, A. M. .N Jers.
Abraham Van Santvoord, A. B. 1865, A. M. 1866.
George West Van Siclen, M. S. Coll. City N. Y.
Edmund Augustus Ward.
Francis H. Weeks, A. B. William's.
James Keappoch Hamilton Willcox, A. B. Univ. N. Y. C.
William Henry Williams, A. B. Brown Univ.
William Clitus Witter, A. B. Yale.

77

## 1868.

Osmin W. Atkins, A. B. Wesleyan Univ.
Marshall Bell, A. B. 1866.
Emile Beneville, A. B. Coll. City N. Y. and A. M. Coll. C. N.Y.
William Warwick Bliss, A. B. Brown Univ.
Morris Mumford Budlong, A. B. Yale.

George Noyes Burt, A. B. Union Coll.
Albertson Case, A. B. Harv. Univ.
Newton Henry Chittenden.
Simeon Baldwin Chittenden, Jr., A. B. Yale.
Elihu Church.
George Clinton.
Henry Kiersted Coddington, M. S. Coll. City N. Y.
Edmund Coffin, Jr., A. B. Yale.
Arthur Douglas Collins.
Edward Donaldson Cowman, A. B. Hobart Coll.
Julien Tappan Davies, A. B. 1866.
Henry Sprong Davis, A. B. Hobart Coll.
Charles Willoughby Dayton.
John Ambrose Deady, A. B. Amherst Coll.
Theodore F. C. Demarest, A. B. 1864, A. M. 1867.
Frederick Nevins Dodge, A. B. Yale.
Franklin Woodward Earl.
Wilberforce Freeman, A. B. Coll. New Jersey.
Michael Emanuel Goodhart.
Daniel Edward Hervey.
William Monefeldt Howland, A. B. Harv. and A. M. Harv.
Walter Langdon Kane.
John Vincent Kernan, A. B. Seton Hall Coll.
James King Lawrence, A. B. Brown Univ.
Theodore Akerly Lord, A. B. Yale.
James A. McCreery, A. B. Mt. St. Mary's Coll.
George Souter McKay.
Payson Merrill, A. B. Yale.
Ormond Tucker Middleton.
Fordham Morris, A. B. Trin. Coll.
Henry Lewis Morris.
Max Moses.
David Judson Newland, A. B. Middleb. Coll.
Edward Holland Nicoll, A.B. 1866, A. M. 1869.
William Greenly Nicoll, A. B. Yale.
William Franklin North.
Robert Hunter Patton.
George Jones Peet, A. B. Kenyon Coll.
James Lyman Price, A. B. 1865, A. M. 1868.
Thomas Bond Raynolds.
Henry Hutchinson Reid.
Thomas Rogers, A. B. Union Coll.
Henry Andrew Root.
Edward Whelan Searing.
Thomas Parish Sherman.
William Edwin Smalley, A. B. 1866, A. M. 1869.
Frank Sherman Smith.
George Putnam Smith, A. B. 1866.
Asa Adams Spear, A. B. Amherst Coll.
Stephen Dover Stephens, Jr., A. B. 1866, A. M. 1869.
Henry Croswell Tuttle, A. B. 1869.
Samuel Hempstead Valentine, A. B. Amherst Coll.
Thomas Sedgwick Van Valkenburgh, A. B. Yale.
John Waring Weed.
John Brandagee Wood, A. B. Yale.

60

## 1869.

William Henry Andrews.
James Knox Averill.
Walton Peckam Bell, A. B. 1867, A. M. 1870.
Charles Wyllys Betts, A. B. Yale.

James Lord Bishop, A. B. Amherst Coll.
Henry Herrick Bond.
Charles Henry Burtis, A. B. 1867, A. M. 1870.
Charles Goodrich Coe, A. B. Yale.
Duane Conant, A. B. Hamilt. Coll.
Thomas Duncan Cottman, A. B. Mt. St. Mary's Coll.
Robert Emmett Cowart.
George Hubert Cowell, A. B. Yale.
James Ambrose Deering, A. B. Manhattan Coll.
George Gosman De Witt, A. B. 1867, A. M. 1870.
John J. Du Bois, A. B. Yale.
Patrick Gavan Duffy.
Frank J. Dupignac.
George Ozro Emerson, A. B. Rochester Univ.
Charles Emmett.
John Barnard Fairbank, A. B. Amherst Coll.
Louis Fellows, A. B. Coll. City N. Y.
Francis Forbes, A. B. Rochester Univ.
Louis William Frost.
George Griswold Greene.
Edward Graham Haight.
George Henry Hansen.
Thomas Hedge, Jr., A. B. Yale.
John Homer Hildreth.
Pierre Van Buren Hoes.
George Chandler Holt, A. B. Yale.
William Warner Hoppin, Jr., A. B. Brown and A M. Brown, M. D. 1864.
Clarence Melville Hyde, A. B. 1867, A. M. 1870.
William Halsey Ingersoll, A. B. 1867, A. M. 1870, E. M. 1875.
George Landon Ingraham.
Henry Whitman Kennedy.
Henry Thomas Lee, A. B. Lafayette Coll.
Hamilton Wright Mabie, A. B. William's Coll.
William Hector McAllister.
John Thomas McDonough.
Dennis McMahon, Jr., A. B. Manhattan Coll.
Charles Anson Maltby.
George Manierre, A. B. Yale.
Francis Elston Marsh, A. B. Coll. N. Jers.
Abram John Miller.
James Appleton Morgan, A. B. Racine Coll.
James Edward Morrison, A. B. Coll. City N. Y.
William Pitt Mudgett, A. B. Bowdoine Coll.
George Francis Murray, A. B. Georgetown Coll.
Henry Loomis Nelson, A. B. William's Coll.
Cadwalader Evans Ogden, A. B. 1867.
Courtlandt Palmer, Jr.
Richard Wayne Parker, A. B. Coll. N. Jers.
Charles Ewing Patterson.
Walter Pell.
Caleb Purdy.
Rudolph Frederick Rabe.
Theodore Ritter.
Charles Roberts, A. B. Coll. City N. Y.
Charles Hall Rockwell.
Francis Markoe Scott, A. B. Coll. City N. Y.
William Henry Secor.
George Preston Sheldon, A. B. Yale.
Frederick Isaac Small, A. B. Yale.
Charles Edward Souther, A. B. Harvard Univ.
Calvert Spensley.
Ernest Gordon Stedman, A. B. Yale.

Francis Lynde Stetson, A. B. William's Coll.
Horace Stetson, A. B. 1866.
Solomon Thayer Streeter, A. B. Amherst Coll.
Charles Avery Tracy, A. B. Coll. City N. Y.
Edgar Abel Turrill, A. B. Yale.
Waldemar Jonas Tuska.
Aaron Ernest Vanderpoel, A. B. 1867, A. M. 1870, Trustee Col. Coll.
Philip Van Rensselaer Van Wyck.
Frank Ward Wessels.
Charles Warren West, A. B. William's Coll.
George Peabody Wetmore, A. B. Yale.
Ezekiel Webster Whipple, A. B. Dartmouth Coll.
James Henry Work, A. B. 1867, A. M. 1870.
William Wilson.
Edward Marshall Wright, A. B. Yale. 81

## 1870.

George Augustus Adee.
Edward Knapp Anderton.
Lemuel Hastings Arnold, Jr.
Theodore Aub.
George Augustus Baker, Jr., A. B. Coll. City N. Y.
Henry Beadel, Jr., A. B. 1869.
Edward Wells Bell, A. B. Yale.
James Michael Brady, A. B. 1868, A. M. 1871.
Alfred Douglas Brush.
Peter Vincent Burtsell.
Charles Kinsey Cannon, A. B. Yale.
Samuel Cardwell, Jr.
Timothy Pitkin Chapman, A. B. Yale.
Henry Abel Chittenden, Jr., A. B. Yale.
John Chorlton.
Edgar Bradford Clark.
John Henry Clayton.
Stacy B. Collins, Jr.
Le Baron Bradford Colt, A. B. Yale.
John Christopher Connor, Jr.
William Edgar Conover.
Gilbert Holmes Crawford, A. B. Coll. City N. Y.
Charles Edward Crowell.
Albert Delafield, B. S. Coll. City N. Y.
Leo Charles Dessar.
Francis Charles Devlin, A. B. St. Francis Xavier's Coll.
George Gillespie Dickson, A. B. Keny. Coll.
William Palmer Dixon, A. B. Yale.
John Holmes Prentiss Dodge.
Charles Arthur Doten.
George Williams Ellis, A. B. Middlebury Coll.
George Washington Flaacke.
William Riley Foster, J. D. Heidelberg.
J. Henry Fowler, Jr.
Robert Ludlow Fowler.
Andrew Gilhooly, A. B. 1868, A. M. 1871.
Joseph Warren Greene, A. B. Yale.
Augustus Fraugott Gurlitz.
Lovell Hall, A. B. Yale.
Frederick Robert Halsey, A. B. Harv. Univ.
George Henry Hart.
Walter Howe, B. S. Coll. City N. Y.
William Reed Jerome, A. B. Hamilt. Coll.
Charles Dunn Jones.
Clarence Delafolie Jones.
Samuel Kalish.
James Knox, A. M. Coll. City N. Y.

Samuel Spahr Laws.
Thomas Alphonso McGlade, Jr.
Robert Bach McMaster, B.S. Coll. City N. Y.
William Fleming McRae.
John McLean Nash, A. B. 1868, A. M. 1871.
John Calvin Paulison, A. B. Coll. N. Jers.
Henry Wilson Payne, A. B. Yale.
Duane Livingston Peabody, A. B. 1868, A. M. 1871.
Paul Pelletier, A. M. St. Louis.
Samuel Edmund Perry.
William Franklin Pitschke, B. S. Coll. City N. Y
James M. Poulsen, A. B. Coll. N. Jers.
Arthur Rickards Robertson.
Roderick Robertson.
George Nicholas Sanders, Jr., A B. 1868, A. M. 1871.
Kaufman Simon.
Orrin Skinner.
William Brown Slocum.
Nathaniel Phillips Smith Thomas, A. B. Yale.
William Knapp Thorn, Jr.
Thomas Birdsall Van Boskerck.
Albert Warren Wells.
Henry Simmons White, M.D. 1866.
James Henry Wood, A. B. Yale.

## 1871.

Henry Green Atwater, A. B. Harv. Univ.
George Augustus Baker, Jr., A. B. Coll. City N. Y.
George Baker.
James Baker, Jr.
Joseph Disbrow Baker.
Thomas Glover Barry.
James William Beekman, Jr.
Henry Bischoff, Jr.
Silliman Blagden, A. B. Yale.
Alden Chester.
William Henry Clark, A. B. Coll. City N. Y.
Thomas Newby Cuthbert, A. B. 1869, A. M. 1872.
William Bayard Cutting, A. B. 1869, A. M. 1872.
Adolf Czaki, Dr. Jur. Heidelberg.
Edward Ritzema De Grove, A. B. Yale.
Samuel Gardner Derrickson.
Harrison Downes, A. B. Yale.
William Alexander Duer, A. B. 1869, A. M. 1872.
Thomas Charles Edward Ecclesine, A. B. 1870.
Charles Howard Edwards.
William Fanning, Jr., A. B. 1870.
Charles Henry Farnam, A. B. Yale.
William Whitman Farnam, A. B Yale, Dr. Jur. Heidelberg.
Edwin Bancroft Foote, A. M. Yale.
William Dudley Foulke, A. B. 1869, A. M. 1872.
George Washington Galinger.
Anthony Ambrose Griffin.
William King Hall, A. B. Yale.
Frank Denham Harmon.
71 Monmouth Gedney Hart.
Edward Banker Hilton.
John Henry Hobart.
Francis Huesmann.
James Hurst.
Frederick Guion Ireland, A. B. Harv. Univ.
Alphonse Anselm Jacobi, A. B. and B. S. Coll. City N. Y.
William Henry Kelly, B. S. Coll. City N. Y.

John Pierre Kirby.
William Whitehead Ladd, Jr.
George Cowles Lay, Jr., A. B. Coll. City N. Y.
John Brooks Leavitt, A. B. Kenyon Coll.
William Henry Lawrence Lee, A. B. Yale.
John Henry Livingston, A. B. 1869.
Nathaniel Alexander McBride, A. B. Coll. N. J.
Bernard Edward McCafferty.
M. Milmo McGowan, A. B. elsewhere.
Frank Malocsay.
Martin Sander Meyer.
Charles Philip Miller.
Theodore Frelinghuysen Miller, A. B. Coll. City N. Y.
William Mitchell, Jr., A. B. 1868, A. M. 1871.
Charles Jacob Nehrbas, B. S. Coll. City N. Y.
David B. Ogden, A. B. 1869.
Philip Joseph O'Hanlon, A. M. Mt. St. Mary's Coll.
William Satterlee Packer, A. M. Yale.
Charles Augustus Peabody, Jr., A. B. 1869, A. M. 1872.
Elmer Poulsen, A. B. Wash. and Jefferson Coll. Penn.
James Prendergast.
Samuel Augustus Purdy, Jr., A. B. 1869, A. M. 1872.
William McNevin Purdy, A. B. 1869, A. M. 1872.
Henry Warren Raymond, A. B. Yale.
Henry Remsen.
Frank Reynolds, A. B. Wesleyan Univ. Conn.
Pedro Philip Riotte.
David Solis Ritterband, A. B. Coll. City N. Y.
Platt Rogers.
James Alexander Ross.
John Watts Russell.
Talcott Huntington Russell, A. B. Yale.
Rudolph Sampter.
Charles Miller Schieffelin.
James Cary Sheffield, A. B. Coll. City N. Y.
Charles William Shelton.
Frank Norsworthy Shepard, A. B. 1869, A. M. 1872.
Hiram Watson Sibley, Ph. D. Heidelberg.
William Thomas Simms.
William Bond Skidmore.
Charles W. Sloane, A. B. St. Francis Xavier's.
Edward Bayard Smith, A. B. 1869, A. M. 1872.
Elliot Smith.
Williams Stebbins Smith.
John Henry Staats.
William Strauss.
William Lincoln Swan, A. B. Coll. N. J.
Alfred Taylor, B. S. Univ. Lewisberg, Penn.
Albert Dana Tenney, A. B. Vermont Univ.
Edward Tillou, A. B. 1869.
Theodosius Stevens Tyng, A. B. Kenyon Coll.
M. Bedell Vail, A. B. Rutger's Coll.
James McCall Varnum, A. B. Yale.
Irving Ward.
Edward Francis Weeks, A. B. 1869, A. M. 1872.
Charles Tylden Westcott, A. B. Washington Coll, Del.
Edward Payson Wilder, A. B. Yale.
Howard Payson Wilds, A. B. Coll. City N. Y.
Walter Brune Wines.
Henry Wood.
Thenford Woodhull, A. B. 1869, A. M. 1872.
Gustav Zimmermann.

## 1872.

James Randall Adams.
Charles Beatty Alexander, A. B. Coll. N. J.
Frederic Allis, A. B. Yale.
Henry John Appel, Jr.
Christian Henry Betjeman.
Stephen James Bidlack.
Robert Forsyth Bixby, A. B. Trin. Coll.
Silliman Blagden, A. B. Yale.
Arthur Crossley Bradley, A. B. Amherst Coll.
William Reynolds Brown, A. B. Amherst Coll.
George W. Bryan, A. B. Wesleyan Univ. Kentucky.
George Allen Buffum, A. B. Brown Univ. R. I.
Charles Henry Bullis, A. B. Yale.
Le Grand Sterling Burton, A. B. Racine Coll. Wis.
Morris Byrne.
Patrick Sarsfield Cassidy.
Edward Henry Clark, A. B. Harv. Univ.
Lewis Brainerd Clark, A. B. Hamilton Coll. N. Y.
George Ansel Clement, Jr.
Hugo Ernest Constant.
Willie Horace Corbin.
Arthur Power Crane, A. B. Yale.
John Cropper, A. B. 1870, A. M. 1873.
Robert Weeks DeForest, A. B. Yale.
Edwin Albert Dobbins.
Elbridge Gerry Duvall, Jr.
Robert Duncan Elder.
Charles Henry Ellsworth.
Charles Crook Emott, A. B. Harv. Univ.
Henry Fisher.
Frederick DePeyster Foster, A. B. 1868, A. M. 1871.
James Horn Gilbert, A. B. Yale.
Julius Levi Goldenberg.
Julius Goldman.
Charles William Gould, A. B. Yale.
John James Graham.
Frederick Grasmuck.
Thomas Greenwood, A. B. Yale.
Samuel Bernard Hamburger.
Solomon Hanford.
William James Harding.
Alfred Augustus Houghton.
Edmund Huerstel.
Frederick Hutchings.
John Henry Inness, B. S. Coll. City N. Y.
Edward Jacobs.
Thomas Allen Jobs, A. B. Coll. N. J.
Adrian Hoffman Joline, A. B. Coll. N. J.
Luther Laflin Kellogg, A. B. Rutger's Coll.
Andrew Wesley Kent.
Abraham Kling.
John Mason Knox, Jr., A. B. Coll. City N. Y.
Sampson Simson Leo.
Francis Ellington Loop, A. B. William's Coll. Mass.
David Thomas Lynch.
Thomas McCafferty.
Richard McCloud.
Samuel St. John McCutchen, A. B. Yale.
James Niall McKane.
Nathaniel Marsh.
Benjamin Thomas Marten.
Heyward Glover Meeker.
Charles Meyer.
Frank Halsey Mills, A. B. Coll. N. J.
John Howard Montgomery, A. B. Coll. City N. Y.
Arthur Murphy.
William Nelson Noble, A. B. Amherst Coll.

John Notman.
William O'Donohue.
William Claybourne Owens.
Howland Delano Perrine.
John Hoyt Perry, A. B. Yale.
Wheeler Whitman Phillips.
Franklin Porter, A. B. Yale.
Edwin Augustus Pratt.
Anderson Price.
Robert Livingston Read, A. B. Yale.
James Denoon Reymert, Jr.
Charles Dallas Ridgway, A. B. Coll. N. J.
Benjamin Franklin Romaine, Jr., A. B. 1871.
Moses Sahlein.
George Starr Scofield, Jr., A. B. 1870, A. M. 1874.
Winfield Scott.
Sanford Sidney Smith, A. B. Harv. Univ.
Edward Leavitt Spencer, A. B. Yale.
Samuel Veith Speyer.
Charles Morton Stafford.
Andrew Musgrave Stirling.
Frank Dodge Sturges, A. B. 1870.
Charles Schermerhorn Suydam.
Charles Singleton Sweet, A. B. Univ. of Chicago.
George Henry Thompson.
Thomas Joseph Tilney, A. B. Yale.
Henry Peter Titus.
Eliphalet Williams Tyler, A. B. Amherst Coll.
Robert Anderson Van Wyck.
Leopold Wallach.
Manchester Ward Weld.
Ira Benjamin Wheeler.
Thomas Randolph White, B. S. Coll. City N. Y.
Franke Sherman Williams, A. B. Yale.
Dennistoun Wood, A. B. 1870, A. M. 1873. 102

# 1873.

Alphonse Henry Alker, B. S. Col. City N. Y.
Henry Chandler Andrews, A. B. Harv. Univ.
Henry Clinton Backus, A. B. Harv. Univ.
Gilbert Henry Badeau.
Franklin Bartlett, A. B. Harv. Univ.
Walter Rogers Beach, A. B. Yale.
Winfield Scott Bird.
Arthur Blackwell.
James Armstrong Blanchard, A. B. Ripon Coll. Wis.
John Gordon Blanding, A B. Yale.
Edward Chadwick Boardman, A. B. Harv. Univ.
James Harvey Bradish, A. B. Ripon Coll. Wis.
Albert Porter Bradstreet, A. B. Yale.
Frederic Bronson, A. B. 1871.
William Mansfield Bruce.
Byron Winfield Buell, A. B. Harv. Univ.
Joseph Arthur Burr, Jr., A. B. Yale.
John Adriance Bush.
Vanderbilt Lothian Buxton, Jr.
Ricardo et Casanova.
William Richards Castle.
Edward Willmott Chamberlain.
Frederick Sidney Chase, A. B. Yale.
George Chase, A. B. Yale.
William Edwards Clarke.
Jones Cochrane.
Clarence Rapalje Conger, A. B. 1871, A. M. 1874.
John Francis Connelly.
Cornelius Elting Cuddeback, A. B. Yale.

John Elliott Curran, A. B. Yale.
Edward Provost De Mott, A. B. Amherst Coll.
Edward Hazard Dixon, A. B. Univ. N. Y. C.
Edward Mundy Dixon.
John Henry Dorrity, A. M. St. Xavier's Coll. N. Y.
Rufus Charles Duff.
James Earle.
Eugene Newton Eliot.
Thomas Charlock Ennever.
Julius Morton Ferguson.
Joseph Fischer, A.B. Rutger's Coll.
Hamilton Fish, Jr., A B. 1869, A. M. 1872.
William Platt Fitch.
James Peers Foster.
Samuel Fowler.
Julius Joseph Frank, A. B. and B. S. Coll. City N. Y.
Meyer M. Friend.
Robert Monroe Funkhouser, Jr., A. B. Dartmouth Coll. N. H.
Philip John Geib.
William Erwin Gilhooly, A. B. 1870.
Alexander Graham.
Gordon Grant.
Lewis James Grant.
David Weild Harkness.
Theodore E. Hancock, A. B. Wesleyan Univ. Conn.
Charles Nathan Harris, A. B. elsewhere.
Ashton Harvey.
Charles Lansing Haskell.
William Hays.
Edmund James Healy, A. M. St. Xavier's Coll. N. Y.
Jacob Herrick Henry, A. B. 1871, A. M. 1874.
Henry Morris Heymann.
Richard Cecil Higgins, A. B. Coll. N. J.
Max Clinton Huebner.
Louis Halleck Hurst.
George Ingraham, A. B. Wesleyan Univ. Conn.
William M. Ivins.
Anson Blake Jackson, A. B. Hobart Coll. N. Y.
Harry Madison Jones, A. B. 1869.
De Lancey Astor Kane.
Samuel Nicholson Kane.
John Haskell Keep.
Richard Busteed Kelly, A. B. 1871, A. M. 1874.
Robert Kelly, A. B. Yale.
Cornelius Eugene Kene.
Luther Martin Kennett, Jr., A. B. Trin. Coll. Conn.
Walter F. Kilpatrick.
Joseph Kling.
Joseph Lambrecht.
J. Scott Laughton.
Francis Lawton, Jr., A. B. Brown Univ. R. I.
Newberry Davenport Lawton.
William Kendel Leicht.
Solomon Livingston, A. B. Coll. City N. Y.
Henry Day Loder, A.B. 1871, A. M. 1874.
Charles E. Lydecker, B. S. Coll. City N. Y.
Donald McLean.
Merritt Gilbert McKinney.
James Brander Matthews, A. B. 1871, A. M. 1874.
Edward Willis Mead.
William Millard.
Benjamin Latham Miller, A. B. elsewhere.
George Alfred Miller.
John Hunter Miller, A. B. Wesleyan Univ. Conn.
William Franklin Mott, Jr., A. B. 1864.
John Reed Nicholson, A. B. Yale.
Henry Patrick O'Niel, A. M. Coll. City N. Y.
Edward Alonzo Page.

Frederick Aycrigg Pell, A. B. Coll. N. J.
Lewis Henry Platt, A. B. Coll. N. J.
John Proffatt, A. B. Lond. Univ.
Louis Radde.
Sands Fish Randall, A. B. Yale.
Henry Alonzo Rawcliffe.
Melville Henry Regensburger.
George Lockhart Rives, A. B. 1868 and Camb. Univ. Eng., A. M. 1872.
Andrew W. Rose, Jr.
John David Rossett.
Arthur Ryerson, A. B. Yale, LL.B. Univ. Chicago.
Edward Heartt Schell, A. B. Yale.
Joseph Schwartz.
True Mortimer Seaver.
Eugene H. Sheldon, A. B. Middlebury Coll. N. H.
Charles Stephen Simpkins.
John Woodruff Simpson, A. B. Amherst Coll.
Abraham Stern, B. S. Coll. City N. Y.
Campbell Steward.
William Adams Walker Stewart, A. B. Coll. N. J.
William Rhinelander Stewart.
Henry Shelby Stokes, LL.B. Cumberland Univ. Penn.
Oscar Solomon Straus, A. B. 1871, A. M. 1874.
William Syms.
Edward Thorn.
George McCarthy Troutman.
William Boyd Tullis.
William Turk.
Charles Unangst, A. B. Hamilton Coll. N. Y.
Merit Melbourne Van Wert.
Arthur Dudley Vinton.
Joseph M. Wallach.
James Bradish Wells, A. B. Harv. Univ.
Charles Kingsbury Westbrook, A. B. Coll. N. J.
Charles Whipple Whiley, Jr.
Judson Boardman Wilds, A. B. Harv. Univ.
Charles Albert Wiley.
Edwin Bleecker Williamson, A. B. Rutgers Coll.
John Schenck Williamson, A. B. Harv. Univ.
William Keene Williamson.
Henry Scudder Wood, A. B. Trinity Coll.
George Zabriskie.
139

## 1874.

Jacob Abarbanell, A. B. and B. S. Coll. City N. Y.
George Birch Abbott, A. B. William's Coll. Mass.
William Clark Albro.
John Wallingford Andrews, A. B. Yale.
Alfred John Baker.
John Joseph Balleray.
Sheppard Banks, A. B. Coll. City N. Y.
Joseph Bartlett Barry, A. M. Mad. Univ. N. Y.
Clifford Allan Herrischoff Bartlett, LL.B. Univ. N. Y. C.
Charles Frederick Bauerdorf.
John Rogers Beam, A. B. Brown Univ. R. I.
Edward Bement.
George Alden Benton, A. B. Cornell Univ. N. Y.
Tunis G. Bergen, Jr., A. M. Rutger's Coll., Ph.D. Univ. Heidelberg.
Franklin Bien.
Ernest William Bischoff.
Herrmann Bolte.
Frank Howard Bosworth.
John Bennett Bottum.
John Brice, Jr.

Charles Theodore Arminius Briegleb.
Max Brill.
James Brisbane.
Edwin Henry Brown.
Edward Warner Cady, A. B. Yale.
John Graig Cameron.
Clarence Campbell, A. B. Yale.
Nelson Garrison Carman, Jr., A. B. Yale.
Alexander Thompson Carpenter.
George Washington Carr, A. B. Brown Univ.
Isaac Carrillo, LL.D. Univ. Havana, Cuba.
John Lucien Coxe Caruana, A. B. Seton Hall, N. J.
Edward Benedict Cobb, A. B. Yale.
Louis Cohen.
Fred. Harmon Comstock, A. B. Coll. City N. Y.
Harry Wilton Cragin, A. B. Yale.
George Ticknor Curtis, Jr., A. B. Harv. Univ.
Edwin Burr Curtiss.
Francis Barrett Daniels, A.B. Harv. Univ.
James Edward De Laney.
Edward Collins Devyr.
Henry Clinton De Witt.
Pomeroy Dickinson.
James J. Doherty, A. B. St. John's Coll. N. Y.
James Henry Donaldson.
John Hampden Dougherty, A. B. Coll. City N. Y.
Benjamin Douglas, Jr., A. B. Lafayette Coll. N. Y.
George Washington Drew, A. B. Yale.
Charles Tappan Dunwell.
Clarence Cushing Edgerton, A. B. 1872, A. M. 1875.
Wheeler De Forest Edwards, A. B. Coll. City N. Y.
Nathaniel Ellis.
Ephraim Elias Ephraims.
William Henry Eustis, A. B. Wesleyan Univ. Conn.
William Everett, Jr.
Haliburton Fales, A. B. 1872, A. M. 1875.
Thomas Powell Fowler.
Benjamin Franklin, A. B. Hobart Coll. N. Y.
John Van Emburgh Fredericks.
Henry French, A. B. Hamilton Coll. N. Y.
Alexander Jones Gibson, A. B. St. Stephen's Coll. N.Y.
Samuel Augustine Gleavy, A.M. St. John's Coll. N. Y.
John Sebastian Graber.
Joseph William Greenwood.
Henry Clay Griffin.
William C. Gulliver, A. B. Yale.
Charles Hafey.
William Henry Haldane, A. B. 1872, A. M. 1875.
Frank Lorenzo Hall, A. B. Yale.
Robert Ray Hamilton, A. B. 1872, A. M. 1875.
John Smith Hansen.
Edward Frederick Hassey.
John Handy Henshaw, A. B. Amherst Coll.
John Franklin Herrlich.
Caleb Marriott Hillman.
Loranus Eaton Hitchcock, A. B. Amherst Coll.
Irving Hoagland, B. S. and Ph. B. Cornell Univ. N.Y.
Leicester Pratt Holme.
George Edward P. Howard
Samuel Allen Hull.
Peter Hulme, A. B. Harv. Univ.
Charles Oliver Iselin.
Charles Donohue Jacot.

Edward Johnson.
Henry Smith Johnson, A. B. Harv. Univ.
James Dana Jones, A. B. Yale.
Abner Kalisch.
William Edgar Keyes, A. B. 1872, A. M. 1875.
Charles Francis Kingsley, A. B. Middlebury Coll. Vt.
Herbert Evelyn Kinney, A. B. Yale.
George Henry Kracht, A. B. Manhattan Coll. N. Y.
William James Lacey.
Timothy Edwin Leary.
John Hodge Leupp, A. B. Rutger's Coll.
John Daniel Lewis.
Nathan Lewis.
Clarence Lexow, Ph.D. Univ. Jena.
John Lindley.
Leopold Lithauer, Jr.
Frederick Morton Littlefield, A. B. Yale.
Benno Loewy.
Addison J. Lyon, A. B. Coll. City N. Y.
John Joseph McArdle.
Henry Goelet McVickar.
Abram Bell Malcomson, Jr.
Henry Ferdinand Mander.
Reuben M. Manley, Dr. Jur. Univ. Heidelberg.
Howard Mansfield, A.B. Yale.
Reuben Maplesden, Jr.
Henry B. Mason, A. B. Yale.
Douglas Merritt.
John A. Miller, Jr., B. S. Rutger's Coll.
John Ernest Miller.
Francis Lewis Minton.
James Moncrief More.
Theodore Miles Morgan.
William Patrick Mulry, A. M. St. Xavier's Coll. N. Y.
Arthur Murphy, Jr.
Ambrose Spencer Murray, Jr., A. B. Trin. Coll. Conn.
Thomas Newbold, A. B. Cambridge Univ. Eng.
Joseph Emanuel Newburger.
Edward Nicoll, B. S. Cornell Univ. N. Y.
Rodolph Crocheron Oakley, A. B. Rutger's Coll.
Francis Ludlow Ogden.
Ludlow Odgen, A. B. 1872, A. M. 1875.
James Lawrence Onderdonk, A. B. 1872, A. M. 1875.
Charles Wright Page.
Herbert Claiborne Pell.
Thomas Alexander Phelan.
Waldorf Henry Phillips.
Hugh Reilly.
Albert Reynaud, A. B. Seton Hall, N. J.
John Tredwell Richards, A. B. Coll. N. J.
Henry Augustus Riley, Jr., A. B. Yale.
Abram Heaton Robertson, A. B. Yale.
Henry Scott Rokenbaugh, A. B. Rutger's Coll.
John Ellis Roosevelt.
William Raphael Rose.
Griffith Thomas Rowe.
Charles Howland Russell, A. B. Harv. Univ.
Henry Sacchi.
Edward Stanley Sackett, A. B. Hamilton Coll. N. Y.
William Henry Sage, A. B. 1871, A. M. 1874.
David Salomon, B. S. Coll. City N. Y.
Richard Morris Saltus.
William C. Sanborn.
Adam Emil Schatz.
Francis Schell, A. B. Yale.
John Egmont Schermerhorn, B. S. Coll. City N. Y.
John Henry Scholl.
David Kohler Schuster.

Leo Schwab.
Garrett Putnam Serviss, B. S. Cornell Univ. N. Y.
John Henry Shepherd, A. B. Hamilton Coll. N. Y.
John Thomas Sherman.
Charles Sherwood, A. B. Yale.
John Lewis Shirley.
Samuel Slesinger.
William Lamartine Snyder.
William Henry Spangler, Jr.
James David Spear.
Louis J. Stich.
Adolphus Henry Stoiber, A. B. Coll. City N. Y.
John Hall Stoutenburgh.
William Whitewright Stuart.
Theodore Sutro, A. B. Harv. Univ.
Charles John Taylor.
Whitfield Terriberry.
Eugene Treadwell, A. B. Harv. Univ.
Isaac Untermeyer.
Peter Labagh Van der Veer, A. M. Rutger's Coll.
John Everitt Van Nostrand.
Edward Emerson Waters, A. B. Harv. Univ.
Arthur Delano Weeks, A. B. 1872, A. M. 1875.
Samuel William Weiss, A. B. Yale.
David Johnson Halsted Willcox, A. B. Yale.
Hubert Williams.
Joseph Cæsar Wolff.
George Meech Wood.
William Platt Wood, A. B. Yale.
Amos Edward Woodruff.
Henry Edgar Woodward, A. B. 1872, A. M. 1875.
James Lawrence Woodward, A. B. Coll. City N. Y.
Bernard Zwinge.

184

## 1875.

Frederic William Adee, A. B. Yale.
Louis Adler, B. S. Coll. City N. Y.
Joseph Augustus Adlington, A.B. Wesleyan Univ. Conn.
Frederic K. Agate.
Henry Seely Akin, A. B. Ripon Univ. Wis.
Robert Percy Alden.
William Dunois Allen.
*Robert Arnold, A. B. 1872, A. M. 1875. aet. 23. *1875
Joseph Aspinall.
William Waldorf Astor.
Addison Atwater, A. B. Coll. N. J.
Meyer Auerbach.
Albert Bach, A. B. Coll. City N. Y.
Frederic Harrison Baldwin, A. B. Yale.
Ira Leo Bamberger, A. B. 1873.
Everett Darius Barlow.
William Wade Beebe, A. B. Yale.
William Constantine Beecher, A. B. Yale.
Joseph Francis Beglan.
Hal Bell, A. B. Hamilton Coll. N. Y.
James F. Chamberlain Blackhurst.
Willlam Henry Blain, A. B. William's Coll. Mass.
Albert Barnes Boardman, A. B. Yale.
Henry Conrad Botty.
Henry Hopper Bowman.
Charles Bradshaw.
Charles Bried.
Jacob G. Brinkerhoff.
Francis M. Brown.
Charles Henry Brownell, A. B. Amherst Coll.

William Webb Browning, A. B. Yale.
Augustus Buckingham.
John Frederic Bullwinkel.
George Collinson Burgwin, A. B. Trinity Coll. Conn.
Francis George Caldwell.
William Thomas Carlisle.
Frank Paul Casilear.
John Franklin Chase, A. B. Yale.
Horace Russell Chase, A. B. Trinity Coll. Conn.
James Oliver Clark, A. B. Coll. City N. Y.
John Storer Cobb, A. B. King's Coll. Eng.
John Barriclo Conover, A. B. Coll. N. J.
Edward Boies Cowles.
Francis Ramsdell Culbert.
Solomon WoodwardCunningham, A. B. Amherst Coll.
Charles D'Autremont, Jr.
Charles Casset Davis, A. B. Wesleyan Univ. Ohio.
Edward Augustus Day, A. B. William's Coll. Mass.
James Day, Bonn. Univ. Germany.
Robt. Alex. Baynard Dayton, A. B. Harv. Univ.
Emilio Del Pino, A. B. 1873, A. M. 1876.
Charles Clerc Deming, A. B. Yale.
Paul Desvernine.
Robert Dickey, A. B. Harv. Univ.
Frederic George Dow, A. B. Bowdoin Coll. Maine.
Henry Membry Western Eastman.
Henry J. Eickhoff.
Solomon Alexis Emanuel.
Charles Frederick Estwick.
Charles P. Fagnani, A. B. and B. S. Coll. City N. Y.
William E. Sandford Fales, E. M. 1873.
Frederick Getman Fincke, A. B. Harvard Univ.
James Seely Fitch.
William Francis Foley.
William Henry Forman.
Clarence Marion Foster, A. B. Dartmouth Coll. N. Y.
George Henry Fountain.
John Frankenheimer, Ph. B. Cornell Univ. N. Y.
Walter Smith Fredenburgh.
Theodore Henry Friend.
John Bradbury Frothingham.
William Henry Gibson.
James Knox Glenn, Jr., A. B. Univ. N. Y. C.
Charles Thomas Goadby.
Leo Goldmark.
De Bruce Goodell, Jr.
Joseph Wadsworth Gott, A. B. Yale.
Henry Grasse.
Isidor Grayhead.
Samuel Greenbaum, A. B. Coll. City N. Y.
John Cowan Gulick, B. S. Coll. City N. Y.
John Francis Gulliver.
William Henry Haeselbarth.
George Natt Hale, A. B. Hobart Coll. N. Y.
Andrew Steele Hamersley, Jr.
Henry Clay Harding, M. S. Coll. City N. Y.
Frank Goddard Haughwout, A. B. 1871.
Henry Whiting Hayden.
George Robins Haydock.
Daniel Peixotto Hays.
George Conklin Hendrickson.
Charles Clarke Hendrick, A. B. Rochester Univ. N. Y.
Mitchell Hershfield.
Jacques Henry Herts.
Fred. William Hinrichs, A. B. 1874.

Moses Montague Hobart, A. B. Amherst Coll.
William B. Hornblower, A. B. Coll. N. J.
Frederick Howard.
Thomas Burr Hoxsey.
Joseph Crofoot Hubbard, A. B. Yale.
James C. Hueston.
Loton Sandford Hunt.
George Adrian Iselin, B. S. Cornell Univ. N. Y.
Dudley Lamartine James.
Edwin Augustus Johnson.
Henry Edward Jones, A. B. Cambridge Univ. Eng.
Millard Richmond Jones.
John Innes Kane, A. B. Cambridge Univ. Eng.
John Kean, Jr.
Frank Keck, B. S. Coll. City N. Y.
Edward Kent, Jr.
John Hill Kitchen.
Joseph Kohler.
Solomon Kohn, B. S. Coll. City N. Y.
Isaac Kugelman.
Thomas Richard Lane, A. B. Manhattan Coll. N. Y.
Charles Percy Latting, A. B. Yale.
Frederick Richard Lee.
Henry Leipziger, A. B. and B. S. Coll. City N. Y.
Eugene Howard Lewis, A. B. Yale.
Richard James Lewis.
Charles King Lexow, A. B. Harv. Univ.
George Francis Lincoln, A. B. Yale.
Bloomfield Littell, A. B. Rutger's Coll.
Mortimer Livingston.
Henry Loewenthal, A. B. Coll. City N. Y.
Robert Joshua Lounsbury.
Patrick McCabe, A. M. Seton Hall, N. J.
Henry Macdona.
George Matsell MacKellar.
Percy Hamilton McMahon, A. B. 1873, A. M. 1876.
William Justin Mann.
Adrian Vanderveer Martense, A. B. Rutger's Coll.
Walter Henry Martin.
Henry Metzinger.
Patrick Joseph Mogan.
Casimir De Rham Moore, A. B. 1873, A. M. 1876.
José Gregorio Morales, A.M. Univ. Havana, Cuba.
John Andrew Moran.
Stanley Mortimer.
Thomas Skillman Payntar Mount.
Edward Alonzo Muir.
Samuel Mullen.
Luke Mulvany, A. B. Seton Hall, N. J.
James B. Murray.
Wilhelmus Mynderse, A. B. William's Coll. Mass.
George Baldwin Newell.
Morgan Joseph O'Brien, A. B. St. John's Coll. N. Y.
Stephen James O'Hare, A. B. St. Xavier's Coll. N. Y.
William Creighton Ostrander.
Charles Harrison Otis, A. B. Harv. Univ.
William Henry Paar.
Appleton Downer Palmer.
Adolphus Diederich Pape.
James William Perry.
*Augustus Coe Pirsson, A.B. 1872, A. M. 1875. aet. 24. *1875.
Willard Stanley Pladwell.
William Prall, Ph.D. Univ. Heidelberg.
Tarrant Putnam.
Stuart Fitz Randolph.
David Henry Regensburger.
John Reynolds, A. B. Harv. Univ.

Lucian Haywood Richardson, A. B. Dartmouth Coll. N. H.
Henry Pendleton Rogers.
De Leonard Rugg.
Charles Burnham Sanders, A. B. Harv. Univ.
Frederick Louis William Schaffner.
Herman William Schmitz.
Cornelius Suydam Scott, A.B. Coll. N. J.
Thomas L. Seabrook, Ph.B. Peddie Inst. N. J.
Horace Secor, Jr.
John Ekin Shaw, A. B. Yale.
Harry Higgins Shrope.
Alexander Bethmann Simonds, A. B. 1873.
Angel Jacob S. Simpson.
James Henderson Skidmore, Jr.
John Benjamin Skinner, A. B. elsewhere.
Alexis Cutler Smith.
Arthur Cosslett Smith, A. B. Hobart Coll. N. .Y
James Wessell Smith, A. B. Yale.
Oliver Drake Smith.
Jacob Fonseca Da Silva Solis.
Henry Kittredge Spaulding, A. B. Harv. Univ.
Gilbert Macmaster Speir, Jr., A. B. 1873, A. M. 1876.
Henry Lynde Sprague, B. S. Cornell Univ. N. Y.
Oliver Lloyd Steele.
Seth Thayer Stewart, A. B. Yale.
Silas Moore Stilwell, Jr., A. B. 1873, A. M. 1876.
Lefferts Strebeigh, A.B. 1873, A. M. 1876.
William Stoothoff.
John Ruggles Strong, A. B. 1872, A. M. 1875.
James Francis Swanton, A. M. St. Xavier's Coll. N. Y.
John Patrick Sweeney, A. B. St. John's Coll. N. Y.
Everett Mayhew Swift, A. B. Yale.
Charles Nicoll Talbot.
Sutherland Tenney, A. B. 1873, A. M. 1876.
Thomas Thacher, A. B. Yale.
David Thomson, A. B. 1873, A. M. 1876.
Robert Fingland Tilney, A. B. Yale.
Leopold Turk.
William Gilbert Valentine.
Daniel Babbitt Vermilye, A. B. 1873, A. M. 1876.
Joseph Fenelon Vermilye, A. B. 1871, A. M. 1874.
Henry Walter Webb, E. M.
Samuel Nelson White, A. B. Yale.
Bache McEvers Whitlock, A. B. 1873, A. M. 1876.
Elliot Williams.
Francis Henry Wilson, A. M. Yale.
William Robert Wilson.
Francis Jesse Worcester, A. B. Harv. Univ.

210

## 1876.

John Joseph Adams.
Philip Henry Adee, A. B. Yale.
Shoge Takato Agee.
Spencer Aldrich, A. B. 1874.
Jonathan Cowles Andrus.
Nathan LaFayette Bachman, A. B. Hamilton Coll. N. Y.
Walter John Bagshaw.
Frederick Augustus Baker.
George McCague Baker, A. B. Coll. City N. Y.
James Harris Balston, B. S. Univ. N. Y. C.
Pearce Barnes, A. B. Yale.
Harry Crane Beach, A. B. Coll. N. J.

Perry Belmont, A. B. Harv. Univ.
Eugene Michel Bérard.
Edward J. Bermudez, A. M. St. John's Coll. N. Y.
Franklin Ball Bernard.
Arthur Berry.
William James Courtnald Berry.
John Wales Bissell.
Charles Smith Bloomfield.
Richard Johnson Bolles.
Oliver E. Branch, A. B. Harv. Univ.
John Elmendorf Brandegee, A. B. Trinity Coll. Conn.
John Ernst Brodsky.
Isidore Brooks.
George Selah Brown, A. B. Yale.
Edward Martin Burghard.
James Franklin Burrill.
Richard Busteed, Jr.
George Forrest Butterworth, A. B.
Joseph Byrnes, A. B. Seton Hall, N. J.
Franklin G. Campbell, A. B. Coll. N. J.
Joseph Frank Carlin, A. B. St. John's Coll. N. Y.
Horace Hatch Chittenden, A. B. Yale.
Salter Storrs Clark, A. B. Yale.
Louis Baker Cleveland.
Delphin McLeod Cobb.
Adolph Cohen, B. S. Coll. City N. Y
Samuel Pomeroy Colt.
Frank Bliss Colton.
Le Grand Colton.
Joseph I. Connaughton.
William Wright Conway.
Valentine Cook, Jr.
Ashley Wilson Cooper.
Robert Clifford Cornell, A. B. 1874.
William Nelson Cromwell.
Frank Crowell, A. B. Univ. N. Y. C.
William Truesdell Day, A. B. William's Coll. Mass.
Edward Gibbons Delaney.
Wymberley De Renne.
Edward Devoe.
George Lewis Dickerman, A. B. Yale.
Edward N. Dickerson, Jr., A. B. Trinity Coll. Conn.
Maurice Dillon.
Horace Keating Doherty, A. B. St. John's Coll. N. Y.
Sylvester Spelman Downer.
James Coleman Drayton, A. B. Coll. N. J.
Walton Clarke Dupignac.
William Wells Durkee.
Walter Doumaux Edmonds, A. B. William's College, Mass.
Robert Emmet.
Thomas G. Evans, A. B. Yale.
Harold Faye.
Isaac Fromme, A. B. Coll. City N. Y.
Edward Inglis Frost.
Perry James Fuller, A. B. Rutger's Coll.
Albert Gallup, A. B. Brown Univ. R. I.
Edward Collingwood Garrett, Jr.
Marcus Ames Garrison.
Joseph George Gay.
Edward Winslow Geer, A. B. Hamilton Coll. N. Y.
Walter Clarke Gilson.
Jacob Conrad Goebel.
Henry Francis Göken.
Joseph Goldbacher, B. S. Coll. City N. Y.
Nathaniel Edwards Gouldy.
Hugh John Grant.
Ulysses Simpson Grant, A. B. Harv. Univ.
Samuel Lane Gross, A. B. Bowdoin Coll. Me.

Thomas William Grover, A. B. Yale.
Charles William Hassler, A. M. Columbian Coll. D. C.
Edward Sargent Hatch.
Selden T. Scranton Henry, A. B. 1874.
John W. Herbert, Jr., B. S. (R.)
Harry M. Hiester.
William Hillhouse.
Morris Joseph Hirsch.
Oscar Pomeroy Howe.
Lester Samuel Hubbard, Jr.
Charles Edward Humphrey, A. B. Yale.
Josiah Augustus Hyland, A. B. Hamilton Coll. N. Y.
Augustus Jay, A. B. Harv. Univ.
Edward Rodolph Johnes, A. B. Yale.
William Henry Johnson.
George Howard Jones.
George Washington Keeler.
Michael Joseph Kelly, A. B. St. Xavier's Coll. N. Y.
James Kent, Jr.
James Madison Kerr.
George Christian Kobbé, A. B. 1874.
Samuel Kreizer.
Samson Lachman, A. B. Coll. City N. Y.
George Edwin Lawrence.
William Le Compte.
John Lefferts, Jr.
Henry Masterton Leverich.
Albert Jared Loder, A. B. 1874.
Joseph Edwin Lord, A. B. Yale.
Michael Francis McGoldrick.
William Henry McKee, A. B. Univ. Michigan.
William H. McKeon.
James McNulty.
Henry Hubbell Man, A. B. Coll. City N. Y.
John Richard Manley, A. B. Rutger's Coll. N. J.
Valentine Marsh, A. B. Yale.
Frederic Panet Marshall, A. B. 1872, A. M. 1875.
Isaac Parker Martin, Jr.
Charles Leslie Mead.
Augustus H. Merritt.
Schuyler Merritt, A. B. Yale.
Joseph M. Mestre, LL. D. Univ. Havana, Cuba.
Lamartine Miller.
Grayson Mills, A B. Kenyon Coll. O.
Isaac Newton Mills, A. B. Amherst Coll.
Charles William Minor, A. B. Yale.
Augustin Monroe.
Edward Joseph Mulvany, A. M. St. Xavier's Coll. N. Y.
George Welwood Murray.
John Hoffman Murray.
De Lancey Nicoll, A. B. Coll. N. J.
Lewis Morris Norwood.
Henry Nosser.
Lucien Oudin.
Frederick Sheldon Parker, A. B. Yale.
Joseph Parker, Jr., A. B. Coll. N. J.
William Parkin.
William Henry Parsons.
David Paton, A. B. Coll. N. J.
Edward Townsend Payne.
Henry Silas Payson, A. B. Yale.
John Wesley Peckett, Jr., A. B. Coll N. J.
James Coffin Perkins, A. B. Univ. California.
William Joseph Philbin.
William Augustus Pierrepont.
Robert Leonard Pihlman, Stockholm Coll., Sweden.
Edward Peet Price.

Harrington Putnam.
Edward Sumner Rapallo, A. B. 1874.
Bernard Reilly, Jr., A. B. St. John's Coll. N. Y.
George Richards, A. B. Yale.
Rosell Lewellyn Richardson.
James Adam Robson, A. B. Yale.
Charles B. Rockwood.
George Francis Roesch.
Leopold Gottlieb Rosenblatt.
William Rothschild.
Charles Augustus Runk, A. B. Rutger's Coll.
Edward Russ, Jr.
Louis Johnes Ryerson, A. B. Rutger's Coll.
Peter Ryle.
Abraham Salomon, B. S. Coll. City N. Y.
Benjamin Aymar Sands, A. B. 1874.
Edward Shaffer Savage.
Whipple Owen Sayles, A. B. Yale.
Simon Cleophis Scheeline, A. B. Univ. California.
Edgar Samler Schieffelin.
Delavan C. Scoville, A. M. Wesleyan Univ. Conn.
Robert Senfter.
Ferdinand Shack, A. B., B. S. Coll. City N. Y.
Robert Norsworthy Shepard, A. B. 1870, A. M. 1873.
Thomas T. Sherman, A. B. Yale.
Charles Hurd Sherwood.
Adolph Simis, Jr.
Howard Augustus Smith.
Perry Hiram Smith, Jr., A. B. Hamilton Coll. N. Y.
Wybrants Alonzo Smith, A. B. 1873, A. M. 1876.
William Dunham Snow.
Frank Sperry.
William Reed Spooner.
Frederick Joseph Stone, A. B Harv. Univ.
Frank Storrs, A. B. 1874.
Joseph Walworth Sutphen, A. B. Rutger's Coll.
Merton Gay Swart, A. B. Coll. City N. Y.
Edward Martin Talbot.
Abram Alfred Tappen.
Matthew Hueston Thoms, A. B. Yale.
Henry Neville Tifft, B. S. Coll. City N. Y.
John Newhouse Tonnelé.
Charles De Kay Townsend.
James Mulford Townsend, Jr., A. B. Yale.
George Waite Tubbs.
John Langdon Tupper, A. B. William's Coll. Mass.
John Reynolds Tyler.
Russell Jarvis Uhl.
Wm. James Underwood, Jr., B. S. Coll. City N. Y.
Herbert Valentine.
Henry Van Kleeck, A. B. and B. S. Coll. City N. Y.
Philip Van Volkenburgh, Jr.
Henry Vincent.
Russell Walden, A. B. Yale.
De Lancey G. Walker, A. B. Coll. N. J.
James Montfort Ward.
James Talman Waters, Jr., A. B. Univ. West Va.
James Waters, A. M. Union Univ. Tenn.
Henry De Forest Weeks, A. B. Yale.
George Requa Westerfield.
Charles Whitlock, Jr.
Thomas Parmelee Wickes, A. B. Yale.
Frederick Stanton Wicks, A. B. Yale.
Frederick Beasley Williamson, A. B. Coll. N. J.
George Norman Williamson, A. B. 1873.

Hugh Reginald Willson.
John Seymour Wood, A. B. Yale.
Joseph Simeon Wood, A. M. Coll. City N. Y.
Philemon Woodruff, A. B. Coll. N. J.
William Charles Wotton.
William Edward Wyatt.
Horace G. Yates. 219

# GRADUATES OF THE SCHOOL OF MINES.

E. M.; C. E.; Ph. B.

## 1867.

John Magnus Adams, A. B. 1864, A. M. 1867, E. M.
Samuel Willard Bridgham, E. M. 1868.
Francis Gordon Brown, E. M. 1868.
Edward Stelle Brownson, A. B. 1865, A. M. 1868, E. M. 1869.
John Adams Church, E. M. 1868.
Henry Bedinger Cornwall, A. B. 1864, A. M. 1867, E. M. 1869, Professor of Analytical Chemistry and Mineralogy College of New Jersey, Princeton, N. J.
Edward Everett Giddings, E. M. 1872.
Charles King Gracie, A. B. 1865, A. M. 1868, E. M. 1868.
Albert Ward Hale, A. B. 1853, A. M. 1862, E. M. 1872.
Thomas Hayes Harmer, A. B. 1864, A. M. 1867, E. M. 1872.
David Van Lennep, E. M. 1868.
Frederic Milton Petit, E. M. 1872.
William Wey Tuttle, E. M. 1868.

## 1868.

William Henry Van Arsdale, A. M. elsewhere, E. M.
Augustus Porter Barnard, E. M. 1870, Engineer-in-Charge of the Lighthouse at New Haven Harbor.
George Strong Baxter, A. B. elsewhere, E. M., Division Engineer on the Fourth Avenue Improvement.
James Pettigrew Carson, E. M.
Albert Huntington Chester, E. M., Childs Professor of Agricultural Chemistry, Hamilton College, N. Y.
George Hampton Coursen, E. M., C. E. 1875.
George Jarvis Geer, Jr., E. M.
George Byron Hanna, A. B. elsewhere, E. M., Chemist Geological Survey of North Carolina, Melter U. S. Assay Office, Charlotte, N. C.
Archibald MacMartin, A. M. Coll. N. J., E. M.
Edward Stewart Moffat, A. M. Coll. N. J., E. M.
George Howland Parsons, E. M. 1869.
William Pistor, E. M. 1869, Assistant in Drawing, School of Mines, Columbia College.
Charles Slason Platt, E. M.

Kenneth Robertson, E. M.
Albert P. Shack, E. M. 1869.
Frederick Augustus Schermerhorn, E. M. 1870.
Lenox Smith, A. B. 1865, A. M. 1868, E. M.
William Allen Smith, E. M.
Frederic Stallknecht, E. M. 1869.
Moses Dillon Wheeler, A. B. elsewhere, E. M.

20

## 1869.

*Thomas Monahan Blossom, A. B. 1866, A. M. 1869, E. M., Geologist and Metallurgist Baldwin Expedition.
Frederick Bruckman, E. M.
Alonzo Clarence Campbell, E. M.
William Augustus Hooker, A. B. 1866, A. M. 1869, E. M., Superintendent Cleveland Ironworks, Ohio.
Roland Duer Irving, A. M. elsewhere, E. M., Professor of Geology, Mining and Metallurgy in the University of Wisconsin, Assistant State Geologist of Wisconsin.
Walter Proctor Jenney, E. M. 1871, in charge of the Black Hills Expedition.
Henry Smith Monroe, E. M. (formerly Smith), Assistant Geologist and Mining Engineer to the Government of Yezo, Japan.
Lionel Robert Nettre, E. M.
Henry Newton, A. B. elsewhere, E. M., Assistant in Geology School of Mines Columbia College, Geologist with Black Hills Expedition.
William Bleecker Potter, A. B. 1866, E. M., Professor of Mining and Metallurgy Washington University, St. Louis, Mo.
John Cooper Randolph, A. M. Coll. N. J., E. M.

11

## 1870.

Ogden Haight, E. M.
William Halsey Ingersoll, A. B. 1867, A. M. 1870, LL. B. 1869, E. M. 1875, Assistant in Astronom. Observ.
John Augustus Knapp, A. M. elsewhere, E. M.
John Leo Lilienthal, E. M. 1871.
Stuart Lindsley, E. M.
Edward Moore Parrot, E. M. 1871.
Richard Henry Terhune, E. M.
Theodore Francis Van Wagenen, E. M.
Elwyn Waller, A. B. Harv. Univ. 1867 and A. M. 1870, E. M., Ph. D. 1875, Instructor in Analytical Chemistry School of Mines Columbia College.

9

## 1871.

William E. S. Fales, E. M. 1873, LL. B. 1875.
S. Anthony Goldschmidt, A. B. Coll. City N. Y. 1868, Ph. D. Emory Coll. Georgia 1875, E. M.
John Gordon, Jr., E. M.
Pierre De Peyster Ricketts, E. M., Ph. D. 1876, Assistant in Assaying School of Mines Columbia College.

George Washington Riggs, Ph. B., Chemist Washington University St. Louis, Mo.
Gracie Sayre Roberts, E. M., Assistant in Civil and Mining Engineering School of Mines Columbia College.
Richard Spotswood Robertson, Jr., E. M.

7

## 1872.

Peter Townsend Austen, Ph. B. 1873.
*Frank B. Jenney, E. M., Superintendent Orinoco Exploring Co.
Frederick H. McDowell, E. M.
Thomas O'Connor Sloane, A. B. elsewhere, E. M, Chemist New York Gas Light Co.
Arthur F. Wendt, E. M., C. E. 1875.

5

## 1873.

Frederick A. Canfield, A. M. elsewhere, E. M.
Charles Adams Colton, E. M., Assistant in Mineralogy School of Mines Columbia College.
Henry Augustus Mott, Jr., Ph. B., E. M., Ph. D. 1876.
Henry Walter Webb, E. M., LL. B. 1875.
John Townsend Williams, Ph. B., E. M.

5

## 1874.

William de Liesseline Benedict, E. M.
John Gedney Mott Cameron, E. M., C. E.
Samuel Morris Lillie, E. M.
George Murray, E. M.
Eben Erskine Olcott, E. M., Assistant Superintendent of Pennsylvania Lead Works.
Benjamin Franklin Rees, E. M. 1875.
Francis Bell Forsyth Rhodes, E. M.
Frederick Harrison Williams, E. M.

8

## 1875.

Schuyler Hamilton, Jr., A. B. 1872, A. M. 1875, E. M.
Magnus C. Ihlseng, C. E., E. M., Assistant in Physics Columbia College.
Malvern Wells Iles, Ph. B., Assistant in Analytical Chemistry School of Mines.
Charles Edward Jackson, C. E.
Douglas A. Joy, E. M.
Robert Schuyler Lamson, C. E.
Harry Wenman Leavens, E. M.
Arthur Macy, Ph. B.
William Skaats Noyes, E. M.
Franklin Pool, E. M.
Bayard Taylor Putnam, E. M. 1876.
John Krom Rees, A. B. 1872, A. M. 1875, E. M., Assistant in Mathematics School of Mines 1873–6, Adj. Prof. Maths. Wash. Univ. Miss. 1876–.

Charles M. Rolker, E. M.
Samuel Howland Russell, E. M.
James Simpson Chester Wells, Ph. B., Assistant in Analytical Chemistry School of Mines.
Edwin Atwater Wetmore, E. M.
Albert Allen Wright, A. M., Ph. B.
John Henry Tucker, Ph. B.

## 1876.

Thomas Septimus Austin, E. M.
Frederick Everett Bruen, E. M., C. E.
Francis Sanderson Craven, C. E.
Herbert Carrington Foote, C. E.
Edmund Hyatt Garrison, E. M., C. E.
Louis Benton Gratacap, Ph.B.
Francis Newberry Holbrook, E. M., C. E.
Walter Lowrie Hoyt, E. M., C. E.
Frederick Furneaux Hunt, E. M., C. E.
Frederick Remsen Hutton, A. B. 1873, A. M. 1876, E. M., C. E.
18 Charles King, Ph. B.
Nathaniel Wright Lord, E.M.
Edward Gurley Love, A. B. elsewhere, Ph. B.
John Holme Maghee, A. B. 1872, A. M. 1875, C. E.
William Colman Ross, E. M., C. E.
Albert Francis Schneider, E. M., C. E.
George Cyrus Tilden, C. E.
Augustus Clark Walbridge, E. M., C. E.
James Robert Wardlaw, C. E. 19

# HONORARY GRADUATES,

AND

## GRADUATES OF OTHER COLLEGES

### WHO HAVE BEEN ADMITTED IN COLUMBIA COLLEGE TO THE SAME DEGREE.

## 1758.

*Daniel Isaac Brown, (C.L.), N. Jers. 1753, A. M. and N. Jers., Prothonotary Bergen Co. N. J. 1776, Major H. B. M. Army 1780.

*Samuel Brown, Yale 1749, A. M. and Yale. *1778

*Isaac Browne, (Rev.), Yale 1729, A. M. and Yale. *1786

*Thomas Bradbury Chandler, (Rev.), Yale 1745, A. M. and Yale and Oxford 1753, S. T. D. 1767 and Oxford 1766. *1790

*Leonard Cutting, (Rev.), Cambridge, A. M., Tutor 1756–63. aet. 69 *1794

*Samuel Fayerweather, (Rev.), Harv. 1743, A. M. and Yale 1753 and Oxford 1756 and Cambridge. *1781

*Carey Ludlow, (C. L.), A.M., Mast. in Chanc. N. Y. 1776, Surrogate N. Y. C. 1782.

*John McKesson, N. Jers. 1753, (C. L.), A. M. and N. Jers.

David Matthews, N. Jers. 1754, (C. L.), A. M., Alderman N. Y. C. 1776.

Josiah Ogden, A. B. and N. Jers. 1756.

*Cyrus Punderson, Yale 1755, A. M. and Yale. *1789

*Ebenezer Punderson, Yale 1755, A. M. and Yale. *1809

*Daniel Treadwell, Harv. 1754, A. M. and Harv., Fellow and Prof. Math. and Nat. Phil. 1757–60. *1760

*Timothy Wetmore, (T.), A. M. 14

## 1761.

*John Beardsley, (Rev.), A. B., A. M. 1768.

*William Jackson, A. M. and Yale 1763 and N. Jers. 1771 and Univ. Utrecht. *1813

*William Samuel Johnson, Yale 1744, A. M. and Yale and Harv. 1747, J.C.D. Ox. 1766, LL. D. Yale 1788, Del. to Col. Congr. 1765, Judge Supr. Ct. Conn. 1772, Del. to Congr. 1774, Memb. Council Conn. 1780, Repr. in Congr. 1784–7, Memb. U.S. Constit. Conven. 1787, President 1787–1800, U.S. Sen. 1788. *1819

*Samuel Andrew Peters, (Rev.), Yale 1757, A.M. and Yale, LL. D. elsewhere. *1826

*Samuel Seabury, (Rev.), Yale 1748, A. M. and Yale, S. T. D. Ox. 1777, Bishop P. E. Ch. Conn. 1784–96. *1796

*James Scoville, (Rev.), Yale 1757, A. M. and Yale. *1808

*Agur Treadwell, (Rev.), A. B. and Yale 1760, A. M. Yale. *1763

*Edward Winslow, (Rev.), Harv. 1736, A. M. and Harv. *1784

8

## 1762.

*Samuel Andrews, (Rev.), Yale 1759, A. M. *1818

*Richard Clarke, (Rev.), A.B. and Yale 1762, A. M. 1766 and Yale. *1824

*Robert Harpur, Glasgow, A. M., Prof. Math. and Nat. Phil. 1761–7, Regent Univ. N. Y. S. and Clerk of Board 1784–7, Trustee and Clerk of Board 1787–95, Secy. St. N. Y.

*Bela Hubbard, (Rev.), Yale 1758, A. M. and Yale, S. T. D. Yale 1804. *1812

*Robert McKean, (Rev.), Phila. Coll., A. M.

*Ebenezer Parmele, Yale 1758, A. M. and Yale. *1802

6

## 1764.

*Matthew Cushing, Harv. 1739, A. M. and Harv., Librarian Harv.

*Samuel Giles, A. B., Instr. in Maths. King's Coll.

2

## 1765.

*Jeremiah Leaming, (Rev.), Yale 1745, A. M. and Yale, S. T. D. 1789. *1804

## 1767.

*Samuel Auchmuty, (Rev.), A. B. Harv. 1745 and A.M. Harv. 1746, S. T. D. and Oxford 1776. *1777

*Ephraim Avery, (Rev.), Yale 1761, A. M. *1776

*George Glentworth, M. D. Edinb., A. M.

*Charles Inglis, (Rev.), A.M., S. T. D. elsewhere, Bishop Nov. Scot., Governor King's Coll. aet. 82 *1816

*Hugh Neill, A. M.

*John Ogilvie, (Rev.), Yale 1748, A. M. and Yale, S. T. D. 1770 and Aberd., Gov. King's Coll. 1770–4. *1774

*John Tyler, (Rev.), A. B., A. M. 1769. *1823

7

## 1768.

*Samuel Bard, M. D. and Edinb. 1765, LL. D. N. Jers. 1815, Prof. Theor. and Pract. Med. 1767–76 and of Midw. 1770–6, Prof. Chem. 1784–5, 1786–7, Dean Med. Fac. 1792–1804. *1821

*Samuel Clossy, M. D. and Trin. Coll. Dub., Prof. Anat. 1767–76.

*Myles Cooper, (Rev.), Oxford, LL. D. and Ox., Prof. Mor. Phil. 1762–3, President 1763–75. *1785

*John Jones, M. D. and

Rheims, Prof. Surg. 1767–76. *1791
*Peter Middleton, M. D. and St. And., Prof. Path. and Physiol. 1776–76 and Mat. Med. and Chem. 1770–6, Governor King's Coll.

5

## 1769.

*Ebenezer Kneeland, (Rev.), Yale 1761, A. M. *1777

## 1770.

*Thomas Barton, (Rev.), A. M.
*Robert Blackwell, (Rev.), A. B. and N. Jers. 1768, A. M. N. Jers., S. T. D. N. Jers. and Univ. Penn. 1788.

2

## 1771.

*Jonathan Boucher, (Rev.), A. M.

## 1772.

*Edmund Fanning, Yale 1757, A. M. and Yale and Harv. 1764, J. C. D. Oxford 1774, LL. D. Yale 1803 and Dart. 1803, Surveyor Genl. Prov. N. Y. 1776, Lt.-Gov. Nov. Scot., Gov. Prince Edw. Isl. *1818

## 1773.

*Isaac Hunt, Phila., A. M.
*Joseph Lamson, (Rev.), Yale 1741, A. M. and Yale. *1773
*Harry Monroe, (Rev.), A. M.
*John Stuart, (Rev.), A. M.

4

## 1774.

*Luke Babcock, Yale 1755, A. M. and Yale. *1777
*George Panton, (Rev.), Aberd, A. M.
*James Sayre, (Rev.), Phila. Coll., A. M. aet. 53. *1798
*William Tryon, LL. D., Governor of the Province of New York. *1788

4

## 1787.

*James Hardie, A. B., A. M. 1790.

## 1788.

*Robert Annan, (Rev.), A. M.
*William Cochran, (Rev.), Trin. Coll. Dub., A. M., Prof. Greek and Lat. Lang. 1784–9.
*Robert Charles Johnson, Yale 1783, A.M. and Yale. *1806
*Samuel Latham Mitchill, M. D. Univ. Edinb. 1786, A. M., LL. D. elsewhere, Memb. N.Y. Assemb. 1790–2 and 1797–9, Prof. Bot. 1792–5 and Prof. Nat. Hist. Chem. and Agricult. 1792–1801, Repr. in Congr. 1801–3 and 1810–12, U. S. Sen. 1804–10, elected Prof. Chem. Coll. Phys. and Surg. N. Y. 1807 and declined, Prof. Nat. Hist. Coll. Phys. and Surg. N. Y. 1808–20 and Prof. Bot. and Mat. Med. 1820–6, Vice-Prest. Rutg. Med. Coll. N.Y. 1826–30. *1831
*John W. Watkins, A. M.

5

## 1789.

*Roger Alden, Yale 1773, A. M. and Yale. *1836
*Abraham Beach, (Rev.), Yale 1757, S. T. D., Trustee 1787–1813 and Clerk 1795–1811. *1828
*John Daniel Gross, (Rev.), S. T. D., Regent Univ. N. Y. S. 1784–7, Trustee 1787–92, Prof. Germ. Lang. and Geogr. 1784–95, and Prof. Mor. Phil. 1787–95.
*Jacob Rutsen Hardenbergh, (Rev.), A.M. N. Jers. 1770, S. T. D., Prest. Rutg. Coll. *1790
*Samuel William Johnson, Yale 1779, A. M. and Yale. *1816
*William Linn, (Rev.), N. Jers. 1772, S. T. D., Regent Univ. N. Y. S. 1787–1808. *1808
6

## 1790.

*Henry Maeller, (Rev.), A. M.
*James Proudfit, (Rev.), A.M.
2

## 1793.

*Ebenezer Dibble, (Rev.), Yale 1734, S. T. D. *1799
*Andrew Jaffray, (Rev.), S. T. D.
*William Ogilvie, LL. D., Prof. Human. Univ. Aberd.
3

## 1794.

*Richard Channing Moore, (Rev.), A.M., S. T. D. Dart. 1805, Bishop P. E. Ch. Va. 1814–41. aet. 79. *1841

## 1795.

John Campbell, A. M.
*John Coffin, Dart. 1791, A.M. and Dart. and N. Jers. 1795 and Yale 1798. *1852
2

## 1797.

*James Kent, Yale 1781 and A. M. Yale, LL. D. and Harv. 1810 and Dart. 1819, N. Y. Leg. 1790–94 and 1796, Prof. Law 1793–98 and 1823–47, Mast. in Chanc. N. Y. C. 1793, Recorder N. Y. C. 1797, Judge Sup. Ct. N. Y. 1798–1814 and Ch. Just. N. Y. 1804–14, Regent Univ. N. Y. S. 1800–17, Chanc. N. Y. 1814–23, Trustee 1823. aet. 85. *1847
*Samuel Andrew Law, Yale 1792, A. M. and Yale and N. Jers. 1797. *1845
2

## 1798.

William Best, (Rev.), A. M.
William Scott, (Rev.), A. M.
Andrew Smith, A. M.
Robert G. Wetmore, (Rev.), A. M.
4

## 1802.

William Duke, (Rev.), A. M.
*James Kemp, (Rev.), S. T. D., Bishop P. E. Ch. Maryland 1814–27.
2
2

## 1804.

*Edmund D. Barry, (Rev.), A. M.
Edward Jenkins, (Rev.), S.T. D. and Brown Univ. 1803.
Jacob Larzelere, (Rev.), A.M.
*Peter Stryker, (Rev.),A.M. *1847

4

## 1805.

Clement Meriam, (Rev.), A. M.

## 1806.

*William James Macneven, M. D. and Univ. Vienna 1873, Prof. Mat. Med. Rutg. Med. Coll. N. Y. *1841

## 1809.

Abraham Bronson, (Rev.), A. M.

## 1811.

*John Croes, (Rev.), A. M. N. Jers. 1797, S. T. D., Bishop P. E. Ch. N. Jers. 1815–32. *1832
James Hall, (Rev.), S. T. D.
*William Harris, (Rev.), Harv. 1786 and A. M. Harv., S. T. D. and Harv. 1811, President 1811–29, Trustee 1811–29 and Clerk 1811. *1829

3

## 1815.

*Frederic Beasley, (Rev.), N. Jers. 1797 and A. M. N. Jers., S. T. D. and Univ. Penn. 1815, Tutor N. Jers. 1798–1800, Provost Univ. Penn. 1815. *1845

## 1816.

*John Schureman, (Rev.), Rutg. Coll. 1795 and A. M. Rutg. and N. Jers. 1801, S. T. D., Prof. Eccles. Hist. and Past. Theol. in Theol. Sem. N. Brunsw. N. J. *1818

## 1818.

*Robert Adrain, LL. D., Prof. Math. and Nat. Phil. Rutg. 1810–13, Prof. Math and Nat. Phil. 1813–25, Prof. Math. Univ. Penn. 1827–34. *1843
*Joseph Hopkinson, Univ. Penn. 1786, LL. D. and N. Jers. 1818 and Harv. 1831, Repr. in Congr., Judge U. S. Dist. Ct. Penn. *1842
Samuel Nichols, (Rev.), Yale 1811, A. M.
Andrew Thomson, (Rev.), S. T. D.

4

## 1819.

*Thomas Church Brownell, (Rev.), Union 1804, S.T. D. and Union 1819, LL. D. elsewhere, Bishop P. E. Ch. Conn. 1819–65, Prest. Trin. Coll. 1824–31. *1865

*Philander Chase, (Rev.), Dart. 1796, S. T. D., Prest. Keny. Theol. Sem. 1825–31, Prest. Keny. Coll., Bishop P. E. Ch. Ohio 1819–31 and Bishop Illinois 1833–52, Prest. Jubilee Coll. aet. 76. *1852
John Philip, (Rev.), S. T. D. and N. Jers. 1820.

3

## 1820.

William Forrest, A. M.

## 1821.

*Thaddeus Fiske, (Rev.), Harv. 1785 and A. M. Harv., S. T. D. *1855
*Washington Irving, A. M., LL.D. 1829 and Harv. 1832, J. C. D. Ox. 1831, Memb. of several learned Societies, Regent Univ. N. Y. S. 1835–42, Secy. U. S. Leg. Lond., U. S. Min. to Spain, 1842–46. aet. 76. *1859
Daniel McDonald, (Rev.), S. T. D.

3

## 1822.

*William Lowndes, LL. D., Repr. in Congress, U. S. Sen.
*Thomas Lyell, (Rev.), A. M. Brown 1803, S. T. D. *1848
*Alexis P. Proal, (Rev.), A. M.
John Reed, (Rev.), Union 1805 and A. M. Union, S. T. D.
*Stephen N. Rowan, (Rev.), Union 1804 and A. M. Union, S. T. D. *1835
John Walsh, A. M.

6

## 1823.

John Carroll, A. M.
Abraham N. Halsey, A. M.
*Chauncey Lee, (Rev.), Yale 1784 and A. M. Yale, S. T. D. *1842
*Edward Livingston, N. Jers. 1781 and A. M. N. Jers., LL. D. and Transyl. 1824 and Harv. 1834, Trustee 1793–1806, Repr. in Congr. 1794–1801 and 1823–9, U. S. Dist.-Atty. N.Y. 1801–3, Mayor N. Y. C. 1801–3, Secy. St. U. S. 1831–3, U. S. Min. to France 1833–5. *1836
*John Stark Ravenscroft, (Rev.), S. T. D. Bishop P. E. Ch. N. Car. 1823–30. *1830
*Nathan Sandford, LL. D., U. S. Dist.-Atty. N. Y. 1803–16, Memb. N. Y. Assemb. 1811 and Speaker of the same, N. Y. Sen., U. S. Sen. 1816–22 and 1825–31, Memb. N. Y. Constit. Conven. 1821, Chancell. N. Y. 1823–25. *1838
*John Savage, Union 1799, LL. D. and Union 1829, Ch. Justice Sup. Ct. N. Y.
*Samuel Seabury, (Rev.), A. M., S. T. D. 1837, Prof. Bibl. Learn. and Interp. Script. Gen. Theol. Sem. P. E. Ch. aet. 72. *1872
*Ambrose Spencer, Harv. 1783, LL. D. and Univ. Penn. 1819 and Harv. 1821, Memb. N.Y. Assemb. 1793–5, N. Y. Sen. 1795–1802, Atty.-Gen. N. Y. 1802–4, Regent Univ. N.Y. S. 1805–17, Judge Sup. Ct. N. Y. 1804–19 and Ch.-Just. of the same 1819–23, Repr. in Congr. *1848

9

## 1824.

*Langdon Cheves, LL. D., Repr. in Congr. and Speaker, Supr. Judge S. Car., Prest. U. S. Bank, Ch. Commr. U. S. under Treaty of Ghent. *1857

William A. Clark, (Rev.), A. M.

*James Fenimore Cooper, A. M. *1851

*Thomas Addis Emmet, Trin. Coll. Dub., LL. D., Atty.-Gen. N. Y. *1827

*Ernest Lewis Hazelius, (Rev.), S. T. D. and Union 1824. *1853

*Levi Silliman Ives, (Rev.), Hamilton Coll., A. M., S. T. D. 1831, Bishop P. E. Ch. N. Car. 1831–53. aet. 70. *1867

*James Kirke Paulding, A. M., Nav. Off. N. Y., Secy. U. S. Navy 1837–41. *1860

*Daniel Webster, Dart. 1801 and A. M. Dart. and Harv. 1804, LL. D. and N. Jers. 1818 and Dart. 1824 and Harv. 1824, Memb. of several learned Soc., Repr. in Cong. 1813–17 and 1823–25, Memb. Mass. Constit. Conven. 1820, U. S. Sen. 1826–41 and 1845–50, Secy. St. U. S. 1841–43 and 1850–52. *1852

8

## 1825.

*John Caldwell Calhoun, Yale 1804, LL. D. and Hamilt. 1821 and Yale 1822, Memb. S. C. Leg., Repr. in Congr. 1811–17, Secy. War U. S. 1817–24, Vice-Prest. U. S. 1825–32, U. S. Sen. 1832–43 and 1845–50, Secy. St. U. S. 1844–45. *1850

*Stephen Elliot, Yale 1791, LL. D. and Yale 1819 and Harv. 1822, Memb. S. C. Leg., Prof. Nat. Hist. and Bot. S. C. Med. Coll. *1830

Henri L. P. F. Peneveyre, (Rev.), S. T. D.

*Joel Roberts Poinsett, LL. D., Repr. in Congr. 1821–27, U. S. Min. to Mex. 1828–30, Secy War U. S. 1837–41. *1851

William Shelton, A. M.

5

## 1826.

*William Wirt Phillips, (Rev.), Union 1813, S. T. D., Trustee N. Jers. Coll., Prest. Board For. Miss. Presbyt. Ch. *1865

## 1827.

*Jasper Adams, (Rev.), Brown 1815 and A. M. Brown and Yale 1819, S. T. D., Tutor Brown 1818–19, Prof. Math. and Nat. Phil. Brown 1819–24, Prest. Genev. Coll. 1827, Prest. Charleston S. C. Coll. and Prof. Mor. Phil., Prof. Eth. Milit. Acad. U. S. *1841

William Rollinson Whittingham, (Rev.), A. M., S. T. D. 1837, Prof. in Gen. Theol. Sem. P. E. Ch. N. Y., Bishop P. E. Ch. Maryland 1840–.

2

## 1828.

*Asa Eaton, (Rev.), Harv. 1803 and A. M. Harv. and Brown 1818, S. T. D. *1858
*Charles Taylor Catlin, Yale 1822, A. M. and Yale. aet. 67. *1870
William Buell Sprague, (Rev.), Yale 1815 and A. M. Yale 1819, S. T. D. and Harv. 1848.
3

## 1829.

*Antoine Verren, (Rev.), A. M., Prof. French Lang. and Lit. 1828–39. *1874

## 1830.

*James Marsh, (Rev.), Dart. 1817 and A. M. Dart., S. T. D. and Amh. 1833, Tutor Dart. 1818–20, Prof. Lang. Hamp. Syd., Coll., Prest. and Prof. Mor. Phil. and Met. Univ. Vt. *1842
*Frederic Christian Schaeffer, (Rev.), A. M. N. Jers. 1818, S. T. D., Prof. Germ. Lang. and Lit. 1830–31. *1831
William D. Snodgrass, (Rev.), Wash. Coll. Penn., A. M. N. Jers. 1822, S. T. D.
*William Murray Stone, (Rev.), S. T. D., Bishop P. E. Ch. Md. 1830–38. *1838
4

## 1831.

*Eli Baldwin, (Rev.), S. T. D. *1839
*James Ryan, A. M.
James Shea, A. M.
*George Upfold, (Rev.), Union 1814, M. D. Coll. Phys. and Surg. N. Y. 1816, S. T. D., LL. D. elsewhere, Bishop P. E. Ch. Ind. 1849. aet. 76. *1872
4

## 1832.

*Francis Lister Hawks, (Rev.), Univ. N. Car. 1815, A. M. Yale 1818, S. T. D., LL. D. elsewhere. *1866

## 1833.

*Charles Burroughs, (Rev.), Harv. 1806 and A. M. Harv. and Dart. 1811, S. T. D. *1851
*George Washington Doane. (Rev.), Union 1818, S. T. D. and Trin. 1833, LL. D. elsewhere, Prof Rhet. and Orat. Trin. Coll. 1824–28, Prest. Burlington Coll. N. J., Bishop P. E. Ch. N. Jers. 1832–59. *1859
*James Emott, A. M. Union 1800, LL. D. *1850
*James Hervey Otey, (Rev.), S. T. D., Bishop P. E. Ch. Tenn. 1834–63. *1863
John H. Pinder, (Rev.), S. T. D., Principal of Codrington Coll. Isl. Barbad.
*David Prentice, Yale 1812, A. M. and Yale, LL. D. Union 1839, Prof. Greek and Latin. Lang. Genev. Coll. *1857
6

## 1834.

Orange Clark, (Rev.), A. M.
Thomas Winthrop Coit, (Rev.), Yale 1821 and A. M. Yale 1831, S. T. D., LL. D. Trin. 1853, Prest. Trans. Univ., Prof. Eccl. Hist. Trin. Coll.
Don Thomas Gener, LL. D., Prest. Cortes of Spain.
Robert J. Harvey, A. M.
William Augustus Muhlenberg, Univ. Penn. 1814, (Rev.), S. T. D., Rector St. Paul's Coll. N. Y. and Founder St. Luke's Hospital N. Y. C.
William Sherwood, (Rev.), A. M. 6

## 1835.

*Benjamin Clark Cutler, (Rev.), Brown 1822 and A. M. Brown, S. T. D. *1863
Manuel Fetter, A. B., A. M. 1842, Prof. Greek Lang. and Lit. Univ. N. Carolina.
*William Gaston, N. Jers. 1796 and A. M. N. Jers., LL. D. and Univ. Penn. 1819 and Harv. 1826 and Univ. N. Y. C. 1834 and N. Jers. 1835, N. Car. Sen., Judge Sup. Ct. N. Car., Repr. in Congr. *1844
James Neilson Reynolds, A. M. 4

## 1836.

*Benjamin Hale (Rev.), Bowd. 1818 and A. M. Bowd. and Dart. 1827, M. D. Dart. 1827, S. T. D., Prof. Chem. and Min. and Med. Juris. Dart. 1827–35, President Genev. Coll. aet. 66. *1863
Benjamin Luckock, (Rev.), A. M.
*Jacob Sutherland, Yale 1807, LL. D., Judge Sup. Ct. N. Y. *1845 3

## 1837.

John Bethune, (Rev.), S.T.D.
William Cullen Bryant, A. M. and Will. 1819, LL. D. Union 1853.
*John Duer, LL. D., Memb. N. Y. Constit. Conven. 1821, Trustee 1823–30, Just. Supr. Ct. N. Y. C. 1849–57 and Ch.-Just. same 1857–8. *1858
*George Griffin, Yale 1797, LL. D. *1860
*Fitz-Greene Halleck, A. M. *1867
*Charles Fenno Hoffman, A. M.
Theodore Irving, (Rev.), A. M., LL. D. Union 1851, Prof. Belles-Lettr. Geneva Coll. 1837.
Samuel Allen McCoskry, (Rev.), Dickin. Coll. 1823 and A. M. Dickinson, S. T. D., D. C. L. Univ. Oxf., Bishop P. E. Ch. Mich. 1836–.
*Erskine Mason, (Rev.), Dickins. Coll. Penn. 1823 and A. M. Dickin., S. T. D.
*David B. Ogden, LL. D., Trustee 1815–49 and Chn. of Board 1843–49. *1849
*Thomas House Taylor, (Rev.), S. T. D. *1867
*Samuel A. Van Vranken, (Rev.), S. T. D. 12

## 1838.

*Isaac Boyle, (Rev.), Harv. 1813 and A. M. Harv., S. T. D. and Trin. 1838. *1850
Walter Chisholm, A. M.
*Leonidas Polk, (Rev.), U. S. Mil. Acad. 1829, S. T. D., Bishop P. E. Ch. Ark 1838–41, and Bishop of Louisiana 1841–64. aet. 58. *1864

3

## 1839.

Wm. M. Carmichael, (Rev.), S. T. D.
*Abraham Halsey, A. M. *1857

2

## 1840.

John Watson Adams, (Rev.), S. T. D.
*Stephen Elliott, (Rev.), Harv. 1824 and A. M. Harv., S. T. D., and Trin. 1840, Bishop P. E. Ch. Georgia 1841–66. *1866
Abraham Bruyn Hasbrouck, Yale 1810 and A. M. Yale 1819, LL. D. and Union 1841, Repr. in Congr., Prest. Rutg. Coll.
William Hawkesworth, A.M., Prof. Lang. S. Car. Coll. 1840.
*Hugh Swinton Legaré, (C. L.), S. C. Coll. 1814, LL. D., Memb. S. C. Leg. 1824–30, Atty.-Gen. S. C. 1830–2, Chargé d'Aff. U. S. at Brussels 1832–36, Repr. in Congr. 1836–38, Atty.-Gen. U. S. 1841–43. *1834
*William Hickling Prescott, Harv. 1814 and A.M. Harv., LL. D. and Univ. N. Car. 1841 and Harv. 1843, J. C. D. Oxford 1850, Memb. of many learned societies. *1859

6

## 1841.

*Albert Gallatin, Univ. Genev. Switz. 1779, LL. D., Memb. Penn. Constit. Conv. 1789, Memb. Penn. Leg. 1790–2, Repr. in Congr. 1795–1801, Secy. Treas. U. S. 1801–13, U. S. Commr. at Ghent 1814, U. S. Min. to France 1815–23, U. S. Env. Ex. to Gr. Britain 1826–7, Prest. Council Univ. N. Y. C. 1830, Prest. N. Y. Hist. Society 1843–9. *1849
C. H. Gottsberger, A. M.
*Samuel Nelson, LL. D., Just. Sup. Ct. U. S. aet. 81. *1873
William M. Thompson, A. M.

4

## 1842.

Gustavus Abeel, (Rev.), Union 1823 and A. M. Union, S. T. D.
*James J. Bowden, A. B.
*Charles W. Hackley, (Rev.), U. S. Mil. Acad. 1829, A.M., S. T. D. elsewhere, A. A. Prof. Maths. U. S. Mil. Acad. 1829–31, 1832–33, Prof. Maths. Univ. N. Y. C. 1833–39, Prest. Jeff. Coll. Miss. 1839, Prof. Math. and Astr. 1843–57, Prof. Astr. 1857–61. *1861
*Edward Y. Higbee, (Rev.), A. M., S. T. D. 1843. aet. 70. *1871

George C. Schaeffer, A. M., M. D. elsewhere, Librarian 1839-47, Professor Chem. Georget. Coll. Kent.
John H. Shepherd, A. M.

6

## 1843.

John M. Duncan, (Rev.), S. T. D.
George E. Hare, (Rev.), Union 1826, S. T. D.
Daniel Stone, A. M., Prof. Anc. Lang. West. Univ. Penn. 1843. 3

## 1844.

Edward E. Ford, (Rev.), S. T. D.
Joseph W. Ingraham, A. M.
Charles G. McLean, (Rev.), S. T. D.
*Ambrose Seymour Todd, (Rev.), A. M. Yale 1824, S. T.D. *1861
Charles E. West, A. M. Princ. Rutg. Female Instit. N. Y. C. 1844. 5

## 1845.

*Daniel Dewey Barnard, Will. 1818, LL. D. and Geneva and Brown 1853, Repr. in Congr., U. S. Min. at Brussels. *1861
Edward Cooper, A. M.
Charles Hewitt, A. M.
John W. McCullough, (Rev.), S. T. D.
Horatio Southgate, (Rev.), Bowd. 1832 and A. M. Bowd., S. T. D. and Trin. Coll. 1846, Bishop P. E. Ch. Constantinople 1844-50.
*Bird Wilson, (Rev.), S. T. D. elsewhere, LL. D., Prof. Gen. Theol. Sem. P. E. Ch. 6

## 1846.

William Bayard Blackwell, A. M.
Ezra A. Huntington, (Rev.), Union 1833, S. T. D.

2

## 1847.

William Ingraham Kip, (Rev.), Yale 1831 and A.M. Yale and Trin. 1846, S. T. D., Bishop P. E. Ch. Californ. 1853-.
Joseph Henry Price, (Rev.), Brown 1825 and A. M. Brown, S. T. D.
*John Canfield Spencer, Union 1806, LL. D. and Union 1849, Mast. in Chanc. 1811, Dist. Atty. West. Dist. N.Y., Repr. in Congr. 1817-19, Memb. N. Y. Assemb. 1819-24 and Speaker of the same 1820, N. Y. Sen. 1824-26, Secy. St. N. Y. 1839-41, Secy. War U. S. 1841-43, Secy. Treas. U. S. 1843-44, Regent Univ. N. Y. S. 1840-44. *1855

3

## 1848.

*Francis Vinton, (Rev.), U. S. Mil. Acad. 1830, A. B. Brown Univ. 1833, S. T. D., D. C. L. Will. and Mary's Coll. 1869, elected Bishop P. E. Ch. Indiana 1847 and declined, Prof. Eccl. Pol. and Law Gen. Theol. Sem. P. E. Ch. N. Y. 1869-72. aet. 63. *1872

## 1849.

George Alexander Crook, A. M.
James Stephenson, (Rev.), A. M.
Horace Webster, U. S. Mil. Acad. 1818, A. M. N. Jers. 1824, LL. D. and Keny. Coll. 1842, M. D. Univ. Penn. 1850, Asst. Prof. Math. U. S. Mil. Acad. 1818–25, Prof. Math. Geneva Coll. 1825–48, Prest. Coll. City N. Y. 1848–69.

3

## 1850.

*William Drisler, A. M. *1870
David X. Junkin, (Rev.), S. T. D., Prof. Belles Lettr. and Eng. Lit. Lafay. Coll. 1837–42, Prest. Wash. Coll. Va.
John Barrett Kerfoot, (Rev.), S. T. D. and Trin. Coll. 1865, LL. D. Univ. Camb. Eng. 1867, Rector St. James Coll. Md., Prest. Trin. Coll. 1864–65, Bishop P. E. Ch. Pittsburg 1865–.
*Kendrick Metcalf, (Rev.), Dart. 1829, S. T. D., Prof. Greek and Lat. Lang. and Lit. Hobart. *1872
*Winfield Scott, A. M. N. Jers. 1814, LL. D. and Harv. 1861, Maj.-Gen. and Bvt.- Lt.-Gen. U. S. A. aet. 80. *1866
Timothy D. Williams, A. M.

6

## 1851.

*Francis H. Cuming, (Rev.), S. T. D.
*Martin P. Parks, (Rev.), S. T. D.
John Williams, (Rev.), S. T. D. and Union 1847, LL. D. Hobart 1870, Prest. Trin. Coll. 1848–53, Asst. Bishop P. E. Ch. Conn. 1851–65 and Bishop 1865–.
Octavius Winslow, (Rev.), S. T. D.

4

## 1852.

Stephen Alexander, Union 1824 and A. M. Union, LL. D., Prof. Math. and Astr. N. Jers.
Samuel Gilman Brown, (Rev.), Dart. 1831 and A. M. Dart., S. T. D., Prof. Rhet. and Polit. Lit. Dart. 1840–63 and Prof. Int. Phil. and Pol. Econ. 1863–66 and Prest. 1866–68, Prest. Ham. Coll. 1868–.
William B. Franklin, U. S. Mil. Acad. 1843, A. M., Prof. Nat. Phil. Free Acad. N. Y. C., Maj.-Gen. U. S. V.
*Richard Pulling Jenks, Harv. 1830, A. M. aet. 67. *1872
William McMurray, (Rev.), A. M. Trin. 1846, S. T. D.
John Rowland, (Rev.), A. M.
Jonn Lee Watson, (Rev.), Harv. 1815 and A. M. Harv., S. T. D.

7

## 1853.

Talbot W. Chambers, (Rev.), S. T. D.
*Thomas Frederick Davis, (Rev.), S. T. D., Bishop P. E. Ch. S. C. 1853-71. aet. 68. *1871
Henry D. Erskine, (Rev.), A. M. elsewhere, S. T. D., Dean of Ripon, Eng.

Charles Todd Quintard, (Rev.), M. D. elsewhere, A. M., S. T. D. 1866, LL. D. Camb. Univ. Eng. 1867, Prof. in Medical College, Memphis, Tenn., Bishop P. E. Ch. Tenn. 1865–.
Charles Rogers, (Rev.), LL. D., Fellow Scottish Soc. of Antiquarians, Prof. Eng. Lang. and Lit. Univ. Penn.
Samuel Pratt Strong, (Rev.), S. T. D.

6

## 1854.

William R. Gordon, (Rev.), S. T. D.
Jean Romer, A. M., LL. D. elsewhere, Prof. French Lang. and Lit. Free Acad. N. Y. C.
J. Jackson Scott, (Rev.), S. T. D.
Henry Philip Tappan, (Rev.), Union 1825, S. T. D. Union 1845, LL. D., Prof. Mor. and Int. Phil. Univ. N. Y. C. 1832–38, Chancell. Univ. Mich. 1850-63, Cor. Memb. Inst. of France 1856.

4

## 1855.

John M. Macauley, (Rev.), S. T. D.
Joseph Few Smith,† (Rev.), Yale 1840 and A. M. Yale, S. T. D., Prof. Sac. Lit. Aub. Theol. Sem.

2

† Known subsequently as Joseph Fewsmith.

## 1856.

John Blakely, (Rev.), S. T. D.
George Sharswood, LL. D., Ch.-Judge Dist. Ct. Penn., Prof. Instit. of Law Univ. Penn., Judge Sup. Ct. Penn. 1867–.
Richard Somers Smith, U.S. Mil. Acad. 1834, A. M., Prof. Maths. Eng. and Drawing Brooklyn Polyt. Inst. 1855-59, Director Cooper Union N. Y. C. 1859–61, Major U. S. A. 1861-63, Prest. Girard Coll. Penn. 1863–.
Alfred Stubbs, (Rev.), Yale 1835 and A. M. Yale, S. T. D.

4

## 1857.

Joseph Alden, (Rev.), Union 1829 and A. M. Union and N. Jers. 1832 and Will. 1837, S. T. D. Union 1839, LL. D., Tutor Coll. N. Jers. 1830–32, Prof. Rhet. Polit. Econ. and Hist. Will. 1835-52, Prof. Metaph. and Mor. Phil. Lafay. Coll., Prest. Jeff. Coll. Penn.
Alfred Baury Beach, (Rev.), Trin. Coll. 1841 and A. M. Trin., S. T. D.
Samuel Cooke, (Rev.), A. M. Yale 1847, S. T. D. and Univ. N. Y. C. 1857.
William Ferdinand Morgan, (Rev.), Union 1837 and A. M. Union and Trin., S. T. D. and Trin. 1849.

4

## 1858.

Charles D. Morris, A. M. and Oxford.

Samuel Spring, (Rev.), A. B. and A. M. Yale 1821, S. T. D.

Henry Waterman, (Rev.), Brown 1831, S. T. D.

*Isaac Dyckman Vermilye, (Rev.), A. M.

4

## 1859.

Thomas De Boice Coryell, Univ. Wis., A. M.

*William Armstrong Dod, (Rev.), N. Jers. 1838 and A. M. N. Jers., S. T. D., Tutor N. Jers. 1840–1, Lect. on Architect. and the Fine Arts Coll. N. Jers. *1872

George H. Houghton, (Rev.), S. T. D., Instr. in Hebr. Gen. Theol. Sem. P. E. Ch. N. Y.

*Lot Jones, (Rev.), Bowd. 1821 and A. M. Bowd., S. T. D. *1865

Alexander G. Mercer, (Rev.), Coll. N. J. 1837 and A. M. Coll. N. J., S. T. D , Prof. Ment. and Mor. Phil. Univ. Penn.

Samuel Tyler, LL. D.

6

## 1860.

Charles P. Daly, LL. D., Just. Ct. Com. Pleas N.Y. C., Memb. N. Y. S. Constit. Conv. 1867.

Theodore W. Dwight, Hamilton Coll. and A. M. Hamilt., LL. D. and Rutg. Coll. 1859, Tutor Hamilt. 1842–46, Prof. Law Hist. Civ. Pol. and Pol. Econ. Hamilt. 1846-58, Prof. Munic. Law 1858–, and Warden Law Sch. 1864–, Memb. N. Y. Constit. Conv. 1867, Commr. Appeals N. Y. State.

*John W. French, (Rev.), Trin. Coll. 1832 and A. M. Trin., S. T. D., Prof. Ethics U. S. Mil. Acad.

*Thomas Tompkins Guion, (Rev.), Trin. 1840, S. T. D. aet. 45. *1862

Fordyce Mitchell Hubbard, (Rev.), Will. 1828 and A. M. Will., S. T. D. and Trin. 1860, Tutor Will. 1831–2, Prof. Lat. Lang. Univ. N. Car.

*Matthew Hall McAllister, LL. D., Judge U. S. Dist. Ct. Cal. *1865

William H. N. Stewart,(Rev.), Trin. Coll. Dub., A. M., LL. D. Lafayette 1868.

Charles S. Tripler, M. D. Coll. Phys. and Surg. N. Y. 1827, A. M., Asst. Surg. U. S. A. 1830–38 and Surg. 1838–, Maj. and Bvt. Col. U. S. A.

*Lewis Bartholomew Woodruff, Yale 1830 and A. M. Yale, LL. D. Judge Supr. Ct. N. Y. C., Judge U. S. Circ. Ct. 1870–5. *1875

9

## 1861.

*Alexander Warfield Bradford, Union 1832 and A. M. Union, LL. D. and Union 1852, Corporation Atty. N. Y. C. 1843, Surrogate N. Y. C. 1848–58, Trustee 1855–67. aet. 52. *1867

Charles H. Hall, (Rev.), Yale 1862, S. T. D. and Hobart 1862.

*Abraham Lincoln, LL. D. and Coll. N. J. 1864, President of the United States 1861–65. *1865

*Joseph C. Passmore, (Rev.), S. T. D., Prof. Rhet. Int. Phil. and Pol. Econ. St. James Coll. Md. and Racine Coll. Wis. * 1866

S. Chipman Thrall, (Rev.), S. T. D.

Sullivan H. Weston, (Rev.), S. T. D., Trustee Med. Dept. 1860–.

6

## 1862.

Henry P. Balcom, A. M. Supt. Pub. Sch. Middlet., Conn.

Samuel Buel, (Rev.), Will. 1833 and A. M. Will., S. T. D., Tutor Ken., Prof. System. Divin. Gen. Theol. Sem. P. E. Ch. 1871–.

George Jarvis Geer, (Rev.), Trin. 1842 and A. M. Trin., S. T. D. and Union 1862.

Benjamin Nicholas Martin, (Rev.), Yale 1837 and A. M. Yale, S. T. D., Prof. Phil. and Hist. Univ. N. Y. C.

Henry Joel Scudder, Trin. 1846, A. M. and Trin., Repr. in Congr.

John Cotton Smith, (Rev.), Bowd. 1847 and A. M. Bowd., S. T. D.

6

## 1863.

Samuel Hanson Cox, (Rev.), Univ. N. Y. C., A. M. Trin. 1852, S. T. D.

Samuel Eliot, Harv. 1839 and A. M. Harv. and Trin. 1857, LL.D., Prof. Hist. and Polit. Sci. Trin., elected Prof. Anc. and Mod. Lit. 1857 and declined, President Trin. Coll. 1860–4.

Jared B. Flagg, (Rev.), S. T. D.

Robert S. Howland, (Rev.), S. T. D.

Thomas Ricker Lambert, (Rev.), A. M. Brown 1845 and Trin. 1852, S. T. D.

Henry B. Walbridge, (Rev.), S. T. D.

6

## 1864.

Henry Stephens Cutler, Mus. D.

Joseph G. Fox, C. E. elsewhere, A. M., Prof. Math. Cooper Inst. N. Y. C.

Thomas Hunter, A. M.

3

## 1865.

Samuel Ely, (Rev.), S. T. D.

Richard Graham Hutton, (Rev.), A. M.

*Andrew Johnson, LL. D., Vice-President of the United States 1865 and President 1865–69.

McWalter B. Noyes, (Rev.), A. M.

Samuel S. Shedden, (Rev.), S. T. D.

James Tuttle Smith, (Rev.), A. M., Hosp. Chapl. U. S. A. 1862–65.

William H. Walter, Mus. D.

George D. Waters, (Rev.), S. T. D.

John Freeman Young, (Rev.), S. T. D., Bishop P. E. Ch. Florida 1867–.

9

## 1866.

*Abner Jackson, (Rev.), Trin. Coll. 1837 and A. M. Trin., S. T. D. Trin. 1858, LL. D., Tutor Trin. 1837–38, and Libr. 1837–49, Adj. Prof. Greek and Lat. Lang. Trin. 1838–40, Lect. in Chem. and Nat. Sci. Trin. 1840–51 and Prof. Ethics and Metaphys. 1840–58, Prest. and Prof. Ev. Christ. Hobart Coll., Prest. Trin. Coll. 1867–74. aet. 63. *1874
Charles P. Kirkland, LL. D., Judge Sup. Court N. Y.
James Mulchahey, (Rev.), Trin. 1842 and A. M. Trin., S. T. D.

3

## 1867.

Samuel B. Bostwick, (Rev.), S. T. D.
William Croswell Doane, (Rev.), S. T. D., Bishop P. E. Ch. Albany 1868–.
Ferdinand Cartwright Ewer, (Rev.), Harv. 1848 and A. M. Harv. 1868, S. T. D.
Channing Moore Williams, (Rev.), S. T. D., Bishop P. E. Ch. China 1866–.

4

## 1868.

Philander Kinney Cady, (Rev.), S. T. D.
Benjamin Wistar Morris, (Rev.), S. T. D., Bishop P. E. Ch. Oregon and Washington 1868–.
Charles Franklin Robertson, (Rev.), Yale 1859, S. T. D., Bishop P. E. Ch. Missouri 1868–.

3

## 1869.

Charles Breck, (Rev.), S. T. D.
Theodore Augustus Eaton, (Rev.), S. T. D.
Asa Bird Gardner, (Rev.), Dart. 18—, A.M. and Dartmouth, L. L. B. elsewhere, Prof. Law U. S. Mil. Acad. 1874–.
Thomas Williams Humes, (Rev.), S.T. D., Prest. Univ. East Tenn.
William Quintard Ketchum, (Rev.), S. T. D.
Benson J. Lossing, A. M.
John Carpenter Smith, (Rev.), S. T. D.

7

## 1870.

*Samuel Brazer Babcock, (Rev.), S. T. D. *1873
George Marlow Everhart, (Rev.), S. T. D. and Henry Coll. Va. 1852, Prest. Huntsville Coll. Ala. 1852–57, Rector Kemper Hall Wis. 1871.
Peter Hasbrouck, Rutgers Coll., A. M.

3

## 1871.

George B Andrews, (Rev.), S. T. D.
Edmund De Schweinitz, (Rev.), S. T. D.
John Habersham Elliott, (Rev.), S. T. D.
James Isbell Helms, (Rev.), S. T. D.
Pelham Williams, (Rev.), S. T. D.

5

## 1872.

John Graeff Barton, LL. D., Prof. Eng. Lang. and Lit. Coll. City N. Y.
Howard Crosby, (Rev.), S. T. D. elsewhere, LL. D., Chancellor Univ. City N. Y.
John Watts De Peyster, A. M.
Edward David Hearn, A. M.
William Bell White Howe, (Rev.), S. T. D., Bishop P. E. Ch. South Carolina.
Charles O'Connor, LL. D.
Isaac Lewis Peet, LL. D., Prin. Instit. Deaf and Dumb N. Y. C.
Eliphalet Nott Porter, (Rev.), S. T. D., Prest. Union Coll. N. Y.

8

## 1873.

John Gottlieb Auer, (Rev.), S. T. D., Missionary Bishop Cape Palmas, Afr.
George Beckett, (Rev.), S. T. D.
Aaron Bernstein, (Rev.), A. M., Miss. to the Jews, Bucharest.
William Henry Chandler, A. M., Prof. Chem. Lehigh Univ. Penn.
Henry Augustus Homes, LL. D., State Libr. N. Y.
William Reed Huntington, (Rev.), S. T. D.
Frederic Stengel, A. M., Instr. in Germ. School of Mines Col. Coll.
James Stephenson, (Rev.), S. T. D.

8

## 1874.

E. Edwards Beardsley, (Rev.), LL. D.
Joseph H. Clinch, (Rev.), S. T. D., Chaplain Pub. Instit. Boston, Mass.
Jacob Cooper, (Rev.), D. C. L. elsewhere, S. T. D., Prof. Greek Lang. and Lit. Rutgers Coll. N. J.
Robert N. Merritt, (Rev.), S. T. D.
Clarkson Nott Porter, LL. D., Repr. in Congr.

5

## 1875.

William Spencer Child, (Rev.), S. T. D.
William Kirtland Douglas, (Rev.), S. T. D., Princ. "Bishop Green Training School," Jackson, Miss.
William Porcher Du Bose, (Rev.), S. T. D., Chaplain Univ. of the South, Tenn.
John Nicholas Galleher, (Rev.), S. T. D.
William Andrew Snively, (Rev.), S. T. D.
Thomas Edward Vermilye, (Rev.), S. T. D.

6

## 1876.

John Marshall Kellogg, A. M.
Julius Hawley Seelye, LL. D., Prof. Ment. and Mor. Phil. Amherst Coll., Repr. in Congr., Prest. Amherst Coll.

2

# ENUMERATION.

| | | |
|---|---|---|
| Graduates in Arts | 2242 | |
| Graduates in Medicine | 1437 | |
| Graduates in Law | 1546 | |
| Graduates of the Mining School | 115 | |
| Honorary Graduates, etc | 366 | |
| Total | 5706 | |
| Deduct names repeated | 200 | 5506 |

KNOWN TO BE DECEASED.

| | | |
|---|---|---|
| Graduates in Arts | 1094 | |
| Graduates in Medicine | 41 | |
| Graduates in Law | 20 | |
| Graduates of School of Mines | 2 | |
| Honorary Graduates, etc | 180 | |
| Total | 1337 | |
| Deduct names repeated | 15 | 1322 |
| Presumed to be living | | 4184 |

# INDEX OF OFFICERS.

# INDEX OF GRADUATES.

*h* indicates Hononary Graduates and Graduates of other Colleges who have been admitted to the same degree.

*l* indicates Graduates in Law.

*m* indicates Graduates in Medicine.

*m. e.* indicates Graduates of the School of Mines.

Arcularius,
1868 Philip E. *m.*

Arden,
1844 John B.

Armitage,
1849 William E.

Amstrong,
1864 Richard. *l.*

Arnold,
1864 William P. *l.*
1868 John W. S.
1870 Lemuel H., Jr. *l.*
1872 Robert.

Arrowsmith,
1876 Harold.

Ashmead,
1874 Lehman P. *m.*

Ashmore,
1872 Sidney G.

Aspinall,
1875 Joseph. *l.*

Aspinwall,
1809 Thomas S.

Astor,
1839 John J., Jr.
1849 William.
1875 William W. *l.*

Atkins,
1868 Osmin W. *l.*

Atkinson,
1803 George H.
1808 William.
1869 Clinton. *m.*

Atwater,
1866 Edward S. *l.*
1871 Caleb H. *m.*
1871 Henry G. *l.*
1874 Addison. *l.*

Atwill,
1862 Edward R.

Atwood,
1774† Thomas.
1870 J. Freeman. *m.*
1874 James P. *m.*

Aub,
1870 Theodore. *l.*

Auchmuty,
1767 Samuel. *h.*
1774 Robert N.
1775 Richard.
1775 Samuel.

Auer,
1873 John G. *h.*

Auerbach,
1875 Meyer. *l.*

Auld,
1835 Jedediah B.

Austen,
1872 Peter T. *m. e.*

Austin,
1865 Harvey N. *m.*
1866 David P. *m.*
Thomas S. *m. e.*

Averill,
1869 James K. *t.*

Avery,
1767 Ephraim. *h.*
1832 Walter T.
1866 Edward W. *m.*
1868 William A. *m.*

Aycrigg,
1824 Benjamin.

Ayer,
1866 James M. *m.*

Ayers,
1870 Daniel S., Jr. *m.*

Aymar,
1843 Benjamin N.
1873 José.

Ayres,
1856 William W.
1875 Morgan W. *m.*

Babcock,
1774 Lucas. *h.*
1849 Edward C.
1856 Edwin S.
1862 Francis.
1868 Henry D.
1870 Samuel B. *h.*
1875 William.

Bach,
1875 Albert. *l.*
1875 Thomas C.

Bachman,
1876 Nathan L. *l.*

Backus,
1827 J. Trumbull.
1838 Mancer M.
1872 Henry C. *l.*

Bacon,
1854 George W.
1856 Charles A.
1859 Richard S.
1867 Wilbur R. *l.*

Badeau,
1873 Gilbert H. *l.*

Badger,
1861 George. *m.*
1861 William. *m.*

Bagshaw,
1876 Walter J. *l.*

Bailey,
1802 Joseph *m.*
1813 William.
1829 Theodore A.
1869 Charles H. *m.*

Bainbridge,
1789 John T.
1798 Joseph.

Baker,
1827 Jacob S.
1827 William S.
1862 Cyrus E. *m.*
1864 George W. *m.*
1867 James, Jr.
1870 George A., Jr. *l.*
1871 George. *l.*
1871 James, Jr. *l.*
1871 Joseph D. *l.*
1874 Alfred J. *l.*
1876 Frederick A. *l.*
1876 George McC. *l.*

Balch,
1860 Galusha B. *m.*
1870 Lewis. *m.*
1871 William V. *m.*

Balcom,
1862 Henry P. *h.*

Baldwin,
1831 Eli. *h.*
1856 Albert H.
1860 Daniel P. *l.*
1860 George V. N. *l.*
1866 Silas C. *m.*
1867 Charles H. *l.*
1867 John W. *m.*
1867 Truman H. *l.*

Ball,
1814 John H.
1863 Alonzo B. *m.*
1867 Oglevie D. *m.*

Balleray,
1869 George H. *m,*
1874 John J. *l.*

Balston,
1876 James H. *l.*

Bamberger,
1873 Ira L.

Bancroft,
1840 Charles.

Bang,
1876 Richard T.

Bangs,
1862 Charles W. *l.*
1872 Lemuel B. *m.*

Banks,
1842 William G.
1860 George B. *m.*
1874 Sheppard. *l.*

Barbour,
1865 James E. *m*
1871 Robert.

Barclay,
1766 James.
1772 Thomas.
1796 David.
1867 Frederick S. *m.*
1867 Henry A. W.

Barculoo,
1795 George.

Bard,
1768 Samuel. *h.*
1797 William.

Barker,
1824 Robert.
1827 Thomas H.
1860 Phanet C. *m.*

Barlow,
1875 Everett D. *l.*

Barnard,
1845 Daniel D *h.*
1868 Augustus P. *m. e.*
1874 Walter C. *m.*

Barnes,
1821 William B.
1876 Pearce. *l.*

Barnet,
1771 Ichabod B.

Barnum,
1804 John W.
1865 Edmund B. *l.*

Barrett,
1870 Isaac B.

Barron,
1861 John C. *m.*

Barrow,
1804 William *m.*
1833 James, Jr.
1861 Thomas. *m.*

Barrows,
1870 Arthur A. *m.*

Barry,
1804 Edmund D. *h.*
1820 Edmund D., Jr.
1860 Robert P.
1871 Thomas G. *l.*
1874 Joseph B. *l.*
1875 Daniel E. *m.*

Bartlett,
1833 John S.
1869 Willard.
1873 Franklin *l,*
1874 Clifford A. H. *l.*

Barton,
1770 Thomas. *h.*
1864 Philip H. *m.*
1872 John G. *h.*

Bartow,
1806 John V.
1862 Robert E.
1864 Reginald H.
1869 Evelyn.
1872 George W. *m.*

Bassett,
1786 John.
1862 George P. *m.*

Bates,
1876 Henry W.

Battershall,
1874 Joseph W. *m.*

Bauerdorf,
1874 Charles F. *l.*

Baxter,
1858 Wyllys P.
1868 George S. *m. e.*

Blauvelt,
1801 Abraham L.
1873 Gerritt F. *m.*
1876 Alonzo. *m.*

Bleecker,
1791 Anthony.
1791 William.
1805 Leonard A.
1820 John B.
1865 Edward. *m.*

Bleything,
1871 George D. *m.*

Bliss,
1868 William W. *l.*

Blois,
1867 Eugene S. *l.*

Bloomer,
1758 Joshua.

Bloomfield,
1861 Smith. *l.*
1876 Thomas B. *m.*
1876 Charles S. *l.*

Blossom,
1866 Thomas M.

Blundell,
1861 William. *m.*

Blunt,
1850 Matthew M.

Boardman,
1857 William S.
1863 Daniel F.
1873 Edward C. *l.*
1875 Albert B. *l.*

Bodley,
1875 Harry I., Jr.

Bodman,
1863 Lewis H. *m.*

Boetzkes,
1872 Peter A. E. *m.*

Bogardus,
1815 Archibald R.
1860 John C. *m.*

Bogart,
1790 David S.

Bogert,
1773 Cornelius.
1801 Samuel.
1832 Horatio.
1846 Edward C.
1846 Henry A.
1852 Charles L.
1856 William P.
1861 Ryckman D. *m.*
1865 Sylvester S. *m.*
1875 Albert O. *m.*

Boggs,
1830 John B.

Boise,
1870 Eugene P. *m.*

Bolles,
1876 Richard J. *l.*

Bolmer,
1863 William B.

Bolte,
1874 Hermann. *l.*

Bolton,
1801 Thomas.
1831 James.
1833 Jackson.
1847 John H.
1862 Henry C.

Bond,
1862 Daniel W. *l.*
1868 Thomas S. *m.*
1869 Henry H. *l.*

Bonnett,
1818 Daniel.

Bonney,
1868 Calvin F. *m.*

Boorman,
1860 Robert H.

Borrowe,
1793 Samuel. *m.*

Bosley,
1868 George H. *m.*

Boss,
1864 John B. *m.*

Bostwick,
1867 Samuel B. *h.*

Bosworth,
1874 Frank H. *l.*

Bottum,
1874 John B. *l.*

Botty,
1875 Henry C. *l.*

Boucher,
1771 Jonathan. *h.*

Bowden,
1772 John.
1813 James J.
1840 Samuel.
1842 James J. *h.*
1869 Hector S. *m.*

Bowdoin,
1830 James.

Bowdoine,
1795 James. *h.*

Bowlby,
1862 William W. *m.*

Bowles,
1874 Edward P.

Bowman,
1875 Henry H. *l.*

Bowne,
1803 John.

Boyd,
1787 Samuel.
1797 Robert.
1806 George.
1813 William.
1823 William H.
1832 William L.
1861 William A.
1871 James P., Jr. *m.*

Boyle,
1838 Isaac. *h.*

Boyse,
1840 Gerard S.

Bracken,
1866 Thomas. *l.*

Bradford,
1861 Alexander W. *h.*
1865 Theodore W. *m.*

Bradfield,
1872 Thomas N. *m.*

Bradish,
1873 James H. *l.*

Bradley,
1870 George P. *m.*
1872 Arthur C. *l.*

Bradshaw,
1875 Charles. *l.*

Bradstreet,
1873 Albert P. *l.*

Brady,
1809 John.
1868 James M.

Brailly,
1875 Alfred V. *m.*

Brainerd,
1866 Clarence.

Branch,
1876 Oliver E. *l.*

Brand,
1870 William. *m.*

Brandegee,
1876 John E. *l.*

Brandeis,
1871 Richard C. *m.*

Brashear,
1861 Basil B. *m.*

Brayton,
1861 Samuel N. *m.*
1873 Charles E. *m.*

Bray,
1874 Charles W. *m.*

Breakell,
1873 James A. *m.*

Brennan,
1862 George M. *m.*
1862 John W. *m.*

Brewster,
1867 Edward P. *l.*

Brice,
1874 John, Jr. *l.*

Brickell,
1874† John.

Bridgham,
1867 Samuel W., Jr. *m. e.*
1871 William H.

Bried,
1875 Charles. *l.*

Briegleb,
1874 Charles T A. *l.*

Briggs,
1860 Samuel W. *m.*
1868 Benjamin M. *m.*

Brill,
1874 Max. *l.*

Brinckerhoff,
1798 George.

Brinkerhoff,
1875 Jacob G. *l.*

Brisbane,
1874 James. *l.*

Bristow,
1876 Algernon T. *m.*

Brockway,
1861 A. Norton. *m.*
1873 Charles H. *m.*

Broderick,
1863 John C. *l.*

Brodhead,
1864 Henry. *l.*

Brodsky,
1876 John E. *l.*

Bromley,
1861 Miles S. *l.*

Bronk,
1807 John L.

Bronson,
1809 Abraham. *h.*
1846 Arthur.
1848 Theodorus B.
1863 Willett. *l.*
1869 Edward B. *m.*
1871 Frederic.

Brooks,
1814 James.
1867 John F. *l.*
1869 Lawton S. *m.*
1870 Eugene W. *m.*
1871 Walter A. *m.*
1876 Isidore. *l.*

Broome,
1791 William T.

Brouwer,
1807 John H.
1842 Abraham S.

Candidus,
1872 Pantaleon. *m.*

Canfield,
1862 Robert B.
1873 Frederick A. *m.e.*

Cannon,
1817 John M.
1870 Charles K. *l.*

Cardwell,
1870 Samuel, Jr. *l.*

Carew,
1861 Edmund S. *m.*

Carey,
1839 Arthur.
1839 John, Jr.
1861 George H.
1862 John E. *m.*
1865 George. *m.*
1874 George F. *m.*

Carit,
1864 Adolphe. *m.*

Carle,
1867 Charles A. *m.*

Carleton,
1861 George W. *m.*

Carley,
1864 Eldred A. *m.*

Carlin,
1876 Joseph F. *l.*

Carlisle,
1875 William T. *l.*

Carll,
1870 Lewis B.

Carmalt,
1861 William H. *m.*

Carman,
1874 Nelson G., Jr. *l.*

Carmichael,
1839 William M. *h.*

Carpenter,
1848 Horace W.
1863 Wesley M. *m.*
1874 Alexander T. *l.*
1875 George E. *m.*

Carr,
1874 George W. *l.*

Carillo,
1874 Isaac. *l.*

Carrington,
1860 Charles. *m.*
1862 Edward. *l.*

Carroll,
1823 John. *h.*
1869 Craft C. *m.*

Carson,
1868 James P. *m. e.*
1872 Thomas A. *m.*

Carter,
1829 James A.
1850 Galen A.
1854 Cullen L.
1861 Charles. *m.*
1866 Nathan R.
1867 Frank. *m.*
1872 Henry S. *m.*

Cartter,
1869 William H. *m.*

Carvill,
1832 George, Jr.

Caruana,
1874 John L. C. *l.*

Casalduc,
1874 Eduardo. *m.*

Casanova,
1873 Ricardo. *l.*

Case,
1868 Albertson. *l.*
1869 Charles H. *m.*

Casey,
1834 William B.
1864 Francis P. *m.*
1875 James H. *m.*

Casilear,
1875 Frank P. *l.*

Cassidy,
1872 Patrick S. *l.*

Castle,
1873 William R. *l.*

Caswell,
1861 William H.
1865 John H.

Catlin,
1828 George.
1828 Charles T. *h.*

Chace,
1873 Harrie P. *m.*

Chadsey,
1875 Alonzo G. *m.*

Chalmers,
1861 Matthew. *m.*
1863 George. *l.*
1865 Andrew B. *l.*

Chamberlain,
1871 Charles W. *m.*
1873 Edward W. *l.*

Chambers,
1853 Talbot W. *h.*

Chandler,
1758 Thomas B. *h.*
1774 William.
1862 Thomas K. *m.*
1868 William J. *m.*
1871 Edward B. *m.*
1873 William H. *h*

Chanler,
1847 John W.

Chapin,
1864 Samuel F. *m.*
1873 Frederick W. *m.*

Chapman,
1864 Albert T. *m.*
1869 Curtis. *m.*
1869 James F. *m.*
1869 Sherman H. *m.*
1870 Timothy P. *l.*

Chase,
1819 Philander. *h.*
1860 Seth L. *m.*
1862 Leslie.
1872 Harvey H. *m.*
1873 Frederick S. *l.*
1873 George. *l.*
1875 John F. *l.*
1875 Horace R. *l.*

Chasey,
1875 James. *m.*

Chauncey,
1831 Peter S.

Cheesman,
1874 Timothy M.

Chester,
1868 Albert H. *m. e.*
1871 Alden. *l.*

Cheves,
1824 Langdon. *h.*

Chetwood,
1860 Bradbury C. *l.*

Chichester,
1841 Edward L.

Child,
1810 Francis.
1875 William S. *h.*

Chipman,
1861 John F. H. *m.*

Chisholm,
1838 Walter. *h.*

Chittenden,
1837 Nathaniel W.
1868 Newton H. *l.*
1868 Simeon B., Jr. *l.*
1870 Henry A., Jr. *l.*
1876 Horace H. *l.*

Chorlton,
1870 John. *l.*

Christie,
1799 John.
1863 George A. *m.*

Chrystie,
1806 John.
1828 Thomas W.
1831 James, Jr.
1832 John.

Church,
1859 Frank P.
1868 Elihu. *l.*
1867 John A. *m. e.*
1870 Stewart. *m.*
1872 Dennis, Jr. *m.*

Churchill,
1862 John L.
1876 Stephen E. *m.*

Claflin,
1869 Nelson H. *m.*

Clark,
1824 William A. *h.*
1834 Orange. *h.*
1837 John W.
1840 James F.
1841 John H.
1842 Benjamin F.
1850 James S.
1852 Henry W.
1853 William I.
1856 Charles N.
1863 Paris G. *l.*
1865 Dexter S. *m.*
1865 Lucius D. *m.*
1866 Thomas E. *m.*
1867 Philo W. *m.*
1870 Edgar B. *l.*
1870 Staats V. D. *m.*
1871 William H. *l.*
1872 James S. *h.*
1872 Edward H. *l.*
1872 Lewis B. *l.*
1872 Franklin C. *m.*
1873 Frederick E. *m.*
1875 James O. *l.*
1876 David B. *m.*
1876 Frank P. *m.*
1876 Alexander S. *m.*
1876 Salter S. *l.*

Clarke,
1762 Richard. *h.*
1771 Clement C.
1817 James P. F.
1823 Edward M.
1826 William F. A.
1863 Charles F.
1873 William E. *l.*

Clarkson,
1774† David.
1810 David A.
1860 Howard.
1860 Walter L.
1863 Freeman.

Clay,
1876 H. Ashland. *m.*

Clayton,
1870 John H. *l.*

Clement,
1856 Edward C.
1872 George A., Jr. *l.*

Clemesha,
1866 John W. *m.*

Cleveland,
1871 Clement. *m.*
1876 Louis B. *l.*

Clinch,
1867 Edward S. *l.*
1874 Joseph H. *h.*

Clinton,
1786 De Witt.
1793 George, Jr.
1797 George W.
1868 George. *l.*

Crane,
1866 Albert. *l.*
1871 Horatio N. *m.*
1872 Arthur P. *l.*
1876 John J. *m.*

Crary,
1824 Edward C.

Craven,
1829 Alfred W.
1876 Francis S. *m. e.*

Crawford,
1865 Ten Broeck. *l.*
1867 Samuel O. *l.*
1870 Gilbert H. *l.*

Creelman,
1867 Frederick S. *m.*

Creighton,
1770 James.
1812 William.

Cremin,
1866 Patrick W. *m.*
1875 Michael A. *m.*

Crisfield,
1873 James E. *m.*

Croes,
1811 John. *h.*

Crolius,
1803 Thomas.

Cromwell,
1854 Charles B.
1876 William N. *l.*

Crook,
1849 George A. *h.*
1864 Abel. *l.*

Cropper,
1870 John.

Crosby,
1802 John P.
1827 John P.
1827 William H.
1840 Edward N.
1867 William B. *l.*
1872 Howard. *h.*

Croucher,
1863 Albert E. *m.*

Crowell,
1870 Charles E. *l.*
1873 John B. *m.*
1876 Frank. *l.*

Cruger,
1796 Henry, Jr.
1819 Henry N.
1823 Lewis.
1859 Gouverneur.

Cuddeback,
1873 Cornelius E. *l.*

Culbert,
1875 Francis R. *l.*

Cullen,
1860 Edgar M.

Culver,
1868 Charles. *m.*

Cuming,
1851 Francis H. *h.*

Cumming,
1862 James R. *m.*

Cummings,
1868 Byron. *m.*
1875 George H. *m.*

Cunningham,
1841 Frederick.
1875 Solomon W. *l.*

Curran,
1873 John E. *l.*

Currier,
1864 George W. *m.*

Curtis,
1824 William A.
1855 Benjamin L.
1858 Lewis A.
1862 John H.
1870 Frederic C. *m.*
1870 John G. *m.*
1874 George T., Jr. *l.*

Curtiss,
1874 Edwin B. *l.*

Cushing,
1764 Matthew. *h.*
1871 Ernest W. *m.*

Cushman,
1850 Archibald F.
1859 William F.

Cuthbert,
1869 Thomas N.

Cutler,
1835 Benjamin C. *h.*
1864 Henry S. *h.*

Cutter,
1861 George R. *m.*
1873 Charles B. *m.*

Cutting,
1758 Leonard. *h.*
1793 William.
1830 Robert L.
1856 Robert L., Jr.
1862 Walter.
1869 William B.
1871 Robert F.

Cuyler,
1762 Henry.
1763 Barent.

Cuzner,
1864 A. Thomas. *m.*

Czaki,
1871 Adolf. *l.*

Da Costa,
1855 Charles.

Dake,
1873 Charles R. *m.*

Dakin,
1860 Edward S. *l.*

Daly,
1860 Charles P. *h.*

Dana,
1843 John W.
1857 Richard S.
1874 Alfred S. *m.*

Dandridge,
1870 Nathaniel P. *m.*

Danforth,
1874 Loomis Le G. *m.*

Daniels,
1874 Francis B. *l.*

Danker,
1864 Henry A. *m.*

Darby,
1864 Henry A. *m.*

Darling,
1873 Nathaniel B. *m*

Dastler,
1876 Franz. *m.*

D'Autremont,
1875 Charles, Jr. *l.*

Davenport,
1871 Bennett F. *m.*
1871 James H. *m.*
1873 Silas A. *m.*

Davidson,
1864 Edmund D.

Davie,
1874 George A. *m.*

Davies,
1813 Thomas L.
1857 Henry E., Jr.
1866 Julien T.

Davis,
1798 George.
1814 Cornelius.
1853 Thomas F. *h.*
1863 Rezin P. *m.*
1864 Albert A. *m.*
1868 Henry S. *l.*
1869 Gustavus P. *m.*
1875 Charles C. *l.*

Davison,
1876 David H. *m.*

Dawson,
1822 George W.
1866 Benjamin T. *m.*

Day,
1863 Walter De F. *m.*
1865 James G. *l.*
1870 Henry C. *m.*
1875 Edward A. *l.*
1875 James. *l.*
1876 William T. *l.*

Dayton,
1817 Matthias O.
1868 Charles W. *l.*
1875 Robert A. B. *l.*

Deady,
1868 John A. *l.*

Deall,
1774† Samuel.

Dean,
1853 George W.
1855 William.
1861 Henry M. *m.*

De Blois,
1861 Louis G. *m.*

Decker,
1793 Cornelius.
1867 Samuel. *m.*

Deering,
1869 James A. *l.*

De Forest,
1872 Robert W. *l.*

De Hart,
1873 Henry G. V. *m.*

De Grove,
1871 Edward R. *l.*

De Koven,
1851 James.

Delafield,
1802 John.
1830 John, Jr.
1855 Lewis.
1856 Maturin L.
1863 Francis. *m.*
1866 Augustus F.
1870 Albert. *l.*

Delaney,
1867 John O. F. *m.*
1874 James E. *l.*
1874 James J. *m.*
1876 Edward G. *l.*

Delaplaine,
1833 John F., Jr.
1834 Isaac C.

Delavan,
1875 David B. *m.*

De Leon,
1860 Juan B. P. *m.*

Delile,
1807 Alire R. *m.*

Del Pino,
1873 Emilio Y.

Demaray,
1848 Lyman D.

Demarest,
1804 Cornelius T.
1834 William.
1863 Samuel. *m.*
1864 Theodore F. C.

De Mille,
1848 Richard M.
1875 Henry C.

Deming,
1875 Charles C. *l.*

De Mott,
1873 Edward P. *l.*

Dugro,
1876 Philip H.

Duke,
1802 William. *h.*

Dunbar,
1864 George H. *m.*

Duncan,
1843 John M. *h.*
1843 William C.

Dunham,
1847 Carroll.

Dunn,
1867 N. Gano. *l.*

Dunning,
1871 William B. *m.*

Dunscomb,
1774 Edward.
1806 William E.
1827 Edward.

Dunwell,
1874 Charles T. *l.*

Dupignac,
18?9 Frank J. *l.*
1876 Walton C. *l.*

Durden,
1872 William W. *m.*

Durkee,
1876 William W. *l.*

Duryee,
1795 Philip.
1812 Richard, Jr.
1868 John L. *m.*
1876 George W. *m.*

Dusenbery,
1866 Henry. *m.*

Dustan,
1822 Peter F.

Dutton,
1860 Van Buren. *l.*

Duvall,
1858 Daniel S.
1872 Elbridge G., Jr. *l.*

Duyckinck,
1835 Evert A.
1867 George.

Dwight,
1816 Maurice W.
1860 Theodore W. *h.*
1861 James McL. B. *l.*

Dyckman,
1810 Jacob.
1811 Jacobus.

Dykers,
1819 Peter.

Eacker,
1793 George I.

Eagle,
1863 Clifford F.

Earl,
1868 Franklin W. *l.*

Earle,
1790 Marmaduke.
1865 Frank O. *m.*
1873 James. *l.*

Eastburn,
1816 James W.
1817 Manton.
1827 Edward B.

Eastman,
1862 Barnard D. *m.*
1875 Henry M. W. *l.*

Easton,
1862 Robert T. B. *l.*
1867 Morton W. *m.*

Eaton,
1828 Asa. *h.*
1869 Theodore A. *h.*

Ebbets,
1842 William H.

Eccles,
1788 John.

Ecclesine,
1870 Thomas C. E.

Eckerson,
1864 John E. *l.*

Eddy,
1862 William. *m.*
1870 Herbert M. *m.*
1873 Elmer B. *m.*

Edebohls,
1875 George M. *m.*

Edgar,
1804 William.
1829 William.
1836 Newbold.

Edgerton,
1864 Francis D. *m.*
1872 Clarence C.

Edmonds,
1876 Walter D. *l.*

Edwards,
1850 Edwin W.
1867 Jonathan, Jr. *m.*
1869 John. *m.*
1871 Charles H. *l.*
1873 Arthur M. *m.*
1874 Wheeler DeF. *l.*

Ehninger,
1847 John W.

Eickhoff,
1875 Henry J. *l.*

Eigenbrodt,
1831 William E.

Elberg,
1867 Frederick W. *m.*

Elder,
1872 Robert D. *l.*

Elderkin,
1863 John. *m.*

Eliot,
1863 Samuel. *h.*
1873 Eugene N. *l.*

Ellet,
1824 William H.

Elliot,
1795 Bernard.
1845 George T., Jr.
1871 Henry T. *m.*

Elliott,
1825 Stephen. *h.*
1840 Stephen. *h.*
1871 John H. *h.*
1873 Richmond B. *m.*

Ellis,
1870 George W. *l.*
1872 Barnard. *m.*
1874 Nathaniel. *l.*
1876 Ellsworth S. *m.*

Ellsworth,
1834 Washington W. *l.*
1872 Charles H. *l.*

Elmendorf,
1823 Edmund B.
1845 John J

Ely,
1854 Leicester K.
1860 William S. *l.*
1863 Richard W. *l.*
1867 William S. *m.*
1868 Henry O. *m.*
1874 Edward T. *m.*
1876 Richard T.

Emanuel,
1875 Solomon A. *l.*

Embury,
1828 Edmund.
1853 Daniel, Jr.
1855 Philip A.
1866 William O. *l.*
1867 Clarence U. *l.*
1876 Aymar.

Emerson,
1853 William, Jr.
1860 John H.
1869 George O. *l.*
1869 Nathaniel B. *m.*

Emmet,
1810 Robert.
1824 Thomas A. *h.*
1839 Richard S.
1867 Bache McE. *m.*

Emmett,
1869 Charles. *l.*
1876 Robert. *l.*

Emory,
1831 Robert.

Emott,
1833 James. *h.*
1841 James, Jr.
1872 Charles C. *l.*

Enfield,
1870 Charles. *m.*

English,
1868 David C. *m.*

Engs,
1863 George M. *m.*

Ennever,
1873 Thomas C. *l.*

Eno,
1864 Henry C. *m.*

Ensell,
1872 John E. *m.*

Ephraims,
1874 Ephraim E. *l.*

Epstein,
1871 Moses H.

Erskine,
1853 Henry D. *h.*

Estwick,
1875 Charles F. *l.*

Eustis,
1874 William H. *l.*

Evangeles,
1836 Christodoulos L. M.

Evans,
1864 Lemuel E. *l.*
1870 Edwin. *m.*
1874 George A. *m.*
1876 Thomas G. *l.*

Eveleth,
1866 Edward S. *m.*

Everett,
1864 D. Darwin. *m.*
1874 William, Jr. *l.*

Everhart,
1870 George M. *h.*

Everson,
1864 Duane S.

Evetsky,
1876 Etienne. *m.*

Ewer,
1867 Ferdinand C. *h.*

Exton,
1866 James A. *m.*

Faesch,
1795 John J.

Fagnani,
1875 Charles P. *l.*

Fairbank,
1869 John B. *l.*

Fairfax,
1861 Albert. *m.*

Fairlie,
1818 Frederick.

French,
1860 John W. *h.*
1869 Charles L. *m.*
1871 Thomas R. *m.*
1874 Henry. *l.*

Friedman,
1876 Alfred. *m.*

Friend,
1873 Meyer M. *l.*
1875 Theodore H. *l.*

Fritts,
1875 Crawford E. *m.*

Froeligh,
1799 Peter D.

Fromme,
1876 Isaac. *l.*

Frost,
1846 William J.
1869 Louis W. *l.*
1876 Edward I. *l.*

Frothingham,
1866 Edward. *m.*
1875 John B. *l.*

Fry,
1873 Richard W. *m.*

Frye,
1842 Frederick.

Fuchs,
1875 Jacob *m.*

Fuller,
1861 Winfield S. *m.*
1862 Charles D.
1863 William H. *l.*
1865 Horace S. *m.*
1867 Edward T. *m.*
1876 Perry J. *l.*

Funk,
1817 Seymour P.

Funkhouser,
1873 Robert M. *l.*

Furman,
1801 John.
1864 John H. *m.*

Gage,
1872 George C. *m.*
1875 Eugene F. *m.*

Gaine,
1774† John.

Gaines,
1873 Vivian P. *m.*

Galbraith,
1861 Franklin B. *m.*

Gale,
1863 Edward D. *l.*

Galinger,
1871 George W. *l.*

Gallagher,
1831 John B.

Gallatin,
1841 Albert. *hr.*
1843 Albert, J.
1863 Frederick *l.*

Galleher,
1875 John N. *h.*

Gallup,
1875 Howard.
1876 Albert. *l.*

Ganse,
1839 Harvey D.

Garcelon,
1876 Alonzo M. *m.*

Gardiner,
1863 John L. *l.*

Gardner,
1835 James A. M.
1863 Eugene T. *l.*
1869 Asa B. *h.*

Garner,
1876 Henry B. *m.*

Garr,
1796 Andrew S

Garrett,
1876 Edward C., Jr. *l.*

Garrish,
1866 John P., Jr. *m.*

Garrison,
1810 James C.
1870 Charles M.
1876 Edmund H. *m. e.*
1876 Marcus A. *l.*

Gaston,
1835 William. *h.*

Geer,
1862 George J. *h.*
1868 George J., Jr., *m.e.*
1869 William M.
1876 Edward W. *l.*

Geib,
1873 Philip J. *l.*

Geissenhainer,
1858 Jacob A.

Gelston,
1833 John M.

Gener,
1834 Don Thomas. *h.*
1835 Benigno.

George,
1762 William C.
1865 Charles F. *m.*
1875 Evan P., Jr.

Gerard,
1811 James W.
1843 James W., Jr.

Gerry,
1857 Elbridge T.

Gesner,
1859 John F.

Getty,
1866 Moses D.

Gibbs,
1841 Oliver W.

Gibert,
1821 William N.
1824 James T.

Gibson,
1860 Otis W. *m.*
1868 Charles D. T. *m.*
1874 Alexander J. *l.*
1875 William H. *l.*

Giddings,
1867 Edward E. *m. e.*
1868 Theodore. *m.*

Gifford,
1809 James N.

Gignoux,
1865 John F. *m.*

Gihon,
1861 John, Jr.

Gilbert,
1872 James H. *l.*

Giles,
1764 Samuel. *h.*

Gilfillan,
1862 William J. *m.*

Gilford,
1793 Samuel. Jr.
1824 Jacob T.
1828 George
1835 Thomas B.

Gilhooly,
1868 Andrew J.
1870 William E.

Gillespie,
1834 William M.
1862 George W.

Gillet,
1868 Elmslie M.

Gillett,
1869 Omer T. *m.*

Gillette,
1863 Walter R. *m.*

Gilman,
1865 Charles M. *l.*
1867 Burns. *m.*
1867 Zeeb, Jr. *m.*

Gilnack,
1867 Frederick. *m.*

Gilson,
1876 Walter C. *l.*

Gladstone,
1872 James A. *m.*

Gleavy,
1874 Samuel A. *l.*

Glenn,
1875 James K., Jr. *l.*

Glentworth,
1767 George. *h.*

Glover,
1822 John M.
1867 William E. *l.*

Goadby,
1875 Charles T. *l.*

Goddard,
1861 Josial H. *m.*
1864 William N.

Goebel,
1876 Jacob C. *l.*

Göken,
1876 Henry F. *l.*

Goldbacher,
1876 Joseph. *l.*

Goelet,
1828 Robert.
1860 Robert, Jr.

Goldenberg,
1872 Julius L. *l.*

Goldey,
1866 Charles A. L. *l.*

Golding,
1875 John F. *m.*

Goldman,
1872 Julius. *l.*

Goldmark,
1875 Leo. *l.*

Goldschmidt,
1871 S. Anthony. *m. e.*

Goodall,
1863 Frank W. *m.*

Goodell,
1875 De Bruce, Jr. *l.*

Goodhart,
1868 Michael E. *l.*

Goodridge,
1871 Edwin A. *m.*

Goodwin,
1866 Ralph S. *m.*
1876 Jasper T.

Goold,
1793 Charles D.

Gordon,
1854 William R. *h.*
1871 John, Jr. *m. e.*
1873 William S.

Gosman,
1801 John.
1802 George W.
1806 Jonathan B.
1807 Robert.

Gott,
1875 Joseph W. *l.*

Gottsberger,
1841 C. H. *h.*

Hardie,
1787 James. *h.*

Harding,
1872 William J. *l.*
1874 Edward M. *m.*
1875 Henry C. *l.*

Hare,
1843 George E. *h.*

Harison,
1764 Richard.
1802 Francis L.
1804 Richard N.
1811 William H., Jr.
1842 William H.
1846 William B.
1850 Thomas L.

Harkness,
1873 David W. *l.*

Harley,
1871 John P. *m.*

Harlin,
1862 William H. *m.*

Harmer,
1864 Thomas H.

Harmon,
1855 Edward O.
1871 Frank D. *l.*

Harper,
1848 Joseph W., Jr.
1852 John W.

Harpur,
1762 Robert. *h.*

Harral,
1868 Frederick F. *m.*

Harriman,
1835 Orlando, Jr.

Harrington,
1867 Daniel DeW. *m.*

Harris,
1770 Richard.
1800 Samuel.
1811 William.
1822 Josiah D.
1825 Robert W.
1864 Frank. *l.*
1866 Orrin F. *m.*
1866 Samuel. *m.*
1873 Charles N. *l.*
1873 Philander A. *m.*

Harrison,
1876 Joseph B. *m.*

Harrower,
1874 Pierre P.

Harsen,
1825 Jacob.

Hart,
1811 William H.
1870 George H. *l.*
1871 Monmouth D. *l.*
1873 George. *m.*
1873 James A. *m.*

Harvey,
1834 Robert J. *h.*
1872 Henry P. *m.*
1873 Ashton. *l.*
1875 Chester W. *m.*

Hasbrouck,
1834 Abraham B. *h.*
1862 Solomon E. *m.*
1863 Frank G. *m.*
1863 John C. *m.*
1870 Peter. *h.*

Haskell,
1873 Charles L. *l.*

Haslett,
1867 Audley. *m.*

Hassey,
1874 Edward F. *l.*

Hassler,
1876 Charles W. *l.*

Hatch,
1862 Charles H. *l.*
1876 Edward S. *l.*

Hatfield,
1805 Richard, Jr.

Hathaway,
1867 Henry B. *l.*
1869 George A. *m.*

Haughwout,
1871 Frank G.

Havemeyer,
1823 William F.

Haven,
1857 George G.

Havens,
1862 Jonathan. *m.*

Hawes,
1821 William P.
1866 George E. *m.*

Hawkesworth,
1860 William. *h.*

Hawks,
1832 Francis L. *h.*

Hawley,
1868 George F. *m.*

Haws,
1827 John H. H.

Hayden,
1875 Henry W. *l.*

Haydock,
1875 George R.

Hayes,
1869 Russel T. *m.*

Hays,
1873 William. *l.*
1875 Daniel P. *l.*

Hazelius,
1824 Ernest L. *h.*

Healy,
1872 James J. *m.*
1873 Edmund J. *l.*
1873 Thomas F. *m.*
1876 Joseph. *m.*

Heard,
1832 James, Jr.
1834 John S.
1835 William.

Hearn,
1872 Edward D. *h.*

Heasley,
1869 George W.

Heaton,
1793 Robert, Jr.

Hedge,
1869 Thomas, Jr. *l.*

Heffernan,
1865 John M.

Hegeman,
1862 William A. O.

Hegewisch,
1875 Ernesto M. *m.*

Heine,
1872 Joseph S., Jr. *m.*

Heineman,
1874 Henry N. *m.*

Helms,
1871 James I. *h.*

Hendell,
1791 William, Jr.

Henderson,
1823 William D.
1867 Henry. *m.*

Hendrick,
1875 Charles C. *l.*

Hendricks,
1856 Francis.
1858 Harmon.

Hendrickson,
1875 George C. *l.*
1875 Samuel. *m.*

Henna,
1872 Joseph J. *m.*

Hennion,
1864 Andrew J. *l.*

Henop,
1861 Sidney S. *l.*

Henry,
1800 John.
1849 John V.
1863 Richard M.
1868 Frederick P. *m.*
1871 Jacob H.
1874 Selden T. S.

Henschell,
1872 Edward K. *m.*

Henshaw,
1874 John H. *l.*

Hepburn,
1868 Neil J. *m.*

Herbert,
1876 John W., Jr. *l.*

Herrick,
1854 Carleton M.
1857 James B.

Herriman,
1849 William H.

Herring,
1795 Thomas.

Herrlich,
1874 John F. *l.*

Hershey,
1862 Andrew H. *m.*
1867 William. *l.*

Hershfield,
1875 Mitchell. *l.*

Herts,
1875 Jacques H. *l.*

Hervey,
1868 Daniel E. *l.*

Hewitt,
1842 Abram S.
1845 Charles. *h.*

Heyer,
1814 William H.
1815 William S.
1819 Edward P.
1823 Henry A.

Heyliger,
1774 Nicholas.

Heymann,
1873 Henry M. *l.*

Heyward,
1827 William C.
1829 James.
1830 Nicholas C.
1834 Henry.

Hibbard,
1861 Jerome. *m.*

Hickok,
1869 George B. *m.*

Hicks,
1793 John B. *m.*
1823 John A.
1860 Joseph L. *m.*

Hiester,
1876 Harry M. *l.*

Higbee,
1842 Edward Y. *h.*

Higgins,
1873 Richard C. *l.*

Hildreth,
1869 John H. *l.*

**Hurst,**
1788 William.
1871 James. *l.*
1873 Louis H. *l.*

**Huse,**
1866 Edward C. *m.*

**Hustace,**
1859 E. Treadwell.
1871 Francis.

**Huston,**
1864 Hiram L.

**Hutchings,**
1860 Robert C. *l.*
1872 Frederick. *l.*

**Hutchinson,**
1863 James. *m.*
1866 Edward *m.*
1866 James C. *m.*
1867 Stephen J. *m.*

**Hutchison,**
1875 Nathaniel G. *m.*

**Hutton,**
1823 Mancius S.
1865 Richard G. *h.*
1872 Allen C. *m.*
1873 Frederick R.

**Huyler,**
1800 John.

**Hyatt,**
1862 Stephen B. *h.*

**Hyde,**
1834 William H.
1863 Edwin F. *l.*
1866 Stephen. *m.*
1867 Clarence M.
1876 John E. H.

**Hyer,**
1819 Walter E.
1846 John G.

**Hyland,**
1876 Josiah A. *l.*

**Hyslop,**
1813 Robert.
1856 William R.

**Ihlseng,**
1875 Magnus C. *m. e.*

**Iles,**
1875 Malvern W. *m. e.*

**Ill,**
1875 Edward J. *m.*

**Inderwick.**
1808 James.

**Ingersoll,**
1839 Charles.
1860 William H. *l.*
1867 William H.

**Inglis,**
1767 Charles. *h.*
1795 James.
1821 William.

**Ingraham,**
1817 Daniel P.
1844 Joseph W. *h.*
1869 George L. *l.*
1870 Arthur.
1873 George. *l.*

**Inness,**
1872 John H. *l.*

**Ireland.**
1816 John, Jr.
1830 George, Jr.
1871 Frederick G. *l.*

**Irish,**
1875 Henry L. *m.*

**Ironside,**
1815 William.

**Irving,**
1794 Peter. *m.*
1898 John T.
1821 Pierre M.
1821 Washington. *h.*
1824 Pierre P.
1826 Gabriel F.
1829 John T., Jr.
1837 Theodore. *h.*
1845 George.
1848 Leslie.
1865 Cortlandt. *l.*
1869 Roland D. *m. e.*

**Isaacs,**
1867 Isaac S. *l.*

**Iselin,**
1869 William.
1874 Charles O. *l.*
1875 George A. *l.*

**Isherwood,**
1817 Benjamin.

**Ives,**
1824 Levi S. *h.*
1871 Francis L. *m.*

**Ivey,**
1876 Louis O.

**Ivins,**
1873 William M. *l.*

**Izard,**
1798 Henry.

**Jackson,**
1761 William. *h.*
1809 Samuel.
1814 Allen.
1853 Abram S.
1857 Oliver P.
1859 Charles A.
1862 William H.
1864 Frederick W.
1865 David P. *m.*
1866 Abner. *h.*
1873 Anson B. *l.*
1873 James P. *m.*
1873 John W. *m.*
1875 Charles E. *m. e.*

**Jacob,**
1866 Ephraim A. *l.*
1875 Charles G. *m.*

**Jacobi,**
1871 Alphonse A. *l.*

**Jacot,**
1874 Charles D. *l.*

**Jaffray,**
1793 Andrew. *h.*
1842 Robert, Jr.

**James,**
1862 William M. *m.*
1865 Julian.
1865 Richard D. *m.*
1875 Dudley L. *l.*

**Janeway,**
1794 Jacob J.
1864 Edward G. *m.*
1867 Thomas L. *m.*

**Janvrin.**
1864 Joseph E. *m.*

**Jarvis,**
1837 Benjamin H.

**Jaques,**
1805 Robert.

**Jaume,**
1862 John A. *m.*

**Jauncey,**
1774 John.

**Jay,**
1764 John.
1794 Peter A.
1827 John C.
1836 John.
1859 William, Jr.
1863 Peter A.
1865 John C., Jr. *m.*
1876 Augustus. *l.*

**Jayne,**
1875 Walter A. *m.*

**Jenkins,**
1804 Edward. *h.*
1833 John J.

**Jenks,**
1852 Richard P. *h.*
1860 John W.

**Jenney,**
1869 Walter P. *m. e.*
1872 Frank B. *m. e.*

**Jerome,**
1870 William R. *l.*

**Jessup,**
1869 Andrew J. *m.*

**Jewett,**
1841 Jacob B.
1862 Dan L. *m.*
1868 Charles T. *m.*
1871 Charles. *m.*

**Jobs,**
1872 Thomas A. *l.*
1874 Nicholas C. *m.*

**Johnes,**
1876 Edward R. *l.*

**Johnson,**
1761 William S. *h.*
1772 Uzal. *m.*
1788 Robert C. *h.*
1789 Samuel W. *h.*
1792 John B.
1793 John I.
1819 William L.
1820 Samuel R.
1824 George W.
1831 Bradish.
1832 William T.
1834 Samuel E.
1848 Henry W.
1851 Henry B.
1853 William A.
1862 Eldridge M. *m.*
1863 Woolsey. *m.*
1865 Andrew. *h.*
1865 Parley H. *m.*
1866 Joseph. *m.*
1867 George B.
1867 Samuel. *m.*
1868 Herschel V., Jr. *m.*
1874 Edward. *l.*
1874 Henry S. *l.*
1874 William W.
1875 Edwin A. *l.*
1876 William H. *l.*
1876 Wilmot, Jr.

**Johnston,**
1846 William M.
1875 Charles G. *m.*

**Johnstone,**
1820 James.

**Joline,**
1872 Adrian H. *l.*

**Jones,**
1768 John. *h.*
1890 Samuel, Jr.
1791 Cave.
1795 Nicholas.
1796 David S.
1798 Philip L.
1802 James.
1803 Edward R.
1815 John Q.
1819 Charles.
1819 George.
1822 Henry P.
1827 Joshua.
1830 Edward.
1832 Philip L.
1835 Joshua E.
1836 William A.
1840 Alfred G.
1845 George A.
1845 Samuel T.
1847 Arthur M.
1850 Walter R. T.
1858 Henry L.
1859 Lot. *h.*
1860 Edward R.
1865 Frederick R.
1865 Luther M. *l.*
1869 Henry M.
1869 Shipley.
1870 Charles D. *l.*
1870 Clarence D. *l.*
1872 Samuel B. *m.*
1874 James D. *l.*
1874 Weldon W. *m.*
1875 Henry E. *l.*
1875 Millard L. *l.*
1876 George H. *l.*
1876 Townsend, Jr.

Kobbe,
1874 George C.

Koch,
1865 Joseph. *l.*
1873 Julius. *m.*

Kohler,
1875 Joseph. *l.*

Kohn,
1875 Solomon. *l.*

Korff,
1869 John H. *m.*

Kortright,
1822 N. Gouverneur.

Kracht,
1874 George H. *l.*

Kreizer,
1876 Samuel. *l.*

Krollpfeiffer,
1875 Henry. *m.*

Kuenstler,
1871 Hugo. *m.*

Kugelman,
1875 Isaac. *l.*

Kunze,
1797 Henry.

Labagh,
1827 Abraham B.
1856 Peter I.

Labau,
1844 N. Bergasse.

Lacey,
1874 William J. *l.*

Lachman,
1876 Samson. *l.*

Lacombe,
1859 James P.
1863 Emile H.

Ladd,
1871 William W., Jr. *l.*

Laight,
1767 William.
1793 Edward W.
1802 Henry.
1825 William E.
1836 Edward H.
1853 Edward W.
1862 William E.
1868 Charles. *m.*

Lake,
1836 James P.

Lambert,
1863 Thomas R. *h.*

Lambrecht,
1873 Joseph. *l.*

Lampson,
1867 William. *l.*

Lamson,
1773 Joseph. *h.*

Lane,
1847 John S.
1875 Thomas R. *l.*

Landon,
1876 Newell E. *m.*

Langdon,
1867 Eustis F. *m.*
1874 Charles H. *m.*

Langworthy,
1860 Daniel A. *m.*
1876 William P. *m.*

Lanterman,
1868 A. J. *m.*

Larocque,
1838 Jeremiah.
1849 Joseph.

Larzelere,
1804 Jacob. *h.*

Lathrop,
1862 William G.

Latour,
1869 Isaac P. *m.*

Latting,
1875 Charles P. *l.*

Lauderdale,
1874 Walter E., Jr. *m.*

Laughlin,
1865 James F. *m.*

Laughton,
1873 J. Scott. *l.*

Law,
1797 Samuel A. *h.*

Lawrance,
1840 Edward H.

Lawrence,
1797 Abraham R.
1803 John L.
1812 Augustine N.
1812 Philip K.
1818 William B.
1820 Henry.
1823 Jonathan.
1823 William A.
1841 Joseph E.
1842 Richard M., Jr.
1843 William B., Jr.
1844 Charles W.
1847 Isaac.
1856 Thomas T.
1861 Walter B.
1862 George A.
1864 Joseph B.
1866 Samuel, Jr. *l.*
1868 James K. *l.*
1876 George E. *l.*

Laws,
1870 Samuel S. *l.*

Lawton,
1873 Francis, Jr. *l.*
1873 Neuberry D. *l.*

Lay,
1871 George C., Jr. *l.*

Leaming,
1765 Jeremiah.

Learned,
1865 John B. *m.*

Leary,
1874 Timothy E. *l.*

Leavens,
1875 Harry W. *m. e.*

Leupp,
1874 John H. *l.*

Leavenworth,
1848 Edward.

Leavitt,
1845 John W.
1860 William W. *m.*
1871 John B. *l.*

Le Compte,
1876 William. *l.*

Le Conte,
1797 William.
1799 Lewis.
1803 John.

Ledyard,
1830 Henry.

Lee,
1823 Chauncey. *h.*
1833 Francis P.
1835 Charles C.
1856 David B.
1856 Hermon F.
1861 Benjamin F. *l.*
1863 William. *m.*
1864 Arthur M. *l.*
1865 John L. *m.*
1866 Charles E. *m.*
1869 Henry T. *l.*
1871 William H. L. *l.*
1874 John W. *m.*
1874 Frederick R. *l.*

Lefferts,
1794 Leffert.
1802 Leffert.
1805 Thomas.
1846 John L.
1870 George M. *m.*
1876 John, Jr. *l.*

Legarè,
1840 Hugh S. *h.*

Leggat,
1863 William S.

Leggett,
1837 William H.

Leicht,
1873 William K. *l.*

Leipziger,
1875 Henry. *l.*

Le Moyne,
1850 Adolph, Jr.

Lennox,
1818 James.

Lent,
1795 Adolph C.

Leo,
1872 Sampson S. *l.*

Leonard,
1825 Alexander S.
1866 Algernon S. *m.*
1868 Charles H. *m.*

Le Roy,
1841 Robert, Jr.

Leslie,
1762 Alexander.

Lester,
1863 Elias. *m.*

Lever,
1869 John H. *m.*

Leverich,
1876 Henry M. *l.*

Leveridge,
1835 John W. C.
1840 Benjamin C.

Lewis,
1810 Horatio G.
1843 Edward Z.
1848 Theodore F.
1854 John V.
1861 Thompson B. *m.*
1865 Mordecai. *l.*
1867 Hobart.
1871 Daniel. *m.*
1874 John D. *l.*
1874 Nathan. *l.*
1874 James N. *m.*
1875 Eugene H. *l.*
1875 Richard J. *l.*
1876 Charles W. *m.*

Lexow,
1874 Clarence. *l.*
1875 Charles K. *l.*

Lighthipe,
1863 Lewis H.

Lilienthal,
1870 John L. *m. e.*

Lillie,
1874 Samuel M. *m. e.*

Lincoln,
1861 Abraham. *h.*
1875 George F. *l.*

Lindley,
1869 Newton A. *m.*
1874 John. *l.*

Lindsay,
1866 Walter. *m.*

Lindsley,
1870 Stuart. *m. e.*

Linn,
1789 William. *h.*
1795 John B.

McDougall,
1869 John C. *m.*

McDowell,
1872 Frederick H. *m.e.*

McElligott,
1865 Henry R.

McEwen,
1868 Daniel, Jr. *m.*

McFarlan,
1827 Charles.

McFarland,
1867 William C. *m.*
1871 Arthur H. *m.*

McFarlane,
1861 Carrington. *m.*

McGahagan,
1804 Thomas.

McGay,
1868 Robert J. *m.*

McGill,
1866 Alexander T. *l.*

McGlade,
1870 Thomas A., Jr. *l.*

McGoldrick,
1876 Michael F. *l*

McGowan,
1871 M. Milmo. *l.*

McGown,
1843 Henry P.

McGraw,
1863 Theodore A. *m.*

McGregor,
1810 John.

McGuirk,
1869 John. *m.*

McIlvaine,
1856 Alexis E.

McIntire,
1873 Ansil S. *m.*

McIntyre,
1835 Joseph.
1874 Burnett C. *m.*

Mack,
1807 Daniel.
1867 John A. *l.*

McKane,
1872 James N. *l.*

Mackaness,
1799 Thomas C.

McKay,
1864 William M. *m.*
1868 George S. *l.*
1868 John H. *m.*

McKean,
1762 Robert. *h.*

McKee,
1860 James G. *m.*
1876 William H. *l.*

McKellar,
1875 George M. *l.*

McKelvie,
1866 William H. *m.*

McKim,
1875 William D.

McKeon,
1825 John.
1876 William H. *l.*

McKesson,
1758 John. *h.*

Mackey,
1875 William J. P. *m.*

Mackie,
1794 Jacob O.
1812 Peter, Jr.

McKinney,
1873 Merritt G. *l.*

McKinnon,
1800 John.

McKnight,
1798 Washington.
1808 John.
1846 Charles S.

McLane,
1846 James W. *m.*

McLaren,
1847 John J.

McLaury,
1875 William P. *m.*

McLean,
1844 Charles G. *h.*
1863 Thomas M., Jr.
1869 Malcolm. *m.*
1873 Donald. *l.*

McLeod,
1806 Robert B. A.
1818 Alexander B.
1826 John N.

McLoughlin,
1869 Thomas J. *m.*

McMahon,
1869 Dennis, Jr. *l.*
1873 Percy H.

McManus,
1869 Henry. *m.*

McMartin,
1868 Archibald. *m. e.*

McMaster,
1870 Robert B. *l.*

McMullen,
1837 John, Jr.

McMurdy,
1867 John H. *l.*

McMurray,
1852 William. *h.*

McNamee,
1866 Theodore H.
1867 James.

McNary,
1851 John G.

Macneven,
1806 William J. *h.*
1831 James J.

McNulty,
1861 Albert, Jr.
1876 James. *l.*

Macomb,
1802 John W.
1802 Robert.
1866 Edward. *m.*

McQuesten,
1863 Rockwood.

McRae,
1870 William F. *l.*

McSweeney,
1864 Daniel E. *m.*

McVeagh,
1864 Franklin. *l.*

McVickar,
1802 Archibald.
1802 James.
1804 John.
1809 Henry.
1812 Edward.
1833 Samuel B.
1836 Henry.
1846 William A.
1865 William N.
1874 Henry G. *l.*

Macwithey,
1871 Edward L. C. *m.*

Macy,
1875 Arthur. *m. e.*

Maeller,
1790 Henry. *h.*

Maghee,
1872 John H.

Magie,
1863 David, Jr. *m.*

Magnes,
1849 Charles A.

Maguire,
1871 Philip J. *m.*

Main,
1828 Austin L. S.

Major,
1834 Alexander.
1866 Henry, Jr. *l.*

Malcolm,
1794 Samuel B.

Malcomson,
1874 Abram B., Jr. *l.*

Malocsay,
1871 Frank. *l.*

Mallory,
1873 Maitland L. *m.*

Mallalieu,
1875 Albert W. *m.*

Mallison,
1858 D. Ledyard.

Malloy,
1866 Edward W.

Maltby,
1869 Charles A. *l.*

Man,
1866 Frederick H.
1876 Henry H. *l.*

Mander,
1874 Henry F. *l.*

Manierre,
1869 George. *l.*

Manley,
1799 James R.
1804 Edward.
1808 James R.
1874 Reuben M. *l.*
1876 John R. *l.*

Mann,
1839 Joseph R.
1871 Matthew D. *m.*
1875 William J. *l.*

Mansfield,
1874 Howard. *l.*

Maplesden,
1874 Reuben, Jr. *l.*

Marbury,
1865 Francis F., Jr. *l.*

March,
1826 Joshua S.
1837 Charles D.

Marcley,
1873 James I. *m.*

Marcy,
1860 Thomas K. *m.*

Markham,
1870 William. *m.*

Marrin,
1858 William J.

Marsee,
1871 Joseph W. *m.*

Marselis,
1807 Peter T.

Marsh,
1824 Elias J.
1830 James. *h.*
1854 Elias J.
1864 Joseph A. *l.*
1869 Francis E. *l.*
1872 Nathaniel. *l.*
1876 Valentine. *l.*

Monroe,
1773 Harry. *h.*
1869 Henry S. *m. e.*
1876 Augustin. *l.*

Monson,
1840 Alonzo C.

Montgomery,
1874 Jesse S. *m.*

Montell,
1870 John B.

Montgomery,
1872 John H. *l.*
1872 John A. *m.*

Moore,
1768 Benjamin.
1774† Daniel.
1775† Thomas L.
1794 Richard C. *h.*
1798 Clement C.
1798 Samuel.
1802 Nathaniel F.
1806 David.
1806 Samuel W.
1810 Benjamin.
1842 Clement
1844 William T.
1847 John W.
1856 Richard C., Jr.
1859 James F.
1861 Richard H. *m.*
1866 John. *m.*
1867 Thomas M. *l.*
1872 William O. *m.*
1873 Casimir De R.
1873 Charles H. *m.*

Morales,
1875 Jose G. *l.*

Moran,
1875 John A. *l.*

Morgan,
1831 James M.
1843 William R.
1854 Charles E.
1857 William F. *h.*
1864 John B.
1865 Lawrence O. *m.*
1869 James A. *l.*
1870 John V. *m.*
1874 Theodore M. *l.*
1876 William D. *m.*

More,
1874 James M. *l.*

Morison,
1870 Robert S.

Morrell,
1810 Robert. *m.*

Morrelle,
1849 Daniel.

Morrill,
1828 John A.
1869 Jesse L. *l.*
1876 Frank A. *m.*

Morris,
1768 Governeur.
1775† Jacob.
1813 Nicholas, Jr.
1818 Gerard W.
1826 Henry.
1826 Richard L.
1848 Lewis.
1852 James.
1854 Orlando H.
1858 Charles D. *h.*
1860 Augustus N.
1860 Richard L.
1861 Robert. *l.*
1863 Stuyvesant F.
1868 Benjamin W. *h.*
1868 Fordham. *l.*
1868 Henry L. *l.*
1870 Samuel H. *m.*

Morrison,
1795 John.
1869 James E. *l.*

Morrow,
1876 Cornelius W.

Morse,
1860 Barnett W. *m.*
1863 Sherman. *m.*
1871 James O., Jr.

Mortimer,
1841 John H.
1875 Stanley. *l.*

Morton,
1810 George W.
1810 John L.
1815 Francis.
1824 Hamilton.
1827 Henry J.

Moses,
1841 Israel.
1868 Max. *l.*

Mott,
1806 Valentine. *m.*
1834 William F.
1872 Joseph V. *m.*
1872 Valentine.
1873 Henry A., Jr. *m.e.*

Mount,
1834 Richard E., Jr.
1852 Charles De G.
1872 David H. *m.*
1875 Thomas S. P. *l.*

Mowatt,
1816 John E.

Mower,
1856 Mandeville.

Mudgett,
1869 William P. *l.*

Mudie,
1860 Archibald F. *m.*

Muhlenberg,
1834 William A. *h.*

Muir,
1867 David H. *m.*
1875 Edward A. *l.*

Muirson,
1772 James. *m.*

Mulchahey,
1866 James. *h.*

Mulcahy,
1872 Denis D. *m.*

Mullany,
1866 Frank A.

Mullen,
1875 Samuel. *l.*

Muller,
1822 Adrian H.
1873 Henry C. *m.*

Mulligan,
1791 John W.
1835 William.

Mulry,
1874 William P. *l.*

Mulvany,
1875 Luke. *l.*
1876 Edward J. *l.*

Mundy,
1864 Charles H. *l.*

Munn,
1821 William H.

Munroe,
1871 Chester C.

Munson,
1873 Franklin A. *m.*

Murdock,
1861 Seth M. *l.*
1867 George W. *m.*
1870 Albert J. *m.*

Murfee,
1867 John H. *m.*

Murphy,
1830 Henry C.
1854 Henry C., Jr.
1855 George J.
1867 Philip. *l.*
1872 Arthur. *l.*
1874 Arthur, Jr. *l.*

Murray,
1799 Alexander.
1812 John W. B.
1813 Thomas C.
1863 James.
1866 Nicholas. *l.*
1869 George F. *l.*
1874 Ambrose S., Jr. *l.*
1874 George. *m. e.*
1875 James B. *l.*
1876 George W. *l.*
1876 John H. *l.*

Mursick,
1860 George A. *m.*

Murtha,
1869 Eugene B. *m.*

Muzzy,
1808 Frederick.

Myers,
1874 Charles F. W. *m.*

Mynderse,
1875 Wilhelmus. *l.*

Nash,
1846 Frederick.
1868 John M.

Nathan,
1827 Jonathan.
1861 Gratz.

Naughton,
1872 Thomas J. *m.*

Navarro,
1873 Angel J. *m.*

Nazro,
1863 Hiram H.

Neal,
1810 Ava.

Nealis,
1862 William T. *m.*

Neefus,
1854 Peter J.

Nehrbas,
1871 Charles J. *l.*

Neill,
1767 Hugh. *h.*
1828 George B.

Neilson,
1817 John, Jr.
1847 John.

Nelson,
1804 Joseph.
1841 Edward D.
1841 Samuel. *h.*
1869 Henry L. *l.*
1869 James R. *m.*
1875 John De W. *m.*

Nesbitt,
1875 John H. *m.*

Nesmith,
1860 Robert D.

Nettleton,
1869 Asbel G. *m.*

Nettre,
1869 Lionel R. *m. e.*

Neville,
1876 John J. M. *m.*

Nevins,
1876 Russell H. *m.*

Nevius,
1837 George L.

Newbold,
1874 Thomas. *l.*

Page,
1864 Benjamin M. *m.*
1873 Edward A. *l.*
1874 Charles W. *l.*
1876 Edward W.

Paine,
1875 Arthur R. *m.*

Palache,
1835 Alexander.

Palmer,
1867 William H. *m.*
1869 Courtlandt, Jr. *l.*
1875 Appleton D. *l.*

Panton,
1774 George.

Pape,
1875 Adolphus D. *l.*

Papen,
1874 George W. *m.*

Paris,
1791 Daniel.

Parish,
1841 John H.
1849 Henry, Jr.
1867 Daniel C., Jr. *m.*
1871 Julius L. *m.*

Parker,
1793 James.
1854 James C., Jr.
1864 Henry H.
1866 Willard, Jr.
1869 Richard W. *l.*
1876 Frederic S. *l.*

Parkhurst,
1868 Charles B. *m.*

Parkin,
1876 William. *l.*

Parkman,
1857 Theodore.

Parks,
1851 Martin P. *h.*

Parmele,
1762 Ebenezer. *h.*

Parmly,
1842 Wheelock H.

Parrot,
1870 Edward M. *m. e.*

Parsons,
1861 George H. *m. e.*
1876 Frank. *m.*
1876 William H. *l.*

Partridge,
1875 Edward L. *m.*

Passmore,
1861 Joseph C. *h.*

Paterson,
1812 Matthew C.
1822 Alexander H.

Paton,
1876 David. *l.*

Patterson,
1865 Charles G. *l.*
1869 Charles E. *l.*

Patton,
1861 Robert H. *l.*

Paulding,
1824 James K. *h.*
1812 William J.

Paulison,
1870 John C. *l.*

Payne,
1870 Henry W. *l.*
1876 Edward T. *l.*

Payson,
1876 Henry S. *l.*

Peabody,
1868 Duane L.
1869 Charles A., Jr.
1870 George L.

Pearsall,
1861 Andrew T. *m.*
1861 Robert W. *l.*

Pearsee,
1793 Jonathan, Jr.

Pease,
1862 Edmund M. *m.*

Peaslee,
1875 Edward H. *m.*

Peckett,
1876 John W., Jr. *l.*

Peck,
1841 William L.
1846 Edward M.
1865 George W.
1876 Myrod R. C. *m.*

Peet,
1868 George J. *l.*
1872 Isaac L. *h.*

Peirce,
1870 Henry T. *m.*

Peixotto,
1816 Daniel L. M.

Pell,
1770 Philip.
1806 Ferris.
1840 George W.
1841 William C.
1852 John H.
1858 Benjamin.
1860 Robert T.
1862 Edward M.
1862 Richard V.
1863 James B.
1863 John. *l.*
1869 Walter. *l.*
1873 Frederic A. *l.*
1874 Herbert C. *l.*

Pellet,
1871 Jackson B. *m.*

Pelletier,
1870 Paul. *l.*

Pemberton,
1849 John P.

Pendergast,
1863 Patrick. *m.*

Pendleton,
1805 Edmund H.
1813 Nathaniel G.
1814 James M.

Péneveyre,
1825 Henri L. P. F. *h.*

Pennell,
1852 George C.

Pennington,
1875 John C. *m.*

Penny,
1827 Samuel, Jr.

Percy,
1862 George. *l.*

Perkins,
1824 Henry.
1860 William S. C. *m.*
1876 James O. *l.*

Perry,
1855 William A.
1870 Samuel E. *l.*
1872 John H. *l.*
1873 John E. *m.*
1875 Edward D.
1875 James W. *l.*
1876 Clarence C. *m.*

Perrine,
1872 Howland D. *l.*

Peshine,
1825 William.

Peters,
1761 Samuel A. *h.*
1793 Valentine H.
1826 Hewlett R.

Pettingill,
1876 Edmund L. *m.*

Petit,
1867 Frederic M. *m. e.*

Peyton,
1867 James F. *m.*

Phelan,
1874 Thomas A *l.*
1875 Jeremiah. *m.*

Phelps,
1863 Charles O. *l.*
1863 George D. *l.*
1863 William W.
1864 Henry D. *l.*

Philbin,
1876 William A. *l.*

Philip,
1819 John. *h.*
1843 John C.

Philippe,
1876 Eugene. *m.*

Philipse,
1773 Frederick.
1773 Nathaniel.
1828 Frederick.

Phillips,
1808 John W.
1826 William W. *h.*
1864 James L. *m.*
1866 Edwin. *m.*
1868 Howard W. *m.*
1872 Wheeler W. *l*
1873 David. *m.*
1874 Waldorf H. *l.*

Phinney,
1842 James H.

Phœnix,
1795 Alexander.
1795 Sidney.
1795 Thomas.
1859 Stephen W.

Phyfe,
1825 William.

Pierce,
1861 William B. *m.*
1863 Charles L. *m.*
1869 George P.
1873 Andrew M. *m.*

Pierrepont,
1867 Henry E., Jr.
1876 William A. *l.*

Pierson,
1869 Stephen. *m.*

Piffard,
1864 Henry G. *m.*

Pihlman,
1876 Robert L. *l.*

Pinckney,
1860 Howard. *m.*

Pinder,
1833 John H. *h.*

Pingry,
1868 James O. *m.*

Pinneo,
1865 Joseph O. *m.*

Pirnie,
1839 John, Jr.
1839 Peter B.
1844 Peter M.

Pirsson,
1872 Augustus C.

Pistor,
1868 William. *m. e.*

Pitner,
1869 Thomas J. *m.*

Pitschke,
1870 William F. *l.*

Pladerell,
1875 Willard S. *l.*

1873 Melville H. *l.*
1875 David H. *l.*

Reid,
1845 Aaron B.
1868 Henry H. *l.*
1869 John J. *m.*

Reilly,
1874 Hugh. *l.*
1876 Bernard, Jr. *l.*

Remsen,
1775 Jacobus.
1789 John.
1795 Robert.
1803 William.
1807 Simeon.
1867 Ira. *m.*
1867 Phœnix. *l.*
1871 Henry. *l.*
1876 Robert G. *m.*

Renwick,
1807 James.
1809 Robert J.
1833 Henry B.
1833 William R.
1836 James, Jr.
1839 Edward S.
1876 James A.

Repetto,
1866 Francisco. *m.*

Reuwee,
1864 Albert A. *l.*

Reymert,
1872 James D. *l.*

Reynaud,
1874 Albert. l.

Reynolds,
1835 James N. *h.*
1843 Charles.
1859 Stephen R.
1861 Charles H. *m.*
1862 Jasper G. *m.*
1870 William H.T. *m.*
1871 Frank. *l.*
1875 John. *l.*

Rhame,
1876 William. *m.*

Rhind,
1827 Charles, Jr.

Rhinelander,
1798 William.
1804 Philip.
1808 William C., Jr.
1811 John R.
1815 Frederic W.
1834 Philip.
1847 Frederic W.
1849 Charles E.

Rhodes,
1874 Samuel D. *m.*
1874 Francis B.F. *m.e.*

Rice,
1861 William A.
1864 Charles B.
1874 Arthur H. *m.*
1875 John W. *m.*

Richards,
1858 A. G.
1858 Robert K.
1864 James. *l.*
1866 Jarrett T. *l.*
1867 Joseph S. *l.*
1874 John T. *l.*
1875 Harry E. *m.*
1876 George. *l.*

Richardson,
1875 Lucian H. *l.*
1876 Rosell L. *l.*

Richmond,
1832 Thomas A.

Ricker,
1874 Clinton J. *m.*

Ricketts,
1871 Pierre De P. *m.e.*

Ricord,
1868 Philippe. *m.*

Ridgway,
1872 Charles D. *l.*

Ridout,
1866 William G. *m.*

Rieger,
1872 Joel H. *m.*

Rigby,
1861 Charles D. *m.*

Riggs,
1847 Joseph K.
1869 Benjamin C. *m.*
1871 George W. *m. e.*

Riker,
1799 Samuel, Jr.
1826 Daniel P.
1835 John H.

Riley,
1858 Henry C.
1874 Henry A., Jr. *l.*

Ring,
1842 Zebedee, Jr.
1873 Charles A. *m.*

Riotte,
1871 Pedro P. *l.*

Ripley,
1870 Joseph S. *m.*

Ritter,
1869 Theodore. *l.*

Ritterband,
1871 David S. *l.*

Ritzema,
1758 Rudolph.

Rives,
1868 George L.

Robert,
1762 Daniel.
1864 Charles S. *m.*

Roberts,
1842 Oliver E.

1867 Nathan S. *m.*
1869 Charles. *l.*
1871 Gracie S. *m. e.*

Robertson,
1812 Jacob A.
1813 Alexander H.
1816 John J.
1823 Andrew K.
1823 Noel.
1824 Alexander.
1825 Anthony L.
1868 Kenneth. *m. e.*
1869 Charles F. *h.*
1870 Arthur R. *l.*
1870 Roderick. *l.*
1871 Richard S. *m. e.*
1874 Abram H. *l.*

Robie,
1861 John W. *m.*

Robins,
1860 Edward P.

Robinson,
1773 Beverley.
1826 Beverley, Jr.
1862 John A. *m.*
1863 Robert E.
1865 Thomas. *l*
1866 Edward R. *l.*
1867 George W. *m.*
1867 John W. *m.*

Robson,
1876 James A. *l.*

Roche,
1870 Spencer S.

Rockwell,
1860 Fenton. *l.*
1862 William H., Jr. *m.*
1868 Frank W. *m.*
1869 Charles H. *l.*

Rockwood,
1876 Charles B. *l.*

Rodenstein,
1867 John W. *m.*

Rodman,
1842 Washington.
1850 Erskine. *m.*
1868 Charles S. *m.*

Roe,
1871 John O. *m.*
1875 Jacob I. *m.*

Roebuck,
1772 Peter.

Roesch,
1876 George F. *l.*

Rogers,
1803 Henry F.
1804 Samuel.
1807 George P.
1812 John S.
1817 Edward N.
1817 Samuel D.
1819 George J.
1820 Archibald G.
1827 Henry.
1841 Jones.
1848 Columbus B.

1853 Charles. *h.*
1867 Albert S. *m.*
1868 Thomas. *l.*
1868 William C. *m.*
1869 Orville F. *m.*
1871 Platt. *l.*
1875 Henry P. *l.*
1875 John A. *m.*

Rokenbaugh,
1874 Henry S. *l.*

Rolker,
1875 Charles M. *m. e.*

Romaine,
1806 Samuel B.
1838 Benjamin, Jr.
1840 Worthington.
1871 Benjamin F., Jr.

Romer,
1854 Jean. *h.*

Romeyn,
1774† Nicholas.
1795 John B.
1816 James.
1858 James W.

Romondt,
1872 Charles D. V. *m.*

Roof,
1862 Frank. *m.*
1864 Stephen W. *m.*
1875 Charles B. *m.*

Rooney,
1866 William H. *l.*

Roorbach,
1806 Frederic.

Roosevelt,
1815 James J., Jr.
1819 James H.
1826 William H.
1842 Silas W.
1864 Van Ness. *l.*
1874 John E. *l.*

Root,
1841 George M.
1864 Russell H.
1868 Henry A. *l.*
1875 Samuel C.

Rose,
1873 Andrew W., Jr. *l.*
1874 William R. *l.*

Rosenblatt,
1876 Leopold G. *l.*

Rosenfeld,
1872 Edward L.

Ross,
1795 William.
1795 William M. *m.*
1804 David M.
1808 Henry H.
1843 John H.
1865 Arthur B.
1868 William H., Jr. *m.*
1870 Francis E. *m.*
1871 James A. *l.*
1876 William C. *m. e.*

Scott,
1798 William. *h.*
1850 Winfield. *h.*
1854 J. Jackson. *h.*
1869 Francis M. *l.*
1869 Xenophon C. *m.*
1871 William J. *m.*
1872 Winfield. *l.*
1875 Cornelius S. *l.*

Scovill,
1761 James. *h.*

Scoville,
1861 Frederick. *l.*
1876 Delavan C. *l.*

Scudder,
1862 Henry J. *h.*
1874 Henry T.

Seabrook,
1875 Thomas L. *l.*

Seabury,
1761 Samuel. *h.*
1823 Samuel. *h.*
1856 William J.
1872 John H. *m.*

Seaman,
1774 Benjamin.
1795 Benjamin.
1802 Billopp B.
1804 Robert.
1805 Edward.
1851 George A.
1864 William A. *l.*

Searing,
1868 Edward W. *l.*

Searle,
1771 John.
1866 Dayton W. *m.*

Searls,
1872 Wellington B. *m.*

Sears,
1857 Charles E.
1862 Henry T. *m.*

Seaver,
1869 Horace N., Jr.
1873 True M. *l.*

Sebring,
1771 Michael. *m.*

Secor,
1869 William H. *l.*
1875 Horace, Jr. *l.*

Sedgwick,
1829 Theodore, Jr.

Seeds,
1860 Orin H. *m.*

Seelye,
1876 Julius H. *h.*

Seguin,
1864 Edward C. *m.*

Segur,
1860 Benjamin A. *m.*

Seligman,
1876 Eugene.
1876 George W.

Seney,
1815 Robert.

Senftner,
1876 Robert. *l.*

Senger,
1867 William A. *l.*

Serviss,
1874 Garrett P. *l.*

Seymour,
1826 Daniel.
1836 Charles M.
1850 George F.
1860 Elbridge G. *m.*
1865 Roderick B.
1867 Morris W. *l.*

Shack,
1868 Albert P. *m. e.*
1876 Ferdinand. *l.*

Schater,
1873 James C. *m.*

Shapter,
1840 Peter, Jr.

Sharp,
1868 John. *m.*

Sharswood,
1856 George. *h.*

Shaw,
1774† Jacob.
1862 Samuel F. *m.*
1863 Abner O *m,*
1863 Amos S., Jr. *m.*
1871 Marsh. *m.*
1874 Frank D.
1874 John C. *m.*
1875 John E. *l.*

Shea,
1831 James. *h.*
1837 Charles E.

Shedden,
1865 Samuel S. *h.*

Sheffield,
1871 James C. *l.*

Sheldon,
1868 Charles S. *m.*
1869 George P. *l.*
1873 Eugene H. *l.*

Shelton,
1825 William. *h.*
1867 Charles C. *l.*
1871 Charles W. *l.*

Shepard,
1856 William F.
1869 Frank N.
1870 Robert N.

Shepherd,
1842 John H. *h.*
1874 John H. *l.*

Sherman,
1803 Alpheus.
1868 George H. *m.*
1868 Thomas P. *l.*
1874 Charles. *l.*
1875 George.
1876 Thomas *l.*

Sherwood,
1834 William. *n.*
1849 Ezra K.
1876 Charles H, *l.*

Shippey,
1796 Josiah, Jr,

Shirley,
1874 John L. *l.*

Shoemaker,
1864 Thomas B. *l.*
1866 Murray C. *l.*

Short,
1872 Charles L.
1875 Edward. *l.*

Shrady,
1821 George.
1849 John, Jr.
1863 Jacob. *l.*
1864 William. *l.*

Shreve,
1773 Thomas.
1865 Octavius B. *m.*

Shrope,
1875 Harry H. *l.*

Sibley,
1871 Haram W. *l.*

Sickles,
1792 Jacob.
1804 John J.

Sidell,
1812 John A.

Sill,
1861 Thomas H.

Silliman,
1850 Charles A.

Simis,
1876 Adolph, Jr. *l.*

Simpkins,
1873 Charles S. *l.*

Simmons,
1864 Charles E. *m.*
1875 Arthur R. *m.*

Simms,
1871 William T. *l.*

Simonds,
1873 Alexander B.

Sims,
1873 Harry L. *m.*

Simpson,
1841 Robert G.
1860 Samuel F. *l.*
1864 William V. *l.*
1871 Charles. *m.*
1873 John W.
1874 Edwin D. *m.*
1875 Angel J. S. *l.*

Simson,
1800 Sampson.

Simon,
1870 Kaufman. *l.*

Sinclair,
1869 Alexander G. *m.*
1872 George L. *m.*

Skeene,
1772 Andrew.

Skelding,
1866 Thomas. *m,*

Skellenger,
1875 Edward B. *m.*

Skidmore,
1849 John D.
1871 William B. *l.*
1875 James H., Jr. *l.*

Skinner,
1867 Eugene C. *l.*
1870 Orin. *l.*
1875 John B. *l.*

Slack,
1821 John C.

Slesinger,
1874 Samuel. *l.*

Slidell,
1810 John.

Slipper,
1857 James H.
1859 J. Augustus.

Sloan,
1868 Arthur.

Sloane,
1868 William J. M.
1871 Charles W. *l.*
1872 Thomas O'C. *m.e.*

Slocum,
1864 William E. *l.*
1869 Charles E. *m.*
1870 William B. *l.*

Slosson,
1828 Barzillai.
1833 Edward.

Slover,
1826 Abraham A., Jr.

Small,
1869 Frederick I. *l.*
1873 Sidney I. *m.*
1875 Henry G. *m.*

Smalley,
1866 William E.

Smedberg,
1833 John G.
1852 James R.
1855 Oscar.

Stillwell,
1832 John E.
1875 John E. *m.*
1875 Cleveland S. *m.*

Stilwell,
1862 Thomas H. *m.*
1864 William R. *m.*
1866 Samuel J. *l.*
1872 Samuel D. *m.*
1873 Silas M., Jr.

Stimson,
1868 Daniel M. *m.*

Stirling,
1872 Andrew M. *l.*

Stitt,
1867 John H. *l.*

St. John,
1828 Samuel S.
1848 Thomas P.
1870 Samuel B. *m.*

Stockholm,
1807 Dirck B.

Stoddard,
1864 Freman. *m.*

Stoeckel,
1874 Gustav M. *m.*

Stoiber,
1874 Adolphus H. *l.*

Stokes,
1869 Charles, Jr. *m.*
1876 Henry S. *l.*

Stone,
1830 William M. *h.*
1843 Daniel. *h.*
1847 Archibald M.
1865 Jay S. *m.*
1866 Richard H. *m.*
1876 Frederick J. *l.*

Stoothoff,
1875 William. *l.*

Storm,
1862 John B. *l.*

Storrs,
1866 Samuel J. *l.*
1874 Frank.

Stoskoff,
1869 Louis. *m.*

Stoutenburgh,
1874 John H.

Stoughton,
1810 James.

Stout,
1864 George W. *m.*
1864 John. *l.*
1868 Stephen V. W. *m.*

Straus,
1871 Oscar S.
1871 William. *l.*

Strebeigh,
1873 Lefferts.

Streeter,
1869 Solomon T. *l.*

Stricklin,
1865 David L. *m.*

Stringham,
1793 James S.
1794 John B.

Strong,
1810 Pascal N.
1816 Thomas M.
1825 Oliver S.
1838 George T.
1840 Peter R.
1853 Samuel P. *h.*
1854 Benjamin.
1868 Henry T. *m.*
1871 Alexander. *m.*
1872 John R.

Stryker,
1804 Peter. *h.*
1809 James.

Stuart,
1773 John. *h.*
1808 William.
1864 Sidney H., Jr. *l.*
1874 William W. *l.*

Stubbs,
1856 Alfred. *h.*
1866 Joseph. *m.*

Study,
1866 James M. *m.*

Studley,
1860 William H. *m.*

Sturges,
1861 Frederick D. *m.*
1864 Arthur P.
1867 Frederick W. *l.*
1869 Henry C.
1870 Frank D.

Stuyvesant,
1794 Peter G.
1863 Rutherfurd.

Suckley,
1819 John L.
1820 Rutsen.

Suffern,
1856 Thomas, Jr.

Sugg,
1867 Josiah P. *m.*

Suiter,
1871 Augustus W. *m.*

Summers,
1860 George F. *m.*

Sutherland,
1836 Jacob. *h.*
1874 Douglas R. *m.*

Sutphen,
1876 Joseph W. *l.*

Sutro,
1874 Theodore. *l.*

Suroong,
1873 Vung P. *m.*

Suydam,
1856 Charles C.
1860 Abraham.
1861 Charles H. *m.*
1872 Charles S. *l.*

Swain,
1868 James P., Jr.
1870 George M. *m.*

Swan,
1844 Edward H.
1848 Otis D.
1861 Norman L. *m.*
1868 Benjamin R. *m.*
1871 Henry S. *m.*
1871 Robert, Jr.
1871 William L. *l.*

Swanton,
1875 James F. *l.*

Swart,
1876 Merton G. *l.*

Swarts,
1864 Frederick. *l.*

Swartwout,
1812 John.

Swartz,
1871 Mahlon E. *m.*

Swasey,
1869 Erastus P. *m.*
1875 Charles E. *m.*
1875 George B. *m.*
1875 John H. *m.*

Sweeney,
1875 John P. *l.*

Sweeny,
1840 Owen.

Sweet,
1872 Charles S. *l.*

Sweezey,
1865 John E.

Swift,
1862 John I. *m.*
1872 Samuel. *m.*
1875 Everett M. *l.*

Swords,
1826 Thomas, Jr.
1827 Theodore A.
1829 Charles R.
1834 Robert S.

Sylvester,
1786 Francis.

Sym,
1842 John.

Syme,
1864 William R. *l.*

Symington,
1875 James, Jr. *m.*

Syms,
1873 William. *l.*

Taber,
1863 James A. *l.*
1874 James R. *m.*

Taft,
1866 Charles P. *l.*

Taggard,
1835 William H.
1845 John A.

Taggart,
1860 Charles J. *m.*

Tailer,
1852 Henry A.
1857 James T.

Talbot,
1857 William R.
1866 Augustus.
1866 Richmond.
1875 Charles N.
1876 Edward M. *l.*

Talcott,
1832 Frederick L.
1875 Frederick C. *m.*

Tallmadge,
1845 Frederick S.

Talman,
1811 John N.
1814 George F.

Tappan,
1807 Peter V. C.
1854 Henry P. *h.*

Tappen,
1876 Abram A. *l.*

Taylor,
1792 George.
1792 William.
1793 Willett, Jr. *m.*
1796 Charles.
1831 Edwin M.
1837 Thomas H. *h.*
1861 George L.
1861 Henry A. C.
1868 Robert W. *m.*
1871 Alfred. *l.*
1874 Charles J. *l.*
1876 Phillip. *m.*

Teakle,
1842 Elisha W.

Telford,
1871 William C. *m.*

Temple,
1795 James B.

Ten Broeck,
1834 Anthony.

Ten Eyck,
1874 Cantine H. *m.*

Tenney,
1871 Albert D. *l.*
1876 Phillip. *m.*

Terhune,
1870 Richard H. *m. e.*

1876 Lachlan. *m.*
1876 John R. *l.*

Tyng,
1846 Alexander G.
1862 Charles R.
1863 Morris A. *l.*
1871 Theodosius S. *l.*

Udall,
1772 Richard. *m.*

Uhl,
1876 Russell J. *l.*

Uhle,
1872 Charles P. *m.*

Ulshoeffer,
1856 William G.

Unangst,
1873 Charles. *l.*

Underwood,
1876 William J., Jr. *l.*

Untermeyer,
1874 Isaac. *l.*

Upfold,
1831 George. *h.*

Ure,
1866 Walter. *m.*

Ustick,
1794 Thomas.

Vail,
1869 William H. *m.*
1871 M. Bedell. *l.*

Valentine,
1864 Albert E.
1870 Samuel H *l.*
1871 Obadiah.
1875 William G. *l.*
1875 William A. *l.*
1876 Herbert. *l.*

Vallejo,
1864 Platon. *m.*

Van Alst,
1865 Isaac. *l.*

Van Amringe,
1815 Henry H.
1860 John H.

Van Arsdale,
1868 William H. *m. e.*

Van Boskerck,
1864 Richard T. *l.*
1870 Thomas B. *l.*

Van Buren,
1807 Cornelius.
1829 John D.
1863 Frank R.
1865 Singleton. *l.*
1866 Martin.

Van Buskirk,
1796 Lawrence.

Van Cleef,
1837 George S.

Van Cortlandt,
1758 Philip.
1807 James.
1863 Augustus. *m.*

Van Dalsen,
1876 Spencer. *m.*

Vanderbilt,
1837 John, Jr.

Vanderhoof,
1864 Frederick D. *m.*

Vanderpoel,
1862 John A.
1867 Aaron E.
1867 Augustus G. *l.*
1876 S. O., Jr. *m.*

Vanderpool,
1867 James. *m.*

Vanderveer,
1816 Adrian.

Van Der Veer,
1866 James D. *m.*
1874 Peter L. *l.*

Vandervoort,
1828 John L.

Van Deursen,
1870 David C. *m.*

Vandewater,
1814 Ferdinand.

Van Duzer,
1853 Archibald S.

Van Dyck,
1761 Henry.

Van Giesen,
1866 Henry C. *m.*

Van Harlengen,
1869 John. *m.*

Van Hook,
1797 Isaac A.

Van Horne,
1791 Frederic.
1793 Cornelius A.

Van Houten,
1867 Nicholas B. *m.*
1876 Jacob A. *m.*

Van Keuren,
1874 Cornelius. *m.*

Van Kleeck,
1828 Robert B.
1859 Robert B., Jr.
1863 Frederick B.
1876 Henry. *l.*

Van Lennep,
1867 David *m. e.*

Van Mater,
1808 Daniel.

Van Ness,
1789 John P.
1797 William P.

Van Nest,
1867 James V. D. *m.*

Van Nostrand,
1865 Seymour.
1874 John E. *l.*

Van Pelt,
1799 Peter I.

Van Rensselaer,
1847 Francis.
1867 Philip L. *l.*

Van Riper,
1856 William T.
1866 Cornelius. *m.*

Van Santvoord,
1865 Abraham.

Van Schaack,
1767 Peter
1787 Henry C.

Van Siclen,
1867 George W. *l.*

Van Slyck,
1796 Adrian C.

Van Tuyl,
1844 Otto W. E.

Van Valkenburgh,
1870 Thomas S. *m.*

Van Voast,
1861 Garret W. V. *m.*

Van Volkenburgh,
1876 Philip, Jr. *l.*

Van Voorhis,
1841 Robert D.
1865 Elias W. *l.*

Van Vorst,
1843 Cornelius, Jr.

Van Vranken,
1837 Samuel A. *h.*

Van Wagenen,
1802 Hubert.
1821 Gerrit G.
1826 Gerrit H., Jr.
1828 William W.
1858 Hubert.
1861 William M.
1870 Theodore F. *m.e.*
1871 George A. *m.*

Van Wagner,
1866 Frederick J. *m.*

Van Wert,
1873 Merit M. *l.*

Van Winkle,
1848 Isaac.
1865 Edward H.
1865 Isaac.

Van Wyck,
1795 Pierre C.
1807 Philip G.
1845 Pierre M.
1867 Richard C. *m.*
1869 Philip V. R. *l.*
1872 Robert A. *l.*
1873 Edmund. *m.*

Vardill,
1766 John.

Varick,
1799 Abraham, Jr.
1799 John V.
1807 Theodore V. W.
1813 John.

Varnum,
1871 James McC. *l.*

Vaughan,
1860 Julius. *m.*

Vedder,
1861 Maus R. *m.*

Ver Meulen,
1860 Edmund C. *m.*

Vermilye,
1831 Robert G.
1870 William H. *m.*
1871 Joseph F.
1873 Daniel B.
1875 Thomas E. *h.*

Vermilyea,
1858 Isaac D. *h.*

Verplanck,
1758 Samuel.
1768 Gulian.
1788 Daniel C.
1791 William B.
1801 Gulian C.
1819 Samuel.
1832 William S.
1876 William E.

Verren,
1829 Antoine. *h.*

Vethake,
1808 Henry.

Vincent,
1854 Marvin R.
1876 Henry. *l.*

Vinton,
1848 Francis. *h.*
1873 Arthur D. *l.*

Von Sachs,
1876 William F. A.

Vroom,
1808 Peter D., Jr.

Wackerhagen,
1869 George. *m.*

Waddell,
1821 John H.
1831 Lloyd S.

Waddington,
1860 George.

Wadsworth,
1863 Samuel D. *m.*

Wagstaff,
1822 Alfred.
1866 Alfred, Jr. *l.*

Wainwright,
1845 Henry P.

Whiting,
1864 William L. *l.*
1866 Henry A.
1870 Howard. *m.*
1873 Marshall. *m.*
Whitlock,
1837 Samuel H.
1873 Bache McE.
1876 Charles, Jr. *l.*
Whitney,
1861 Albert B.
Whiton,
1871 Augustus W.
Whittingham,
1827 William R. *h.*
Whybrow,
1870 Charles T. *m.*
Wickes,
1876 Thomas P. *l.*
Wicks,
1876 Frederick S. *l.*
Wiener,
1874 Joseph. *m.*
Wight,
1861 Charles M. *m.*
1864 Thomas. *m.*
1875 Thomas H. *m.*
Wilcox,
1871 Richard D. *m.*
Wilder,
1871 Edward P. *l.*
Wildey,
1860 Pierre W.
Wilds,
1871 Howard P. *l.*
1873 Judson B. *l.*
Wiley,
1873 Charles A. *l.*
Wilkes,
1821 George.
1822 Hamilton.
Wilkins,
1760 Isaac.
Wilkinson,
1872 Robert H.
Willard,
1869 Charles E. *m.*
Willcox,
1867 James K. H. *l.*
1874 David J. H. *l.*
Willett,
1776 Marinus.
1819 Marinus, Jr.
1822 Edward M.
1856 Elbert M.
1864 Marinus, Jr.
Williams,
1822 William R.
1833 James A.
1850 Timothy D. *h.*
1851 John. *h.*
1856 Howell L., Jr.
1860 Augustus P. *m.*
1867 Channing M. *h.*
1867 William H. *l.*
1868 Stephen W.
1871 Pelham. *h.*
1872 Frank S. *l.*
1873 John T. *m. e.*
1874 Cornelius. *m.*
1874 Frederick H. *m. e.*
1874 Hubert. *l.*
1875 Edward P. *m.*
1875 Elliot. *l.*
1876 Leighton.
Williamson,
1807 Charles A.
1872 Nicholas. *m.*
1873 George N.
1873 Edwin B. *l.*
1873 John S. *l.*
1873 William K. *l.*
1876 Frederick B. *l.*
Willis,
1862 Francis.
1862 William H., Jr.
1864 William S. *m.*
Willson,
1876 Hugh R. *l.*
Wilmarth,
1868 Frank. *m.*
Wilmerding,
1868 Lucius K.
Wilson,
1800 George.
1800 Peter.
1818 Abraham D.
1822 Samuel F.
1825 Peter.
1825 William.
1826 Harris.
1835 William H.
1836 James W.
1845 Bird. *h.*
1860 Philip L. *l.*
1861 Benjamin F. *m.*
1862 Merritt H. *m.*
1863 Benjamin. *m.*
1865 Francis F.
1866 James W. *m.*
1869 William. *l.*
1870 John P. *m.*
1872 Robert B. *m.*
1875 Francis H. *l.*
1875 William R. *l.*
1875 James L. *m.*
1876 Claude. *m.*
1876 Howard E. *m.*
Winans,
1840 James W.
1874 Frederick N. *m.*
Winchell,
1865 Alvord E. *m.*
Windsor,
1834 Lloyd.
Wines,
1871 Walter B. *l.*
Winslow,
1761 Edward. *h.*
1857 William B.
1864 Miron, Jr. *l.*
1867 John. *m.*
1873 James M. *m.*
Winston,
1863 Gustavus S. *m.*
1866 Joseph S. *m.*
Winter,
1801 Gabriel.
1827 William.
Winterton,
1772 William. *m.*
Winthrop,
1812 Egerton L.
1827 Grenville T.
1860 Egerton L.
1864 Buchanan. *l.*
1866 Benjamin R., Jr. *l.*
Wise,
1871 Simon P. *m.*
Wissman,
1866 John F.
Witherbee,
1867 Silas O. *m.*
Withers,
1865 Russell. *m.*
Witter,
1867 William C. *l.*
Witthaus,
1867 Rudolph A., Jr.
Wohlfarth,
1866 Augustus. *m.*
Wolfe,
1838 Theodore F. *m.*
Wolff,
1874 Joseph C. *l.*
Wood,
1851 J. Walter.
1868 John B. *l.*
1870 Dennistoun.
1870 James H. *l.*
1871 Henry. *l.*
1872 Henry D.
1873 Henry S. *l.*
1874 George. *l.*
1874 William P. *l.*
1875 Chalmers.
1875 Halsey L. *m.*
1876 John S. *l.*
1876 Joseph S. *l.*
Woodbridge,
1872 Enoch D. *m*
Woodford,
1854 Stewart L.
Woodhull,
1791 Jesse, Jr.
1869 Thenford.
Woodill,
1866 Alfred H. *m.*
Woodruff,
1860 Lewis B. *h.*
1861 Charles H. *l.*
1863 Lockwood D. F. *m.*
1874 Amos E. *l.*
1875 John E. *m.*
1876 Philemon. *l.*
Woods,
1791 James.
Woodward,
1793 Elias B.
1872 Henry E.
1874 James L. *l.*
Woodworth,
1876 D. Sidney. *m.*
Worcester,
1875 Francis J. *l.*
Work,
1867 James H.
1871 George F.
Worster,
1863 Willard P.
Worth,
1829 Fanning S.
Worthington,
1874 Henry. *m.*
Wotherspoon,
1837 Alexander S.
Wotton,
1876 William C. *l.*
Wright,
1799 David.
1830 George W.
1851 David A.
1864 Samuel P. *l.*
1865 George P. *m.*
1866 Joel W. *m.*
1869 Edward M. *l.*
1869 William B. *m.*
1875 Albert A. *m. e.*
1876 William G. *m. e.*
Wyatt,
1809 William E.
1876 William E. *l.*
Wyckoff,
1840 Van Brunt.
1862 Albert. *l.*
Wynkoop,
1819 Richard.
1866 Gerardus W. *m.*
Yale,
1862 Leroy M.
Yates,
1787 John W.
1876 Horace. *l.*
Yost,
1866 George L. *m.*
Youle,
1793 Joseph. *m.*
Young,
1865 John F. *h.*
1866 Charles. *m.*
1866 William H. *m.*
1868 John F. *m.*
1876 Joseph C., Jr. *m.*
Youngs,
1866 Graham.
Zabriskie,
1828 Martin R.
1835 Christian, Jr.
1854 Jeremiah L.
1869 Samuel M. *m.*
1873 George. *l.*
Zborowsky,
1828 Martin.
Zemansky,
1874 Abraham P. *m.*
Zimmermann,
1871 Gustav. *l.*
Zwinge,
1874 Bernard. *l.*

# COLUMBIA COLLEGE.

1754-1876.

www.ingramcontent.com/pod-product-compliance
Lightning Source LLC
LaVergne TN
LVHW020920110826
845150LV00004B/723

* 9 7 8 1 4 2 5 5 5 4 9 6 5 *